WIVES AND DAUGHTERS

Wives and Daughters

Women and Children in the Georgian Country House

Joanna Martin

Hambledon and London
London and New York

Hambledon and London
102 Gloucester Avenue
London, NW1 8HX

175 Fifth Avenue
New York, NY 10010
USA

First Published 2004

ISBN 1 85285 271 2

A description of this book is available from the
British Library and from the Library of Congress.

Typeset by Carnegie Publishing, Lancaster,
And printed in Great Britain by Cambridge University Press.

Distributed in the United States and Canada
exclusively by Palgrave Macmillan,
A division of St Martin's Press.

Contents

Illustrations

Plates

Between pages 108 and 109

Between pages 204 and 205

Text Illustrations

Acknowledgements

I have been working on the Fox Strangways family on and off for thirty years, and it is impossible to thank adequately everyone who has helped me during this time.

For permission to use documents which are still in private hands, I am grateful to Thomas Methuen-Campbell, Ilchester Estates, Sherborne Castle Estates and the Talbot Trust, Lacock Abbey Collection, National Trust Fox Talbot Museum.

The members of staff of the many record offices and libraries in which I have worked have been endlessly patient. These include the librarians and archivists of the County Record Offices of Cornwall, Dorset, Gloucestershire, Suffolk, West Glamorgan and Wiltshire; also the Manuscripts Department of the British Library; Cambridge University Library; the Family Records Centre; the Fox Talbot Museum at Lacock; the National Archives (Public Record Office); the National Library of Wales, Aberystwyth; the Royal Archives; and Swansea University Library.

Many individuals have been generous with their advice and practical assistance. I am particularly grateful to my brother, Thomas Methuen-Campbell, who has found numerous letters and pictures for me at Penrice, and to Susan Rands who has given me a great deal of her time. She has supplied me with information and illustrations, and has encouraged me at every stage. I would also like to thank the following: John Adams, Ted Cockayne, Joy Cooke, Lord Digby, Kate Fielden (Bowood), Mary Frampton, Michael Gray, Madeline and Christopher Heal (Redlynch), the Marquess of Lansdowne, Michael McGarvie, Susan Morris (Debrett Ancestry Research), Timothy Mowl, Richard Morris, Pat Murrell, the Earl of Oxford and Asquith, Adrian Pearse, Ann Smith (Sherborne Castle Archives), Lilian Swindall (Dorset County Museum), Janet Todd, the Hon. Mrs Townshend, Roger Waine, John Wingfield Digby, Helen Trompeteler (the National Portrait Gallery) and Thomas Woodcock (Norroy and Ulster King of Arms).

Martin Sheppard at Hambledon and London, who encouraged me to write this book in the first place, has given me invaluable help throughout. His advice on the organisation of the book has been especially helpful.

Finally, I would particularly like to thank my husband, Edward Martin, who has supplied me with background information on family history, on heraldry and architecture, and on gardens. He has travelled around south-western Britain with me in search of the houses and churches connected with the Fox Strangways family, and has photographed many of the portraits and other illustrations used in this book.

Illustration Acknowledgements

Most of the illustrations were photographed by Edward Martin or supplied by the owners of the images. The author and publisher are also grateful to the following for supplying illustrations: the National Portrait Gallery, London (7–9, 14, 15, 17); the National Trust, Fox Talbot Museum, Talbot Trust Collection (22); and Dorset Archives Service (p. 263).

Editorial Notes

Writing a book about a group of women presents one immediate problem. How should one refer to a woman if, as almost invariably happened in the past, she changed her surname when she married? If she and her husband acquired or inherited a title there would be further changes. Wherever possible, I have used the names by which these people were known by their contemporaries. Thus, a woman is referred to by her maiden name before she marries, and by her married name thereafter (and by her second husband's name if she remarried). Cross-referencing in the biographical notes (pages 357 to 364) should enable readers to keep track of these changes. For the sake of simplicity – and also because this is how they usually signed their own names – I have generally preferred Strangways to Fox Strangways, even where the latter is technically correct.

The daughters of barons and earls were usually addressed as 'Lady': *Lady* Susan Strangways, *Lady* Mary Strangways and so on. Again, to make the names as simple as possible, I have omitted this title in most instances.

All dates before 1752 are New Style, with the year beginning on 1 January.

In quotations from original documents, I have used italics where words are underlined in the original texts, and have modernised the punctuation and use of capital letters. Ampersands have been expanded.

I have not attempted to metricate the imperial quantities and measurements given in the original documents. For those who are unfamiliar with the old money, it may be useful to note that there were twenty shillings (20s.) in one pound (£1), and twelve pence (12d.) in one shilling. One guinea was £1 1s. In the eighteenth century the pound sign (£) would usually have been written after, or above, the number, but I have followed the modern convention of placing it first.

One pound (1 lb.) in weight is approximately 0.45 kilograms, and there are sixteen ounces (16 oz.) in a pound. A hundredweight is 112 lbs. One foot (1 ft) is 30.5 centimetres: there are twelve inches in a foot, and three feet in a yard. A gallon is approximately 4.55 litres, and there are eight pints in a gallon. A bushel was a dry measure of eight gallons, used for commodities such as coal and grain.

The names of counties, where given, are those that were in use before reorganisation in 1974.

Abbreviations

Add. MS	Additional Manuscript
BL	British Library (Manuscripts Department)
DRO	Dorset Record Office
GEC	George Edward Cockayne, *The Complete Peerage* (new edn, edited by Vicary Gibbs and H. A. Doubleday, 13 vols, London, 1910–59)
PP	Penrice Papers
PRO	The National Archives: Public Record Office, London
RCHME	Royal Commission on Historical Monuments, England
RO	Record Office
WSRO	Wiltshire and Swindon Record Office

In Memory of
Evelyn, Lady Blythswood
'Penrice Granny'
1870–1958

Introduction

Amongst the books in Thomas Hardy's reconstructed study in the Dorset County Museum in Dorchester are the four volumes of the author's own copy of John Hutchins's *History and Antiquities of the County of Dorset*, which was first published in 1774. Annotations and pedigrees added to these books by Hardy himself bear witness to his fascination with the colourful lives of the ladies of the Fox Strangways family of Melbury House in the parish of Melbury Sampford, which lies twelve miles north west of Dorchester.[1]

Melbury is one of the great houses of Dorset, and its owners have been prominent in county society for four centuries. The death of the last male Strangways owner in 1726, and inheritance by two heiresses in succession, meant that women played an unusually important part in shaping the destiny of the house and estate in the eighteenth century. This book tells the story of the ladies of Melbury, their friends, relations and servants, and the houses they lived in, over a period of a hundred years, from 1730 to 1830. The story is told as far as possible through the women's own words, recorded in their letters, journals and memoirs. They belonged to the landed elite, the wealthiest and most influential group of families in eighteenth- and nineteenth-century Britain, whose exploits were observed by their less exalted contemporaries with 'fascinated admiration, deferential respect, scandalized horror, amused condescension and lofty disregard'.[2] Though they made up less than one per cent of the population, such families owned perhaps 40 per cent of the land, and it was this land that gave them their pre-eminent social status and political power.[3]

Thomas Hardy drew much of his material from Hutchins, whose volumes recount the history of the Strangways, Fox and Horner families, the owners of Melbury in the Georgian age. And though, as Hardy himself wrote, such accounts can appear at first sight to be as dry as dust, they hint at 'palpitating dramas'. As a young man, Hardy found himself 'unconsciously filling into the framework the motives, passions, and personal qualities' which lay behind these dramas.[4] He was able to supplement the information that he found in Hutchins's *History* with his own family's recollections, for his maternal ancestors had been tenants and employees of the inhabitants of Melbury for several generations. Melbury House is King's Hintock Court in Hardy's short story 'The First Countess of Wessex', a fictionalised account of the marriage in 1736 of Stephen Fox (Stephen Reynard) of Redlynch in Somerset and Elizabeth Strangways Horner (Betty Dornell), the heiress of Melbury. The story of this union, which brought together the two families and their estates, first appeared in *Harper's New Monthly Magazine* in 1889, and then (with some amendments) formed one of the chapters in Hardy's book, *A Group of Noble Dames*, first published in 1891. Hardy's mother, Jemima Hand, came from Melbury Osmond, just a mile or two from Melbury House, and her great-grandfather Joseph Childs had been the Melbury estate carpenter for many years in the mid eighteenth century. Jemima worked for the Fox Strangways family when she was a young woman, and her last employer, the Revd Edward Murray, was related to them by marriage. Murray was vicar of Stinsford (Hardy's Mellstock) near Dorchester, and it was at Higher Bockhampton in the same parish that Thomas Hardy was born in 1840. In later years Hardy also visited Melbury and the Horner family home, Mells in Somerset, whose owners told him about their forebears.[5] Hardy wrote fiction, based on fact, but the true history of the 'First Countess of Wessex' and her relations is dramatic enough. Their stories also touched the lives of many people to whom they were not related by blood – for in addition to being wives, sisters, mothers and daughters, these women were also landlords, patrons, employers and friends.

Wives and Daughters tells the story of four generations of women in an extended family. It begins with Susanna Strangways of Melbury, who was born in 1689 and outlived five brothers and three sisters to become the sole heiress of one of the largest landed estates in Dorset. Susanna married Thomas Horner of Mells in Somerset in 1713, and eventually inherited the whole of her family's extensive West Country estates. The Horners – or Strangways Horners, as they became in 1726 – had just one surviving child, their daughter Elizabeth (1723–1792), who married a local landowner, Stephen Fox of Redlynch near Bruton in Somerset, in 1736, when she was only thirteen. Stephen was never prominent in public affairs, but his younger brother Henry (later Lord Holland) made a vast fortune for himself out of government service, holding the offices of Secretary at War from 1746 to 1755 and Paymaster General from 1757 to 1765. Lord Holland's younger son was the well-known politician Charles James Fox, and relations between members of the Fox Strangways family and their cousins at Holland House remained close for several generations.

Stephen and Elizabeth Fox (who became the first Earl and Countess of Ilchester in 1756) spent much of their married life at Redlynch, and they continued to live there for part of each year after inheriting Melbury on

Susanna Strangways Horner's death in 1758. Of their nine children, the most interesting is the eldest, Lady Susan Fox Strangways, who was born in 1743, and died in 1827 at the great age of eighty-four. Susan was a rebel. She eloped with an actor, lived for several years in America, and eventually returned to Dorset, where she spent the remainder of her long life at Stinsford House, where Thomas Hardy's mother was later to work. A highly intelligent woman, Susan was a prolific letter writer, and she also kept a detailed journal for almost sixty years.[6]

In the fourth generation, the focus of the book moves from Somerset and Dorset to South Wales. Lady Mary Lucy Fox Strangways, a granddaughter of the first Earl and Countess of Ilchester and the niece of Susan O'Brien, was born at Redlynch in 1776 and spent her early years there and at Melbury. She went to live at Penrice Castle in Glamorgan in 1794 after her marriage to its owner, Thomas Mansel Talbot. Mary was the mother of eight children, and the aunt of the photographic pioneer William Henry Fox Talbot (1800–1877), who spent much of his childhood at Penrice and Melbury with his aunts, uncles and cousins.

In addition to telling the story of the lives of these women and their families, *Wives and Daughters* describes life in four large country houses in the Georgian period. Until the twentieth century, when so many large estates were broken up, a country seat was the administrative centre of a family business, which would usually be based on renting out tenanted land, combined with operations such as farm management, property development and the exploitation of natural resources such as coal and iron. It was these activities that provided landowners with much of the money that they needed to contruct and furnish their mansions, and gave them the power base that enabled them to pursue their social and political ambitions. A large country house and its ornamental grounds stood as a symbol of the owner's influence and superior social position. Its symbolic significance was particularly great if the family had been in the same area for many decades, or even centuries, so that the house itself was filled with the portraits and coats of arms of relations and powerful friends, and the nearby church was dominated by the tombs of valiant and pious ancestors.

Though contemporaries complained about the decay of hospitality in the eighteenth century, the owners of great country houses continued to entertain important visitors – including members of the Royal Family – and many gave money and food to passers-by and to their poorer neighbours. Nor should the economic importance of a fully staffed and inhabited mansion be underestimated: many people from the surrounding area were employed in the house itself and on the estate, and earned a living by providing the landowner and his family with goods and services of all kinds.

The country house was also the landowning family's home – the place where they felt they belonged, even if they also had a house in London. It was at the family seat that many of them were born, where they grew up and reared their own children, and where they eventually died.

Thomas and Mary Talbot were my four-times-great grandparents, and I spent a part of of my own childhood at Penrice. Since the house has never been sold, nobody has ever cleared out the miscellaneous debris that every family accumulates over the years. When, as a history undergraduate, I had to write a dissertation, I had a largely unexplored archive all to myself. Instead of travelling to libraries and county record offices to look at books and documents, my research trips in the summer of 1973 involved spending many hours in the attics at Penrice, burrowing into packing cases, boxes and trunks, brushing off the dust, dead flies and bird-droppings that had accumulated since the eighteenth century, and trying to avoid the disintegrating corpses of birds and bats. Occasionally I would emerge triumphant with a bundle of letters, a volume of household accounts, or a book of faded photographs. There was far more material than I needed, and I always hoped that I would be able to do something more with it one day.

Most of the documents at Penrice were collected together in the mid nineteenth century by Charlotte Traherne, a daughter of Thomas Mansel Talbot and Mary Lucy Fox Strangways. Many of these papers had been sent to Mrs Traherne by her aunts, uncles and cousins, and I was therefore in the unusually fortunate position of having letters that had been written by the inhabitants of Penrice as well as those that had been sent to them. Of particular interest, too, were the letters and journals of Agnes Porter, the governess to the children of two generations of Lady Mary's family. These were edited by me and published in 1998 as *A Governess in the Age of Jane Austen.*

Since the 1970s I have worked on several more groups of family papers which complement those at Penrice. By no means all of the material relating to Penrice itself is in the house: there are collections of manuscripts in the West Glamorgan Record Office in Swansea, and in the National Library of Wales in Aberystwyth. The archives of the Fox Strangways family are divided, in a somewhat arbitrary manner, between the British Library (Holland House collection) and the Dorset County Record Office (Fox Strangways/Ilchester). Most of the family letters are in the British Library, and most of the estate papers and household accounts are in the Dorset Record Office. The Digby family archives at Sherborne Castle and in the Dorset Record Office provided useful material, as did the Lacock Abbey manuscripts. Some of the latter are now in the Wiltshire Record Office in Trowbridge, whilst others are in the Fox Talbot Museum in Lacock. The Holland House, Fox Strangways/Ilchester and Lacock Abbey collections are all vast, and none has been properly catalogued. Where the manuscripts in the Dorset and Wiltshire Record Offices are concerned, the researcher has to take pot-luck and order any boxes that look as if they might contain something of interest. This is very time-consuming, and it is not surprising that so few of the documents used for this book have been studied in any detail by previous researchers.

Taken all together, the amount of material that has survived is almost overwhelming. Thousands of letters, and several journals and memoirs, make it possible to build up a detailed picture of day-to-day life in these four country houses, from the accession of George II in 1727 to the death of George IV in 1830. In each one of these generations, daughters outnumbered sons, so a large proportion of the surviving letters and journals were written by women. I have therefore chosen to concentrate on the subjects that these women wrote about most frequently. These revolved mainly (though not exclusively) around their homes and their families: they exchanged information on medical matters; they worried about their children's education; and they described their journeys and visits to friends and relations. A love of flowers and gardens also united the women of successive generations of the Fox Strangways and Talbot families.

The subject-matter of the book also reflects my own interests: having been brought up in a Georgian house, and having also spent many hours as a teenager poking around museums and country houses with my grandparents, I have always been fascinated by the practical details of country house life. What did the houses look like? Who lived in them? How were the rooms used? How was the household organised? How many servants were there, and what did they do? What did people eat – and how did they spend their time? In an attempt to provide answers to these questions I have used a variety of additional documents, in particular a series of extraordinarily detailed eighteenth-century household accounts from Melbury, Redlynch and Penrice. The nature of these sources means that less attention is given to the role of these houses as 'temples of the arts' than is usual in accounts of country house history.[7]

Men are not entirely ignored, though a second book would be required to do justice to the subjects to which their letters most frequently refer, summarised by Amanda Vickery, in the introduction to her book *The Gentleman's Daughter*, as 'My gout is still bad; here is the gun dog I promised you; have you finished the will?'[8] The gentlemen of the eighteenth and early nineteenth centuries wrote mainly about politics and local administration, about estate management, and – most of all – about hunting and shooting. Their female contemporaries were not totally uninterested in these topics, but it is certainly true that they occupied a great deal less of their time and attention.

PART ONE

Daughters

1

Susanna

The parish of Melbury Sampford lies in west Dorset, about five miles from the border with Somerset, where the chalk downland which covers much of the centre of the county of Dorset begins to give way to a region of fertile, well-watered valleys, separated from each other by low limestone hills. In this area, on high ground to the north of the village of Evershot overlooking the Vale of Blackmore, the medieval owners of Melbury laid out a deer park and built their mansion house in what was, for the period, an unusually prominent position. Most great medieval houses, in Dorset as elsewhere, occupied sheltered valley sites.[1]

The house and estate have belonged to the Strangways family since 1500, when Henry Strangways bought the reversion of the manor of Melbury Sampford for £400, after marrying the widow of its previous owner, William Browning.[2] The Strangways line can be traced back to Thomas Strangways, who was born around 1430 and died in 1484. His family came from Strangeways, a hamlet in the parish of Cheetham near Manchester,[3] and he acquired Stinsford and other property in Dorset as a result of his marriage with Alionor Talboys, the heiress of the Stafford family of Hooke.[4]

It was under Henry's son Giles Strangways (*c.* 1486–1546), who held Melbury for more than forty years, that the family rose to the highest ranks of Dorset landowning society. After receiving a legal training,[5] Giles became an Esquire of the Body to the new King Henry VIII in 1509, and he spent most of the remainder of his life in the service of the Crown, both at Court and in the West Country. He fought in several campaigns in France between 1514 and 1544, and was present at the Field of Cloth of Gold in 1520. At home in Dorset, he was a Justice of the Peace from 1509 onwards, and he represented his native county in Parliament in 1529 and 1539.

Having become the owner of Melbury Sampford after his father's death in 1504, Giles Strangways also inherited Melbury Osmond around 1530. A few years later he was well placed to make further additions to his estates as one of Henry VIII's commissioners for the dissolution of the monasteries in Dorset. In 1543–44 he was granted the site of the recently dissolved monastery at Abbotsbury, together with the manors of Abbotsbury and East Elworth, for which he paid almost £2000.[6] Abbotsbury, which lies on the coast, about fifteen miles from Melbury, was a desirable acquisition in economic terms, but it was of sentimental value too, for Giles's father and grandparents had all been buried in the monastery's Lady chapel.

There were many gentlemen in the early sixteenth century who found that they needed a new house to reflect their family's recently acquired wealth and the enhanced social status that went with it, and Sir Giles Strangways (he was knighted in 1514) was no exception. He rebuilt the Brownings' medieval house next to the church at Melbury Sampford, using three thousand loads of golden limestone from the Ham Hill quarries nine miles away. When John Leland visited Melbury in 1542, he noted that 'Mr Strangeguayse hath now a late much buildid at Mylbyri *quadrato* [in the form of a quadrangle] advauncing the inner part of the house with a loftie and fresch tower'. The new house, square in shape and, for its day, unusually regular in its plan, was mainly on two storeys, with attics. It enclosed a central courtyard around which ran a corridor giving access to each of the rooms. The hexagonal prospect tower, which rose in two stages above the rest of the house, gave wide views over the fine deer park and the fertile and well-wooded countryside described by Leland.[7]

The descendants of Sir Giles Strangways continued to hold Melbury and Abbotsbury through the sixteenth and seventeenth centuries. His grandson, Sir John Strangways, died in 1666 aged eighty-two, having spent more than three years in the Tower during the Civil War, as a result of his steadfast support of the Royalist cause. The Parliamentarians had stormed his house at Abbotsbury in 1644, and Sir John had been taken prisoner and fined £10,000 for his 'delinquency'. His son and heir, another Giles Strangways, who had been imprisoned with his father, outlived Sir John by only fifteen years, dying in 1675 at the age of about sixty. At this time three of Giles's sons were alive: John, the eldest, aged about forty; Thomas, aged thirty-two; and Wadham, the youngest son, aged twenty-nine.[8] Thomas had just married an heiress, and the future prospects for the family appeared bright. But in a little over fifty years, after seven males of the family had died unmarried or without producing a surviving son, there were no male descendants of Sir John Strangways left.

John Strangways, Giles's eldest son, outlived his father by only ten months. He had done his best to produce an heir: following the death of his childless first wife in December 1675 he had waited only three months before marrying again, but had died just three weeks later. His heir was his recently-married brother Thomas, who moved into the old house at Melbury with his young wife Susanna Ridout.[9] Their family grew steadily: Susanna bore a total of five sons and four daughters. One boy and one girl died under the age of five, but the others survived the early years of childhood.

In 1676, therefore, Thomas Strangways inherited an estate that gave him an income of approximately £5000 a year.[10] A loyal Tory and a faithful supporter of the Church of England, he represented Dorset in the House of Commons for over thirty years without having to fight a single election. He finally stood down in favour of his elder son shortly before his death in 1713.[11] In 1692, with sons aged fifteen, ten, five and one, and a daughter of two, Thomas set about modernising and extending the old family home at Melbury.[12] They lived there together until 1713, when Thomas died at the age of seventy, leaving a widow, two sons and three daughters.

A series of further deaths in the next two decades was to have profound and far-reaching consequences for the Strangways family and the Melbury estate. The first death, in 1716, was that of John, the younger of Thomas and Susanna Strangways's two surviving sons. John was twenty-nine years old and a bachelor. Susanna's death in 1718 was followed in 1722 by that of a daughter, Judith Strangways, aged twenty-four. Another four years passed and the remaining members of the family went into mourning again after the death of the only surviving son, Thomas Strangways. Thomas was forty-four years old and had been married for sixteen years, but he and his wife had no children. The death of Thomas Strangways junior in 1726 changed everything, for it left his two surviving sisters, Susanna and Elizabeth, as the owners of the Melbury estate.[13]

In aristocratic families the birth of a daughter was not always greeted with undiluted joy. Whilst few parents would have expressed themselves quite as forcibly as Lord Hervey, who told Henry Fox in 1733 that 'Lady Hervey is brought to bed of a nasty, shabby girl',[14] many made it quite clear that they would have preferred a boy, especially if they already had several girls. In 1748 Charlotte Digby congratulated her brother, Lord Ilchester, on the birth of 'a pretty little girl' (his fourth daughter), but added, 'I dare say ... it would have been more welcome if it had been another [boy], but you will be fond of it when you are acquainted with it'. When yet another girl was born a little over a year later, Charlotte's son told his uncle, 'I wish with all my heart Lady Ilchester had brought forth a son instead of a daughter, for they are much more convenient things'.[15] Five years later Lord Ilchester was again 'in great hopes' of a son, but reported sadly that 'I have nothing but a little Frances Muriel'.[16] Lord Ilchester did at least have two sons by this time. His granddaughter Mary Talbot gave birth to no fewer than five daughters before her only son appeared on the scene. After the birth of the second girl, Mary's husband wrote to tell his cousin Henrietta Maria Hicks Beach that he intended to 'dance merrily all the night long on Thursday next', at a party to celebrate the baby's birth, but confessed 'if it was a boy I should hop around more nimbly'. Eighteen months later, shortly before another baby was due, Thomas tried not to be too optimistic, and told Mrs Hicks Beach's husband: 'Our little girls are both so very entertaining … that my wish for a son is not so very great as it has been, and if another of the wrong sort comes I shall not be in the dumps, but shall hope for better times in future.'[17] When the long-awaited son was at last born, Thomas was reported to be 'the happiest of men'.[18]

Every landowner hoped for a son and heir – preferably 'an heir and a spare' (or two) – who would inherit his name and coat of arms and take over the family estates. If he had no son, but several daughters, there was a risk that the property would be divided, or the family's wealth dissipated as a result of legal disputes. Various measures could be taken to avoid this. The estate might be entailed on a brother or nephew, bypassing the landowner's daughters altogether, though if this happened the girls would expect to receive generous dowries. When Thomas Strangways Horner of Mells died in 1741, leaving one daughter but no sons, his estates passed, according to his marriage settlement, to his brother. Under the settlement, which had been made in 1713, the sum of £7500 had been set aside to provide portions for younger children. One version of Thomas's will, made in 1724, specified that his only daughter Elizabeth should have an additional £9500 if she had no brothers. This would have given her a total dowry of £17,000, though this was reduced to £11,000 in another will made four years later. In the event, Thomas Horner left his daughter just ten guineas, after she had married without his consent.[19] Sometimes, the son of a daughter or sister might be chosen as the heir, often with the condition that he should take the surname and arms of his benefactor. Thomas Mansel Talbot, who married Mary Strangways in 1794, inherited the Penrice and Margam estates through his grandmother, a daughter of the first Lord Mansel.

Daughters had to be provided with dowries, so they took wealth out of the family. How well a girl married depended on her own physical attractiveness, her family's connections and the size of her dowry. In order to prevent the payment of daughters' portions from becoming too much of a burden on a family's resources, a maximum amount would usually be specified in the parents' marriage settlement. So, the more daughters a couple had, the smaller the dowry that each one would receive. The smaller her dowry was, the less likely it was that a girl would make a marriage that would extend her family's network of useful connections. A landowner who had several daughters was clearly at a disadvantage.

The vast majority of young women in eighteenth-century Britain (and their parents) saw marriage as their ultimate goal. Daughters were educated to be good wives, and very few girls chose to remain single. Marriage gave social status and a degree of financial independence. Even if a woman did not get on with her husband, there was a strong possibility that she would outlive him. If she had children of her own, she would have someone to look after her in old age. A spinster would probably have to remain in her father's or brother's house: even if she was entitled to a financial settlement, she might well find it difficult to extract the money due to her from her male relatives. Very few paid occupations were open to ladies at this time: some became housekeepers, paid companions or governesses, but such a loss of status could not normally be countenanced for the daughters of the landed elite.

For both men and women, the ideal marriage partner was physically attractive, wealthy, well-connected, good-natured and of at least equal social status. Georgian aristocrats lived most of their lives within a restricted circle in which everyone knew (or had a friend who knew), and gossiped about, everyone else. The family and friends of a young woman of marriageable age would make sure that they found out everything they could about potential suitors. When Edward Digby, son of William, Lord Digby, proposed to Charlotte Fox (the sister of Stephen and Henry Fox) early in 1729, Charlotte's family were concerned because Edward's elder brother, John Digby, was known to be mad. He had been disinherited as a result, but the Foxes were afraid that he might recover, in which case Edward would not inherit his father's estates. They were also worried that John might be suffering from some hereditary illness. So Dr John Wigan, the former tutor to Charlotte's two brothers, made enquiries about the Digbys, as he informed Henry Fox:

> Remembring his [Edward Digby's] elder brother's case, I was immediately inquisitive about the whole family, and am perswaded there is no reason to apprehend that one will recover, or the other lose his senses. Neither My Lord (what My Lady was, I don't hear) nor any of the other children, who are all long ago grown up, being in the least disordered proves the illness not hereditary.

Wigan believed that John Digby's illness 'was from mercury', which was commonly used to treat syphilis.[20]

In 1762, when Charles Bunbury was courting Lady Sarah Lennox, the girl's relations exchanged information about the young man and his family. Sarah told her best friend Susan Fox: 'My sister has heard that his father has an odness in his temper a little like madness. That's a shocking circumstance if it is realy like madness, but it may be only an odd temper, and that makes a great difference, you know.'[21] A few weeks later the sister,

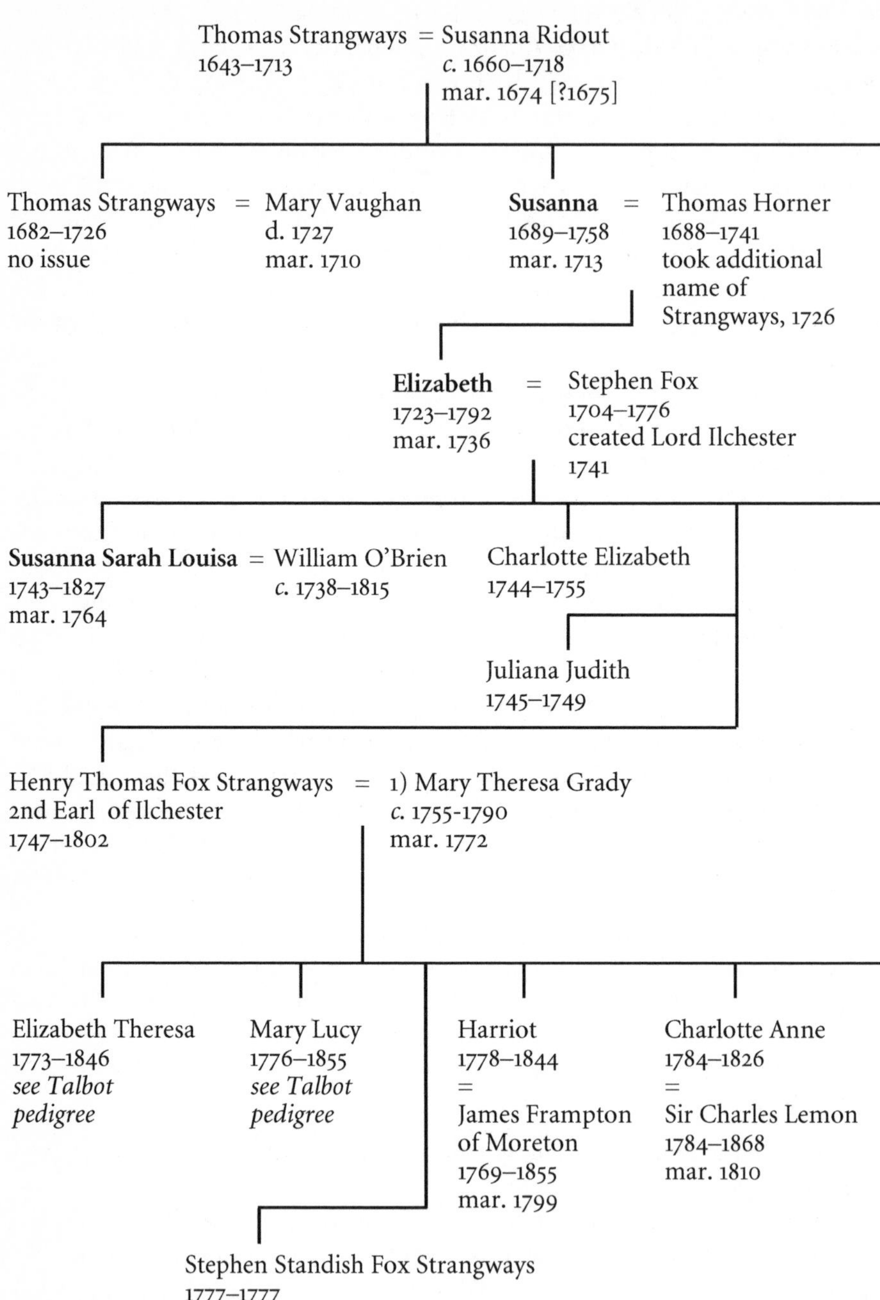

The Fox Strangways Family

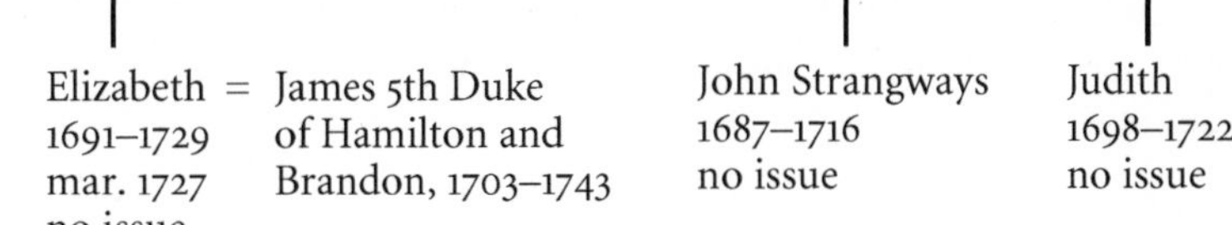

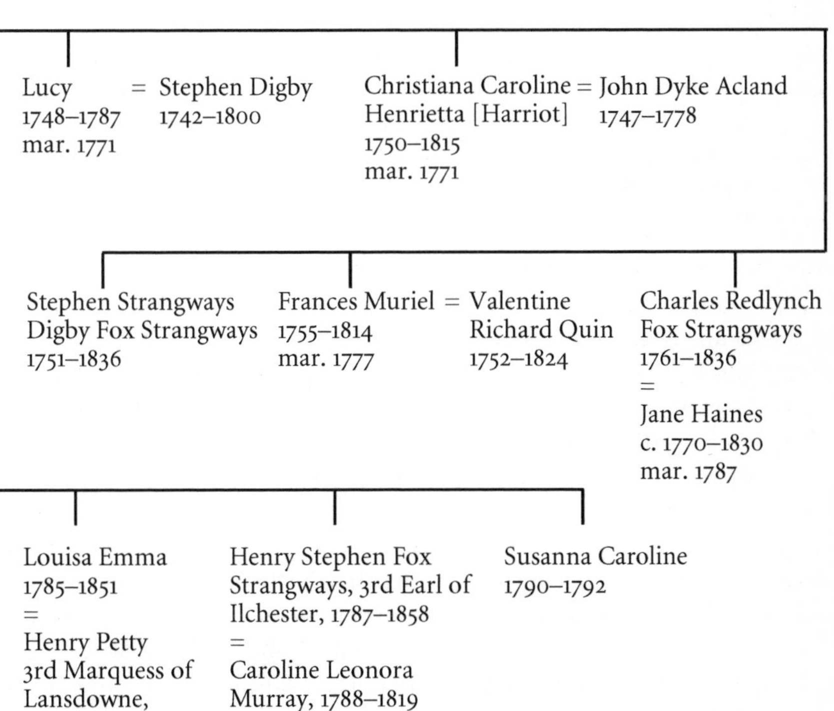

Louisa Emma
1785–1851
=
Henry Petty
3rd Marquess of
Lansdowne,
1780–1863
mar. 1808

Henry Stephen Fox
Strangways, 3rd Earl of
Ilchester, 1787–1858
=
Caroline Leonora
Murray, 1788–1819
mar. 1812

Susanna Caroline
1790–1792

Caroline Fox, still had doubts about Bunbury, but was determined to be optimistic about the (ultimately disastrous) match:

> Everybody speaks well of the young man. Lord Shelburne says he has an elegant, beautiful mind – I wish he could have added a plentiful fortune ... One should have wished pretty Sal a greater match, but there is enough to live with frugallity and she likes him, so I think one can't put her off ... following her own inclination.[22]

A young woman would be warned by her friends and parents to be wary of a man who was blatantly hunting for an heiress, and a wealthy woman of any age who chose to give herself to someone who had no money at all was likely to be condemned. In 1731 it was reported that the widowed Duchess of Cleveland, aged nearly seventy, was about to marry Philip Southcote, 'the Duke of Norfolk's cherry-cheeked Lead-Captain'. According to Lord Hervey:

> Such an exploit will make Her Grace's name ... as proverbial for ideocy as her defunct spouse's of foolish memory. The selling herself once to a fool with a great title and a great estate was a common, and consequently excusable, prostitution, but to buy a fool without either title or estate, and deprive her age of the comforts for which she sacrificed her youth, is a madness, a weakness, and an infamy which nobody can forgive her.[23]

Most people thought that it was important that two people who intended to marry should at least like, if not love, each other. In 1765 Susan O'Brien's friend Susanna Mackworth married John Hotham, 'a King's Messenger with a pretty good preferment, but not great, a small fortune, a very agreeable man and much in love with her, so that 'tis thought a pretty match for her'. A few months later, Susanna's sister Fanny married the only son of Lord Montagu, 'a very agreeable, good sort of man, an extreme good match for her, and they were in love with one another'.[24] Pleasant manners and an equable temperament were desirable attributes for both sexes, but for a woman it was particularly important that her husband should be good-natured. As Sarah Bunbury told Susan O'Brien when reporting the marriage of Frances Greville and John Crewe in 1766, 'I am sure you will be glad, for ... he is a very amiable man, and there is no harm in his having £10,000 a year, you know'.[25] It also helped if the bride's parents liked their future son-in-law. Susan O'Brien thought that there was a good chance that the marriage of Sophia Pitt and Lord Marsham in 1806 would be a success, because the groom suited Sophia's father, William Morton Pitt, 'as well as his daughter'. Both men had 'the same sentiments on all subjects of importance, the same religious principles, the same desire of doing good'.[26] Lord Marsham does, indeed, appear to have been the ideal son-in-law:

> He is extremely respected and very respectable; has good sense, good humour and good principles, all necessary ingredients to make the marriage state happy, and which do not often meet in the same person. He appears greatly attached to her and will, I trust, know how to value her many good and valuable qualities.[27]

Looks were of less importance for a man than for a woman. When the Dowager Duchess of Leinster married her children's tutor William Ogilvie in 1779, Sarah Lennox (the Duchess's sister) wrote 'I ... think him a very good sort of man ... but she certainly did not marry him *pour l'amour de ses beaux yeux*, for he is very ugly and has a disagreeable manner'.[28] Where a girl was concerned, however, a beautiful face and good manners could help to make up for a modest dowry. Conversely, a large dowry could make up for a lack of physical attractiveness. In 1732 Sarah, Duchess of Marlborough, described the kind of girl that she would like her grandson the Earl of Sunderland to marry:

> What I wished him was a woman with good sense, good humour, and good education; of a creditable family; not a flaming beauty, nor an Assembly-Lady, but she should be genteel and healthy; and for money, 'twas not a matter whether she had anything or nothing.[29]

The Earl ignored the Duchess's advice and married Elizabeth Trevor, who brought with her a dowry of £20,000. Sarah was horrified, and commented acerbically (and, no doubt, with some exaggeration):

> I think it a very improper match for a man that might have had anybody, without being at all in love with the person, to marry a woman whose father is a mighty ridiculous man, a family of beggars, and all very odd people. The woman herself... has been bred in a low way, and don't know how to behave herself upon any occasion, not at all pretty, and has a mean, ordinary look. As to the behaviour, if she has any sense that may mend. But they say she has very bad teeth, which, I think, is an objection alone in a wife. And they will be sure to grow worse in time.[30]

Life was certainly easier for a new bride if her husband's family liked and approved of her. Like the Earl of Sunderland, Ste Fox, the son of Lord and Lady Holland, chose his own wife – his match with Lady Mary Fitzpatrick was, in his mother's words, 'entirely his own doing'. Lady Mary was not a great heiress but, as a sister of the Earl of Upper Ossory and a niece of the Dowager Duchess of Bedford, she was well connected. A few weeks after the wedding, in April 1766, Lady Holland told her niece Susan O'Brien how delighted she was with her new daughter-in-law, 'A most amiable girl [who] has a universal good caracter, a superior understanding and a sweet temper'.[31] On the other hand, it was not unknown for a suitor to be put off by the behaviour of a girl's parents. In 1766 Lady Harrington, a woman who, according to Mrs Delany, had 'given her whole life up to vanity and folly',[32] was known to be on the look-out for a husband for her daughter Isabella. But, according to Sarah Bunbury, the dislike of Isabella's mother was 'so prevalent that it hurts her, and none of the young men have spirit enough to take her out of her mother's hands'. A few weeks later Lady Harrington was said to be 'as mad as a dog' because John Crewe had proposed to Frances Greville, instead of her daughter.[33]

During the last decade of the twentieth century much was written about the rise of 'affective individualism' in the eighteenth century. It was claimed that parental influence over the selection of a marriage partner was declining by the end of the century. As a result, men and women were more likely to be drawn to each other by personal attraction, and were beginning to be less concerned with the social and economic advancement of their family as a whole.[34] Other historians, however, disagreed, asserting that romantic attachments were by no means unknown in the first half of the century, whilst practical concerns were never entirely disregarded by later generations.[35] A study of the marriages of the Fox Strangways family and their friends certainly suggests that affection between husband and wife was always thought to be important. In 1734 Lord Hervey reported that Sir William Wyndham had recently married Lady Blandford, adding the comment that he could not understand why the bride had agreed to the match, since Sir William was 'neither young enough to be married for love, nor rich enough to be married for interest'.[36] In 1776 after the suicide of John Damer, the son of Lord Milton, Sarah Lennox thought that 'he had no more business to marry a girl he did not like than she had to accept a man she was totally indifferent to'.[37] As will be seen in the following chapters, people continued to marry for all kinds of reasons throughout the Georgian period – as they always have done – and love was rarely the only consideration.

In 1726 Melbury was inherited jointly by the two surviving sisters of Thomas Strangways junior. Susanna, the elder of the two, had married Thomas Horner of Mells in Somerset in 1713, a few weeks before her father's death.[38] At the time, the match had appeared to be a suitable one: the bride's father was wealthier than his new son-in-law, but he still had two other daughters and two sons to provide for. At nearly twenty-four, Susanna was of more than marriageable age,[39] and, judging from later portraits, she was no great beauty. Her husband, a colonel in the Somerset militia, had inherited the Mells estate on his father's death in 1708. According to a contemporary source,[40] Thomas Horner 'wanted money to pay his brother's fortune', and vowed that he would not marry a woman with a dowry of less than £10,000. Having been disappointed in his hopes of marrying Margaret Hippisley, the heiress of the Ston Easton estate, he had paid court to a number of prospective brides, including Miss Strangways, 'But when he found that the fortune would not rise to his expectations, he desisted from repeating his visits in hopes that the Lady Mother, who ruled all, would add a brace of thousands to the young lady's fortune'. Horner was back at Melbury a year later. Not surprisingly, he was greeted somewhat coolly by his bride-to-be, who displayed even at this early stage the independence of spirit that was to characterise her attitude to life in her later years. According to a story told by Susanna's maid:

> Miss Strangways made the tea, but it was contrived that the cup and saucer to be given Mr Horner was scalding hot. On receiving it into his hand 'Zounds', says he, 'it is damned hot!' 'I thought', says the lady in a very mild tone, 'it was very cold.' Every one present was sensible that the gentleman meant the tea; the lady meant the lover.

The marriage nevertheless took place shortly after this incident, and Thomas Horner had to make do with the not inconsiderable dowry of £7500.[41] It seems that money, convenience and the establishment of useful connections were the main considerations here. Love, affection even, hardly came into it.

It soon became evident that Thomas and Susanna Horner had little in common. Thomas Horner was, according to family tradition, 'a mere fox-hunter and spent his time between hunting and drinking'.[42] Susanna was clearly bored by her husband's hunting companions, preferring the company of her own friends and relatives, such as her cousin Charlotte Clayton. Charlotte, who was about ten years older than Susanna, had useful connections at Court: she was a Woman of the Bedchamber to Queen Caroline and subsequently became Mistress of the Robes. She knew John, Lord Hervey and Sarah, Duchess of Marlborough and was probably responsible for bringing Susanna into their circle.[43] An additional problem was Susanna's failure to present her husband with a male heir. Two sons were born and buried as infants: Thomas in 1717 and Strangways in 1721. Then, in February 1723, a daughter was born. She was named Elizabeth, after her father's mother and her mother's younger sister, and she alone survived.

Thomas and Susanna Horner took the additional name of Strangways in 1726 when Susanna and her sister Elizabeth inherited Melbury. Elizabeth was thirty-six years old, and still unmarried, at this time, but her new status as a wealthy heiress ensured that she did not remain a spinster for much longer. And the successful suitor on this occasion was not a country squire, like her brother-in-law, but a duke. Elizabeth Strangways became the second wife of James, fifth Duke of Hamilton and Brandon in 1727. The duke, who was several years younger than his bride, appears to have been an unpleasant man, and Elizabeth was apparently 'very miserable' with him.[44] But not for long: within two years she too was dead.

Until 1882, when the Married Women's Property Act was passed, a woman's estates usually passed to her husband when she married, and she would forfeit the right to make a will unless she was widowed. Under certain circumstances, however, a married woman could retain the right to bequeath any property that she had inherited, and the Strangways family had ensured that this would happen if Elizabeth predeceased her husband. Elizabeth, Duchess of Hamilton and Brandon, made her will on 24 October 1729, ten days before she died. Perhaps significantly, her husband is not mentioned at all, though Elizabeth left £300 a year each to his youngest brother and sister. Otherwise, apart from some minor bequests, everything was to go to her sister Susanna. The property was to be held for Susanna by three trustees, and the income from it was to be paid to her 'as if she were sole and unmarryed'. Thomas Horner was not to 'intermedle or have any power to dispose of or incumber the same or any part thereof'.[45] Thomas still had the power to 'intermedle' in his wife's original share of the Melbury estate, but her sister's death gave Susanna an unusual amount of financial independence for a married woman.

It was not long before Susanna Strangways Horner took advantage of her new-found freedom and left the West Country – and her dull, irascible husband – behind. Her travels are not well documented, but she and her daughter Elizabeth seem to have spent most of their time between 1731 and 1735 on the Continent. A letter written by Susanna to her cousin Charlotte Clayton in 1730 or 1731 gives an account of her first trip across the Channel. At this stage she was accompanied by her cousin Sir Robert Long of Draycot Cerne, Wiltshire, who was fifteen years her junior. There is no hint of any impropriety, and it seems most likely that he was merely a travelling companion. Their party landed at Dunkirk and then travelled through Flanders and Holland, stopping on the way to see the sights of Brussels, The Hague and Utrecht. Susanna enjoyed her trip through the Low Countries, and was particularly impressed by the Roman Catholic churches in The Hague, which, she thought 'cannot be exceeded by human art'. In later years she was to try to recreate some aspects of these buildings in the churches on her estate in Dorset.

In Utrecht Susanna consulted one Dr Boerhaave, who told her that 'All my illness proceeds from a humour still left and fluctuating in my liver, with a total relaxation or weakness'. He recommended 'the Spa water, if it agreed with me, as much exercise as my strength will bear, and a warm climate where the perspiration is free and open'. After Utrecht, therefore, the party turned south to the village of Spa in the Ardennes. Susanna's initial impressions of Spa were not favourable, as she told Charlotte Clayton:

> The situation of this place is romantic and wild, but the most detestable little village I ever saw. The regimen everybody keeps that drinks the waters, I fancy you will not envy. We rise at five in the morning, drink the waters three miles from the village, and starve with the cold. Reading and writing is prohibited ... One must not sleep, though the effects of the waters are such as make it hardly possible to avoid it. If one does sleep, it is a chance if ever one wakes. At dinner, we are to eat nothing but roast meat, as dry as a stick; at supper a little weak broth with bread, pretty thick. Go to bed at nine, dine at twelve, sup at seven. Thus us poor mortals breathe, for living it is not. Thinking, too, is debarred, so that however incoherent this letter is, or tedious, as a water-drinker I hope not to be blamed.[46]

In spite of its obvious discomforts, Spa was the most popular continental watering-place for British tourists at this time, and the visitors were able to enjoy a lively social life in addition to the benefits of taking the waters. Susanna told her cousin that she had spent the first few afternoons after her arrival there 'in receiving visits, from the gentlemen as well as ladies, from people known and people unknown; amongst the rest are a vast many English, as well as Scotch'. In August 1732 it was reported that there were nearly a hundred English gentlemen and ladies in the town.[47]

By the summer of 1732 Susanna and Elizabeth had been joined by Henry Fox, the younger son of Sir Stephen Fox, who had died in 1716 at the great age of eighty-nine, having made an vast fortune as a financial entrepreneur and government servant. Susanna and Henry had known each other for several years before 1732: Henry was a regular visitor to his elder brother Stephen Fox's house at Redlynch in Somerset, which is only four or five miles from Milton Clevedon, where Susanna's mother and her two unmarried daughters had gone to live after the death of Susanna's father in 1713. Henry became a trusted friend of Susanna's sister the Duchess of Hamilton and Brandon, and he was named in October 1729 as one of her trustees and executors. His duties as a trustee of part of the Melbury estate would have brought Henry into regular contact with Susanna over the next few years. His first known visit to Mells took place in January 1730, when he wrote to his brother Stephen complaining of his lack of success during a shooting expedition, but he may well have been there before.

Henry's stay in Spa did not last long, for he was back in England by the middle of September. Susanna and her daughter also left Spa, but they travelled next to Italy, the most popular destination for British tourists at this time. They were in Naples by January 1733, when Susanna wrote to Lord Hervey describing an earthquake, and they seem to have stayed there for several months. They were certainly in Naples for long enough to have a double portrait painted by a local artist, Francesco Solimena.[48] In this portrait, which is still at Melbury, Susanna – aged forty-three – appears confident and relaxed. She looks robust, even though she was still supposed to be travelling for health reasons. Susanna stares determinedly at the onlooker, unlike her ten-year-old daughter, who looks pale and delicate. Elizabeth seems shy, her gaze withdrawn, both from her mother and from everyone else.

Henry Fox left England again in July 1733. This time his destination was Paris, where he was joined by his sister Charlotte and her husband, Edward Digby – and Susanna Strangways Horner. After a few weeks in Paris, Susanna and Elizabeth went to Nice in the south of France, where they were to stay for almost two years. Henry Fox was with them for much of this time. One reason for Henry's prolonged stay on the Continent may well have been the need to evade his creditors, but it was widely believed that he and Susanna were lovers. Lord Chesterfield described Susanna as 'a very salacious Englishwoman, whose liberality restored [Mr Fox's] fortune, with several circumstances more to the honour of his vigour than his morals'.[49] Whether he could best be described as her lover or her protégé, Susanna appears to have been trying to 'improve' Henry. She wrote in January 1735 to tell Stephen Fox that 'he studys very hard, and I don't know but I may make a great man of him'.[50] A few months later they all returned to England. Henry had to take up his duties in the House of Commons, having succeeded his brother as Member of Parliament for the notoriously venal borough of Hindon in Wiltshire in February,[51] whilst Susanna had other matters on her mind. Her daughter was now twelve years old, and potential suitors (and their parents) were already beginning to show an interest in the girl – or, more accurately, in her fortune.

2

Elizabeth

Elizabeth Strangways Horner was born in 1723. When she was an old woman, she told her grandchildren about her early upbringing, which had been somewhat unusual:

> She was the youngest child. The seven others had all died infants, and poor Mrs Horner, in despair at her repeated losses and seeing the keeper's wife at the high lodge at Melbury with a good half dozen of rosy children, determined to entrust her darling with this woman and made a vow not to interfere. Accordingly, the little Elizabeth was transferred to the lodge, with strict instructions that she was to be treated in all respects like one of the woman's own children. Mrs Horner went to see her every day, and had often great difficulty in keeping her vow when she saw her darling with a dirty, greasy pinafore, sucking a long bit of bacon or a bone. However, the child remained there till two years old, and came home very stout and well.[1]

Elizabeth had spent the next few years at Mells and Melbury with her parents. Then, from the age of about seven, she had trailed around Europe in her mother's wake, with little or no opportunity to spend time with other children. As her own daughter Susan O'Brien later wrote:

> Never having passed her youth with equals or companions of her own age or rank [my mother] knew nothing of the intimacies and friendships of children and youthful minds ... An only child, and heiress of a large fortune, she was much indulged and flattered by inferiors to whom she was consigned and by whom she was surrounded.[2]

Susanna Strangways Horner and her daughter returned to England from their continental travels in the summer of 1735. Though Elizabeth was only twelve years old, her parents were both keen to find a husband for her. Unfortunately for the young girl, the subject of her marriage soon proved to be an explosive source of conflict between Thomas and Susanna, whose already strained relationship cannot have been improved by Susanna's dalliance with Henry Fox. Each wanted a son-in-law whom they could control, and who would be an ally in the internecine war that was bound to follow.

In July, Susanna took her daughter to see the Queen – dressed in a 'coat', as she did not have a suitable gown. Thomas Horner joined his wife and daughter in London, and the quarrels soon started. As Susanna told Lady Sundon:

> Mr Horner ... is just the same man he ever was, and in the morning will marry his daughter immediately; at night will not marry her till she is between twenty and thirty. My constant and steady purpose is to close in with any match he will approve of likely to make her happy, and to wait with patience till such a temper of mind shall, among the great variety, begin to appear.[3]

In another letter, written ten days later, Susanna reported, 'Mr Horner has the oddest intention now, which is not to marry his daughter but to somebody that will live in the house with *him*'.[4] Surprisingly, the suitors were not all frightened off by the behaviour of the girl's parents. One possible husband was the Duke of Leeds; another was Lord Middlesex, the son of the Duke of Dorset. Both young men were in their early twenties, and the fact that they could even be considered as prospective husbands for Elizabeth, whose father had no title, underlines the attractiveness of the girl's fortune.

By mid November Susanna had set her sights on a potential son-in-law, and negotiations had begun. The man in question was Stephen Fox, Henry's elder brother, who was thirty-one years old. Susanna had begun to correspond with Stephen whilst she and Henry were in the south of France,[5] and it may well have been Henry who suggested the match in the first place, but the proposal to Stephen seems to have been made by Susanna. She also consulted her friend Charlotte Digby, the sister of the Fox brothers. Charlotte, who seems to have had some doubts about Elizabeth's suitability, spent several weeks in Bath with Susanna and Elizabeth towards the end of 1735.[6] In the meantime, the hostilities between Elizabeth's parents continued. Thomas does appear to have been a particularly difficult man: he visited his wife and daughter in Bath and told them that there was a smallpox epidemic at Mells and that he was glad that Elizabeth was not there. He then returned to Mells and sent for the girl three days later. When her mother asked him to make sure that Elizabeth had no contact with the people in the village, Thomas wrote her a 'harsh, unreasonable, angry letter' and said that he could take care of his daughter as well as her mother. Elizabeth went to Mells, but her father saw her for only half an hour on the day she arrived, and then took her back to Bath on the following day. At least she had some fun whilst she was in Bath: Susanna felt unable to visit the Rooms or Assembly Houses, where balls and other social gatherings took place, but Elizabeth was able to go there with Mrs Digby. In a letter to Lady Sundon, Susanna expressed the hope that 'seeing so much of what is called entertainment now will make her less eager for public places when she is first married'.[7]

Thomas certainly knew something of the negotiations with Stephen Fox, and he was implacably opposed to the proposed match. So Susanna simply ignored him. The Strangways version of the subsequent events, as written down by a member of the family in the nineteenth century, tells how Susanna, fearing that her husband might 'take a freak' of marrying his 'little treasure' to 'one of his boon [hunting and drinking] companions', decided to forestall him and make sure that Elizabeth was safely settled before her father knew anything about it.[8]

It was on 15 March 1736 that Susanna Strangways Horner pulled off a dramatic *coup* when her daughter Elizabeth, now aged just thirteen, was married to Stephen Fox. The marriage took place in secret in 'the library below stairs' of Fox's London house in Burlington Street.[9] Before entering the house, little Elizabeth 'was lifted up to knock at the door of her future husband with her own hand by way of proof of voluntary consent'.[10] The ceremony was performed by a tame clergyman, Peter Lewis Willemin,[11] and the witnesses were John, Lord Hervey; the bridegroom's sister, Charlotte Digby; and the bride's mother. Once the ceremony was over, the bride returned with her mother to their house in Grosvenor Street.

After the wedding, Susanna set about covering her tracks. Amongst the Fox Strangways family papers are copies of three letters, all apparently written by Susanna on 20 March 1736. We cannot be sure that they were actually sent, but they show how her mind was working. In one letter (intended, presumably, to be seen by Thomas Horner), she wrote to tell Stephen Fox of her husband's answer to Fox's proposal to her daughter. She had, she said, not expected the answer to be favourable, but it was 'more the contrary than I could have imagined'. There was no hope of alteration, and Susanna asked Fox to 'desist from any future thoughts of this kind' and not to attempt to see her or Elizabeth 'till she may be settled'. At the same time Susanna sent Fox another letter, but this one was clearly not for her husband's eyes. 'If', she told Fox, 'you don't keep your word with me, I will in earnest never pardon you.' With this second letter Susanna enclosed a draft of a letter that her son-in-law was to send to her. In it he was to inform Susanna that he and Elizabeth were married. He was then to continue as follows:

> I hope in God you had no objection but Mr Horner's not consenting. I knew you would not get over that, and therefore did not sollicit yours after he had not only refused, but in so rough and uncivil a manner denyed his consent. I saw there were no great hopes of ever gaining him to alter his opinion of me which I may, however, flatter myself is not thoroughly well-grounded, and I will, by my behaviour to his daughter, make it my business to shew that, if

I do not quite deserve her, I have some more merit towards it than he will allow me.

Fox was directed to send this letter on the 'night of the enterprize'. The 'enterprize' concerned was a second ceremony, which took on 22 March, also at the house in Burlington Street, but in 'the red damask room up one pair of stairs'. Susanna presumably hoped that her husband would believe that Fox had eloped with Elizabeth, but she also needed to rule out any possibility of the marriage being declared illegal – anticipating, no doubt, that her husband would do his best to ensure that this was exactly what happened. So Susanna does not appear as a witness on 22 March, nor does Charlotte Digby. The second marriage was witnessed by four close friends of the Fox brothers: John, Lord Hervey; Lucius, seventh Viscount Falkland; Thomas Winnington; and Charles Hamilton, the youngest son of the sixth Earl of Abercorn.[12]

Within a couple of days everyone knew about the wedding. It was reported in the *Daily Advertiser* of 24 March, and soon afterward Lord Gower wrote to tell a friend:

The Town is at present very much entertained with little Stephen Fox's wedding, who on Monday night last run away with the great fortune Miss Horner, who is but just thirteen years old and very low and childish of her age.[13]

On 28 March Stephen Fox wrote again to his father-in-law, assuring him 'that I did, and do, love your daughter extremely' and vowing to be 'a good husband to your daughter, ever full of dutyfull regard to you [and] ready to come into what ever settlement you and Mrs Horner shall think proper'.[14] Again, it is not known if the letter was actually sent, but it is difficult to believe that Susanna had no hand in it. Predictably enough, Thomas Horner was furious when the news of his daughter's marriage reached him. He had been made to look a fool: his opposition to the match was well known, and the fact that the bridegroom was the brother of the man who had cuckolded him served only to rub salt into his wounds.

On the face of it, the match was not a bad one. The bride was, admittedly, unusually young, though it was legal for a girl to marry at the age of twelve with a parent's consent. Where wealth was concerned, Stephen Fox had inherited property which might be expected to produce about £6500 a year,[15] an income which placed him on approximately the same level as the Strangways family. Moreover, the Fox estates in Wiltshire and Somerset complemented the Strangways lands in Dorset and Somerset very nicely. As it turned out, Fox did not benefit greatly from the Strangways properties during the first twenty years of his marriage, whilst Susanna was still alive. Under their marriage settlement, the newly-married couple were to receive the income from the Duchess of Hamilton's share of the estate, but this was heavily encumbered with debts and legacies. In return Elizabeth, would be paid a jointure of £1500 a year from her husband's estates if she were to become become a widow, and the sum of £20,000 was set aside to provide portions for younger children.[16]

But there were other difficulties. The Strangways and Horner families could both be traced back to the fifteenth century, and Elizabeth's ancestors had been substantial landowners and leaders of county society for many generations. The Foxes, on the other hand, could only be described as nouveaux riches. Stephen's father had been born in almost complete obscurity at Farley in Wiltshire, one of ten children of a couple who were respectable but apparently living in near poverty. Sir Stephen Fox (as he became in 1665) had risen from the position of page boy to become the contemporary equivalent of a millionaire due to an extraordinary combination of first-rate ability and good luck. Having been appointed to manage the finances of Charles II in 1654 whilst the Court was in exile in France, Fox had returned to England with his royal master in 1660, and had been largely responsible for managing the nation's finances over a period of more than twenty years, occupying the position of Paymaster of the Guards from 1661 to 1680, and eventually becoming First Lord of the Treasury for a brief period. It is highly likely that he turned down the offer of a peerage on more than one occasion. Nevertheless, Fox's contemporaries never forgot his humble origins, even though his reputation for rectitude and integrity remained unblemished. Elizabeth Horner's new husband was rich, but he was not quite respectable.[17]

Then there was the problem of Lord Hervey. Hervey, born in 1696, was the eldest son of John Hervey of Ickworth in Suffolk (who became Baron Hervey in 1703 and Earl of Bristol in 1714) by his second wife. On the death of his elder half-brother Carr Hervey in 1723, John succeeded to the courtesy title of Lord Hervey. A Whig, he was elected Member of Parliament for Bury St Edmunds in 1725 and soon joined the influential circle around Sir Robert Walpole and Queen Caroline, the wife of George II. It was not long after this that he became friendly with the Fox brothers and their sister Charlotte. Hervey had been a nervy, sickly child, and he suffered from ill-health (real or imagined) on and off throughout his life. Promiscuous, effeminate in appearance and bisexual, marriage in 1720 had not prevented him from engaging in extramarital relationships with both men and women. He paid frequent visits to Bath, and it may have been there that he first made the acquaintance of Henry Fox, probably in 1726. It was not until some months later that he first met Stephen.

In many ways Hervey had more in common with Henry Fox than with his brother. Henry was good-looking, gregarious and an opportunist like Hervey, whilst Stephen was shy and totally lacking in ambition. He aimed to pass his life 'with tranquillity and obscurity', and he was content to spend his time in the country, planning improvements to his house and grounds, riding around his estates, and hunting and shooting with his friends.[18] He was not greatly interested in politics or in London gossip – subjects which absorbed much of Hervey's attention. Henry was attractive to, and attracted by, women, whilst Stephen was not so obviously masculine. Physically, he gave the impression of being much less robust than his brother. Like Lord Hervey, Stephen was slightly built, with small bones and a rather delicate appearance. Lord Hervey appears to have fallen for Stephen almost immediately. Much later, in 1737 he told his friend, 'I have loved you ever since I knew you ... much better than most people are capable of loving any thing'.[19] There is some evidence that the friendship between Lord Hervey and Stephen Fox developed into a physical relationship, though the exact nature of this is necessarily obscure.[20] Stephen's letters to Lord Hervey have not survived, and it is therefore impossible to tell exactly what his feelings towards the older man may have been. He was, in any case, much more reserved than Hervey, and it seems unlikely that his letters would have been filled with tender expressions of love, as Hervey's were. But when Hervey fell ill in the autumn of 1727 it was Stephen, rather than Lady Hervey, who looked after him, taking him first to Redlynch and then to Bath. During the next few years the two men spent as much time together as their different commitments would allow.

Lord Hervey and Stephen Fox were on the Continent together from July 1728 to September 1729, travelling to Spa, Paris, Rome, Naples and Florence. The reason – or excuse – for their journey was Hervey's poor health: he fell seriously ill whilst they were in Naples, and Stephen nursed him devotedly – so much so that Hervey was certain that his friend had saved his life. After their return to England, Hervey pursued a political career in London, whilst Stephen retreated to Somerset. Lord Hervey's letters over the next few years are full of complaints about Stephen's reluctance to come to Town, but the two men still saw a good deal of each other, and Hervey continued to exert a powerful influence over the younger man. Stephen's father had been a Tory and Stephen had himself first entered the House of Commons as a Tory in 1726. But, after 1730, he – like Hervey – became a supporter of Walpole's Whig government. Henry Fox, too, saw that the opportunities for advancement as a Tory were few and far between and went over to the Whigs, following the same route as another close friend, Thomas Winnington, the MP for Droitwich. Winnington, who like Lord Hervey was known for his loose morals, made friends and enemies in equal numbers. Horace Walpole wrote in his memoirs of Winnington's good humour and wit, but also of his lack of principles. It was, he said, 'impossible to hate or trust him'.[21] Other members of the same set were Charles, Earl of Sunderland,[22] grandson of the Duchess of Marlborough, and his brother-in-law William, Viscount Bateman.

Given the company that he kept, and his change of political allegiance, it is hardly surprising that the idea of having Stephen Fox as a son-in-law was abhorrent to Thomas Horner. Horner was an old-fashioned, backwoods Tory with Jacobite sympathies. Although he was a Member of Parliament for Somerset on and off from 1713 to 1741, he spent little time in London and 'left no mark on Commons proceedings'.[23] He was most at home in the country: he and his hunting companions might have read of the activities of effete London-based aristocrats such as Hervey with horrified fascination, but they would certainly not have wanted a daughter to marry one of them. Stephen Fox and Elizabeth Strangways Horner were, however, legally married.

Stephen's motives in agreeing to the match with Elizabeth were not entirely mercenary, for he was wealthy in his own right, and – unlike his younger brother – he had not lost money at the gaming-tables. His relationship with Lord Hervey had cooled by 1735, though they were still close friends. It was, perhaps, in recognition of the weakening of his hold over his friend that Lord Hervey chose to promote the match with Elizabeth. He acknowledged that Stephen 'wanted that domestic appurtenance to a married life called *a home to go to*'. Hervey – who had married, apparently for love, a woman who had brought him only a small fortune – recommended that Stephen should look for a wealthy bride. He may have betrayed his own disappointment when he told his friend's sister:

> The first thing that ought to be considered by those who marry, merely because they choose a married life, is fortune. I never said, if one knew anything very bad of a woman's temper or morals, that money in one scale ought to be looked upon as a balance to any qualities you could put into the other ... But I did say, and continue to say, that the fortune may be a certainty, and that for the rest you must take your chance, for there is no getting a wife bespoke – you must take her ready-made.[24]

Stephen may have hoped that he had a better prospect of happiness with a young bride, whose character he could mould to suit his own, than with an older and more experienced woman. It seems unlikely that anyone really bothered to consider what Elizabeth thought of all this. An apologetic letter to her father, written a week or two after her wedding, must have been dictated by Susanna:

> I don't know what to say for myself, dear Papa, but I assure and promise you that if you can forgive me what I have done I will never again willingly offend

you. I know I have done wrong, but if you and Mama could forgive me, my fault would turn to my own happiness and I could never be tempted to do wrong any more, since, by doing right towards you, I shall now equally please my Mama and you and Mr Fox. Indeed, Papa, if you can forgive this want of duty, you shall never have another instance to complain of in your most affectionate and most humble daughter and servant, E. Fox.[25]

In a recent account of the Horner family, the clandestine marriage of Stephen Fox and Elizabeth Strangways Horner is described as 'a family tragedy'.[26] A tragedy it may have been for the Horners, for they lost any claim to the Melbury estate, but Susanna's choice of Stephen Fox was a stroke of genius from her own family's point of view. Ever conscious of her responsibilities as 'the last of her family and name' as she was,[27] she secured the survival of her family name and estates by selecting a son-in-law who had plenty of money, but lacked an illustrious pedigree stretching back into the middle ages. There can be no doubt that the expectation that he and his wife would eventually inherit Melbury helped to secure a peerage for Stephen in 1741. This was acknowledged after Susanna's death in 1758, when her son-in-law changed his surname to Fox Strangways, and took the Strangways coat of arms.[28] For visitors to Melbury in the second half of the eighteenth century, the importance of the Strangways inheritance was underlined by the many family portraits hanging in the principal rooms of the mansion, and by the coats of arms of Susanna's ancestors, which were prominently displayed in the house and church. Significantly, descriptions of the interior of Melbury at this time include few references to the Horner arms.[29] Had Elizabeth Strangways Horner been married to a duke, as her aunt had been, the importance of her own lineage would have been diminished.[30]

For the first three years after the wedding the newly-married Mrs Fox continued to live with her mother, seeing her husband occasionally – but only when her father was out of the way. During this time Stephen and Elizabeth communicated mainly by letter. Elizabeth's earliest surviving letter to her husband, written in October 1736, shows a romantic, if somewhat naive, attachment to him. She addresses him as 'My dearest dear Mr Fox', and tells him that 'to be kept seperate from you afflicts me more than you can possibly imagine'. The letter finishes with the words 'I am in a melancholy way, and can add no more than that I am happy only in being yours, which I am most fondly and faithfully'.[31] In another letter, written in 1736 or 1737, Elizabeth assures her husband:

My heart and inclination is honestly, fondly and intirely yours, and in me you may always be sure of the full possession of my love, and it will not be a vast

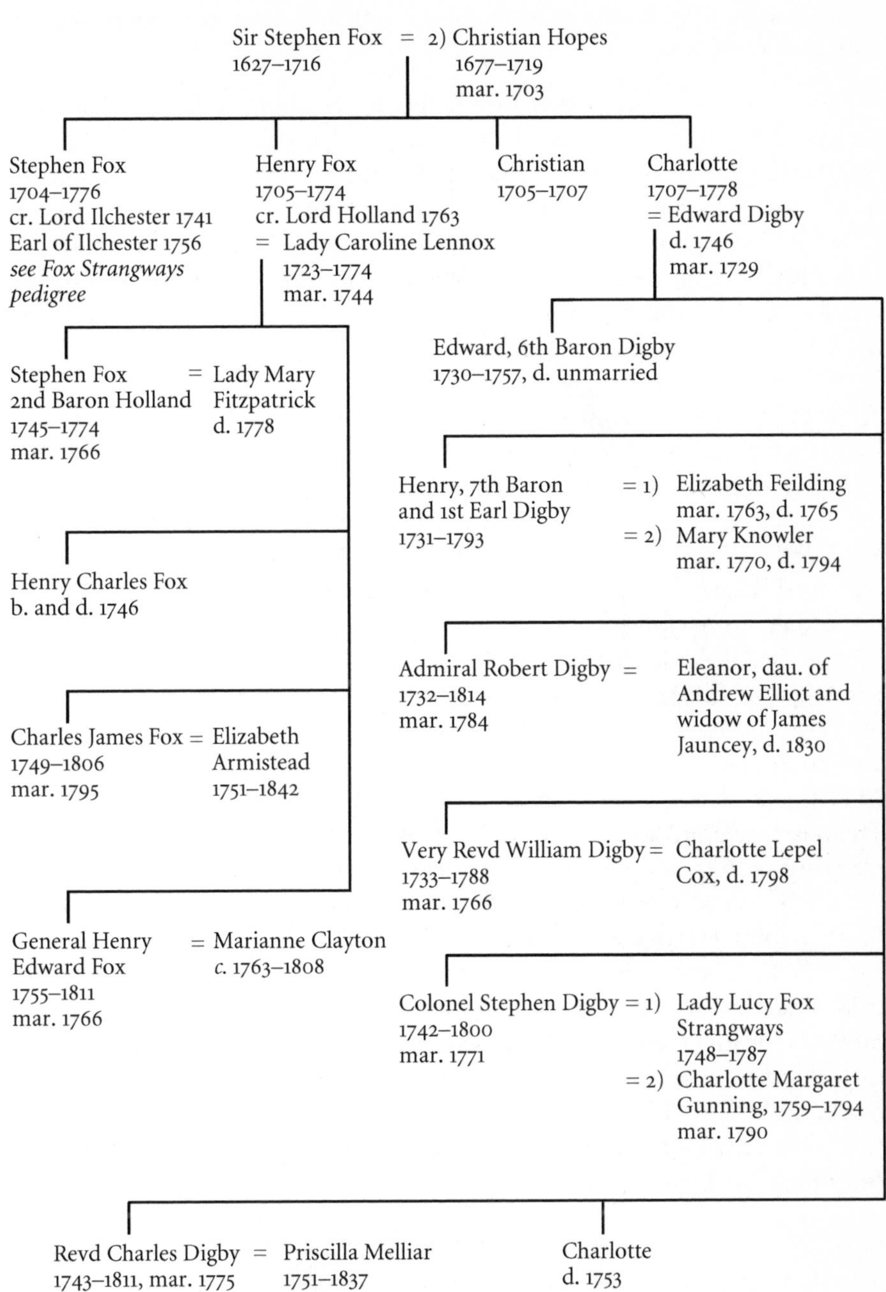

The Fox and Digby Families

> while I hope before, with Mama's consent, we shall be every thing we wish to be to one another.[32]

If Stephen Fox ever wrote any love letters to his child-bride, they have not survived. He later commented on Elizabeth's capriciousness, as did her eldest daughter Susan, who wrote of the misery that this had brought to those closest to her.[33] As early as 1742, Stephen told Lord Hervey to 'remember that opposition is like matrimony: scarce anyone ever embarked in it without being heartily tired'.[34] Stephen Fox's relationship with his wife was founded on mutual interest and some affection, but it could certainly not be described as a love match.

Thomas Strangways Horner and his wife continued to live largely separate lives after their daughter's wedding.[35] Horace Walpole later claimed that 'rich Mrs Horner' had 'kept' Henry Fox until about 1741.[36] This may or may not have been true: as Susanna's granddaughter wrote many years afterwards, Walpole 'was not a school of good nature',[37] but they certainly remained friends. Thomas never forgave his daughter for marrying against his wishes. In a vindictive will, written a year before his death at the end of 1741, he directed that, unless Elizabeth agreed to forego the dowry of £7500 out of the Mells estate to which she was entitled under her parents' marriage settlement, 'all the plate, furniture, pictures, paintings, drawings and household goods which shall be at the time of my decease of any of [the] houses late of the Strangways' should be sold after Susanna's death. Thomas could not even bring himself to mention his daughter by name, referring to her as 'my daughter, the wife of Stephen Fox Esq.' He left Elizabeth precisely ten guineas. In contrast, each of the daughters of his brother John Horner was to receive £1000 when she married or came of age.[38] In the event, this clause was deemed to be invalid, and John Horner paid £7500 to his niece and her husband within a couple of years of his brother's death. He also paid his sister-in-law the jointure of £800 a year to which she was entitled. Wrangling over Susanna's claims on the Mells estate, and the division of the family silver (which included some items on which the arms of both the Horner and Strangways families were engraved) continued for many years.[39]

In the summer of 1739, when she was sixteen, Elizabeth Fox left her mother's household at Melbury and moved into her husband's mansion at Redlynch in Somerset. Redlynch was to be her home until her mother's death twenty years later. The estate lies in well-wooded country on the eastern edge of the Vale of Blackmore, two miles from Bruton. Sir Stephen Fox, Stephen's father, had bought the property in 1672, paying £8700 for the manor of Redlynch, with a substantial mansion and over 480 acres of demesne land, in addition to a large number of smaller holdings and cottages which were leased out to tenants. The house was pleasantly situated overlooking a valley, with meadows, pasture and woodland, but it was old-fashioned and apparently in poor condition when Sir Stephen acquired it. One bedchamber is named the 'Castle of Sparrows' in an inventory of 1683, which suggests that it may have been semi-derelict.[40] Sir Stephen never lived in the house, and he lost interest in building up his West Country estates in the 1680s when it became apparent that Charles Fox, his only surviving son by his first wife, was unlikely to produce an heir. He contemplated selling Redlynch, but eventually changed his mind and decided to keep the house and estate after all.[41]

Sir Stephen's second marriage, to Christian Hopes in 1703, was followed by the birth of two more sons, Stephen and Henry, in 1704 and 1705. This led him to take a new interest in Redlynch. If, as he hoped, the elder of these sons was eventually to take his place in society as the owner of a great landed estate, he would need a suitable country seat. The old house at Redlynch, which had been neglected for so many years, was therefore to be rebuilt, apparently under the direction of Thomas Fort, son of Alexander Fort, the Master Joiner in the Office of Works, who had worked at several royal palaces and had also been employed by Sir Stephen for building projects at Chiswick, and at Farley in Wiltshire.[42]

In 1708 or 1709 work began on a new west-facing building of local limestone, for which Thomas Fort was paid at least £1400.[43] Most historians have assumed that the old house at Redlynch was demolished at this time,[44] but contemporary records suggest that much of it remained standing, and that the new block was attached to its western front. A 'particular' of Sir Stephen Fox's estate made in 1712 refers to 'the mansion house at Redlynch newly erected, together with the antient buildings thereunto adjoining'.[45] The estate accounts show that the old house was being repaired in 1714 and 1715, when windows were mended, curtains were cleaned, the old beds were refurbished, and new beds were sent down from London. Payments to plumbers at this time suggest that the gravity-fed piped water supply to the house and offices was being installed, or possibly extended.[46]

The new building at Redlynch was still unfinished when Sir Stephen Fox died in 1716. Stephen, his elder son and heir, was a twelve-year-old schoolboy at Eton, and he would not need a country house for several years. As a result, work seems to have come to a virtual halt, though some money had to be spent to prevent the structure from falling down: in 1718 Richard Baker was paid £1 16*s*. 'for iron cramps, [and] rings and sprigs to fix on the said cramps, to support and strengthen the timber work over the new buildings at Redlynch'. The house remained largely unoccupied whilst its young owner completed his education at Oxford and on the Continent, though repairs were carried out when necessary: there are payments to tilers and carpenters, and to a plumber and glazier for mending the water pipes, the cistern in the brewhouse, and windows in the house, chapel and stables. In 1723 the sum of £29 10*s*. was paid to 'Mr Ireson ... for securing Redlinch house from fire, by taking out the beames in the chimnys'.[47] This is the first reference to the master builder Nathaniel Ireson, who was living at Stourton at the time, working on Stourhead House for Henry Hoare. Ireson was to be employed at Redlynch on and off for the next thirty years.[48]

In 1725 Stephen Fox came of age, and from this time onwards he spent an increasing amount of time in Somerset, making a home at Redlynch for himself and his younger brother and sister. In 1729, at the age of twenty-one, his sister Charlotte married Edward Digby, the son and heir presumptive of William, fifth Lord Digby.[49] With both parents dead, Charlotte was free to choose her husband, and a dowry of £13,000 ensured that she had received plenty of offers. In the event, she chose a man whom both of her brothers knew and liked, and who (barring an unexpected recovery by his lunatic brother) was the heir to the Sherborne Castle estate, only twelve miles from Redlynch. In 1729 Dr John Wigan wrote that Edward Digby was 'so unexceptionable that I shall find Miss mad if she don't accept of him'.[50] The marriage seems to have been a happy one, and Charlotte was devastated when her husband died in 1746, writing shortly afterwards, 'Nothing can add to my present misery. It is too great to continue in this state: it must either abate or I must sink under it.'[51]

By 1727, Stephen Fox had begun to alter and extend his father's house at Redlynch, and the work continued after his marriage, as his family grew and needed more space.[52] There were nine children altogether: Susan (born in 1743), Charlotte (1744), Judith (1745), Henry (1747, known as Lord Stavordale from 1756), Lucy (1748), Harriot (1750; also known as Kitty), Stephen (1751; known as Tangy), Frances (1755; known as Fanny), and Charles (1761). Charlotte and Judith both died young (in 1755 and 1749 respectively), but the others all survived. Most seem to have inherited their mother's fair complexion (Henry Fox called Elizabeth 'the white peacock'), for their aunt Caroline Fox referred to them in 1751 as 'the pretty little white fairy children of Redlynch' and compared them unfavourably with her own son Charles, then two years old, who was dark, like his father, and 'a fine, noble-looking child ... vastly well and infinitely beautifull'.[53]

After Susanna Strangways Horner's death in 1758, Lord and Lady Ilchester began to spend more time at Melbury, and Lord Ilchester considered selling Redlynch – mainly, it would appear, to save money. He tried to persuade his brother to buy the house. Henry Fox's refusal clearly caused a certain amount of ill-feeling between the two brothers, for Stephen wrote some years later:

> You had an opportunity of doing an extreme advantageous thing to your own family, and a very kind one to mine, in preventing me having two seats and gardens and parks to keep. I reckon I should save £1700 a year by living only at Melbury and having no servants at Redlynch, which I will say is as pleasantly situated, and as compleat, as any in these parts: the furniture new, the plantation of my planting near forty years old, and all the woods thriving ... When I offered it you said 'Let Peter Taylor buy it', but my view and intentions were that a place I had laid out so much money upon, and which had been a hundred year in the family, should remain in it, and there is scarce an instance of a younger brother in great circumstances refusing the purchase of the family seat, especially such a one as Redlynch.[54]

A few years after the birth of their youngest child, Lord and Lady Ilchester's circumstances changed again, as their elder children began to marry and set up households of their own. Susan married an actor, William O'Brien, in 1764 and was packed off to America in disgrace. By 1770, when the O'Briens returned from exile, negotiations were under way for the marriage of Susan's younger sister Harriot to John Dyke Acland, the elder son of a West Country baronet, Sir Thomas Dyke Acland of Killerton in Devon. The groom-to-be was eminently suitable, and he was an old friend of Harriot's elder brother Lord Stavordale, who had written three years earlier to his father, 'I wish indeed with you that [Mr Acland] would like either of my sisters, for he is a most worthy young man'.[55] Everyone approved of the match: Lord Digby wrote to his uncle to say that he was 'extremely glad to hear that [Lady Harriot] was likely to be married and settled so much to your and Lady Ilchester's satisfaction', and Lord Bristol thought the alliance 'in every respect a most eligible one'.[56]

John Dyke Acland and Lady Harriot Strangways were married early in January 1771, and Lord Ilchester gave his daughter a dowry of £8000. John and Harriot seem genuinely to have been in love, and their union – which was to last for only seven years – was a happy one. Acland got on particularly well with his father-in-law, and wrote a light-hearted letter to him a few months after the wedding, describing his new wife as 'my little tyrannical plaything' and 'the little toad'.[57] The marriage was ended by John's death in 1778, a short while after his return from Canada, where he had been serving in the army. His wife – as independent-minded in her own way as her elder sister – had insisted on accompanying him on this expedition.[58]

In May 1771, four months after the Aclands' marriage, Harriot's elder sister Lucy received a proposal of marriage from her first cousin Stephen Digby, a captain in the Twenty-Fourth Regiment of Foot. The fifth of six sons, Stephen had inherited only £2000 from his father,[59] and he had to make his own way in the world. He was only too well aware that Lucy, with a dowry of £8000, could have found a wealthier husband, and wrote to Lady Ilchester to say that he knew that his proposal was disadvantageous to her daughter, but that 'Lady Lucy still has my affections'.[60] Lady Ilchester sent a copy of her reply to her husband, with the comment 'Young people and love are sad things'. It is clear from this letter that the 'affair' had already been going on for some time. Lady Ilchester told Digby:

> I can have no objection to you, as I always thought your disposition amiable, but fear and think you will both terribly feel the smallness of your income after you have been some little time married, [but] love is blind.[61]

Lord and Lady Ilchester gave Stephen permission to marry their daughter, and the wedding took place on 1 October. This marriage, too, was a success, and Stephen turned out to be 'the tenderest and [most] faithfull of husbands'.[62] Lucy, however, died of breast cancer in 1787, and Stephen remarried three years later – after a brief flirtation with the authoress Fanny Burney, who was at the time Keeper of the Robes to Queen Charlotte.[63]

In 1772 it was Lord Stavordale's turn to marry. Whilst the marriages of their daughters had taken money away from the family, Lord and Lady Ilchester might reasonably have expected that their eldest son and heir would bring in money by choosing a bride with a substantial dowry. But this was not to be. Described by Sarah Bunbury in 1766 as 'a sad, wild young chap, [who] drinks and keeps bad company',[64] he was addicted to gambling, as were his cousins Ste and Charles Fox.[65] He also showed a worrying predilection for unsuitable women. As a sixteen-year-old schoolboy at Eton in the summer of 1764 he had begun to correspond with Anne Murray of Brownlow Street, Drury Lane, whom his father suspected of being 'a bawd or a young whore'. Two years later, when he was an undergraduate at Oxford and still under age, Lord Stavordale had nearly become engaged to an unidentified young lady. His parents hastily sent him off to The Hague, on the first stage of a continental tour which would keep him out of England for a year or two.[66] By February 1770 he was back in London, gambling at Almack's.[67] Three months later he joined the army as a cornet in the First Regiment of Horse, which was stationed in Ireland. His parents no doubt hoped that this would keep him out of trouble for a while, and they cannot have anticipated the principal consequence of their son's stay in Ireland, for he fell head over heels in love with the penniless daughter of an Irish gentleman and announced that he wished to marry her.

Mary Theresa Grady, the object of Lord Stavordale's affections, was one of five daughters of Standish Grady of Cappercullen in the parish of Abington, county Limerick. Of native Irish stock, the Gradys had been Catholics until the seventeenth century, when they had converted to Protestantism. In the middle of the eighteenth century they had settled at Cappercullen, eight miles east of the city of Limerick. The house, which dated from the seventeenth century with eighteenth-century additions, was neither grand nor very large, though there was a deer park with red and fallow deer. By English standards the Gradys were a minor gentry family, and under normal circumstances Standish Grady would not have expected to marry one of his daughters to the eldest son and heir of an English earl. Lord Stavordale's family and friends tried to persuade him to change his mind, suspecting that the young lady was a gold-digger. His brother-in-law, John Dyke Acland, begged him not to be too hasty, and warned him:

> Have you well considered the advantages and disadvantages of an alliance with an Irish family whose friends, connections and interests are perfectly unknown to your friends here [in England]? Have you well considered, love apart, the light they stand in in their country, and the light which you may be able to present the lady and her relations to your friends here? ... Are you tolerably certain ... that a little time would not make you of a different disposition, or that it might not offer you a woman that might be more suitable to your situation, and that you might like as well? ... It is my decided opinion ... that Lord Ilchester will be violently against it on account of fortune.[68]

Lord Stavordale refused to change his mind, and he and Mary Grady were married at Cappercullen on 26 August 1772.[69] Lord and Lady Ilchester were reassured by good reports of their new daughter-in-law's character, and her beauty, intelligence and kindness quickly removed their remaining reservations when they eventually met her. For a few years the newly-married couple moved around, living partly in Ireland and partly in England, but in 1775 Lord Stavordale left the army and they settled at Redlynch. In the following year the first Earl died, and Lord and Lady Stavordale became the second Earl and Countess of Ilchester.

The next to marry was the youngest daughter, Fanny. Fanny was given a dowry of £10,000 – two thousand pounds more than her elder sisters, in recognition of her 'affectionate and dutifull behaviour' to her father during his last illness.[70] The circumstances of Fanny's engagement and marriage in 1777 to Sir Valentine Richard Quin of Adare, County Limerick (twenty miles from Cappercullen), are unknown. The couple had four children, and

Fanny was said to be well and very fond of her home in 1792 when her brother visited Adare.[71] In the autumn of 1793, however, she left her husband and children and fled to England, never to return to Ireland. Quite what precipitated this drastic step is unclear. The only hint is given in Susan O'Brien's journal:

> About the end of March [1794] I went to see my sister Fanny at Bristol. Penitence and misery seemed personifyed in her figure, her manner, her words, her actions. Such a lesson to her sex was hardly ever given, of every virtue and amiable quality lost to herself and her family by imprudence, unjustifiable imprudence, and *fear*, for that occasioned all her errors.[72]

Susan does not say what Fanny was afraid of. News of the Reign of Terror in revolutionary France had reawakened fears of an uprising in Ireland, but if this was the reason for her flight it seems surprising that she left her children behind. She may have been scared of her husband, who was evidently a difficult man. In 1799 his niece Elizabeth Talbot thought that he was 'as mad as a March hare', and a decade later one of Sir Richard's daughters described him as 'the most miserable man in the world'. According to Susan O'Brien 'his temper would always have made him unhappy in any situation'.[73] He did, at least, allow Fanny to see her children in England, and this was by no means inevitable in such cases. But his provision for her maintenance was certainly not generous. In 1801 Susan O'Brien found that her sister was 'obliged to deny herself every enjoyment, nay almost necessarys, from the smallness of the income Lord Adare [her husband had acquired this title in 1800] allows her'.[74] Fanny died in 1814, and Lord Adare married again two years later at the age of sixty-four. The new Lady Adare, born Margaret Mary Coghlan, was a twice-married widow of no particular social status or wealth. Within a year this marriage, too, had broken down, and Lord Adare was involved in an acrimonious dispute with his second wife's family for several years thereafter.[75]

The last to marry was Charles, Lord and Lady Ilchester's youngest child by six years. He went into the church, and his eldest brother presented him to the living of Maiden Newton in Dorset in 1787. In the same year he married Jane Haines, the seventeen-year-old daughter of a local clergyman. It seems unlikely that she brought a substantial dowry with her. Charles had inherited £5000 when he came of age, and his father also left him an annuity of £100, but he and his wife – who went on to bear him eight children – were never well off. When Susan O'Brien died in 1827 she left what money she had to Charles and his family.

Only one child of the first Earl and Countess of Ilchester lived into middle or old age without marrying at all. This was Stephen, the second son. In

1767, when he was fifteen, Stephen entered the army as a cornet in the Fifth Regiment of Dragoons, and he served in Ireland and America before going onto half-pay in 1783 when his regiment, the Seventy-Sixth Foot, was disbanded. By this time he was a lieutenant-colonel. He remained on half-pay until his death in 1836. The provision for Stephen was more generous than that for his younger brother: he inherited a total of £5000 from his father, together with an annual income of £450 from rents. After leaving the army, Stephen took up farming, and settled down in the country at Godminster, not far from Redlynch. A shy, awkward man, he became quite close to his eldest sister Susan O'Brien in later years. Though he never married, he did have an illegitimate son, Charles White, to whom he left the residue of his estate when he died in 1836.

The second Earl and Countess of Ilchester had eight children: two boys and six girls. The eldest was Elizabeth (born 1773, and called Lily by her sisters), then came Mary (1776), Stephen (born and died in 1777), Harriot (1778), Charlotte (1784), Louisa (1785), Henry (Lord Stavordale, born 1787, and usually known as Harry) and Susan (born in 1790; died in 1792). Mary Theresa, the second Countess, disliked London and spent as much time as possible in the country with her children, often without her husband. In later years her daughters looked back with longing to their happy childhood at Redlynch. As the third daughter Harriot wrote to her sister Mary: 'Perhaps my liking [Redlynch] so much may proceed from the same reason yours does, viz. my having spent so *many, many* happy hours, and some *very, very* miserable ones [there].'[76]

Susan O'Brien described her sister-in-law as 'the best of wives, often in very difficult situations',[77] and it is clear that the second Earl was not always easy to live with. He continued to gamble away his fortune, and he is known to have fathered two illegitimate children after his marriage.[78] Poor health added to his Countess's troubles, and she died in 1790 aged about thirty-five. The eldest of her seven surviving children was then sixteen; the youngest only six weeks old.

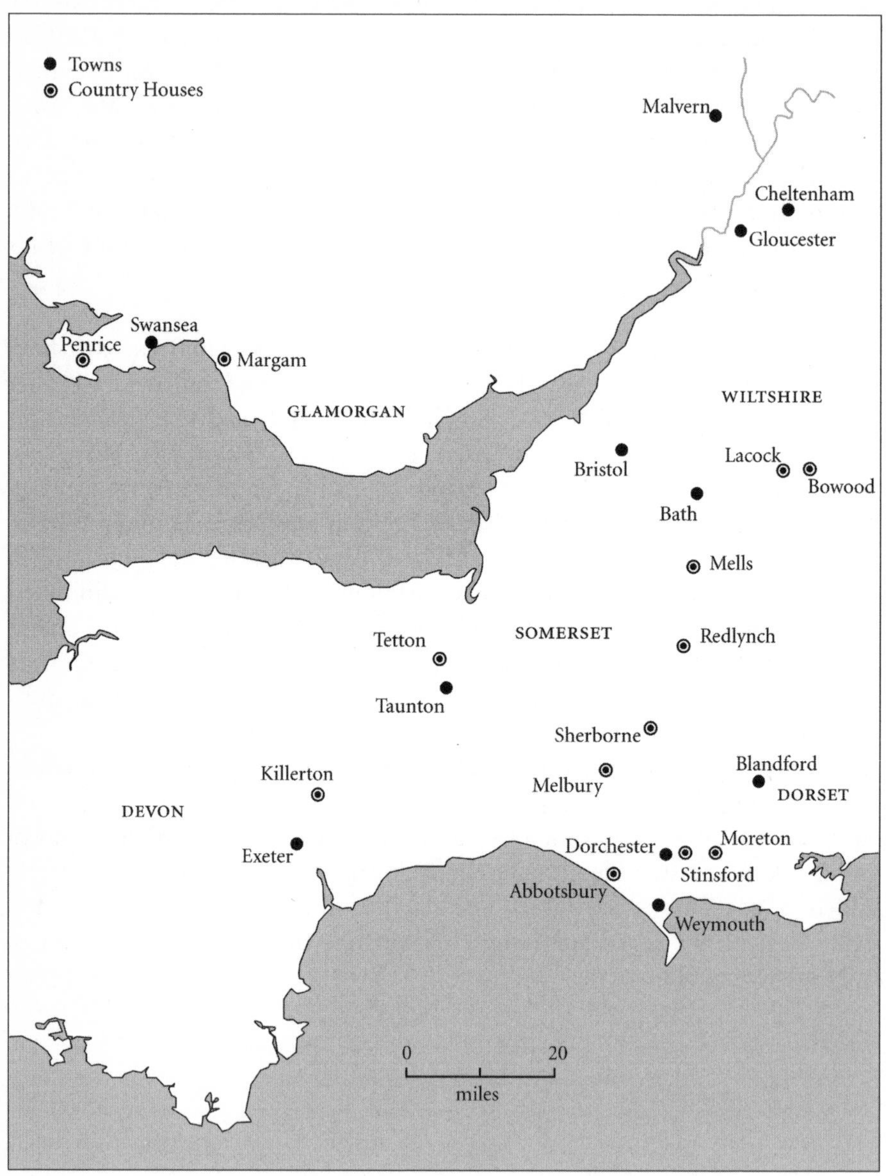

The country houses of the Fox Strangways ladies and their families.

3

Susan

On 9 April 1764 Horace Walpole wrote to his friend Horace Mann, the British Resident in Florence, to tell him about the latest London scandal:

> A melancholy affair has happened to Lord Ilchester. His eldest daughter, Lady Susan, a very pleasing girl though not handsome, married herself two days ago at Covent Garden church to O'Brien, a handsome young actor. Lord Ilchester doted on her and was the most indulgent of fathers.'Tis a cruel blow.[1]

Lady Susan Fox Strangways, who was born in 1743, had been the centre of attention during the first years of her life: a pretty, intelligent little girl, she was indulged by her parents, and her early letters to her father indicate that her relationship with him was particularly close. She signed herself 'yours to death' and assured him that she was 'now yours, and ever yours, till I am someone else's'.[2] Susan also occupied a special place in the affections of her uncle and godfather Henry Fox, who had no daughters of his own. When Susan was eighteen months old, her uncle described her in the Melbury game books as 'the loveliest, liveliest and best humoured child that ever was yet born'.[3] A letter from Susan, written for her by her father when she was very young, is addressed to 'Dear Uncle Harry' and signed 'your own niece, Susan Fox':

> Pray send unto me a good many yards of red tape, and [I] will love you dearly. Pray send enough for me to give some unto Charlotte. Papa will call me gimcrack, but I am his own daughter Susan. Pray, uncle, don't forget to send the red tape unto me. This is all my letter unto you.[4]

Henry Fox had married in 1744, a year or two before this letter was written. He was nearly forty, whilst his bride Lady Caroline Lennox, the eldest daughter of the Duke and Duchess of Richmond, was just twenty-one. By the time of the marriage Henry was a Lord of the Treasury, and a rising star in the government. No doubt he hoped that the Duke's support would enable him to rise further, but he also seems to have been genuinely in love with Caroline, as she was with him. Caroline's parents were, however, quite certain that they did not want Henry as a son-in-law. As a young man Henry had gambled away much of his inheritance, and he was known to have been involved with several women, including his brother's mother-in-law. His father's humble origins were well known, whilst Caroline was a great-granddaughter of Charles II. So the two eloped and married in secret, in the Conduit Street house of Henry's friend Sir Charles Hanbury Williams. Four days before the ceremony Caroline voiced her fears in a letter to her husband-to-be:

> I am vastly frightened to think of what I am going to do. I dare not reflect upon it, I fear they will never forgive me. I hope you won't suspect me now of being altered but, believe me, this is the greatest proof of love it is possible for me to give you.[5]

Four years passed before the Duke and Duchess were reconciled with their daughter and her husband.

In 1746 Henry Fox was appointed Secretary at War, a post that he was to hold until 1755. In 1746, too, he took a lease of Holland House, a Jacobean mansion in Kensington, which was then on the outskirts of London. It was there that he and Caroline lived for most of the year, and there that they brought up their children, Stephen (born in 1745), Charles James (born 1749) and Henry (born 1755).[6] Lord and Lady Ilchester and their children were frequent visitors, and their daughter Susan spent much of her time at Holland House with her cousins. As she grew up, she remained close to her uncle Henry, who told his brother in 1760: 'Lady Susan is more agreeable the more one sees of her. My admiration and love was allways great, but they increase.'[7] Two years later he sent his love to 'Lady Sweet Suke'.[8] By 1759 Susan was often at Court, appearing regularly at the royal drawing rooms and birthday celebrations. It was at this time, when she was sixteen, that Susan met Sarah Lennox, the fourteen-year-old sister of her aunt Caroline Fox, for the first time. At first, Sarah was not impressed by her new acquaintance, writing to her sister Emily at the end of January 1760:

> Lady Susan Strangways is come to Town. She is not pretty. She is very fat, has a good complexion, large heavy eyes, a wide mouth, and very fine light hair. I don't know her yet. As to her manner, you may know it as well as me, for she [is] exactly Lady Caroline Russell without that queer voice, or at least not so bad. But she does up her mouth exactly like her, and walks just the same.[9]

Nor was Susan's mother immediately struck by Sarah's own supposed beauty, writing to tell her husband early in February that the girl had small eyes and was 'a bad likeness of her mother'. Lady Ilchester did, however, concede that Sarah 'looks merry', and she also reported that 'she [Sarah] and Susan are famous for joking'.[10] This was the beginning of a close friendship which was to last until Sarah's death, sixty-seven years later.

During the winter of 1760 to 1761 Sarah and Susan both took part in the amateur theatrical performances that were a regular feature of life at Holland

House. On 16 December Lady Ilchester wrote to tell her husband that the two girls were to act in the play *The Distressed Mother* during the following week. After the performance Susan informed her father 'we had a very small audience, but we did pretty well'.[11] Susan's uncle was certainly impressed, for he referred in a letter to his brother to 'Minx's [Susan's] most extraordinary performance of Hermione'. He continued 'I never saw a part so well acted in my life'.[12]

Horace Walpole saw Susan and Sarah in another play early in 1761, when he wrote to tell his friend George Montagu that he had been 'excessively amused', and that the two girls 'were delightful, and acted with so much nature and simplicity that they appeared the very things they represented'.[13] By this time everyone in London was talking of the partiality of the new King George III for Sarah. The two had first met when Sarah was presented at Court in November 1759, shortly after her arrival in London. Henry Fox began to dream of a marriage which would make his sister-in-law Queen of England, and would greatly enhance his own power and influence. Susan, too, began to believe that her friend might really become Queen and, as she noted many years later, 'I almost thought myself Prime Minister'.[14] In the summer of 1761, however, the King decided to marry Princess Charlotte of Mecklenburg-Strelitz. When the marriage took place, on 8 September, the ten bridesmaids (all the daughters of dukes and earls) included Sarah and Susan. Susan was fortunate to be asked, for her father had been made an earl only five years earlier. As Henry Fox told his brother, 'It is a great (though expensive, and possibly troublesome) compliment to come down to my dear Lady Susan – possibly the lowest in rank that is capable'.[15] Two weeks later, on 22 September, Susan also attended the coronation of the new King and Queen in Westminster Abbey. In later years she remembered the event as having been 'a very fine sight, but much less interesting to me than I expected it to be'.[16]

Although she was still only sixteen, Sarah's family decided that they had better get her married off as quickly as possible. Even her nephew Ste Fox, only a few days older than Sarah herself, advised her 'Don't refuse a good match when you can get it, and don't go to plays and operas too often'.[17] The Duke of Marlborough was looked on as a possible husband, but he preferred Lady Caroline Russell, and married her in 1762.[18] The recently-widowed Earl of Erroll was keen, but Sarah refused him. Another suitor then appeared on the scene. This was Charles Bunbury, son of the Suffolk landowner Sir William Bunbury and Whig MP for Bury St Edmunds. Bunbury was reasonably good-looking and would become a baronet on his father's death, but the family's Suffolk estates were worth only £5000 a year, and Charles and his wife could expect no more than £2000 a year whilst

Sir William and Lady Bunbury were still alive. Nobody was very enthusiastic about the match, but nevertheless Lady Sarah Lennox and Charles Bunbury were married at Holland House on 2 June 1762. Susan was, of course, present. Bunbury took Sarah back to his house at Great Barton in Suffolk after the wedding, but Susan had little time to miss her friend, for she was already deeply immersed in a flirtation of her own – one that was to prove, in the eyes of the world at least – to be her downfall. For she was in love with William O'Brien, an actor of whom no member of her family could possibly be expected to approve.

William O'Brien's origins are, to say the least, obscure. The best evidence that we have is a biographical note written by O'Brien himself around 1808. His information is somewhat vague, and it is clear, for example, that he did not know exactly when he had been born. It is possible that he deliberately gave incorrect information. It seems, however, that his great-great-grandfather had been one of the 'Wild Geese' – Irish Catholic gentlemen who had supported James II, and had fled to the Continent after the fall of Limerick to the forces of King William in 1691. O'Brien's father had been a recruiting officer for one of the Irish brigades in the service of the French monarchs. It was in Ireland that he had met his wife, a member of the gentry family of Macarthy of Spring House, County Tipperary. Their only child, William, had been born in London, *circa* 1740, and his mother had died two days later. His father had died (or disappeared) soon afterwards, and William had been brought up, apparently in London, by people whose surname was O'Brien, but to whom he was not actually related. A delicate child, he had been educated at home by a Catholic priest, who had taught him French and Latin and a little Greek. After this, in O'Brien's own words:

> I was thought so lively and animated as to be trusted with a character in a comedy to be performed by some young people of the neighbourhood. My admiration of Garrick at that time was unbounded, the proposal was accepted. I played my part so well, and obtained so much applause, that it certainly gave me that violent inclination to the stage which, when afterwards I got into embarassed circumstances by prematurely setting up for a smart fellow about Town, I hastily and most thoughtlessly adopted.[19]

David Garrick took the young man under his wing, and O'Brien appeared on the London stage for the first time in 1758. As a good-looking, popular young actor, he was invited to help with the amateur theatrical performances at Holland House, and he probably met Susan Strangways in the winter of 1760 to 1761. Susan later told her aunt Charlotte Digby that 'she dated her passion ... or at least the discovery to herself that it was one', from the time of her being bridesmaid to the Queen in the autumn of 1761.[20] It was during the latter part of 1762 that the two declared their love to each other by exchanging poems. In William's first composition he said that he had been 'struck by the dart of love' on seeing Susan, after which: 'Well pleased, the nymph beheld my pain, And blushed acceptance of my heart'.[21] Susan later admitted that she had initiated the correspondence with William, and that 'besides many encouraging looks, he had received a note from her before he presumed to speak'.[22]

The problems of arranging meetings without arousing suspicion are hinted at in a poem written by William in the summer of 1763:

> My time, O ye Muses, was happily spent
> When my Susan I met with wherever I went,
> At the play, at the Gardens, wherever I could,
> I always was happy when near her I stood.[23]

It was easier to keep in touch during Susan's visits to Sarah Bunbury in Suffolk, well away from the inquisitive eyes of her family and their servants. In a letter written on 21 July 1763, William begins by referring to 'Such exquisite marks of your affection as I received some time ago from Barton', and continues:

> I see you love me, and that with an ardour mixed with such prudent tenderness that, had I the whole world to give away, you of all the world should command it. Every circumstance of your letter has endeared you to me so much that I am continually tormenting myself with ideas of our being prevented in our share of felicity. Good God! What would become of me should any of my letters to you miscarry, should any trace of our connexion be discovered?[24]

The meetings and exchange of letters lasted about a year before Susan's family discovered what was going on. They were horrified by Susan's determination to ruin her reputation by a love affair with an actor. Though William O'Brien was an educated man, handsome, charming and with good manners, his origins were obscure and his parents unknown. He had no fortune of his own, and he had to depend on his own wits and talent to earn a living. To make matters worse, he had come to the attention of people in high society in the worst possible way – as an actor. For actors were considered to be little better than servants, whilst actresses were barely distinguishable from prostitutes. It may have been socially acceptable for a gentleman or aristocrat to set up an actress as his mistress, but it was social suicide for a lady to enter into a relationship with an actor. She would compromise herself and bring disgrace on her family, damaging the marriage prospects of her sisters. How much of this Susan realised at the time is unclear, for she was used to being indulged and admired. Many years later, when they were both old women, she and Sarah looked back on this crucial period in their lives, and reflected on their uncle's influence:

> She [Sarah] agreed with me in thinking no young person could be much with my uncle Holland without being the worse for it. His excessive praises and flattery excited our vanity, made us many enemies, and unfitted us for any society that was not *superfine*. His maxim that young people were always in the right, and old ones in the wrong, could not, and did not, fail to give us a contempt for those to whom all deference was due, and, when these maxims operated, his anger and displeasure was heightened by the disappointment of our not succeeding in the scheme he had laid for us.[25]

Henry's plans for Susan had included marriage with 'a handsome lord with £10,000 a year'.[26]

When they found out about the love affair, Susan's relations did their best to hush the matter up. Lord Ilchester subsequently complained that his errrant daughter had met with 'the kindest treatment and most gentle usage on the discovery of this shocking affair'. She had promised not to see O'Brien again, and the family had 'extricated [her] out of the situation she was got into, and [saved] her reputation ... by the greatest care and nicest delicacy'.[27] On 12 February 1764,[28] however, Susan came of age, and she and William decided to marry in secret. It was arranged that Susan should visit Katherine Read, the fashionable society artist who was working on a pastel portrait of her, on the morning of Saturday 7 April, and then find some reason to send her servants away. She would then slip away and meet William, or one of his friends, who would take her to St Paul's, Covent Garden, where the ceremony was to take place. They are said to have gone first to O'Brien's 'villa' at Dunstable in Bedfordshire, but by early May they were just outside London, in Hendon.[29]

The storm broke immediately after the marriage. Lord Ilchester refused to meet, or even to communicate with, his daughter at all, and wrote to Sarah Bunbury to ask her not to see or correspond with 'that base and treacherous wretch my ungratefull daughter'. Susan, he continued, had 'deliberately ruined herself, disgraced her family, acted a cruel part towards her sisters, and broke her father's and mother's heart by matching herself with a scoundrel of so vile a profession that there are no possible means left to retrieve her'.[30] Fortunately for Susan, Sarah ignored Lord Ilchester's requests. Lord Holland who felt that his niece had betrayed him, wrote on the back of a letter that Susan had written to him just before her wedding: 'Lady Susan, April 6. She ruined herself Saturday the 7, 1764'.[31] In the following month Susan's friends persuaded her to write to her mother, to ask for her forgiveness. Lady Ilchester – who had herself been in a similar position twenty-eight years earlier – agreed to forgive Susan, but signed herself 'your unhappy mother' and told her ungrateful and undutiful daughter:

> You have put it out of my power, or any one's, to make you happy in this world. I pray to God you may be so in the next. I can with truth say it has been, from your earliest dawn of reason, your father's and my greatest pleasure to make you so … You have given up most affectionate parents, and many loving relations, in short, what have you not given up as to situation in life? [32]

Sarah Bunbury's sister, Louisa Conolly, was more sympathetic, telling Susan: 'If you consider marriage in its true light, surely you have fulfilled what I reckon the happiest end of it, and that is marrying the person you love best … For real happiness does certainly consist in spending your days with a person you love.' [33]

The immediate problem was to decide what should be done with the new husband and bride. Susan's relations were all adamant that William should give up his acting career, but he had no other means of earning a living. Lord Ilchester and his brother both agreed that the best course would be for William and Susan to go abroad. [34] This would get them out of the way, and deprive the gossips of London society of fresh material that could bring 'disgrace and uneasyness' to the rest of Susan's family.[35] They might also be able to make an independent fortune for themselves.

Various proposals for their future provision were put forward during the summer of 1764. It was suggested that O'Brien might become British Consul at Cadiz, or that he might find employment with the East India Company. By July, however, Susan's relations had turned their eyes to America:

> Where they have thoughts of procuring or purchasing for the husband [William O'Brien] some employment of sufficient salary for their immediate support, and obtaining a grant of lands as an establishment for their family.[36]

With her family prophesying her ruin if she refused to go, Susan had little choice in the matter. She tried to be optimistic, and to show her gratitude to Lord Holland, the main instigator of the American project, realising that he was trying to do his best for her. In August she wrote to tell her uncle:

> I have heard the most favorable accounts possible of New York and the people which, if true, is a very happy circumstance. I hope we shall be able to make the lands turn out as well as we are flattered with the hopes of. It shall be no fault of ours if we do not, for I'm sure we are determined to persist in as much frugality and resolution to go through with every thing that is proper for the management of them that is possible.[37]

All notions of frugality disappeared, however, when William and Susan began to prepare for their voyage. Lord Holland's agent Samuel Touchet was given the unenviable task of keeping their expenditure within reasonable limits, but he was totally unsuccessful. When he told Susan that her uncle thought that she could require 'no extra stock of cloaths', the young lady replied that Lord Holland was 'much mistaken in that particular'. And when Touchet 'remonstrated against dressing tables, sophas etc. etc. as expensive in cost as well as freight', Susan said she would not go abroad without them. A Chippendale table cost £247; a chariot was purchased, with clothes, books, guns and watches for William O'Brien. The O'Briens also took with them lengths of cloth 'checks for furniture and counterpains … fustians for his own and servants' wear; ginghams for waistcoats and her morning gowns; dimitys etc.' It was, as Touchet wrote in one letter, 'to no purpose to restrain them'.[38] Lord Ilchester had been persuaded to give the couple £1000 to equip themselves for their stay in America, and it was expected that they would need another £1000 for 'improving' the American lands that were to be granted to them.[39] By the time they sailed they had already spent over £2000.

According to a letter written by Samuel Touchet at the end of August, the O'Briens were to leave London on 7 September, and travel to Falmouth via Staines and Stockbridge, then south through Blandford and Dorchester. Poor Susan was 'much cast down in passing through Dorsetshire without seeing one friend or relation'.[40] From Dorchester they were to travel to Exeter, via Honiton. The journey from London to Exeter was expected to take three days, and Touchet had been told that the final stage, from Exeter to Falmouth, would take another two days 'on account of hills'.[41] On 17 September William and Susan O'Brien finally boarded the packet at Falmouth. The 'best accommodations' had been reserved for them, and they took three servants with them, in addition to their clothes and furniture. After a comparatively quick crossing, lasting thirty-four days (during which Susan was 'vastly ill the whole way'), they eventually reached New York.[42]

The arrival of the young couple created quite a stir in New York, where earls' daughters were few and far between. The leaders of the colonial town's society were, however, worried that Susan's example might induce their own daughters to 'take husbands at their own hands'.[43] Susan's own impressions of the place that was to be her home for the next five years were not favourable. And it became evident almost immediately that her family's hopes that she and her husband would make their fortune in America were wildly over-optimistic. Three weeks after arriving in New York Susan wrote to tell her uncle:

> I'm sorry to be obliged to say we were very much deceived in the accounts we have had of this place. Far from being one of the pleasantest in [the] world, all I have yet seen of it is barren and uncultivated even to the gates of the town, and our disappointment in regard to the lands is even greater, for all those we

> were told of at Konajahory on the Mohawks River are granted long ago, and all settled above twenty miles back, nor are there any ungranted nearer than between Ticonderoga and Crown Point. There is a surveyor gone up to see if any there are good, and we are told by the Lieutenant Governor ... that these are as good as any we should go to a greater expense for. But as to going there ourselves and attempting to settle them, it is an absolute impossibility, and would be madness to think of. The people here all endeavour to get as much land as they can, and indeed all the most considerable people have large tracts of very good land, for as they have got it for a trifle they think it advantageous for their familys two or three generations to come, whenever this happens to be the seat of Empire. But no one attempts laying out anything themselves, as they have the impossibility of ever gaining the least advantage by it ... The finding this certainly to be the case is a very great disappointment to us, as we had flattered ourselves in England that by coming here we should have it in our power, by pains and industry, to gain from them an agreeable maintenance, and we now find ourselves as far from it as ever, nay farther, for at home we had the hopes that by coming here we should, and now after the misery of a long voyage we find those hopes to be entirely groundless.[44]

William and Susan were certainly an unlikely pair of pioneers, for both had spent much of their previous life in London, and neither had any experience of farming, or of manual work of any kind. Lord Holland was not, however, inclined to sympathise with his niece in her uncomfortable situation, for by the time he received her letter he had begun to discover how much she had spent before leaving England. He blamed Samuel Touchet for the lack of restraint, and Touchet wrote to tell Susan that her uncle was 'so much displeased with me I dare scarcely go near him'. Lord Holland said that he saw no prospect of anything but the O'Briens' ruin, that 'it was vain for him to think of serving' them, and that 'he expected to hear Mr O'Brien is in a jail at New York before the year comes round'.[45] Sarah Bunbury advised her friend to show 'true repentance' and to 'give up all pleasure etc. for to keep up a caracter of patience and the strictest integrity'. Showing a distinct lack of sympathy, she also told Susan:

> I am monstrous sorry you have found New York so bad, but it's an ill wind that blows nobody good, for the worse the town and the vulgarer the folks, the less occasion you have for expence, and what is nothing to you will make you live *en reine* there, so don't introduce anything finer than you need, for you may yourself set the fashion, and 'tis your fault if 'tis an extravagant one.[46]

It was not long before Susan told her family that she wanted to come home. Her aunt Charlotte Digby wrote to beg her not to 'give up the only chance of your being independant and returning with a fortune in some measure equal to your birth'.[47] Though the O'Briens were in America for several more years, they never did get the long-anticipated grant of lands. They stayed in New York until 1769, making a few friends and living on an annuity of £400 from Susan's uncle, with £100 a year from Lady Ilchester. From 1765 the O'Briens also received £90 a year from William's salary as Barrack-Master at Quebec, a post which Lord Holland obtained for him.

Susan seems to have had no communication with her brothers and sisters whilst she was in America, though she received occasional letters from her mother, from her aunt Charlotte Digby and from Sarah Bunbury. Nor did she have any direct contact with her father, who refused to give her any further assistance, saying that 'she has ruined herself, and all attempts to help her are in vain'.[48] Susan did receive goods from home from time to time – in 1765 Samuel Touchet promised to send 'porter and Cheshire cheese by the next ship, together with the tambour needles and gold thread'. Later in the same year he sent 'malt liquor and Cheshire and Gloster cheeses' and promised to let Susan have 'the pickles and groceries, and also the grate and ironing stove by the first opportunity'.[49] Sarah Bunbury even sent a chaise to New York for her friend in 1766.[50] The O'Briens seem to have lived fairly comfortably, though on a much more modest scale than Susan was accustomed to at home – in 1765 she said that she would be unable to invite Lord Holland's friend Clotworthy Upton to her house as it had only one bedchamber.[51]

It was presumably in connection with William O'Brien's position as Barrack-Master at Quebec that the couple travelled to Canada in the spring and summer of 1766, visiting Niagara Falls and Montreal on the way. Sarah Bunbury, marooned in the Suffolk countryside, wrote enviously to her friend: 'I long to hear something of your journey. I know you delight in the thoughts of doing what no other woman ever did or will do.'[52] But the O'Briens did not stay in Quebec for long, and they were back in New York by the beginning of August, still hoping that their fortunes would be improved by a grant of land, or by a more lucrative post for William. Such a post was eventually procured in 1768, not by Lord Holland but by Susan's mother, who used her interest with Lord Hillsborough, Secretary of State for the Colonies. The new post, of Secretary and Provost Marshal of Bermuda, added only £100 to the O'Briens' income, however, as they chose to stay in New York and pay a deputy to carry out the work in Bermuda.

By the spring of 1769 William and Susan were again threatening to come home. After almost five years in America, Susan told Lady Holland:

> [We] find by experience that it is impossible for us to live within our income. We see the flattering views with which we came here have intirely disappeared. We have not one inducement to remain in a country vastly expensive [and] vastly disagreeable, in which we cannot make a usefull friend or even a pleasant

acquaintance, and of which we know so much as to be convinced [it] can never be the least advantage to us.[53]

As soon as she found out about her daughter's plans, Lady Ilchester wrote to dissuade her from returning to England, telling Susan:

> You are, I fear, plotting a scheme which, if put into execution, will be the ruin of both you and Mr O'Brien. If you come to England this year, or before you have tried the living on your new appointment, depend on it I will never see your face or do the least thing for you.[54]

Her mother's threats had the desired effect, at least for the time being. Through Lord Holland's influence, William was appointed storekeeper in the ordnance department at Quebec at an annual salary of £150, and in September 1769 the couple set off for Canada again. Almost twenty years later, Susan began her journal with an account of their journey:

> The 14 of September 1769 left New York for Quebec. We took our passage on board a sloop, and in three days sailed up Hudson's River to Albany. Nothing can be more delightful than the navigation of this beautiful river ... We arrived ... at Albany on the 18 of September and left it early the next morning to proceed on our journey. There is nothing in this place worthy the curiosity of a stranger and, though the second town of so large a province as New York, [it] is but a very poor one – its inhabitants altogether Dutch, and so attached to their old customs and manners that much less improvement has been made here than in most other places considering that it was settled so long ago. The rest of our journey was not so pleasant or easy as its begining had promised. Though we left Albany in a chaise of our own, we were soon obliged to quit it and mount our baggage carts.[55]

Susan grew up during her years in America, and she learned a great deal from her years overseas. She soon realised that the people who held power in England had little idea of the true state of affairs in the colonies, and responded indignantly when her correspondents in England failed to take her seriously:

> My accounts, I see plainly, are not believed, though I am not such a foolish, nonsensical girl as to write a parcel of lies because I don't like the country ... I assure you. There are a thousand ... good reasons why somebody of some consequence should come to this country to give the government some more true notions. The people of substance complain that the ministers at home have their accounts all from prejudiced people – either from officers who have suffered great hardships and are consequently violently prejudiced against it, or from others who have some particular attachments, and from that discribe it as the garden of the world and are as far wide of truth the other way. In short, the general cry is that the English ministers don't know the condition or interest of the colonys, and that sensible people who have a knowledge of affairs ought to

> come and enquire into the true state of things, and that it would be of infinite service both to England and America.[56]

Many years after her return to England, Susan wrote of 'the most astonishing ignorance of those in England about everything in America', and the inevitable failure of the money-making projects which had been promoted by her friends and family in England, including 'raising flax, ironworks, and other equally impracticable schemes, which every packet brought out for us to make a fortune by'.[57]

The O'Briens were no happier in Quebec than they had been in New York, and they returned to England in September 1770, having utterly failed to make the hoped for fortune, or to obtain a sufficiently lucrative post for William. They were therefore penniless, and entirely dependent on the goodwill of Susan's relations. Their reception was less than ecstatic. Negotiations were under way for the marriage of Susan's younger sister Harriot to John Dyke Acland, and Lord and Lady Ilchester were afraid that the reappearance of their prodigal daughter would ruin Harriot's chances of making a match that was, in their opinion, eminently suitable. Susan's father still refused to see her, and it was made quite clear that she and her husband were not welcome in Burlington Street or at Holland House.

A month after her wedding in January 1771 Harriot wrote Susan a letter which led to a serious rift between the two sisters:

> As I am now settled, and consequently have new connexions and relations to consult, I hope you will not think it unkind if I acquaint you with the conditions ... on which I can see you on your return to Town. As long as my father remains in his present way of thinking, I should esteem myself unpardonable in my conduct to him, did I see you in any but the privatest manner possible ... On these conditions ... I shall be glad to see you, at your own house, privately, alone and by appointment. I hope you will not think these conditions hard, since they are unalterable.[58]

Not surprisingly, Susan was greatly upset by her sister's words, and replied 'As I never receive any company I am ashamed of, so I never intend to receive any who are ashamed of me'. She dismissed her sister's 'frivolous excuse of not behaving decently towards me while my father remains in his present way of thinking', blamed her aunt Charlotte Digby for turning her sister against her, and accused Harriot of being 'unnatural and cruel'.[59] But Harriot was in an impossible position, unable to respect the wishes of her parents, her husband and her new in-laws, and at the same time to receive openly a sister with whom she had had little or no communication for six years. Sarah Bunbury was sure that Harriot had been put up to writing the letter by the Aclands, especially Sir Thomas, whom she described as 'old, proud and *hérissé de préjugé* [bristling with prejudice]'.[60] It was to be another seven years before Susan and Harriot were on speaking terms again – seven years during which the other members of the family took Harriot's side. When Susan saw her father in 1772 – for the first time since her marriage – she found that 'his affection was wholly alienated from me'.[61] Lord Holland, who had been out of power since 1765, was in poor health by this time, his attention fully occupied by the activities of his two eldest sons, who were doing their best to disperse the vast fortune that he had built up for himself during his years in office.

In 1771 the O'Briens went to live at Winterslow in Wiltshire, close to the house that Lord Holland had bought for his son and daughter-in-law Ste and Mary Fox. But the Foxes' house at Winterslow was burned down early in 1774; Lord and Lady Holland died within three weeks of each other in the following July, and Ste outlived them by only six months. Since the O'Briens' only reason for living at Winterslow had been 'the pleasure of his [Ste's] neighbourhood', they began to look for another home. In the summer of 1774 they spent six weeks at Weymouth, on the Dorset coast about twenty miles from Melbury, and five or six miles from Abbotsbury, where Susan's mother had built a new house a few years earlier.[62] One day they drove over to Stinsford, a village just outside Dorchester where, as Susan later wrote, they saw:

> A house belonging to my mother's estate, which had been long inhabited and was in very bad repair. We both were much pleased with it, and Mr O'Brien was so struck with the place that he immediately became desirous of living there.[63]

The old manor house of the Stafford family which stands next to Stinsford church had been the home of Susan's ancestors Thomas and Alionor Strangways, who were living there when Thomas died in the winter of 1484 to 1485.[64] Their descendants lived mainly at Melbury, but Stinsford was used from time to time by younger members of the family. It was a substantial building of local stone with no great architectural pretensions, and in the second quarter of the seventeenth century the house was said to be 'nowe something decayed'.[65]

According to Hutchins, Stinsford House was 'much repaired and beautified' by Thomas Strangways junior, Susanna Strangways Horner's brother, who lived there with his wife Mary after their marriage in 1710.[66] They continued to use the house after 1713, when Thomas inherited Melbury from his father. Sixteen years later, when Thomas made his will, he left to his wife 'the furniture of Stinsford House' for her life. When Mary

Strangways made her own will a few months afterwards, she was living at Stinsford.[67] After her death, in February 1727, Stinsford seems to have gone to sleep for almost fifty years. Susanna Strangways Horner and her daughter were there briefly in 1736, a few months after the latter's marriage to Stephen Fox, and an inventory drawn up in the following year suggests that little had changed in the intervening decade. After 1736 there is no indication that any member of the family visited Stinsford until the mid 1770s, though occasional payments for maintenance work in the house and gardens there are recorded in the estate accounts. Whether it was leased out from time to time or looked after by a caretaker is unclear, but many of the furnishings seem to have remained in the house.

In London, during the winter after the O'Briens' visit to Stinsford, they discussed the possibility of taking over the old house with Susan's family. Everyone approved of the idea. Stinsford was out of the way enough to be suitable for William and Susan, whose social rehabilitation still had a long way to go, and it would be cheaper for them to live in the country than in London. Stinsford was, moreover, only fifteen miles from Melbury. With Susan's father now in poor health, her mother was anxious to have her eldest daughter close at hand:

> My mother was quite eager that I should be near her and live at a place of hers which she thought it was in her power to improve and, at the same time that she was amusing herself, be of real use to us by making it every day more and more comfortable and convenient for us.

At first, however, Susan was not too sure that the move to Stinsford was a good idea. Admittedly, the place was 'excessively pretty, and the spot in the kingdom I prefered as a residence'. On the other hand, she could see difficulties ahead, due to 'Mr O'Brien's disposition to expence and my mother's total incapacity for business'. Old George Donisthorpe, the Melbury estate steward, foresaw that the repairs were going to cost a great deal more than anyone expected. But Lady Ilchester was not to be dissuaded, and she sent workmen into the house to make it ready for her daughter and son-in-law, thinking that it could be made 'comfortably habitable' for about £50. George Donisthorpe estimated that the cost was likely to be nearer to £1500:

> The difference was considerable. However, no builder was consulted, or any plan formed, and by the extreme of bad management, after a thousand pounds has been laid out [the house is] still so out of repair as to be unfit either to let or inhabit.

Nevertheless, the O'Briens were able to move in during the summer of 1775. They found 'agreeable acquaintances' in the neighbourhood, and were soon happily occupied with plans for the future. Many years later Susan remembered how they would sit in the porch on fine evenings, to watch the sunset and 'contrive our little improvements',[68] though they had barely enough money to live on, and almost nothing to spare for further work on the house. In 1777 Susan's mother agreed to pay for some repairs and alterations, which were expected to cost £250. When the bill was presented, however, it came to more than £800. Lady Ilchester was not pleased, and told her daughter and son-in-law that their overspending 'would ultimately fall on us, as we could not expect her to provide for us in future if we spent her money in such a manner at present'. But she 'both generously and kindly paid the bill, and said it should be no more mentioned'. Susan continued to worry, but she and William stayed at Stinsford, patching the house up as best they could, sometimes moving out in the winter when it became too cold and damp. Occasionally, when they were even shorter of money than usual, they moved in with Susan's mother at Melbury for a few months. They both grew to love Stinsford, and Susan did her best – with limited success – to 'have Mr O'Brien settle as a country gentleman and live within his income'.[69]

The O'Briens' income in the early 1790s was approximately £800 a year, which included annuities of £200 from Susan's father and £400 from her mother.[70] The latter payment ceased when Lady Ilchester died in the autumn of 1792, and William and Susan's money problems immediately grew worse again. They were now dependent on Susan's brother, with whom relations were often difficult.

The second Earl of Ilchester was four years younger than his sister, and the two had never been close. As his parents' eldest son and heir, Lord Ilchester had inherited by far the greatest share of his family's wealth and power, and it was probably inevitable that this should lead to resentment from some of his siblings. Sarah Bunbury, who had been dependent on her own brother after leaving her first husband in 1769, had summed up the difficulties of such a situation in 1775:

> An elder brother of a family is *commonly* reckoned to be looked upon with respect merely because he is the head of the young part of the family and, though he may treat his brothers and sisters with unkindness and deserve great blame, yet he seldom is looked upon as obliged in decency to take any notice of any of his family more than common civility if he don't like them. These are my notions of subordination, which I know you will laugh at, for I know you have too much American spirit to understand it.

Subordination – to anyone, but least of all to her siblings – was a concept that Susan found difficult to grasp. As Sarah (who knew her friend as well as anyone) added later in the same letter: 'You know too … your manner is apt to set people against you: you toss up your head (a great crime in many people's eyes, for it denotes contempt), you have a directing way'.[71] In a later letter Sarah referred to Susan's 'tough, oaklike mind'.[72] Susan refused to defer to her brother, and he, in return, showed little affection towards her. As she wrote many years later:

> My brother's reserve chilled my heart out of all freedom, confidence and ease. Yet he was good natured – but he never loved me. I was older than he was, I thought myself fitter to advise and govern than to soothe and cultivate him. My sisters were younger: they looked up to him; he loved them.[73]

Susan found it difficult to discuss business with her brother after their mother's death, and he remained uncommunicative during the years that followed. He did, however, continue to support his sister, and gave her a present of £200 when she was ill in 1799.[74]

The O'Briens were away from Stinsford for three years from July 1800, following William's appointment to a government board. A month after their arrival in London they were horrified to receive a letter from Lord Ilchester, asking if they intended to return to Stinsford. If they did not, he wished to demolish 'the greatest part' of their home and convert the remainder into a house for the tenant who farmed the land. Even if they did return, the dilapidated state of the house meant that much of it would have to be taken down. Susan wrote that 'We are so attached to [the house], the happiness of our lives depends so much on our living there, that we cannot give it up without expressing with how much regret it must be'. Fortunately, Lord Ilchester changed his mind, and the house was saved.[75] Susan was homesick for her Dorset home, writing in April 1801, 'Oh Stinsford, Stinsford! When shall I regain happiness, liberty and health. When shall I return to your beloved shades?'[76]

Lord Ilchester died in 1802, and the O'Briens returned to Stinsford in the following July after William had been appointed Receiver General for taxes in Dorset. Their own financial situation had improved considerably, and Lord Ilchester's brother Stephen, his trustee and executor, was willing to spend some money on their house. Within a week of William and Susan's return to Stinsford, they were 'very busy with workmen of all sorts putting things in order'. From past experience, however, Susan anticipated that the work would not be properly managed: 'Mr Field [the agent] and a carpenter will settle everything, and afterwards everything will be wrong and found fault with'.[77] Her forebodings were only too well founded, for the work continued, on and off, for at least two more years. In October 1804 William O'Brien wrote to Susan, who was staying with her sister in Somerset, to tell her that the carpenters had taken up all the skirting boards, and had

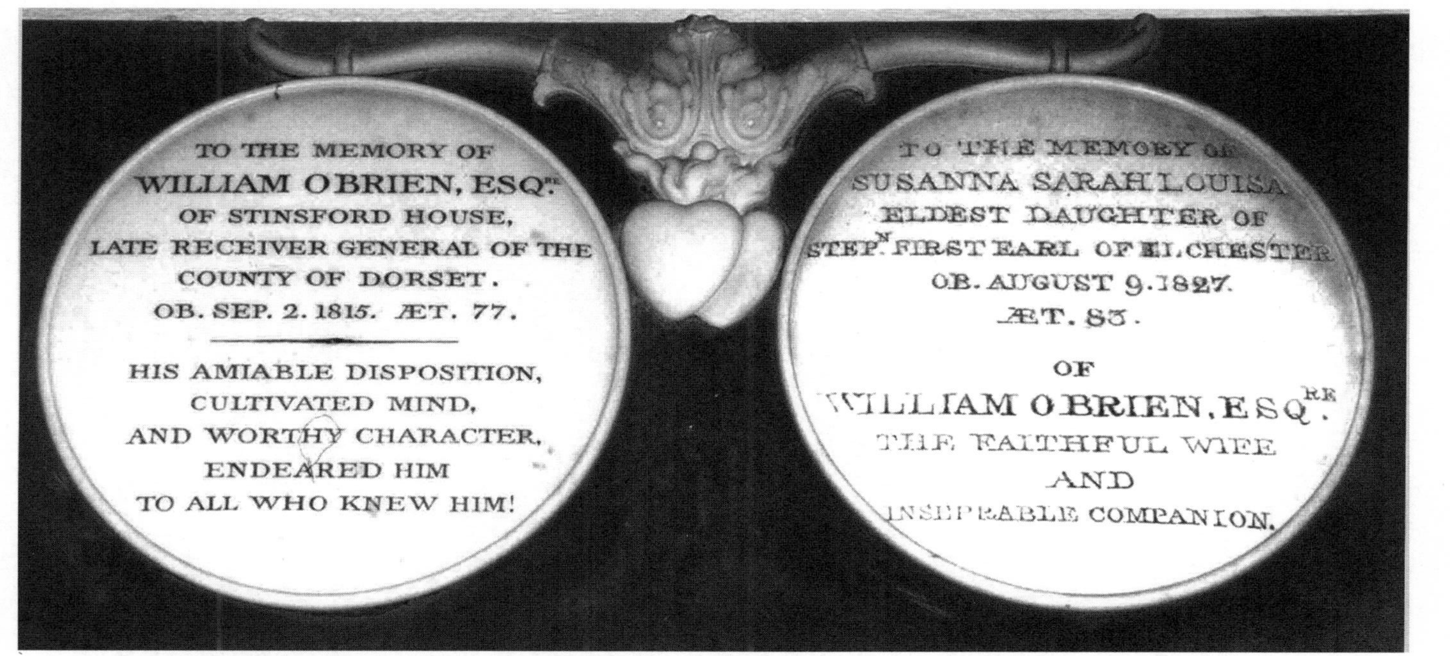

The memorial to William and Susan O'Brien in Stinsford church 'filled all vacant spaces chock-full with broken glass, that not a rat can put his nose in anywhere'.[78] By the end of the year the main structural repairs had barely been started, and Susan wrote that 'the ruinous state of the house, admitting rain in every part, has occasioned much to be spent, even to patch it up for the winter'.[79]

The builders eventually returned in the spring of 1805. Extracts from Susan's journal for the following few months will ring only too true with anyone who has had work done on their own house in later times:

1805

25 March: A load of sand came for the building. I did not ever think to see it begin.

8 April: Workmen came to begin the repairs. Long looked for, comes at last, though a month later than was intended.

9 July: Driven out of the drawing room. The roof over it much worse than the workmen expected.

31 July: All the latter part of the month at home without company, and plagued to death with the workmen and all the discontent they occasion.

21 September: Returned to Stinsford [after a visit to Sherborne Castle]. Work little advanced – ill-managed from first to last.

31 December: The work about the house hardly done yet, and very ill done ... and very, very provoking. Altogether it has been an odious jobb, but now at least we shall be dry in the house.[80]

Whilst the men were at work, Susan was busy choosing new furnishings, writing in May to her niece Elizabeth Feilding 'our riches will only authorise the purchase of new window curtains and chair covers, the present having more holes than anything else – but papering, sashing etc. are deferred for some time, perhaps *sine die*'. In September she wrote, again to Elizabeth, to say that they were now dry and comfortable 'and able to get rid of our magnificent rags, and put clean linnen curtains and chair covers, which, you know, is a great event here'.[81]

In the long term, the O'Briens' marriage turned out much more happily than anyone could have expected. William and Susan were together for over fifty years, and there is no indication that William was ever unfaithful. They had no children.[82] Susan was overcome with grief after her husband's death in 1815, telling her niece Mary that he had been 'the object of my thoughts, affections and anxieties since nineteen years old, and must till death be the object of my regrets'.[83] She stayed on at Stinsford, and died there in 1827 at the age of eighty-four. Susan remained active in mind and body until almost the end, and was remembered with great affection – and a certain amount of awe – by her nephews and nieces and their children.

After Susan O'Brien's death Stinsford House was occupied by Edward Murray, the vicar of Stinsford and brother-in-law to the third Earl of Ilchester. It was as a maid to the Murrays that Thomas Hardy's mother, Jemima Hand, first came to Stinsford, having previously worked for Susan O'Brien's brother, the Revd Charles Fox Strangways. Many people in the village still remembered 'Lady Sue' when Hardy was a boy: his grandfather (another Thomas Hardy) had built the vault in which she and her husband were buried, and he had also erected their monument on the north wall of Stinsford church. In his disguised memoir, first published in 1928 in his wife's name, Hardy tell us that he felt 'a romantic interest' in 'the occupants of the little vault in the chancel' at an early age.[84] The hours that he must have spent gazing at the O'Briens' memorial during the long Sunday sermons of his childhood are remembered in the poem 'The Noble Lady's Tale', which was inspired by their story:

A yellowing marble, placed there
Tablet-wise,
And two joined hearts enchased there
Meet the eyes;
And reading their twin names we moralize.

Stinsford House still stands today. Much of the surviving structure is of one principal storey, with basements and attics. This unusual design is traditionally believed to be the result of rebuilding necessitated by a fire in the early nineteenth century which, it is said, 'seriously damaged the house'.[85] There is, however, no indication that the house was affected by a fire during Susan O'Brien's lifetime. There was a fire close by, and this may be the origin of the story. In March 1825 two barns at the nearby farm were set on fire, and the flames spread to Susan's stables and coach-house. Susan noted in her journal: 'I received kind offers and enquirys from all in Dorchester. The inns sent chaises and offers of all kinds, thinking it was the house.'[86] Fortunately for Susan, the conflagration was extinguished before it reached the house itself.

4

Mary

William and Susan O'Brien had no children of their own, but Susan's journals record regular visits to Stinsford by her nephews and nieces, whom she also saw at Melbury and in their own homes. She was closest to the daughters of her brother, the second Earl of Ilchester, and to Kitty Acland, the only surviving child of her sister Harriot.

The second Earl was not able to be as generous to his daughters as his father had been. The first Earl's wife had been an heiress, and he had inherited the Redlynch estate free from substantial debts. Nevertheless, the payment of more than £30,000 to his daughters and younger sons between 1764 and 1782 must have placed a considerable strain on the resources of the Redlynch and Melbury estates. By the end of the eighteenth century the family's financial situation had deteriorated, and the girls of the next generation had to make do with portions that were much smaller than those paid to their aunts. The second Countess, Mary Grady, brought little or no money to her husband's family, and her own relations were therefore not in a position to negotatiate a marriage settlement that would provide generously for her or her children. Before the marriage took place, Lord Stavordale asked his parents what he could expect in the way of a home and income for himself and his bride-to-be. Lady Ilchester replied that they 'might do greater things ... if it was a desirable match'. As she commented in a letter to her husband, 'as it is, they will gladly come into anything we please'.[1] Under the settlement, which was eventually drawn up in 1782, ten years after the marriage, the sum of £16,000 was allocated for the portions of daughters and younger sons.[2] Five daughters survived to marry, so this gave them £3200 each. In a codicil added to his will in 1790, the second Earl said that his daughters 'cannot have very large fortunes according to the original settlement, there being so many of them', and asked his son to increase the dowry of each of them by £2000 if he was able to do so. The second Earl also referred to his own debts, in part the result of his continuing addiction to gambling, regretting that his son 'will justly have to accuse me for my follies which will, during his lifetime, I fear, much contract his income'.[3] When he died in 1802 the Earl owed at least £37,700.[4]

Susan O'Brien's niece Mary Strangways was the first of her generation to marry. Mary, the second daughter of the second Earl and Countess of Ilchester, was very like her lovely, dark-haired mother: reserved, serious-minded and unselfish. When, early in 1792, Lord Ilchester made the long journey to western Ireland to visit his sister Fanny Quin and the parents of his late wife, it was fifteen-year-old Mary that he took with him, rather than her elder sister Elizabeth, who was to be presented at Court that spring.

Lord Ilchester left Redlynch on 12 January 1792, with Mary and her little brother Harry, Lord Stavordale. Three days later they arrived at Penrice Castle, which stands on the Gower peninsula in South Wales, only twelve miles from Swansea, one of the stopping-points on the principal route from southern England to Milford in Pembrokeshire, the port most commonly used by the passage-boats to Ireland. Lord Ilchester had known Penrice's owner, Thomas Mansel Talbot, for several years, perhaps since his Oxford days, for the two men had been at the university at the same time, though at different colleges. Both were aged forty-four when Lord Ilchester visited Penrice, having been born within a few days of each other in July 1747.

Unlike Melbury, Redlynch and Stinsford, Penrice Castle was a modern house, having been built less than twenty years before Lord Ilchester's visit. Today Gower is a popular holiday area, but in the eighteenth century it was wild and remote, and backward compared with the West Country, or even with the more accessible parts of South Wales. Thomas Talbot's ancestors had first acquired property in Gower in the twelfth century, and they had lived in castles at Penrice, and then in the nearby parish of Oxwich, until the mid sixteenth century when Sir Rice Mansel of Oxwich had bought the buildings and estates of the dissolved abbey of Margam, near the coast about twenty-five miles away. Sir Rice Mansel converted the abbey buildings into a mansion that was to be the family's seat for the next two centuries. Thomas Talbot had inherited the Penrice and Margam estates in 1758 when he was ten years old. After coming of age in 1768 he had spent several years travelling on the Continent, mainly in Italy. By 1772, when he returned to Britain, he had both the money and the inclination to build himself a new house. He never seems to have liked the old mansion at Margam, which was, by this time, rambling, inconvenient and neglected. It had changed little, and had been used only intermittently, since the death of the first Lord Mansel in 1723. Thomas eventually began to demolish the old house in the late 1780s.

Impressed by the classical villas that he had seen in Italy, and filled with the contemporary enthusiasm for uncultivated, romantic scenery, Thomas Talbot commissioned the Gloucestershire architect Anthony Keck to design a totally new house for him, below the walls of the thirteenth-century stone

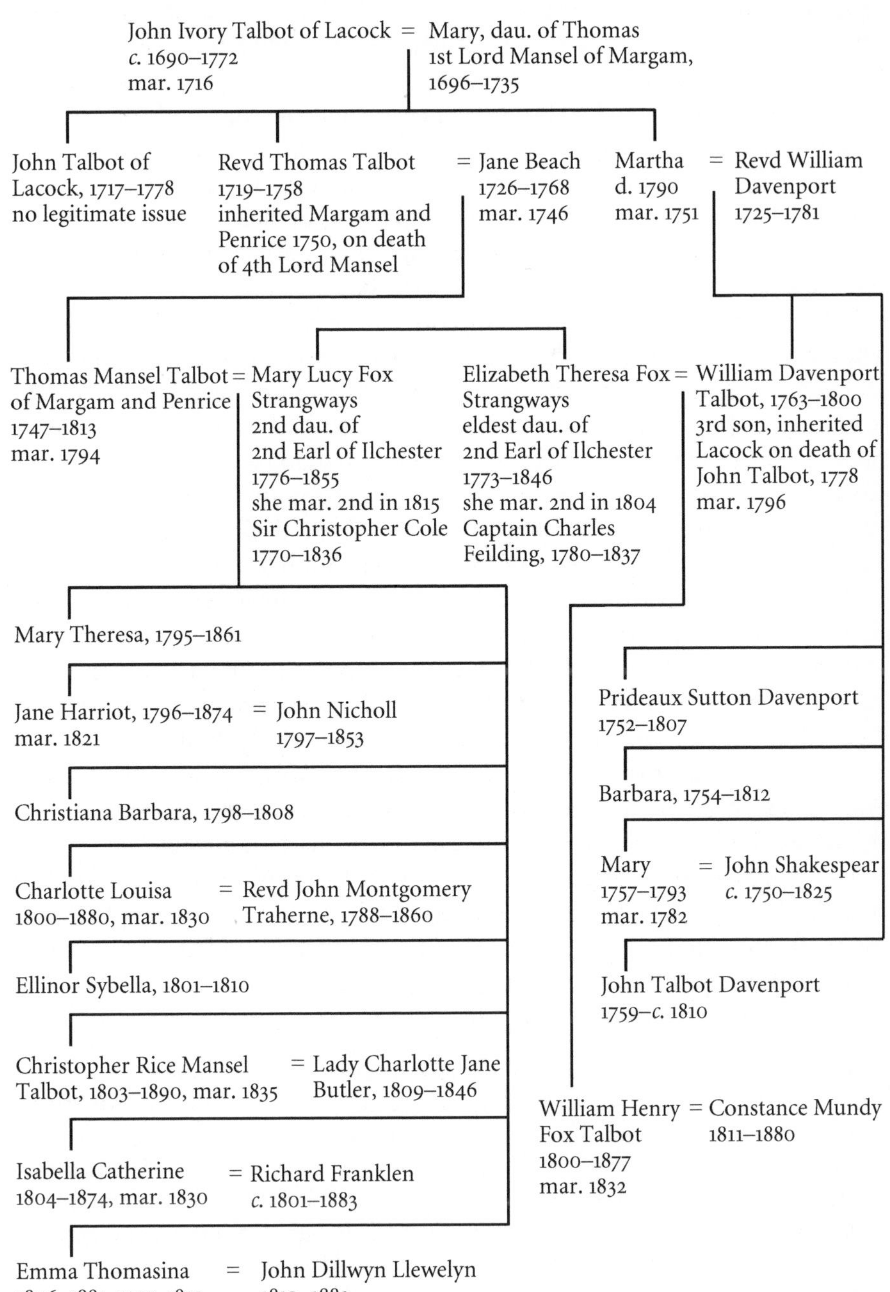

The Talbot Family

castle at Penrice and overlooking the Bristol Channel – a situation which Thomas described in 1773 as 'the most romantic spot in all the county'.[5] Work on a new neo-Classical 'shooting box' began in 1773 and continued for three or four years. The house, which is built of stone and bricks faced with ashlar Bath stone, specially shipped from Bristol, is plain – even severe – in its plan and exterior elevations.[6] It is at its most impressive when seen from the south or south east. There are three and a half storeys in addition to the garrets, and the principal rooms all have spectacular views over the park and lake to the marshes and Oxwich Bay.

In 1776, whilst the work on the interior of the house was still in progress, Thomas Talbot turned his attention to the creation of an ornamental park by landscaping the woods and pasture grounds around the old castle. Whilst it had been the natural beauty of the site which had prompted Thomas to built at Penrice in the first place, he felt that this could be enhanced. Extensive work was carried out at a cost of several hundred pounds during the period 1776 to 1779 under the direction of the landscape designer William Emes. This included the enlargement of the small stream below the house to form a chain of lakes, the planting of groups of trees including two hundred poplars, sixty pines and a variety of fruit trees, and the creation of paths and shrubberies. The walled kitchen gardens in the south-east corner of the park also appear to have been laid out at this time. Emes, who came from Derbyshire and was greatly influenced by Lancelot 'Capability' Brown, had previously worked mainly in the Midlands and North Wales. His work at Penrice added to the naturally romantic appearance of the grounds around the house, and showed the new building off to its best advantage.

The reactions of contemporary visitors to the new Penrice Castle were mixed. The house and grounds were praised, but a number of people clearly found it difficult to understand why their owner should have chosen to build at Penrice in the first place. Henry Skrine, who toured Wales in 1798, was probably not untypical when he commented:

> [Gower] is in general a rocky and uninteresting district except where the sea view enlivens it; yet has fancy or some other cause or predilection disposed Mr Talbot to create a highly ornamented villa, with all its luxurious appendages, at Penrice, near the extremities of this tract ... The house is an elegant modern structure, and the diversities of lawn, wood and water, introduced with much taste and design, strongly contrast the asperities of the surrounding district and surprise the stranger with a degree of refinement he could little expect in such a tract. Yet may an observer, without too critic an eye, deem the trim aspect of this park, with its smooth sheet of water, inconsonant with the rough outline of the coast and country ... Still more must he wonder that its owner should desert the noble seat of Margam, in the midst of a populous and plentiful country, to form a

> fairy palace in a dreary and desolate wild, far from the haunts of man, and near the extremity of a bleak peninsula.[7]

It must, however, be remembered that, when he planned and built Penrice in the 1770s, Thomas Talbot did not think of it as his principal seat: it was to be a shooting box rather than a family home. Until he became too old and ill to undertake further projects, Thomas always intended to replace the old mansion at Margam, though he never got further than clearing the site. It was left to his son, Kit Talbot, to build the house that eventually took over from Penrice as the centre of his family's estates.

Thomas Talbot continued to travel during the 1780s, living at Penrice for only a part of the time. The house remained only sparsely furnished, as its owner became involved in other building projects, most notably the construction of the longest orangery in Britain on his estate at Margam between 1786 and 1790. He also had a spacious new coaching inn built at Pyle, a mile or two from Margam, at a cost of at least £1000. It provided comfortable accommodation for travellers, and also for Thomas, who had his own apartment there.[8] It was probably at the Pyle Inn that Thomas met Lord Ilchester and his party in 1792, so that he could show them his collection of orange trees and then conduct them to Penrice.

The original plan seems to have been for Lord Ilchester and his son and daughter to spend a few days at Penrice before travelling the remaining seventy or so miles to board their ship for Ireland, but their stay was to last longer than they expected. The bumpy Welsh roads were too much for the springs of Lord Ilchester's carriage, which broke and had to be sent to Bristol to be repaired. In addition, Lord Ilchester's gout flared up, and it was a month before he was well enough to set out again. During these weeks Thomas Talbot fell in love with Mary Strangways. Mary, who celebrated her sixteenth birthday whilst she was at Penrice, was upset and confused by his attentions, though her romantic sensibilities were awakened by the older man, who appeared shy and lonely in his remote but beautiful home. Whether Thomas proposed then and there is unknown, but the letters written by Mary to her younger sister Harriot during the following months suggest that some unsettling event took place whilst she was at Penrice.

On 19 February the visitors left Penrice and continued on their journey to Ireland. In the meantime, Thomas Talbot was galvanised into action by the faint hope that Mary Strangways might eventually return to Penrice as his bride, and he began to refurbish and redecorate his long-neglected home, and improve the park and gardens. The work continued after Lord Ilchester's return from Ireland in September 1792. In the meantime, Mary's life resumed its old course for a while: there were lessons with her governess and visits to Melbury and Abbotsbury. She spent part of the winter of 1792 to 1793 in London, and in the following spring she was presented at Court – the formal recognition that she was now an adult. During her stay in London Mary apparently received marriage proposals from two 'young smarts' – one the Earl of Thanet and the other 'a man of good fortune, and handsome in his person'.[9] She turned them both down, and Thomas waited with increasing impatience to find out if he would be able to marry her. Mary's friends and relations advised caution, as her suitor was so much older than she, and Mary was extremely reluctant to commit herself. To Fanny Richards, the sister of Mary's governess Agnes Porter, the girl's behaviour was 'a mystery', though she believed that Mary would be 'much happier with Mr Talbot than with a younger and more gay husband'. She also understood that the 'bar to the union' did not proceed from Lord Ilchester, not least because 'Lord Ilchester wishes not for grown-up daughters to inspect his conduct'.[10] Mary finally accepted Thomas's proposal in December, and he wrote to her, begging her to name the day when the ceremony might take place.[11]

Strictly speaking, Mary was marrying beneath her, for she was an earl's daughter and Thomas had no title. In theory, too, her father was much wealthier than her future husband, with mansions at Melbury, Redlynch and Abbotsbury, a shooting box at Maddington in Wiltshire, and a rented house in London. The Ilchester estates produced an annual income of approximately £16,000 in the 1790s, whilst Thomas's gross income from his Welsh estates was about £8000 a year, and he had only one comparatively small house, in Glamorgan. In terms of disposable income, however, the difference was not so great, for the interest and annuities due out of Lord Ilchester's annual income came to £6000 a year in the 1790s, whilst Thomas was paying only £1500.[12] Thomas seems to have received only £500 of Mary's dowry at the time of their marriage: Lord Ilchester paid him interest at the rate of 4 per cent a year until his death in 1802, after which his executors handed over a further £3000.[13]

Mary's relations agreed that Thomas was 'a very amiable man' and 'a man of excellent character',[14] but the age difference continued to worry them. As her aunt Susan wrote, 'her choice was thought extraordinary, as his time of life was very unsuitable to hers'. Susan added, however, that Mary was 'so amiable and good a girl that I think, and sincerely hope, she will be happy'.[15] Her elder sister Elizabeth (Lily) tried to persuade Mary not to marry a man who was so much older than she was. According to the memoirs of Mary's son Kit Talbot, her reply was 'you have not seen that beautiful garden at Penrice!'[16] It would probably be true to say that

Mary was drawn by the attractions of Penrice itself, as well as those of its owner.

By the end of the first week in January 1794, Thomas and Mary were both in Town. Mary was busy choosing her trousseau, telling Harriot: 'What with Circassian-Turkish-Polish dresses etc. etc ... I have been as busy as a bee since I came to London'. Meanwhile, her husband-to-be (whom she christened 'Gustavus') showered her with presents, including 'the *pretiest* watch you ever saw', pearl bracelets and earrings, a diamond ring, and 'heaps of books and plants'.[17] Mary's father gave her a Welsh dictionary. Mary, not surprisingly, was suffering from cold feet by this time. On 13 January she informed Harriot, 'I have been today to see all my fineries completed. I like my day apparel very much, but ... [*sic*] – perhaps you may guess what I mean. If not, I will explain it to you when my eyes may delight themselves with your dear face'. She also told her sister that she wished that the marriage ceremony was over 'for, like a dark cloud, it overshadows all my prospects'.[18]

The marriage duly took place at Melbury on 1 February, and the new bride and groom set off for Penrice. Mary, who was not yet eighteen, was extremely homesick at first, but she was determined to make the best of her new situation. In a letter written from Penrice five days after the wedding she assured Harriot 'I have so many things to amuse me, and I have followed your advice so strictly "not to think" that I am in very good spirits'. She liked her new home, telling her sister 'You would be astonished if you was to see the beauty and comfort of everything inside this house'.[19] The transition from daughter to wife was, nevertheless, a difficult one, as Mary told Harriot in another letter written during the early days of her marriage:

> All my troubles and turmoils are, I am afraid, going to begin. I have already been seeing (a little) into my affairs, and must presently go about them again. Everybody intends coming to see me, and we are [so] far from most of them that they cannot go back the same day, and therefore, as they are total strangers, I shall not know what to do with myself to entertain people for so long together. Adieu, all snugness up in my own room! Adieu, all my dear, cherished reverie! I must now always be present, both body and mind, and as I am not very much used to that, I don't know how to begin.[20]

Mary became more confident as time went on, and she settled happily into her role as mistress of Penrice. Her first child, a daughter named Mary Theresa after Mary's mother, was born at Penrice in August 1795. Four more daughters followed: Jane in 1796, Christiana (Tina) in 1798, Charlotte in 1800 and Ellinor in 1801. Then, in 1803, Christopher (Kit), the only son, was born. After him came two more girls: Isabella (Bella) in 1804, and

Emma, the baby of the family, in 1806. Thomas Talbot was devoted to his wife and children, telling Mary in one letter:

> Kiss the dear children for their fond father. I think him one of the very fondest that ever lived, at least I know that there is only one being on earth that he loves with sincerer affection, and must do till death us do part: my ever dear wife, Mary Lucy Talbot.[21]

The Revd Sydney Smith, who visited Penrice in 1799, gave his impressions of Thomas and Mary Talbot in a letter to Henrietta Maria Hicks Beach:

> I like your cousin Mr Talbot. He is good-tempered, unaffected and civil. I should think him, too, to be generous, hospitable, expensive and passionate, fond of his wife and children to dotage. Lady Mary seems to be an amiable, valuable woman, who uses her influence over her husband to the best purposes. She is shy, a little rural – for which I like her not the worse – and very handsome.[22]

Thomas's health deteriorated as he grew older, and within a few years it was Mary who was the 'commanding officer' in the household. As her son wrote many years later: 'My reminiscences [of my mother] are of one who was unceasingly active, ubiquitous, vivacious [and] energetic, ruling and managing everything and everybody, from her husband downwards.'[23]

The happiness of family life at Penrice during these years is reflected in the memoirs of Mary Talbot's daughter Charlotte Traherne:

> What a blessing it is to be born into a family: to open one's eyes for the first time among people who are all ready to love and serve you, without waiting for merit on your part, merely because you are the child of their sister, their friend, and whose love is ready to bear the neglect and ingratitude of thoughtless childhood without taking offence, so that it is not an easy matter, even for a very faulty child, to get rid of the friends Providence has supplied him with at the very outset. This blessing and unmerited mercy I enjoyed in common with the generality of human beings born into this world, but the degree of it was more than common, and we have to thank God for a mother whose love and care was so unceasing, so enlightened, so individual, as I may say, that each of her six children felt beloved, appreciated, understood, warned and directed as though she had been the sole object upon which that mother's love was concentrated.[24]

Amongst the most regular visitors to Penrice during the early years of Thomas and Mary Talbot's marriage was Thomas's cousin William Davenport Talbot, who had inherited the heavily-indebted Lacock estate in Wiltshire from his uncle John Talbot in 1778 whilst he was still under age.[25] Unable to afford to live at Lacock, William had entered the army as a cornet in the Second or Queen's Regiment of Dragoon Guards in 1783. William's relations commented on his headstrong behaviour,[26] and by 1790 he already owed over £2600 on his own account, including £55 still due from his time as an undergraduate at Oxford, and £1000 for his transfer from the Dragoons to the Royal Fusiliers.

After serving in Holland, Gibraltar and Canada, William Davenport Talbot eventually left the regular army in 1795, by which time he was a captain in the Eighty-Eighth Regiment of Foot or Connaught Rangers. It was probably ill-health that eventually made him give up his commission. He was at Penrice for several months from December 1794: Thomas Talbot had been William's guardian during his minority, and the two had always been close. Then, early in 1795, William Davenport Talbot met Mary Talbot's sister Lily Strangways, whom Thomas and Mary had brought back from Melbury for a visit that was to last for several months.

William was unwell during the first months of 1795, and Lily helped to nurse and entertain him. Lily was two years older than Mary, and quite unlike her sister. Mary was shy and enjoyed solitude, whilst Lily was an extravert, who always liked to be the centre of attention. Mary was the prettier of the two, but Sydney Smith, who met Lily when he visited Penrice in 1799, thought that she had 'a countenance that is dangerous and interesting and intelligent'. He also admired her 'pretty little figure and her bewitching smile'.[27] Attractive and intelligent as she was, Lily was also stubborn, self-centred and volatile. Susan O'Brien, who loved her niece, recognising that her character showed many similarities to her own, told Lily in 1792: 'You have no pliability in your temper, and less of the good nature that proceeds from sentiment and a desire to oblige than any young person I ever met with'.[28] The differences between the two sisters were summed up many years later by Mary's son Kit Talbot, who wrote:

> My aunt required society, and knew how to make it; she could converse equally well with all sorts of people and make herself agreeable to all, and never was so happy as when she was doing so. My mother, on the other hand, would have exhibited unmistakable symptoms of being bored, and her conversation would have shewn signs of effort, with the same society that came so naturally to my aunt Lily ... How could such diverse branches have come from the same root? Yet they resembled each other in warmth of heart and love for their own family, and also in power of mind and capacity of understanding, if in nothing else.[29]

Unlike Mary, who had married the first man to propose to her, Lily had broken many hearts before she met William Davenport Talbot. In the summer of 1793 Agnes Porter told her sister that her eldest pupil had 'an attachment which I neither will, nor ought to, hear of'.[30] The identity of this suitor is unknown, but one of his rivals was certainly Sir George Paul of Rodborough, Gloucestershire, a friend of Lord Ilchester, who was thirty years older than Lily. Exactly what happened at Penrice in the spring of 1795 is unclear, but William was soon said to be 'infatuated' with Lily. Thomas Talbot wrote some time later that 'this retired spot was never the occasion of such mischief before, and I hope I shan't live to see the like again'.[31] By the end of the year William was pressing Lily to marry him.

Whilst Lord Ilchester seems to have been happy with his second daughter's marriage to one of his old friends, he most certainly did not consider that William Davenport Talbot was a suitable husband for Mary's elder sister. The age difference was not so great – William was ten years older than Lily – but he had no money and few prospects; he was in poor health; and he had two elder brothers who had been disinherited because they were mentally handicapped. William did not even have a house of his own to take Lily to, for Lacock Abbey had been leased to the Dowager Countess of Shrewsbury. Susan O'Brien sympathised with her niece, for she knew only too well the problems that would follow if Lily insisted on marrying a man of whom her family disapproved. In December 1795 she wrote to Mary:

> I am now at Melbury, where I find our dear Eliza[32] under great uneasiness and embarassment. I most sincerely feel for her situation and pity her, as indeed I do my brother, who doats on her and feels as much distress as I do on this very unpleasant occasion, but it is impossible to wonder that, in such times as these are, the kindest parent should not approve a choice where fortune is so circumscribed. I feel my own life at present so embittered by narrowness of circumstances that I cannot but wish most anxiously that one I love as dearly as I do your sister should not suffer the many deprivations I do, and I most sincerely hope both partys will reflect in time with coolness and prudence on what equally concerns the happiness of both.[33]

But coolness and prudence were qualities that Lily conspiciously lacked, and she accepted William's proposal, telling her father that, whilst she was 'entirely unblinded by the illusions of love' and had no 'romantic attachment' to her suitor, who was 'much more deeply interested' than she was, she was too fond of him to see him miserable, and to know that she was the cause of that misery.[34]

Lord Ilchester eventually relented, and William and Lily were married in London on 17 April 1796. Agnes Porter was present at the ceremony, which she described in her journal:

> At two the company assembled in the drawing room [of Lord Ilchester's London house, 31 Old Burlington Street]. Mr Charles Strangways, her uncle, performed the ceremony. Her father gave her away; her voice trembled, but she did her best

> – did not articulate the word 'obey', but behaved on the whole very prettily – was dressed in a green riding habit, black hat and feather; a long white veil fell down over her face.[35]

After the ceremony 'all wished them joy and drank their health', and the newly-married couple then set off for Bath, where they spent a fortnight with Lily's aunt Catherine Gumbleton before travelling on to Wales. In her journal, Susan O'Brien contrasted this marriage with that of her niece Kitty Acland, who married Lord Porchester (later the second Earl of Carnarvon) a week later:

> In April [1796] my two nieces were married. Miss Acland with compleat approbation of her friends, great riches, great rank, and every probabillity of happiness. Lady Elizabeth, against every representation that the prudence and affection of her family could suggest to prevent it. What will be the consequence? Will prudence and foresight, or foolish *entêtement* be productive of the most happiness to these two girls?[36]

Why did Lily marry William Davenport Talbot? He was certainly handsome and he had a good deal of charm. The fact that her family disapproved of him so strongly no doubt increased her determination to defy them. Probably, too, she was a little jealous of her younger sister, already comfortably established in her own home, with a baby daughter born in August 1795. Life at home had also become more difficult after her father's second marriage in August 1794. The new mistress of Melbury was a cousin, Maria Digby, a girl only two years older than her new daughter-in-law.

Three of Lord Ilchester's daughters now remained unmarried. Harriot, born in 1778, was lively and good-natured, but she had neither Mary's beauty nor Lily's wit and elegance. Lord Ilchester told Thomas Talbot that his only reason for going to London in the spring of 1798 was 'for the annual chance of Harriot's getting a good husband'.[37] This comment highlights the importance of the London Season as a marriage market. Girls 'came out' into society at the age of seventeen or eighteen, and were then shown off by their parents, relations and friends to potential suitors, most of whom knew exactly how much they were worth. Social events in other towns such as Bath, Tunbridge Wells and Weymouth performed a similar function. Harriot had a suitor with £12,000 a year by the summer of 1798, and Susan O'Brien thought that she 'had better not aspire to the glory of refusing, but to the wisdom of accepting'.[38] But Harriot's sisters did not think much of the man, and he soon disappeared from the scene. In November it was reported that Lord Ilchester was planning to go to Bath to try pumping 'and begin the winter campaigne for Harriot'.[39] Harriot eventually became engaged in the following summer, when she was twenty-one. Her husband-to-be was a country gentleman, James Frampton, who was thirty years old and had inherited the Moreton estate, not far from Dorchester, on his father's death in 1784. The match was not a brilliant one for Harriot, but her relations seem to have been pleased to welcome Frampton into the family. As Susan O'Brien wrote when the engagement was announced, 'Mr Frampton is an agreeable man of the greatest respectabillity and, though his fortune is not large, may make her [Harriot] very happy'.[40] Ten days later Susan added:

> On the whole, all circumstances considered, it is a desirable match for Harriot. Here is love and prudence in unison: tranquil love, if such there be, *sans délire, sans craint, sans agitation* and, as Rousseau would perhaps say, *sans amour* – but enough, I trust, for happiness.[41]

An interesting comment from a woman who had herself married for love!

At the end of August Harriot was taken to London to buy her trousseau. Within a week 'everything was bought and made up'. Susan O'Brien reported that Harriot's new clothes were 'very elegant and well-chosen and, according to Harriot's taste, a great deal of lace'. The O'Briens were at the ceremony, which took place at Melbury on 9 September. This was evidently a much bigger affair than the weddings of Harriot's two elder sisters had been:

> [We were] a pretty good posse, but Harriot persevered in liking a good, jolly, old-fashioned wedding. We have been unlucky with the weather, which spoiled the beauty of the procession, as some went with umbrellas, some (and the bride herself) in the sedan chair. Charles performed the ceremony, and all behaved very well. She kept up her spirits to the last, and looked very pretty in her finery.[42]

Afterwards, the guests feasted on 'a fine cake, fruits etc. etc.' and then 'after salutations and congratulations were over', the bride retired to disrobe. Her bridal dress 'of embroidered India muslin, the finest possible, with [a] veil of Honiton lace', was changed for a riding habit,[43] and Harriot and her new husband set out for Redlynch, where they spent a few days before settling in at Moreton. Harriot's fourteen-year-old sister Louisa wrote to tell her brother Harry about the wedding, and informed him 'it was the most melancholy day I spent *in all my life*'.[44]

Harriot's marriage seems to have been a particularly fortunate one. It lasted for forty-five years, ending with her death in 1844. Moreton is only five miles from Stinsford, and the O'Briens saw the Framptons often. Susan O'Brien thought that Harriot and her husband suited each other pefectly, and wrote in 1805 that Harriot 'is placed exactly where she should be, in a family that adore her, and of which she is the life and pleasure, and where her activity of mind and disposition is considered as a perfection and a virtue'.[45] Many years later Kit Talbot remembered his aunt with great affection:

> Lady Harriot Frampton, as I recollect her first, was fat, fair and forty, of the most kindly and genial disposition. My visits to her hospitable house in Dorsetshire every winter are among the most agreeable of my reminiscences of early life.[46]

Five months after Harriot's wedding, Lily's first child, a son, was born at Melbury. He was baptised William Henry Fox Talbot, but was always known as Henry. By the time of his son's birth, however, William Davenport Talbot was seriously ill. In July Lily left him at her father's house in London, whilst she travelled to Wales with her baby son. A few days later Susan O'Brien found William 'wretchedly ill, and so forlorn it quite shocked me'. She wondered how Lily could possibly have left him: 'She is much to blame – it sets everyone against her ... I wish I had come ... a few days sooner – I might have prevailed with her to have stayed and spared her conscience and character. What they will suffer should this poor man die – and they in Wales.'[47] Five days after this was written, on 31 July 1800, William Davenport Talbot died. None of his own relations was present and he was nursed during his last hours by Susan O'Brien and a friend of the family, Alicia Campbell. He asked repeatedly for his sister Barbara Davenport, but she eventually arrived after his death, 'in a dreadfull way'. Susan O'Brien commented:

> What a melancholy end is this poor man's! Not a friend with him ... so destitute as to be obliged to Mrs Campbell and I for the last attentions he could be sensible of. No one even to order his funeral; Mr O'Brien obliged to order things that were of the first necessity.[48]

A few days later, news came from Penrice that Lily was 'in a deplorable state' and quite unfit to travel.[49] On 6 August the funeral procession set out for Lacock. When word came that neither Lily nor Thomas Talbot intended to leave Penrice, Barbara Davenport was 'so affected and so hurt' by their neglect that she resolved to travel to Lacock herself, 'though hardly able to make such an effort'.[50] She never forgave Lily for her failure to attend William's funeral. Her own family, too, thought that Lily had acted very badly and they were shocked by her behaviour. Harriot Frampton, who hurried to Penrice as soon as she heard the news of William's death, told Susan O'Brien that 'from the moment I first saw Lily to the last, I never perceived the smallest shadow of regret for poor Mr Talbot. What she did feel was certainly remorse for having left him, and having been always ungrateful for his kindness.'[51] Susan summed up her own feelings in a letter to Agnes Porter, who was at Penrice with the Talbots:

> Indeed ... I heartily pity, as well as blame, her. I have loved her as my own child, and therefore I feel the more hurt at all that has happened, and the more alarmed at the situation she is in – a trying one to any woman at her age ... My hopes now are that her vanity, which has led her into many errors, may now take a different turn, and that she may have the idea ... that more celebrity and more admiration is to be got by a steady and good conduct in a difficult situation than by being followed by fashionable profligates, or talked of by fashionable wits.[52]

The next few years were difficult for Lily, for she still had no house of her own, and her husband's death had left her and her baby son very badly provided for.[53] She was barely on speaking terms with her sister-in-law Barbara Davenport, and showed little inclination to face up to the realities of her position. The situation only really began to improve when Lily remarried. Her second husband, whom she married at Penrice in April 1804, was Captain Charles Feilding, a naval officer six years her junior. Feilding, who had first gone to sea as a captain's secretary at the age of thirteen, was not wealthy, but he was well connected, being a great-nephew of the fifth Earl of Denbigh. On hearing of the wedding, Susan O'Brien wrote in her journal 'may this marriage prove more fortunate than her former – but it is almost as extraordinary'.[54] In spite of Susan's forebodings, however – and also despite the fact that Feilding's mother made it all too obvious that she heartily disapproved of her new daughter-in-law – the union turned out well. Two years after the wedding Susan wrote that Charles was very fond of Lily, and 'very handsome and pleasing'. Susan hoped that Charles would 'fix her weathercock head'.[55] Charles Feilding was indeed a steadying influence on his wife, and he was also an exemplary stepfather to her young son, Henry Talbot, who spent much of his childhood at Penrice with his aunt Mary and his Talbot cousins.[56]

After the second Earl of Ilchester's death in 1802, his widow took over the responsibility for finding husbands for her two youngest stepdaughters, Charlotte and Louisa. Inevitably the girls spent a good deal of time with their Digby cousins, who included several young clergymen and naval officers. Susan O'Brien, who noted that the Digbys 'generally marry relations', wrote in 1803 that her two nieces were 'so surrounded by Digby connexions that speaking to them is speaking to the whole family'. 'I shall be very much mistaken', she continued, 'if there is not something going on between some of the captains and Charlotte or Louisa sooner or later.'[57] A few months later Susan was dismayed to hear that Captain Henry Digby, the eldest of Lady Ilchester's three brothers, wished to marry Louisa. Henry was thirty-four, whilst Louisa was only eighteen:

> [The proposal] surprised and concerned me. Not that Captain Digby may not be called as good a match as Louisa's fortune entitles her to expect, but that, so young and beautiful as she is, she should have no chance out of the Digby family does seem a pity. I do not think Lady Ilchester had any plan or contrivance to bring this about ... but she must be very short-sighted, if she did not wish it, to imagine girls who see nor hear of anything, male or female, but Digbys, will not fancy themselves in love and accept the first offer made, especially when backed, as this will be, by all those she has much intimacy with. He is too old for her, has not either figure or manner that is pleasing – yet, having money, it is better than Captain Stephen or Captain George would have been.[58]

Susan's sister Harriot Acland agreed that the match was a bad one, though Digby had won fame and a substantial fortune as a result of his naval exploits. A week later the news was all over Dorset, and soon everyone in London knew about it as well. Then, at the end of April, William O'Brien returned to Stinsford from a trip to London and informed his wife that everything had been deferred for six months. Not long afterwards, Susan heard a 'strange account of Captain Digby's very improper behaviour and conversation about Louisa'.[59] By July the marriage was off and Lady Ilchester was barely on speaking terms with the rest of her family, who blamed her and Louisa's aunts for the turn of events. Relations between the Digby and Fox Strangways families remained difficult for some time, not least because of Henry Digby's own 'unfeeling and gentlemanlike behaviour'. Unwilling to accept that it had been Louisa's own decision to break off their engagement, he put himself in her way as often as he could.[60] National events, however, intervened: Henry went back to sea and won further fame for himself at the battle of Trafalgar. When, in 1806, he married the widowed Lady Andover, Susan O'Brien commented somewhat sarcastically 'A hero of Trafalgar must be irresistible'.[61]

In 1804 Maria, Countess of Ilchester, became a Lady of the Bedchamber to Queen Charlotte, and in the following year her great friend Alicia Campbell was appointed sub-governess to the Queen's granddaughter, Princess Charlotte. As a result, Lady Ilchester's two stepdaughters found their social life transformed, and they spent much more time in Court circles, both in London and in Weymouth. Towards the end of 1806 a Dorset landowner, Sir William Oglander of Parnham, was said to be 'smitten with Louisa'. Susan O'Brien thought him 'a sensible, agreeable man' who was 'quite in love'. She felt, however, that he was 'not a match for her in any respect whatever'.[62] Exactly why Sir William was so unsuitable is not clear.

By this time, however, another suitor had appeared on the horizon. This was Lord Henry Petty, the heir to the Marquess of Lansdowne and a Member of Parliament, who had been appointed Chancellor of the Exchequer in 1806 when he was only twenty-six.[63] In January 1807 Lord Henry was said to be 'very partial' to Louisa,[64] but he was more cautious than Henry Digby had been. As Louisa confided to her sister Mary Talbot in May, the strain of waiting to find out if he would declare himself began to tell:

> I can't be happy here [in London]. The whole of a London life is so contrary to every wish and taste of mine that trying to appear not discontented in company only makes me more unhappy when alone. I hate being shown like a horse for sale every night of one's life, particularly as no one will buy me. I know, indeed, but one person I would be sold to, and he would as like think of being hung as me, for he hates me, I'm sure.[65]

In July Louisa wrote that she was beginning to think 'he has a sort of tiny liking for me',[66] but that she was still not sure of him. Eventually, in November, Lord Henry proposed and was accepted. Everyone was delighted, for this was an excellent match for Louisa. Lord Henry was wealthy and extremely well connected, he was reported to be 'amiable and sensible', and he and Louisa were in love with each other.[67] As Louisa told Mary on her wedding day, 'No one ever had, I am sure, so fair a prospect of happiness as I have, for he improves upon me every day.'[68] And the marriage does seem to have been successful, though Kit Talbot thought that his aunt 'would have been happier in a humbler position than that of a marchioness, the wife of a leading politician'. He found her rather distant, and liked her the least of his aunts, for 'she was so exclusively devoted to her husband that it always seemed to me that the rest of the world was a blank to her'.[69]

Now only Charlotte remained with her stepmother. Less robust than Louisa, she was sensitive, and her health was thought to be 'lamentably dependant upon her mind'.[70] But Charlotte, too, was a beauty, and she had several admirers. In 1806 Colonel Bathurst was showing an interest. Susan O'Brien did not like the young man, finding him 'rather *dashy* – as well let alone'.[71] In the following year Charlotte was 'a good deal annoyed by a correspondence with Lord Charles Townshend',[72] and she also seems to have rejected her brother's friend George Eden at this time.[73] Another suitor, a Captain Moore, was turned down in 1809. In the summer of 1810, however, Charlotte became engaged to her brother's friend Charles Lemon, the Member of Parliament for Penryn, and son and heir of Sir William Lemon of Carclew in Cornwall. The Lemons were not an ancient landed family – Charles's great-grandfather had made a fortune from mining and smelting

Cornish tin and copper – but Charlotte's relations seem to have been pleased with this match. Susan O'Brien summed up their opinion of Charles:

> He has been long a great admirer, seems a very amiable young man, is a great friend of her brother's, has a good character and a good fortune, and as they have been much together they must know more of each other than the generallity of young people have any opportunity of doing before they marry. There is, therefore, I trust, a good prospect of happiness for them.[74]

The marriage was, indeed, a happy one so long as it lasted. The Lemons were 'comfortable and agreeable' together,[75] and they had many interests in common. But their lives were soon clouded by tragedy: their first son died as a baby in 1812; their only daughter was in poor health for several years before she died in 1825; and their only surviving son was drowned in the following year. This final blow was too much for Charlotte, and she died a few months later 'of a rapid decline'. As her nephew Kit Talbot wrote, 'her disposition was too affectionate to enable her to bear up against the misfortunes of this world'.[76]

The last of this generation to marry was the only son, Harry, who became third Earl of Ilchester on his father's death in 1802. He, too, seems to have married for love. His wife, Caroline Murray, was a cousin of his stepmother and he had known her for some time. One of nine children whose father George Murray, Bishop of St David's, had died aged only forty-two, Caroline was not pretty and she had no fortune, but she was 'remarkably pleasing', and 'had been brought up in such good principles and was quite the character and disposition that would suit him'.[77] They married in 1812, and seem to have been happy together, but this marriage also ended in tragedy, for Caroline died in 1819, shortly after the birth of her fourth child.

By the time of Harry's wedding, his sister Mary had been married to Thomas Talbot for eighteen years. Thomas was now aged almost sixty-five and a virtual invalid. He died in 1813, leaving his widow with six children, of whom the eldest was almost eighteen.[78] Mary grieved for 'the loss of an affectionate heart, to whom she could contribute all the happiness it was capable of enjoying',[79] but the last few years of Thomas's life had clearly been difficult for her. In 1815 she married again. Her second husband, Sir Christopher Cole, was a very different man from her first. He was a Cornishman of comparatively humble birth, a naval officer who had made a name for himself by capturing the islands of Banda Neira in the East Indies in 1811. Six years older than Mary, Sir Christopher had spent most of his adult life at sea and he had not been married before. He had been introduced to the Talbots by Charles Feilding, probably in 1811, and had visited them in Wales in the spring of 1812. He seems to have gone to Penrice again in September 1814, but he and Mary do not appear to have come to any kind of agreement at this stage. A few weeks later, however, Mary was surprised and horrified to receive a proposal from her husband's old friend Dr John Hunt, the incumbent at Margam. Hunt was about sixty-five years old, and had married late in life, at the age of fifty. He had lost his wife in 1813, and evidently thought that Mary would be an ideal replacement, telling her: 'We thoroughly know each other, we entertain a mutual esteem and attachment. This I presume to say for both – for myself I could add much more, and I think a confession will not surprize you.'[80] It is evident from Mary's reply that this was not the first time that Hunt had made known his feelings towards her: she had turned him down in the previous year, and had been accused of 'cold family reserve'. Her response to his second declaration was unambiguous. She told Hunt that 'Though known to you for many years, you have proved your little knowledge of my disposition. Therefore, the seldomer we meet, the less liable I shall be to misconstruction.'[81]

At the end of the year Sir Christopher Cole wrote to Mary, offering her 'a warm and affectionate heart' and describing himself as 'a friend already bound to you by every sentiment of affection and esteem'. He did not actually propose at this time, but was clearly hoping for some encouragement.[82] Mary raised some objections, reminding him that she was thirty-eight years old and might not be able to give him any children, but it was not long before she agreed to marry him. Sir Christopher's proposal seems to have taken most of Mary's relations by surprise. She consulted her brother, who advised caution, thinking that the man might be a fortune-hunter, and telling her 'I shall be anxious to know how far he may have explained his circumstances to you for you to form an opinion as to the propriety of the measure, viewing it in a prudential light'.[83] But, as a widow whose first husband had left her well provided for, Mary could afford to please herself, and she married Sir Christopher Cole in April 1815. Susan O'Brien thought that her niece had made a mistake, writing in her journal '[I] hate a second marriage. Did not think she would marry again – feel disappointed.' Her first impressions of Sir Christopher, whom she met for the first time a few weeks later, were not good: 'A stout, hard-looking man, not handsome, about fifty. Well spoken of and said to be good-tempered – that he may prove so is much to be wished, as married happiness depends so much on it'.[84] Kit Talbot who was, perhaps inevitably, jealous of his stepfather and resented his influence over his mother, wrote that Sir Christopher:

> Was a very remarkable man, both in personal appearance and in mental qualities ... When I first knew him his manners, though courtly to his equals

> and superiors, were often brusque and unpleasant to others, and he was both dictatorial and unconciliating. But all this wore away with time, and in his latter days he was always an agreeable companion, and had quite lost the objectionable demeanour of which I speak.[85]

Sir Christopher does seem to have improved on closer acquaintance, for when Susan O'Brien met him again in 1821 she found him 'more chatty and agreeable than I have ever seen him', and thought that he seemed good-natured.[86] Whatever her relations may have thought of him, however, Sir Christopher was undoubtedly the love of Mary's life. If she wrote any love letters to her first husband, they have not survived, but her usual reserve disappeared in her letters to Sir Christopher. In 1821 she signed herself 'your dutiful, affectionate, obedient, faithful, chearful and loveing wife', and in 1823 'your foolishly, passionately attached wife'.[87] Kit Talbot noticed how his mother changed (not, he thought, for the better) as a consequence of her second marriage. She was no longer the commanding officer in the household: 'after she married Sir Christopher Cole, the leading characteristics of [her] manner were indicative of entire submission to his will [and] languid acquiescence in his wishes, and she seemed to think even only through the medium of his mind'.

Mary was inconsolable after Sir Christopher's death in 1836. According to Kit:

> It is not too much to say, that sorrow for the loss of her second husband was the secret spring of all her actions in later life, and more or less leavened all her feelings ... She had lost the only friend to whom she could communicate her real feelings and thoughts.[88]

Mary's garden helped to distract her from her grief, as did her son and daughters and their rapidly expanding families.

Thomas and Mary Talbot had five daughters who lived long enough to marry. Four of them did so, none spectacularly well. The reason for this was probably not financial, for each girl was entitled to a dowry of £10,000 – almost three times as much as their mother had received. But Mary's fondness for the countryside and her reluctance to spend time in Town meant that her girls were relatively unsophisticated, and were never really launched onto the social scene in London. All four found husbands among the Glamorganshire landed gentry: all quite respectable, but none as wealthy as their brother.

Jane, the second daughter, was good-natured and friendly. As a girl, she was a tomboy, and she was close to both her brother and her cousin Henry Talbot. In 1810 her former governess Agnes Porter thought that Jane was 'a compound, at present, of whim, indolence and genius' who had, however, 'hitherto made very little progress in what is called learning'.[89] In 1821, when she was twenty-five, Jane married John Nicholl of Merthyr Mawr in Glamorgan. They had ten children, and Jane died in 1874. After Jane's wedding it was to be another nine years before there were any more marriages in the family. Bella, a stout, boisterous girl, who was described by Agnes Porter, with a marked lack of enthusiasm, as 'a nice child in her way',[90] married Richard Franklen of Clemenstone, Glamorgan, in 1830. She, too, was twenty-five at the time and, like Jane, she died in 1874. The Franklens had seven children.

Charlotte, Bella's elder sister, also married in 1830, at the comparatively advanced age of thirty. Charlotte (often known as Charry) was the most academic member of the family: in 1810 Agnes Porter wrote that she had 'a decided inclination for literature, which merits the greatest cultivation'.[91] She was also a talented amateur artist. Charlotte and her husband the Revd John Montgomery Traherne of Coedarhydyglyn, an eminent local antiquarian, shared interests in archaeology, heraldry and genealogy, and had known each other for several years before their marriage. They had no children, and it was Charlotte who, in later years, kept the widely-scattered members of her family together by 'constant correspondence'.[92] She died in 1880, aged eighty.

The last girl to marry was the youngest girl, Emma, who was twenty-six when she married John Dillwyn Llewelyn of Penllergaer in 1833. Known as 'Morning Star' as a child, Emma was bright, lively and pretty. She and John had known each other since childhood: Penllergaer is twelve miles from Penrice, and Thomas and Mary Talbot had been friendly with John's parents, Lewis Weston Dillwyn and Mary Adams. John and Emma Llewelyn had seven children, and Emma died in 1881.

The only daughter who remained a spinster evidently chose to do so. In 1827 Mary informed a cousin that her eldest daughter, Mary Theresa, 'will not accept any of the good offers she has received, chusing, she says, to let well alone'.[93] Mary Theresa 'railed against matrimony' and could not understand why her sisters wanted to marry. Her brother Kit found this attitude incomprehensible, as he told her:

> Assuredly, I think it is you that are crazy, instead of Bella and Charry who, like the wise ants, are laying up something for their old age when, in the course of nature, their older friends may be gone. With *men* it is different – they do not depend so entirely on their families, and besides can marry at whatever age they like, as the world at present goes.

Kit tried to persuade Mary Theresa to lend him her dowry at this time, but she replied that 'she wished to have it in her power to give away'.[94] She was fortunate, for she could choose to remain single and still retain a significant degree of financial independence: many women would have found it difficult to withstand pressure of this kind and would thus have lost control over the fortune to which they were entitled.

Kit wanted to borrow his sister's dowry because he had started to build a new, Tudor-style mansion at Margam, close to the site of the old house that his father had demolished forty years earlier. The new family seat was planned for Kit by the fashionable London-based architect Thomas Hopper, though Kit and his sisters also made significant contributions to the design. Margam Castle, as the house became known locally, incorporated many elements from family houses such as Lacock and Melbury. Even today, one of its most notable features is a tall octagonal tower, which was modelled on the Tudor prospect tower at Melbury. In 1835, whilst work on the house was still in progress, Kit married Lady Charlotte Butler, the daughter of an Irish peer, Richard Butler, first Earl of Glengall. They had four children, one son and three daughters, but Lady Charlotte died in 1846, aged only thirty-seven.

Once it was habitable, Margam Castle became the family's main residence in Glamorgan. In 1836, Kit's mother and her second husband moved to Llanelay near Cowbridge, to be closer to the rest of the family, and Penrice was then used mainly for summer holidays and shooting parties. The central portion of the house was completely rebuilt in the 1890s by Kit's daughter, Miss Emily Charlotte Talbot, mainly to provide additional accommodation for visitors and servants. After Miss Talbot's death in 1918 the Penrice and Margam estates were separated for the first time since the mid sixteenth century: Margam went to her only nephew, Captain Andrew Mansel Talbot Fletcher, whilst Penrice was inherited by one of his sisters, Evelyn, the wife of the fourth Baron Blythswood. In 1967–68 the late Georgian and Victorian extensions were largely demolished, so that the house now appears more or less as originally built.[95]

PART TWO

Wives

5

Country Houses

The four houses in which the Fox Strangways ladies lived – Melbury, Redlynch, Stinsford and Penrice – were all very different. Contemporary descriptions of these buildings, together with inventories of their contents and household accounts, tell us how they were altered and adapted to meet the changing needs of their inhabitants during the eighteenth and early nineteenth centuries. An increasing desire for privacy meant that servants became confined, as far as possible, to the back of the house, or even to service buildings that were separate from the main structure. At the same time, less formal patterns of everyday life, combined with different requirements for the entertainment of visitors, led to the introduction of new ways of arranging the principal rooms of the Georgian country house.

In 1692 Thomas Strangways began to modernise and remodel the Tudor home of his ancestors at Melbury. As a Member of Parliament and leader of county society, he wanted a house in which he could receive important guests. The formal grandeur of the Baroque style, which was the height of fashion in the 1690s, suited this purpose very well. Under the guidance of 'Mr Watson', an otherwise unknown provincial architect, the old mansion, which had previously been approached from the north, was turned round. Visitors now drove or rode up to the house from the east, across a newly-built stone bridge over a small natural stream.[1] Watson also embellished the house's new entrance front with a classical pediment and columns, balustraded parapets and modern sash windows.[2] At the same time the central sections of the north and south fronts were redesigned. The interior of the house was refurbished, and a new staircase hall and corridors were constructed. The chimney-pieces in several rooms were ornamented with carved wooden festoons of musical instruments, fruit, flowers, birds and fishes for which, Horace Walpole was later told, Grinling Gibbons was responsible. Once most of the work was finished, probably in 1698, Thomas Hill was employed to adorn the main staircase with a vast portrait of Thomas Strangways accompanied by his wife and six of their children. The ceiling over the staircase was covered by a large painting of the Council of the Gods by the prolific Flemish artist Gerard Lanscroon, who also decorated the landing on the first floor.

An inventory of the contents of the house, drawn up in 1727 after the death of Thomas Strangways junior, gives us a detailed picture of Melbury as it was in the early eighteenth century. It was comfortably fitted out, with all the luxuries that the Strangways family's considerable wealth could buy. The rooms on the ground floor included the marble hall, which had 'Scotch pladd' window curtains (perhaps indicating their late owner's Jacobite sympathies), together with fourteen walnut chairs with seats of Spanish leather, an Indian punch bowl and cover, and an oval Dutch table. Other rooms included the prayer hall, and the great drawing room which had white damask window curtains, a sofa covered with blue damask, and several chairs and tables including a walnut card table. An eating parlour and a smoking room are also listed. As was usual at this time, several of the principal rooms were grouped in apartments, and the larger bedrooms all had closets next to them. These closets would sometimes have been used by servants, but at Melbury in 1727 none, apart from the closet next to the nursery, had a bed in it. Two contained close-stools, but the others seem to have been used largely as sitting rooms. Thomas Strangways and his wife Mary shared a bedchamber, but each also had a dressing room and closet of their own.[3]

The most elaborately furnished rooms were set aside for the accommodation of important visitors. These included the inlaid bedchamber, which was hung with damask lined with white embroidered satin and had green mantua silk window curtains. The furnishings of this room included an India japanned table, gilt sconces and two alabaster figures. There was also the inlaid drawing room, with crimson velvet chairs, crimson mantua silk window curtains and an India card table; and the inlaid dining room with green mantua silk curtains, twelve chairs and a marble sideboard. The sumptuousness of the furnishings of these rooms is indicated by the values set on their contents: those of the inlaid bedchamber were worth £109 10*s.*, compared with £26 10*s.* for the furnishings in the bedchamber of the master and mistress of the house; and the contents of the inlaid drawing room were valued at £137 10*s.*, against £49 10*s.* for the great drawing room. The total for the contents of the inlaid dining room, which did not include a table, was £41 10*s.*, whilst the furnishings of the other eating parlour were worth a modest £11 15*s.* Such a suite of rooms was described by Charlotte Smith in her book *The Old Manor House*, set in the 1770s. The manor house of the title, Rayland Hall, had been built in the 1690s like Melbury, and since then it 'had not received the slightest alteration, either in its environs or its furniture':

> It was the side of the house formerly set apart for company, but now was very rarely inhabited. The furniture was rich, but old fashioned: the beds were of cut

The north front of Melbury House (1732). The service rooms are on the left, and the stables on the right. (*Private Collection*)

The east front of Melbury House by B. Pryce for the first edition of John Hutchins's *History of Dorset* (1774). (*By permission of the Syndics of Cambridge University Library*).

> velvet or damask, with high testers, some of them with gilt cornices. The chairs were worked, or of coloured velvets, fringed with silk and gold, and had gilt feet. Fine japanned cabinets, beautiful pieces of china, large glasses, and some valuable pictures, were to be seen in every room, which, though now so rarely inhabited, were kept in great order, and the oak floors were so nicely waxed that to move upon them was more like skating than walking.[4]

Other rooms at Melbury in 1727, probably on the first floor, were the library and a music room. No musical instruments are listed in the latter room, which held a bed with yellow mohair hangings, yellow sarsnet window curtains and a japanned table. The walls of the principal rooms were hung with silk, tapestry or gilt leather. The total value of the contents of the house at this time came to £982 16*s*.[5]

On the north side of the main house there was a courtyard flanked by two ranges of buildings dating from the late seventeenth century, each consisting of two storeys with attics. The eastern block contained the the 'offices' or service rooms, with bedrooms for servants over them. Facing this block, on the western side of the courtyard, were the stables, with a further range of offices behind them.[6] The service rooms listed in the inventory of 1727 include the preserving room, still-room, brewhouse, bake-house, dairy, wash-house and kitchen, but it is not known where each of these was located.[7]

Thomas and Susanna Strangways Horner appear to have carried out little, if any, new work at Melbury during their joint ownership of the house, which lasted from 1729 to 1741, when Thomas died. Susanna was abroad for several years in the 1730s, and Thomas seems to have spent as much time as possible at his own house, Mells in Somerset. He was involved in the management of part of the Melbury estate, but he seems to have done his best to make life as difficult as possible for his ungovernable wife. By 1739 he was trying to lease part of Melbury House to a tenant, and the steward George Donisthorpe wrote to tell his mistress that that 'All the furniture at Melbury is now taken down and packed up in cases, as are the family pictures in the best dining room'. He also commented, 'Mr Horner does not seem to care what becomes of any thing provided his designs succeed'.[8]

After 1741 Susanna had a free hand at last, and she immediately set about restoring and improving the house and grounds, which had probably seen few changes since her father's day.[9] By the middle of 1742 George Donisthorpe was able to send his mistress a report on the work which was already well under way. The exterior stonework of the main house was being cleaned and repaired and the roofs were being retiled. The stonework of the offices around the north court was also repaired at this time, and the court itself was pitched and levelled. Some of the work on the house was organised by the master builder Francis Cartwright (*c.* 1695–1758) of Bryanston, near Blandford, and the Melbury accounts show regular payments to 'Mr Cartret, builder', from May 1743 onwards. Inside the house, new marble chimney-pieces were installed, some of the pictures were cleaned, and the floors in the best dining room and the 'chintz room and closet' were relaid. Payments in July 1742 include £8 to the carpenter Joseph Childs (the author Thomas Hardy's great-great grandfather) for 'wainscoating the gallery, 120 yards'.[10] Several plumbers and glaziers were also at work in the house in the mid 1740s, and by 1747–48 a water closet had been installed.[11] Most members of the household, however, had to make do with close-stools and chamber pots or, in the case of the servants, the 'offices' or 'bog-houses' (probably earth closets) in the north court.

Susanna Strangways Horner died in 1758. In her will, she directed that all her possessions at Melbury, such as plate, pictures, and furniture, should be listed after her death and should remain in the house as heirlooms. They were to be held by trustees, who were given the power to exchange or dispose of any plate or furniture that became 'old or decayed or unfashionable', but only on the condition that any goods that were disposed of were replaced by new pieces of equal or greater value.[12] Horace Walpole, who visited Melbury in 1762, described the house as 'a sumptuous old seat in a fine situation', and wrote that 'the apartments are most richly and abundantly furnished with pictures, tapestry, fine tables and the finest old china and japan collected by Mrs Horner, and many family pictures'.[13] After this, Melbury seems to have remained virtually unchanged until the death of Susanna's daughter, the first Countess of Ilchester, in 1792.

By the 1790s the grounds and gardens were too formal for contemporary tastes, and the mansion itself appeared old-fashioned, with furnishings that were shabby and out of date. In a letter sent from the house in the mid 1790s Elizabeth Strangways begged her father, the second Earl, to let her and her sisters go to London, telling him 'It would be better to be *imprisoned* in Burlington Street than to range in this gloomy mansion of our forefathers, with no other society than the Wadhams and the Ayliffes'.[14] Lord Ilchester seems to have initiated some changes before his mother's death in November 1792, for the estate accounts record the payment on 14 October of £331 16*s.* for various works, including 'disbursements by Your Lordship's direction about the ... new drive and other alterations at Melbury'.[15]

The second Earl subsequently turned his attention to the interior of his family seat, and in October 1801 some of the contents of Melbury were sold at an auction held in the house. These included many of the objects which had been collected by his mother and grandmother, such as 'household furniture, pier and chimney glasses, tapestry, china, pictures, prints and drawings, books, sideboard of plate about six hundred ounces and sundry plated articles, greenhouse plants, a billiard table, three clocks, japan cabinets, a set of mahogany dining tables, carpets, carvings in wood, and miscellaneous curious and useful domestic articles'. The items that were sold at this time included the wooden carvings by Grinling Gibbons from the tapestry room and south drawing room, which went for £64 7*s.* 6*d.* and £48 6*s.* respectively.[16]

Lord Ilchester's alterations were still unfinished when he died, less than a year after the sale. When Susan O'Brien visited Melbury in August 1803, for the first time in over three years, her reaction to the changes was one of 'pain and uneasiness':

> We cannot see that place so changed without feeling the numberless losses we have sustained and all the alterations that have happened. Hardly anything that used to give us pleasure remains: the shrubbery, the old grove, the flowers, the neatness, even nicety, of my mother's time all gone. All appearance of grandeur, the old fashioned grandeur, gone. The house, from striking everyone by its suits [*sic*] of rooms of different sizes, its fine old furniture so suitable to its stile, and its delightful greenhouse at the end, now appears contracted and reduced, to look like a common gentleman's house. All faults are now remarked, as there is no longer the deception of antiquity to disguise them. The unhappy interruption of all my poor brother's plans renders everything so confused that even what were his plans are not to be judged of from what appears. It is a sad reflexion that all was unnecessary to anybody's real comfort.[17]

Little more could be done until Susan's nephew, the third Earl, came of age in 1808. Four years later, Susan found Melbury much improved. She looked back at the changes that the house had seen during the previous century:

> Greatly does it add to the pleasure of this last stage of my life to reflect that all our ancestors, from those in the family picture to the last that we have lost, must look down with approbation and pleasure on their present representative, who unites good principles, good sense and pleasing manners with a love for the place which he inherits from them, improving it, as they had done before, according to the tastes and improvements of the times they lived in.[18]

After this time, there do not appear to have been any major alterations until the second half of the nineteenth century, when the house was greatly enlarged for the fifth Earl of Ilchester, by Anthony Salvin in 1872 and George Devey in 1884–85.

When George III visited the second Earl and Countess of Ilchester at Redlynch in 1789 he expressed 'Great surprise at the odd manner in which

Penrice Castle, Glamorgan, by Thomas Rothwell (1792). (*Private Collection*)

[the mansion] was built'. The King asked the name of the architect 'and said he deserved a patent for building extraordinary houses'.[19] The somewhat unusual plan of the house, which consisted of two quite separate buildings, was probably due to the fact that it had been constructed in several distinct phases. It seems, however, to have worked well enough for the occupants. Redlynch was home to the children of the first and second Earls and Countesses of Ilchester, who all seem to have preferred it to Melbury. Life at Redlynch was simpler and more relaxed than at Melbury, a stiff, rather formal household, where their widowed grandmothers – first Susanna Strangways Horner and then Elizabeth, Countess of Ilchester – lived, and where they had to behave themselves.

Exactly how much of Redlynch was built by Sir Stephen Fox, and how much by his son, is unclear, but it was the latter who finished the house and made it really habitable for the first time. As he wrote in 1746, 'Ever since I came of age [in 1725] I have been doing something [at Redlynch], which is an expence I should have quite saved had I had a house finished in any country'.[20] Stephen's growing interest in rural matters after he settled at Redlynch is underlined by Lord Hervey's comment in 1727, when he offered to send some books to his friend: 'If your studys are to be of a piece with your other occupations, I should think Switzer's Compleat Gardener, Hubbard upon Agriculture, and Hales upon Vegetation would not be unwelcome.'[21] Another letter from Hervey, written a year later, refers to the alterations and improvements to the buildings and grounds that were under way at Redlynch:

> You are by this time at Redlinch and finding your park-wall advanced, the foundations of your new building lay'd, your slopes improving, your puddles filling, and your plantations thriving.[22]

Henry Fox kept an eye on the builders whilst his elder brother was on the Continent with Lord Hervey in 1728–29, and a letter written at this time shows that the work in progress included the library and a bedchamber.[23] The improvements continued after Stephen's return to England in 1729. An upholsterer, Mr Green, was paid £190 in May 1731; in 1732 Lord Hervey refers to the completion of 'the slope and the piece of water'; and in 1734, in a letter to Henry written at Redlynch, Hervey says that the place is 'extreamly improved' and that he has been sitting in 'your new alcove room, which has a thousand beautys and *agrémens*'. In 1735 Stephen Fox paid £45 16*s.* to the builder Nathaniel Ireson, who had first worked at Redlynch twelve years earlier.[24] By this time the main house (known as the 'great house') consisted of two equal storeys, with a hipped roof. On the west-facing entrance front there were nine bays, of which the central three projected slightly beneath a pediment adorned with the Fox family's coat of arms. On the north and south fronts the centre was recessed between two short wings. To the north west of the house were two short ranges of buildings: one housed the stables and the other the kitchens and other service rooms.

After 1739, when Stephen and Elizabeth Fox first began to live together, the building work at Redlynch started again, still under the direction of Nathaniel Ireson.[25] A new stable-block was constructed in 1740–41, and additional accommodation was provided within a building known as the 'offices', built between 1741 and 1745. This two-storeyed structure was almost entirely detached from the original house, to which it was joined only by a covered passage. A plan which is undated, but was probably drawn in the mid eighteenth century, shows that the rooms on the ground floor included a laundry, wash-house, housekeeper's room, store and still-room, steward's room, steward's dining room, servants' hall and waiting room. There was also an apartment for Mrs Fenn, the housekeeper. All of these rooms could be reached via a corridor, which ran the length of the building. The plan of the upper floor or 'chamber storey' was almost identical.[26] These chambers were not, as one might expect, used only by the servants: in a letter written in 1746, just before a visit to Redlynch, Henry Fox asked if he and his wife could 'lye in the offices'. They did not wish to sleep 'so far off as the library apartment', especially as Henry was likely to get up earlier, or go to bed later, than his wife. He asked his sister-in-law to 'indulge us in this little timourousness'.[27] This suggests that, whilst the apartments which were usually given to guests were in the older part of the house, most members of the family slept in the newer building.

A number of new garden buildings were also constructed in the early 1740s.[28] By the summer of 1745, however, Stephen (now Lord Ilchester) was short of money and the work had come to a temporary standstill, as he told his brother:

> With regard to the building at Redlynch, I heartily wish it had never been begun because it has cost a great deal of money ... Though Redlynch has been the business of my life, and I am come within a year or two of seeing it compleatly finished, yet I am putting a stop to it, and it will probably for ever remain unfinished, which is one of the things that half breaks my heart.[29]

Parts of the house appears to have been uninhabitable at this time, as a visitor commented: 'It was melancholy to me to see all the rooms, especially the library, in rubbish and workmen's dirt'.[30] The work was delayed for only a short time, however. By the spring of 1746 Henry Fox was writing to his brother about designs for chimney-pieces for the saloon, parlour and eating room which had been supplied by Henry Flitcroft, an architect who was particularly popular with Whig patrons.[31] Henry, who commented that Flitcroft had 'no taste', had discussed the designs with Charles Hamilton of Painshill, an old friend who had been a contemporary of the Fox brothers at Oxford and was a regular visitor both to Redlynch and to Stephen's shooting lodge at Maddington on Salisbury Plain.[32]

The building work at Redlynch continued in the 1750s. Most of this was again directed by Nathaniel Ireson, though Henry Flitcroft also seems to have been involved. Inside the house, some of the chimney-pieces were altered. Outside, a new lodge with round embattled towers was constructed at the western entrance to the park in 1754–55. Another building, described as a 'venison house', was built at the same time. Then, in 1759, a total of £136 18*s.* 8*d.* was spent on bricks for the 'feasant court', an aviary for ornamental game birds.[33] In the same year, £3 1*s.* 6*d.* was paid for 'diging the place for the bogg-house and building and finishing ditto, making the steaps and pitching etc.' The last-named building may have replaced the 'sarvants' bog-house', which is mentioned in 1749, when the sum of 11*d.* was paid for a lock for the door. As at Melbury, there was also a water-closet in the house by this time.[34]

Between 1746 and 1750 a London upholsterer, Samuel Severn, provided furnishings for Redlynch. Severn and his men were also working in Lord and Lady Ilchester's London house at the same time, and it is sometimes difficult to work out exactly which items were destined for which house, but he supplied large quantities of cloth for curtains and wall-hangings at Redlynch, including canvas, hessian and 'brown Scots cloth'; green silk and damask, and crimson harateen.[35] Severn was also paid for making 'the Belzmozeen hangings for the dressing room and bedchamber at Renclinch'. Exactly what these were is unclear, but the material seems to have been a form of silk, and the hangings were apparently in the Whig colours of blue and buff. Severn also sold frames for beds and chairs, upholstery materials of all kinds and other items such as mattresses, quilts, bolsters and pillows.[36] In May 1747 £10 15*s.* was paid 'to Holmes, painter, for guilding and clening picturs', together with 14*s.* 'for leaf gould for guilding'.[37] By the summer of 1750 the house was ready to receive visitors, and Lady Ilchester wrote to her husband, who was already at Redlynch, to tell him where everyone was to sleep:

> Our own room for Mama; the Balsmarine for Miss Long; the green Miss Rachel; the secret appartment for us; the middle room in the offices for Mr Fever, and the little bed to be put within Mama's room for Hester. All the windows to be left open till we come, and other rooms will be wanted for Mr Canel, etc. I think Miss Long's servant should lye in the little yellow room by the secret appartment.[38]

In 1762 Horace Walpole wrote that Redlynch was 'a comely dwelling, a new stone house with good rooms and convenient'. He described the interior of the main house in some detail:

> You enter the house by a handsome stone hall. Over the chimney a bas relief, a sacrifice to Diana, taken from one in the hall at Houghton, and that from the antique. Next is a good eating room ... Thence you enter the salon, a double cube of twenty feet. The cieling from the great room at Wilton, but the ornaments lighter. It is hung with green damask and pictures. The chimney-piece from one of Inigo Jones ... The next is a drawing room, hung with tapestry of the months, manufacture of Mortelack. Ebony table, glass and stands, ornamented with silver ... Dressing room hung with green damask and pictures ... Great bedchamber, very handsome room with an alcove supported by columns, dressing table of gilt plate, and a rich bason and ewer, in good taste. In the passage, some busts, one of John, Lord Hervey, by Bouchardon. Above, a large library. [There is also a] billiard room hung with portraits.[39]

Sale particulars of 1912 give a little more information about the decoration of the principal rooms. The entrance hall had a stone-flagged floor, a 'beautiful ceiling', and a stone carved mantelpiece. The ceiling and cornice in the billiard room were 'beautifully moulded'. The south-facing saloon had an oak floor 'and richly decorated and gilded ceiling and cornice, the cove ornamented with octagonal gilded roses and bosses arranged to give additional perspective to the room'.[40]

An inventory of the contents of Redlynch, taken a few weeks after the family moved out in 1793, shows how the house had changed in the previous three decades. In the entrance hall, which had red curtains at the windows, was a large marble table on a gilt frame, with twelve stools. The billiard room, which had been on the first floor when Horace Walpole visited, was now downstairs, apparently in what had formerly been the 'eating room'. In most of the principal rooms on the ground floor the curtains and upholstery were green,[41] unlike Melbury, where blue was the predominant colour. In the south-facing saloon at Redlynch was a harpsichord, together with mahogany sofas and chairs upholstered in green damask, with striped cotton covers, and two marble side-tables on gilt frames. The tapestry room next door (called the drawing room by Walpole) had a pier table 'plated and japanned' with a large plated pier-glass over it, a silver-plated lamp, a mahogany side-table and eight mahogany armchairs, covered with the same material as the chairs in the saloon. There was also the green room, with a couch and chairs, a mahogany table, and green damask curtains at the windows; and a dining room with a large mahogany dining table and mahogany chairs. The curtains in this room were of green stuff or woollen material. On this floor, too, were a room for a valet, which had a bed in it, and a waiting room for the other servants.

Whilst the billiard room was moved downstairs between 1762 and 1793, the 'great bedchamber' was moved upstairs. Most of the bedrooms had one or two closets attached: several of these had beds in them, whilst others held a night-stool or commode and a wash-stand. In the 'green room above stairs', the most elaborately furnished of these bedrooms, the four-poster bed and the windows were hung with green damask curtains. In the Belmazine bedroom the hangings were now of blue damask. In this, as in the other bedrooms, most of the furniture was of mahogany. There was also a chintz bedroom, with its own dressing room and closet. Also in this part of the house, over the saloon, was a room described as the 'old nursery'. In 1793 this was used as a bedroom.[42] Above the bedrooms in the main house were eleven garrets. All had four-poster beds in them – some had two – with cotton hangings. These rooms, which were simply furnished, would have been used by the servants.

There were eleven rooms on the first floor of the offices. Most had four-poster beds in them, many with corded dimity (cotton) hangings. Unlike the chambers in the older part of the house, none of these rooms had a closet attached. Whilst less richly furnished than the chambers on the first floor of the main house, they were more comfortable than the servants' garrets, and they appear to have been used by the younger members of the family. In one, there was a child's 'cribb bedstead' in addition to a four-poster bed with white cotton furniture. Several rooms had green baize floor-cloths, and there are references to writing tables, inkstands and bookshelves. Two of the rooms had no bed in them, and these may have been used as sitting rooms.

The ground floor of the offices does not appear to have been altered greatly between the 1740s and 1793. The rooms listed are the laundry, wash-house, still-room, housekeeper's room, steward's room, footman's room, a pantry (which had a bed in it), and the servants' hall, from which a passage led to the main mansion. The kitchen, dairy, brewhouse and bakehouse appear to have been housed in another group of buildings behind the main block of offices.[43]

Redlynch was the home of the second Earl of Ilchester and his family until July 1793, when they all moved to Melbury, eight months after the dowager Countess's death. The family never lived in the house again after this, though they visited occasionally in the early years of the nineteenth century. Like his father, the second Earl considered selling the house but failed to do so. Some of the furnishings, including chimney-pieces, green silk damask wall-hangings and the Mortlake tapestries seen by Horace Walpole, were taken to Melbury.[44] Many of the remaining house contents were sold at auction in July 1801, three months before the Melbury sale.[45] Susan O'Brien, who visited Redlynch in 1804, was sad to see how the place had deteriorated, as she told her niece Elizabeth Talbot:

> It affected my spirits a good deal ... So would [it] you, to find poor Redlynch, the seat of your former glorys, look so abandoned and forsaken, the house unfurnished and the shrubbery quite overgrown and ruinous, and though the time of my glorys is more remote, yet I assure you I could hardly stand it.[46]

Redlynch was eventually sold by the Ilchester estates in 1912. By this time the main house, which had been used as a farmhouse for many years, was largely unoccupied. Most of the accommodation was in the service block (the offices), having been converted into a house by Sir Edwin Lutyens in 1901. Two years after the sale, in 1914, the former service block was badly damaged by a fire thought to have been started by suffragettes. Soon after this, the old mansion was demolished.[47]

Penrice Castle was quite different from both Melbury and Redlynch, having been built by Thomas Mansel Talbot on an entirely new site in the 1770s. By this time the most important rooms in large country houses were no longer arranged in formal suites as in a baroque house such as Melbury: at Penrice the large dining room, drawing room and study or breakfast room can all be reached from a central hall. Similarly, the arrangement of the bedrooms on the first and second floors reflected the modern taste, for they lacked the closets which had been thought essential seventy years earlier. At the very top of the house were the garrets where the servants slept, and the semi-basement contained pantries, and the housekeeper's room and servants' hall. As at Redlynch, the 'kitchen offices', with the brewhouse and laundry, were in a separate building, attached to the main house by a covered corridor.

The new house at Penrice was provided with modern comforts such as a piped water supply from a nearby spring, installed by the plumber Benjamin Grazebrook in 1783.[48] The house was not fully furnished at this time, but those rooms that were finished were fitted out in the latest fashion. Two of the chimney-pieces had been purchased in Rome during Thomas Talbot's travels, but most of the others were provided by the architect of the house, Anthony Keck, who also supplied many of the internal fittings, such as cupboards and shelves for the butler's pantry, housekeeper's room and larder; tables and benches for the servants' hall; bedsteads for the servants; an ironing board, drying horses and mangles for the laundry; a pepper mill and coffee mill; a bench for salting bacon; and even the 'floors and seats in the common privies'. An upholsterer, Henry Hill of Marlborough, presented a bill for £425 13*s.* 5*d.* in 1778. Hill provided only sun-blinds for the main bedrooms and for the dining room and drawing room, which were not to be properly furnished for another decade. For the study or breakfast room he supplied a mahogany oval breakfast table, six mahogany wheel-back chairs and two elbow chairs to match, all with green leather seats, together with pea-green damask curtains and strawberry-pattern Wilton carpet. The hall was furnished with four further mahogany wheel-back chairs and a set of mahogany dining tables. The 'attic' bedrooms on the second floor were papered, carpeted and furnished, to provide accommodation for visitors and perhaps also for Thomas himself. One room had 'straw ground paper with green sprigs', curtains with a narrow blue Manchester stripe and 'yard wide Scotch carpet', and was furnished with a mahogany night table with a stool to draw out, a four-poster bedstead with curtains to match those at the windows, a 'neat mahogany chest of drawers of good wood', a square mahogany 'bason stand' and four 'died elbow chairs' with stuffed seats covered with blue Manchester stripe. Another bedroom had 'stoco ground paper with blue stripes and sprigs' and red and green Manchester stripe curtains, and another was decorated with pearl ground paper with green and red sprigs, with orange and black Manchester stripe bed furniture and curtains.[49] The general effect would have been light, pretty and modern.

Little new work was done at Penrice after the early 1780s, as Thomas Talbot was occupied elsewhere and visited the house only occasionally, usually with shooting parties made up of small groups of male friends. After Lord Ilchester's visit with his daughter in 1792, however, Thomas embarked on a large-scale programme of restoration. The interior of the house was repainted, and the remaining rooms were fully furnished for the first time. The London upholsterer and decorator Quentin Kay of Hatton Garden supplied a large number of goods, including 'a patent apparatus for a water closet complete' for £13 5*s.* 5*d.*, also chairs, wardrobes, mirrors, washstands and other bedroom furniture, including 'a very large four-post bedstead with handsome mahogany carved and reeded feet posts' and chintz cotton bed-hangings. For the main dining room Kay supplied 128 yards of buff-coloured moreen,[50] and 130 yards of green satin lace for curtains, also 'twelve very handsome mahogany chairs, the seats double stuft with the best materials and covered with fine red morocco leather' and 'two very neat folding fire screens covered with fine green stuff'; and for the breakfast room a sofa, six more mahogany chairs, and a mahogany Pembroke table with an inlaid border.

In the spring of 1793 Thomas ordered furnishings for a lady's dressing room, again from Quentin Kay. This was somewhat optimistic since Mary Strangways had not agreed to marry him at this time.[51] Later in the year the furniture for the drawing room at Penrice arrived: 'ten very handsome cabreole elbow chairs ... richly japanned ... all double stuft with the best materials in brown linen, and covered with rich variegated silk damask finished with a rich silk guimp'; also two sofas to match the chairs, two 'very large, handsome French plated pier-glasses in rich carved frames, gilt in burnished gold', 'a pair of handsome satinwood card tables with neat painted border, lined with fine green cloth', and 'a very fine handsome satinwood Pembroke table to match, with a painted border, two leaves and a drawer'. These items, too, were all supplied by Quentin Kay. In addition, Kay provided cornices, silk damask window curtains and valances, and 'a very fine large Axminster carpet'. Penrice was now fully habitable at long last, and Mary Talbot described her first impressions of her new home in a letter written shortly after her marriage in 1794.

> My dressing room ... is of a light blue ... The drawing room is likewise painted of a very pale blue, and there are some *very fine* pictures in it – of them, you know, I am no judge. The furniture is green satin, and there is some of the prettiest satinwood tables in it that can be. The dining room is very large and is green, it has got red morocco chairs and very pretty salmon-colour curtains. The rest of the rooms are very comfortable, but it is time enough for you to have an idea of them when you come here yourself.[52]

As the Talbots' family grew during the years that followed, conditions at Penrice became increasingly cramped. In 1804 one visitor, the traveller Benjamin Heath Malkin, commented that the house was 'scarcely large enough for [Mr Talbot's] own family'.[53] Two years later a visitor had to sleep in a bed in the housekeeper's room 'for want of a better'.[54] Eventually, therefore, it was decided that an extension was needed. The family moved out of the house in April 1812 and work began under the direction of the Swansea architect William Powell. At the same time some rooms in the older part of the house were repainted. The Talbots eventually returned to Penrice early in the spring of 1813. On 17 March, Mary Theresa Talbot wrote from the house to her brother Kit to tell him about the changes:

> The people are putting down the floors in the new building. The walls are all plastered, but very wet. They say that it will not be dry enough to paper till next summer twelvemonth ... The drawing room is a very pretty green colour, and the dining-room and breakfast parlour are a greyish-green; the hall and staircase a blue-grey.[55]

The alterations included a small three-storeyed extension to the main house, with a new set of back stairs. New bedrooms were added above the offices, and the passage joining the house to the offices also appears to have been reconstructed. Thomas Talbot barely lived to see the work completed, for he died in May 1813, a few weeks after he and his family had moved back into Penrice. Very few further changes were made in subsequent years: in 1836, after his widow and her second husband Sir Christopher Cole moved out, her son was reported to be putting the house in order, as it was 'quite *dégradée*', and filled with furniture that was forty years old, and 'much *usé* and *tombant en lambeaux*' (much used and falling to pieces).[56]

By the early nineteenth century, only Stinsford remained as a reminder of a bygone age. The O'Briens never had enough money to restore or refurbish the house properly, and they probably used at least some of the furnishings which had been bought by Susan's forebears a hundred years earlier. An inventory of the contents, made shortly after the death of Mary Strangways in 1727, shows that it had once been very comfortable in spite of its relatively modest scale. The rooms listed include the hall, best parlour, little eating parlour, little drawing room (with silk hangings), and the great drawing room. The last-named was furnished with eight japanned chairs, several stools, a sofa covered with blue velvet, and a walnut card table. There were tapestry hangings on the walls, and blue mantua silk window curtains. The most expensively decorated room in the house was the chintz bedchamber, with its chintz bed and window curtains lined with white Turkey silk, chairs and stools covered in the same material, and tapestry hangings on the walls. Of the other bedchambers, one had yellow calico hangings; one had 'crimson cheney[57] furniture lined with thread satting'; and the other had 'blew cheney furniture lined with printed silk', with window curtains and wall-hangings of the same material. Much of the furniture in the principal rooms was japanned or made of walnut. At the top of the house were six garrets, and there was also a servants' hall, in addition to a room for the steward, a kitchen, a brewhouse and pantry.[58]

To an imaginative girl like Charlotte Talbot, who stayed at Stinsford with her great-aunt Susan O'Brien early in the nineteenth century, the old house was highly atmospheric. Some parts of it bore a distinct resemblance to Sleeping Beauty's castle:

> As a child, I wandered [at Stinsford] in all the luxury of realized romance, imagination peopling the stone halls and suites of unused, but furnished, rooms with all the fair ladies and fringed Grandissons, who might last have looked at themselves in those mirrors, or sat on those chairs, or sung to the harpsichord, strung so curiously with quills to make the notes sound. Not a curtain, fire-iron or footstool added or removed since their days. Bright sun, entering at the

> windows, kept the rooms from feeling damp or looking gloomy. The inhabited sitting rooms had beautiful china ... worked chairs [and] wood fires on *dogs*.[59]

Thomas Hardy's father, who was born in the parish of Stinsford in 1811, could remember the house in Susan O'Brien's day. As a boy, he had gone with the other members of the village choir to sing carols to the old lady, and he recalled that Susan would listen from the top of the stairs, whilst he and the other singers stood below her in the hall by the terrace door.[60]

6

Country House Life

In the eighteenth and nineteenth centuries few aristocratic landowners stayed in the same house all year round. Many families had more than one country seat, and most also had a house in London where they spent several months in the winter and spring.[1] Their movements from one residence to another were dictated in part by the weather, for nobody wanted to be marooned in a cold, draughty mansion in January and February, when the countryside was 'dismal ... and covered with snow',[2] the roads were bad and visitors were few and far between. But other factors were of equal, if not greater, importance. These included the parliamentary calendar, for even the least politically active landowner would feel the need to attend one or other of the Houses of Parliament from time to time. If he was at all ambitious, he and his wife would be obliged to put in regular appearances at Court, and be seen at the royal assemblies, or drawing rooms, and balls. Politics apart, the main interests of the Earls of Ilchester and their Digby cousins – as of many of their male contemporaries – were field sports of various kinds, especially hunting and shooting. This meant that they were very reluctant to leave the country between September and January.

The parliamentary sessions usually began in mid November.[3] Lord and Lady Ilchester sometimes went to London at this time, but they, and their cousins at Sherborne Castle, generally preferred to stay in the country for Christmas. They would set off for London after the men had stopped shooting, in January or February. By this time, as a contributor to the *Gentleman's Magazine* commented in 1738, many women had had quite enough of country life:

> I consider January as the general Gaol-Delivery of the fair sex: then they come to Town, flushed with the health, and irritated with the confinement, of the country ... Every fine woman who comes to Town in January comes heartily tired of the country and her husband. The happy pair have yawned at one another at least ever since Michaelmas.[4]

The timing of their departure would depend on the weather, since heavy rain or snow could make the roads totally impassable for days, or weeks, at a time. In 1775 Lord Digby's servants set off from Sherborne Castle with the luggage waggon on 24 January, but it was another week before the family was able to leave Dorset 'having been delayed by bad weather'.[5] In January 1814 Susan O'Brien wrote that they were 'entirely snowed in' at Stinsford. Travel was impossible: 'The mails come on horseback and even the grandees of this world cannot proceed. Lord and Lady Cholmondely have passed the last week at the Antelope [in Dorchester] and ... they are snowed in likewise at Melbury and Abbotsbury.'[6]

Transporting the family, with their servants and baggage, to London was a major undertaking. In January 1734 the Redlynch house steward paid £9 5*s.* 8*d.* for the expenses of four days on the road to London with twelve servants and eleven horses, and in June 1744 he claimed £6 5*s.* 2*d.* for 'my expenses from London with Miss Charlot, a coach and six, and six saddle horses, twelve servants, three days on the road'.[7] Lord and Lady Ilchester and their children travelled in carriages – usually one or more coaches and post chaises – accompanied by a few servants, some of whom would be on horseback to act as security guards and outriders. In the mid eighteenth century a local carrier, Joseph Clavey, was regularly employed to convey the remaining servants, and the luggage, from Redlynch to London. In January 1751 his load consisted of seven trunks, fifteen boxes, two bundles, one hamper, a hat-box, one box belonging to the servants, and 'five servants passengers'.[8]

Most London residences were rented, rather than owned outright. In 1730 Stephen Fox bought the lease of 31 Old Burlington Street from Lord Hervey for £4000.[9] Friends and relations who lived close by in this, the most fashionable area of London in the mid eighteenth century, included Susanna Strangways Horner in Albemarle Street, and Henry and Caroline Fox in Conduit Street. These London houses were designed for entertainment and display, and they were richly furnished. An inventory of the Albemarle Street house made in 1741 refers to hangings of silk damask, furniture of walnut and mahogany, gilt sofas, Turkey and Persian carpets, and large quantities of china and japanned objects. There was a 'great picture room', a tapestry room, a dining parlour (with paintings by Canaletto, Poussin and Claude), and a Chinese room (with India-paper hangings).[10] Houses such as this were filled with the tenant's own furniture, and might be held for many years – the Earls of Ilchester occupied the Burlington Street house until about 1870. Many families, however, did not need – or could not afford – a permanent London base, though they might come to Town for a few weeks at the height of the Season. In the last quarter of the eighteenth century the Framptons of Moreton generally went to London 'for two or three months once in two years'.[11] William and Susan O'Brien did not go to London every year either, but when they could afford to make the journey they would spend a month or two there in the spring. They sometimes slept in Old Burlington Street, but they also used nearby hotels: in 1807 they were in a hotel in Cork Street; in 1808 and 1814 they slept at the Clarendon Hotel; and in 1810 they were in 'a very good hotel' in Sackville Street. During Susan's last stay in London, in May and June 1825, she took lodgings in Bruton Street.

Thomas and Mary Talbot had no London house of their own, though this was due not to a lack of money but to their own dislike of city life. In a letter written early in 1794 Thomas referred to London as 'this truely disagreeable town', and informed Michael Hicks Beach: 'My better half ... I thank God, instead of being passionately fond of this town, detests it, if possible, more than I do.'[12] At the same time Mary told her sister Harriot, 'I feel great joy at leaving this hateful town which, you know, never suited either my body or my mind'.[13] Nevertheless, the Talbots did visit London from time to time, though they did not stay for the whole of the Season. In 1797 they had a house in Brompton, which was still semi-rural but within an easy carriage ride of Mayfair. In 1814, the year after her husband's death, Mary and her daughters rented 34 Lower Brook Street, near Grosvenor Square. This seems to have been an experiment, to see how Mary's daughters took to 'the World'.[14] In 1815 they were in London again, this time at 11 Berkeley Square. Mary's sisters and aunt did their best to convince her that her daughters needed to broaden their horizons and spend more time away from Penrice. As Susan O'Brien wrote in 1816, 'I think a little of the world is a good thing for young ladies to see before they make their choice. It corrects romantic ideas, so natural or pleasant in youth, but anything romantic, or even elevated sentiments, are not of the present day.'[15] Two months later, however, Susan had to admit to Elizabeth Feilding that the visit to London had not had the desired effect: 'Mary ... and all of them seem very happy, but speak with horror of London. Indeed, they hate it so much, and give such good reasons for their dislike, that it's almost a pity they would go.'[16]

The Talbots were by no means alone in their dislike of London, which Lord Hervey described in 1735 as 'this disagreeable scene of dirt and politicks'.[17] The city was generally felt to be unhealthy: in a letter written around 1760 Lady Ilchester complained to her husband that 'I am not so well as in the country, want exercise and feel stuffed',[18] and few years later Sarah Bunbury wrote: 'I would not for thousands live the whole year round where I could not smell the fresh air ... I have the fidgets and grow to hate London.'[19] The second Countess of Ilchester (Mary Talbot's mother) had spent the early years of her life in the Irish countryside and never seems to have felt at home with the *beau monde* of London, much preferring to spend her time at Redlynch with her children and garden. Sarah Bunbury and Susan O'Brien both agreed that:

> The less Lady Ilchester is in London, the better, since she hates it so much, for it is the silliest of all things for us poor mortals, who have plenty of real misfortunes, to coin unnecessary ills out of form and rule, as we see so many simple people do every day.[20]

In May 1785 Sarah summed up her own objections, telling Susan that she would not bring her sickly daughter to London: 'For a hot journey, a close air, no shade to sit in, no good milk to live on, would be evils that would outweigh the good of having her pulse felt by a London doctor instead of a country one'.[21] Not everybody thought that London air was unhealthy: in 1810 Louisa Lansdowne advised Mary Talbot to spend the winter in the neighbourhood of the capital, because 'the coal smoke softens the air so much'.[22]

Many women, however, were bored and lonely in the countryside and would have agreed with Elizabeth, Lady Holland, who wrote in 1798 that 'the sight of a country residence fills me with gloom. I feel escaped from some misfortune when I get out of its precincts'.[23] In Februrary 1794 Kitty Acland compared her own social life in London with that of her cousin and friend Lily Strangways in Dorset in a letter to Susan O'Brien:

> I hear there has been a large party at Melbury. I hope it has engaged poor Lily, who must, I think, be tired of the country before this, and impatient to partake of the gaieties of this dear town. We have been out but little: several times to the opera, and a few assemblies, but nothing like a dance. There are to be four publick balls next month, at the Festini Rooms, Hannover Square, under the direction of Lady Townsend, the Duchesses of Gordon and Rutland, and Lady Salisbury. I expect them to be delightfully pleasant. We have got our names down.[24]

Lily, meanwhile, was begging her father to 'take us out of this dreary solitude' at Melbury. 'If we were in London', she continued, 'we might be at least *improving* ourselves, and not *wasting those precious hours which can return no more in fruitless regrets and anticipations.*'[25] With so many friends and relations gathered together in London, the months of the Season usually passed in a whirl of social activity. There were assemblies and balls, visits to the theatre and opera and to pleasure gardens such as Ranelagh and Vauxhall, and numerous private dinners. When William and Susan O'Brien spent three weeks in London in June 1807 they dined in their hotel only three times. On several occasions they dined with one friend, and then went on to a concert or another private house in the evening. Susan also went shopping, for visits to London were an opportunity to buy clothes, new furniture, books and other luxury goods that were not usually available in country towns.

For many people, attendance at Court was an obligation that was to be endured rather than enjoyed. The most important events included the ball held every year to celebrate the King's birthday. The last Birthday ball for George I, held in May 1727, was described by Lord Hervey in a letter to Henry Fox:

> The occurrences of all Birthdays are alike. There was a great croud, bad musick, trite compliments upon new garments and old faces in the morning, feasting and drinking all day, and a ball with execrable dancers at night.[26]

A year later, in a letter to Henry's brother, Hervey wrote after another engagement at Court: 'There was dice, dancing, crowding, sweating and stinking in abundance, as usual'.[27] But Hervey had seen all of this many times before. In 1758 everything was new and exciting to Susan Fox Strangways, aged fifteen:

> Mama and I have this day been at Court, and her hands and feet [are] so tired she could not write herself ... I have been presented to the King and the Prince and Princess of Wales. I like Leicester House much the best, as there was more people. Mama was likewise presented.[28]

A girl's first presentation at Court was a necessary rite of passage, a sign that she was grown up (and ready to be launched onto the marriage market). Mary Strangways, who was presented in 1793, was terrified at the prospect, though her aunt was informed that she 'looked vastly well, was dressed vastly well and held yourself vastly well'.[29] The importance attached to the choice of clothes for this special occasion is underlined in the following account written by the governess Agnes Porter in April 1797:

> Lady Harriot Strangways, my third dear pupil, was presented at Court. Lady Ilchester, Lady Elizabeth Talbot, and Miss Lily Digby ... accompanied her. They were all most elegantly dressed and looked extremely well indeed. Lady Harriot's dress was a crape white petticoat trimmed with silver flowers, a wreath of pearls in her hair, large pearl earrings, and a laylock gown; Lady Elizabeth's was simple: elegant white and silver. Lady Ilchester, a pale yellow gown and a white petticoat, large emerald earrings set in diamond; a diamond feather in her hair of remarkable lustre. They all had feathers. Miss Digby's dress was laylock and white with bugles – she looked perfectly delicate and neat, but was eclipsed by the blooming Harriot, the elegant Eliza and the tall and (in full dress) the graceful-looking Lady Ilchester. Lord Ilchester was in purple and silver.[30]

Lord and Lady Ilchester usually took several children to London with them, though some might be left in the country with their nurses and governess.

Even if the whole family was away, the servants who remained at Melbury and Redlynch had plenty to do. The house steward and the housekeeper would ensure that the whole house was thoroughly cleaned, and the chimneys swept: the sweep at Redlynch was paid £1 4*s.* in March 1752 for sweeping thirty-two chimneys at 9*d.* per chimney, and John Barfoot was paid two guineas a year in the 1750s and 1760s for sweeping the Melbury chimneys. In 1748–51 he also received 18*s.* a year for the chimneys at Abbotsbury and Stinsford.[31] At this time, too, any repairs to the building or its furnishings were carried out, linen was mended, china dusted and washed, and silver cleaned and polished. Much of the furniture was covered up to keep it clean and prevent damage and fading. Upholsterers would often supply two sets of covers for chairs and sofas at this time: one for best and one for everyday use. The inventory of the contents of Melbury in 1727 includes references to calico covers for the tapestries in the inlaid drawing room, and loose covers, also of calico, for damask-covered chairs and sofas throughout the house. At Stinsford in 1727 the chairs and sofas in the great drawing room all had loose covers of shalloon (a light woollen material) in addition to their velvet covers, and at Mells in 1741 there were chairs with walnut frames upholstered in blue damask, with blue serge covers.[32] When Lord and Lady Ilchester bought new chairs from Samuel Severn in 1748, the upholsterer supplied covers of 'Belzmozeen' and silk damask, and also chair cases made of blue and white check material. At Redlynch in 1793 the mahogany armchairs in the tapestry room had upholstery of green damask, covered with striped cotton. The Redlynch accounts for 1745 include a payment of 18*s.* 9*d.* for 'twelve and a half yards of chequed linnen for chaier covers, at 18*d.*', and at Melbury 14*s.* was paid in 1768 for '13 yards of check at 13*d.* per yard for covering the pewter in the kitchen etc. when the family is absent'. The servants were also expected to keep the house aired by opening and closing windows regularly, and lighting fires when necessary. Payments made by the housekeeper at Redlynch in 1741 included 7*s.* for 'a masheen to aier beds etc.',[33] but in some houses it was one of the maids' duties to keep the beds throughout the house aired by sleeping in them from time to time.[34] The housekeeper would check her storerooms and cupboards and order any provisions that would be needed when the family returned to the country. At the same time the gardeners and workmen would be busy cutting grass, repairing and rolling paths and drives, and planting, weeding and tending flowers, fruit and vegetables.

With the end of the parliamentary session, usually in May or June, landowners and their families began to think about leaving London for the countryside. Once again, whole convoys of vehicles were needed to carry them and their possessions (including items which had been purchased in Town) back to their estates. In 1750 the 'Miss Foxes' arrived at Redlynch on 31 March, followed by their parents on 13 May. Joseph Clavey was paid for carrying two loads, the first consisting of six cases, six trunks, eight hampers, six soap-tubs, one table-stand, one pair of iron dogs, two passengers and four parcels, and the second of one box, four trunks, five cases, one bundle, one block, one stand and three passengers.

By the last week in July everyone who could possibly do so had left London, and country-dwellers found their neighbourhood 'thickening for the summer season'.[35] The travellers did not necessarily head homewards at once, but might take the opportunity to visit friends on the way or stop for a few weeks in a watering-place such as Bath. In the 1780s Sarah Napier, who was forced to stay in London during the summer and autumn, informed Susan O'Brien that 'The Town is perfectly empty, and not the worse for it, as the solitude one lives in gives an idea of a country life', and 'There is not a living soul in London, so I can tell you no news'.[36]

Once they were in the country, the ladies settled down to a routine of dinner parties and visits to neighbours, walks in the garden and drives to see local sights. The Earls and Countesses of Ilchester moved regularly between their houses at Melbury and Redlynch, with less frequent visits to Abbotsbury and Maddington. The Talbots sometimes spent a few days at Margam. Though the Mansels' old mansion there had been demolished, the gardens were kept up, and a pavilion at the end of the orangery was used as a library and daytime sitting room. The family slept nearby in a 'cottage' which, according to Agnes Porter, was 'a snug house, small when compared to Penrice, but containing ... a family of twenty persons'.[37]

Visitors came and went, many of them staying for several weeks. In the summer of 1751 Lord and Lady Ilchester arrived at Redlynch from London on 6 June. Twelve days later Lord Ilchester's sister Charlotte Digby and her daughter came to stay. They were there for seven weeks. On 3 July Henry and Caroline Fox reached Redlynch with their friend John Calcraft.[38] Calcraft left for London three days later, and the Foxes stayed for only three more days before they, too, set off back to Town. Other guests at Redlynch in the early 1750s included Lord Digby and his brothers, Robert Colebrooke, Lord and Lady Bateman, Dickie Bateman, and Charles Hamilton of Painshill.

Any visitor who undertook the journey to Penrice from England would be expected to stay for some time. Lord and Lady Ilchester and Lord Stavordale came on 6 February 1798. They eventually left on 19 April, five days after the birth of the Talbots' third daughter. A cousin, Barbara Davenport, arrived on 25 May and stayed until 21 July. In the early nineteenth century Mary Talbot's nephew Henry Talbot was often at Penrice for several months at a time, sometimes with his mother and sometimes without. In 1804 Lily Talbot and Henry arrived on 8 March. They were joined on 20 April by Charles Feilding; Lily and Charles were married at Penrice church on 22 April, and they then set off on their honeymoon, leaving Henry at Penrice. Lily eventually returned on 13 November, remaining at Penrice for the birth of Mary's sixth daughter, and left again on 16 December without Henry, who stayed with his cousins until the middle of the following May. Then, at the end of September 1805, Agnes Porter was sent to collect Mary's younger sisters Charlotte and Louisa from the Passage over the Bristol Channel.[39] The girls were at Penrice until the end of December, when everyone set out for England: Charlotte and Louisa for Melbury, and the Talbots for London. William and Susan O'Brien undertook the journey to Penrice only once, in 1811, when they stayed from mid January until the second week in May. Visits such as these, with shorter stays by friends from Swansea and further afield in Glamorgan, helped to relieve the isolation of Mary Talbot's day-to-day life.

Stinsford was on the way from Melbury and Maiden Newton to London, and the O'Briens were sometimes overwhelmed by visitors, though many of these stayed for only one night. Susan O'Brien complained that her house was 'considered as an inn', and told one visitor bluntly that she should stay for longer next time she came.[40] As she wrote in her journal:

> My young relations find better amusement than coming here but as *passengers*, or for balls or races etc. My older ones content themselves with having a great regard for me, liking my company, praising everything, but never coming near me but as *passengers*.[41]

When she told her sister-in-law Maria, Countess of llchester that 'a little more society, and not so many calls, would be much pleasanter', Susan was mortified to be informed that 'If I did not live in the way, I should not see so many of my family'. She thought that then, at least, 'those few that did come, would have come really to see me, and not for the various other reasons that now prevail'.[42] More welcome were the longer visits by Susan's brother Stephen and her sisters Harriot and Fanny.

The O'Briens also saw a good deal of Susan's brother Charles and his family, who lived only ten miles away, at Maiden Newton. Every June from 1806 to 1824 several of them came to Stinsford on a fishing trip. These parties, which usually lasted for about a week, were clearly something of a strain. In 1816, after everyone had left, Susan wrote in her journal: 'I should have been disappointed if they had not come, but am disappointed that their being here afforded me so little pleasure and amusement.' The number of participants grew from year to year: in 1822 there were nine of them, together with four servants and four horses, and in 1824 eighteen people had to be accommodated. Susan, now aged over eighty, found this too many:

> It was unlucky in all respects – the weather unfavourable and the sport very bad. The whole stile of this very different from the former partys, when a few came, amused themselves at the river, and came home to a sociable supper with us. It was now too numerous for the house or family.[43]

After William O'Brien's death, Charles and his wife seem to have decided that it was their duty to provide companions for Susan, and their daughters were sent to stay at Stinsford on a regular basis. Unfortunately, Susan found these nieces poor company, for they were dull and had little to say for themselves, writing in 1818, 'they all want more to animate them than any conversation that I can furnish, therefore no great amusement on either side'.[44]

By the 1820s there were many more opportunities for socialising in the countryside than there had been a hundred, or even fifty, years earlier. In the first half of the eighteenth century people entertained select groups of friends and acquaintances at home, in a rather formal style. Whole suites of rooms, such as the inlaid rooms at Melbury, were set aside for the reception of important guests, but were rarely used by the family at other times. By the middle of the century the internal layout of houses was changing, with the provision of more rooms where large numbers of people could be entertained: a grand saloon or ballroom for parties, with room for people to dance; a large dining room; and several smaller sitting rooms where the inhabitants of the house could sit and chat, read, draw or play cards. New houses, such as Penrice Castle, were planned with this more relaxed way of life in mind, and the second Earl of Ilchester's alterations at Melbury (of which Susan O'Brien so disapproved) were intended to produce the same effect. In January 1811 Susan found 'a vast number of people under the same roof' at Melbury, 'some of all ages, in partys all over the house'.[45]

A typical event of the late eighteenth century was the ball held at Stourhead in December 1791, during the visit of the celebrated authoress Madame de Genlis and her 'pupils'. Mary Strangways and her sister Lily were invited, though Mary was only fifteen, and neither girl had yet officially 'come out'. Mary described the party to her younger sister Harriot, who was at school in Weymouth:

> The ball at Stourhead … was very pleasant to *me*. There was only eight ladies that danced, so of course we did not dance much – only six before dinner and

> six after. Madame Genlis ... would not let her three pupils dance after supper, so we made Lady Digby and Mrs C[harles] Digby dance instead. We staid there all the next day, and at night Madame Genlis and Mademoiselle d'Orléans played on the harp delightfully. Afterwards we all played blindman's buff till after two. The next day ... we play hopscot all the morning, and hoped [*sic*] up and down (upon on leg) the steps before the hall door.[46]

There were more family parties too, and better transport made it possible to gather groups of friends and relations together for a weekend of shooting or sight-seeing. A special occasion, such as a christening or coming of age, would bring many visitors. In August 1803, the baptism of the heir to the Penrice and Margam estates was celebrated with 'much festivity'. The little boy's uncle Lord Ilchester and his great-uncle Colonel Stephen Strangways travelled to South Wales from the West Country, a number of local friends came to dinner, an ox was roasted for the 'country people', and there was a dance in the evening.[47] Lord Ilchester's coming of age in 1808 was celebrated in style at Melbury by family, friends and estate workers and tenants:

> The park was full of people from all the neighbouring villages. Great plenty of meat and beer distributed, Evershot Volunteers keeping regularity and order. At three o'clock a dinner in the saloon and eating-room for three hundred people: two tables the length of the room and one cross one at the top, where Lord Ilchester sat and did the honours very well in a pleasing and popular manner ... There were several young men of Lord Ilchester's acquaintance in the house, as well as almost all his near relations: two aunts, five sisters, three brothers, and Lady Ilchester. Everything was well-arranged: each lady sat between a gentleman and a tenant, so that all partook of the company and conversation suitable to the day. The evening was turbulent, but altogether, considering the number of people present and the abundance of victuals and drink, everything was conducted with great propriety and good humour.

The evening ended with fireworks. Another large party was held two days later at Redlynch, and there were further festivities at Somerton and Abbotsbury.[48]

Similar gatherings, involving both family members and the country people, were held to celebrate national events. In July 1814 feasts were organised in honour of the Peace of Paris and Napoleon's abdication. At Stinsford the local farmers gave a supper for their work people, and the O'Briens entertained the rest of the inhabitants of the parish. It rained, so the guests could not sit outside and 'were forced to be stuffed into our servants' hall, where between eighty and ninety were seated and enjoyed a very good meal', consisting of strong beer, beef and pudding.[49] On Coronation Day in 1821 there was a feast for the children of the village. Susan O'Brien's friend Mrs Floyer gave 'gooseberry pies, enough for near a hundred, on a long table in her field'. Afterwards there was dancing and singing 'and perhaps more happiness, certainly more joy, than in Westminster Hall'. A month later there was a dinner for all the people of the parish, given to celebrate the birth of an heir to the local landowner, William Morton Pitt.[50]

The eighteenth century also saw the transformation of country towns such as Sherborne, Blandford and Dorchester. New town halls and assembly rooms were built, and inns were enlarged to provide large spaces where public parties and dances could be held. The Sherborne Castle game books record that 'Lord and Ladies Digby etc. went to the Sherborne assembly' in November 1763. A month later they saw two plays, *The Conscious Lovers* and *The Honest Yorkshireman*, which were acted 'by command of Miss I. Feilding'.[51] The shops were improving too: in 1813 Susan O'Brien and her friends 'walked about [Dorchester] shoping [*sic*] and seeing fashions'. Susan later wrote in her journal:

> It's quite amazing how so many milliners can find employment and proffit in such a town as Dorchester, but it's the same, I believe, in most others and, whatever else fails, dress goes on with everybody, and our farmers' ladys are smarter than anybody, even from London.[52]

A few years later, however, Lady William Russell described Dorchester as 'a very melancholy town, surrounded by trees like boulevards'.[53]

By the 1790s there were numerous public entertainments in Dorset during the summer and autumn, many of which were attended by the Melbury family and their friends. Everyone went to the Blandford Races in July or August, and several parties were held whilst the judges were in Dorchester for the summer assizes. In 1803 Susan O'Brien attended 'a grand dinner' for the assize judges at Milton Abbey on 28 July. The assizes started on the following day, and a party went from Stinsford to watch the court proceedings, after which everyone went to 'Mrs Frampton's law party' in Dorchester. On 30 July Susan went with her nephew Lord Ilchester and his sister Charlotte 'to hear Captain Wolfe's trial for pressing men in Portland'.[54] Dances were also held during the annual meetings of the local volunteer regiment, the Dorset Yeomanry, and other social events were enlivened by the presence of large numbers of officers of the army and navy, who were stationed in Dorchester and Weymouth during the wars with France in the 1790s and early 1800s. For the young, unmarried girls of the area they were an irresistible attraction. Nor were their charms lost on the older women: Susan O'Brien thought that the officers of the King's German Legion, whom she met in 1804, were 'many of them, well-informed, sensible and agreeable men – Colonel Bock in particular'. The O'Briens held a 'great dinner' for the Hanoverian officers at Stinsford.[55] Eight years later Harriot Frampton was 'captivated by General Jones, who commands at Weymouth, and who is so handsome, and so bald, and has the most beautifull profile that ever was seen'.[56]

Weymouth, which began attracting 'polite' visitors in mid century, became even more fashionable after 1789 when the Royal Family began to make regular visits in the summer and autumn, and the town developed rapidly. Visitors could meet their friends in the assembly rooms, and there was a theatre, several libraries and a wide range of shops. There were also many social events: assemblies or drawing rooms, fêtes and balls, and dances on board the ships anchored in the harbour. The presence of the royal visitors could, however, be a mixed blessing: in 1809 Susan O'Brien went to a ball in Dorchester which was attended by the Duke of Cambridge, and found it 'excessively full and disagreeable' because of the numbers of people who had come to see the Duke.[57] For some people it was all too exhausting, especially as they could not leave the parties, or even sit down, whilst the royal visitors were present. As Susan O'Brien commented after the King's departure from Weymouth in October 1804, 'It has been a fatiguing, bustling season for the neighbourhood. The Royal Family feel no fatigue.'[58] Susan's niece Louisa Strangways, at Weymouth with her stepmother in September 1805, wrote of balls and plays and shooting parties, but admitted to her sister Mary, 'Between ourselves, I hate it all. I used to be ten thousand times happier when we lived quietly at Melbury and never saw any but people I loved.'[59] Many girls could not afford to be so choosy: if, like the daughters of the Revd Charles Strangways, their parents could not afford to take a house in London during the Season or, like Thomas and Mary Talbot, did not wish to do so, these local entertainments did at least give them a chance to mix with new people – and, perhaps, find a husband. When, in 1819, Charles Strangways appeared to be reluctant to let his family go to the Blandford Races, his sister commented that this was a pity, as 'A little amusement and change of scene is necessary for Mrs Strangways, as well as desirable for the girls'.[60]

South Wales saw no royal visitors, and lacked resident aristocratic families, but the facilities of Swansea were also improving at this time, even though the town's attempts to turn itself into a genteel seaside resort were ultimately doomed to failure by the proximity of the copper works, coal mines and other industrial enterprises. Swansea's first theatre opened in 1785. By 1789 there was a bathing house on the Burrows, close to the sea, with rooms for dancing and dining, in addition to sleeping accommodation. Race meetings began in 1803, when the stewards were Thomas Talbot and his friend

1. Thomas and Susanna (Ridout) Strangways of Melbury and their children, by Thomas Hill (*c.* 1698). Susanna (Strangways Horner) is seated, front right. (*Private Collection*)

2. A Strangways lion at Melbury. In 1698 a pair stood before the east front of the house; they are now on gate-piers at the entrance to the park.

3. Melbury House, Dorset, south front (2003).

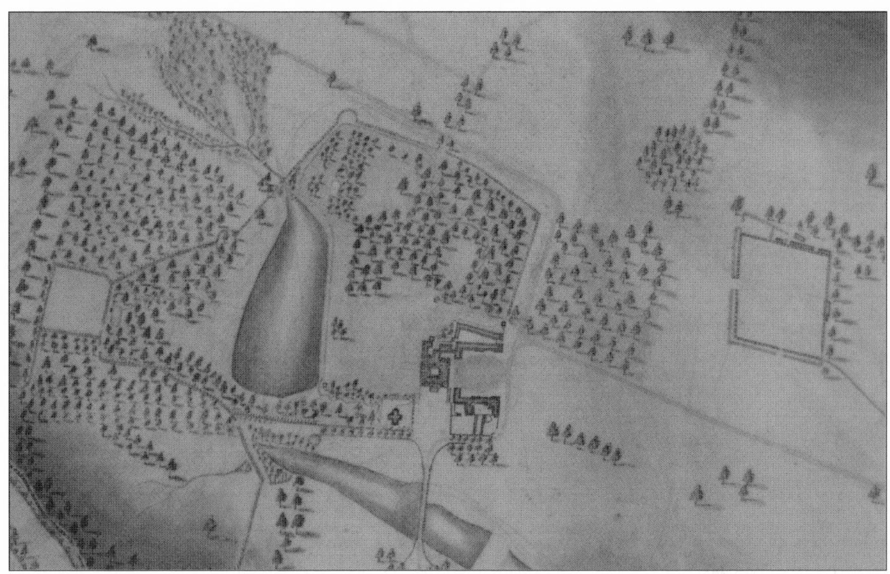

4. Melbury House and grounds from an estate map (*c.* 1790). (*Reproduced with the permission of Ilchester Estates and the Dorset Archives Service, ref. D/FSI, MC9/4*)

5. Susanna Strangways Horner and her daughter Elizabeth in Naples, by Francesco Solimena (1733). (*Private Collection*)

6. Elizabeth, first Countess of Ilchester, by John Giles Eccard (*c.* 1760). (*Private Collection*)

7. Lord Hervey and his Friends by William Hogarth (*c.* 1742). The sitters are (left to right) Peter Lewis Willemin (?); Stephen Fox; Henry Fox; John, Lord Hervey; Charles, Duke of Marlborough, and Thomas Winnington. (*Private Collection*)

8. Stephen, first Earl of Ilchester, by Francis Cotes (*c.* 1755). (*Private Collection*)

9. Henry Thomas, second Earl of Ilchester, by Thomas Beach (1778). (*Private Collection*)

10. Redlynch House, Somerset, the old mansion, from the sale catalogue of 1912. (*Reproduced with the permission of Ilchester Estates and the Dorset Archives Service, ref. D/FSI, box 340*)

11. Redlynch House, Somerset, stables, offices and mansion house (*c.* 1910). (*By kind permission of Adrian Pearse*)

12. Charlotte and Louisa Fox Strangways, daughters of the second Earl of Ilchester, by John Westbrooke Chandler (*c.* 1800–5). Charlotte is on the left and Louisa on the right. (*Private Collection*)

John Llewelyn of Penllergaer, who gave 'balls and breakfasts' for the race-goers.[61] A new library opened in 1804, and in the same year Thomas Talbot subscribed £200 towards the construction of a new set of assembly rooms in the town, though these were not completed until 1821.[62]

The ladies probably saw more of their husbands during the summer than at any other time of year, for the latter had neither political affairs nor sport to distract them. In the first week of September, however, partridge shooting started. Later in the month the sportsmen would go after pheasants as well. The Sherborne game books show that they generally stopped shooting partridges at the end of October, and went after woodcock instead. Lord Ilchester would spend some time shooting at Sherborne with his Digby cousins, and he and the Digbys, together with other friends, would also stay at Maddington for a few weeks, generally in September. The house at Maddington, 'that little Trianon, sacred to sweat and spaniels', as Lord Hervey called it in 1731, had only two beds to begin with, but it was later enlarged.[63] Elizabeth Fox was there for the first time in September 1739 – a development that was not appreciated by her husband's old friend Sam Hill, who wrote sourly in the Redlynch game book that nobody had been out shooting on 6 September, and that this represented the 'first fruits of women coming to Maddington'.[64] Elizabeth (now Lady Ilchester) was, however, back again in 1744 with her baby daughter Susan. In the 1780s the second Earl and Countess would travel to Maddington together, taking several of their children with them. Their granddaughter Charlotte Traherne recorded her mother's memories of these happy times:

> The journey [to Maddington] was performed in two carriages – the coach and the phaeton. The latter was driven by my grandfather with his wife sitting beside him and my mother stuck up in the head – a very happy seat she said – and enjoy the views, for it was very high. At Maddington they had ponies and country rides, few studies and a great many pets.[65]

There were also shooting trips to Abbotsbury in the autumn and during the weeks after Christmas. In the first half of the eighteenth century such expeditions might consist of a handful of shooters with a keeper or two, but they gradually became larger and more organised. By the nineteenth century there was a regular round of shooting parties, on Lord Ilchester's own estates and on the estates of friends and relations, such as Sherborne Castle and Moreton. Fox-hunting also became increasingly popular, extending the sporting season well into the spring. A few women went out hunting, but in general their role was confined to looking after the men when they returned from their day out in the field, and entertaining any female visitors.

On 7 September 1764 at Sherborne Castle 'Lord Stavordale, Mr Stephen and Charles Digby went a-shooting towards Wooten and West Hall. Lord Digby rode round the park with Lord Winchelsea; the ladies drove round in a carriage'.[66] When the Royal Family visited Melbury in October 1817, 'the gentlemen went out shooting and the ladys walked and drove about the park'. Susan O'Brien, who had a bad cold, stayed indoors 'to talk and play at whist'.[67]

In December the family would begin to gather at Melbury for the Christmas season. Christmas Day itself was celebrated quietly: everyone went to church and there were mummers and carol singers. At Christmas in 1760 the singers from Evershot and Melbury were given 7*s.* 6*d.*, and nine years later the housekeeper paid a shilling 'to bread for Evershot and Melbury singers'.[68] The first Earl and Countess sometimes spent Christmas at Redlynch, where they would also be entertained by local singers and musicians. On 1 January 1747 they gave 10*s.* 6*d.* to 'the maskeraders' from Batcombe. Smaller sums to singers from Redlynch (5*s.*), Bruton (2*s.* 6*d.*), Shepton Montague (5*s.*), Batcombe (5*s.*) and Kilmington (5*s.*) are recorded at Christmas 1759. At the latter date Ann Scott was paid 5*s.* for cleaning the chapel at Redlynch, ready for the Christmas service.[69] On Christmas Eve 1782 the Redlynch choristers were given 10*s.* 6*d.*, and those from Bruton, Shepton Montague and Yarlington received 5*s.* Two days later choristers from Brewham, Charlton Musgrove and Bruton turned up, and each group received 5*s.* On 28 December 'Mr Loader (musician)' and his band 'consisting of four persons' were paid four guineas for playing for two evenings.[70]

By the end of the eighteenth century the Christmas parties had increased in size and there were numerous balls and assemblies for the visitors to attend. Plays were put on – there are references to 'theatricals' at Dunraven Castle in Glamorgan in 1794 and 1795, and at Penllergaer in 1799.[71] Susan O'Brien described one family Christmas at Melbury, in 1809:

> Sir George Paul, Lady Elizabeth and Mr Feilding and several of Lord Ilchester's young friends, Lady Ilchester and her three sons, three children of Lady Elizabeth's, made a house-full and a merry Christmas. Singers, ball and mummers as usual, but the mummers are become politicians and, instead of St George and his dragon, have got Bonaparte, the Duke of York, and the OPs [?opposites] for their *dramatis personae.* This spoils the simplicity and merriment of the whole thing.[72]

The O'Briens sometimes spent Christmas at Stinsford, where they would be visited by the carol-singers immortalised by Thomas Hardy in *Under the Greenwood Tree.*[73] In 1810 the weather was so bad that the singers were unable to go on their rounds on Christmas morning, but they sang on Christmas Day in 1819, and Susan gave them 'their supper, beef and beer' in the evening.[74] The largest and most elaborate party would be held on Twelfth Night, when there was 'dancing and merriment'. Everyone would eat a specially decorated cake, and 'draw for names'. Jane and Mary Theresa Talbot were at Melbury for the party held on 6 January 1813, and Jane wrote afterwards to tell her younger sister Charlotte about the occasion:

> We danced till three in the morning. My name was 'Lady Lappet' – rather a stupid name, I think. Mary was – I forget what. Aunt Harriot Ackland was queen and Giles [Strangways], king. I could not save you any mottos because everybody broke theirs.

According to Mary Theresa's letter, written at the same time, her name was 'Lady Danglecub'. She kept one of the ornaments from the 'twelfth cake' for Charlotte – 'a little leg of mutton [which] will do for the baby house'.[75] Two years later Kit Talbot was at Bowood, where the celebrations clearly did not come up to the Melbury standard:

> We had a very bad twelfth cake, not worth the name. It was about the size of this half-sheet [of paper], all brown, with not a single ornament, motto, or a morsel of ice! It was as heavy as could be, and nobody eat any but Bella [his sister] and I. There was no kinging and queening, nor any sort of merriment.[76]

Once Twelfth Night was over, the lure of London soon became irresistible to most landowners and their wives.

For the servants, the country house day began early. Long before the family was awake, the housemaids would be up and about, opening the shutters, dusting, sweeping and polishing, cleaning the grates and laying and lighting fires. Fires had to be lit in the kitchen, too, both for cooking and for heating water. Soon, other servants would be busy preparing breakfast for the family. This was usually a light meal, consisting of bread and butter, toast, small cakes and warm rolls, with honey or marmalade. To drink there would be tea, coffee or chocolate.[77] Georgian ladies and gentleman were not, in general, early risers, though they got up earlier in the country than in the town. When Lady Caroline Lennox was planning her elopement with Henry Fox in London in 1744, she told him that her parents and sister were never up until twelve or one.[78] In the country breakfast was usually between nine and eleven, though this varied according to the season and the day's programme. On one morning in the summer of 1790 Agnes Porter rose at six, read for an hour and then walked out before breakfast before settling down with her pupils for several hours.[79] But the ladies of the household might not appear downstairs before midday, preferring to breakfast in bed or in their dressing rooms. In 1763 at Sherborne Castle the decision of the ladies to rise at eleven o'clock and 'honour the gentlemen with their company at breakfast' was so unusual as to be worth noting in the game book. Visitors quite often arrived early to join the family for the first meal of the day. The Dean of Wells breakfasted with the Digbys in September 1764, and in December 1772 Lord Ilchester and his daughter Fanny rode over from Redlynch to breakfast between eleven and twelve o'clock.[80]

At Penrice the first meal of the day was usually taken in the breakfast room or parlour, which was smaller and more convenient than the dining room. In the early 1800s breakfast was usually at ten or ten thirty, by which time Thomas and Mary Talbot had often been up for some time. Mary sometimes wrote letters before breakfast, whilst her husband went out for a walk. On one morning in March 1806 Thomas walked out to inspect his workmen on Oxwich marsh, and found them all 'buisily at work'. A month or so later he 'took a glass of Spa water soon after getting up ... and then took a walk before breakfast'.[81] In later years breakfast at Penrice was usually at nine.[82] In 1813 Kit Talbot had to breakfast by himself whilst he was staying at Melbury, as the other boys did not appear downstairs until eleven or twelve.[83]

The children and their attendants would usually be up well before the adults. How much time the children spent with their parents varied: in the eighteenth century many children were with maidservants for much of the day, though some households also included a woman – often a poor relation – who acted as a companion to the mistress of the house and as a minder for her children.[84] By the nineteenth century parents were more likely to employ a professional governess. Agnes Porter, who was governess at Penrice from 1799 to 1806, generally rose at seven, and she was with her pupils for most of the morning, though they also saw a good deal of their mother.

The limited amount of evidence that is available suggests that children in the Georgian period were not usually housed in a special part of the house, as was often the case in the nineteenth century. Instead, they were given rooms wherever it happened to be convenient, usually on an upper floor.[85] There was a nursery at Melbury in 1727, with a small room next door for a servant. These two rooms appear to have been on the first floor, and they are listed between 'the white cloth roome over the marble hall' and 'the blew damaske room'. The nursery was comfortably, but not luxuriously, furnished, with a 'plad stuffe bed', a looking-glass and table, a square breakfast table and six matted chairs. The window curtains were made of white calico. There were, however, also 'two peeces of gilt leather hangings'. The Redlynch inventory of 1793 includes a reference to an 'old nursery' above the saloon, on the first floor of the original mansion. This nursery was also furnished as a fairly simple bedroom: the four-poster bed had blue and white hangings, and the room also contained a mahogany chest of drawers, a mahogany table, five chamber chairs and a 'toylight table'. The window curtains were made of muslin. This room was next to the chintz dressing room, bedroom and closet, which were probably used by the second Countess of Ilchester, and may have housed her children whilst they were very young, especially when they were still being breast-fed. The child's nurse may have slept in the nursery, or in a closet next to it. The older children (and some adults) appear to have slept, and spent most of their time, in the rooms over the offices.[86] At Penrice the children slept in the bedrooms on the second floor, which were more simply decorated than those on the first floor.

During the shooting season most of the men would be up early, ready to spend several hours out with their companions and gamekeepers. At other times a landowner might ride out to inspect his estate, or spend the morning discussing business with his stewards and bailiffs, or reading and writing letters at home. He might do this in his dressing room – in 1727 there was 'a walnutt scrutore' or writing-desk in Thomas Strangways's dressing room at Melbury – or in the library. There was a library at Melbury in 1727, probably upstairs, hung with gilt leather. The contents included a walnut chest of drawers, a black-japanned card table and six walnut chairs, in addition to 'a blacke japanned burow with booke case and glass doores' and three plaster heads.[87] One of Stephen Fox's first alterations at Redlynch was the construction (or fitting out) of a new library, where he wrote letters to Lord Hervey in 1730. By this time such libraries were being used increasingly as informal sitting rooms – in November 1731 Lord Hervey told Stephen that he wished that they were 'all together in the cold library [at Redlynch] where pens and ink are so scarce',[88] and in 1748 Stephen described a typical morning in the country to his brother:

> I am called at half an hour past eight; seldom rise till half an hour past nine; am in the library before ten; stay there chatting with Julian and Harry [his children] 'till half an hour past eleven. Then to the forest for four or five hours.[89]

The mistress of the household would often spend the morning in her dressing rooom or in an upstairs sitting room, sometimes known as a boudoir. She would summon the housekeeper or cook to her to give them their orders for the day, and she might also inspect the household accounts and play with, or instruct, her children. Any spare time before her maid came to do her hair and help her to dress would be filled by sewing, reading, writing letters or playing cards. Because they functioned as informal sitting rooms where visitors (including men) might be received, ladies' dressing rooms were comfortably, often lavishly, furnished. At Melbury in 1727 Mary Strangways's dressing room held 'a cabinett with some china on topp', an oval writing table of walnut, two velvet elbow chairs and four velvet-covered stools. In the adjoining closet, to which only the most favoured visitors would be admitted, were a velvet easy chair, two velvet stools, one japanned writing table, an inlaid cabinet and a large china jar. Mary Strangways also had a dressing room next to her bedroom at Stinsford, with 'a walnutt buroe with a booke casse att top with glass doores' and four square stools with black frames, covered with red flowered silk.[90]

At Penrice, the room which was to become Mary Talbot's dressing room was probably left unfurnished (apart from some sun-blinds) until 1793 when Thomas Talbot ordered furnishings from Quentin Kay. These included 'a very fine handsome ladies satinwood secretary with a writing drawer, with bookshelves at top and sundry drawers complete' and 'a very large elegant satinwood library bookcase, richly inlaid with various sorts of wood'.[91] Mary described this room in a letter written shortly after her arrival at Penrice as a bride, early in 1794:

> My dressing room, which I shall begin with as the most charming room in the whole house, is of a light blue with white dimity cushions to the chairs. There is a tapestry picture over the chimney-piece, and the rest of the room is hung with drawings of ruins about Rome. There is a beautiful satinwood bookcase full of all sorts of delightful books ... I have a remarkable sweet-toned pianoforte in it, and am now writing at the prettiest escritoire that can be.[92]

Staying at Penrice in January 1811 Susan O'Brien wrote 'We have established ourselves very comfortably ... We go and settle in Mary's room after breakfast, where Mr O'Brien reads till nunch time, then the children, or going out, or anything one has to do.'[93] Twenty-five years later, Kit Talbot wrote that he hoped that his new wife would 'never adopt the family habit of hiding herself all the morning' and told his mother that he had furnished their bedroom at Margam 'purposely to prevent its being snapped up for a morning sitting-room'.[94]

The first Countess of Ilchester does not seem to have been a great reader, but she could happily spend all day playing cards. Indeed, Susan O'Brien later recalled that her parents had often spent much of the day apart: 'my father in one room reading, my mother in another playing at cards'.[95] In August 1750 Lord Ilchester wrote from Redlynch that 'Mrs Digby, Lady Ilchester [and] Miss Cheeke are now at ombre, and have been so many hours this week.'Tis computed to be a game at least fifty times prettier than brag.'[96] Ombre and brag are both card games, the latter being similar to poker. Forty years later, when card games (usually cribbage) were Lady Ilchester's main entertainment, life could be difficult for her visitors. Susan O'Brien wrote an account of one particularly uncomfortable stay at Discove, a farmhouse near Redlynch where her mother stayed from time to time:

> Mr O'Brien [was] almost confined to his room to avoid every sort of altercation, which it was impossible for him to do if he played at cards with [my mother]. That fertile source of ill-humour has become her only occupation, and I have frequently this year played eight hours a day with her.[97]

The ladies did not always spend the whole morning indoors. If the weather was fine they might drive out before dinner. Often this was purely for pleasure, but there were also certain formal calls that had to be paid, even in the country. On 30 November 1770, three weeks after Lord Digby's second marriage, 'Lord and Lady Ilchester, Lady Lucy and Lady Harriot came [from Redlynch to Sherborne] in the coach to make their first visit to Lady Digby. They arrived a little after one o'clock in the afternoon and returned about three o'clock.'[98] They did not stay for dinner. At Stinsford, the O'Briens sometime drove out to call on friends in the neighbourhood, and they often had visitors in the morning. One day in November 1824 Susan 'went out to visit Lady William Russell ... Lord William having left a card here'. She added that she 'could not avoid it without incivillity, though much surprised at his having done so, being quite unacquainted'.[99] Leaving cards was more common in London, where etiquette demanded that someone who wished to inform a neighbour of their arrival should should first call and leave a card. The recipient of the card would then return the call. Susan later discovered that her cousin Lord Holland had suggested that the Russells, who had recently come to live in Dorset, should contact her. Susan found, rather to her surprise, that she liked Lady William, and she and the Russells saw a good deal of each other during the following months, though the newcomers were young enough to be her grandchildren. Two months after their first meeting, Lord William told Lady Holland: 'Old Lady Susan keeps us all alive by her gaiety and anecdotes of our grandmothers and their sweethearts. She is a prodigy, and a most amusing prodigy.'[100] At Penrice Mary Talbot was usually occupied with her children and household affairs for much of the morning, but if the weather was fine she would often work in the garden, or walk or drive out with the children and any visitors who might be staying. Occasionally she went in the carriage to Swansea (twelve miles away) to shop and pay visits, returning in the late afternoon.

The most important meal of the day, and the one to which guests were most likely to be invited, was dinner. Numerous Digby and Fox Strangways cousins dined at Sherborne Castle, and the Digbys were regular visitors to Redlynch and Melbury. Some people merely stopped for dinner before travelling further: on 28 August 1755 Susanna Strangways Horner dined at Sherborne Castle 'in her way from Redlynch to Melbury',[101] whilst others dined and then stayed overnight. At Stinsford the O'Briens often dined with their neighbours at the rectory and with the Pitts at Kingston Maurward, both houses being within walking distance. Friends and relations who were close enough to Stinsford for regular dinner visits included the Framptons at Moreton, Lord Dorchester at Milton Abbey and his cousins at Came House, and the Brownes at Frampton Court. At Penrice the Talbots dined out quite frequently, and they often entertained friends at home. With no resident aristocrats in South Wales, they socialised mainly with the local gentry and clergy: families such as the Collinses of Oxwich, the Lucases of Stouthall and the Kings of Marino near Swansea. John Collins, the rector of Oxwich, sometimes came to dine alone, continuing a tradition that had begun whilst Thomas Talbot was still a bachelor. Elizabeth Talbot clearly thought that her sister's acquaintances were not select enough, though her own neighbours at Lacock, where she spent a year or two in the 1790s, do not seem to have known quite what to make of her, as she told her sister Harriot:

> I am going to be plagued with some of my neighbours at dinner. I hope you pity me, as you know how I hate to be civil, particularly in hot weather. They are good souls however, some of them, and when I compare them with some people's neighbours I think myself very well off. They are elegant and refined in comparison of Mary's and many others, though they think me deranged for liking moonlight walks and drives. However, *entre nous* ... I rather like being abused than otherwise, and it is a sort of notoriety *qui me sied à merveille* [which suits me very well].[102]

In 1801 and 1802 Thomas and Mary Talbot also held regular dinner parties at Penrice for officers stationed locally. These were usually held on Friday evening, and up to eight men would be invited at a time.

The Talbots occasionally took picnic dinners to local beauty spots when they had visitors. One day in May 1802 they set out in open carriages with some friends to visit the cliffs at Worm's Head, about six or seven miles from Penrice. They dined under a tent, but this did not protect them from the rain, which began to pour down. When the party eventually returned to Penrice at seven in the evening one of the guests, Mr King, told Agnes Porter that 'there was nothing like *pleasuring*', but his wife was 'quite defeated', and Mary Talbot had to go to bed at once, 'wet to the skin'. Agnes, who had declined an invitation to accompany them, being 'apprehensive of bad weather', commented rather smugly in her journal: 'I love pleasure, but not when "the bitter overbalances the sweet".'[103] Another trip to Worm's Head two years later was more successful. Agnes went too on this occasion, and they had 'a charming day': 'We pitched our tent at pleasure where the prospect was most varied and extensive. We dined with appetite on a cold collation and then wandered about as fancy enclined us.'[104]

Wealthy families took great pride in their ability to keep a good table, and this meant offering generous quantities of food and drink of the best possible quality. When Thomas Horner of Mells visited Melbury in 1760 to claim the silver that belonged to his family, he and a friend dined at the house with the steward George Donisthorpe. Dinner consisted of ten dishes, and a further five dishes were served at supper at ten o'clock. The three men got through six bottles of port, and Donisthorpe eventually left for his bed in Evershot between three and four in the morning.[105]

For formal dinners there would usually be two or three courses, each consisting of a selection of dishes, both sweet and savoury, all of which would be laid out on the table at the same time. Finally, dessert would be served. Informal family dinners were much simpler and were not necessarily eaten in the principal dining room. At Moreton in the 1780s the Framptons 'lived entirely in one of the worst rooms in [the house], where we breakfasted, dined and supped; and even with company in the house, excepting on the rare occasion of a large party'.[106] In 1727 Melbury had an 'eating parlour', which appears to have been the everyday family dining room. The contents of this room were valued at £11 15*s*. High-status guests would presumably have dined in the inlaid dining room. On the grandest occasions such as royal visits, when large numbers of people had to be fed, the guests would sit down to dine in the hall or saloon. Stinsford had a 'little eating parlour' in 1727, furnished with ten cane chairs, 'a wainscott oval table, a square table, a Dutch breakfast table ... and a hand tea table'. There was no best dining room at Stinsford at this time but the hall, in which there were twelve chairs, a 'wainscott ovall table' and a marble sideboard on iron brackets, was probably used for this purpose.[107] Tables would be moved around as necessary, for it was not usual until the latter part of the eighteenth century for everyone to sit around one table. In 1793 the dining room at Redlynch held 'a large mahogany dining-table with seven leaves occasionly', and also a smaller mahogany table, in addition to twelve chairs.[108] At Penrice it is difficult to believe that the large dining room, at the opposite end of the house from the kitchen and a cold room at the best of times, with three exterior walls and four windows, was ever used on a day-to-day basis unless there were too many people to fit into the cosier and more convenient breakfast room.

For most of the eighteenth century the usual time of dining at Melbury and Redlynch, and also at Sherborne Castle, was three o'clock. There were variations, however. In 1731 Lord Hervey, at Kew, refers to dining at five '*à la* Redlynch', and in 1748 Stephen Fox, at Redlynch without his wife, would dine at five after a day's shooting.[109] Dinner was usually later in London, and became later still during the eighteenth century – the result, according to Susan O'Brien, of changes in parliamentary hours. In 1760 the sittings were over in time for everyone to sit down to dinner at four o'clock; by 1820 Parliament did not meet until four or five o'clock, the speeches were longer than they had been sixty years earlier, and the men were not ready for dinner until seven or eight o'clock. In the country, too, the dinner hour gradually became later, though the Talbots often dined at three when they were at Penrice, especially if any of the children were to eat with them. Thus, on 20 October 1801, Mary noted in her pocket-book 'little Mary dined with us in parlour [at] three'.[110] In 1804, however, Agnes Porter wrote that the adults at Penrice generally dined at five, and the children (who had already dined at one) came in at dessert. In 1825 Susan O'Brien complained about 'great dinners, and at the London hours' whilst she was staying at Moreton.[111]

When there were guests, dinner might last for two or three hours. Afterwards the ladies would move into the (with)drawing room, leaving the men to continue drinking by themselves. Eventually, however, the men would join the ladies, and tea and coffee would be served. Guests were sometimes invited to come after dinner, to take tea and then spend the rest of the evening with their hosts – when Agnes Porter went to visit her mother in Salisbury in 1791 she arrived to find that her sister Elizabeth was 'from home on a tea visit'.[112] In 1802, when Thomas and Mary Talbot were away, the rector's wife, Mrs Collins and her two daughters dined at Penrice with Agnes Porter and the Talbot children, and the other five Collins children came to tea afterwards.[113] In the winter the guests would often have to return home in the dark. This does not seem to have been a problem, though moonlit nights were appreciated. One day in December 1770 Lord and Lady Digby set out from Sherborne a little after midday with Charles Digby, 'to make a dining visit at Redlynch'. The journey took them a little under two hours. They had 'a very fine, light evening' for their return, and arrived back at Sherborne at half past nine.[114]

As dinner time became later, many families began to fit in an extra meal in the middle of the day. This was luncheon – often referred to as 'nunch' or 'nuncheon'. To begin with this was an informal snack, usually cold, available for anyone who happened to be around. In fine weather it might be eaten outside – on one day in April 1802 Mary Talbot noted that she had 'gardened all day and nunched in the garden'.[115] At Penrice nunch, which was usually at one o'clock, could be the main meal of the day for the younger children. The meal became more important in the nineteenth century, and luncheon parties were introduced. In 1817 the Duke and Duchess of Gloucester, who were staying at Melbury for a few days, drove over to Sherborne, where Lord Digby entertained them with 'a handsome luncheon'.[116]

There were changes later in the day too. When dinner was at three, another meal would be fitted during the evening. This was supper, a light and usually informal meal, which was usually set out around ten o'clock. One Sunday in May 1802 at Penrice, three neighbours dined with the Talbots and Agnes Porter after the church service, which was at half past three. They then had tea at eight and 'supper, a cold collation, at ten'.[117] The children would not eat as late as this: in July 1791 Agnes Porter sent her pupils with their maid to supper at seven o'clock, whilst she 'supped on water gruel *par préférence*' around ten. Sometimes, supper was omitted altogether. In 1793 Harriot Strangways (aged fourteen) informed her sister Mary: 'We keep charming hours: breakfast at nine, dine at three, drink tea at six, eat no supper, and go to bed from nine to eleven.'[118] In 1804, however, Mary Theresa Talbot was allowed to sit up to supper with her parents and Agnes Porter as a special treat on her ninth birthday.[119]

What everyone did after dinner depended on the time of year, and whether they had company. Left alone at Redlynch in August 1790, Agnes Porter and her pupils 'walked, read and had a little musick' after dinner one day. On the following afternoon, the girls' uncle Colonel Strangways arrived after dinner, 'drank tea with his nieces and me, after which we took a beautiful walk. At our return we read some extracts and spent the evening very pleasantly'.[120] When Lord Ilchester was at home, his daughters would spend the evening with him, whilst Agnes read, wrote letters or practised on the piano or harpsichord alone. If there were visitors the evening would often be spent playing cards, or there might be a dance or an impromptu concert. In September 1823 Susan O'Brien dined with her neighbour Mrs Floyer, the widow of the vicar of Stinsford: 'A large party, and the best arranged and best appointed that I have seen a long time. We had a very good dinner, music, cards, no form and pleasant chearfull conversation.'[121] A quiet evening at home could be spent listening whilst one of the company read out loud – or simply sitting around and chatting.

At night, Agnes Porter always looked in on her pupils before retiring to bed, usually at eleven. The personal servants of the ladies and gentlemen in the house would have to stay up until their employers went to bed, so that they could help them to undress. Finally, the house steward, housekeeper, butler or footman would make their rounds, to see that the doors and windows were secure for the night, make sure that the fires were safe, and extinguish any lamps or candles that were still burning.

7

Servants

A large Georgian country house was a community, of which the owner and his family made up only a small part. They were outnumbered several times over by a horde of servants, many of whom lived in the house, together with an ever-changing group of visitors and dependants. In the medieval and Tudor household many of the most visible attendants were of high social status, due to the practice of sending the adolescent sons and daughters of noble and gentry families to live with a friend or relative for a few years, to finish their education and, it was hoped, to set them on the road to a lucrative profession or advantageous marriage. These young gentlemen and gentlewomen were themselves waited on by other servants, most of whom were male. A few maidservants were employed in great medieval houses – in 1501 Alionor Strangways of Stinsford bequeathed legacies to two women: Agnes, to whom she left 6*s.* 8*d.*, and Margaret, who was to have 3*s.* 4*d.*[1] Such female servants were, however, largely invisible at a time when a family's position in society was measured by the number of men in livery available to greet and wait on visitors, or accompany their master and mistress when they were away from home. Female servants, who did not wear livery, remained in the background, attending to the needs of the ladies of the family in their private quarters, nursing their children, and washing the clothes and household linen.

The composition of noble and gentry households changed during the seventeenth century, most particularly after the Restoration of 1660. The aristocratic waiting women and gentlemen of the Tudor period disappeared, to be replaced in most instances by employees who came from humbler backgrounds. These servants fell into several distinct groups. There were the indoor domestic servants, who were supervised by the house steward or housekeeper. They were usually paid an annual salary, in addition to which they received food or board wages, and they were expected to live in. Some of them moved from house to house with their employers. The indoor servants also included the personal servants of the master and mistress such as valets and ladies' maids, who usually travelled with their employers, to whom alone they were answerable. In most households, too, were a number of people whose precise position within the domestic hierarchy was ambiguous. They were usually of a higher social status than most of the other employees, and included poor relations, chaplains, tutors, governesses and companions. Some of these people might perform specific duties, with the men acting as stewards and the women as housekeepers and ladies' maids. There were also the outdoor servants. The 1727 inventory of Melbury includes chambers for the shepherd, huntsman, bailiff and carters, and all of these rooms had beds in them. Such men became less and less likely to live in as the eighteenth century progressed, so that by the second half of the century most of the male outdoor staff lived in cottages on the estate, though the coachman, grooms, postillions and stable-helpers were generally accommodated near to, or over, the stables.

The number of servants employed at any one time varied according to the circumstances of the owner of the house: anything from twenty-five to fifty for a wealthy peer, and approximately twenty for the average large county family in the eighteenth century.[2] If a landowner was short of money, he would try to reduce his household expenses, and this usually meant dismissing some of the servants. The total number also varied according to the age, marital status and social commitments of the owner. Bachelors and widows generally needed fewer servants than married couples with several children. Elderly or reclusive owners might have few visitors, whilst others would need enough people to wait on an ever-changing group of friends, relations and acquaintances. Some of these servants would be male, but the proportion of female servants increased after 1660. When Sir John Strangways of Melbury made his will in 1664 he left legacies to a total of twenty-three servants, of whom only four were female. A list of the servants at Melbury drawn up in 1715 also lists twenty-three, but by this date the number of women had risen to seven. By the 1740s, if not earlier, most of the more menial positions within the house were filled by girls and women, working as maids in the scullery, kitchen, nursery and laundry, and keeping the house clean. François de La Rochefoucauld noted in 1784 that some English noblemen had thirty or forty menservants, 'but usually it's the women who do the cooking and all the housework that isn't seen, while the menservants are employed only on those duties that have to be performed in front of everyone'.[3] In the second half of the eighteenth century there were generally between twenty-one and twenty-seven servants at Melbury, and approximately half of them were female.[4] The Earls of Ilchester also maintained a separate household at Redlynch until 1793, and some of the servants moved from one house to another with their employers. Thirty-four servants are listed at Redlynch in 1764 (eighteen male and sixteen female), but a much smaller number stayed there when the family was away. Around 1800 the O'Briens probably had approximately half a dozen servants at Stinsford, a much more modest household. At Penrice the Talbots usually employed ten to twelve female and eight to ten male servants in the early nineteenth century. The comparatively high proportion of girls and women in this household is probably due to the fact that the Talbots had eight children. In addition to two nursemaids, they needed two laundry maids to cope with the family's washing.

In large houses such as Melbury and Redlynch the servants were supervised by a steward. In the Tudor household the house steward had been at the top of the domestic hierarchy. Such men – for they were always male – had become less widely employed during the Stuart period, and by the end of the seventeenth century they were found only in the mansions of the richest families.[5] House stewards were employed at both Melbury and Redlynch during the first half of the eighteenth century. They took charge of the day-to-day running of the household and some also had a supervisory role in the management of the family's estates. A steward had to be educated, for he was responsible for keeping the accounts and was expected to write regularly to his employers when they were away from home. The steward was addressed as 'Mr', and his father might have been a servant, a tradesman, or even a country gentleman.

The steward at Melbury in 1713 when Thomas Strangways died was John Biddell, who was paid £20 a year.[6] John's wife, Anne Biddell, was also employed by the family: in 1718, when Thomas Strangways's widow died, she left all her clothes to Anne, together with a suit of mourning.[7] Biddell's accounts for the years 1726–28 show that he was responsible for paying bills for items as diverse as 'crawfish, lobsters, lamb and other things' used at the funeral of Thomas Strangways junior in 1726, seeds for the garden, and medicines for the servants. He also paid the wages of his fellow servants and sent cash to his master and mistress. In May 1727 he sent £105 to Thomas Horner 'att Somerton cock-match'.[8]

John Biddell's successor as steward was George Donisthorpe, who arrived at Melbury in 1729 and was still steward there when he died fifty years later. His origins are unknown. He was not a local man, and his ancestors probably took their name from a village on the borders of Leicestershire and Derbyshire. Donisthorpe wrote a fine, clear hand until the very end, and he could spell and express himself with ease, so he was evidently well educated. He also knew how to ingratiate himself with Susanna Strangways Horner. In his first surviving letter he complained about the behaviour of her husband's employees, and ended:

> The desire I have of acquainting you with all occurrences happening at, or in

> any ways concerning, Melbury, will I hope plead my excuse for this tedious epistle, with which I would not have presumed to have troubled you, could I have reconciled my silence with my duty, to which I shall on all occasions endeavour to shew a regard in some measure meriting the great trust, confidence and favour which you have been pleased to repose in, and confer on, me.[9]

Donisthorpe was a general steward, responsible for collecting the rents and overseeing the bailiffs and other estate employees, and also for preparing the estate accounts. He ran the household at Melbury, and paid the servants' wages, the taxes and most of the household bills. He supervised the building works and the alterations to the garden there in the 1740s, paying the workmen and writing long, detailed letters to tell his mistress how they were getting on. Donisthorpe's position gave him a considerable amount of power in the local community, and he seems to have been thoroughly disliked by the tenants of the estate. An epitaph in the church at Melbury, composed by a local farrier, apparently read as follows:

> To this quaint corner we bequeath
> George Donisthorpe, esquire,
> His body here is underneath
> And we much fear from what we hear
> His soul is not much higher.[10]

The steward might well have a home of his own – George Donisthorpe and his wife had a house in Evershot. He was, however, expected to sleep in the mansion from time to time, and his duties would frequently take him to the family's other country houses, and also up to London. Usually, he would have an office or sitting room close to the most commonly used entrance to the house, from which he could observe any visitors and keep an eye on the servants as they went about their work. At Melbury in 1727 the steward's room held ten leather chairs, two oval tables, two corner cupboards and a 'Dutch table'. The contents of the steward's chamber are also listed: there was a feather bed and bedding, and also six old chairs, three stools, an oval table, a fire shovel and tongs, a pair of fire dogs and an oak cabinet. In 1727 the steward (Mr Biddell) had a bedchamber at Abbotsbury too, and the inventory of the contents of the house there also lists the 'steward's hall', which contained six leather chairs and a round table. A steward's room is also listed at Stinsford in 1737.[11]

Edward Hiett, the house steward at Redlynch, served the Fox family for at least fifty years. Bequests made in Hiett's will suggest that he probably came from Cirencester in Gloucestershire, where he owned the Fleece Inn.[12] He first appears in the records in 1713, when he was Lady Fox's footman in London, with an annual salary of £5. Two years later he was still earning

£5 a year, but was described as a 'footman and butler'.[13] Hiett had evidently been promoted by 1728, when William Dounie, the steward at Melbury, paid 2*s.* 6*d.* 'to Mr Haiet's servant that brought a present of a leash of pheasants'.[14] By 1735 Hiett's annual salary was £30, and he was keeping the household accounts at Redlynch.[15] Like George Donisthorpe at Melbury, Edward Hiett continued to work for the family until shortly before his death in 1764. His wife, Mary, was also employed by the Fox family for many years. She was a nursery maid to Sir Stephen Fox's children at Chiswick and subsequently became a housekeeper at Redlynch. The Hietts seem to have been totally loyal to Lord Ilchester, who depended on them to keep the household at Redlynch running smoothly.

Edward Hiett's responsibilities were similar to those of George Donisthorpe with the difference that Hiett appears to have had little to do with the running of the estate. He was, however, in overall charge of the stables and gardens as well as the house. He also supervised the building works at Redlynch in the 1740s. In 1745, when he was trying to reduce his household expenses, Lord Ilchester wrote that:

> Hiett's account comes every year to about £2900, which account takes in horses, dogs, housekeeping, travelling expences, board wages and, in short, everything but Lady Ilchester's, mine and the children's expences.[16]

A list of 'businesses that might be performed by the *Domi Senschallus*', which was drawn up in 1764 for Hiett's successor, summarises his duties:

> Mornings, to walk through the servants' hall etc. and see how things are, or were left there the last evening. Anything found amiss to give necessary instructions to be avoided in future. Do the same after breakfast, a little before and after dinner or supper if necessary, but do not appear too officious, for that may create a jealousy and hatred amongst the servants. A cursory view with a discerning eye may be sufficient.
>
> To regulate broils and quarrels (if any), but if that cannot be appeased, after forbearance and repeated admonitions, then to take a proper opportunity to lay it before My Lord.
>
> As there is no clerk of the kitchen, he should superintend the weight of the butcher's meat, groceries etc. etc. To examine the bills of parcels with goods, and ... pay such tradesmen's bills as come under his cognizance to examine.
>
> If he understands measuring and artificers' work, he should have the direction of repairing the mansion house and offices thereto belonging, and it may be the neighbouring farm-houses, cottages etc.
>
> To examine the housekeeper's book weekly or monthly, if necessary and required.
>
> To take a turn now and then in the stables, common cellars, brew-house, wash-house, laundry, dairy, bake-house, the gardens etc.

> If necessary to inspect the bailiffs' and woodwards' accounts.
>
> To measure timber, wood, artificers' work etc. etc.
>
> To pay all the servants' wages, but dismiss none without the Lord and Lady's directions and commands.
>
> To pay the home rates and taxes, unless that be more proper for another person.
>
> He should receive from the head steward, or else, sufficient monies to discharge all those things under his cognizance to pay.
>
> He should have an under lock-up room with a fireplace in it for his office, if convenient to be had; otherwise a room above stairs, besides his bedchamber, except his bedchamber be a large room, sufficient to be made into two rooms, for he is supposed to be frequently, or at certain stated hours, at his office, which should be stamped with His Lordship's authority. These things will give him weight, for if he is to have no other weight than a bare word, or order [it] is but wind, that would soon vanish and be evaded. He would be blowed upon, despised, and become as sounding brass or a tinkling cymbal. His office would be precarious and soon become not worth filling.
>
> He should have a boy, or an inferior servant, at his command to send in errands in His Lordship's business.[17]

It is not clear whether the Hietts had a house of their own at Redlynch, but Edward certainly had his own accommodation within the mansion. The plan of the 'offices' made in the mid eighteenth century shows the steward's room and the steward's dining room next to each other on the ground floor. The position of these rooms, in the south-eastern corner of the building, would have given their occupant an excellent view of the entrance front of the main house. In 1762, when Edward Hiett made his will, he left some of the furnishings of his room to his friend and fellow servant Molly Fenn. Molly was to have 'some old bed and table linnen, my books, two easy chairs, a strong box and several other things which may be accounted as lumber, being but of little value'.[18] Some of these pieces of furniture are mentioned in Molly Fenn's own will, which was written ten years later.[19] At the end of the eighteenth century the contents of the steward's room at Redlynch included a bedstead with blue furniture, six walnut chairs, a mahogany armchair, a large clothes press, a corner cupboard, a 'wash-hand stand bason and glass', ten pictures, eight glazed prints, a Bath stove, two oak tables and a boot jack.[20]

Men like George Donisthorpe and Edward Hiett were hard to replace. Reynier Tiler, who was employed at Redlynch from October 1782, was described as a house steward. He kept the accounts as Hiett had done, paying for items as diverse as 'musick on Lady Elizabeth's birthday' in 1782 (10*s.* 6*d.*); 'two mugs for toast and water etc.' in 1783 (1*s.* 11*d.*) and 'a padlock for Lady Ilchester's woman' (1*s.*, also in 1783). Tiler's salary of £42 a year in 1784–85 was not inconsiderable.[21] He seems, however, to have stayed for five years at the most. In general, the house steward was a rare creature by the second half of the eighteenth century, found only in the most conservative of great households. His duties had been taken over by a number of different servants, especially the land steward, who kept the estate accounts, collected rents and other revenue, paid the salaries and wages and sent cash to his employer, but had little to do with the day-to-day running of the house, and the (female) housekeeper, who supervised the domestic staff, ordered and distributed supplies, and kept the household accounts. Other duties were performed by the butler and personal servants such as valets and ladies' maids.

In smaller households the roles of the servants were less precisely defined. At Stinsford William and Susan O'Brien usually had two upper servants, one male and one female, each of whom had a variety of duties. Thomas de Borgi, who was with them from about 1770 to 1797, was succeeded by William Parkinson. Parkinson, who was paid £30 a year, combined the roles of butler, house steward and valet. He was expected to go to market to order provisions, and to 'have an eye over the other men servants and give an account of their behaviour, and to receive from them applications for whatever may be wanting'. As William O'Brien's *valet de chambre*, he tied and powdered his master's hair and looked after his clothes and linen.[22] After Parkinson came St John Jourdan 'a native of Geneva', who died in 1826.[23] Borgi's wife, Hannah, appears to have started work as a maid at Redlynch in the 1750s. She went with the O'Briens to America in 1764, and then returned to England and settled with them at Stinsford.[24] Hannah, who died in 1797, is described on her gravestone as 'housekeeper in the family of William O'Brien Esquire', but both she and her successor, Sarah Carter, also did much of the work of a personal maid. Later on, in 1822, Susan O'Brien had a cook-housekeeper, who 'fell down in an apoplectic fit' and died four days later.[25]

In earlier times the butler had presided over the buttery and the wine and beer cellars, and his main responsibility had been the provision of drink for the household. The eighteenth-century butler bottled the wine and decanted and poured it for the family and guests. He also looked after the glasses and was responsible for keeping the plate secure and making sure that it was cleaned properly. In some households he performed some of the duties of a valet, including shaving his master. The butler's pantry at Mells Manor in 1741 had several cupboards in it, including an oaken napkin press, together with a table, a japanned copper cistern, a large hone or whetstone with a case, four tortoiseshell razors, a Windsor chair, an iron plate-stand and a pipe-burner.[26] The butler would be expected to sleep in, but he might travel around with his employer. The butler's chamber at

Melbury in 1727 was between the chambers allocated to the cook and the coachman, and was well furnished. There was a bed with furniture of yellow stuff (woollen material), two Turkey worked chairs, a square table and a writing desk. There was also a butler's chamber at Stinsford at this date.

The duties of butler and footman might well overlap, though the former was usually paid more than the latter. At home, the footmen fetched coal and wood for the fires, carried water up to the bedrooms, and looked after the candles and lamps. They cleaned and polished the plate, brought food from the kitchen to the eating-room, and waited at table. At Redlynch in 1745 there were three footmen: Charles Swyer, Abraham Peirce and Silas Kerslake. Each of them earned £6 a year.[27] Footmen usually accompanied their employers when they went from one house to another. If Lady Ilchester stayed in Bath without her husband, she would take one or two footmen with her, to wait on her, carry messages and assist the other servants. Footmen rode on the back of the coach, walked before the sedan chair in Town, and accompanied their master or mistress when they went on foot. They wore livery, and were expected to be smartly turned out, for they were amongst the most visible of the servants. Edward Hiett was paid £5 a year in 1715 when he was Sir Stephen Fox's butler and footman at Chiswick. In 1764 the butler at Redlynch was Abraham Pierce, who received £8 a year. William Adams, who had been a footman at Melbury (at £7 a year) in 1754, became butler there in 1766. He stayed until 1787 when he and his wife were both discharged. As butler, Adams was paid £10 a year in 1784. Unlike most other butlers he wore livery, and his status was clearly inferior to that of the house steward, who was paid more than four times as much. The butler would sometimes have an under-butler to help him. Ellis Dawe senior was Susanna Strangways Horner's under-butler from 1742 to 1758, whilst his son (also called Ellis) was a footman at the same time.[28] Both received £7 a year. Joseph Coward was under-butler at Redlynch in 1791, with an annual salary of £15.[29]

At Penrice Thomas Mansel Talbot employed no house steward, and it was the butler who supervised the other servants and went to market and paid bills for his employers. Few butlers at Penrice lasted long. One, Jourdan, was dismissed in 1800. Another, John Mayor, was at Penrice from about 1804 to 1806. He was paid £47 5*s*. a year, as was his successor Christopher Sievers 'a German [who has] lived in England eighteen or nineteen years'. Sievers only stayed for about a year. After him came Abraham Wintle, who arrived in the spring of 1807. By the beginning of 1809 the Talbots again needed a butler, and they asked Mary's sister Louisa Petty to try to find one for them in London. She replied that she had heard of a servant who might be suitable, and that her husband had asked about his character:

> He is a respectable-looking middle-aged man, and Alderman Coombe, whom [he] has just left says he understands all that a butler should understand perfectly. He had not the care of the wine, as Alderman Coombe always took care of the cellar himself, but he thinks him quite fit to be trusted with it, or anything else … His wages are sixty guineas. You must now decide whether you will have him or not. His name is Quantril.[30]

The Talbots decided to engage George Quantrille, and he arrived at Penrice three or four weeks later. He was paid £63 a year and he seems to have been a success, for he stayed at Penrice until a few months after Thomas Talbot's death in 1813.

Male cooks were employed whenever possible, though female cooks were found in some kitchens. The latter were always paid less. The best-paid cooks travelled from house to house with their employers, and might well have been engaged in London in the first place. In 1744 Susanna Strangways Horner asked Henry Fox to enquire about a cook whom she thought of employing, and Fox replied with some information on the woman, who had evidently moved around a good deal:

> The cook you recommended to me has left Lord Berkley's and was here on Monday. I gave her £15 a year, and so did Mr Wollaston whom she next lived with. Lord Berkley gave her £20. She is willing to come to you, and when I proposed £15 a year only to her she said she must know what kitchen perquisites there were before she could tell whether she could come at those wages. If you have a mind to take her, be so good as to let me know your terms and when you would have her come, and then I'll enquire why she left her last two places, and if I hear no harm of her I'll hire her for you.[31]

Hannah Timms, who was cook at Redlynch in 1749, was paid £12 a year; in 1761 Tamer Hurd was paid £18, and in 1783 another cook, Margaret Blackburn, received an annual salary of £25.[32] A male cook could earn much more than this: Hugh Sawley, the cook at Redlynch from 1736 until his death in April 1743, was paid £25 a year. His replacement, William Thomas, was paid £35, whilst the annual salary of another cook, Christopher Wiseman, who was discharged in 1745, was £42. French cooks could usually demand comparatively high salaries. John Debrett, who arrived at Melbury early in 1749, is said to have been born in France in 1724, and was probably of Huguenot origin. His annual salary was £35 when he was engaged, but this was increased to £40 later in the same year. After the death of Susanna Strangways Horner he continued to work for the family until 1793, when he was finally discharged. By this time his salary was £50.[33] In 1796 Thomas Talbot wrote that he had been unable to get a cook at fifty guineas a year 'which I was in hopes of'. Instead, he engaged a sixty-year-old Frenchman, 'not an emigré, as he has lived twenty years in England, and is a man of my own age, staid and steady'. This man was to be paid sixty guineas a year.[34] After three months, however, Thomas reported 'My Geneva cook is going, and I expect an English one every day who has just left the Marquis of Stafford's family'.[35] In 1799–1800 the cook at Penrice was called Boucher. He may have been another Frenchman and he, again, was paid sixty guineas a year. In 1806 yet another new cook travelled down to Penrice from London. This one was a woman, and the Talbots appear to have employed female cooks from this time onwards. There is a memorial in the churchyard at Penrice to Elizabeth Ace, who 'lived twenty-eight years as cook in the family at Penrice Castle. Honest, chearfull and kind-hearted, she suffered under a severe disease with Christian patience and humility'. She died in 1832, aged fifty-eight.[36] Predictably, Elizabeth Ace was paid much less than the male cooks had been – in 1809 her annual salary was fifteen guineas.

The housekeeper's status was roughly equivalent to that of the female cook, and in smaller houses the two positions would be filled by the same woman. Female housekeepers were becoming quite common in great houses by the beginning of the eighteenth century, taking over many of the duties that had formerly been the responsibility of the lady of the house or the house steward. Eighteenth-century writers of books on female education thought that a woman should be capable of running her own household, and the genteel women of the minor landed gentry and professional classes of Lancashire and Yorkshire evidently continued to take pride in their ability to manage their own households during this period.[37] There is, however, little indication that the first Countess of Ilchester had either the knowledge or the inclination to do more than give general instructions to her upper servants and check their accounts from time to time. Susan O'Brien remembered that her father had treated his wife very much as a child, and she thought that her mother had, 'no knowledge of business': 'Her economy was of the worst kind, that is to say in trifles present, without looking to consequences future'.[38] Susan, who had comparatively few servants, had to take a much more direct part in the management of her own household at Stinsford. In 1796 she advised her niece Elizabeth, who was about to marry William Davenport Talbot, and was likely to be in similarly straitened financial circumstances:

> It is absolutely necessary for every woman to attend in some degree to her ménage. With a large fortune this attention need not be employed on every minutia, but in a general superintendence of the whole establishment. The scale you will set out upon will not allow of negligence in any article of expence, therefore

> attention is indispensable, notwithstanding any repugnance you may feel *pour les détails domestiques.* A short time every day, and a regular account kept, will make it an easy duty.[39]

For those who could afford professional help, the ideal housekeeper was a middle-aged woman, probably a widow, with experience in looking after her own household. In addition to ordering food and other supplies and keeping accounts, she was expected to supervise the other female servants and ensure that the house was kept clean and well-aired. Unlike some of the other servants who moved from place to place with the family, the housekeeper would be responsible for one house, and she would stay there all year round. The housekeeper was generally given the courtesy title of 'Mrs', even if she had never been married. A list of servants at Melbury in 1715 is headed by Mrs Macie the housekeeper, with a salary of £8 a year. This was at least twice as much as the other female servants, most of whom were paid £2 or £3 a year, but much less than the male steward John Biddell, with £20. Mrs Elizabeth Huxley, the housekeeper at Melbury in 1726, was paid only £7 a year; at Redlynch Mrs Hiett received £10 in 1735–48; but Mrs Hayes, who came to Melbury in 1748, was given an annual salary of £16. There was evidently some dispute over the salary due to Mrs Louche, who took over as housekeeper on 1 April 1751, as the Melbury house steward recorded in his book:

> N.B. Mrs Louche told me 24th of August that it was agreed her wages should be £30 per annum from her first coming. N.B. By Mrs Strangways Horner's orders, per Mrs A[inslie], Mrs Louche is to have per annum £21. Paid off 26th September 1752; went away 25th October 1752.[40]

The housekeepers at Sherborne Castle in the 1760s received an annual salary of £20, and Mrs Shaw, who was at Redlynch from 1748 to 1764, was paid £16 a year.[41] A letter from Lady Ilchester to her husband, written around 1750, gives some information on the housekeeper's duties:

> Mama proposes to be at Redlynch next Wednesday evening, that is, I imagine, about nine o'clock, at which time I should wish supper to be ready and the beds well aired, and some boiled chickens for supper, the nicest that can be got. [Tell her] to get ... some fruit [and] to bespeak some very brown household bread ... If you will let Mrs Shaw know all this, I fancy she will understand what I mean.[42]

Twenty years later the salaries paid to the housekeepers at Melbury and Redlynch had increased significantly. Mrs Ann Hayes, who may previously have been employed at Melbury, was paid £30 a year at Redlynch from 1782 to 1789, and Mrs Elizabeth Field, who was at Melbury for at least ten years from 1781, earned £32 10*s.* a year. She was the wife of John Field, the estate steward, and she had evidently taken over some of the duties that had formerly been performed by her husband's predecessor, George Donisthorpe.[43] The housekeeper's salary continued to creep upwards in later years: in 1814 Mrs Crawford, also at Melbury, was paid £36 15*s.* a year. This was quite a high salary for a woman at the time, but much less than a man would have been paid for a position with similar responsibilities. Housekeepers in smaller houses, where the family was only occasionally in residence, had fewer responsibilities and would earn much less. The women employed at Abbotsbury were paid about £4 a year in the mid eighteenth century for what was essentially a caretaking job.[44]

In the early nineteenth century the housekeepers at Penrice were often left in charge of the household whilst the butler travelled with the family. Housekeepers at Penrice, like butlers, tended not to stay for very long. They were paid less than their contemporaries at Melbury: Mrs Oke, the housekeeper at Penrice in 1800, received £26 5*s.* a year: the same salary as the coachman, but less than was paid to the gardener, male cook and butler. A later housekeeper, Mrs Ellen Sandford, was with the Talbots from about 1809 to 1815. When she left around the time of Mary's marriage to Sir Christopher Cole, Mary asked her sister Louisa to look for another housekeeper for her. Louisa wrote to enquire if Mary wanted 'a manager like Mrs Sandford, as it has occurred to me that Sir Christopher's servant is perhaps your head, and that would make it a much easier thing to find one for you'.[45] Two years later Mary was looking for a housekeeper again. This time Sir Christopher made enquiries in London, and reported back to his wife:

> Mrs Llewelyn is in great dismay, for she thinks if she offers thirty guineas per annum to a housekeeper she shall get her face slapped! Mrs Grenfell is of totally different opinion and thinks thirty or twenty-five guineas full enough.[46]

The housekeeper was usually expected to sleep in the house. The housekeeper's chamber at Melbury in 1727 contained a corded bedstead with calico furniture, three chairs, a chest of drawers and a looking-glass. No other room at Melbury was allocated to the housekeeper at this date, but in later years she would usually have a room in the basement or on the ground floor, close to the steward's room, which would be used as an office and a sitting room. In 1793 the housekeeper's room at Redlynch, on the ground floor of the 'offices' between the stillroom and the steward's room, held a four-posted bedstead with check furniture, a mahogany clawed tea-table, two dressing tables, a 'turnup' bedstead, an oak chest and drawers, a dinner bell, a night-stool, several chairs, two pictures, a wash-hand basin and glass, and a Bath stove.[47]

The housekeeper supervised the lesser female servants, such as housemaids and chambermaids, nursery maids, and the women and girls who worked in the laundry, dairy, brewhouse, kitchen and scullery. The lower servants waited on their superiors: at Melbury in 1715 Mrs Macie had a maid of her own, as did the Redlynch housekeeper in 1736.[48] In 1758 a list of expenses paid for mourning for the servants on the death of Susanna Strangways Horner included a payment for 'the housekeeper's maid at Abbotsbury'.[49] Many of the maids were young girls, and the housekeeper was responsible for training them and seeing that they behaved themselves. Some stayed for only a year or two, whilst others gained promotion to more responsible positions. Their salaries were very low. In 1715 Lydia Northover, the under dairymaid at Melbury, received £2 10*s*. a year; the dairymaid Grace Forse £3, and the brewing maid Grace Browning, £4. In the 1740s most of the maids at Redlynch were paid from £4 to £6 a year, though a few earned only £3. Indoor male servants, such as footmen, generally received a pound or two more than the women. This differential was maintained in later years: in the 1780s the lowest-paid male at Melbury was William Chandler the under groom, at £6 a year, whilst few of the the females were paid more than £5 or £6.[50] At Penrice Castle around 1800 the lowest-paid servant was the scullery maid, at four guineas a year. The salaries of the other maids were from six to eight guineas a year, whilst the inferior male servants received twelve to eighteen guineas a year.

The removal of the outdoor male staff from sleeping accommodation in the house in the eighteenth century was probably not unconnected with the increasing tendency to employ young female staff. Houses did not usually have separate servants' quarters at this period: the lower servants would usually sleep at the top of the house in the garrets, or over the service rooms such as the laundry or bakehouse, and it was not always possible to accommodate the men in a different part of the house from the women. At Melbury in 1727 the dairy maids' chamber (with four beds in it) appears to have been next to the grooms' chamber. At Penrice Castle at the end of the century more effort was made to separate the sexes: the maids slept in the garrets at the top of the house, whilst the menservants' accommodation was over the offices.

In addition to the maids who lived in and were paid by the year, a number of women were employed on a casual basis, especially when the master and mistress were at home with their children and a large party of visiting friends and relations. At Redlynch in April 1745 Ann Cook and Betty Porter were each paid 6*d*. a day for helping in the house and kitchen, and for washing and ironing. A few years later, in January 1749, Betty Porter was paid 8*s*. for helping in the house and kitchen, and another maid was paid 'to milke, the maid being sick'. At Melbury Betty Toogood was paid 5*s.* 5*d.* to wash and iron in September 1760. Grace Bartlett was employed on a casual basis for several years in the 1760s. She usually received 5*d.* a day for helping in the scullery or laundry, 8*d.* a day for washing and scouring, and 9*d.* a day for ironing. In September 1761 she was given 3*s.* for 'getting fowls and mushrooms for Redlynch and [Melbury]', and in 1763 she received 8*d.* a day for picking apples. Grace was sometimes called in if one of the other maids was ill, or had left unexpectedly: she was paid 12*s.* in April 1763 'for three weeks work at 8*d.* per day helping Mary Addams to clean the rooms because the other maid was gone'. Later in the same year the housekeeper paid 5*s.* 'to Grace's foolish boy to buy him stockings and shoes'. Betty Childs is also mentioned several times: she was paid 5*d.* a day to wash and mangle, and 9*d.* a day for helping to brew. Another woman, Mrs Humphreys, came in to help with the sewing: in October 1761 she received 12*s.* for 'three weeks working to mend the office beds, bolsters etc. and several in the house', at 8*d.* a day. Women and girls also did outdoor work from time to time: in 1785 at Redlynch Honor Shears and Grace Martin were paid 15*s.* 6*d.* and 18*s.* respectively 'for work done in the garden'.[51]

Of the servants who worked outside the house, the gardener was usually the best paid. The list of servants at Melbury in 1715 shows that William Franklin, the gardener, earned £12 a year. Only the steward, Mr Biddell, earned more than this. The gardener's room at Melbury in 1727 had a bed in it, together with a Spanish table, a leather chair and 'an old fashion clocke', but, like the other male outdoor servants, later gardeners seem to have lived out of the house. Samuel Guy, who worked at Melbury for over fifty-three years, died in 1775 aged seventy-nine 'leaving behind him (that which he worthily deserved) the character of a faithful servant and a very honest man'.[52] In 1746 Guy was earning £16 a year; this had been increased to £17 a year by 1754. Guy was able to sign his name, but his wife Bridget, a maid at Melbury, signed with a cross when she received her salary of £3 in 1754. John Eaton, who was gardener at Redlynch in the 1740s, received £18 a year. Another Redlynch gardener, John Philips, who was discharged in 1756, was paid £30 a year, though his successor John Woodman, received only £21. In general, the gardeners' salaries increased gradually during the rest of the century. In 1781 Mr Fraser was paid £25 a year at Melbury. His successor, Joseph Eaton, was paid £21 a year when he took over in 1783, but by 1792 this had been raised to £24 3*s.* There was often an under gardener as well, though much of the work in the gardens was done by labourers who were paid by the day.

The coachman, who had his own room over the stables, was usually paid a little less than the gardener. Matthew Wilde, the Melbury coachman in the 1740s and 1750s, was paid £10 a year, as were Thomas Lamberd, the coachman at Redlynch in 1764, and George Stocker, who was coachman at Melbury in 1784. In addition to driving the family's coaches, the coachman supervised the grooms, postillions and stable-boys, and he was ultimately responsible for the management of the horses and the maintenance of the carriages and harness. The coachman had to be literate so that he could submit his accounts to the house steward. These included the money that he had paid out on his master's behalf, together with any charges incurred when he was on the road.

Some carriages would be controlled by a postillion riding the front nearside horse, rather than by the coachman sitting on a box. Postillions, who seem to have earned roughly the same amount as coachmen, also acted as guards and outriders, and they were often sent ahead of the coach, when the family was on the road, to order meals and fodder for the horses and find accommodation. Beneath the coachman and postillion in the stable hierarchy came the grooms and under grooms, who were paid between £5 and £7 a year in the 1760s. The grooms would usually share a room: the grooms' chamber at Melbury held three half-headed bedsteads with bedding. It was possible for a diligent servant to be promoted from one position to another: at Penrice David Jones is listed first as a stable boy in 1799, when he was paid 1*s.* 6*d.* a week (£3 18*s.* a year). He was aged about sixteen at this time. In the following year Davy became a postillion, earning £12 12*s.* a year. He was still a postillion in 1813, but by this time his wages had been increased to £15 15*s.* a year. Two years later he was the coachman.

Every large house had a servants' hall where the employees would spend their limited free time. The contents of the servants' hall at Stinsford in 1737 were typical: there was a long table with three forms, a chair, a chest, two warming pans, 'one of them of little value', and – a more unusual item 'a block to dress wiggs on'.[53] At Redlynch in the second half of the eighteenth century the servants' hall was in the north-eastern corner of the offices, behind the steward's rooms and next to the passage which led to the old mansion. In this room in 1793 were three large dining tables 'with stools, etc. etc.', several other tables, two large iron candlesticks, a toasting-fork, a plate-warmer and seven pictures. Next to the servants' hall was a smaller room, which was called the waiting room in the middle of the century and the footman's room in 1793, when there was a four-posted bedstead in it, together with five chairs, an oak table, a fire grate and six pictures. There was a servants' hall at Stinsford too. This must have been quite a large room, for in 1814 Susan O'Brien recorded that between eighty and ninety people had sat down to dinner there.[54] Most of the servants would eat their meals in the servants' hall. In the list of instructions for the house steward at Redlynch, drawn up in 1764, it was suggested that:

> To have but one table for the servants to dine altogether appears to be good œconomy. But the house steward, the housekeeper, and one or two other of His Lordship's upper servants ... should have liberty at some convenient hour at night or evening, at least three times a week, to set down together in a room by themselves, to talk over and consult His Lordship's domestic affairs, or other matters.[55]

The upper servants included the personal attendants of the master and mistress of the house. They remained somewhat aloof from the rest of the household, and were usually engaged and paid directly by their employers rather than by the house steward or housekeeper. Many a lady's maid stayed with her mistress for several decades, becoming a friend and confidante. The maid's duties included helping her mistress to dress and undress, arranging her hair, and looking after her clothes, in addition to fetching and carrying and, on many occasions, acting as her employer's eyes and ears within the household. She would also nurse her mistress if she was ill. Judith Pearce was left £20 a year for life in the will of the second Earl of Ilchester, which was written in 1780. This generous bequest was made in recognition of Judith's 'unwearied attention and care of Lady Ilchester during her very long illness'. In a codicil of 1781 Judith was given £50 a year more 'for the continuation of her unremitted attention and the great fatigues she has gone through during the very long sickness Lady Ilchester has for such a length of time struggled with'.[56]

Ladies' maids and valets were on call at all hours of the day and night. Before the mid eighteenth century this meant that they had to be within earshot of a bell that could be operated by hand or by means of a simple pulley, but from the 1760s onwards more complex systems were introduced. The use of bell-wires, plumbed in around the house, made it possible to summon servants from more distant parts of the building. It was therefore no longer necessary for servants to sleep in, or close to, the bedrooms of their masters or mistresses. The 1727 inventory of Melbury suggests that the ladies' maids and valets were probably sleeping in the garrets over the main bedchambers, which were presumably accessible via back staircases. Servants sometimes slept in closets, but whilst most of the bedchambers at Melbury had adjoining closets at this time, none had a bed in it. At Milton Clevedon (a much smaller house) two years later, one of the two closets adjoining the Duchess of Hamilton's chamber had a bed in it, and the 'ladies' women's room' was next door to the 'young ladies' chamber'.[57] In Susanna Strangways Horner's London house in Albemarle Street in 1741 her 'woman's room', with a bedstead hung with crimson damask, two walnut chests of drawers, a walnut dressing table, a mahogany dining table and three old walnut chairs, was next to Susanna's own bedchamber and dressing-room.[58] Ten years later, when Lady Ilchester wrote to her husband about the preparations for her arrival at Redlynch with her mother, she asked for 'the little bed to be put within Mama's room' for Susanna's maid Hester.[59] In 1759 Lady Ilchester asked her husband if he would like to sleep in her dressing room in their London house, and told him 'my servant lyes in the closet'.[60]

A lady's maid was paid roughly half as much as housekeeper, but she, too, was often addressed as 'Mrs'. Hester Harding, who was Susanna Strangways Horner's maid, was paid £8 a year from 1746 to 1754. When Susanna died in 1758 she left Hester £10, and an annuity of £10 for life. A memorial in the church at Melbury, erected by Susanna's daughter after Hester's death in 1767 at the age of seventy-nine, records that Mrs Hester Harding had 'lived above thirty years a very faithful servant to Mrs Susanna Strangways Horner'. Another long-serving lady's maid was Elizabeth Andrews, who was with the first Countess of Ilchester from the 1750s. She seems to have helped with the children to begin with, for in January 1759 Lady Ilchester wrote from London to tell her husband that 'Betty Andrews comes with the boys, and Mrs Shaw and I have contrived even when you come none of the servants shall lye out of the house'.[61] Mrs Andrews received £16 a year from 1781 to 1791. Mr Andrews, who may have been her husband, was Lord Ilchester's valet at this time. As usual, his salary was higher: he received £20 a year from 1781 to 1787, and this was then raised to £30 when the butler William Adams was discharged and his responsibilities increased. In recognition of her maid's long service, Lady Ilchester left Elizabeth Andrews an income of £50 a year when she died in 1792.

Caroline Fox was heavily dependent on her maid Milward, who had been with her since before her marriage. Milward wrote letters for Caroline and read to her, she managed the household when her mistress was in Bath, and she was often left with the children when their mother was away. Caroline was evidently somewhat shocked when, early in 1748, she discovered that Milward (aged forty) had secretly married Mr Fannen the house steward. In a letter to her employer, the new Mrs Fannen told him that the only reason for the secrecy 'was to escape jokes and questions'. 'For', she continued, 'as My Lady and you both agreed in approving of Mr Fannen as a servant, I thought you would not be angry at my choice of a friend.'[62] The newly-married couple decided that they would like to stay on in the Fox household. Their mistress gave her opinion of their behaviour in a letter to her husband:

> Don't you think it is rather silly in Milward to marry? I do. I did not think she would have been guilty of anything so silly at her age. Fannen is younger, a little, than her. I wonder to [*sic*] at him, don't you? I reckon you aprove of their staying in the family.[63]

Henry, who was highly amused by the whole affair, replied:

> You ask me my thoughts on their marriage. In the first place, I never wonder at a marriage. In the next, I am always inclined to esteem people that please themselves. So, upon the whole, you see I approve it.[64]

He tried to persuade his wife to ask if the marriage had been consummated, but she replied: 'I can't possibly find out what you would know. I ... don't at all care to attempt it, because she [Mrs Fannen] would be mad'.[65] In the event little changed. Mr Fannen seems to have spent much of his time in London or at Holland House, whilst Mrs Fannen continued to travel with her mistress. The Fannens moved into their own house in 1766, but Mr Fannen continued to act as steward and Caroline still sought Mrs Fannen's help and advice, writing:

> I frequently walk to see her. Sometimes one of my sons and I dine with her snug. She always comes if I want her, which I do when I want to alter, change or settle anything in the house with regard to servants, furniture etc.[66]

Other maids who were with their mistresses for many years were Susan O'Brien's servant Hannah Borgi, and Edith Shears, who was employed first at Redlynch and Melbury, and then moved to Penrice with Mary Strangways when she married Thomas Talbot in 1794. Edith seems to have started work as a housemaid in 1784, when she was paid £6 a year. By 1785 this had been increased to £7, and in 1787 she received £8 2*s*.[67] Around this time she became a nursery-maid, for she was left an annuity of forty pounds in a codicil added to the will of the second Earl of Ilchester in 1792 'for the care she has taken of Charlotte and Louisa'.[68] At Penrice Edith was known as 'Mrs Shears'. She was Mary Talbot's personal maid and was paid twelve guineas a year. Although her annuity probably became payable in 1808 when the third Earl of Ilchester came of age, Edith was still at Penrice in 1813.

At Redlynch and Melbury, as in many other country houses, there were also several women whose position within the household hierarchy is hard to define. These included friends and distant relatives who acted as companions, amanuenses and chaperones. From time to time they might also do some of the work of a lady's maid, a housekeeper or a governess. Such a woman was Mary (Molly) Fenn, who lived with the first Earl and Countess of Ilchester for almost forty years. Molly Fenn was a great-granddaughter of one of Sir Stephen Fox's brothers, and she was therefore her employer's cousin. She was probably born in the early 1720s, and she was orphaned in 1731 when her parents both died within a few weeks of each other. Molly then appears to have been looked after by her father's spinster sister Ann Fenn. A receipt for six months' wages of £4 10s., paid by 'Mrs Fox' to 'M. Fenn' early in 1737, suggests that Molly may have gone to live with Elizabeth (Strangways Horner) shortly after the latter's marriage to Stephen Fox.[69] The two girls were roughly the same age. In these early years Molly seems to have travelled with her employer, for there is an account for her washing at Wandsworth and Goodwood, together with travelling expenses, dating from 1742.[70] She is usually described as 'Lady Ilchester's woman', and her duties were those of a companion and lady's maid. She also helped to teach Elizabeth's eldest daughter to read.[71] That she was expected to work for her living is indicated in a letter to her sister-in-law, which Molly left with her will:

> Though I have a grateful heart, 'tis not in my power to make the least return … to my good Lord and Lady, but to pray for them, which I do daily. My ill-health long prevented me doing my business as I ought.[72]

Personal maids were usually given their mistresses' cast-off clothes, and Molly refers in her will to 'clothes unmade up that was My Lady's'. During the latter part of her life, when she was at Redlynch for much of the time, Molly also performed some of the duties of a housekeeper. In her will she left a guinea each for a ring to 'all my friends at the steward's table'. This underlines her position as a servant. Had she been seen as a full member of the family, Molly would have eaten alone when the rest of the family was away, not with other employees – even if they were the upper servants. Nevertheless, Lord and Lady Ilchester were both very fond of Molly, and were both 'grieved and alarmed' by her death in 1774. Elizabeth was not the most demonstrative of women, but she told her son: 'I suffer greatly for [Molly's] loss. She was my sincere friend and almost constant companion for many, many years.' In another letter Elizabeth told her daughter-in-law that Molly had 'lived with me from our youth up, and was a most worthy person'.[73]

Equally difficult to categorise is Joanna Cheeke. Born in 1722, Joanna was the daughter of one of the estate stewards at Redlynch, and references to her in the letters of Lord Ilchester's brother and sister and some of his oldest friends suggest that she had visited Redlynch regularly when she was still very young. She was just a year older than the first Countess of Ilchester, and was to remain a friend of the family for over seventy years, dying in 1819 aged ninety-seven. Entries in Lady Susan O'Brien's journal give some indication of the family's affection for their old friend:

> 25 September 1803
>
> Mrs Melliar [Joanna Cheeke] came from Abbotsbury. Very glad indeed to see her so well and so chearfull at her great age. A happy temper and pleasing manners have made her a general favorite wherever she was, and she still continues to be so, though eighty years old.
>
> 1 April 1817
>
> I am often reminded by Lord Ilchester [the third Earl] and Mrs Campbell of my father and Miss Cheeke. Everybody wanting her company, giving a sort of playfull life. Lord Ilchester joking and tricks, as was formerly with the Chick-sey [Miss Cheeke's nickname]. Everybody glad when she came, sorry when she went. Never making any mischief in the family, though sometimes perhaps envyed.[74]

The first reference to Miss Cheeke comes in December 1747, when she was in London with Lady Ilchester and two of the latter's children. Miss Cheeke helped to amuse the children, and accompanied Lady Ilchester on visits to the theatre and opera. The two women went to see *The Tempest*, and Lady Ilchester wrote afterwards 'I don't think it is a pretty play. At the begining of it Miss Cheeke was in a great fright and wanted to go home again. We were misserable creatures, had no bean to attend us.'[75] Early in January there was a masquerade, for which Miss Cheeke made 'pretty conceits' for herself and Lady Ilchester.[76]

Lady Ilchester went to London again in the autumn of 1748. Miss Cheeke did not go with her this time, but it was suggested that she might go in January, as Lady Ilchester was due to give birth and would be 'much alone during her lying in'. From a letter written by Lord Ilchester to his brother, it is clear that there had been some tensions within the household during the summer:

> I make no question [Lady Ilchester] would have asked [Miss Cheeke] to be with her, if Mrs Horner had not taken all the pains imaginable this whole summer to set her against her.'Tis incredible how she is prejudiced against [Miss Cheeke] and with what malice she pursues her. I don't find there is the least crime laid to her charge, but only general discourse against companions, and how improper it is for Lady Ilchester to keep company with a person of so low a rank, upon which subject a vast deal of egregious nonsense has been talked – that Miss Cheeke was put upon too high a footing last year, that some people were very blamable to make a great fuss with her ... Lady Ilchester has told me since we

> came here [to Redlynch], one thing has been much insisted on, that if she should go to London now, she would think she had a right always to go ... It is exceeding cruel in Mrs Horner to pursue anybody so inveterately that has in no shape deserved it, and vastly impertinent in her to interfere in my family.[77]

It seems clear from this and another letter, written ten days later, that Susanna Strangways Horner was jealous of Miss Cheeke's friendship with her daughter. When Miss Cheeke's name was mentioned, Susanna had exclaimed 'Miss Cheeke! I hear of nothing but Miss Cheeke's going to every public place last winter.' The line between a companion who was a servant and one who was a friend was a very fine one, and it is difficult to say exactly where Joanna Cheeke belonged. Lord Ilchester, who liked Miss Cheeke and enjoyed her company, was hopeful that his wife would soon miss her former companion:

> Lady Ilchester, as you know, is capricious, and nobody that I know ever continued so long in favour as Miss Cheeke, nor will she allow her to be out of favour, though her behaviour of late has been quite different, and in no degree so frank as formerly ... I am much mortified at Miss Cheeke's not going to London ... because I am very partial to her and delight in her company, which considering the life I lead in London is a vast resource to me.

He had, however, been unwilling to insist that Miss Cheeke should go to London:

> Not only because it might be liable to misinterpretation, but likewise because ... if Lady Ilchester had consented with great reluctance and unwillingness, she could easily have contrived that Miss Cheeke will lead a most miserable life.[78]

Whether Miss Cheeke went to London at all during the winter of 1748 to 1749 is unknown. Her fall from favour was, however, only temporary. In August 1749 Henry Fox asked his brother if Miss Cheeke could be sent to Bath, as a companion to his wife, who had threatened to 'hang herself ... unless Miss Cheeke will meet her there'.[79] Lord Ilchester, replied, however, that his wife was reluctant to let Miss Cheeke go:

> You say Lady Caroline will hang herself if [Miss Cheeke] does not go to Bath immediately. Lady Ilchester says she will hang herself if she goes from hence ... [but] I have contrived [she] should go to Bath the latter end of next week.

Miss Cheeke was reported to be 'in a most prodigious fidget' about this unexpected summons, complaining that 'her gown is not made, her things are unwashed'.[80] Nevertheless, she duly went to Bath, and Caroline wrote to tell her husband:

> Miss Cheke and I shall do very well together, only she is too complaisant and

won't do her own way enough. It would make it pleasanter to me if she would, but I believe she is used to study other people's way[s].[81]

Another letter, written by Caroline a few days later, is interesting for the light that it casts on Lady Ilchester's treatment of Miss Cheeke:

At first Miss Cheke thought it necessary to tag everywhere after me and to fast 'till I breakfasted, but I have insisted upon her eating some breakfast before me in a morning, for 'tis impossible anybody can chuse to fast two hours after they are up. Now I know she likes lying abed, but I can't persuade her not to get up for to go with me in a morning ... I believe you'l agree with me, 'twould be pleasanter to have anybody take their way in such things, but I believe she does not dare at Redlynch.[82]

Joanna Cheeke continued to spend a good deal of time with both Lady Ilchester and Caroline Fox in subsequent years. She played cards for hours on end with Lady Ilchester, and wrote letters for her. She also acted as her lady's maid from time to time – in January 1755 Lady Ilchester complained to her husband that that 'Miss Cheeke has dressed me French, which makes my dubble chin appear, and that I don't like'.[83] Joanna stayed in Bath with Caroline Fox in 1756 and 1758, and again in 1761. Many years later, after Caroline's death, Sarah Lennox asked Susan O'Brien to give her love to Joanna for 'there is none of our family who do not think themselves bound by the strongest ties of [obligation to her] for her goodness to my sister'.[84] Joanna's relationship with both Fox brothers was certainly quite informal, though there is no evidence that she was the daughter or mistress of either, as has been claimed.[85] In 1756, when she was thirty-four, Henry teased Joanna about becoming an old maid. There were fears at this time that the French might invade England, and Henry told his wife:

Pray tell Miss Cheke that the French are the gallantest people in the world, and understand that matter so well that they will make ravishing quite easy to her ... She should try a little how it is before they come, and whether they come or not, it will have been worth her while, I can assure her.[86]

A week later Henry said that he had heard that 'Miss Cheke has got some chastity drops, and is not afraid of the French now'.[87]

Joanna Cheeke did not remain an old maid for the rest of her life. In 1763, at the age of forty-one, she married a widower, William Melliar, an attorney who lived in Castle Cary, about five miles from Redlynch. Parson Woodforde, an old friend of William Melliar, did not take to Joanna, finding her pretentious and insincere. It is clear that she made the most of her connnection with the family at Redlynch, and thought herself above those of her neighbours who came from a similar background to her own. In 1768, when Lord and Lady Ilchester's eldest son came of age, she gave a 'public breakfast' in the vicarage garden at Castle Cary 'where there was coffee, tea, chocolate and all kinds of cakes etc. proper for the above; a very good band of musick, bells ringing; eighty loaves given to the poor of Cary'.[88] In later years Joanna continued to spend a good deal of time at Redlynch, especially after her husband's death in 1772. Her ties to the Fox Strangways family were reinforced in 1775 when her stepdaughter Priscilla Melliar married Lord Ilchester's nephew Charles Digby. Although she did not receive a salary, Joanna was given money by Lord Ilchester and his family from time to time. In a letter written in the 1750s Lord Ilchester asked his cousin Lord Digby to 'speak kindly' to Miss Cheeke if he happened to meet her at Melbury or elsewhere. 'And', he continued, 'if you could contrive to make her some trifling present, I should think myself still more obliged.'[89] When he died in 1776, Lord Ilchester left Joanna a hundred guineas in his will.

Both Molly Fenn and Joanna Cheeke helped to look after Lord and Lady Ilchester's children, performing some of the duties of companions, governesses and, in later years, chaperones. The professional nanny was a Victorian invention: in earlier times children in wealthy households were looked after on a day-to-day basis by nurses and nursery maids, who were paid only a little more than the other maids. In a list of projected expenses for her five-year-old son Henry, Elizabeth Talbot claimed in 1805 that she needed £16 16*s.* a year to pay the wages of a nursery maid, and £14 for a cook-maid, in addition to £27 6*s.* for the board wages of each of these servants for a year.[90] By this time, however, many parents were becoming uneasy about allowing their children to spend too much time in the company of their servants. The influential writers on education Richard and Maria Edgeworth taught that 'familiarity between servants and children cannot permanently increase the happiness of either party', and that 'if children pass one hour in a day with servants, it will be in vain to attempt their education'. Children, who should learn by example, would be damaged by 'inferior society'.[91] Since few wives of landowners had the time – or inclination – to spend every hour of the day with their children, they turned increasingly to professional governesses. Some households employed two such women: in 1806 Mary Talbot wrote that she would like to have two governesses at Penrice, so that the sub-governess could supervise the children when the superior governess was otherwise occupied 'to prevent their ever being with servants'.[92]

Within the household, the governess occupied a position that was uneasily poised between the family and the servants, and it was inevitable that she should suffer from the anomalies of her situation. A governess had to be a lady and, whilst socially inferior to her employers, she would invariably consider herself to be superior to the main body of servants. The maids at Redlynch and Melbury waited on Agnes Porter, the governess to the daughters of the second Earl of Ilchester. Agnes usually ate her meals with her pupils, or alone in her room. She never ate in the servants' hall, and the only other female employee with whom she socialised was the housekeeper. In London in 1791 Agnes occasionally drank tea with Lady Harriot Acland's housekeeper Mrs Churchyard, whom she described as 'a very sensible, worthy person'.[93]

Even if a governess was employed, the Edgeworths' advice about keeping children away from servants was often impracticable. Kit Talbot wrote in his memoirs that he had feared his mother, and had looked upon his nurse 'as my only real friend in the world'.[94] The servants at Penrice in 1800 included Anna Green, nursemaid, who was paid ten guineas a year, and Jennet Flew, under nursemaid, who was paid five guineas. Anna may previously have worked at Redlynch, for her mother lived in Wincanton, only three or four miles away.[95] By 1802 she had apparently been replaced by Susan Tatham (Sukey), who was then about twenty years old. In 1809 Sukey was earning fourteen guineas a year. She continued to work for the Talbots after her marriage to the postillion (later coachman) David Jones in 1811. In 1815 Sukey accompanied three of the girls when her husband drove them from Bath to London. According to Charlotte Talbot's account of the journey, they arrived at their rented house in London before the other servants, 'so Sukey was the footman, and we had some coffee'.[96] After Sukey's death in 1832 the Talbots erected a gravestone in Penrice churchyard 'in grateful and affectionate recollection of her fond and unremitting affection to the children commited to her care'. The inscription also records that Sukey had been the 'faithful ... and much respected nurse of the family of Penrice Castle' for nearly thirty years'.[97] When Jennet (or Jenny) Flew, who had been under nursemaid in 1800, married Thomas Ace the gardener at Penrice, Mary Theresa Talbot wrote to tell her brother about the presents that they were giving to the bride-to-be:

> Your fender is green, and looks very nice. Jane gave her [Jenny] a thing to hang upon your fender to keep her toast hot upon; Mama has given her a warming-pan, and I am going to get her some dinner china, for she has not got *a dish or a plate* to eat her dinner on ... Jenny has got a very pretty carpet and rug, she has got plenty of tea-things and two tea-trays and a tea kettle, candlesticks and a bed which I have not seen.[98]

Jenny was literate, though her spelling was somewhat erratic. She wrote to the Talbot children when they were away from Penrice, telling them in 1814 that 'Penrice is very dull withought your good Mama and all her darlings', and in the following year 'It as bin a very dull winter here withought you. I long to see all your merry faces'.[99] The Talbots were all very fond of her.

The relationship between servants and their employers was one of mutual dependence, and sometimes of genuine affection, and wealthy people who ignored the needs of their servants were censured. When John Damer, the heavily indebted eldest son of Lord Milton, committed suicide in 1776, his wife Anne (who later became a well-known sculptress) had to leave her house almost immediately. As Sarah Lennox wrote:

> Even the poor servants are owed fourteen months wages, which I think is one of the most melancholy reflections, for, you see, they are in absolute want of bread if they are unlucky in not getting a place immediately. She [Anne Damer] paid ... those servants who were in absolute want; the rest were too generous to take any, and absolutely refused to take more than would serve them for immediate use. The are all very fond of her, and cried bitterly at her leaving the house in such a way.[100]

Susan O'Brien noted that her mother had been 'much in the hands of servants', and had been fortunate 'to have those that were honest and attached to her and to her family'.[101] In 1797, when she was temporarily without a maid, Susan told one of her nieces who had asked how she was getting on, 'I do very badly, and am perfectly uncomfortable'.[102] When her housekeeper Hannah Borgi died in 1797, Susan mourned the loss of a woman who had been with her for almost forty years, whom she described as 'a true and faithfull servant of the old sort, not now to be met with'.[103] Almost twenty years later, after the death of St John Jourdan, 'a good and faithfull old servant', Susan reflected that she had, on the whole, been fortunate in the people who had worked for her:

> A good character and good treatment have made me pass on with few strangers, and those now remaining are what may be depended on for honesty and doing truly their duty.[104]

Servants were generally given mourning clothes and at least a quarter of a year's wages when their employer died. In 1726 Thomas Strangways left two years' wages to most of his servants, and three years' wages to three of them. Susanna Strangways Horner left sums varying from £5 to £50 to a long list of servants in 1758. Some were also to receive a year's wages, and others were given annuities. Mourning clothes were also given to twelve male servants and fifteen female, at a cost of £42 3*s.* 1*d.* for the men and £50 8*s.* 3*d.* for the women.[105] The second Earl of Ilchester, who died in

1802, left sums of money and annuities to some of his servants. Each of the others was to receive a year's wages and a suit of clothes.

In addition to their salaries, which were usually paid annually in arrears, indoor servants would be given board and lodging in their employer's house, as would some outdoor servants. François de La Rochefoucauld thought that English servants lived well: 'feeding them is a tremendous business: they never leave the table, and there are always cold joints of meat, and tea, and punch, from morning till night'.[106] When the family was away from home, those servants who stayed behind were usually given board wages, out of which they were expected to pay for their own food. Employers had visions of their servants living a life of luxury whilst they had the house to themselves; board wages were thought to be more economical, and to reduce the opportunities for pilfering. Some, however, argued that board wages gave servants too much independence, and presented them with 'a constant excuse to loiter at public houses'.[107] Upper servants invariably received higher board wages than their inferiors; and men usually received more than women, presumably on the basis that women ate less. At Melbury in the 1740s Mrs Phillips the housekeeper had 5*s.* a week; most of the men (including the gardener and coachman) had 4*s.* a week; whilst the maid-servants had 3*s.*[108] There was only a small increase during the next thirty years, for in the 1770s the upper male servants (including the cook and steward) at both Melbury and Redlynch were given board wages of 7*s.* a week each; the lower male servants were given 5*s.*; and the women 4*s.*[109] By 1814, however, the board wages paid at Melbury had approximately doubled, with the housekeeper receiving 14*s.* a week, whilst most of the menservants had 10*s.*, and the maids 8*s.* These sums appear to have been close to the average for servants in country houses, though their contemporaries in London would probably have received more, as the cost of living in the city was higher.[110] In the mid eighteenth century the male servants from Melbury and Redlynch (such as coachmen and postillions), travelling to and from London or from one house to another, would usually receive 1*s.* 6*d.* a day (10*s.* 6*d.* a week) for their board.[111]

Conscientious employers also thought it their duty to look after any servants who fell ill. The owners of Melbury and Redlynch seem to have been quite generous in this respect. In 1734 Lord Ilchester 'was pleased to allow Mrs Hiatt hir expenses at the Bath'. He was clearly fond of Mrs Hiett,[112] his former nursemaid, who was a housekeeper at Redlynch for many years. She was in Bath for seven weeks in 1734, at a cost of £9 10*s.* 2*d.* Mrs Hiett also spent six weeks in Bath in the following year. This visit cost Lord Ilchester £11 4*s.* 7*d.*[113] In 1745 Mrs Hiett visited Bath again: Lord Ilchester paid a total of £14 3*s.* for her to spend six weeks and four days there. This was made up of miscellaneous expenses of 15*s.* a week; £3 5*s.* for lodgings; 11*s.* for washing; 5*s.* 'to the maids'; 10*s.* 'to the pumps'; stagecoach to London £1 4*s.*; travelling expenses on the road 15*s.*; chariot and four horses from Redlynch to Bath £2 5*s.*; and 15*s.* expenses for a night at the Old Down Inn on the way.[114] More than half a century later, in 1817, Susan O'Brien paid for her maid Carter to spend five months in Bath 'for medical advice and assistance'. Susan noted in her journal that this was 'a great inconvenience, but not to be compared to the loss of a valuable life'.[115] Considerable sums of money were also paid out for medical treatment for the servants at both Melbury and Redlynch. At Melbury, Mr Meech, a local apothecary, was paid £72 7*s.* 6*d.* 'by a bill for medicines for Mrs Strangways Horner's servants, paupers etc.' from 6 July 1749 to 8 December 1750.[116] At Redlynch the local apothecary, Thomas Clarke, was paid £27 1*s.* 3*d.* for treating the servants in 1750. In 1751 Clarke's bill included £16 15*s.* 'for My Lord and family'; £10 12*s.* 11*d.* for the servants; and £14 0*s.* 7*d.* for Mrs Hiett, and in 1752 he was paid £19 19*s.* 8*d.* for the family, and £23 16*s.* 4*d.* for the servants. A year later 'B. Sanger and J. Fye's nursing and lodging in the small pox' cost £2 3*s.* 6*d.* They were both servants, and were no doubt moved out of the house to prevent them from infecting the other occupants. In 1764 'the expences of the landry maid [at Sherborne Castle] having the small pox' came to £5 5*s.*[117]

Servants also received other payments and benefits over and above their annual salaries. Male servants were usually given their work clothes and liveries. Female servants, who wore no uniform or livery, generally had to provide their own working clothes. Even Dr Johnson was unable to explain why this should be so, since women servants worked much harder than the men.[118] The Redlynch accounts do, however, include a payment of 10*s.* 2*d.* in 1748 for 'a milking cloke for the dairey maid'. At Melbury 7*s.* 6*d.* was paid for 'a cloake for the dairy maid's use' in 1763.[119] Mary Talbot occasionally gave gowns to her former governess, Agnes Porter, and to the maids at Penrice. There was also plenty of scope for extracting money or gifts in return for favours: the servant might put in a good word for a boy or girl who wanted a place in the household, or suggest that a particular tradesman should be patronised. In 1742 the steward George Donisthorpe claimed that he always refused to countenance 'the sinister hope of gratuities on payment of bills' at Melbury, 'esteeming the same dishonest as well as dishonourable'.[120] By no means all stewards and housekeepers were so fastidious. Perquisites were also attached to many posts: ladies' maids were given their mistresses' cast-off clothes, and cooks were allowed to sell 'kitchen stuff' such as dripping, bones, and lumps of fat. Molly Fenn was given clothes by Lady Ilchester, and the cook whom Henry Fox interviewed for Susanna Strangways Horner in 1744 enquired about kitchen perquisites.[121]

Nursemaids were given 'christening money': when Susan, the youngest child of the second Earl and Countess of Ilchester, was baptised in January 1792 her nurse Edith Rawlins received four guineas.[122] At Penrice in 1801 Anna Green and Jennet Flew were given ten and four guineas respectively when Charlotte Talbot was christened.[123] Beer was usually provided, and many female servants also expected to be given tea or an allowance in lieu. The Redlynch household accounts include a payment of 2*s.* 2*d.* for 'tea for the nurses' in March 1751, and 1*s.* 2*d.* was paid at Melbury in 1762 for 'a quarter of a pound of common tea for Mrs Humfris'. In 1768 the sum of 6*s.* was paid 'to common tea, two pounds for Mrs Humphris etc. etc.' Mrs Humphreys was a casual female servant, who was paid 8*d.* a day for sewing. In 1781 Mary Rutter, a cook at Redlynch, was given £3 19*s.* 'for tea and traveling expences'. After the death of Thomas Talbot, Susan Jones was paid £4 18*s.* 'for two years four months allowance for tea during her service as nursery maid at Penrice Castle'.[124]

Servants would also expect to receive tips, known as vails, from visitors, and payments of this kind to other people's servants often appear in the household accounts. In August 1728 the vails paid by (or on behalf of) the Duchess of Hamilton included:

To the groom at My Lord Digby's [Sherborne Castle] – 1*s.*
To the butler at My Lord Paulet's [Hinton St George, Somerset] – 5*s.*
To the groom there – 2*s.* 6*d.*
To the groom at My Lord Digby's – 1*s.*
To the groom at My Lady Inchingbrook's – 1*s.*[125]
To the groom at Esquire Hervie's[126] – 2*s.* 6*d.*
Paid the groom at Madam Stroud's [Parnham] – 2*s.* 6*d.*
Given to the groom at Mr Seymer's [Hanford House] when My Lady dined there – 2*s.* 6*d.*
Given to the groom at My Lord Digby's when My Lady supped there – 2*s.* 6*d.*
To the keeper there at the park gate – 2*s.* 6*d.*

At the same time, several tips were paid to servants who called at Melbury with gifts for the Duchess:

Paid to Colonel Chidley's servant that brought a present of a brace of carps – 2*s.* 6*d.*
Paid to Mr Gifford's servant that brought a present of two brace quails – 2*s.* 6*d.*
Paid to Mr Haiet [Hiett]'s servant that brought a present of a leash of pheasants – 2*s.* 6*d.*
To Madam Stroud's servant that brought a present of four brace quails – 5*s.*
To My Lady Phillips [Phelips]'s servants that brought a present of walnuts – 2*s.* 6*d.*[127]

Female servants, who had less contact with visitors, had fewer opportunities for earning money from tips than their male contemporaries. Mary Talbot's pocket-books do, however, record payments, usually ranging from 2*s.* 6*d.* to 10*s.* to the maids in the houses where she stayed in the early nineteenth century.

At Melbury and Redlynch in the eighteenth century the hiring and firing of servants seems to have been left largely to the house steward or, in the case of the lower female servants, the housekeeper. At Penrice, however, it is clear that both Thomas and Mary Talbot were directly involved. Before his marriage Thomas had lived in what he himself described as 'a very irregular kind of manner', and he had made do with a handful of servants. He therefore wrote from London in January 1794, two weeks before the wedding, to ask his friend Michael Hicks Beach for advice:

> I have had great difficulties in hiring servants and am as yet unprovided with an under-butler. I don't at first mean to trouble myself with more than three servants in livery, viz. William, an under butler and a handy boy. The coachman and old Mr Porter to wait at table besides, occasionally, and also the postillion (who is a decent looking fellow) if wanted ... My *better half* is not desirous of a great family of servants ... Do also, my dear friend, tell me what wages you give such servants as are in livery and what cloaths you give them ... I should not be thus particular did I think you would have any scruple to direct me for the better, and say what is really proper and decent to give, which if your having had so regular and good establishment for so many years did not through experience enable you to do, I would not ask it.[128]

Employers believed that servants were corrupted by city life, and most preferred to recruit maids and the lower male servants in the country. Such servants often came from the families of tenants of the estate, or from an area with which the family already had contacts. Some of the servants at Penrice came from Somerset or Dorset. These included the nurse Anna Green and Mary Talbot's maid Edith Shears. Mary also took a housemaid to Penrice with her when she married. Harriot Strangways thought that the maid, who arrived at Melbury just before the wedding, was 'a nice little girl [who], though very young, can be quite a maid of all works'.[129] Upper servants were more of a problem, and they often had to be engaged in London. It was particularly difficult to find good servants to work at Penrice, since there were so few other large houses in the Swansea area. Thomas and Mary Talbot tried to employ servants who had at least been interviewed, if not personally recommended, by friends or relations, but this was not always possible. In 1796 Thomas complained to Michael Hicks Beach:

> I have been a good deal plagued lately about servants and, being obliged to take such as are sent to me from tradesmen in Town without my first seeing them, have

frequently been disappointed. It now so happens that I have wrote to Reddish[130] about a footman in the room of one I have now in my old servant William's place, who is of all the stupid footmen or other servant I ever saw the most stupid. Do me the favour of permitting your servant to see a man that Reddish has wrote to me about, who has lived with Lady Gormanston, and favour me with your opinion if he is such as will suit me so as to be serviceable when Lady Mary is in Town to wait on her with the carriage etc. etc. I expect to hear from Reddish every day. I am not in a great hurry for a servant, and would not wish to hire another dull blockhead, as I am by no means fond of changing my servants.[131]

Mary Talbot usually took responsibility for engaging the female servants. In 1803 she asked Mrs Hicks Beach for help:

I am going to plague you with a commission, which is to enquire for a good laundry maid for me. The wages must depend on what she asks, as I cannot expect to meet with a good one without paying for it, and it is one of the essentials without which we cannot go on.[132]

The turnover of servants in great households was often high. Many remained in one place for less than a year, and few stayed for more than five years.[133] This was particularly true of the younger maidservants.[134] Some were sacked because they were pregnant; others for insolence or for neglecting their duties. Some just left or ran away. For the majority of lower female servants in particular, domestic service was not a long-term career, but simply a way of supporting themselves and accumulating savings so that they could marry and set up a home of their own. The household accounts do not usually state how long each servant stayed, but it is possible to work out that eight of the female servants earning from £3 to £6 a year at Melbury during the period 1747 to 1753 were there for an average of between fourteen and fifteen months. Nor did the upper servants necessarily stay for much longer. Inevitably, some had to be sacked: Mrs Trengrouse, who was employed at Redlynch as a governess and chaperone for Lord and Lady Ilchester's daughters, was dismissed in 1764 when Susan eloped with William O'Brien. Conscience-striken, Susan tried to persuade Lord Holland to help the woman, writing to ask her uncle: 'As I have been unfortunately the cause of her losing an agreeable maintenance, I think it incumbant on me to use the little interest I may still have with you to procure her some little place to help keep her.'[135] Lord Holland replied that he 'could, and would with pleasure, go to see [Mrs Trengrouse] hanged at Tyburn'.[136] Other servants were dismissed for drunkenness, insolence or dishonesty – or all three. In 1800 Thomas Mansel Talbot had to sack his butler Jourdan:

I was obliged to discharge Jourdan for drunkeness when at home and when he went to Swansea to market, besides being a very great liar and leaving things

> unpaid at Swansea, which is certainly much to my discredit ... Jourdan's uncivil ways had nearly been the cause of our housekeeper's going away.[137]

Keeping servants was particularly difficult at Penrice, where butlers, cooks and housekeepers came and went in rapid succession. Some found that the house was simply too remote, especially as the Talbots paid only infrequent visits to London. As Thomas Talbot wrote in 1796, 'always in the country won't do with many of them'.[138] Similarly, in 1817, when Mary Cole was looking for a housekeeper, her husband told her that it might be difficult to find one 'who will agree to live constantly in the country'.[139] It was probably due to the difficulty of finding reliable servants that Thomas Talbot took personal responsibility for ordering many household goods and paying the bills for them.

The servants worked hard and had little time to themselves. Contemporary commentators tried to encourage them to use their limited leisure for self-improvement, though their advice was often ignored. In her book, *A Present for a Servant Maid*, which was first published in 1743, Eliza Haywood gave the following advice:

> In all well-governed families a servant-maid has the liberty every Sunday, or every other Sunday at least, in the afternoon, of going to church, which if she neglects, it discovers she has little sense of true religion, and may well be suspected of failing in her duty to an earthly master or mistress, when she fails in that to her Maker. And yet, how many of you had rather walk in the fields, go to drink tea with an acquaintance, or even lie down to sleep?[140]

The monotony of the life of the Penrice servants was occasionally relieved by a dance. On the first day of February 1798, the fourth wedding anniversary of Thomas and Mary Talbot, 'The servants had a dance. The gentlemen drank and the ladies mumped [sulked].'[141] In a few houses servants were also given opportunities to improve themselves. At Redlynch there was a servants' library, to which Agnes Porter donated a copy of an 'excellent book', *The Whole Duty of Man ... With Private Devotions*, in 1790.[142] Whether the servants actually read this, or other improving works, is of course another matter. Some, but by no means all, servants were literate. The fact that someone could sign their name does not, of course, necessarily indicate that they could read and write, but the information given in the household accounts from Melbury and Redlynch does indicate a comparatively high level of literacy. Approximately 60 per cent of men and 40 per cent of women in the general population may have been literate in the mid eighteenth century.[143] Of twenty-three servants at Melbury whose wages were paid at Michaelmas 1754, ten males (90 per cent) signed their names in the receipt book, and only one did not. There were twelve female servants, and nine of them (75 per cent) signed.[144] Sixty years later, in 1814, twenty-nine servants are listed, fifteen male and fourteen female. This time six signed with a cross, four of them female. These figures, with 86 per cent of the men and 71 per cent of the women able to sign, suggest that literacy did not increase greatly in the late eighteenth century. It may even have declined. Whether the servants could read and write before they were taken on, or were taught by their fellow employees, is unknown, but some of the Melbury servants were probably former pupils of the charity school in Melbury Osmond funded by the owners of the estate.[145]

8

Household Management

The management of a large household in the eighteenth and nineteenth centuries was a complicated business, with twenty or thirty servants to supervise and an enormous range of supplies to be obtained from many different sources. The owners of great country houses were heavily dependent on their upper servants to carry out most of this supervisory work, especially during the weeks – or months – when they were away from home.

The stewards and housekeepers at Melbury and Redlynch were required to keep detailed accounts, showing exactly how they spent their employers' money. The household accounts list items as diverse as sealing-wax and writing paper, canary seed and mousetraps, but most of the purchases were connected with the provision of food and drink. There would often be forty or fifty people to be fed every day, including the family and household staff, together with any guests and visiting servants. In one typical week in June 1748, Susanna Strangways Horner's household at Melbury consumed 23 pounds of beef, 13 pounds of mutton, 6 pounds of veal, 10 pounds of lamb, half a flitch of bacon, 5 young turkeys, 3 young geese, 10 ducks, 46 fowl and chickens, one hare, 12 rabbits, 50 pounds 8 ounces of butter, 2 raw milk cheeses, 8 skimmed milk cheeses, and 170 eggs. They drank three-quarters of a hogshead (40½ gallons) of strong beer, half a hogshead (27 gallons) of ale, and two hogsheads (108 gallons) of small beer.[1] A great deal of advance planning was required, for many supplies were not available locally. They had to be ordered in bulk from large towns such as London or Bristol and sent into the country by carrier's cart.[2]

The inhabitants of Melbury, Redlynch and Penrice Castle certainly ate well, and much of their food was home-produced, for they had extensive vegetable gardens and orchards. The Redlynch accounts show that Lord and Lady Ilchester's gardeners were sowing a wide variety of seeds in the 1750s, including 'shortlep' radish, salmon radish and common radish, globe artichokes, white mustard, cress, savoy cabbage, cauliflower, carrots, Dutch turnip, red beet, spinach, cucumber, endive, Spanish onions, chervil, curled parsley, sweet basil, sweet marjoram, purslane, sugar peas, 'nunparells pease', 'Charlenton pease', 'marrow pease', 'golden hotts peas',[3] Windsor beans, and long-podded beans.[4] Landowners expected to eat their own fruit and vegetables whilst they were in the country, and baskets of fruit, flowers and vegetables were often sent to London too.

Melbury, Redlynch and Penrice had glasshouses and hothouses where the choicest fruits, such as melons, grapes and peaches, could be cultivated. In 1756 Edward Hiett, the steward at Redlynch, paid £11 11*s.* for 'melon glasses from Bristol'.[5] Pineapples, which were particularly highly prized, were being grown at Melbury by 1749.[6] There were orange trees at Melbury and Redlynch by the mid eighteenth century, and Susan O'Brien also had some at Stinsford. In South Wales the Talbots had a vast orangery at Margam and a smaller one at Penrice. Throughout the summer and autumn friends, neighbours, and anyone who hoped for a favour, would bring gifts from their own gardens. In the 1760s Lord Digby's servants brought fruit from Sherborne to Melbury every summer (including pineapples in 1770), and the rector of Melbury, Marrian Feaver, often sent his servants to the house with gifts of asparagus, grapes and honey. In October 1761 the housekeeper paid 2*s.* 6*d.* 'to a man for grapes, who used to bring them every year', and in 1766 'Mrs Houlton's grandson' was given 2*s.* 6*d.* for bringing apples. Two years later 5*s.* was given to 'the old woman at Melbury for cherreys, by My Lady's order'.[7] There were other gifts of food, too, including the occasional turtle. At Sherborne Castle there was a turtle for dinner one day in October 1772. It had been given to Lord Digby by Mr Bristed. Susan O'Brien was given some turtle in 1826 by her friend Mrs Field, and she invited some friends to share this great delicacy.[8]

Many estates also had home farms, which produced mutton, pork, beef and poultry for the table. An 'account of Mrs Horner's stock of cattle' at Melbury, drawn up in March 1748, shows that Susanna Strangways Horner had two bulls, six steers, two bullocks, six heifers, seventeen milch cows, two 'calves to rear up' and an unspecified number of ewes and lambs. In 1750 the steward paid £10 10*s.* for thirty Portland sheep, and two years later Richard Miller, the farm bailiff, spent a total of £352 on farm stock, including thirty-five 'fat weather sheep', and some dairy cows. Miller also bought cattle and oxen at the fairs in Dorchester, Exeter and Barnstaple. In April of the following year five more cows were bought, together with four heifers and a bull 'of the sparked sort', all for £39 1*s.*[9] At Redlynch the steward paid £1 14*s.* for 'two Welch piggs' in 1736. 'Pide' (pied) cows and heifers were bought for Redlynch in 1738 and 1759.[10] 'Alderny' cows bought in March 1760 cost £29 8*s.*, and the expenses of fetching them from Southampton came to an additional £1 0*s.* 8*d.*[11]

In 1762 Horace Walpole admired Lord Ilchester's cows at Redlynch:

> The park is filled with a particular breed of cows, which have a pretty effect.

> Their whole fore and hinder parts are black or brown, and the bodies milk white, divided in such strait lines that they look as if they had a sheet flung over them, whence they are called Sheet-Cows.[12]

Sheeted Somerset cattle were found in a number of parks in the eighteenth and nineteenth centuries.[13] The Redlynch farm stock sold in 1801 included lambs and ewes, two pigs, and milch cows called Blossom, Cherry and Motley.[14] In the early nineteenth century Thomas Talbot was buying 'Scotch oxen' to be fattened at Penrice. Sometimes a butcher would be brought in to slaughter the animals and prepare them for the kitchen: at Melbury in 1750 a man was paid £1 7*s.* 6*d.* for 'killing, dressing and cutting up eleven beasts at 2*s.* 6*d.*'; with 9*d.* for killing and dressing three sheep at 3*d.* each, and 3*d.* for 'cutting up a burned pigg'. Some of the meat produced on the estate would be salted and cured at home, but bacon, butchers' meat and poultry were also purchased from time to time. Melbury and Redlynch also had poultry yards: in the late 1740s the chicken houses at Melbury were given new tiled roofs at a cost of £20 7*s.* 6*d.*[15] In 1736 Mary Pressey was employed as a 'poultry woman' at Redlynch at an annual salary of £3. In 1761 the 'chicken maid', Mary Smith, was paid £4. Payments in 1753 include £1 7*s.* for ten bushels of 'barly meal for the chikens'. In 1761 the housekeeper at Melbury paid 4*s.* 6*d.* for 'six couple of large white fowls for to breed', and in the following year she bought 'oatmeal for little chickens to eat'. Purchases in 1767 included 'pork bread and gurgings to feed fowls with' (14*s.* 6*d.*).[16] Turkeys were also reared: in 1758 John Beaumont was paid 9*s.* 11*d.* for making a turkey coop for Redlynch, and in the following year a boy was paid a shilling a week for looking after the turkeys there.[17] In 1770 at Melbury 'a hen turkey kept for breed' cost 2*s.* 6*d.*[18]

Most great estates had lakes, which were kept stocked with fish such as trout, carp and tench. Payments at Redlynch in 1738 included £3 19*s.* for '232 brace of store tench' at 3*d.*, with a guinea to the men who brought them from Shaftesbury. In 1741, 8*s.* was paid for '100 brace of carp and tench'.[19] Some fish were caught with rod and line; others were netted. At Sherborne Castle on 11 November 1766:

> [They] began to fish the canals, and made an end about 4 o'clock. It is supposed there was near a ton weight of pikes catched, the largest of which weighed 28 pounds, and several about 15 or 16. There were an immense quantity of fine tench; 40 or 50 brace of exceeding fine carps, but very few large perch. All turned in again, except the pikes and 40 brace of tench and 8 of carps.[20]

Redlynch had a rabbit-warren, and Melbury, Redlynch and Sherborne Castle all had deer-parks which provided venison, both for the household and for gifts to friends and neighbours. There were no deer at Penrice, but venison was sent there regularly from the Talbots' park at Margam. There was a pigeon-house at Abbotsbury: this was leased to Corbet Pitman in the mid eighteenth century, and his rent included twenty-five dozen (300) pigeons a year. In 1748–49 Susanna Strangways Horner bought an additional 236 pigeons from Pitman at 4*s.* 6*d.* a dozen. Pitman also supplied Melbury with fish, and shellfish such as prawns, lobsters and crabs. Other men brought fish on a regular basis. During the week of 12 to 18 June 1748, the household at Melbury bought 2 bass, 5 salmon peals (young salmon), 6 doreys, 30 mackerel, 57 herrings, 50 mullets, 9 plaice and dabs, five dozen whiting, a dozen gurnards, one pilchard, and an unspecified number of trout.[21] The total cost was approximately 7*s.* Some kinds of fish were prized particularly highly: in July 1761 the housekeeper paid 10*s.* 6*d.* 'to the man that brought the turbot by My Lord's orders', and 2*s.* to 'the man that brought a sturgeon from Abbotsbury'.[22] In 1798 the housekeeper at Penrice bought a turbot for 15*s.* and a codfish for 3*s.* 6*d.* At this time brill cost 4*d.* a pound in Gower; three lobsters and nineteen crabs cost 2*s.*; and a pint of sand eels cost a penny. During the shooting season, at Penrice as elsewhere, there would be plenty of pheasants, woodcock, partridge and wild duck for the family and their visitors to eat. Melbury was also supplied with wildfowl trapped in the decoy at Abbotsbury.

The household inventories list the rooms in which much of the food was processed and prepared. There was a preserving room at Melbury in 1727. The contents included a brass preserving pan, various pots and skillets, two pairs of brass scales with weights, an iron stove, two marble mortars and two sweetmeat cupboards. Whilst the mistresses of less wealthy households took pride in their skill at preserving and pickling,[23] it is clear that it was the housekeeper who presided over the Melbury preserving room. Indeed, the housekeeper seems to have used it as her own private sitting room, for it also held seven chairs and four tables. Next door, and also within the housekeeper's domain, was the still-room, where there were two cold stills and two copper hot stills, which would have been used to distil herbal medicines and waters of various kinds – cordials and alcoholic drinks for the household, and flower waters (especially rose-water) for medicinal, culinary or cosmetic use. By the middle of the eighteenth century many of these were bought in, and less distilling was done at home. In 1741 there was a pewter limbeck or still in the still-room at Mells, but the room seems mainly to have been used to store china and the equipment needed for making tea, coffee and chocolate.[24] The still at Melbury was apparently in working order in 1749, when a brazier was paid 5*s.* for 'tinning and mending

1762	Disburements bro^t Forwards .	93	9	4¾
Aug. 28	To 3 Load of Straw .	1	11	6
	To Thomas Martin as ℘ Bill His expences at Lyme .	2	8	8
30	To the Labourers Bill for 4 Weeks to the 22d Instant .	14	11	11
	To the Garden Bill to the same time .	5	17	3½
	To Richard Linscom the Mason in full of his Bill .	1	12	8
	To the Postman for 7 Weeks & 3 Journeys due the 28th .	.	18	.
	To Mr Dawe in full of his Bill for things bo^t in London	21	5	2
	To 6 Mops 6d and 6 beasoms 1s 9 .	.	7	9
	To 6 Balls of twine .	.	2	3
	To Lord Digbys Servant for bringing Fruit .	.	2	6
	To Mrs Dawe what she gave a poor Woman by my Ladys Ord^r .	.	5	.
	To Joseph Childs Joiner in full as ℘ Bill .	2	1	5
	To Mr Skodes Servant for bringing rails .	.	5	.
31	To the Poors allowance .	.	16	.
	To old Francis the same .	.	4	6
	To Mugs 2d and rosin 2d .	.	2	2
	To John Parsons Expences to Sherborn and hoice to Bridport &c as ℘ Bill .	.	11	3
	To John Pitchers Expences &c as ℘ bill .	.	18	2
	To James Gales wife by my Ladys Order .	.	5	.
	To John Barnes Expences &c as ℘ Bill .	.	5	8
Augst ye 31 1762 alowed by me Eliz Ilchester	To Thomas Chinnoths wife by my Ladys Order .	.	5	.
	To Mr Feavers boy by my Ladys Order .	.	2	6
	Total of Disbursments from the 31st July 1762 to the 31st Augt inclusive	148	8	9¼
	To Payments in the Housekeeping Book as by the same appears .	89	2	8½
		237	11	5¾
	To Cash received as by Account appears .	252	8	6½
	Ballance from Mrs Cooper .	14	17	0¾

A page from the Melbury household accounts for 1760 to 1770. The payments include £2 1s. 5d. to Thomas Hardy's ancestor, Joseph Childs. (*Reproduced with the permission of Ilchester Estates and the Dorset Archives Service, ref. D/FSI, box 217*) a stillhead'.[25] No still is listed in the still-room at Redlynch in 1793, but there was a coffee-pot, a chocolate-pot and two tea-kettles, with a spice-mill, five jelly-moulds and various implements for making sweetmeats. The products of the Melbury still-room and preserving room in the mid eighteenth century included cherry brandy and cowslip wine, 'mango' (a kind of pickle, often made with melons or cucumbers), preserved apricots, preserved damsons and elder syrup.

The preserving room and still-rooms were usually within the main body of the house, close to the housekeeper's room. Other service rooms – especially those requiring their own chimneys, or where strong smells or steam were likely to be produced – were often built around a series of courtyards at the back. Of these rooms the most important was the kitchen, where the cook was in charge, assisted by a number of maids who worked in the kitchen itself and in the sculleries. Most of the cooking was done on coal-fired ranges: at Melbury in 1727 there was a 'range grate', with several spits, turned by a jack. A new range at Redlynch cost £5 6*s.* in 1738. The mid eighteenth-century household accounts include regular payments for cleaning and repairing the kitchen jacks. In 1754 at Redlynch 'reparing the jack with new wheels' cost 7*s.* 6*d.* There were cranes and hangers so that large pots could be suspended over the fire, and trivets to hold other pots and pans. The cook at Melbury also had 'a boyler fixt in the wall' in the kitchen. At Redlynch a 'new coppar boylar for the kitching' cost £3 13*s.* 6*d.* in 1744.[26] For smaller-scale cooking operations which did not require the intense heat generated by a range, the cook would use a charcoal burner or chafing-dish. One of these, probably of iron, is listed in the Stinsford inventory of 1727. The charcoal was burnt on the estate, and brought to the kitchen on a regular basis. By the end of the eighteenth century chafing-dishes had been superseded by built-in cast-iron stoves of iron, heated by charcoal or coal. The cooking pots were placed on trivets above the fire, and the temperature was regulated by using a register to control the draught. Kitchen equipment purchased from Oldham's Manufactory and Warehouse for the kitchen at Penrice Castle in 1792 included 'a very large polished steel register stove'. This, with 'a double beaded steel fender and set of shovel and tongs all complete', cost £26 5*s.*[27]

Much of the equipment used in the eighteenth century can still be found in modern kitchens: every country house cook had a pestle and mortar, a pair of scales and a chopping-block, and every kitchen contained a variety of cooking pots and pans made of of copper, brass and iron, such as saucepans, frying pans, stewpans, fish kettles and tea kettles. In 1761 a tinker was paid 8*s.* for mending pots, pans and kettles at Melbury. There were also patty pans, skimmers and ladles, spoons of metal and wood, toasting forks, graters, colanders and chopping knives, and large quantities of ceramic and pewter dishes and plates. In 1745 'a large claver [cleaver] for the kitching' at Redlynch cost 9*s*., whilst 'three kitching knives and [a] steel' cost 8*s.* 6*d.*[28] 'Earthen ware for the use of the housekeeper, larder or kitchen' bought for Melbury in 1763 cost 8*s.* 2*d.*, and at Penrice in 1799 'earthing where for the kitching' cost 3*s.* The scale of food production is illustrated by the Redlynch inventory of 1793: there were twenty-two 'stew pans of different sizes with covers' in the kitchen, also six fish kettles, eleven saucepans with covers, and four frying pans. Each house also had a number of sculleries and larders, which were used in conjunction with the kitchen. In 1737 the larder at Stinsford had in it a lead cistern to salt meat in, and the wet larder at Mells in 1741 held two lead-lined salting troughs.[29] Mells also had a dry larder at this time, containing a variety of cupboards, tubs and barrels, all of which were described as 'old and broken'.

Food was preserved by drying, salting and pickling. In the mid eighteenth century the household at Melbury was using approximately a hundredweight of ordinary salt a month, at a cost of 10*s.* or 11*s.* a hundredweight.[30] Ice was also used to keep food fresh, and Melbury, Redlynch and Penrice Castle all had ice houses. The ice to fill the house was usually taken from a lake nearby, though compacted snow could be used as well. As the ice house was filled, salt was mixed into the ice, which was then pounded and rammed into a solid block, since this would melt more slowly than smaller lumps. In 1762 the housekeeper at Melbury paid 13*s.* for 114 pounds of salt 'for the ice house'. Salt for the ice house at Redlynch in January 1784 cost £2 2*s.*[31] The supply of ice to fill the house each winter was uncertain, being dependent on the weather, so the estate workers would be summoned as soon as the temperature fell far enough. At Melbury on 17 December 1768 the sum of 2*s.* 6*d.* was paid for 'bread for the labourers … when the first ice was put in'. At Penrice in 1807 it began to snow unusually early, on 4 November, and there were heavy snowfalls on and off for the rest of the month. On 28 November there was 'A very severe frost for one night. The water below the house froze over so hard that the geese walked on it without breaking the ice'. On 30 November and 1 December the men filled the ice house.[32] They were just in time, for it began to thaw on the next day. In the following year the ice house was filled on 23 December. The ice in the house would not normally be edible, and its main use was to cool wine and refrigerate meat, fish and dairy products. It also enabled the cook to make ice-cream and other frozen desserts.

Vast quantities of beer were drunk, by both the family and servants.[33] The beer was stored in the cellars: in 1737 Stinsford had one cellar for strong beer and another for small beer. So did Mells in 1741, when the strong beer cellar held 29 hogsheads, 14 of which were full of beer, whilst the other cellar held 4 hogsheads, only one of which was full. In March 1748 the cellars at Melbury held 27½ hogsheads (1485 gallons) of strong beer brewed in 1746; 22 hogsheads (1188 gallons) of strong beer brewed in 1747; 6½ hogsheads (351 gallons) of ale; 10¼ hogsheads (553.5 gallons) of small beer, and 26 bottles of cider.[34] The beer and ale were brewed at home, using malt and hops which were usually bought from local merchants. Small beer, which did not keep long, was made when it was needed during the year. Strong beer and ale were brewed less frequently, and several hundred gallons would be made at a time.[35] This was skilled work, and the brewer – usually a man – would be brought in specially and would stay for up to a month. At Redlynch James Hileard was paid £1 11*s.* for thirty-one days' brewing in January 1742. Payments were also made at this time to a cooper for 'heading the caskes etc. and for 4 new buks' (£9 10*s.* 6*d.*); and to the miller for grinding 303 bushels of malt (£2 10*s.* 6*d.*). Raw materials purchased for the brewing included a bag of hops (£6 16*s.*) and 302 bushels of malt (£77 11*s.*). Hileard was back at Redlynch again in December 1742, when he was paid £1 4*s.* for another twenty-four days' brewing.[36] At Melbury, most of the brewing was done in March: in April 1761 the housekeeper paid £1 'to Mr Daw's eating for three weeks when he was here brewing and before'. At the same time Betty Childs was paid 12*s.* 'for helping to brew 16 days at 9*d.*' William Holt, who came to brew at Redlynch in 1785, was paid £2 12*s.* 6*d.* for twenty-one days' work. He also received board wages of £1 1*s.*, as the family was away, with his travelling expenses of 6*s.*

The brewhouse was at the back of the house, next to the bakehouse. These two rooms are listed together in the Melbury inventory of 1727, and they probably shared a chimney. The contents included two furnaces: one large and one small; several vats and tubs, a meal trough and a lead pump. The Redlynch household accounts include numerous payments for equipment for the brewhouse, including a hop-strainer in 1749; 'a huckmuck and baskett for brewing' in 1751; and a hop-basket in 1754. At Melbury in 1762, a large wooden bowl for the brewhouse cost a shilling, and 'a seeve for the use of the brewer', 6*s.*[37] Stinsford had a brewhouse too at this time, though no bakehouse there is mentioned. They were still brewing beer at Stinsford in the early nineteenth century. In 1808 Henry Talbot wrote from his preparatory school at Rottingdean to ask his mother to send him 'some more Stinsford beer'.[38] Whether the headmaster would have welcomed this is debatable: one of the under gardeners at Stinsford told Thomas Hardy many years later that the O'Briens had 'kept a splendid house' with 'a cellarful of home-brewed strong beer that would almost knock you down.

Everybody drank as much as he liked [and] the head-gardener was drunk every morning before breakfast'.[39] There was also a brewhouse at Penrice, and Thomas Talbot's pocket-books show that he made regular purchases of hops (from Bristol) and malt. Cider, too, was made at Melbury in the 1760s: 'a rope for the cyder wring' cost 5*s.* 9*d.* in 1763, and in April of the following year John Swetman was paid 4*s.* 2*d.* for making cider.[40]

Every great house employed at least one dairymaid, whose duties included milking the cows and making butter and cheese. How much was produced depended on the time of year: at Melbury in the mid eighteenth century the dairymaid started making butter and cheese in March, and the work continued until November. During most of the summer of of 1748 the dairy produced between ten and twenty-two pounds of butter a week, together with seven or eight 'skim cheeses'. No cream is mentioned in the accounts for this year, but in the following year the cook had up to twenty pints of cream a week.[41] There was a small brass furnace in the dairy at Melbury in 1727, with two brass skillets, five lead-lined cisterns for milk, five tubs and a long table. The contents of the 'dairyhouse' at Mells in 1741 included a cheese press, a butter churn, a lead milk-cistern and two milking pails. At Melbury in 1749 the cooper was paid 1*s.* 4*d.* for making 'two new pails for the dayry maid'. Pans for the dairy cost a shilling in 1760 and new 'cheese vates', bought at the same time, cost 4*s.* Purchases in 1763 included 'tape and cheese clouts for the use of the dairy' (1*s.* 2*d.*) and 'panns for ditto, wooden spoon and dish' (2*s.* 9*d.*). In 1768 the housekeeper bought 'milk pans and butter pots' for £1 1*s.*[42] The surplus produce was sometimes sent to the market: in August 1768 the housekeeper at Melbury recorded that she had received £6 14*s.* 4*d.* 'for butter and household cheese sold'.[43] In previous generations the dairy, like the still-room, had been the province of the lady of the house, and eighteenth-century ladies – including Queen Charlotte and Marie-Antoinette – liked to play at being dairymaids in specially-built ornamental dairies. A Gothic dairy was built at Sherborne Castle in the 1750s, and a passing reference in the Redlynch accounts to the payment to a glazier of 4*s.* for 'two squares [of glass] in My Lady's dairy' in 1762 suggests that the first Countess of llchester may have had a dairy at Redlynch too, though none is mentioned in the inventory of 1793.[44]

Considerable quantities of food also had to be bought in. Basic products, including some fruit and vegetables, and supplies of butter, flour, cheese and meat, could be obtained from local towns such as Dorchester, Sherborne and Yeovil. In November 1728 the steward at Melbury paid 9*d.* 'to the cooke's man when to Dorchester for provisions' and 2*s.* 'to Bettie Vincent for her horse from Dorchester with provisions'.[45] Some produce also came from local farmers. In 1747–48 Farmer Abram supplied the household at Melbury with fat cows, fat pigs, poor pigs and porkers, white fowls, wether sheep, butter (at 5*d.* or 6*d.* a pound), oats and barley, and in November 1763 Farmer Burden was paid £3 10*s.* 11*d.* 'for butter, cream etc. had before the family left Melbury'.[46] Seasonal delicacies such as mushrooms, samphire, apricots and black cherries were also bought from local people from time to time. At Melbury in 1728 the steward paid 5*s.* 4*d.* for 800 'gurkins' at 8*d.* per hundred.[47] At Penrice the Talbots bought laver (edible seaweed), and they also sents pots of it to friends in England. But most of the more exotic goods – especially those imported from foreign countries – came from grocers, usually in Bristol or London. In the late 1740s goods sent to Melbury by Mr Houlton, a Bristol grocer, included sugar (in loaves, powder and lumps), currants, raisins, coffee (5*s.* 6*d.* or 6*s.* a pound), green tea (10*s.* 6*d.* to 16*s.* a pound),[48] ginger, mace, cloves, cinnamon, nutmegs, saffron, black pepper, white pepper, sweet almonds, bitter almonds, Jordan almonds, common almonds, 'pestatia nuts', candied oranges and lemons, Seville oranges, rice, pearl barley, 'vermagilly' (vermicelli), vinegar, anchovies (at £1 15*s.* a barrel), capers and isinglass (gelatine). Chocolate was bought from a Mr Smith, who was probably in London: it cost 5*s.* 6*d.* a pound, and the bill for the period from November 1748 to June 1750 came to £41 14*s.* In January 1749 Mr Francis Skull was paid £1 12*s.* for 'eight bottles of fine mushrooms'. London grocers such as Tolson and Lewis of New Bond Street supplied the household at Penrice with tea, coffee, cocoa and other luxury goods in the early nineteenth century, though 'coarser articles' were sent from Bristol by Mr John Ambrose, whose bills came to approximately £80 to £100 a year.[49] Extra provisions would be needed at Christmas. Purchases for Melbury early in December 1761 included 'three lemons to put in mince pye', and 'cranberries for tarts' cost 2*s.* 6*d.* at the beginning of January 1765. There are references to turkeys in 1761 and 1763, but they were not necessarily eaten at Christmas. In 1814, however, the O'Briens, in lodgings in Weymouth, dined on 'a turkey and chine'.

Wine and spirits were also purchased to supplement the home-brewed beer. They were usually bought in barrels and bottled at home. Port (red and white) was supplied by the hogshead or the pipe:[50] in 1748 a wine merchant, Mr Harbin, was paid £40 for two and a half hogsheads of port wine sent to Melbury. A year later Mr Harbin sent a hogshead of white port, for which he charged £16. A further order a few months later was made up of 'a pipe of old port' (£32), and a hogshead of Lisbon wine, though the latter was subsequently returned. In 1751 John Willett of Bristol sent 'two baskets of exceeding good wine' by carrier to Redlynch. The baskets contained twelve gallons of white Lisbon wine, at 5*s.* 6*d.* a gallon, and Willett also charged 8*s.* for four dozen quart bottles.[51] In the same year the wine merchants Collingwood and Holford sent 'two dozen of the best claret', costing £4 16*s.*, to Melbury. In the early nineteen century Thomas Talbot was buying port from Messrs Sealy and Co. of Bridgwater and Mr T. Grant of Bideford. He bought a pipe at a time, at costs varying from £96 to £115. In 1806 Grant supplied twenty gallons of brandy, at 19*s.* 8*d.* a gallon, and Talbot also ordered butts of sherry and 'Bucellas white wine' from Sealy at different times.[52] Whilst most of these liquors were shipped in barrels to Swansea or Oxwich, some wine was sent in bottles: in May 1808 Talbot paid Sealy and Co. a total of £342 16*s.* 6*d.* for a number of shipments, including 'wine sent in bottles, sixty dozen of port'.

The housekeeper's responsibilities included looking after the household linen and overseeing the work of the maids who cleaned the house and worked in the wash-house and laundry. The wash-house at Melbury had two brass furnaces in it, together with six washing tubs. The mid eighteenth-century plan of the offices at Redlynch shows that the laundry and wash-house were behind the housekeeper's room. The equipment there in 1793 included a copper boiler, with sixteen washing tubs and several baskets, pails and pans. Much of the equipment was made of wood: in the 1740s a cooper was paid for hooping tubs and pails for the wash-house at Melbury.[53] The laundry was used for mangling, and then drying and airing, the washing (though as much drying as possible was done out of doors: there were 'drying yards' at Melbury and Redlynch), and also for ironing. The Redlynch laundry had a 'hat-stove' in it to heat the irons. In 1744 the housekeeper at Redlynch paid £5 17*s.* for 'Sleseia holland, ironing cloth, etc.', and 10*s.* for 'a line for the landrey drying frame'.[54] In 1761 a hundred yards of rope were bought for the 'landry horse' at Melbury.[55] Laundry goods such as starch and blue for both Redlynch and Melbury came from grocers in Bristol: in February 1747 Mr Houlton sent Poland starch, common starch, 'best blew' and 'best smelt' to Melbury.[56] Purchases by the housekeeper there in 1762 included 'one yard of flannen for blew bags etc.'[57]

Essential supplies for the housemaids included materials such as lead for blacking the grates and ranges, and a wide range of cleaning equipment. Payments at Melbury in 1728 included 12*s.* for '24 pound of drums to make mops'.[58] In 1743 John Pearcem of Sherborne supplied two hair brooms to Melbury, together with 'one brush called a pope's head'.[59] In 1750 the housekeeper paid 3*s.* 6*d.* for two large 'dust panns', and 2*s.* for four brushes, and in 1769 'hard brushes for the use of the housemaids' cost 8*s.* 6*d.* In

1793 there were two brass housemaids' pails, two brushes and two 'dust shovels' in a closet in the offices at Redlynch. Payments in 1762 included 3*s.* 6*d.* for 'cloth for dishclouts'. In 1765 the housekeeper bought seventeen yards of towelling at 4½*d.* a yard, and sixteen yards of Irish cloth at 1*s.* 3*d.* a yard for use in the kitchen at Redlynch from a 'Scotchman' or pedlar. In 1784 at Redlynch a yard of flannel was bought 'to polish wax candles'. Some soap was bought from local tallow chandlers, but the better quality supplies came from further afield. Thomas Talbot bought soap for use at Penrice from Messrs Tripp and Co., a firm of soap boilers in Bristol, at a cost of approximately £30 a year.

For most of the eighteenth century candles and rush lights were the only available source of artificial lighting. At Melbury in 1727 the main living rooms had pairs of glass sconces or bracket candlesticks (probably fixed to the wall). The sconces in the inlaid bedchamber were gilt, whilst the inlaid dining room had 'six cheney sconces'. There were also large numbers of portable candlesticks: iron for the servants, brass for the family. The Stinsford inventory of 1737 lists eight brass candlesticks, and three 'flat ditto', with two pairs of snuffers and stands. In 1744 the steward at Redlynch paid £1 for five 'lantorns for the pasiges', and 7*s.* 6*d.* more for glazing them.[60] Tinder-boxes were used to light the candles: one was bought for Melbury in 1751 at a cost of 6*d.* Lighting was expensive: in the 1740s and 1750s Mr Cornelius Pye was paid approximately £30 a year for supplying spermaceti candles to Melbury. These were good quality candles for use by the family: at 20*d.* a pound they were a little cheaper than wax candles, but they cost much more than the tallow candles and rush-lights used by the servants.[61] 'Rush candles' were supplied by local tallow chandlers, John Mullins and (from 1743) James Hull, who charged 6*d.* or 6½*d.* a pound. The kitchen at Melbury supplied Mr Hull with some raw materials, for which he allowed a discount: 2*d.* a pound for kitchen grease, from 2½*d.* to 4*d.* a pound for tallow, and 6*d.* a bushel for ashes. In the early nineteenth century Thomas Talbot bought wax candles from Mr A. Romano of Mount Street near Berkeley Square in London. In 1804, after making one payment, he noted in his pocket-book 'Memorandum: when I write for more to say those sent last were very bad and eventually want snuffing'. By the end of the eighteenth century oil lamps were also widely used. The Redlynch inventory of 1793 refers to several 'globe glass lamps', and there were other lamps which were described as 'mahogany framed and glazed'. The valet had a 'tin framed and glazed lamp' in his lobby. Lamps were also used at Penrice: in 1806 Thomas Talbot paid £34 12*s.* for fifteen and a half gallons of spermaceti oil from Messrs Sanders and Co. of Bristol. This oil, from sperm wales, was the best quality available, but at eight shillings a gallon it was expensive. Colza, or rape-seed, oil became increasingly popular in the early nineteenth century.

A good supply of fuel was also needed, for warming the rooms, heating water and cooking. Each estate had woodland which provided a ready supply of firewood, and references to fire-dogs in the Melbury inventory of 1727 suggest that most of the rooms had wood-burning hearths at this time.[62] In the library, however, there was a 'stove grate', which would have used coal. Coal became increasingly popular in the eighteenth century. It was more satisfactory than wood in many ways: it gave out more heat and required less attention, since it burned more slowly and produced less ash. Most of the main rooms at Stinsford already had stove grates by 1727 – the result, perhaps, of the improvements carried out by Thomas and Mary Strangways a few years earlier.[63] No stoves are mentioned in the Mells inventory of 1741, when the hearths all had fire-dogs for burning wood. At Redlynch in 1793 there were coal grates in the entrance hall, saloon and dining room, but the billiard room, tapestry room and green room had fire-dogs. Upstairs, most of the main bedrooms had coal-fired Bath stoves by this time. Coal was much more expensive than wood, especially at Redlynch and Melbury where it had to be brought some distance by cart or packhorse. The coal used at Melbury was carried in carts from Weymouth, twenty miles away. In the 1760s the household used a cartload every two weeks or so during the winter whilst the family was at home. In February 1768 Thomas Trent's 'expences to Weymouth for coals, and on the road on account of the wheels breaking twice', came to £1 1*s*.[64] It is not clear where the coal used at Redlynch came from, but the bill for coal used in the house during the last six months of 1744 came to £45 1*s*. 6*d*.[65] Coal was much cheaper at Penrice, as there were pits a few miles from the house.

9

Health

Of all the topics discussed by the ladies of the Fox Strangways family in their letters, those connected with health occur most frequently. The well-being of members of the household was traditionally the women's responsibility, and it was they and their female servants who looked after babies and small children and nursed them when they were sick. They entertained and waited on the bed-ridden, and, when they could possibly do so, helped their daughters and sisters through the difficult and dangerous hours of childbirth. In their letters these women exchanged news about their own ailments and those of their friends and relations; they supported and sympathised with each other in times of difficulty; they reported on the effects of medicines and other remedies; and they gave their opinions on the doctors whom they had consulted. Belonging, as they did, to one of the wealthiest and most influential families in the country, they could afford to seek out the best available medical advice, whether in London, Bath or even further afield, on the Continent. A study of the health problems suffered by successive generations of the family, and of the various ways in which they were treated, thus gives us a good view of the capabilities – and failings – of medicine in the Georgian period.

The country gentlewoman of the sixteenth and seventeenth centuries made medicines, ointments and pills in her still-room for her family and servants, and also for the poor people of the neighbourhood. During the eighteenth century, however, the housekeeper took over much of the work in the still-room from her mistress, and many home-made remedies were replaced by preparations purchased from local apothecaries. Apart from the occasional recipe, such as one for 'Sir Stephen Fox's eye-water' and another for blackcurrant lozenges, there is little indication that the Fox Strangways ladies were actively involved in the production of medicines. In the early 1750s the Bruton apothecary Thomas Clarke supplied the household at Redlynch with a wide variety of preparations, including elderflower water, orange-flower water, spirits of lavender, syrup of violets and syrup of roses,[1] all of which would have been made at home a few decades earlier. Home-distillation and the domestic manufacture of medicines continued for longer in less grand households – at Catchfrench in Cornwall in the mid eighteenth century the ladies exchanged 'receipts and prescriptions' and they were still 'eminently skilled in cooking and medicine' and the production of 'pills and potions',[2] and at the same period the Norfolk sisters Barbara Kerrich and Elizabeth Postlethwaite discussed distilling and the best way to make 'pennyroyal water' in their letters.[3] Eliza Haywood's *A New Present for a Servant Maid* includes recipes for hysterical water, plague water, treacle water and 'wonderful water'. The last-named was said be 'a pleasant, good cordial [which] greatly breaks the wind of the stomach, and disperses flatulence'.[4]

In the eighteenth century, as in the twenty-first, women were more likely to seek medical advice than their male contemporaries. There were, however, some problems that were more likely to affect the latter. Men and boys, being physically more active, were more often injured as a result of accidents – usually involving horses or guns, or both. Riding accidents were common – Lord Stavordale broke a rib in a fall in 1766, and his father was reported to be 'much bruised and in a good deal of pain' following a similar mishap three years later. In 1788 William O'Brien fell from his horse and broke his collar-bone, after which he was 'only' confined for a month, and in 1807 Stephen Strangways 'had a fall from his horse and hurt his head'.[5] Thomas Talbot had several accidents – in 1801 he came home 'his head tied up and very lame owing to a bad fall', and in 1808 he fell down the ha-ha at Margam.[6]

In 1808, too, the third Earl of Ilchester was seriously injured whilst he was out hunting. His horse failed to clear a ditch and fell, crushing Lord Ilchester underneath it. Lord Ilchester's thigh was broken, and he was carried the three miles back to Melbury by relays of men, on a gate covered with coats. Three surgeons were already waiting for him when he reached the house, as his friends had gone 'different ways' for medical assistance. The bone was set by 'Mr Palmer and Mr Lamb of Bedminster' and the patient was confined to his bed for almost two months. Relations and other visitors to Melbury rallied round to entertain him: a looking-glass was fixed up so that he could 'see down the park to amuse himself', and four ropes with handles were attached to his bed to help him to move. Three weeks after the accident, Charlotte Strangways reported that her brother was 'so well that I almost live in dread of his growing unmanageable. We sat by his bed last night and played a rubber of whist with him ... He is now netting some cherry nets, which amuses the end of his fingers'. Lord Ilchester was still lame, and in some pain, five months after the accident.[7]

The women of the family were less accident-prone, though they, too, were occasionally hurt. Susanna Strangways Horner fell down the stairs at Melbury in 1746 and was 'much brused in her face and hurt her arm, but no bone broke'.[8] In March 1761 Sarah Lennox fell from her horse at Maiden Bradley in Somerset and broke a leg. She was first carried three or four miles to Stourhead, and then 'upon men's shoulders, in a very pretty bed made for the purpose' another four miles to Redlynch. It was almost two months before she was able to return to London.[9] Carriages sometimes overturned, injuring the occupants,[10] and several other minor accidents are recorded: Mary Talbot sprained her ankle in 1805, as did her cousin Lady Porchester in 1810. Louisa Lansdowne complained in 1811 that she could 'neither walk nor dance' as a result of a similar mishap.[11]

Gout was a disorder that was thought mainly to affect men, largely because of its association with hard drinking. In the absence of any reliable diagnostic test for gout, it was a label that was liable to be attached to pains affecting many different parts of the body, including the joints, the stomach and the head. Several men of the Digby and Fox Strangways families suffered from it. The Revd William Digby died in 1788 aged fifty-four, 'a martyr to the gout'.[12] The second Earl of Ilchester suffered from recurrent attacks of the gout in his hands and feet, and it was one of these, in 1792, that prolonged his first stay at Penrice and led eventually to the marriage of his daughter Mary to Thomas Talbot. During the last years of his life, Lord Ilchester was carried around in a sedan chair when he was unable to walk. His death, in Buxton in 1802, was thought to be due to 'gout in the head'.[13]

Women's pains and swellings were less often attributed to gout. In 1803, when she was governess at Penrice, Agnes Porter was seriously ill for almost three months. In August she was 'confined to my chair – feet and hands seized by the harpy claws of the gout'. Ten days later she was 'In limbo – continued very ill six weeks. Could not turn myself in bed to the right or left – quite stationary where placed, whether in bed or on a chair. Quite a cripple – could not stand, nor move.' At the beginning of October Agnes could 'walk a few steps and scrawl a few lines', but she then suffered a relapse and was 'almost in despair of recovering my limbs'. An old friend, Dr Malcolm Macqueen, advised her to 'bathe and rub the afflicted parts in tepid salt water, as also to eat solids and drink a glass or two of sound wine every day'. Within a few days Agnes was on the mend, though whether this was due to the tepid salt water or the 'sound wine' is unknown.[14]

Rheumatism and arthritis afflicted both men and women. In the 1750s the first Countess of Ilchester spent some time in Bath, where she was treated for a painful hip. In old age, according to her great-granddaughter, she was 'so crippled by rheumatism' that she walked 'pushing a light stool before her instead of a crutch'.[15] The O'Briens also suffered from severe rheumatism in old age, but this may have been due in part to the poor state of their house at Stinsford, which was cold and damp for much of the year. In 1811, after a visit to her niece Mary in Wales, Susan wrote, 'We came strait home, pretty well but both rheumatic. Such a wet season was never known, so it's no wonder old bones should feel its effects.'[16] In the autumn of the same year Susan was unable to attend the Yeomanry Ball in Dorchester because she was 'seized with such violent pains in my hip and back that at first I could not move without screaming'. The doctor diagnosed 'a violent rheumatick seizure'. Susan found this depressing, telling her niece Elizabeth, 'After what I saw my poor mother suffer so long from that complaint, I confess it lowers my spirits a good deal'.[17]

Almost everyone was affected by digestive problems of various kinds. By contemporary standards the Earls of Ilchester and their families ate extremely well. They were never short of food – indeed, many of their disorders were no doubt caused by eating and drinking too much. For women, tight corsets and a lack of exercise probably did not help. As with gout and rheumatism, however, it is impossible to determine exactly what did cause the many internal disorders from which Georgian ladies and gentlemen suffered. In 1749 Susanna Strangways Horner was said to be 'very ill with a violent complaint in her bowels', and in 1774 Molly Fenn died of 'a short but painfull disorder in her bowels'.[18] In the following decade William O'Brien suffered from a 'bilious disorder', which meant that he 'could not spend the night without opium, or spend a day without the most excruciating pain'.[19] Everyone had their own remedy for stomach upsets. In 1796 Thomas Talbot, suffering from 'a diarrhoea' was recommended to try burnt cork mixed with quince marmalade. He found it effective to begin with, but soon reported that 'it now rages as bad as ever'. 'I don't', he continued, 'mean to try any more experiments unless absolutely needfull.'[20] Probably more effective was oxide of bismuth, which Dr Fowler recommended to Mary Talbot in 1813 as being 'of so efficacious and yet so innocent a nature ... that I cannot but earnestly entreat you to give it a trial'.[21]

Problems with teeth were also common, and many people suffered terribly. In 1811 Louisa Lansdowne said that she was 'half crazy' with toothache, and Harriot Acland was very ill a few years later, due to 'a broken tooth, which ... occasioned so much pain, swelling and inflamation that it could not in a long time be extracted'.[22] In most cases the only possible remedy was to have the tooth pulled out, though William O'Brien had a tooth filled in London in 1808.[23] In 1811 Ann Fowler's grandmother, aged eighty-eight, had 'at three different times within a fortnight ... *ten* teeth (all large and firm in her head) drawn'. Afterwards she was reported to be 'quite well, except the inflammation you might suppose, which has been very great'.[24] Two years later Kit Talbot told his sister Jane about a tooth-drawer in Blandford, who was supposed to be skilled: 'But some of the boys whose teeth he has drawn say he had two or three tugs at it, and pulled out a piece of gum at last.'[25] Bribery reconciled children to the necessity of having teeth extracted: in 1805 Henry Talbot told his cousin Mary 'I am very sorry my tooth is not drawn, because of my six shillings I was to have had, that is if I had two teeth drawn', and in 1818 Mary Cole assured her daughter Emma that she had not forgotten her debts 'one shilling for the loose tooth, and half a crown for the tight tooth'.[26]

Infectious diseases, which mainly affected children and young adults, were quite often fatal. In the mid 1740s Bobby Digby (later Admiral Robert Digby), aged about fourteen, was sent to sea 'with the meazles out upon him',[27] which cannot have been popular with his shipmates. In the early nineteenth century there was a widespread belief that the constitutions of delicate children could be improved if they caught the measles. In the summer of 1810 the Talbot children spent some time in Salisbury under the care of Dr Richard Fowler, where they were deliberately infected. Mary Talbot was assured by her stepmother that 'My sister ... tells me [the measles] often do delicate children a great deal of good'.[28] During the months of May, June and July one child after another was infected. All survived, though Kit later claimed that the after-effects of the measles had 'nearly carried me off'.[29]

Many children also caught whooping cough, which was particularly dangerous to infants. Little Harry Fox, the baby son of Henry and Caroline Fox, died in 1746 of 'a hooping cough'.[30] Less than two years later, in the summer of 1748, Lord and Lady Ilchester's children all had the whooping cough, and there were fears that their only son, also called Harry, aged only eleven months, would not survive. Lord Ilchester wrote to tell his brother:

> Mr Thornton [the doctor] says, and I believe with great truth, that Harry will not live long. His cough ... is settled upon his lungs, and by what he spits up Mr Thornton thinks an abcess is formed there, and that 'tis next to impossible he should recover. He imagines he may live a month or two.

Harry's elder sister Susan, who was five years old, was also seriously ill, and her father thought that she was 'going very fast into a consumption ... she looks like a shadow and has a wretched cough'.[31] Ten days later, the children's aunt reported that 'Mr Thornton is always telling them it must terminate in death. Miss Fox looks very thin and ill'.[32] There was not a great deal that the doctors or parents could do, though a change of air was recommended and the children were taken first to Abbotsbury, near the sea (where they grew worse) and then to Redlynch. In spite of Mr Thornton's gloomy predictions, however, none died. In 1804 Thomas and Mary Talbot's four youngest children, whose ages ranged from eighteen months to six years, all had the whooping cough. Mary reported 'though they are not as bad as many are in it, yet it is terrible to see'.[33] The two eldest girls escaped this time, having had the disease in infancy, but by early October they and one of their sisters were suffering from a 'putrid fever'. This could mean typhus or diphtheria, but it seems likely to have been something less serious in this instance. In mid November they were all sent, with their governess, to the Swansea bathing-house, 'for change of air to them after the whooping cough and fevers' and also to clear the house of infection, as their mother was about to give birth to her seventh child.[34]

Even more feared than the measles and whooping cough was scarlet fever or scarlatina, an acute infectious disease characterised by a high fever and a sore throat, with a red rash on the skin. When two of Lord and Lady Ilchester's daughters had scarlet fever in London early in 1748, their brother and sister were sent to their uncle's house in the hope that they would escape the infection. This disease, which Caroline Fox thought 'a sad distemper for children or any body',[35] was quite often fatal – in 1836 Mary Cole reported that it had killed over fifty children in one small town in Glamorgan.[36] Complications following scarlet fever were also common. In 1814 James Frampton, aged twelve, caught scarlet fever at school, and several other children were sent home as a result. James never really recovered, and he died four years later.[37] In 1816 scarlet fever broke out at Harrow when Kit Talbot was pupil at the school. Kit wrote on 19 July to say that Dr Butler, the headmaster, was trying to keep the outbreak a secret, that his boarding house had been 'thoroughly fumigated' four times, and that half the school had already gone home. The remaining boys went on the following day. Kit seems to have been unconcerned by the dangers of the disease, informing his mother, 'It is a great pity that the scarlet fever came so suddenly to Harrow, because if it had not I should in all probability have brought home a prize book.'[38]

Less easy to identify from contemporary descriptions, but also fatal in many cases, was tuberculosis, or consumption as it was usually known at this time. Tuberculosis had been around for centuries, but it did not become a mass killer until the first quarter of the nineteenth century.[39] This was mainly due to the effects of the Industrial Revolution, which brought vast numbers of people from the countryside into the towns and cities where they lived in appallingly overcrowded and insanitary conditions. Though the poor were the most likely to be affected, consumption was no respecter of class divisions, and the disease also killed many children and young adults in wealthy households. It is possible that some of the early deaths of members of the Fox Strangways family in the eighteenth century were due to tuberculosis, but it may be significant that the most easily identifiable case is that of Ellinor Talbot, who died in 1810 aged eight – at precisely the time when the disease was at its peak. Ellinor may have been infected by Miss Smith, a governess who arrived at Penrice Castle in May 1807 and fell ill almost immediately. Early in August, Miss Smith went to her mother in Swansea. She was well enough to return to Penrice towards the end of November, but a month later Mary Talbot noted 'Miss Smith worse'.[40] The governess went back to her mother's house early in the following year, and Mary Talbot went to visit her there on 18 April. Four days later Miss Smith was dead. It was not generally understood at this time that tuberculosis was an infectious disease. Most people believed, instead, that those who developed tuberculosis had a predisposing inherited constitution which could be aggravated by an unwholesome life.[41] As a result, no attempt was made to keep Miss Smith away from the Talbot children. In October 1807, five months after Miss Smith's arrival, six-year-old Ellinor developed a fever. The little girl had never been strong, and she had almost died when a few weeks old. Her health deteriorated during the following year: in May 1808 she was 'very ill', and in December 'very poorly'.[42] By February 1809 Ellinor was 'much worse',[43] and the Talbots decided to take her to Salisbury, to consult Dr Fowler. Susan O'Brien saw Ellinor in April, and thought that she looked 'very ill indeed'.[44] She had a cough, and suffered from intermittent attacks of the ague or fever – classic symptoms of consumption. A reprieve in late April and early May was followed by a relapse. In an undated letter, written at some time in 1809, Mary Talbot told her sister Harriot Frampton:

> Ellinor is very ill with an every day ague, which is worser and worser every day, but I live in hopes of its giving way again to the ague drops, but I cannot help dreading that the shade of an Ellinor, which is now all that is left, will soon depart for [a] mansion more suited to the innocence and patience of such little angels.[45]

Ellinor's fevers were treated with bark.[46] Other remedies were suggested too: in July 1809 Dr Fowler told Mary to stop the bark for a time, and to try 'three or four drops of diluted vitriolic acid twice a day if she perspires at night more profusely than the weather may account for'.[47] But nothing had any lasting effect. In the desperate hope that a change of air would help her, her parents took Ellinor to Clifton early in December, but six weeks later, on 16 January 1810, her father noted in his pocket-book, in the

Greek letters which he reserved for particularly significant entries, 'My dear, dear daughter died'.[48]

After Ellinor's death, Mary watched anxiously over her surviving children, for she had now had good reason to suspect that there was a 'family tendency to consumption'.[49] Her youngest daughter, Emma, was less than three years old when Ellinor died, and Emma, too, was thought to be delicate. Twenty years after a visit to Penrice in 1811, Mary's friend Mrs Burgh remembered Emma's 'delicacy of chest', which had 'made a Welch flannel cloak necessary upon leaving the drawing room [at Penrice] to go to bed'.[50] Mary Talbot and her friends seem to have had great faith in the therapeutic effects of flannel. In fact, none of Ellinor's remaining five sisters[51] appears to have suffered from consumption. Emma died in 1881, aged seventy-five, and her brother and sisters all lived into their sixties, seventies or eighties. But other members of their extended family certainly did suffer from the disease, including Mary Talbot's first cousin and near contemporary Lilley Digby, who died in 1820 aged forty-two, 'her lungs being seriously affected'.[52]

Many children and young adults in the early nineteenth century suffered from tuberculosis. But at least they and their parents had less to fear from another disease that had brought disfigurement and death to so many – both young and old – a century earlier. Smallpox, like tuberculosis, affected all classes of society, and in some years it is thought to have accounted for a tenth of all deaths in Europe. One of Sir Stephen Fox's sons (James) had died of smallpox in 1677 at the age of twelve, and Queen Mary of England died of the disease in 1694, as did the seventeen-year-old Duchess of Grafton in 1742.[53] Those who caught smallpox and recovered could be blinded or permanently scarred. For a girl this could mean the end of all hopes of making a good marriage. The disease became less of a threat in the eighteenth century as a result of the introduction of inoculation. The preventative effect of inducing a mild attack of smallpox, which would immunise the sufferer against more severe forms of the disease, had been known in the East for some time, but the practice was first introduced to England by Lady Mary Wortley Montagu, the wife of the British Consul in Constantinople. In 1717 she had her four-year-old son inoculated by an old woman who was Constantinople's 'General surgeon' for inoculation,[54] and her daughter Mary was then successfully inoculated in London in 1721 at the age of three. The efficacy of the new practice was hotly debated, but several London doctors subsequently adopted and refined the technique with the support and encouragement of the Royal Family.

By the 1740s the children of aristocratic families were inoculated almost as a matter of course. This was usually done when they were between three and five years old, so there was always a risk that the child would be infected before it was thought old enough for the procedure. In 1746 Caroline Fox was 'teized with ... melancholy apprehensions', one of which was the fear that her son Ste – not yet two years old – might catch the smallpox, as the disease was 'vastly about'.[55] Inoculation could be dangerous, and careful preparation of the inoculee was thought to be necessary. This involved fasting and bleeding and the administration of vomits and purgatives to bring the patient to a 'low' condition, which, it was thought, would aid their eventual recovery. Children were usually brought to London to be inoculated – in 1746 Lord Ilchester mentioned 'the inoculation of the children' as one of his reasons for wishing to maintain a house in Town.[56] Susan Fox and her younger sister Charlotte were inoculated in 1747, aged four and three respectively, and they seem to have suffered no serious ill-effects. In the spring of the following year there were plans to inoculate their cousin Ste Fox, but the operation was put off because his mother was pregnant, and it was thought inadvisable that she 'in her condition' should 'undergo so great a flutter and anxiety as that operation must necessarily give her'.[57] There were also fears that the unborn child might catch the disease from his or her brother. Ste was eventually inoculated in the autumn of 1749, without suffering any ill effects. Just over a year later, Lord and Lady Ilchester's son and heir was inoculated at the age of three and a half. In a letter to her brother-in-law, Lady Ilchester referred to the period of the inoculation as 'that melancholy time', and continued: 'I begin to tremble at Harry's operation. I can't help it, though really I believe there is no danger, and hope in God he will do as well as Susan and Cha did.'[58] Again, the inoculation appears to have been a success.

The incidence of smallpox was reduced in the eighteenth century, but it remained a serious threat, and patients would occasionally contract a fatal form of the disease as a result of inoculation.[59] Immunisation became safer at the end of the eighteenth century when Edward Jenner, a country doctor in Gloucestershire, discovered that vaccination with cowpox gave a patient immunity against smallpox. Since cowpox was a mild disease in humans, vaccination was much safer than inoculation with smallpox itself. The discovery was made in 1796, and the practice was taken up remarkably quickly. By 1799 over 5000 people had been vaccinated in England and abroad.[60] In September 1800 Harriot Frampton reported that her sister Lily had decided to take her six-month-old son Henry to Cheltenham 'to Dr Jenner, to have [him] inoculated with the cow pox'.[61] Children were now immunised at a much younger age than fifty years earlier. Thomas and Mary Talbot's children were inoculated at ages ranging from six months to two years. In 1805 Isabella Talbot, aged a little less than a year, was 'innoculated with the cow pock' by the Swansea surgeon John Charles Collins.[62]

For most of the women included in this book, pregnancy and childbirth, and their associated health problems, were the dominant features in their lives for at least ten years after their marriage. Many women did not marry until they were in their mid twenties, but those who married younger had the largest families. Elizabeth, the first Countess of Ilchester, was married at the age of thirteen, but she gave birth to her first child in 1743, ten days before her twentieth birthday. Two years later Lord Ilchester reckoned that his wife was 'likely to lay in once in fifteen or sixteen months'.[63] Lady Ilchester's ninth and last child was born in 1761 when she was thirty-eight. Mary (neé Grady), the second Countess of Ilchester, was also less than twenty years old when her first child was born in 1773. The last of her eight children was born in 1790, a few weeks before her own death at the age of thirty-five. Mary Talbot gave birth to her first child in 1795 when she was nineteen, and to her eighth and last in 1806, when she was thirty. In 1815, when she was nearly thirty-nine and about to marry for the second time, she warned her husband-to-be that she might not have any more children.[64] None of the Fox Strangways ladies had any children after the age of forty, but Lady Sarah Napier was forty-four when she gave birth to her daughter Cecilia, and her mother, the second Duchess of Richmond, bore her last child at the same age. The Duchess had been married at the age of thirteen and had begun to live with her husband in 1722 when she was sixteen. Her first child was born in 1723 and her last in 1750.[65] The Duchess's eldest grandchild, Ste Fox, was born in 1745 and her youngest, Cecilia Napier, in 1791.

Whilst aristocratic couples were usually delighted to discover that a baby was on the way, this was by no means always the case. Pregnancies which came too close together were not good for the mother – in 1785 the health of the second Countess of Ilchester was said to be good 'though she does breed so fast'.[66] When Susan O'Brien heard that her sister-in-law Jane, the wife of the Revd Charles Fox Strangways, was pregnant for at least the fifth time, she commented, 'I am very sorry for … poor Mrs Strangways … on account of her own health, which suffers, and the heaps they already have to provide for'.[67] Contraception was not unknown, and condoms were used, though mainly in order to avoid the clap, or venereal disease. In 1750 Neddy Digby wrote from Rome to tell his uncle Henry Fox: 'Since I have been here I divert myself with an exceeding handsome whore, but *non sine cundum* [not without a condom], for I am grown vastly prudent.' Neddy's prudence did not last long, and most of his letters from the Continent are full of descriptions of the women he had bedded, and the diseases that they had given him.[68] The only other means of preventing conception to which there is a direct reference in the Fox Strangways letters is abstention, which was probably more common. In a letter sent from Bath, perhaps in November 1752, Lady Ilchester told her husband that she missed him, and commented, 'The fear of breeding is the reason given for our not being together, and I will assure you my bed is very narrow'.[69]

Of greater significance, it seems, was the number of children lost as a result of miscarriage and still-birth. Occasionally a miscarriage was brought about deliberately. Early in 1747, suspecting that she might be 'breeding', Caroline Fox complained that she would lose 'a whole summer's comfort again'. A week later she 'took a good dose of physick ... in hopes to send it away, but it has only convinced me my fears prove true'. On the following day, however, she reported 'I am not breeding – is not that clever?' Whether Caroline had really been pregnant is uncertain, but she was certainly prepared to take steps to reverse the situation.[70] More often, however, the reaction to a miscarriage was one of sorrow. The second Duchess of Richmond, mother of Caroline Fox and Sarah Napier, was pregnant twenty-seven times, but fifteen of these pregnancies seem to have ended in miscarriages.[71] Mary Talbot was unusual in that she gave birth to eight healthy babies in twelve years. Her pregnancies are comparatively well documented, and there is no indication of any miscarriage. Other women in the family were less fortunate. Most suffered at least one or two miscarriages, and many lost a succession of babies before they reached their full term.[72]

The first Countess of Ilchester had a miscarriage in late July or early August 1746, about a year after the birth of her daughter Juliana. By the end of November she was pregnant again. Two months later there was another scare. Lord Ilchester told Henry Fox that they were worried that Lady Ilchester would again miscarry, and that she had stayed in bed for a few days. Fox replied 'I am sorry for Lady Ilchester's alarm. They have so often proved no false ones.'[73] This suggests that the previous year's miscarriage had not been the first one. In the event, Lady Ilchester gave birth to a healthy boy – her first son – at the end of July in 1747. Another baby, a girl, was born dead in 1759. When he heard the news, Lord Ilchester's friend Dickie Bateman commented: 'I could have wished it had been ... a boy and that it had lived, but as she [Lady Ilchester] is safe and well I dare say you are satisfied.'[74]

Two generations later, at least three of the daughters of the second Earl of Ilchester lost babies. Harriot Frampton had one miscarriage in 1805 and another in 1807. A premature daughter born in 1814 lived for only two hours. The doctor told the family that the baby had been 'so weak and small ... it was impossible it should live'. A letter written by Harriot's aunt suggests that there may have been other miscarriages too:

> Poor Harriot bears the loss with great firmness and composure, as she always has done all her trials and former disappointments, and I hope after a time will not feel it as a misfortune.[75]

Harriot's two younger sisters also lost several children. In an undated letter Charlotte Lemon wrote in the early stages of one pregnancy that:

> I am going to try what profound quiet will do ... My repeated miscarriages have so weakened me, and I have so little recovered my strength from the last, that I feel nothing but great care will make me go on now.[76]

The other sister, Louisa, suffered one miscarriage just over three months after her marriage to Henry Petty in 1808. She was 'taken *ill* at Holland House' early in July and ordered to rest. A few days later she went to Court, 'but could not get through it' and nearly fainted. She lost the baby. By the end of November Louisa was pregnant again, and she complained, 'I am not allowed to walk or exert myself at all, which is a very new state to be reduced to'.[77] Two weeks later she was 'laid up on the sofa'.[78] She was also 'very sick' and said that she felt 'very fat, lazy, stuffy etc.'[79] In spite of all her care, however, Louisa lost this baby too, in May or June of the following year. Yet another miscarriage followed, before Louisa's first surviving child, a son, was born in March 1811.

Once a pregnancy had been confirmed, the parents had to take a decision about the best place for the mother-to-be to give birth. The country was in general considered to be healthier than the town, but medical assistance was closer at hand – and possibly more skilled – in London, and many women chose to lie in there. It became usual in the Georgian period for a woman to be attended by a professional man-midwife or accoucheur when she gave birth, rather than the old-fashioned 'granny midwife' who would have helped her own mother or grandmother.[80] When in 1771 Harriot Acland's first child was born unexpectedly early at the house of an acquaintance in Devon, a man-midwife, Mr Patch, was sent for.[81] Harriot's mother did not approve of Mr Patch, but she was assured by the Aclands that he 'would not suffer by being put in competition with a Hunter or a Hawkins',[82] and that he was 'an exceeding clever man in his profession'.[83] Most of the children of the first Countess of Ilchester were born in London, and in 1746 her husband mentioned 'Lady Ilchester's breeding' as an additional reason for keeping a house in Town.[84] Timing was important, to ensure that the journey from the country did not endanger the mother-to-be and her unborn child. In November 1746, when Lady Ilchester was just a few weeks pregnant, her husband wrote from Redlynch to tell his brother:

> Lady Ilchester does not go to Melbury as was designed, but will stay here till she is quick. It was thought the journey thither might hurt her … Her Ladyship's pregnancy makes an alteration in our journey to London. I did intend coming up to the meeting of Parliament after Christmas; she won't move till the latter end of February.[85]

Lord and Lady Ilchester's first son was born in London on 29 July 1747. In mid October 1751, pregnant again, Lady Ilchester had an uncomfortable journey to Town, suffering from 'terrible' rheumatic pains, and thinking with 'great uneasiness … of what I must go through before I can expect any perfect ease'.[86] Her second son was born in London early in December.

By the mid eighteenth century the medical advice that was available in country towns had improved significantly, and there was less incentive to make the journey to the capital. The first Countess of Ilchester's two youngest children, Fanny and Charles, were born at Redlynch, in 1755 and 1761. Most, if not all, of the children of the second Earl and Countess of Ilchester were born (from 1773 to 1792) in the country, at Redlynch. In the next generation, Mary Talbot's children were all born at Penrice. In 1801 Mary's sister Lily, with no permanent home of her own, chose to give birth to her first child at Melbury, where plenty of help and advice was available, as her stepmother had two small sons. Another sister, Louisa Petty, told Mary in April 1809 that she wanted to be confined at her country house, Bounds in Kent, as she would be 'baked alive' if she stayed in London during the summer.[87] At least two of Charlotte Lemon's children were born in Dorset, at Deans Leaze near Blandford, and Harriot Frampton's children were probably all born at her Dorset home, Moreton.

Most births were uncomplicated. In 1749 Henry Fox described the birth of his third son, who was to grow up to become the politician Charles James Fox:

> After a safe quick labour, which lasted but from a little after nine till within a few minutes of twelve last night, Lady Caroline was brought to bed of a boy. He was a good deal wasted and is weakly, but likely to live. His skin hangs all shrivelled about him, his eyes stare, he has a black head of hair, and 'tis incredible how much like a monkey he looked before he was dressed … He now looks like other children do, and crys like a cat as other children do.[88]

In 1771 Harriot Acland was 'brought to bed of a fine, jolly boy'. The Aclands were unprepared for this event, which took place sooner than they had expected. As the baby's father informed his mother-in-law:

> She [Harriot] ate last night a great supper, was in remarkable spirits, and went to bed with as little expectation of what happened as ever she did in her life. This morning about 4 o'clock she complained to me of what she called a colic,

> but I, luckily guessing what it was, sent instantly for Mr Patch [the man-midwife], who in about three hours arrived, and in an hour more all was over.[89]

Even the wealthiest and best-attended woman could, however, die in childbirth. Every eighteenth-century woman would have known of a friend or relation who had died in this way – as Louisa Petty wrote in 1809 when she was pregnant: 'Life is always uncertain, and in my state doubly so'.[90] The first wife of Henry, Lord Digby died in this way early in 1765, after less than eighteen months of marriage. She had just come to London from the country.

> [She] was so tired with her journey and so feverish she went to bed, but got no sleep. Her fever went off but she was so nervous that she had fits of convulsions so strong and so frequent that she died in a fortnight.[91]

Lord Digby's mother told her niece Susan O'Brien that 'Poor Harry' was 'indeed most excessively shocked with her death, and had a very great loss, for she was perfectly agreeable to him in every respect'.[92] Mary Talbot usually remained 'charmingly well' during her pregnancies, and recovered quickly after the births of her children, but she almost died in 1803. Six weeks after her only son was born she began to suffer from 'nervous spasms'; she could not sleep and grew weaker and weaker. Her sister Harriot Frampton hurried from Dorset to Penrice to nurse Mary, and – according to family tradition – thereby saved her sister's life. But Mary's sister-in-law, Caroline, Countess of Ilchester, died quite unexpectedly in 1819, two hours after the birth of a daughter. As Susan O'Brien, who was at Melbury at the time, wrote in her journal 'This happy house [became] in a moment a house of desolation'. She told Mary Talbot:

> Poor Caroline's wish was to have a girl, but short was her joy ... Her death is wholly unaccounted for by anything belonging to her situation, and the only conjecture that can be made is that some blood vessel had burst in her head ... It is the saddest and most bitter misfortune to us all.[93]

There are few references in the letters to the experience of giving birth, though Mary Talbot did complain in 1795 that her stepmother had not told her what to expect:

> Pray tell Maria she gave me but a poor idea of what I was to suffer at *the time*, and several things disapointed me very much, particularly as she told me it was not a sickening pain, but I was *dreadfully sick* for many hours before, every *paroxysm* brought on violent sickness.[94]

In 1764 Sarah Bunbury informed Susan O'Brien that 'the Duchess of Marlborough is come to Town to pig, and Lady Warren also'.[95] This was not, however, an expression that would have been used in polite society to refer to a woman who was about to give birth. For most of the eighteenth century the most usual terms were 'lying in' or being 'brought to bed'. In 1818, however, Susan O'Brien noted, in a list of changes since 1760, 'No one can say *breeding* or *with child* or *lying in* without being thought indelicate. *In the family way* and *confinement* have taken their place'.[96] The first use of *confinement* in the sources used for this book comes in 1796, when Thomas Talbot told Michael Hicks Beach that 'my dear wife expects to be confined every day'.[97] *Confinement* was an appropriate term, because the new mother would be expected to stay at home for at least a month after the birth of her child. In 1771 Lady Ilchester accused her son-in-law John Dyke Acland of imprudence and indecency in proposing to move his wife ten miles to Killerton, the family home, less than a month after she had given birth to their first child. Acland replied that he could not see the difference between 'going ten miles from one house to another' and 'going ten miles on the turnpike road airing'.[98] More often, however, the new mother barely went beyond her bedchamber and dressing room, where she would receive close relatives or female friends. It was not unusual for these rooms to be redecorated in anticipation of a birth – in 1742, before the birth of her first child, the first Countess of Ilchester wrote from London to tell her husband, 'I am quite happy to have my room furnished by the time I lye in, because all the Town will see it then'.[99]

The ceremony of 'churching' (formally named the 'Thanksgiving of Women after Childbirth') traditionally marked a new mother's re-emergence into the outside world.[100] In 1798 Mary Talbot went to church for the first time a month after the birth of her third daughter, Christiana. On 16 September 1801 she gave birth to her fifth daughter, Ellinor. Nine days later she went into her dressing room (which was also used as a sitting room) for the first time, and on 2 October she went out 'airing'. Vistors arrived on 7 October, and on the following day Mary went downstairs and sat with them in the evening. On 18 October – a month after the birth – Mary intended to go to church, but was prevented from doing so by bad weather.[101] Mary's only son was born on 10 May 1803. Five days later she dined in her dressing room for the first time, and on 20 May her husband reported 'My dear wife ... is able to walk into her dressing room, and back again into her bedroom at a *proper* hour in the evening'.[102] On 28 May, Mary went out 'airing', but she was then taken ill. According to her stepmother, 'her illness was entirely owing to a cold caught by airing too soon after her confinement'.[103] Mary was unable to go out again until the end of June. It was still usual in the early nineteenth century for a new mother to wait for at least month after giving birth before travelling. In February 1800, after the birth of her son, Elizabeth Talbot was said to be intending to stay at

Melbury (where the child had been born) 'until after the month is up and she is fit to travel'.[104] In 1808 Elizabeth was 'preparing for Melbury' a month after the birth of her first daughter in Weymouth.[105]

If possible, a woman's mother or other female friends or relatives would stay with her for several weeks before and after the birth. In 1748 Joanna Cheeke was asked to go to London to keep Lady Ilchester company, 'as [she] will be much alone during her lying in'.[106] The daughters of the second Countess of Ilchester particularly regretted the early death of their mother at such times. Their stepmother, who was only two years older than her eldest stepdaughter, was not a satisfactory substitute. In 1796 Elizabeth wrote to Harriot:

> I am quite pleased with Lady Ilchester for having offered to attend Mary's *accouchement*. It is *for the first time* trying to replace the person whose place she occupies in maternal care, and though Mary must feel the difference *infinite*, yet it is still doing all that lays in Lady Ilchester's power, and as such she has the thanks of *my* heart. I hope you will go, for though you would be of no *use* at the *moment*, you would be a much greater comfort, both before and after, than anybody.[107]

In 1801 Mary had her aunt Harriot Acland to nurse her when Ellinor was born, and her sister Harriot Frampton travelled from Dorset to look after her when she became ill after Kit's birth two years later. Another sister, Elizabeth Feilding, was at Penrice when Isabella and Emma Talbot were born, in 1804 and 1806. A quarter of a century later, Mary spent much of her time hurrying from one married daughter's house to another to assist at the births of her numerous grandchildren.

A monthly nurse was usually employed to look after the new mother and her baby. At the births of her first children, Mary Talbot was helped by 'Nanny' Longford, who came from Redlynch and had nursed Mary's mother during her last illness. On 19 March 1798 Thomas Talbot wrote from Penrice to say that he had just sent a servant to the New Passage (across the Bristol Channel) 'to meet the old nurse that has always attended my dear Mary on these occasions'.[108] Christiana Talbot was born on 14 April, and the nurse left again in the Talbots' coach on 14 May.[109] Such nurses were often passed on from one sister to another. In 1809, three months before the expected birth of her baby, Louisa Petty told Mary Talbot, 'I am to have Harriot's nurse, and I hope I have got Anna Green to take care of it [the baby] when it arrives, dear little thing'. But Anna's mother persuaded her to change her mind, and Louisa wrote again a couple of weeks later, 'I am so vexed ... I don't know what to do. It was so comfortably settled, and I felt so sure she would have taken as good care of it whether I lived or not, which I should never feel with a stranger.'[110] Later in the year, when she was pregnant again, Louisa told Mary that Harriot had offered her 'a delightful nurse'.[111] Once the monthly nurse had gone, other nursemaids would usually take over: in 1811 Charlotte Lemon wrote before the birth of her first child that 'Nurse Whitcombe arrived yesterday, and I am provided in all other respects, so my mind is quite easy. The other nurse is not young, and I like what I hear of her'.[112] Nurse Whitcombe was also with Charlotte for the birth of her daughter in 1816. Her arrival, a fortnight before the baby was due, reassured Charlotte, who wrote that it was 'a great satisfaction to have her in my power'.[113]

Before the 1760s it was usual for aristocratic women to employ wet-nurses to suckle their babies. Convention prevented them from feeding their own infants, and no satisfactory alternative to human milk existed.[114] It seems unlikely that either Susanna Strangways Horner or the first Countess of Ilchester breast-fed any of their own children. In a codicil to her will, written in 1789, Lady Ilchester left three guineas to Nurse Bollman who had suckled her youngest daughter, Fanny.[115] By the next generation, however, things were changing, and the fashionable physicians in London were beginning to recommend that the mother herself should breast-feed her newly-born child if at all possible. In 1768 Sarah Bunbury was the first woman of her family to breast-feed.[116] Whether the second Countess of Ilchester breast-fed her babies is unknown, but her sister-in-law Harriot Acland certainly fed at least one of her own children – in 1774 Harriot's mother commented, 'I am glad she succeeds in being a nurse'.[117] Most, if not all, of the daughters of the second Earl and Countess of Ilchester breast-fed their children as a matter of course, if they were able to do so. In September 1795, a month after the birth of her first baby, Mary Talbot wrote to her sister:

> [She] has a pretty nose for a baby, and a *beautiful mouth*, which Mon Ami [the baby's father] is afraid will be quite spoiled by sucking, as he thinks it widens her mouth ... I hope nothing will happen to prevent my suckling Mary till long after Christmas, else I think she might as well be brought up by hand.[118]

Mary went on to ask if her stepmother, Maria, Countess of Ilchester, was suckling her own little son William, who had been born in May. All did not, however, go smoothly during the next few months, for Mary wrote again at the beginning of February in the following year:

> I was to have begun this letter with an account whether my affairs went on right again. They have been very well ever since, one day excepted, when we had some tremendous thunder and lightning, which happened suddenly while the little darling was sucking and startled me so much that my milk went away, every drop, but all came right again in the evening.[119]

Shortly after this letter was written, Mary's husband began pressing her to wean the baby. Soon, little Mary was being given 'pudding', and Thomas wrote to tell his wife 'I rejoice to hear she takes it [the pudding] so kindly, and hope you'll let her have nothing else. Do, my dear life, be mindful of what is to come, and let my dear darling be content with her pudding.'[120] Presumably Thomas was anxious for his wife to stop breast-feeding in the hope that she would soon produce his much-wanted son. In fact, Mary must have become pregnant around the time when this letter was written, for her next baby, another daughter, was born in mid November 1796. This one was breast-fed until well into the next year. Harriot Strangways wrote in August 1797 to ask if the baby had been weaned yet. The Talbots were planning a visit to Ireland, and Harriot commented that 'it must be impossible to go any voyage with a child that is nursing'.[121] In July 1806, when Harriot had a baby of her own, her aunt Susan O'Brien informed Elizabeth Feilding, 'Harriot concludes her nursing this month, and the next, I suppose, will issue forth, resplendent for her long seclusion'.[122] A lady would not be expected to breast-feed in public, and she would therefore stay at home with the baby until it was weaned. When this took place would depend to some extent on personal preference, but between three months and a year old was usual.[123] Early in November 1748 Charlotte Digby wrote to her brother Lord Ilchester, 'I am glad the dear little white man bore his weaning so well and continues so well after it'.[124] The 'dear little white man' was Lord Ilchester's first son, Lord Stavordale, who had been born on 29 July 1747. The child's first artificial food would be pap, made of bread or oatmeal moistened with water or milk. Cows' milk was generally used, though asses' milk was also thought to be good for babies. In a letter which was probably written early in 1774, the first Countess of Ilchester reported that her little granddaughter Elizabeth 'sucks a great deal, eats a little pap, and crows'.[125]

If a mother was unable to breast-feed her baby, she would have to find a wet-nurse. Mary Talbot's son was born on 10 May 1803. By the end of the first week in June Mary was seriously ill and too weak to feed the baby, so a wet-nurse was brought in. The nurse continued to feed the baby until April 1804, when she was paid £26 5*s*. for her services. Mary seems to have fed her youngest daughter, Emma, for three months, after which a wet-nurse was again employed.[126] By the early nineteenth century, however, artificial methods of feeding had become more reliable and a wet-nurse was not always thought to be necessary, even if the mother could not feed the baby herself. The little son of the third Earl of Ilchester and his wife was born at Melbury on 7 January 1816. His mother fed him to begin with, but on 21 February Susan O'Brien reported: 'The nursing here did not succeed and little Stavy [Lord Stavordale] has been fed for some days. Lady Ilchester's milk did not agree with him.' A fortnight later, Susan wrote again, 'Dear little Stavy has no wet-nurse, but is going on as well as possible without one, as [he] eats and sleeps and laughs and grows'.[127]

Even in the wealthiest families, most parents at this period could expect to lose one or two children in infancy or early childhood. Many lost more. Some survived the perils of childhood and grew into young adults, but died before marrying and starting families of their own. Sometimes the cause of death is clear – smallpox, whooping-cough and consumption were comparatively easily diagnosed, but many children endured months and years of illness, without anyone really knowing what was the matter with them, or what should be done to help them.

Susanna Strangways Horner gave birth to several children, but all died young apart from her daughter Elizabeth. Elizabeth, the first Countess of Ilchester, bore nine children, three boys and six girls. The second and third daughters died young: Juliana in 1749, aged three, and Charlotte in 1755 at eleven. In neither case is there any indication of the cause of death, and neither child seems to have been particularly sickly. In the next generation, the second Countess of Ilchester gave birth to six girls and two boys. Of these, two died in infancy. The first son, Stephen, died in 1777 when he was only a few months old, and the youngest daughter, Susan, lived for twenty months. Even though her mother died a few weeks after her birth, little Susan was said to be 'a thriving child' at the age of five months.[128] Six months later, however, she was 'very poorly, does not grow at all better, has bad nights'. 'I believe', wrote her grandmother 'her disorder is in her head, as she cannot sit up and holds her hands to each side of her head.'[129] In the summer of 1791 Susan's condition improved, but she was ill again in December, and in January 1792 her governess wrote:

> We had the misfortune to lose our dear little child Lady Susan Strangways. She died after fifteen days' illness, at five in the morning ... aged one year and eight months. I watched her almost constantly, that is eighteen hours of the twenty-four. Much affected at her loss – God preserve the other six to be a blessing to themselves and to all that know them![130]

Charles Fox Strangways, the youngest brother of the second Earl of Ilchester, and his wife had six sons and two daughters, all of whom lived at least into their late twenties, most into their fifties or sixties. Charles's sister Lucy and her husband Stephen Digby had three sons and two daughters. All of them survived childhood, but Kenelm, who seems always to have been sickly, died in 1809 at the age of twenty-four. Less fortunate was Lucy's sister Harriot Acland. She and her husband John Dyke Acland had four children, two girls and two boys. The first-born son and one daughter died in infancy. The second son, who was named after his father, died in 1785 at the age of seven. Only one daughter, Kitty, lived long enough to marry and have a family of her own – and she died two years before her mother. Fanny, the youngest daughter of the first Earl and Countess, also had two sons and two daughters. Three lived into middle age, but the eldest, Eliza, died at the age of sixteen, having been ill for some time. Her cousin Mary Talbot commented 'she was a good-hearted little girl, but I hear she suffered so much that it was quite a release'.[131] The survival rate of the children of the second Earl of Ilchester and his siblings therefore varied considerably from family to family – from a quarter (Harriot Acland) to all (Charles Fox Strangways).

In the next generation, too, some families were more fortunate than others. Lily, the eldest daughter of the second Earl and Countess, had three children by two husbands, and all lived. The three children of Lily's younger sister Louisa, who became Marchioness of Lansdowne, also survived, as did the four children of their only brother, the third Earl of Ilchester (though the elder of his two sons died unmarried at the age of twenty-one). Harriot Frampton, another sister, had four children, but lost one son, James, in 1818 when he was sixteen.[132] Mary Talbot had the largest family. Like her mother and paternal grandmother, she gave birth to many more girls than boys – seven daughters and only one son. One daughter, Christiana (known as Tina), died in 1808 aged ten 'after a most lingering and painful illness, which she bore with patience worthy the imitation of those of riper years, and which will ever impress the hearts of her family with the tenderest regrets'. Exactly what was the matter with Tina is unclear, but she had suffered a good deal over the years. In 1804 her parents took her to Bath to have 'an excrescence' removed from her face. A caustic substance was applied on 4 December, and on 24 January 1805 Mary Talbot noted in her pocket-book that 'Poor Christiana had her lump taken off'. By the end of February she was 'almost entirely well'. Early in 1808, however, Mary was again anxious about Tina, who had begun to cough. It is possible that she was suffering from tuberculosis. By 8 March she was 'speechless, but sensible'. She died two days later. 'Her last draught', wrote Mary, 'was from my hand, and her last kiss on my cheek.'[133] Two years after Tina's death her sister Ellinor died, probably of consumption. But the others all survived, and Agnes Porter thought that the Talbots were lucky to lose so few children.[134]

The most unfortunate parents were Mary Talbot's sister Charlotte and her husband Sir Charles Lemon. They had three children, all of whom died young. Charley, the first-born, survived for only a year. In November 1812 his father wrote sadly:

> We have lost our darling child. He had latterly acquired so many little engaging ways of interesting any body who took notice of him, and had occupied so much of our time and happiness, that his loss has made us feel very desolate. It was so like a dream that our happiness was complete but three days ago, and has now arrived so sudden a shock that it is difficult to believe it has really passed away so rapidly ... Our dear boy had been some days extremely feverish from a cold caught and irritation from his teeth, in recovering from which he fell into a stupor from which nothing could raise him, and yesterday morning at nine o'clock expired without a groan or convulsion, and with the placid countenance of an angel.[135]

Charlotte was already pregnant again when Charley died, and another son, also named Charles, was born in the following May. Then, in 1816, Charlotte gave birth to a daughter, Augusta. At first the baby thrived. When Augusta was nine months old her mother described her as 'the nicest fat little ball you ever saw, with a very pretty mouth and brilliant eyes, and a lovely complexion and *so* good humoured'. But two years later Augusta had 'an eruption' on her face, and in the following year her health deteriorated:

> Her neck shewed symptoms of inflammation, and it has risen *most* rapidly, which they say shews great strength of constitution. She has suffered much pain from the utter inability of moving her head or being able to bear the least jerk ... She is much weaker and grown very thin.

For a year the little girl was unable to sit up, or even to lift her head. She then seems to have recovered to some extent, thought she continued to suffer from what was thought to be rheumatism. At about eight years old she was reported to be 'quite stout' and her mother had begun to worry about her for other reasons:

> She is grown so imperious in her manner, and so fond of power and aware of her own consequence from the fuss that naturally has been made about her health after such dreadful illnesses, that she sometimes poses me how to act, as I find constant finding fault (which really she unfortunately deserves at present) only makes her hard.[136]

But Augusta's recovery was short-lived, and she died in May 1825 at Aix-les-Bains, apparently as a result of 'a dysentery, from a cold caught on her journey'.[137] Just under a year later Augusta's brother Charles, who was now his parents' only surviving child, was tragically drowned in 1826 whilst swimming in the schoolboys' bathing place at Harrow.[138] The boy's parents were devastated and Charlotte, who was already ill when the news of Charles's death arrived, outlived her son by less than six weeks. She was nursed during her last illness by her sister Mary, who 'saw her sink into her grave with the utmost resignation to the will of God, though unable to support the grief of losing her two children'.[139]

In the third quarter of the seventeenth century almost 40 per cent of the children born to English peers died before the age of fifteen. By 1830 the proportion had fallen to less than 20 per cent.[140] The reasons for this 50 per cent decline in mortality are not clear. There seems to have been no great medical advance, apart from the introduction of inoculation against smallpox, which undoubtedly saved a large number of lives. But while smallpox killed fewer children, more began to die as a result of contracting tuberculosis. It has been suggested that more children in aristocratic families survived after the mid eighteenth century because their mothers were becoming more directly involved in their day-to-day care.[141] In addition to better parental supervision, improved nutrition and hygiene undoubtedly helped as well. Amongst the poorer inhabitants of the countryside – and, to an even greater extent of the towns – the mortality rate was much higher.

Once the dangerous years of childhood were past, life-expectancy improved dramatically. In the eighteenth and nineteenth centuries, as in the twenty-first, women tended to live longer than men. If they survived the years of child-bearing they could reasonably expect to live into their sixties. With one or two exceptions, the female members of the Fox Strangways family lived even longer, with an average age at death of around seventy for the eighteenth-century generations. Susanna Strangways Horner lived to the age of sixty-eight, and her daughter Elizabeth to sixty-nine. The average rose in the nineteenth century: Mary Talbot was seventy-nine when she died, whilst her daughters lived an average of seventy-three years.[142]

Elizabeth, Countess of Ilchester, spent much of her time with her mother during the latter's last years – an experience that she often found extremely trying, though she attempted to do her duty, writing to her husband from Bath in 1752, 'I feel sorrier for her than for myself, for she is so often confused she must suffer extremely, and that vexes me'.[143] Forty years later, Elizabeth's daughter Susan O'Brien experienced similar feelings when she stayed at Melbury with her mother, who had been crippled by rheumatism for many years:

> The situation we found her in at Melbury in November, and in which she has continued ever since, is a most melancholy one – suffering and helpless in every thing. Life must be a burthen and misery, so it appears to me in health, but how different to the sufferer. Every thing comes on by degrees, and we are used to one distress before another comes on. Nature's love of existance still makes life on any terms desirable.[144]

Lady Ilchester's health improved a little after this, and she lived for another year. Susan noted with relief that her mother had appeared to suffer no pain, and that she had come downstairs 'and passed her time in her usual manner' on the day before her death.[145]

Some women lived into extreme old age in surprisingly good health. In 1810 Susan O'Brien visited her parents' old friend Joanna Melliar when she was nearly ninety years old, and found her 'very well, very lively, reads without spectacles, not in the least deaf and seems to enjoy herself very much'. Nine years later, however, Joanna was 'quite gone – quite a miserable object'. After seeing her, Susan commented:

> Poor woman! The sight of her would, I think, prevent one wishing to live to be a hundred – unable to walk, no memory left, and a most melancholy, withered and wretched appearance.[146]

On hearing the news of Joanna's death a few months after her visit, Susan described it as 'a happy event for her and her friends'.[147] Susan herself, the first-born of her family, outlived all her sisters. In 1815, after the death of Harriot Acland, she wrote 'Older than any, ought to have gone first, but have such good health that I may be (as an old woman once said) left at last like a pollard in the copse'.[148] Five years later, feeling 'very unwell and very old', Susan thought that 'A short illness like this would be a most happy termination for me ... A helpless old woman is a dismal prospect.'[149] In particular, Susan dreaded losing her independence. In 1824 she wrote:

> I hope my eyes won't fail. If not, I may do pretty well, else I shall be very sorry to live and have a companion to read and take care of me for a salary. A hired companion has long been my dread.[150]

In the following year she wrote, 'I dread having someone to take care of me. I dread being left alone to servants. I can only say "le plus grand bonheur des mortels est d'être mortel" [the greatest good fortune of mortals is to be mortal].'[151] Alert and active almost to the end, though her sight and hearing were failing, Susan continued to write regularly in her journal until three weeks before her death in 1827. She was not 'left alone to servants', and instead complained about the never-ending stream of female friends and relations who came to 'look after' her, when she would much rather have been left alone. In 1826 she told Mary Cole, 'I am rather tired of being ... an invalide, or reckoned so. I have been so little used to being taken care of and told when it's too cold or too windy to go out that I don't relish it at all'.[152]

Several women also had to look after elderly and sick husbands and other male relations. Charlotte Digby seems to have had a terrible time in the early 1750s after her ninety-year-old father-in-law Lord Digby suffered two strokes. Physically, he was in a bad state, and almost totally deaf, so that it was very difficult to talk to him. He had deteriorated mentally, too, and Charlotte hardly dared to leave him for fear that his youngest son, Wriothesley, would persuade Lord Digby to leave a large share of his estates to him, thus disinheriting Charlotte's sons. By the 1770s Charlotte's brothers were both in poor health. Lord Holland was 'become almost childish' by the spring of 1772, and in 1774 his elder brother was 'seized with the palsy' – in other words, he had a stroke. This led to 'great interruption of business' with him or with Lady Ilchester.[153] For the next two years Lord Ilchester's life was 'continually declining'. By the time he died in 1776, 'the sad situation he was reduced to, and what he suffered, could alone reconcile his family to his loss'.[154] Mary Talbot nursed her first husband through many years of illness. He was almost thirty years older than she was, and suffered many attacks – perhaps epileptic fits or small strokes – in his last years. Thomas's son remembered him as

> More or less an invalid, and suffering occasionally from dreadful attacks of the head, which produced temporary insensibility accompanied by contortions of the eyes and countenance painful to look at.

By 1806 – seven years before his death – Susan O'Brien found Thomas 'in a sad state, his intellect going, his memory gone'.[155] Kit wrote that his mother had treated her husband 'much like a child', and that he was 'not allowed' to do many things that he wished.[156] William O'Brien's health also declined for several years before his death: he became unsteady on his feet and suffered several bad falls. He also became depressed, writing to Mary Talbot in 1810:

> I am ... so nervous that I am hardly myself. I am, when once I begin, so sensitive that I smart and agonise at every pore, and I fancy every thing that I most abhor, and am given up to all manner of horrible imaginings. Then I go a-fishing for affronts and plans and designs against me, and I have a dreadful casting-net that, when it once goes into the Slough of Depond, never fails to draw up every thing that can dismay or disgust.[157]

In October 1813 William was very ill, and his wife wrote that she hated 'to see him suffer so much'. She felt 'it is only by him that I hold to this world or to happiness in it, and I see his health sensibly so declining that it almost breaks my heart'.[158]

Without any of the diagnostic tools used by doctors today, such as X-ray machines and scanners – or even thermometers or stethoscopes – it was often extremely difficult for the medical men of the eighteenth and early nineteenth centuries to discover what was wrong with their patients. Physical examinations were usually perfunctory: the doctor would ask about the patient's medical history, and he would study their outward appearance, observing the colour of their skin and looking for signs of spots of a rash, or of any swelling or inflammation. He might take the patient's pulse and listen for any cough or breathing problems. He might also examine the patient's evacuations – phlegm, urine and faeces, which were thought to give the best evidence of inner health or sickness. In the mid 1740s Lady Ilchester told her husband 'Harry [their son] is grown prodigiously and looks delightfully. His stools are quite right, I never saw anything so fair.' At about the same time Caroline Fox was worred about her son Ste, because his stools appeared 'slymy'.[159] In 1748 Charlotte Digby wrote to Henry Fox about the latter's son and Lord Ilchester's children, who all had bad coughs:

> Mr Thornton won't allow your boy's to be a hooping cough but a consumptive one, and thinks the lungs ulcerated from the flegm he brings up being a little discolored ... Miss Fox was by all accounts very ill a few hours at Abbotsbury – My Lady thought the black stools were occationed by a great quantity of elder-root she had taken for her cough, but Mr Thornton says they are not.[160]

Exploratory surgery was, in most cases, out of the question, though post-mortem operations were sometimes carried out. The cause of Charlotte Digby's daughter's death in 1753 was unknown until her body was opened, and the surgeon discovered a tumour weighing three pounds.[161] And after the death of William Davenport Talbot in 1800:

> Dr Fraser and Mr Rust proposed opening the head. As the family had been afflicted with epileptic fits, they thought it ought to be done for the sake of the child he has left.[162]

In general, surgery of any kind was seen as a last resort, to be avoided if at all possible. When Lord Ilchester fell from his horse and broke his leg in 1808, his stepmother and friends decided not to send for a London doctor to make sure that the medical men had set his leg properly, because 'it most probably must renew the whole business by opening and examining the injured part, which would occasion much pain and other inconveniences'.[163] Where men were concerned, the most commonly performed operation was 'cutting for the stone' – lithotomy, or the removal of stones or gravel from the bladder. The Sherborne game books record that in 1756 'Edward, Lord Digby, was cut for the stone – and recovered'.[164] The London doctors John Truesdale and John Ranby had recommended Mr Hawkins, who used a newly improved version of a surgical instrument known as a gorget, and 'cut with so much certainty that he did not lose one patient in fifty ... [Mr Truesdale said] his practice at present was very great and that he cut at least once a week'.[165]

In the absence of any effective anaesthetic, all kinds of surgery were acutely painful. Poor Joanna Cheeke suffered agonies when she had problems with one of her legs in 1750. Lord Ilchester wrote to his brother:

> I am excessively shocked to think what poor Miss Cheeke suffers. Her leg has been cut deep into the bone in pursuance to Mr Ranby's advice which, I believe, was good advice; the operation excessive painfull, so are the dressings, and as I understand the meddling with the bone, as Mr Clarke is forced to meddle with it, is a most horrible sensation.[166]

In 1799 Susan O'Brien went through an operation to remove a lump from one of her breasts. She was extremely reluctant to submit to the knife, but she remembered only too well how her sister Lucy had suffered before she died of breast cancer in 1787, even though she had had 'the best advice'. Susan had been ill in the spring of 1798, and had consulted the surgeon Adair Hawkins about a swelling in her breast. Hawkins had prescribed leeches and a warm salt-water bath, but these had done no good. In October he warned Susan that she might have to go to London for advice 'though ... he does not profess himself an advocate for operations of *the knife* when they can be avoided'. Susan decided to try alternative medicine first:

> We had the strongest recomendation from Mrs Drax of a Mrs Hobson, who had done a surprising cure of a complaint in the breast in her family ... I was the more inclined to try her as I understood her methods were gentle and would not occasion much suffering. I feel more willing to consult a quack than a surgeon, who has but one thing to propose – and that too terrible to bear the thoughts of. How foolish this is! To prefer ignorance and an old woman's nonsense to science, skill and good sense, yet I cannot help it. I cannot look at my complaint fairly as what it probably is, but still dream on and flatter myself that the well-informed are mistaken and that the ignorant will perform wonders. I hate myself for such folly, yet without the old woman I should never have been perswaded to go to London.

So Susan left Stinsford on 8 December, to stay with her cousin Colonel Stephen Digby at his house in Richmond Park. She hardly expected to see her home again. A week later she saw Mrs Hobson, 'who thought my complaint not bad, and gave me her medicines, which she said would soon cure me'. The doctors, Adair Hawkins and Sir Walter Farquhar, were surprisingly tolerant, and 'were not against my trying [the medicines] and thought they might be harmless, if not useful'. Early in March Susan saw Mrs Hobson again. The old woman 'seemed surprised at the little effect [her medicines] had had in so long a time' and gave Susan some more.

Later in the same month, when the medicines were still failing to work, Susan consulted another surgeon, Charles Blicke. A few days later Blicke, Hawkins and Farquhar met together:

> After a great deal of talking and examination [they] decided *my fate*. That I must have my breast cut or expect the swelling, which they consider as a cancer, to encrease and occasion me greater suffering than the operation, which Mr Blicke says will be without difficulty. That is to say, without difficulty to him – but for me! Thus am I dashed from the hopes of Mrs Hobson's cure to the worst state of suffering mortality, or to a dreadful operation.

Susan was unable to make a decision, but her husband went to London 'To find a house for me to end my life in – for I have but little hopes of life, nor any great wish for it, if I become a maimed, mutilated wretch'. 'And how', she continued, 'can I be otherwise if I consent to such an operation?' She was persuaded to consult Mr Stott, who used electricity to treat his patients. Susan had no great hope that Mr Stott would be able to do anything, commenting before she saw him that 'it will either be *kill* or *cure*'. She did not like Mr Stott when she met him, taking 'quite an antipathy to him and his odious, impertinent behaviour'. Susan had 'not the plague of any doubt' that she did not want to be treated by the unpleasant Mr Stott, who 'gave no great hope of success, or any encouragement to put myself under his care'. She understood that she would 'suffer great pain and confinement, and after living a twelvemonth near him in Bloomsbury [would] be perhaps as well as I am now'.

Susan finally agreed to the operation. Unlike Fanny Burney, who was to go through a similar ordeal twelve years later, she was given several days' advance warning. She talked to her family and settled her affairs, commenting: 'it is like ordering one's own funeral'. Susan was particularly worried about what would happen to her husband if she were to die as a result of the operation, but her sister Harriot assured her that 'They looked on him as one of themselves, and that he should experience every sort of attention and assistance from her in case of my loss'. On the morning of 22 April 1799, the day of the operation, she wrote in her journal, 'I am sure I feel exactly like a person preparing for execution'. She then wrote no more until 1 May, the first day on which she was able to hold a pen again.

Susan's account of her operation is less detailed than Fanny Burney's, but she nevertheless tells us much about the horror of undergoing surgery without any kind of anaesthetic:

> My suffering was very great and very long, though the operation was performed by Mr Blicke with the greatest skill, humanity and tenderness. The assistance of Sir Walter Farquahar and Mr Adair Hawkins afforded me all the comfort the

> nature of my situation would admit. I was much shocked at the proposal of being blinded before I went into the room appointed, as I had no idea that, after the resolution I had brought my mind to adopt, it should be supposed I could be frightened at the sight of the instruments and aparatus necessary, and as I had a fixed determination rather to die than scream and lament or make any resistance, or even that they should see a tear of mine, I combated it as long as I could, but at last submitted to Mr Blicke's instances, as he said he could not answer for doing his duty if he was to see the countenance and the looks of his patient in such a situation. I was therefore blinded by Sir Walter Farquahar and Mr Adair Hawkins to my execution, for nothing less did it appear to me, who felt at that moment quite free from pain and in all respects in health and strength. I think I have now a perfect idea of what is felt on such occasions, at least by those who are executed without thinking themselves criminals, as in party or religious disputes. A kind of self-confidence, an exaltation in doing what you ought – for doing well – a haughty, indiscribable indifference about life or death, and a determination of going through any part well that you had undertaken – these were the sentiments that supported me through this great effort.

The operation was a complete success, and on 17 June Susan returned to Stinsford after an absence of six months. It was, as she said 'a pleasure I did not much hope ever to have again'.[167]

Other remedies, though less unpleasant, were only sporadically effective. Eighteenth-century doctors and their patients assumed that sickness was caused by poisonous substances within the body, so most treatments were designed to rid the body of these toxins by purging or vomiting, blood-letting, sweating or removing phlegm and pus. In 1813 when William O'Brien was taken with a 'violent pain in his bowels', the doctor feared 'inflamation'. Susan reported:

> He ordered him to go to bed, and all sorts of evacuations and a hot bath, which had some effect and made us rather easier ... Dr Cooper dined with us, which enabled him to judge what more might be necessary, and he did judge bleeding necessary, which surprised me very much. It had, however, instantaneous good effect, and he seemed to mend immediately.[168]

Laxatives or purgatives were widely used. Many of these included mercury – in 1748 Ste Fox was given a 'mercurial purge'.[169] Magnesia was a popular, relatively mild purgative. The second Countess of Ilchester, who suffered many years of poor health, had 'a stomach complaint' and it was thought after her early death that she had taken too much magnesia. Her granddaughter was told that it had 'formed a ball in her stomach'.[170] In the nineteenth century several different saline purgatives were used, of which the best-known today is Epsom salts, or magnesium sulphate. Also popular were Cheltenham salts. Thomas Talbot took regular doses of salts, and in

1806 he was taking Rochelle salts (tartrate of sodium and potassium). They worked, he said, 'very bad'.[171] Castor oil and calomel (mercurous chloride) were also popular purgatives in the nineteenth century. Susan O'Brien thought calomel 'the only thing effectual in obstructions', and in 1807 calomel was prescribed for Isabella Talbot, who was 'very ill'. Poor William O'Brien, suffering in the year before his death with 'a shortness of breath so painful as almost amounted to suffocation', was treated with calomel by the doctors, 'who thought it proceeded from the bowels being loaded'. Susan O'Brien was not totally convinced, and she was probably right in her belief that her husband's problems 'may proceed from other, and more dangerous, causes'. Calomel was sometimes taken in the form of 'blue pills', and these appear to have been a novelty in 1812 when Maria Burgh told Mary Talbot that she had never heard of them before, 'but suppose them quite fashionable'.[172]

Emetics such as ipecacuanha were also frequently used, and were generally referred to as 'vomits'. In 1747 Lady Ilchester wrote to tell her husband '[tonight I] am to take a vomit for a giddyness in my head and sickness in my stomach'.[173] Sometimes people overdid the vomits, which were often self-prescribed. In 1750 Charlotte Digby informed Henry Fox:

> I have had [Dr Smith's] advice all along, since My Lord Digby was ill. Before, I managed myself, and I believe hurt myself by too much vomiting. I am better, but extremely weak, and have disagreeable nervous pains.[174]

In smaller doses, ipecacuanha was also used as an expectorant, as was tartar emetic. In 1810, when Kit Talbot had a cold, Dr Fowler recommended that his mother should give him emetic tartar – or, alternatively, castor oil. The latter was probably marginally less unpleasant than the former.[175]

Another popular remedy was blood-letting, which was used to treat a wide variety of ailments. It was seen as a way of cleansing the body by removing 'stale' blood and stimulating the production of new blood, and was used to relieve any pain that appeared to be the result of pressure, such as a headache, and also to reduce the overheating produced by a fever. Regular blood-letting was thought to alleviate the problems caused by over-indulgence in food and drink. The blood was drawn off by opening a vein, by scarifying the patient's skin, or by applying leeches. Patients often reported that they felt much better after blood-letting. In the 1740s Joanna Cheeke told Lord Ilchester 'Mrs Horner has been blooded this afternoon, which relieved her very much', and around the same time Joanna herself was blooded, though she 'did not much like the opperation'. Susanna Strangways Horner seems to have been particularly keen on blood-letting, for in 1750 her daughter reported: 'Mama has again been blooded. I really am very uneasy at her bleeding so very often'. Later in the same year Susanna was to be blooded with leeches, which were often used for headaches and eye problems. In 1807 Charlotte Strangways told her sister Mary: 'My eyes are much better. I had leeches on again, and Phipps put me to great agony, but certainly did me good. I still have two leeches in attendance on my person.' In 1813 Susan O'Brien had a bloodshot eye, and her friend Mrs Floyer 'came to help put leeches on it'. A couple of months later Susan felt very ill, and 'put leeches to my head'. She continued to use leeches regularly in later years, usually to relieve a headache.[176] But bleeding did not always work: in 1764, when he had problems with his eyes, Lord Ilchester was blooded 'many ounces', but 'to very little purpose'.[177]

Cupping was often used in association with blood-letting. Two methods were used: dry-cupping and wet-cupping. Both involved the application of a cupping-glass to the skin of the patient, so that a vacuum was created. This was done to draw blood to the surface of the skin in order to relieve deep-seated congestion. It was also used to ease the breathing of a patient who was suffering from asthma, bronchitis or heart disease. In 1808 William O'Brien was 'seized with ... rushing in his head', and the doctor was summoned. He 'applied leeches and cupping glasses and a blister' and the patient soon felt better. Cupping, too, could be overused. In 1811 William O'Brien was again cupped, though 'only by way of prevention', as he was not ill. His wife thought 'he does it too often'.[178]

Blisters, poultices and plasters were also used to 'draw out' internal problems. A blister was an irritant substance, such as mustard or tincture of iodine, which was applied to the skin. In 1808 Susan O'Brien had a blister applied when she was suffering from bronchitis, and Dr Fowler thought that blisters were 'always particularly useful' for Kit Talbot in similar circumstances.[179] In some instances sores (also known as 'issues') were deliberately created, or prevented from healing, so that the pus which formed in them could be drawn off, thus removing poisonous substances from the body. In 1748, after she had been inoculated, Susan Fox 'had an issue cut again, hers having been dryed up after the smallpox, which was not so well for her'.[180] Such sores were also produced by the use of a seton: a few strands of silk or some other fibre were passed through the skin with a needle and left hanging out at each end. In 1804 Thomas Talbot was 'strongly recommended' to try a seton between his shoulders, but, very sensibly, 'he would not hear of it'.[181]

Such treatments were supplemented by measures designed to build up the patient's strength, such as fortifying medicines and a strictly controlled diet. In 1777 the second Countess of Ilchester asked her husband to bring her 'some analeptick [restorative] pills' from London.[182] Rhubarb was used in large doses as a purgative, and in smaller quantities to aid digestion. Bitters and bark were prescribed in small quantities to stimulate the appetite: in 1745 Henry Fox told his brother that 'Lady Caroline trys bark and rhubarb, and if that don't do, go's to Bath in March'.[183] Three years later, when she was in Bath, Caroline's doctor 'Ordered me a preparation of bark and bitters to take besides the water, my stomach being even too weak to bear the Bath water without something else to strengthen it'.[184] In 1777 the second Countess of Ilchester wrote that she had been prescribed 'another bitter instead of bark, which has been lately discovered, but the name of which I cannot this instant recolect'.[185] In 1813 William O'Brien took bitters, and two years later 'Dr Cooper ordered bark. O. [William O'Brien] took a great deal, with seeming good effect'. In 1819 Charlotte Lemon reported that her invalid daughter Augusta was taking 'Iceland moss and bark to keep up her strength'.[186] Preparations containing iron (known as steel) were also used: in 1810 Louisa Lansdowne informed her sister Mary, 'I am taking the bark as an agreeable variety, and mean to return to the steel, which has agreed so famously with me'. Kit Talbot and Augusta Lemon, too, were both given steel.[187]

Asses' milk, being easily digestible, was thought to be particularly suitable for invalids. When Ste Fox was recovering from the whooping cough early in 1747, his mother wrote:

> When I come to Town … I propose he should drink asses' milk and ride a-horseback before a man … I'm told there is some danger of a hooping cough falling on the lungs, which makes air, exercise and asses' milk necessary for a long time after the violence of the cough is abated. The child is not so much loaded with phlegm since his vomit. He has had no blister.[188]

In 1749 John Edwards was paid 2*s.* 6*d.* for 'bringing his ass and fole' to Redlynch, and in the following year the first Countess of Ilchester asked her husband to 'Desire Mr Hiet to get an asse for Mama against she comes, for she drinks the milk every morning'. A decade later Lady Ilchester's daughters Susan and Harriot were both drinking asses' milk. In 1814, when William O'Brien had a bad cough, Dr Cooper was said to trust to 'change of air and asses' milk' to restore him to health.[189]

Alcoholic drink was quite frequently prescribed by the doctors. In 1748 Caroline Fox said that she was giving her three-year-old son Ste claret every day 'and he shall leave off his pudding for some time and take his physic'.[190] Ellinor Talbot, always a delicate child, was reported to be eating meat and drinking wine every day when she was two years old,[191] and a few years later a friend wrote that Charlotte Strangways, who had recently been ill, 'rides, wears flannel and drinks claret'.[192] In 1814 Mary Talbot advised her fourteen-year-old nephew Henry about his diet whilst he was away at school:

> My chief anxiety is about your appetite, and I hope you will exert some self-denial – in the first place by denying yourself trash of all sorts, which your stomach is not now strong enough to dispose of, and secondly by not indulging any indolence when you should be nourishing yourself. If *really* strong beer is to be had at Harrow, your Mama will furnish you willingly with money to buy it.[193]

Less fortunate patients were told to abstain from alcohol: in 1801 Susan O'Brien noted that her husband had given up wine, and that one 'very agreeable' effect was 'that of taking off a somnolency that was become alarming to me, as well as melancholy and uncomfortable'.[194]

In 1766 Lord Holland, whose health had been deteriorating for some years, was said to 'mend very much' on a diet of 'strawberrys, peas and minced meat'.[195] A vegetarian diet was sometimes recommended: in 1811 Dr Fowler told Mary Talbot to give her daughter Emma 'no animal food so long as she goes on well without it'.[196] Patients did not, however, always follow the recommendations of their physicians. In 1748 Caroline Fox was advised to drink viper broth, but she told her husband that she could not possibly swallow it 'unless I'm very bad indeed'. The recipe for this concoction directs the cook to 'kill a viper, skin it, take out the entrails and cut the flesh into small pieces'.[197]

Most doctors and patients recognised the benefits of a regular lifestyle, and plenty of fresh air and exercise. Exercise might be taken on foot or on horseback – or even in a carriage. In 1748 Henry Fox offered to find a horse for his wife to ride, and told her 'in the meantime use a post chaise or your coach, which on Somersetshire roads is likely to be exercize sufficient'.[198] In 1810 Dr Fowler told Mary Talbot that he was sure that her health had been injured by 'that pernicious habit of sitting up late' and that 'both your health and your comfort will much depend on going to rest and rising early'.[199] In the following year he told her 'the best thing you can possibly do is bathe, and live in the open air without fatigue, and as much as may be without anxiety'.[200]

The doctors could do little to relieve severe pain. Laudanum (tincture of opium) was widely used, in spite of the risk of addiction. In 1729 Dr John Wigan, a friend and former tutor of the Fox brothers, warned Henry Fox against 'the ill custom I hear you are got into to taking laudanum':

> I am certain, if you continue using opium it will destroy ... in you all those good qualities from which my affection towards you took its rise, besides the prejudice it will do to your constitution. You must expect your memory to fail; your

> judgment to grow irresolute; your temper to be indolent at best, and uneasy by intervals; your apprehension slow; your company irksome. There is some difficulty in leaving it off at first, but if you will use a good deal of exercise, as I'm glad to hear you do, so as to amuse and tire you, I'm confident within a few days you will neither want spirits nor sleep without it … If you leave the laudanum off all at once, you'll suffer more for two or three days, but that will be the only struggle. If you sometimes take a little and sometimes not, the work will be endless, and your courage fail you.[201]

Medicines supplied to the household at Redlynch in the 1750s include paregoric elixir (which contained opium) and laudanum.[202] In 1798 William Davenport Talbot was confined to his bed with a sprained ankle, and his wife reported that he was 'in a high fever … with pain and laudanum'.[203] A shopping list in Mary Talbot's pocket-book of 1804 includes a reminder to buy 'paregoric'.

At least as effective as most of the remedies that were available – and certainly more pleasant – was a visit to a spa or watering-place, or to a seaside resort. There was an explosion in the number and popularity of such places in the eighteenth century, and small provincial towns such as Weymouth and Cheltenham were transformed, becoming fashionable holiday resorts, popular with the middle classes as well as the gentry and aristocracy. Visitors to these places could consult the most skilled – or, at least, the most expensive – medical practitioners, who would prescribe a range of therapies. Most patients would come to drink the mineral waters in order to cleanse their systems and ease their digestive problems. Other visitors bathed in the waters, for hot baths would make the patient sweat and help to rid the body of toxic substances, and also ease rheumatic pains. Cold baths were believed to stimulate and strengthen the constitution. In 1811, when Mary Talbot expressed some doubts about the usefulness of bathing, Dr Fowler encouraged her to persist, telling her that he had known many who 'appeared indebted to cold bathing for much of their vigor, though their lungs were tender'.[204] But whatever the benefits of the waters themselves may have been, for most visitors to these places the opportunities for entertainment and socialising – combined with a little shopping – were at least as attractive.

Bath, where the therapeutic effects of the mineral waters from the hot springs had been appreciated since Roman times, was by far the most popular resort in the eighteenth century. By the 1730s the transformation of the cramped, insalubrious and still largely medieval provincial city visited by Samuel Pepys in 1668 into 'the hub of the fashionable world' was already well under way.[205] Bath is approximately forty miles from Melbury and twenty-five from Redlynch. From both houses the journey could be accomplished fairly easily in one day. Members of both the Fox and Strangways families were visiting the city by the late 1720s, and Stephen Fox spent several weeks there with Lord Hervey at the end of 1727 'drinking the waters, playing quadrille and attending the assemblies'.[206] Susanna Strangways Horner was also in Bath in 1727,[207] and her younger sister Elizabeth, Duchess of Hamilton, died 'on the road from Bath' in 1729.[208] After their return from the Continent in 1735, when relations with Thomas Horner were difficult, Susanna and her daughter often took refuge in Bath, and Susanna continued to visit the city regularly in later years. Elizabeth sometimes accompanied her, though with a certain amount of reluctance, writing to her husband in the early 1750s, 'I am just come home from Mama's, which I do with as much pleasure as many people would go to the prettiest entertainment in the world'.[209] It was perhaps during the same visit to Bath that Lady Ilchester told her husband, 'I had rather be at home with you and the children than at all the Baths in the world',[210] but she did at least find that bathing in the hot spring-water helped to relieve a painful hip. She was less sure if it did anything for her other health problems, writing:

> I bathed this morning at nine. Now it's two and I am pretty well, but allways very faint with it. I go to bed and lie some time, but can't sleep, though I am quite hevey. I stood on the hotest spring. The days I bathe, my body swells a good deal. I can't say whether it does me service or no. God grant it may, for I really am wore out with complaints ... Of late my ear is vastly troublesome from a continual noise in it.[211]

Another letter, which was probably written during the same visit, was much more cheerful:

> I have been in pain of late, but not very bad. In the whole I am greatly mended ... I like Bath vastly: I do just as I like, and lead a very peaceable life, not so much cards, and yet I often play, but more moderately in point of time and money than usual.[212]

A few years later, however, Lady Ilchester found the Assembly Rooms 'a most forlorn place – only one whisk table, and a few stragling, misserable-looking men and women'.[213]

The Fox Strangways ladies continued to visit Bath in the second half of the eighteenth century. In 1774 Lady Ilchester's daughter Fanny was 'not at all well', suffering from 'an indigestion' and 'rather nervous'. Fanny and her sister Lucy were therefore sent to Bath. A few years later the second Countess of Ilchester was 'in a very weak state' after a serious illness, and she was ordered to spend the winter in Bath. She stayed there with her mother-in-law and with the O'Briens.[214] By the end of the century, however,

Bath was less popular with the aristocracy, who found that the society there was not exclusive enough – in 1799 Catherine Gumbleton told her niece Harriot Strangways 'You and I agree perfectly in our ideas of Bath, for I never was in a place I dislike more, though it always did me so much good'.[215] In 1810 Susan O'Brien, staying in Bath for her husband's sake, found 'the plays good, the balls out of fashion, and the card partys humdrum'.[216] But even if Bath was no longer so fashionable, many of the best doctors were still to be found there, and the town was more accessible than London for those who lived in the West Country and Wales. It was in Bath that the 'excrescence' was removed from Christiana Talbot's face in 1804, and Mary Talbot went there in 1815, suffering from rheumatism and hoping that the waters would help her. In 1816 Susan O'Brien had thoughts of visiting Bath to see a dentist, and she continued to go there occasionally. She was in Bath in 1819 – more than sixty years after her first visit to the city as a little girl – but she did not like it:

> London is far preferable *for me* [and] I think but little more expensive. Bath wants a companion – London does not. Everybody that I know is in London, few at Bath, which is full of *semi-fine ladys*, which I dislike more than anything.[217]

Even in the eighteenth century, when Bath was still the height of fashion, some people preferred to go to other, less highly developed watering-places. Hotwells near Bristol was popular by the mid eighteenth century – Lord and Lady Ilchester were there with three of their daughters in 1754, staying in 'an extreme pretty neat house, and a very fine situation ... very quiet'. Lord Digby, who was there too, was however said to be complaining that he 'has not yet found any good by the watters'.[218] The nearby village of Clifton grew rapidly after 1790, and it was popular with later generations of the family. Thomas and Mary Talbot took their consumptive daughter Ellinor to Clifton at the end of November 1809, and the child died there six weeks later. The Talbots and several of their daughters were in Clifton again in the winter of 1812 to 1813, a few months before Thomas Talbot's death.

Jane Austen lived in Bath from 1801 to 1806, and quickly grew to dislike the town. When she fell ill in 1816 it was to Cheltenham, rather than Bath, that she went.[219] The spa there had been founded early in the eighteenth century, but it did not become fashionable until 1788 when the Royal Family spent five weeks in the town. The Talbots liked Cheltenham, and they also stayed in Malvern. Both towns were quiet and surrounded by pretty, hilly countryside. Although only twenty miles apart, Cheltenham and Malvern were quite different. As the Talbots' friend John Hunt wrote in March 1812:

> At the present season of the year, I should think Cheltenham a better situation for invalids in general than Malvern, which is better suited to the warm than the

> cold months. No two places within a morning's drive can be so different, and therefore tried with [so] little inconvenience.[220]

Two years earlier, George Eden had described Malvern as the 'only place I ever was at where breathing air and drinking water are sources of positive pleasure'.[221] Cheltenham was 'gayer' and more developed than Malvern. Maria Burgh thought that the Talbots would prefer the latter:

> I did not think [you] would like Cheltenham for more than a short [time] as there is great sameness in most watering-places. It has often astonished me how many persons, generally considered sensible and not apparently wild after pleasure, could leave their lovely places and enjoy the stupid, and often impertinent, stare of strangers. I never walked at Cheltenham without a veil, as I am particularly embarassed by daring scrutiny ... From all I have heard of Malvern, I am not surprised you should feel it particularly delightful and free from *form* after Cheltenham. The air is most salubrious and the water singularly pure. I am sure your daughters admired the lovely views from the hills.[222]

But the family continued to visit Cheltenham. When she went there with her daughters in 1822 Mary Cole found 'the walks very much encreased ... and spas built'. Mary told her husband that the town was 'still enlarging but, I think, not improving'. Nevertheless, they all enjoyed the music provided to entertain the visitors:

> We have found out now that there is a third band playing every day at the Sherborne Spa and, as it consists of a harp and flageolet very nicely played, and indulges us with all manner of Scotch airs and soft music, we have in a manner forsaken the others and abandoned the gawdy parterre, to patronize this violet in the shade.[223]

As with Bath, many visitors to both Cheltenham and Malvern came for a holiday, rather than for strictly medical reasons. When pressed to go to Malvern in 1812, Susan O'Brien refused, saying:

> We are too far gone in the way of all flesh to travel about the world for waters or airs, though I hear an old friend of ours is just gone there – not, I believe, in search of either, but to *passer son temps* in the London vacation.[224]

The eighteenth century also saw the development of seaside resorts where the visitors could bathe in the sea or in salt-water baths. Sea air was generally considered to be particularly beneficial – though not by the first Earl of Ilchester, who wrote in 1748 that his wife had taken the children to Abbotsbury for a week 'upon a supposition that the sea air is good, which to be sure is nonsense'.[225] But Lord Ilchester was in the minority. Weymouth, on the Dorset coast, is only twenty miles from Melbury, and Harriot Strangways was sent to a boarding-school there in 1787. She had a problem with one of her knees, and it was hoped that sea-bathing would help. In May 1789 Susan O'Brien, who had been 'advised sea bathing',[226] spent a fortnight in Weymouth, a few weeks before George III and other members of the Royal Family visited the town for the first time. Weymouth remained popular with the Royal Family and the Court for the next twenty-five years, and the facilities available for 'polite' visitors expanded rapidly. In addition to immersing themselves in the sea, from a bathing-machine, visitors could also use a hot sea-water bath. There was much less to do in Weymouth than in Bath, but the social life was lively enough, as Harriot told Mary in 1792:

> Lady Digby took me to the play once, and to the Rooms once, and the King took a great deal of notice of me, and the Queen and princesses too, but I like the Princess Amelia best, though I did not speak to her. I have not bathed for some time now. I left off the hot bath on account of a bad cold about three weeks ago, and have not begun again as Mr Warne expects every day to hear from Mr Hunter about going into the sea, so I don't know which I am to do yet, but my knee continues very well and, I think, is much smaller.[227]

Twenty or so years later, in 1815, Harriot was in Weymouth with her son James, in the hope that the warm sea bath would help him to recover after scarlet fever.[228]

Resorts such as Weymouth, Bath and Malvern were all within reasonably easy reach of the West Country and South Wales. Occasionally, however, members of the family ventured further afield. In the spring of 1802 it was suggested that the waters of Buxton might help the second Earl of Ilchester. Mary Talbot was not convinced that this was a good idea, telling her brother, 'I think Penrice air would do my father a great deal more good than Buxton waters'.[229] Lord Ilchester, however, was persuaded to make the long journey to Derbyshire, though he was reported to be 'very low, and much averse to going', believing that if he did so, he would never return. His presentiment was correct – he died at Buxton, as a result, it was thought, of 'very improper treatment by an ignorant physician'.[230] Some people travelled to Europe in the hope of a cure: Susanna Strangways Horner and her granddaughter Susan O'Brien both visited Spa. Susanna apparently 'found benefit by the Spaw-waters' during her stay there in 1732, though the experience was not totally enjoyable. Other members of the family also visited Spa in later years.[231]

Both the Fox Strangways family and the Talbots also had bathing facilities much closer at hand. There were bath-houses at both Redlynch and Melbury by the mid eighteenth century: in September 1740 Betty Ponter was paid £1 7*s.* for 'attending Mrs Fox' in the cold bath at Redlynch.[232] In 1791 the second Earl built a 'neat bathing-house' close to the beach at Abbotsbury, which was 'accommodated with hot and cold baths, dressing room etc.'[233] In Gower, the Talbots had 'an excellent bathing-machine with an umbrella' on the beach at Oxwich,[234] and Mary and the children bathed there regularly during the summer. There was also 'a tub made on purpose for warm sea bathing' at the gardener's house at Penrice. This had been used by William Davenport Talbot (who died in 1800) and it was still there in 1804.[235] Attempts were also made in the early nineteenth century to turn Swansea into a genteel watering-place. A bathing-house was built on the sand dunes to the west of the town, and in 1804 Mary Talbot told Mrs Hicks Beach that the facilities there included 'hot salt baths and very comfortable dressing-rooms'. Agnes Porter, who spent four weeks at the bathing-house in November and December 1804 with the Talbot children, who were recovering from whooping-cough, did not, however, enjoy her stay very much:

> A most bleak situation: no trees, no houses. Close on the sea; the *dwelling* poor; windows ill-fastened; the bed curtains shaking with the wind; the sea roaring with 'hollow blasts'. But we must hope it will be salutary.[236]

Nor was it necessary to go to Bath or to another spa to drink the waters. Mineral water could be drunk at home, though without the extra benefits of a visit to a watering-place. Bottles of water from Bath, Bristol and Cheltenham were sent to Redlynch in the early 1740s, and the Melbury household accounts for the years 1748 to 1750 include numerous payments for bottles of Bath water, Bristol water and Hotwell water. Bath water was the most expensive, costing up to 6*s.* 9*d.* for a dozen bottles, whilst bottles of Hotwell water cost between 3*s.* 4*d.* and 4*s.* 2*d.* per dozen. Baskets and packaging cost 2*s.* for a load of three or four dozen bottles.[237] At the end of the century, in 1791, William O'Brien drank Spa water at home 'which was of great use to him'.[238] Some doctors persuaded their patients to drink sea-water, which must have been useful as an emetic, if nothing else. In the early 1750s Lady Ilchester, who was staying in Bath, told her husband that she was to start drinking sea-water, and a few years later the same treatment was used for her son, Stephen, at school at Wandsworth, on the advice of Mr Truesdale. Truesdale seems to have been particularly keen on sea-water, which he also recommended for Ste Fox.[239]

The Earls of Ilchester and their friends and relations could afford to pay for the best medical advice available. They often used London doctors, though the growth of provincial medical services in the eighteenth century meant that a journey to the capital was not always necessary. Wealthy people

13. Susan Fox Strangways (later O'Brien), by Katherine Read (*c.* 1760). (*Private Collection*)

14. William O'Brien, by Francis Cotes (*c.* 1762). (*Private Collection*)

15. Susan O'Brien, by Francis Cotes (*c.* 1764). (*Private Collection*)

16. Stinsford House, Dorset. (*c.* 1980)

17. Sarah Lennox, Susan Fox Strangways and Charles James Fox, by Sir Joshua Reynolds (*c.* 1762). Susan hated the picture: 'Lady Sarah and I were disfigured and insipid, which we were not'. (*Private Collection*)

18. Mary Theresa, Countess of Ilchester, with her daughters Elizabeth and Mary, by Sir Joshua Reynolds (*c.* 1778). (*The Trustees of the Bowood Collection*)

19. Penrice Castle, Glamorgan (2003).

20. Mary Talbot and her son Christopher (?), artist unknown (1806). (*Private Collection*)

21. Thomas Mansel Talbot, artist unknown (1806). (*Private Collection*)

22. William Henry Fox Talbot, aged three, artist unknown (1803). (*The National Trust, Fox Talbot Museum, Talbot Trust Collection*)

23. Charlotte Traherne (*née* Talbot) (*c.* 1870–75). (*By kind permission of Richard Morris*)

24. Two domestic scenes, water-colours by one of the Talbot daughters (*c.* 1815). (*Private Collection*)

25. Mary Cole (*née* Fox Strangways) and her daughter Emma Llewelyn (*c.* 1850). (*Private Collection*)

had access to several different kinds of medical practitioners at this time. The most prestigious – and therefore the most expensive – were the physicians. These men, who were entitled to be called 'Doctor', would have received a university education, and, if not themselves from a gentry background, would have acquired a gentlemanlike manner that would inspire confidence in their wealthy patients. Their function was to diagnose the complaint, advise the patient on a suitable course of treatment, and prescribe the necessary medicines. In most cases a consultation with such a man involved little in the way of physical examination or active treatment, though in 1799 when Susan O'Brien found a lump in her breast, both Sir Walter Farquhar and the surgeon Charles Blicke examined 'the part'.[240]

Most physicians serving the elite were to be found in London. In 1783, out of a total of just over 3000 medical practitioners in provincial England, only 363 were physicians.[241] The majority of these were based in the larger provincial towns and the spas, such as Bath. When Thomas Strangways junior was dying at Melbury in 1726 his wife and sister sent for Dr John Freind, a well-known London physician. Freind arrived at Melbury after Thomas Strangways had died, but he was nevertheless paid £105 for his 'journey and trouble'.[242] There are occasional references to other physicians in the eighteenth century. In the mid 1740s Lady Ilchester, who was at Melbury and pregnant, consulted 'Doctor Heale', who was probably Henry Hele, MD (1700–1778), a physician who practised in Poole and Salisbury. A few years later Susanna Strangways Horner, in Bath, was blooded and took 'strong physicks by Dr Fruin's advice'.[243] In the 1790s Walter (Sir Walter from 1796) Farquhar, physician to the Prince of Wales, looked after Lady Digby; he was called in to see both Harriot Strangways and Agnes Porter; he advised Mary Talbot when she brought her two eldest children to London to be inoculated against smallpox in 1797; and he assisted at Susan O'Brien's operation in 1799. At the end of the century William Davenport Talbot was treated by Farquhar, and also by Dr William Mackinnon Fraser of Lower Grosvenor Street, London, who was subsequently consulted by Talbot's widow, Elizabeth, about her son Henry, who was thought to be delicate.

In the early nineteenth century the O'Briens often consulted a Dorchester physician, Dr Christopher Cooper, who soon became a friend. Cooper came from a gentry family, and his personality and background made him a valued dining companion. Other members of Susan's family consulted him too. When Lord Ilchester broke his leg in 1808, Dr Cooper was summoned to Melbury to give his opinion on the treatment that had already been given. He also treated the families of Lord Ilchester's uncle the Revd Charles Fox Strangways, and of his sisters Harriot Frampton and Charlotte Lemon.[244]

Dr Cooper supported Susan during William O'Brien's last illness and he continued to visit her during her widowhood. She did not, however, believe that he was infallible, writing in 1823 when urged to ask him to call, 'I defer [Dr Cooper's visit], as I feel rather better, and when I did consult him last year it was to no purpose, as he did not know what the complaint arose from, nor what to do for it'.[245] Three years later, feeling ill and depressed, she complained, 'A week since he [Dr Cooper] deigned to see me, but I don't believe he can do me any good, I am the less desirous of a visit, though I think so indifferent a doctor seldom falls to anybody's lot but here'.[246] Dr Cooper did see Susan a few days later. He continued to practise in Dorchester 'with much reputation' until he died there in 1842, 'much esteemed and lamented'.[247]

Another doctor who was popular with the family was Dr Richard Fowler, who in 1796 was elected physician to the infirmary in Salisbury, a position that he held until 1847. He built up an extensive and lucrative private practice, and was consulted by many of the Talbots' aristocratic connections such as Lord Holland and the Marquess of Lansdowne. Fowler, who died in 1863 at the great age of ninety-seven, was a man of wide interests, a Fellow of the Royal Society and a founder member of the British Association for the Advancement of Science, on friendly terms with most of the political, literary and scientific men of his time. He was also an entertaining companion:

> His conversational powers were of a high order, and literally overflowed with knowledge, playfulness, and anecdote; in a word, he was a philanthropist, a scholar, a scientific man, and a cosmopolitan in the largest sense of the word.[248]

Mary Talbot seems to have met Dr Fowler for the first time in 1808 when he was called to Melbury to see her daughter Christiana a few days before the child died. In the following year the Talbots took their daughters Ellinor, Jane and Charlotte to Salisbury, where they rented a house in the Cathedral Close. The purpose of their prolonged stay was to enable Dr Fowler to observe the little girls and advise on a course of treatment. He was also consulted about Thomas Talbot's own health. Mary had great faith in Dr Fowler's judgement, and got on well with both him and his wife. She valued their friendship and support, for her husband was in poor health by this time. After her return home in July 1809 Mary kept up a regular correspondence with both Dr and Mrs Fowler, and their letters helped to sustain her whilst she was at Penrice with only her children as companions. With Mrs Fowler she discussed gardening and mathematics. Mrs Fowler recommended the study of Euclid for therapeutic reasons, writing that 'You cannot think how much mathematics takes off pain of the body, and I am sure it would have the same on mental pain'.[249] Dr Fowler did not patronise Mary, and he wrote to her as to another rational human being whose opinion he valued. He reassured her about the health of her husband and children and, more particularly, about her own care of them, asking her in one letter, 'Why will you continue to fritter away the comfort that you might enjoy by keeping your mind perpetually on the hunt for subjects of self-accusation?'[250] The Talbots returned to Salisbury in 1810, and when Mary wrote to thank Dr Fowler for his help, he replied:

> I really wish you would never again think of thanking me for what it is my daily duty to do for Tom, Dick or Harry. I am a mere Hackney coach on its stand, and if I carry safely through their difficulties those who chuse to call me, I am glad both for my own sake and theirs, but this certainly gives neither me nor the coach any claim to thanks.

Mary was still consulting Dr Fowler twelve years later, when she asked for his advice about her daughter Charlotte. Whatever the value of his medical advice may have been, his moral support was invaluable during a difficult period of her life.

Much more numerous than the physicians, though lower in status, were the surgeons and surgeon-apothecaries. In 1783 the county of Dorset had nine physicians, one surgeon and fifty-nine surgeon-apothecaries. The corresponding numbers for Somerset were twenty-nine, eighteen and ninety-three. Both surgeons and apothecaries received their training during an apprenticeship, which usually lasted for seven years, rather than at an university. Their status was lower because their expertise was thought to be manual and practical, rather than intellectual. The surgeon treated external complaints such as wounds and injuries, together with boils and other skin conditions, and he also set broken bones and performed simple operations. The apothecary was initially allowed only to dispense the medicines prescribed by a physician, but after Rose's Case in 1701 he was also able to visit patients and prescribe medicines for them. He could not charge anything for giving advice, however, and his income was earned from the preparations that he supplied.

In spite of their supposedly inferior status, many surgeons and apothecaries were quite grand and accumulated substantial fortunes. There was, for example, John Ranby (1703–1773), the son of an innkeeper, who was elected a Fellow of the Royal Society in 1724. Ranby, a friend of the artist William Hogarth, was 'a man of strong passions, harsh voice, and inelegant manners'.[251] He was appointed surgeon-in-ordinary to the King's household in 1738, and became principal sergeant-surgeon to George II in 1743, and surgeon to the Chelsea Hospital in 1751. He also established a large private surgical practice. John Ranby's aristocratic patients included Lord Ilchester's family, the Digbys and the family at Holland House. Ranby seems to have treated Lord Ilchester for an urinary infection in 1737, and he was asked to help in 1750 when Robert Digby's gum would not stop bleeding after two teeth had been extracted. Perhaps surprisingly, Ranby (who does not appear to have visited the patient, being 'confined with the gout') ordered him to be 'immediately blooded ten ounces', and also to take bark every two hours. Even more surprisingly, this treatment was reported to have stopped the bleeding, and the boy was said to be 'pretty well' afterwards.[252] In the following year Ranby, who clearly made the most of his connections with high society, was reported to be going 'a fox-hunting' at Euston, and in 1753 Henry Fox told his nephew Lord Digby that he had given Ranby some venison for his daughter 'to save yours'.[253] Venison was a high-status gift, which was given only to close friends and family, or to people on whom the giver wanted to confer a particular favour. In 1756 Ranby was consulted about the advisability of Lord Digby's being 'cut for the stone'.

Whilst they were in London, Lord Ilchester's family also used the services of 'Mr Truesdale', who must be John Truesdale, apothecary, of St James's Street, London, one of two 'apothecaries to the King's person' in 1779.[254] He was personable (in 1751 Joanna Cheeke said that he looked 'as handsome as ever, but not quite so fat'),[255] and he had a good bedside manner. Truesdale was consulted by the Duke and Duchess of Richmond in 1750, and also by Henry and Caroline Fox. In 1759 both Truesdale and Ranby were called in to treat the Foxes' son Stephen during a serious illness.[256] The Sherborne Castle accounts also record payments to Mr Truesdale in London in the mid 1760s.[257]

A surgeon who appears to have practised in both London and Dorchester was Adair Hawkins, who supported and advised Susan O'Brien at the time of her operation in 1799. Hawkins, together with Sir Walter Farquhar, assisted at the operation, which was performed by the surgeon Charles Blicke of South Lambeth, whom Susan described as 'one of the most skillfull [surgeons], a very humane and feeling man'.[258] Hawkins was also a good friend to Susan, refusing to take any money for his professional advice and attendance. He continued to treat members of the family for many years: in 1813 Susan asked him to come to Stinsford to see her husband, and several years later both Hawkins and Dr Cooper were called in to see Augusta Lemon.[259] Another surgeon with Dorset connections was James Nooth, who appears to have practised in Dorchester to begin with, but later moved to Bath. He attended Henry Talbot, and he also removed the growth on Christiana Talbot's face during the winter of 1803–4. Nooth's career clearly prospered, for he then went to London. By April 1805 he had settled in Cavendish Square, and had secured the position of surgeon to the Duke of Kent.[260]

Medical practitioners of all kinds were plentiful in London. In a country town such as Dorchester or Bruton, however, there might be only one or two. Most such men, therefore, had to be able to turn their hands to all aspects of medicine, diagnosing and treating their patients' complaints, delivering their babies, and also prescribing and supplying the medicines that they needed. The provincial surgeon-apothecary was thus the eighteenth-century equivalent of the modern general practitioner. Such a man was Thomas Clarke of Bruton, who was regularly called in to treat the family at Redlynch and their servants in the 1750s. The accounts presented by Clarke give a fascinating insight into the work undertaken by a country doctor at this time. For the year to 22 January 1750 his bill came to a total of £37 0*s.* 4*d.* Of this, £3 6*s.* 7*d.* was for the horses; 15*s.* 6*d.* for the dogs; £5 17*s.* for the family (who were not in residence for the whole of the period covered); and £27 1*s.* 3*d.* for the servants. The expenditure on medical attention for the servants was always comparatively high, for looking after dependants well was a matter of family pride. A nobleman who was known to be a good master would attract the best and most loyal servants.

In the months of April, May, June and July 1750, the following payments were made to Thomas Clarke for members of the family at Redlynch:[261]

		s.	*d.*
14 April	Sea water, Miss Charlott	01	00
25 April	Sea water	01	00
26 April	Tincture rhubarb	02	00
24 May	An embrocation and plaister, My Lord's leg	05	00
27 May	Tincture of rhubarb, My Lord	02	06
28 May	Purging pills	02	00
3 June	Bleeding Master Fox	10	06
4 June	A journey, Master Fox	02	06
	A rhubarb apozem [infusion]	02	00
5 June	A journey, Master Fox	02	06
6 June	A journey	02	06
7 June	Elderflower water	00	06
8 June	6 powders, Miss Charlott	02	00
	A spermaceti mixture, Miss Charlott	02	04
19 June	Drawing Miss Fox's tooth	05	00
23 June	A purge, Miss Fox	01	00
	Syrup of roses	00	06

25 June	A purge, Miss Fox	01	00
1 July	A purge, Miss Fox	01	00
3 July	Issue plaister, Master	01	00
4 July	Issue plaister, Misses	01	00
12 July	A quart medicat' wine,[262] Miss Lucy	05	00
	A paper, fumigat'[263] powder	03	00

Clarke was also paid as follows for looking after the servants in April and May:

2 April	Spirits [of] lavender	02	00
4 April	2 oz. spirits[of] hartshorn [ammonia]	02	00
6 April	Bleeding the coachman	01	00
	A balsamic mixture [for] his cough	02	00
8 April	An oily mixture, Mrs Hiett	02	00
	1 1/2 oz. spirits hartshorn	01	06
9 April	Rhubarb, Patty	01	00
10 April	A box of pills, Mrs Hiett	02	00
13 April	A journey and bleeding Mrs Delafonse	02	06
14 April	An opening [laxative] electuary	02	04
30 April	A journey and bleeding Mrs Delafonse	02	06
8 May	A blister, the landre [laundry] maid's ear	00	06
10 May	A journey and bleeding Mrs Shaw	02	06
13 May	A journey to Mrs Hiett	02	06
14 May	A bottle spirit tincture	02	04
15 May	Bleeding James Wallis	01	00
16 May	A lambative [medicine], his cough	02	06
	A purgative electuary, Mrs Shaw	02	03
25 May	A purge, Mrs Fenn	01	00
	A purge, Charity	01	00
30 May	Liquorish [a laxative], Charles Swyer	00	02
31 May	Liniment, Mrs Hiett's knees	02	04

Lord and Lady Ilchester appear to have had great faith in Thomas Clarke. In 1750 when Henry and Caroline Fox's son Charles was seriously ill at Redlynch, Lord Ilchester told his brother that the local surgeon had saved the child's life 'by putting him on blisters on his back and plaisters on his feet'. Clarke died in 1762,[264] to be succeeded as the family doctor at Redlynch by Thomas Sampson, another Bruton surgeon and apothecary. Sampson, of whom the family also had 'a great opinion' supplied medicines in 1763, and he treated the first Earl of Ilchester during his last illness ten years later.[265] In 1784, again at Redlynch, William O'Brien's recovery from an apparently fatal illness was thought to be due to 'the unremitted care of Mr Samson', whom Agnes Porter described a few years later as 'a very well-informed, intelligent person'.[266] Sampson continued to look after the family until they moved from Redlynch to Melbury in 1793.

Fashions in medical treatment came and went during the eighteenth and early nineteenth centuries. Doctors and their patients all had their favourite remedies, from sea-water to steel. In 1805 Susan O'Brien wrote to Elizabeth Feilding about the latter's son Henry, who had recently been ill: 'I hope you don't play tricks with him and dose him, as you did yourself, with every new thing you heard of'.[267] The impact of certain illnesses changed over time – smallpox, a major cause of mortality in the early eighteenth century, had been partly replaced by tuberculosis a hundred years later. The overall impression, however, is that there were no major advances in medical knowledge in this period, apart from the introduction of inoculation against smallpox. Nothing much changed until the mid nineteenth century: the first real improvement in diagnostic techniques came with the introduction of the stethoscope after 1819; anaesthetics (ether and chloroform) were used from the 1840s onwards; and antiseptics (carbolic and boracic acids) from the 1860s. But the real changes came in the twentieth century, with the discovery of the diagnostic possibilities of X-rays before the First World War, followed by the introduction of sulpha drugs, then antibiotics, from 1935 onwards. For the first time doctors could give their patients medicines that really did overcome fevers and bacterial infections. At last, treatment of the sick was becoming less unpleasant in its administration, and more beneficial in its outcome.

10

Education

The principal aims of female education in the early nineteenth century were much the same as they had been a hundred, or even two hundred, years earlier: to produce girls who would be a credit to their parents, and would eventually make good marriages. But the ways in which these aims were achieved were changing, and the education given to Mary Talbot's daughters was very different from that of their great-great-grandmother Susanna Strangways, or their great-grandmother Elizabeth Strangways Horner.

In the sixteenth and seventeenth centuries a well brought up girl was trained to be a dutiful wife and mother, capable of managing her household and looking after her husband and children. A few ladies, such as Sir Thomas More's three daughters and Queen Elizabeth I, received a highly academic, classical education, but they were exceptional. For most girls, practical skills such as needlework, preserving fruit, making medicines for the household and keeping accounts were much more important. A certain amount of book-learning was thought necessary, since a mother was usually responsible for teaching her children – both boys and girls – until they were about seven. It was her duty to instruct them in the principles of the Christian religion, and for this she would need to be able to read the Bible and other improving works for herself. But reading and academic interests were not supposed to occupy too much of a woman's time, as this would lead her to neglect her other duties. Equal importance was attached to behaviour: a gentlewoman was expected to have good manners, and she had to be able to teach her children how to conduct themselves. Above all, she had to be chaste, obedient, discreet and prudent – and she was expected to ensure that her daughters followed her example.[1]

Susanna Strangways was born in 1689, so her education would have begun around 1695. According to her epitaph, she was 'born and bred in the country'.[2] Susanna may have been taught by her mother to begin with, and she may also have had some lessons with a private tutor – perhaps a local clergyman or schoolmaster, or her parents' private chaplain, for the 1727 inventory of Melbury mentions 'the chaplinge's roome'.[3] Like her contemporary Mary Pierrepont (later Lady Mary Wortley Montagu) and many of her female descendants, Susanna was probably at least partly self-educated, having the advantage of access to her father's library at Melbury.[4] Susanna was evidently highly intelligent, and her surviving letters are fluent and clearly expressed. According to a distinctly obsequious 'Character' written shortly after Susanna's death in 1758, 'Her sense was of the first rate, improved by a large acquaintance with the polite world, the best books, and the most refined company'.[5] In one respect, however, it is clear that her education had failed. Above all, girls were expected to be dutiful – towards God, towards their parents and, ultimately, towards their husband and children. Susanna was, however, stubborn and self-willed, unwilling to defer either to her husband or, in later years, to her son-in-law. She showed signs of her independent attitude, even before her marriage to Thomas Horner, when she made it quite clear that she felt that he had not pursued her with sufficient enthusiasm. Nor does chastity, another essential requirement, seem to have come very high on Susanna's list of essential qualities. Whatever her relationship with Henry Fox may have been, it is evident that her contemporaries believed that they were lovers.

Thomas and Susanna Horner's daughter Elizabeth was born in 1723. According to her eldest daughter, Elizabeth received 'the education usual at that time – reading, writing and the principles of religion'.[6] An entry in a Melbury account-book indicates that Elizabeth's first tutor was the local schoolmaster:

> Paid Mr Edward Godfrey, schoolmaster in Melbury Osmond ... as well for teaching Miss Horner and Aminta, as also for teaching children in Melbury Osmond, for one whole year ending at Christmas last: £13 13s.[7]

This entry was made in March 1728, a few weeks after Miss Horner's fifth birthday. Who Aminta was is unknown.[8] Two or three years later Elizabeth's studies were interrupted when her mother set off on her travels on the Continent. Susanna and her companions presumably gave the little girl some lessons, and she may have had some instruction from tutors along the way, but the stilted language and poor spelling of Elizabeth's later letters suggest that her education was somewhat sketchy. Nor does she ever seem to have been particularly interested in reading or self-improvement. Henry Fox did make some attempts to fill in the gaps in her education during his stay with Elizabeth and her mother in the South of France in the mid 1730s. He encouraged the child to write to him whilst he was away, and in his replies he pointed out her errors of spelling and grammar. He also corrected her French, and instructed her in the art of letter-writing. In his final letter, written shortly before Susanna and her household left Nice, Henry also gave his young pupil some advice on her future conduct – advice which he would have done well to follow himself. Henry suggested that the child should write down her thoughts on different subjects, and recommended that she should 'make the folly of all vice the frequent subject of this exercise'. 'Doing wrong' was, he continued, 'the way, almost the inevitable way, to be miserable here as well as hereafter', whilst doing right was 'the pleasantest and shortest, as well as the surest, road to temporary as well as eternal happiness'. If Elizabeth looked around her she would find that those who were covetous were 'unhappy from those very riches which they wretchedly and uncharitably hoard or by wicked means attain'.[9]

Unfortunately for Elizabeth, the competing demands of her parents soon made it impossible for her to 'do right' and obey both of them. Her mother proved to be the stronger and more determined of the two, and it was she who married her daughter off to Stephen Fox at the age of thirteen. She even persuaded Elizabeth to take some of the blame for the clandestine marriage. It seems unlikely that Elizabeth was given any academic tuition after she became Mrs Fox. According to her daughter, she had, however, 'a good plain understanding, great rectitude of principle and desire of doing right'.[10]

By the middle of the eighteenth century less attention was paid to household management, and more to the development of refined manners and the cultivation of good taste. An idea of the improved education that some girls received at this time may be gained from Lady Sarah Pennington's book *An Unfortunate Mother's Advice to her Absent Daughters*, which was published in 1761. Lady Sarah laid great emphasis on the importance of religious instruction, believing that this was much more valuable than the 'polite education' that her daughters were certain to receive. She hoped that her daughters would learn to 'speak correctly and write grammatically', and thought that they should be well acquainted with French and, perhaps, Italian. They should learn geography and natural philosophy, and acquire 'a good knowledge of history', both of their own country and of other European nations; they should be 'perfect in the first four rules of arithmetic', but not more, as they would not need it and 'the mind should not be burthened with needless application'.[11]

Many parents gave much less thought to the upbringing of their daughters than Lady Sarah Pennington, and continued to educate them in what Lady Mary Wortley Montagu described as 'the greatest ignorance'.[12] Jonathan Swift complained that the daughters of great and wealthy families were either left entirely to their ignorant mothers, or sent to boarding schools, or put into the hands of English and French governesses, who were 'generally the worst that can be gotten for money'.[13]

Writing in the early nineteenth century, Susan O'Brien thought that her own education, and that of her sisters in the mid eighteenth century, had been neglected, due to their mother's belief that 'the same [education] she had received was sufficient for [her daughters]', though women's education was, in general, 'much advanced'.[14] Susan did, however, have a governess: Mrs Mary Delafons, who was engaged towards the end of 1747 and stayed with the family at Redlynch until the summer of 1753.[15] Mrs Delafons, who was paid £20 a year, was a Londoner. She was probably the widow of a French Huguenot, and she had a son, John Delafons, born around 1739, who went into the navy. Many years later, in 1808, he wrote to Susan O'Brien, asking her to recommend a school which his wife and daughters had recently established for the education of 'a limited number' of girls, in which 'both attention and care will be paid to the education and morals of the young ladies, as well as a strict and particular regard to their life and comfort'.[16] Whether Mrs Delafons was herself of French origin is unknown, but she was probably employed because she could speak, and teach, the French language. French governesses were fashionable at this time – the Duke and Duchess of Bedford employed a French mademoiselle to 'guard and chaperon' their daughter Lady Caroline Russell, who was just a couple of weeks older than Susan Fox (and a fellow bridesmaid at the wedding of George III). This woman's teaching duties seem, however, to have been fairly limited.[17]

Shortly after Mrs Delafons left Redlynch, another governess was engaged. This was Mrs Trengrouse, presumably another widow, who was paid £21 a year. Nothing is known about her qualifications or teaching abilities, but she stayed with Lord and Lady Ilchester's daughters until 1764, when she was dismissed after Susan's elopement with William O'Brien. Susan was also taught French by Madame Le Prince de Beaumont, a French refugee who was a well-known authoress and educationalist of the time. Madame de Beaumont's best-known work, *Le Magasin des Enfants*, was 'practically a treatise on education, perhaps the first of such modern treatises'.[18] In it, she included characters based on some of her pupils. Fifty years later, when asked by one of her nieces if a character named *Lady Spirituelle* had been based on her, Susan wrote:

> I always understood that *Lady Sensée* was Lady Sophia Carteret, who was Madame de Beaumont's heroine and pattern of perfection. *Lady Mary* was supposed to be Lady Mary Hill.[19] As for me, I was never *Spirituelle*, only solid raisoneuse and argumentation. She called me *Lady Sincère* – I believe because I often contradicted her nonsensical notions about balls and other such pastimes, which she thought too *mondain* to occupy young and innocent minds, in which I had the honor of differing entirely.[20]

Susan may have thought Madame de Beaumont's ideas 'nonsensical', but these lessons, which came to an end in 1759, made her into 'a very good French scholar and a most agreeable converser'.[21]

Writing-masters were commonly employed to teach both girls and boys at this time, and several of Lord and Lady Ilchester's younger children had lessons with Thomas Moore, a local schoolmaster at Redlynch. Moore was first employed in 1753 to teach 'Master Fox' to read. From 1756 to 1759 his pupils were 'Master Strangways, Lady Lucey and Lady Christian [Harriot]'. Moore was paid 5*s.* a week, and he taught the children to read and write. He was brought in again (this time at 6*s.* a week) in 1762 and 1763 to teach Fanny, who was then aged seven.[22] Unlike Susan, who was educated entirely at home, Lucy, Harriot and Fanny all attended schools in London at various times between 1757 and 1765, and for at least some of this time they were pupils at Mrs Sheeles's fashionable school in Queen Square, Bloomsbury. Fanny Burney, whose father was music master at the school from about 1760 to 1775,[23] later remembered two of the Strangways girls: Fanny, who had been unsympathetic when her mother was ill in 1761 or 1762, and Lucy, who had been 'the reverse in kindness and consideration'.[24]

This somewhat haphazard programme of education did at least ensure that the girls learned to read and write well, in both English and French. Whether Susan and her sisters acquired many of the ornamental accomplishments that were becoming increasingly important at this time is unclear. Lady Sarah Pennington gave some excellent advice on this subject – advice which was, unfortunately, not always followed:

> Musick and drawing are accomplishments well worth the trouble of attaining, if your inclination and genius lead to either. If not, do not attempt them, for it will be only much time and great labour unprofitably thrown away, it being next to impossible to arrive at any degree of perfection in those arts by the dint of perseverance only, if a good ear and native genius are wanting.[25]

In addition to learning French and Italian, Lady Caroline Russell was taught to play the harpsichord and guitar, to sing and to dance.[26] Many young ladies also learned to draw. Susan and her sisters must have had dancing lessons; there was a spinnet at Redlynch by 1747 and a harpsichord at Melbury in 1769,[27] but there is no indication that the girls' musical or artistic abilities were developed to any great extent.

The main aim of a girl's education was still to enable her to find a suitable husband, and to prepare her for married life. In practical terms, this meant that she should know how to run a large household. Lady Sarah Pennington thought that 'the management of all domestic affairs is ... the proper business of woman', though she admitted that such an assertion might be thought to be 'unfashionably rustic':

> 'Tis certainly not beneath the dignity of any lady, however high her rank, to know how to educate her children, to govern her servants, to order an elegant table with œconomy, and to manage her whole family with prudence, regularity and method.[28]

There is, however, little indication that the first Countess of Ilchester took a great deal of interest in household management. Nor was she very successful in teaching her eldest daughter how to behave. Mary Frampton probably echoed the general opinion of Susan's upbringing, when she wrote that 'her principles and education ... had been neglected'.[29] Susan's early letters to her father are signed 'your dutyfull daughter' or 'your most dutyfull daughter', but it was felt that she had ignored her duty to her parents when she eloped with William O'Brien in 1764. As her mother wrote shortly afterwards:

> Though the death of a beloved child is terrible, yet how far preferable to their being disgraced, abandoned. Consider of these things – you can't plead want of sense or, thank God, want of strict instruction in the principles of your duty to God, your neighbour, and yourself.[30]

Though it was too late for Elizabeth to help Susan after she had 'ruined herself', she does seem to have tried harder with her younger daughters. In 1766 Sarah Bunbury told Susan: 'your mother is very strict in her resolution of going everywhere with her girls, which I suspected she would grow tired of'.[31]

The young ladies of the mid eighteenth century may have been more accomplished than their mothers, but their education still left a great deal to be desired. In recognition of this, an increasing number of conduct books, addressed to girls and young women, began to appear. These were written by both men and women, who usually stressed the importance of duty and obedience. Some of these books, such as James Fordyce's *Sermons to Young Women* (first published in 1765) and John Gregory's *A Father's Legacy to his Daughters* (1774), remained in circulation for fifty years or more. Agnes Porter, the governess at Redlynch and Melbury and later at Penrice, was familiar with Fordyce's sermons, which the oleaginous Mr Collins reads aloud to the Bennet sisters in Jane Austen's *Pride and Prejudice.* Jane Austen mocked conduct books, with their 'pictures of perfection', and said that they made her feel 'sick and wicked'.[32]

Within the Fox Strangways family there are definite signs that more attention was being paid to the girls' education by the last quarter of the eighteenth century. In the first instance this was largely due to the efforts of the second Countess of Ilchester, who was born around 1750. Little is known of Mary Grady's own childhood, though her mother was said to be 'a charming woman' who had educated her children well and had set them a good example.[33] Susan O'Brien wrote of her Irish sister-in-law that she did not have 'all the high accomplishments beginning to be common in this [country]', having been 'educated in another kingdom [Ireland]', but her judgement, manners and feelings were impeccable. The best music and dancing masters may not have been available in western Ireland, but young Mary Grady enjoyed reading, and she had 'a heart stored with good principles and an understanding to direct the use of them'. Though her health was poor, she was nevertheless 'active and attentive to the care and improvement of her children'.[34] Not content with the mixture of schoolmistresses and tutors who had taught her sisters-in-law – and unable, due to illness, to do a great deal herself – she chose to employ a governess, who would take general responsibility for the children's welfare, in addition to instructing them.

Governesses had occasionally been employed to teach the children of wealthy families since the Tudor period. Some were poor relations, and few had themselves received more than the perfunctory instruction given to the majority of their female contemporaries. By the last quarter of the eighteenth century, however, the demand for private governesses was rising, for the second Countess of Ilchester was not alone in feeling dissatisfied with the education that had been thought adequate for earlier generations. Finding a suitable woman – or rather lady, as a governess had to be a gentlewoman – was, however, not a simple matter. As Anna Jameson, herself a former governess, wrote in 1846, there were in the eighteenth century 'few women either inclined to the task or by education qualified for it'. Anna Jameson thought that governesses had become a numerous 'class' only since the turn of the century, due in part to the fact that there were more such women available, since increasing numbers of women were having to support themselves, having, for various reasons, failed to find husbands.[35] The first governess at Redlynch proved to be 'unsatisfactory'. She was Miss Jane Arden, the daughter of a Yorkshire schoolmaster and a friend of the radical writer Mary Wollstonecraft.[36] Miss Arden started work in 1780 and left in July 1783, when the sum of 8*s.* 2*d.* was paid for her chaise and driver. The children also had some lessons with a writing-master at this time: John Penny was paid £7 6*s.* in February 1783, and in January of the following year the household accounts record the payment of £6 17*s.* 6*d.* to 'Mr Penny, writing-master to the ladies'. A further payment of 2*s.* 3*d.* for 'three slates for the ladies' was made on the next day.[37] These were the last payments to Mr Penny, for it was at this time that another governess arrived. This was Agnes Porter, who was to stay with Lord and Lady Ilchester's children for thirteen years. She then spent several years at Penrice Castle with the Talbots and their children, returning regularly until shortly before her death in 1814 to help when the parents were absent.

In some respects Agnes Porter was the archetypal governess. She was born in Edinburgh around 1750, the eldest daughter of the Revd Francis Porter and his wife Elizabeth. Lacking an influential patron, Francis Porter did not gain a parish of his own until 1778, when, at the age of sixty, he became the vicar of Wroughton near Swindon. When he died, only four years later, he left little, if any, money to support his widow and three unmarried daughters. Agnes, who was by this time living with the Ramey family of Great Yarmouth,[38] probably as a companion to Mrs Ramey, now needed to earn enough to support herself and help her mother. She therefore entered the only respectable paid profession that was open to a woman in her position: she became a governess. She went first to look after the daughters of Ambrose Goddard of Swindon House, MP for Wiltshire. Agnes stayed with the Goddards for less than two years, and in January 1784 she went to live at Redlynch, as governess to Lord and Lady Ilchester's daughters. She stayed with them until 1797 when she was invited to live with a friend, Elizabeth Upcher, in Great Yarmouth. After Mrs Upcher's unexpected death in 1799 Agnes settled at Penrice Castle with the Talbots, and she remained there, as governess to the children and companion to their mother, until she retired in 1806.

Of Agnes's own education we know nothing. There is no indication that she ever went to school, and it seems likely that she and her sisters were largely educated at home. Agnes wrote easily and fluently, and she loved books. She had a lively and enquiring mind, and continued to educate herself throughout her adult life, attempting at various times to learn Italian, Latin and German. Her French was good, as she and her sister Fanny had spent some time in Boulogne in their youth. She sang and played the piano and harpsichord, but her few surviving attempts at sketching suggest that she could not draw well. Her teaching skills were certainly adequate, but her moral qualifications were of equal importance to her employers. Agnes was highly respectable and, as the daughter of a clergyman, she could be expected to give her pupils a thorough grounding in the Christian religion. She also differed from many other governesses in two important respects: she actually liked children, and she was a good teacher. From the beginning it was obvious that she was different from the previous governess at Redlynch. Mary Talbot later told her daughter Charlotte that she had been 'a very naughty, sulky child' until Agnes Porter came, and 'with her sweet good sense and discernment of character used to charm her out of her obstinacy'.[39] Her pupils gave Agnes the affectionate nickname 'Po', and she was 'Po' to the children of the next generation as well.

Agnes taught her younger pupils to read and write. With her, the children studied history, geography, classics (in translation), the French language and French and English literature. In August 1790 one morning was spent 'relating passages from ancient and modern history', and on the afternoon of the same day 'we entertained ourselves with a play of Shakespeare's, *Richard II*'.[40] Moral education was not neglected: Agnes's pupils read the Bible and other religious books, and they were taught to say their prayers and recite the catechism. Although needlework was less important than it had been fifty or a hundred years earlier, the girls were still taught sewing and embroidery. Agnes was also responsible for supervising the children when their lessons were over: she walked with them in the gardens and shrubbery at Redlynch, or watched them as they played indoors. In 1796, after the family had moved to Melbury, the youngest of Agnes's pupils described a typical day with her governess:

> I generally get up about half past six. At seven I go to Po and read the day-book and Bible, and sometimes one of Gay's fables. At eight I go out till nine, and if it rains I play with my dolls or do anything I like. At nine we breakfast in the square drawing-room, and at ten begin studying with Po till two. At three we dine, and after dinner sometimes we study a little, and sometimes ride, walk or work in our gardens. We go to bed about half past eight.[41]

Agnes Porter was responsible for the girls' academic education, but other teachers were also employed from time to time, especially when the family was in London. Early in 1791, when they were all at Old Burlington Street, she noted: 'At home all day with my pupils and their various masters. What a pleasure it is to me to see them daily improve in person, manners and elegant accomplishments'.[42] When the family left London at the end of April, after a stay of three months, Agnes 'settled with my pupils' ... masters', paying them a total of £79 18*s.* 3*d.*[43] The 'elegant accomplishments' for which specialist tutors were required included music and dancing. Agnes could supervise the girls whilst they practised, but in 1788 her pupil Elizabeth had some lessons with 'M. Helmandel'. This was probably the well-known music teacher Nicolas Joseph Hüllmandel, who had been a pupil of C. P. E. Bach. A further payment to 'Hulmandel' is recorded in 1793. At the same time a total of £31 10*s.* was paid to other, unspecified, masters in London. In 1788 a Frenchman, M. Chapui, was employed as a dancing-master, and six years later 'Hills, drawing master' was paid £5 19*s.* 6*d.*[44] During a stay in London in the spring of 1796 Lord Ilchester's younger daughters 'made great progress with their masters in music, drawing and dancing'. Agnes, in the meantime, 'supervised as well as I was able, and made them practise in the intervals'. On this occasion Lord Ilchester gave Agnes £60 to pay his daughters' masters before the family left London.[45]

Lord Ilchester and his family had a high opinion of Agnes Porter. In 1790, shortly after Lady Ilchester's death, Charlotte Digby (the second wife of Colonel Stephen Digby) wrote to Mary Strangways:

> It is a great comfort to me to think that you have so valuable and amiable a friend about you as Miss Porter, so able and qualified to form and cultivate your mind and improve and open every virtuous and amiable disposition, and so really and truly interested about you.[46]

For all his faults, Lord Ilchester was fond of his children, and he appreciated the care that Agnes had taken of his daughters after their mother's death. In the first years after her arrival at Redlynch, Agnes's annual salary was eighty guineas (£84) – but in 1790 this was increased to a hundred guineas (£105).[47] Agnes was thus unusually well paid – most governesses would have thought themselves lucky if they had earned half this amount. In recognition of her exceptional devotion, Lord Ilchester also remembered Agnes in his will, leaving her an annuity of thirty pounds for life. Half a century later, Lord Ilchester's grandson, Kit Talbot, also recalled with affection the woman who had taught him during his earliest years:

> My poor children want someone who would love them and feel an interest, not merely in 'doing themselves credit' but in seeing their little charge happy ... In these days there do not exist such people as Miss Porter. Formerly, servants and dependants remained for half a century in a family, but now these things are changed, and the old feelings of attachment and affection have yielded to a more commercial view of the connection between employer and employed.[48]

In addition to being comparatively well paid, Agnes was also much better treated than many nineteenth-century governesses. She had a room of her own at Redlynch (many governesses had to sleep in the same room as their pupils), and she also expected to have a bedroom to herself, with the use of a parlour where she could entertain friends, whilst the family was in London. She spent most of the day with her pupils, though maids were available to dress them, give them their meals, bathe them and put them to bed. There were also maids to wait on Agnes herself. When Lord Ilchester was away from home, Agnes dined with her pupils, and she was able to invite friends and relatives to join them. When her pupils' father was at home, however, her inferior status was more obvious. As Agnes wrote in her journal: 'When Lord Ilchester is from home I spend the evenings with his daughters; when he is at home I pass them alone.'[49] At Penrice Agnes was treated much more as a member of the family: the house was smaller and life there was less formal. In such an isolated situation, moreover, Mary valued the friendship of a woman whom she had known for so many years. The Talbots paid Agnes £100 a year, and they continued to give her £30 a year after her retirement in 1806. Until shortly before her death in 1814 Agnes was able to live quite comfortably: she corresponded with her former pupils and saw them from time to time. She was spared the poverty-stricken old age that awaited so many spinsters at the time.

Finding an adequate replacement for Agnes Porter at Penrice proved to be an almost impossible task. More women were seeking to become governesses by this time, but many of them were ineffective and underqualified. In 1800 Harriot Frampton told Susan O'Brien what she thought of Mrs Jones, governess to a sixteen-year-old cousin, Harriot Quin:

> Harriot Quin is ... a very good-humoured, unpretending girl, very uninformed, and not at all accomplished. Mrs Jones (though I think her remarkably well calculated for her situation, as she seems to know a good deal of the world and has lived in very good company) is extremely ignorant herself. Even if Harriot had the inclination to inform herself, which she certainly has not, [Mrs Jones] would not be able to give her much assistance.[50]

Wherever possible, mothers preferred to base their choice of a tutress for their children on personal recommendation. When she knew that Agnes Porter was planning to leave Penrice, Mary Talbot asked her husband's cousin Henrietta Hicks Beach to help her to find a new governess:

> As I know you feel interested in such near relations, and likewise feel the great importance it is to have a proper governess to assist me in laying a good foundation of their youthful minds, I do not hesitate to request you to enquire *far and near* for a religious and well-educated woman who has no objection to *many* pupils. French and English grammatically, and the fundamental part of music, I think are very necessary accomplishments, and to as many other acquirements as I can meet with in the same person I shall have no objection.[51]

Mrs Hicks Beach suggested one woman, but Mary doubted that she would be able to cope. She decided that she might need to employ two governesses instead of one:

> Our children are so numerous now that they are in each other's way at study-time, and therefore I have thought [this] plan would be a good one: the superior governess as head, and a person under her direction capable of bringing the little ones on in reading etc., and to whom I could entrust them when the governess is out of the way, at dinner with us or elsewhere, to prevent their ever being with servants. I am withheld from enquiring about the person you mentioned,

> as I think such extreme timidity as is represented would not suit Mr Talbot or my little Welsh goats, supposing French to have been omitted by mistake from the list of acquirements you enclosed ... As to salary, that must depend on what the person asks. We give Miss Porter a hundred a year, and she always breakfasts, dines and sups with us and is our companion in the evening, but in the mornings we of course follow our different avocations.[52]

A few weeks after Agnes Porter's departure in October 1806, two new governesses, Mary Pryor and Jane Elborough, arrived at Penrice. The rector of Oxwich, John Collins, commented that 'they seem rather young, but genteel women'.[53] For some reason, however, they proved to be unsatisfactory, and in March 1807 Mary Talbot noted in her pocket-book 'Had an explanation with Miss Elborough and Miss Pryor'.[54] The two women left a few weeks later. They were replaced by two half-sisters, Miss Emily Raines and Miss Smith, whose mother lived in Swansea. They may have been recommended by the educational writer and philanthropist Sarah Trimmer, whom Mary Talbot certainly consulted. Mrs Trimmer, a pioneer in the founding of Sunday Schools, was well known and widely respected, and so many people wrote to her for advice that she became known as 'an unofficial employment exchange for young governesses'.[55] The Talbot children liked the consumptive Miss Smith, whom John Collins thought 'amiable and well-informed',[56] but she fell ill less than three weeks after her arrival at Penrice. Miss Smith struggled on for several months, staying with her mother from time to time, but she eventually became too ill to work. During her absences, Mary Talbot did her best to cope with her eight children. Agnes Porter was clearly worried about her, writing in October 1807:

> In the absence of any tutress, it is not your children who are losers, but yourself. You have so much patience and intelligence that they cannot fail to improve, but then the fatigue might be too exhausting both for your health and spirits.[57]

Miss Smith died in April 1808 and Miss Raines, who was also in poor health, left Penrice in the autumn of the same year. The Talbots were sorry to see Miss Raines go. Agnes Porter, who visited Penrice in the summer of 1808, approved of her, and thought that she was 'as attentive to the darlings as can possibly be'.[58] Shortly before she and her mother left Swansea, Miss Raines wrote to her former pupil Charlotte Talbot:

> I shall always remember your affectionate behaviour to me with sincere pleasure. I hope you will never forget me, for I shall always love you all dearly where ever I may be ... I should be very unhappy to leave this place without seeing you all once more.[59]

Mary Talbot seems to have had no governess at all during the winter of 1808 to 1809. Her sister Louisa wrote to say that she was afraid that 'you will wear yourself out with so much upon your mind', though she told Mary 'you are *perfectly capable* of educating your children'.[60] By May 1809, however, another governess had been engaged. This was Mary Bere, who was to stay with the Talbots for five years. Agnes Porter thought Miss Bere 'old enough to be careful, and young enough to be playful'.[61] She taught the children French, but the Talbots also appear to have employed a French governess, Madame Purivaux or Puirvaux, for a few months. This woman, who may previously have taught Mary Talbot's younger sisters, was paid £42 in August 1809. Little is known about Madame Puirvaux, but she may have been one of the many impoverished émigrées who were forced to flee from France at the time of the Revolution. In a letter written in 1796, Thomas Talbot commented: 'I suppose that at this time there is a greater choice of French governesses than ever was known, and possibly of the highest rank, good sense and respectability'.[62] Miss Bere was succeeded at Penrice by a Miss Fry, but she stayed for only a year. After her came Mademoiselle Allemand, who was more successful, though Susan O'Brien doubted that she would suit the Talbots:

> I hope your present governess will answer your expectations, but you must not expect too much. You will find few foreigners who understand your abstruse subjects, even in their own language. I hope she is more agreeable than Miss Fry.[63]

Unlike their brother Kit, none of the Talbots' daughters was ever sent away to school. Girls' schools were beginning to fall out of favour at this time, for many wealthy parents feared that the intake of such institutions was not exclusive enough, and that their daughters would fall into 'vulgar' company. The quality of the instruction in such schools was frequently poor; the girls were often inadequately supervised, and insufficient attention was paid to moral education. In 1796 Thomas Talbot, who disapproved of girls' boarding schools, advised Henrietta Hicks Beach not to send her daughters away, but to keep them at home with a governess instead:

> I can't here refrain from giving my opinion that [your girls] should not go to any school. The sweet, engaging and delicate manner they have been hitherto bred up in might possibly suffer from bad example ... As to schools for girls, it is as unserviceable as and dangerous as keeping boys at home: the one is liable to be run away with by the dancing master, and the other fall in love with the kitchen maid.[64]

Mary Talbot's own attitude to boarding schools was no doubt coloured by the experiences of three of her sisters. Harriot, who was Mary's junior by two years, had been at school in Weymouth on and off from 1787 to 1792, having been sent away for the first time when she was about nine years old, apparently for health reasons. She had an injured or deformed knee, and it was hoped that regular sea-bathing would be beneficial. At first Harriot was at a school run by 'poor dear gouty Mrs Morris',[65] where the fees for her board and education amounted to approximately £120 a year.[66] In March 1791 she was moved to Mrs Hepburn's school, which went rapidly downhill over the next year or so. Harriot told Mary that Mrs Hepburn's husband had 'gone so far as even to beat (in a slight degree) his wife in one of his passions', and Susan O'Brien wrote, after visiting Harriot in the summer of 1792, 'The school goes on as badly as possible. [Harriot] thinks it will not do half a year more, even if Mr Hepburn does not kill his wife, of which there is nightly apprehensions.' Harriot's father finally removed her from the school shortly before Christmas of the same year.[67]

Harriot's letters from Weymouth certainly suggest that contemporary doubts about girls' schools were only too well founded. The girls had lessons in French, music and drawing, but much of their time was spent gossiping and playing games. Agnes Porter had a poor opinion of the standard of Harriot's schooling. In December 1790, when the girl was at Redlynch for a while, Agnes noted in her journal 'My dear Lady Harriot good and amiable. I hope I shall enable her to make up for her school-days' indolence, and consequently small progress.'[68] A year or so later Lily wrote to her younger sister:

> You cannot think, my dear love, how vexed and mortified I have lately been to hear from several people such dismal accounts of the state of your education and improvements. As long as it remained unnoticed I flattered myself it was not so bad, but now it is not only observed but repeated to me, it must be *affreuse* indeed. I do not consider it as entirely your fault, considering the disadvantages you are under, but what is worst of all, and perfectly inexcusable, is that you not only do not improve, but absolutely go backwards, for instance spelling, in which you used to excel, is now very indifferent.[69]

It was left to Agnes Porter to repair the damage as best she could when Harriot finally came home.

After Agnes left Melbury in 1797, one of her pupils, Charlotte (aged thirteen), was sent to the London boarding school that her aunts had attended thirty year earlier. The school in Queen Square, which was known as the 'Young Ladies' Eton' was now run by Mrs Ellen Devis, a well-regarded schoolmistress who had published textbooks on geography and English grammar. The pupils were taught history, geography and other academic subjects, and they also 'learned to speak and read French with a very good accent, and to play the harpsichord with taste'. According to Frances Power Cobbe, whose mother attended the school in the 1790s:

> It was not considered in those times that packing the brains of girls with facts, or even teaching their fingers to run over the keys of instruments, or to handle pen and pencil, was the *alpha* and *omega* of education.

Instead, the main emphasis was on manners and deportment:

> *Decorum* … was the imperative law of a lady's inner life as well as her outer habits; and in Queen Square nothing that was not decorous was for a moment admitted. Every movement of the body in entering and quitting a room, in taking a seat and rising from it, was duly criticised.

They even kept the body of a carriage in the school, so that the pupils could 'practise ascending and descending with calmness and grace, and without any unnecessary display of their ankles', and the girls were all dressed 'in the full fashion of the day' with powdered hair and rouged cheeks.[70] Mary Talbot did not think that Mrs Devis's school would be good for her younger sister, as she told Harriot in 1798:

> *Entre nous*, I wish you could warn [Charlotte] a little against the bad examples she may meet with at school, particularly what I heard they endeavour to teach her and all the newcomers to that seminary, which is to despise *disgrace*, which is the only punishment made use of there, and which you must be sensible is a very bad thing for her to learn, who is already so hard to govern.[71]

How long Charlotte stayed at the school is unknown. A year later she and Louisa were to have some lessons during the school holidays with their brother's tutor, as Lady Ilchester wrote to tell her stepson:

> Monsiur Richard is to be with us during your holidays to teach you French and geography, and I make no doubt you will like him as much as his other pupils do. He is very good-humoured as well as clever, and I trust that you, Charlotte and Louisa will gain much useful knowledge from him.[72]

Like any twentieth-first-century mother, Mary Talbot was interested in contemporary theories about children's education. She and Agnes Porter studied books on the subject, and Mary and her sisters exchanged their own thoughts and experiences. Towards the end of the eighteenth century the conduct books which had been so popular a few decades earlier were beginning to be replaced by books which looked at girls' education in more general terms, with less emphasis on duty and obedience. Many of the educational writers of the time were influenced by the French philosopher Jean-Jacques Rousseau, who had emphasised the necessity of devising a plan of education which treated each child as an individual, and brought out their own innate talents and abilities. Despite the radicalism of his ideas on education and society, Rousseau was deeply traditional in his attitude to women, believing that they were naturally inferior to men, and that girls should be educated only to be useful and pleasing companions for members of the opposite sex.[73]

One of the most influential followers of Rousseau was Stéphanie Felicité, Madame de Genlis, whose book *Adèle et Théodore: or Letters on Education* was published in London in the 1780s. Lily and Mary Strangways met Madame de Genlis at Stourhead in 1792, and at the same time Charlotte Digby gave Agnes Porter a copy of one of the Frenchwoman's other well-known works, *Leçons d'une gouvernante à ses élèves.*[74] Madame de Genlis was beginning to fall out of favour by the end of the eighteenth century as a result of her stress on the importance of acquiring ornamental accomplishments, which had become so widespread that their value had decreased. As Richard and Maria Edgeworth wrote in 1798, '[Accomplishments] are now so common that they cannot be considered as the distinguishing characteristic of even a gentlewoman's education.'[75] Nevertheless, Madame de Genlis was still widely read in the early nineteenth century, and there are many of her books in the library at Penrice.

Agnes Porter and Mary Talbot both approved of the Evangelical writer Hannah More. Now one of the 'forgotten women of England's cultural history', More was among the most eminent and influential female writers of the late eighteenth and early nineteenth centuries.[76] Though deeply conservative in her emphasis on propriety, Hannah More did at least believe that women should be given a more rigorous academic education. In 1786, two years after her arrival at Redlynch, Agnes copied a paragraph from More's *Essays on Various Subjects* into her extract book:

> A lady may speak a little French and Italian, repeat passages in a theatrical tone, play and sing, have her dressing room hung with her own drawings, her person covered with her own tambour work, and may notwithstanding have been very badly educated. Though well-bred women should learn these, yet the end of a good education is not that they may become dancers, singers, players or painters, but to make them good daughters, good wives, good Christians.[77]

Mary Talbot acquired a copy of More's *Strictures on the Modern System of Female Education* in 1799.[78] Her sister Lily read the book at Penrice and recommended it to another sister, Harriot, who was about to marry, telling her 'Whenever I have a daughter I shall read it every day in the year'.[79] Agnes Porter read, and enjoyed, More's *Cœlebs in Search of a Wife* soon after the book was published in 1808, and she also read *Hints towards Forming the Character of a Young Princess* around the same time.[80] Hannah More was in favour of an improved system of education for women primarily because they would then be better equipped to influence the people around them – especially their husbands and children – and make them better people. Like her near-contemporary, the poet William Cowper, she advocated a life of quiet domesticity, preferably in the countryside where it was easier for the individual to concentrate on the development of their relationship with God. Rousseau, too, had condemned the corrupting effects of society and extolled the benefits of untouched nature, encouraging parents to keep their children in the country, where they could run free and benefit from healthy outdoor occupations such as gardening.[81] These ideas coincided perfectly with Mary Talbot's own dislike of London society, and her preference for a quiet country life. Whilst she was at Penrice in 1811 Susan O'Brien noted in her journal:

> I am frequently reminded since I have been here of many scenes that are described in *Adèle et Théodore*: les enfans et les gouvernantes font toute la society. They are the most amiable and pleasant children I have ever been with, and I feel interested in every thing that concerns them – yet it is too remote, too solitary ... Mary's conversation the only thing rational or pleasant.[82]

Another extremely popular author at this time was Maria Edgeworth, who was later to become a friend of Mary Talbot's sister Louisa Lansdowne. In June 1802, when she was at Penrice, Agnes Porter read *Practical Education* by Maria and her father, Richard Lovell Edgeworth, which had been published four years earlier.[83] Agnes commented 'Between theory at night and practice all day, I should do *something*'.[84] The Edgeworths, who were also influenced by Rousseau, believed that children were rational human beings, whose natural gifts might be brought out by education, but they were rather more interested in the needs of girls than Rousseau had been. Both boys and girls, they argued, should be taught by example, and they should be reasoned with, rather than punished. Girls should, however, be taught to be more restrained than boys 'because they are likely to meet with more restraint in society', and because 'much of the effect of their [girls'] powers of reasoning, and of their wit, when they grow up will depend on the gentleness and good-humour with which they conduct themselves'.[85] For both boys and girls, the Edgeworths stressed the importance of fresh air and exercise. Children were to be encouraged to use their hands, and to play with toys that 'afford trials of dexterity and activity', such as 'tops, kites, hoops, balls, battledores and shuttlecocks, nine-pins and cup and ball'. They could be taught chemistry and mineralogy, and they might also study living plants and fossils. Gardening was a particularly suitable occupation for children, as it combined academic study with fresh air and exercise. In later years the Edgeworths were criticised for their emphasis on practical work at the expense of the cultivation of a child's mind and imagination, but they did allow girls to study a much wider range of subjects than had hitherto been thought necessary or desirable.

Mary Talbot also consulted Mrs Hicks Beach, whose first three daughters were several years older than Mary's own. In the late 1790s the Beaches employed a Mrs (or Miss) Williams as a governess for their girls. She must be the Mrs Williams who was recommended by the Revd Sydney Smith (tutor to the two Hicks Beach sons from 1798 to 1803) as being 'extreemly good tempered and perfectly well bred'.[86] Mrs Hicks Beach gave a copy of Mrs Williams's manuscript 'Plan on which I should wish my daughters to be educated' to the Talbots. As might be expected, Mrs Williams laid particular emphasis on religious and moral training. She believed that children should have religion 'so interwoven in their hearts and souls as to prevent their ever being contaminated by any bad examples they may meet with, or led astray by any of the prevailing errors or follies of the times'. Their minds should be well informed: they should learn history, geography, botany, natural history and astronomy, as well as being 'perfectly mistresses of ... the historical and natural history of their own country and its antiquities'. They should be well acquainted with the best authors in the English and French languages; they should be excellent accountants, able to organise their own household, and should have 'some notion of the value of landed or funded property, repairs of estates and expences of building'. They should be able to manage without servants and make their own clothes if necessary. Such a programme, if rigorously followed, can have left little time for ornamental accomplishments, but the girls were also to be 'well acquainted with the rudiments of drawing and musick' and they should be able to sing and dance.[87]

Every well-educated young lady was expected to be able to read and speak French. Some girls had Italian lessons, but few had the opportunity to study Latin or Greek. Agnes Porter tried to teach herself Latin, German and Italian, and she was not alone in wanting to learn new languages. In 1804 and 1805, when the King's German Legion was stationed in Dorchester, Susan O'Brien attempted to learn German, though without much success. Susan's niece Charlotte was learning Latin in 1808, and two years later Charlotte wrote that she and Caroline Murray were 'most busily studying Italian, reading, drawing etc.'[88] The Talbot girls also knew a certain amount of Latin. They seem to have taught themselves, with some help from their brother Kit and cousin Henry, for whom Latin and Greek were an important part of the school curriculum. In 1816 Kit wrote to Jane:

> I think that you would soon obtain a sufficient knowledge of the Latin language to understand the botanical names etc. if you were to regularly and attentively begin at the Latin grammar, which I will explain to you next holidays.[89]

Another incentive to learn Latin was the girls' desire to read the old family papers at Penrice. About 1820 Jane Talbot wrote to her sister Charlotte:

> *Sciant omnes presentes at futures quod ego* am much better today. At least, rather better. I have been occupied with those foul deeds all day, and have found great treasures for you to help decipher. And considering I have had no help, I made out a good many, and I think the language comes easier to me.[90]

Lord Ilchester had given Mary a Welsh dictionary shortly before she married Thomas Talbot in 1794,[91] and most of the younger Talbots picked up a certain amount of Welsh. None of them became fluent, though Kit claimed in 1818 that 'the [Welsh] grammar, as far as concerns the parts of speech, appears very easy to be acquired when compared with the Latin and Greek grammars'.[92]

The girls of the nineteenth century studied a wider range of subjects than their grandmothers had done, but the more traditional female accomplishments were not entirely neglected. The young ladies of the late Georgian period were still expected to be competent needlewomen. Inevitably, some were better at sewing than others. In 1792 Susan O'Brien wrote to her niece Mary:

> I am glad you have finished your grandmama's apron. I have finished myself one like yours, and intend to hansel it at the race ball, which is to be this week. Harriott has been labouring hard at some ruffles for her, and to her great discomfiture one of them has been lost – or, as she says, stolen, for she is so carefull, I suppose, that nothing of hers can be lost.[93]

When a new baby was due, the aunts, sisters and other female relations would busy themselves making presents for it. In 1811 Louisa Lansdowne made 'a basket cradle ... covered with knotted muslin and prettily furbelowed' for her sister Charlotte's first child.[94] The sisters also made clothes for each other – in 1815 Charlotte asked Mary, 'I have never had a certain green muslin worked in orange chenilles. Where is it? Do not you think you could finish it some fine day?'[95] At Penrice in the early nineteenth century the girls made dolls' clothes and learned patchwork and cross-stitch with their mother. They also worked at other crafts – Mary Talbot bought netting pins and needles, a 'twister to make cord', a straw-splitter, and sheets of coloured pasteboard. She painted on velvet and tried her hand at japanning. She bought 'boxes to paint' and spent time painting work-boxes, vases and screens for her sisters. Paper-cutting was also popular – in 1813 Mary Theresa Talbot wrote:

> Charlotte has been cutting out all sorts of droll things this evening, and I have

> been cutting out tea-trays, fly-boxes, baskets, pocket-books, ships, pockets and four-pocketed baskets for Isabella and Emma.[96]

Many of the products of their labours, such as housewives (small pocket-cases for sewing equipment), pincushions and 'platted cases for sticking plaister',[97] were destined for charity fairs and bazaars. In 1821 Susan O'Brien was at Melbury when the Talbot girls held a fair. Susan commented rather disparagingly:

> They amuse themselves with making a variety of toys, like a repository for charitable uses, and getting their friends to buy them. Useless things, but it makes them ingenious and industrious, and fitted for all trades *en cas de revers*.[98]

In 1811 visitors to Penrice found Mary Talbot and her children absorbed in a new occupation. Thomas Talbot noted in his pocket-book that he had paid £24 6*s.* 6*d.* to Mr Hotzapfel for 'a lathe for dear Mary, and a tool-case with tools, sent to Penrice'.[99] In the following year he paid nine guineas for 'a chimney-piece for dear wife's turning-room'.[100] The lathe at Penrice seems mainly to have been used for turning dolls, but at Melbury, where Lord Ilchester and his family had a lathe at the same time, they were more ambitious, producing 'beautiful beads for necklaces, bracelets etc. etc.' made from the bark of a Scotch fir tree.[101] A few years later Mary was given 'the most beautiful set of chess-men of his own turning ... all different, and all pretty' by her brother.[102]

Drawing lessons were an essential part of a young lady's education by the end of the eighteenth century. Harriot Strangways learned to draw 'in black and white crayons' at her boarding school in Weymouth in the 1790s,[103] and when Mary Talbot arrived at Penrice as a bride she found in her new dressing-room 'two of the nicest little painted work-tables, and the most compleat paint-box with water-colours and body colours, crayons and colours in bottles, saucers and pallats'.[104] Artists had to mix their own paints, and in later years Mary's children enjoyed helping her with this task, as she wrote to tell Kit when he was away at school:

> We have been very busy grinding paints today. I bought the colours in powder and mixed them up with gum-water and white sugar-candy till they were like paste, and then put them in little saucers ... We made eighteen sorts, and I thought you would have liked to be of the party, as it was such nice dirty work.[105]

In 1804 Mary wrote that she hoped that one of the Hicks Beach daughters continued to take 'views from nature' as 'it is so amusing both to take them and, afterwards, to look at them over and over again'.[106] Some members of the family were talented amateur artists, but Mary's own artistic abilities seem to have been somewhat limited – in a letter written during her honeymoon with Sir Christopher Cole on the Isle of Wight, she said that she wished that she could draw, so that she could record the scenery of the island. It appears that Henry Talbot could not draw well either. It was his frustration with his own inability to record the scenery of the Italian Lakes whilst he was on his honeymoon in 1834 that led him to experiment with 'photogenic drawings' and then to discover a practical system of negative-positive photography.

Music was also important. The daughters of the second Earl of Ilchester learned to play the harpsichord – in September 1792 Mary noted that she had 'played on the harpsichord by moonlight'.[107] A few years later Harriot and Charlotte were 'learning to sing and play the tamboureen', and their stepmother planned to buy a triangle for Louisa. 'I think', she wrote, 'we shall have a charming concert'.[108] In 1795 Lily Strangways, who was staying at Penrice, described the musical activities there:

> There is a Welsh harper living in the house, who plays to us whenever we are in the humour, and there is a pedal harp on which Mary and I practise ... Mary's dressing room is a charming room, the pleasantest, I think, in the house. It has all sorts of comforts in it, nor is the least of them a very sweet-toned pianoforte and a *choisie* collection of books and prints.[109]

Ten years later, when her daughters were busy with their music lessons, Mary's pocket-books record regular payments for tuning the piano, and in 1807 her husband paid £82 to the well-known piano-makers Messrs Broadwood and Co. for 'a new grand pianoforte with additional keys and three pedals'. Another piano was bought from Broadwoods for £99 12*s*. in 1812.[110] In 1811, after a visit to Penrice, Mary's Irish friend Mrs Burgh commented on the musical skills of the eldest Talbot daughter:

> Will you give my kind love to Miss Talbot and tell her *now*, what I intended to have done the morning I was leaving Penrice Castle, which is that I am certain she will be a most excellent pianoforte player if she accustoms herself to *count*, and to play *rather* slower than all learners are inclined to do. She has a nice finger and a powerful hand, therefore Nature has done her part, and surely a little mechanical attention will not be withheld.[111]

Mary Theresa and her sisters also learned to play the harp. They sang too: their mother was fond of Scottish songs, and in 1809 a visitor to Penrice was entertained during dessert by the two youngest children, who sang duets and were 'as blooming and gay as larks'.[112] A few years later a cousin, William Digby, was sorry to find that Emma, the youngest daughter, had 'grown too big to sit upon his shoulder and sing the donkey song'.[113]

The Talbot children had dancing lessons at Penrice, in which they were sometimes joined by their neighbours, the Lucases of Stouthall.[114] For several years in the early nineteenth century Mr William Hart came weekly from Swansea when the family was at home. In addition to dance steps, such masters taught deportment, which was particularly important for young ladies. In 1814, when Charlotte, Princess of Wales, was at Moreton, everyone noticed her 'awkward walk and manner, which will be a great disadvantage in future, as in her publick situation gentle and pleasing manners enhance favors and cover a multitude of faults'.[115] During the Talbot family's visits to Clifton in 1810, 1812 and 1813 the 'ridiculous' Mr Harrington was employed to teach the children music and dancing. Charlotte Strangways reported, 'He is so extraordinary a man, both in looks and manner, that it is impossible to keep one's countenance'. With Mr Harrington the children learned to perform 'evolutions' or exercises, one of which Charlotte Talbot described to her mother thus: 'Put your feet together in the first position, then lift up your heels … and go "jig, jig, jig" without letting them down, doing your circles at the same time'.[116] It seems that the results of such tuition were not always thought to be beneficial, for in 1810 George Eden wrote to tell Mary Talbot that he had seen the latter's eldest daughter, who was staying with her aunt in London:

> I saw Lady Elizabeth … yesterday. She consulted me as to what dancing master would teach Miss Talbot how to enter a room in the most graceful manner. I am sadly afraid they are going to spoil all that you and nature and Penrice had between you brought to great perfection.[117]

Susan O'Brien, however, thought that the Talbot girls would have benefited from a little more polishing:

> [Lady Mary's] daughters are amiable and sensible, with much information of various kinds, but they have not the *manners* and *tournure* [appearance] required in the world – they inherit their mother's absence of mind and total abstraction from surrounding objects, which don't make them such agreeable companions as they are valuable friends.[118]

Mary Talbot's education of her children was widely admired by her friends and relatives, who thought that '[her system] was not to be surpassed for its sound judgement and tact'. The only dissenting note was struck, many years later, by Mary's son, who felt that this system 'gave rise to mutual distrust and, on my part, to occasional duplicity'. After two years at Harrow, Kit decided that he wanted to be moved to another school, 'being then fourteen years old and well capable of forming and supporting my opinions', though he knew that 'to express those opinions openly and without reserve would lead to no result'. Kit recognised, however, that his mother's apparent hard-heartedness resulted from her fear that he would be 'too puffed up' by his position in life, and would 'too soon [become] the great man'. As a result, she 'carried her caution to an extreme which resulted in want of confidence on both sides'. So Kit embarked on a campaign which was designed to ensure his removal from Harrow:

> I took care to fill all my letters with descriptions of the novels and romances I was reading, and took care that it might appear my principal friends were certain boys who, I knew, were considered undesirable companions for me.[119]

Kit understood his mother only too well, and he was duly moved to a tutor in Fulham.

Many nineteenth-century writers on education continued to repeat the advice given to previous generations. In 1801, for example, Elizabeth Hamilton thought that the most desirable female attributes were:

> Meekness, gentleness, temperance and chastity; that command over the passions which is obtained by frequent self-denial; and that willingness to sacrifice every selfish wish, and every selfish feeling, to the happiness of others, which is the consequence of subdued self-will, and the cultivation of the social and benevolent affections.[120]

There had, nevertheless, been significant changes, as Susan O'Brien acknowledged when she spent a few days at Melbury in 1813 with her nieces, together with the new young Lady Ilchester and the latter's sisters. According to Susan, the drawing room was 'like an academy of arts – not trumpery arts of box-making and cutting paper, but painting and music to please the most knowing connoisseurs'.[121] Caroline, Countess of Ilchester, who had been carefully educated by her formidable mother, Lady George Murray,

> knew all that it was desirable for a woman to know on every subject, and on many subjects her information was very great. She had all the accomplishments of the time she lived in – music, drawing, natural history in many of its branches [and] modern languages.[122]

Susan, who had been well educated by the standards of her day, felt somewhat out of her depth when in company with her younger relations. In 1821 she noted in her journal:

> Went to Moreton. All Lady Mary's family there, and Lady Charlotte and hers. All so informed, and conversant in every branch of the fine arts and fashionable sciences and learning that I feel as ignorant as an Iroquois amongst them, notwithstanding I passed a very agreeable week with them, who are all charming girls – good sense, good feelings, good principles – everything good about them.[123]

Nor did Susan think that all this new learning was necessarily a good thing, writing in her journal after a visit to Melbury in 1823:

> It was not long ago suggested in company that conversation was not as lively or, as it was termed, witty as formerly. People paused a little, but in the main assented to this opinion. It was attributed to the great encrease of scientific learning now taught to everybody, women and children, which gives a learned and serious turn to everything – everything is to be *approfondi*, and the great fear of using an ungramatical expression, or of not being acquainted with the subject talked of, prevents lively and unpremeditated sallys, and quick answers are seldom heard. Without knowing much of music, geology or botany, doubts and fears keep the young silent, and, with great knowledge on these subjects, conversation is edifying, but not entertaining, universally. The very newspapers teach Latin and Greek and a little Hebrew – enough, perhaps, for the young ladies.[124]

The Hicks Beaches' governess Mrs Williams summed up the attitude of the majority of her contemporaries when she wrote that girls should not become 'So absorbed [in their studies] as to induce them to neglect their more essential duties'.[125] In the early nineteenth century most people still agreed that, however well educated girls might be, it was undesirable for them to be too studious, or to show off their learning. In 1809, when Charlotte Talbot was nine, Agnes Porter commented 'I hope [she] makes merry and dancing, playing, dolls etc. If she reads too much she will be called a book-worm – that will never do'.[126] A year later, Elizabeth Talbot told Susan O'Brien that she thought her sister Harriot:

> very clever and entertaining, but would be thought more so by most people … if she did not engross the conversation so much as she does, for be a person ever so well-informed and pleasant, everyone likes to have a share, which makes her less liked than she ought to be.[127]

Susan O'Brien felt that there had been both losses and gains during her lifetime, reflecting in her journal a year or so before she died 'Il faut vivre avec son siècle. It seems to me the *siècle* I lived in was a *siècle* of pleasure; and this is a *siècle* of arts and sciences, reason and dullness.'[128] For the rest of the nineteenth century, educational opportunities for women improved only slowly. The prejudice against learned women persisted, and marriage and motherhood were still seen as the ultimate goals.

11

Literature and Science

It is difficult to overestimate the impact that the availability of books of all kinds had on the lives of the ladies of the late Georgian country house. Novels and romances, together with quantities of non-fiction books, were devoured by both men and women, but the latter spent much more time at home than their brothers and husbands. Most boys were sent away to school and university, and many, as they grew up, became involved in politics and public life: spheres from which women were, for the most part, excluded. Books, which could be sent for, or borrowed from a friend or even a public library, were an invaluable resource for women, providing instruction and entertainment, and topics for discussion with friends and relations.

The eighteenth century saw a dramatic increase in the number of books being published, and in the range of subjects that they covered. When Lady Christian Fox died in 1718 there were thirty-one books in her closet at Whitehall, including three Bibles and a prayer book. Of the remaining volumes, at least twenty were mainly concerned with religion. The others were all serious works, on subjects such as 'ecute diseases' and 'politicall arithmeticke'.[1] If one compares this with the fifty-seven books read by Lady Christian's granddaughter Susan O'Brien in 1793, 1794 and 1795, the contrast is striking. These included few, if any, religious books, but numerous novels. Susan read several historical works, including an account of the French Revolution and a history of the Plague of Marseilles. She read travel books, accounts of the American states of Virginia and Kentucky, and several volumes of memoirs and letters. Susan also studied 'Mrs Woolstoncraft on Education' – Mary Wollstonecraft's *Thoughts on the Education of Daughters*, published in 1787.[2]

Novels began to appear in increasing numbers after 1740, when the first part of Samuel Richardson's best-seller *Pamela* was published. Word soon got round if a book was worth reading. Early in 1751 Caroline Fox wrote from Bath to ask her husband to 'Send *Peregrine Pickle* (as it can't be had here) in all haste'.[3] Smollett's picaresque novel *The Adventures of Peregrine Pickle* had just been published. A list of books bought by Lord Ilchester between April 1760 and March 1762 includes Samuel Johnson's novel *The Prince of Abyssinia: A Tale* (later known as *Rasselas*), first published in 1759, and Laurence Sterne's *Tristram Shandy* (1760). Sarah Napier recommended Fanny Burney's *Cecilia* to Susan O'Brien in 1782, the year of the book's first publication.[4]

Commentators soon began to express their concern about the popularity of novel-reading among women, believing that the time thus spent was wasted, and that novels would corrupt feminine minds and hearts. In 1761 Sarah Pennington advised her daughters not to give herself 'the trouble of reading … novels and romances' – 'though many of them contain some few good morals, they are not worth picking out the rubbish intermixed'.[5] There is, however, no indication that the girls at Melbury and Redlynch were discouraged from reading novels. Agnes Porter, the pious daughter of an Anglican clergyman, read books of sermons and other devotional works, but she also enjoyed works of fiction, especially Gothic novels. Agnes copied out an extract from *The Prince of Abyssinia* in 1786. Three years later Harriot Strangways wrote from her school in Weymouth to beg her sister Mary to send her '*The Prince of Abyssinia*, which I have a longing to read'. She also asked for 'The two volumes of *The Preambulation of a Mouse*, which I want very much, indeed *any* pretty book you can get, of *any* sort or any kind'.[6] In 1792 Harriot was reading Ann Radcliffe's Gothic novel *The Sicilian Romance* (published that year), commenting in a letter to Mary 'How shocking it is! It has given me a sort of languid feel that is very, very disagreeable'.[7] Susan O'Brien read *The Sicilian Romance* in the same year, and *The Mysteries of Udolpho*, Mrs Radcliffe's most successful book, two years later. Agnes Porter knew *Udolpho*, and she owned a copy of Radcliffe's book *The Romance of the Forest.* Another novelist who was popular at this time was Charlotte Smith: Agnes Porter owned *Ethelinde: or The Recluse of the Lake*, and Susan O'Brien read *The Old Manor House* in 1795. A few years later everyone was reading the works of Walter Scott. The O'Briens read *Waverley* in 1815, the year after it first appeared. Susan commented '[I] did not like *Waverly* as much as my sister does. Don't think O. [O'Brien] likes it at all'.[8] Susan was entertained by *Guy Mannering*, which she read two years later, but she did not like *Ivanhoe*, finding 'the incidents so very unatural that even the times [they] are supposed to represent can't reconcile them with probabillity, even with possibillity'.[9] Nor did Susan like Maria Edgeworth's novel *Patronage*, finding it 'not near so entertaining' as some of the writer's other novels. It was 'too didactic':

> Instruction should be given, but not shewn so plainly. As a novel it is too soon apparent how it must conclude: every branch of one family is so good and so wise; of the other so bad and so foolish that it hurts the interest.[10]

In 1816 Susan asked her niece Mary if she had read Lady Caroline Lamb's book *Glenarvon*, a sensational novel which had just been published. Susan had been lent it by her friend Mrs Pitt, who thought it 'the worst book that ever was'.[11]

Too much novel-reading was thought to be bad for boys as well as girls. In 1812 Alicia Campbell wrote of William Fox Strangways, who had fallen in love with a girl who was thought to be unsuitable:

> Had poor Lady Ilchester checked his taste for romance and, indeed, depraved reading, and induced him to store his mind with rational and solid studies, she would not have had those silly notions to combat.[12]

Kit Talbot knew, when he listed the books that he had been reading at Harrow, that his mother would think that he had been wasting his time:

> I have read *Evelina, Wakefield Castle, The Three Monks, The Faro Table, The Black Tower, The Mysterious Penitent, The ditto Hand, The Recluse of Norway, Tom Brown, The Mysteries of the Castle, Ditto of the Forest, The Towers of Ravenswould, The Castles of Athlin and Dunboyne, Sebastian and Isabel*, and *The Witch of Ravensworth*. I like *The Recluse of Norway* very much, and *The Castle of Wakefield*. As to the others, they are merely romances, except *The Faro Table*, which is a satire I cannot understand.[13]

Henry Talbot also read *Evelina* by Fanny Burney, which, he said 'did not come up to my expectation, having heard it much praised'. But he enjoyed '*Persuasion* by Miss Austen, which is very pretty and interesting'.[14]

People read both for amusement and for instruction. Susan O'Brien sought comfort in her books after her husband died: on a February day in 1817, when she was at Melbury, she 'sat and read all the morning to avoid talking on subjects I don't understand'.[15] In 1819 Susan spent 'Several days stuffing my head with novels and nothings. Filled the loneliness I wished for while ill, without *ennui*'.[16] At the end of 1826, a few months before her death, Susan spent several days alone, reading beside the fire in the library at Stinsford:

> These two solitary days, and some books that I used to feed my imagination with, though reading melancholy as well as pleasurable scenes, pleases me. They always did. I can absorb myself, and even think I see and hear the people I feared; the people I loved; and even those I cared not much about; even the scenes themselves.[17]

Susan enjoyed books on travel and history, and read the occasional sermon. She read poetry, commenting after seeing some 'beautiful verses' by Lord Byron that 'it seems hardly possible that anyone that can write such singular and amiable feelings can be so bad, so worse than bad, a man'.[18] Agnes Porter, who enjoyed poetry too, distinguished between reading for pleasure and for educational reasons. In 1790 she read in *The Whole Duty of Man* 'a most excellent instruction', but she also 'treated' herself with 'Tasso and an hour of *Ormond's Life*' and read *Gaudentio di Lucca* 'to amuse me'. Later in the same year she was still reading *The Whole Duty of Man*, for improvement, together with *Gil Blas* for entertainment. In 1794 she enjoyed the works of Marie Jeanne Riccoboni and, for her 'more serious reading', the *Life of Gustavus Adolphus* by Walter Harte. In 1804, when staying with her sister and brother-in-law in Swindon, Agnes and her companions read 'Dr Lyttelton *On the Articles* and the Bishop of London's lectures'. Their 'amusing reading' was *The Infernal Quixote* by Charles Lucas.[19]

Mary Talbot read some novels, but she preferred more informative books. She took her reading very seriously, and sought advice from friends such as Townshend Selwyn and Dr Richard Fowler. In 1809 Selwyn wrote:

> Shall I tell you my secret for making reading interesting? *Never* read too long at a time. Make choice of such books as are applicable to your present state of mind; when you meet with a passage that particularly strikes you, either shut your book and suffer your mind to dwell upon it, or make an extract of it to which you may recur when you have done reading. Thus you will by degrees form in your mind a new set of ideas and impressions which, if they cannot efface the old ones, will at least divert your attention from them occasionally ... But I well know Dr Fowler will be a much better superintendant of your studies than I can, who am just come from digging for sense in huge volumes of old divinity ... I do not believe you would find much pleasure in [light reading] just now – the heart must be gay and the spirits buoyant to enable one to enjoy the effusions of fancy and trace with satisfaction the ideal scenes of fiction and romance. You want rather to be interested and amused.[20]

In addition to a collection of books on natural history that was waiting for Mary when she arrived at Penrice after her marriage in 1794,[21] she had 'all Shakespear's works, and all the poets bound so prettily', together with 'all sorts of history, ancient and modern'.[22] In subsquent years she continued to read widely on scientific subjects, and listed books that she had read, or wished to read, in her pocket-books. In 1802 these included Mackenzie's *Voyages in North America in 1789 and 1793*, Lee's *Theory and Practice of Botany and Walker's Lectures on Natural Philosophy.* In 1792 Mary noted that she was reading 'psalms and *Sacra Privata*', and religious works continued to be important to her. In 1802 she listed Isaac Watts's *Psalms and Hymns* and his *Guide to Prayer*, in addition to *The Practice of True Devotion* by Robert Nelson.

Books on conduct and education formed an important part of many women's libraries. Much of Mary Talbot's reading was for self-improvement, to enable her to educate her own children. In this she was following the Edgeworths' advice:

> One of the best motives which a woman can have to cultivate her talents after she marries is the hope and belief that she may be essentially serviceable in the instruction of her family.[23]

Mary's books included *An Enquiry into the Duties of the Female Sex* by the influential Evangelical author Thomas Gisborne, who argued that the duties of women were 'to care for their relatives, to improve their menfolk and to bring up their children on a Christian path'.[24] The Talbots also bought large numbers of books aimed specifically at younger readers. Such works had barely existed in the mid eighteenth century, but they were published in vast numbers fifty years later. In 1800 Thomas Talbot bought his little girls 'quite a library' in London.[25] In 1809 he wrote a note to remind himself to 'buy more nursery books at Tabart's and Co., no. 157 New Bond Street'.[26] The books listed by Mary Talbot in 1802 included *Poetry for Children* by Miss Aikin (Anna Laetitia Barbauld) and Thomas Day's didactic novel *The History of Sandford and Merton.* A few years later she wanted *Wonders of the Microscope, Wonders of the Telescope, Ladies Arithmetic,* Robinson's *Pleasing Instructor or Entertaining Moralist,* and Elizabeth Helme's *Maternal Instructions, or Family Conversations.* Madame de Genlis remained popular – Mary also hoped to have all her works 'bound uniformly'.[27]

Many books were given as presents; others were borrowed from friends and relatives, or bought on their recommendation. In 1808 Louisa Petty wrote to tell Mary Talbot:

> There is a little book of Mrs Hamilton's which you will like, lately come out: *The Cottagers of Glenburnie*; and *Memoirs of Captain Carleton* you would also like, it is short and very interesting. When you want a *very* amusing book read Malthus, as I was very much amused, interested and improved by it, and it is not fair to dislike a book whithout [sic] reading it.[28]

Two years later George Eden sent Mary *Cicero on Old Age* with the comment that it was 'a book you can certainly have no occasion for for many years, but I hope you will live long enough to find the use of it'. He had tried to find *Comte Alfieri* for her, but it was 'not to be had in all London'.[29] Later in the same year Eden recommended 'Huskisson's pamphlet on the depreciation of banknotes' with the comment that 'it requires almost as much attention, and is more practically useful than Euclid, and I do really think that if you set it before you, and put your two elbows on the table, you will like to study it'.[30]

Women also read newspapers and periodicals. Some of these might be bought locally, but most would be sent from London when the family was in the country. In January 1748 Caroline Fox wrote from Bath, asking her husband to send her 'the *noos*paper' from London.[31] The *Annual Register* and the *Gentleman's Magazine* were popular sources of gossip and information. Such periodicals also included reviews of books, which could be ordered from booksellers in London or Bath. In 1806 Thomas Talbot paid £31 19*s.* to the bookseller Mr J. Dedman of 12 New Store Street, Bedford Square, for 'newspaper 52 weeks, books, letter-paper etc.'[32] In 1779 Sarah Lennox asked Susan O'Brien if she had read 'the new weekly paper called *The Englishman*', which was 'excessively clever and true, and has the merit of plainess and no spite but at Lords North, Sandwich, and Germaine'.[33] Thirty years later 'reviews and newspapers', together with books about travels in Persia and Iceland, kept Susan and her husband 'pretty well employed in the reading way'.[34]

Reading aloud was a popular diversion in the evenings, and during the daytime when the weather was bad. Each member of the family would take their turn, whilst the others sewed, sketched or dozed. In March 1801 Mary Talbot noted in her pocket-book 'Mon Ami read some of *Park's Travels*, as it was raining', and on the following day 'Mon Ami read two hours to me in *Park's Travels*, then I went gardening'. In the following year 'Mon Ami read to me all evening in the most agreeable manner', and in the summer of 1804 'Mon Ami read to me in the garden and I worked'.[35] In October 1808, a few months after her marriage, Louisa Petty informed Mary, 'We have just finished reading Gibbon. Lord Henry [her husband] has read it out to me of an evening. It is twelve volumes – don't you think we have been very diligent?' After Gibbon, the Pettys moved on to Adam Smith's *Wealth of Nations*.[36] When the O'Briens were at Penrice early in 1811 they all read Dr Clark's *Russia*, followed by a life of Lord Charlemont, which, Susan thought, was 'certainly a heavy and laboured performance'. Next, they worked their way through Madame du Deffand's correspondence with Horace Walpole. Susan found these letters 'inferior to Madame de Sévigné's'.[37] The O'Briens also read to each other every evening at home when they were not otherwise engaged. In the summer of 1811, when Lady Adare was at Stinsford with her sister and brother-in-law, William O'Brien wrote to tell Mary Talbot:

> There is a very sensible book of travels in Spain by a Mr Jacob, who was a Dorchester man, a dissenter, and in Parliament. He gives the latest account of that country and people, and I think may be depended on. That sort of reading, when

well-written, amuses me more than almost any other. The contemplation of one's fellow creature is always interesting and improveing. There is a very interesting and, to me, entertaining book by a Mr Pasley upon the military institutions of this country, which I am reading to your aunts whom it amuses and, I dare say, would you, as it treats the subject historically, and I think of most people I know you have the least objection to knowlege and information.[38]

The ladies of the late eighteenth century were certainly better read than their mothers and grandmothers had been. They also wrote much more – both for publication and for private consumption. None of the Fox Strangways ladies had anything published before the mid nineteenth century, though a children's book by Agnes Porter was printed in 1791. But they all wrote hundreds of letters, many of which were carefully preserved, and later sorted and annotated, by their nineteenth-century descendants. With such a widely-scattered family, exchanging letters was an essential means of keeping in touch with relations and maintaining friendships, of discussing and passing on information about mutual acquaintances, and of finding out what was going on in the outside world. The usually short, stilted, factual style of the earlier letters gave way to epistles which covered many pages, and expressed the writer's hopes and fears. The composition of letters was an art – one in which Agnes Porter tried to instruct her pupils. In 1793 she commented on the brevity of the notes that she had received from Mary Strangways, and told her former pupil that she was 'rather mistaken' in her idea of letter writing. Agnes then gave her opinion on the subject:

> A letter to a friend seems to me simply this: giving them an hour of your company, notwithstanding whatever distance separates you. To do this is to convey your thoughts to them while you are writing. It little signifies what scenes surround you or what company you see – no, it is *yourself* your friend requires, and extraneous circumstances have no farther weight than as they affect and interest *you.* It is what you do; what you think; what you hope, fear, expect or wish, that forms matter for a friendly correspondence.[39]

Sending letters was expensive in these days before the introduction of the penny post. The cost was usually paid by the recipient, but letters sent to, or by, peers and Members of Parliament went free under certain conditions. Such people would give franked and post-dated covers to their family and friends. Agnes Porter could send her letters without payment whilst she was living with Lord Ilchester's family, and in later years she was sometimes able to obtain covers from acquaintances.

Many women – including Agnes Porter, Susan O'Brien and Mary Talbot – also kept commonplace books in which they wrote down their thoughts, and into which they copied extracts from books and poems that had attracted them. Mary later burnt 'the book in which the thoughts of her early years had been entered'. This was regretted by her son, who had always found his mother unwilling to confide in him. To him, the writings of her later years showed 'a monotony of sadness'. The subject-matter, which was devoted principally to 'serious thoughts', indicated a general 'dissatisfaction at her own want of firmness, decision etc., and constant self-accusation of a want of sufficient thankfulness to the Giver of all Good'.[40] Several of Mary's pocket-books from the early nineteenth century have, however, survived. Most of the entries are a factual record of the family's activities, with lists of books and plants and other things that Mary wanted to buy, but there are a few more personal notes: 'How thankful ought I to be, who have the use of all my faculties! May I never abuse them' (1798, after visiting an invalid); 'Mon Ami would be perfect if he was not so passionate. I must set him a good example' (1798); 'A melancholy prospect and retrospect considered' (1801); 'How dull the time passes when debarred society and employment' (1806, after the birth of her youngest child).

Rather more communicative was Agnes Porter, whose journals for much of the period from 1790 to 1805 have survived. For Agnes, her journal was a means of self-examination, in addition to a record of day-to-day events, of her hopes and fears, of the plays and books that she had enjoyed, and the journeys and visits that she undertook. Agnes cannot have expected that her journals would ever be published, but they were read by the families of her pupils during her lifetime. In 1812 she sent Mary Talbot a parcel of letters, together with two volumes of her journals, with the hope that they would amuse and interest her former pupils.[41] Unfortunately for later readers, the expectation that her journals would be seen by other people led Agnes to delete some words and to cut out sections or whole pages. In most cases these sections appear to have included material that Agnes felt to be too personal, painful or revealing.

The most assiduous record-keeper of the family was Susan O'Brien. She started to write her journal at Redlynch on 9 April 1787, beginning with an account of the years since 1769. At the beginning of the first volume, Susan set out clearly her reasons for writing this account of her life:

> Having frequently wished to recollect past occurences, as well for the amusement of my mind (tired of the dulness and uniformity of my way of life) as for a means of correcting any faults or errors which my judgement or my temper may have led me into. To procure myself this advantage I have determined to set down to the best of my recollection whatever of any consequence has happened to me for some years past, and though most of the events I shall have to remember will be probably very trivial, they may furnish subject for my observation and

> improvement, and by presenting to my mind at one view the motives of my actions, as well as their consequences, shew me whether I have erred in my choice of them, or whether it is to another cause that I must impute the constant ill success that has hitherto attended all my schemes of ease and happiness.[42]

For the next forty years, Susan kept a detailed record of her everyday life and of the comings and goings of the family. She commented on the characters of her relations, and recorded her reminiscences of past times. The journal became a confidant, especially after William O'Brien's death in 1815, when she was often lonely and depressed. Susan tried to be cheerful when she was with other people, but wrote in her journal 'I hope my eyes won't fail – if not, I may do pretty well, else I shall be very sorry to live and have a companion to read and take care of me for a salary. A hired companion has long been my dread.'[43] Susan's worst fears were not realised and she retained her faculties and her independence almost to the end. The last entry in the journal was written on 18 July 1827, three weeks before she died.

The children at Penrice Castle benefited greatly from the fact that their mother enjoyed their company and was reluctant to be parted from them or to leave Penrice. Highly intelligent and comparatively well educated as she was, Mary continued to read widely long after she had left the schoolroom. She was interested in scientific subjects, chiefly natural history and, more particularly, botany. She shared these interests with several members of her family – both male and female – and with many of her contemporaries. Women, who were generally excluded from the male preserve of classical studies, were positively encouraged to take up scientific pursuits at this time. Science, which was so intimately involved with 'mechanical and menial matters', was thought by many to be 'too contemptible and too trivial' to deserve serious study by gentlemen. This feeling is echoed in Susan O'Brien's comment in 1813 that, although her nephews Henry Talbot and William Fox Strangways were 'wonderfully clever', she feared that they might use their talents 'too scientifically for their fortunes'.[44] Three years later, when she heard that William was to go to Russia as a diplomat, Susan wrote to Mary Cole: 'If I may say so to you, his mind is so occupied with botany, mineralogy, geology, choncology etc. etc. that politicks, dates and treatys will be but dull and dry studys, though much more necessary for his improvement in his present line.'[45] Susan was probably right, for William's letters suggest that he spent much of his time abroad plant-hunting.

Educational writers such as the Edgeworths thought that girls could usefully spend time on scientific experiments, as they involved some of the same techniques as domestic cookery. 'Scrutinizing lower forms of life through a microscope' was, moroever, felt to be 'more womanly than vain attempts to master the complexities of Latin and Greek'. An interest in science could have other beneficial effects for female students: it was felt that such studies 'encouraged domesticity and curtailed flightiness [and] offered a harmless hobby, a curative for depression and a corrective to the evils rife in society'.[46] Many of these 'scientific ladies' of the late Georgian period passed their interests on to their children – and not only to their daughters, for boys and girls were commonly taught together until the boys went away to school at the age of eight or so. John Stevens Henslow (born 1796), who was Charles Darwin's tutor at Cambridge, probably inherited his taste for natural history from his mother, 'an accomplished woman' who was 'a great admirer as well as a collector of natural and artificial curiosities'. Henslow's father's library contained many books on natural history, as did the library of Charles Darwin's father. Darwin (born 1809) spent his early life in a house full of older sisters, and began his education with one of them.[47] And Mary Talbot's own scientific studies were to influence the developing interests of her nephew Henry Talbot, who spent much of his early life with her at Penrice.

William Henry Fox Talbot had been born at Melbury in 1800, a few months before his father's death. His mother, Mary Talbot's elder sister Lily, had no permanent home at the time, and her financial situation was precarious. Preferring London to the country, and unwilling to be encumbered with a small child, she left Henry with his aunt and cousins at Penrice, or with his half-uncles at Melbury, for weeks, or months, at a time. Until he was sent away to school in 1808, Henry probably spent more time at Penrice than anywhere else, and he continued to return there in his school holidays.

Of Thomas and Mary Talbot's eight children, four were born before Henry and four after. Charlotte, the fourth daughter, was just six days older than her cousin, who shared his birthday (11 February) with Charlotte's mother. It is hardly surprising, therefore, that Jane Talbot referred to Henry in 1811 as 'our *seeming* brother'.[48] In some ways Henry seems to have got on rather better with his aunt that he did with his mother, whose love for him was both intense and demanding. Mary returned her nephew's affection, writing to him around 1820:

> I cannot describe how much we miss you, my dear Henry, nor my own regret at the long time it will be before I have another friendly visit. To find your mind in the same teachable habit or, in other words, free from the self-sufficiency that clouds so frequently the best abilities where there is not a wish for self-knowledge, was a great pleasure to me ... I have been so bothered with conversation since I have been writing this that I am afraid you will find it difficult of comprehension,

> but you will understand that you are my beloved nephew and I your affectionate aunt, Mary L. Cole.[49]

There seems to have been a certain amount of rivalry between the two sisters for the affections of their sons. In the summer of 1814 Mary wrote to tell her aunt Susan that Henry was coming to Penrice for his holidays, and commented: 'It is flattering to me to find that those who differ from me in outward theory approve me in positive practice'.[50] At the end of these same holidays Henry wrote from Penrice to his mother: 'I am so tired of Harrow that I think going there is like leaving the Garden of Eden'.[51]

Although Henry Talbot is now remembered mainly as one of the inventors of photography, he was interested in a wide variety of subjects, including chemistry, astronomy, geology, mathematics and etymology. Botany and horticulture were lifelong passions – passions that he shared with many of his mother's relations, though not, it seems, with his mother herself.[52] Instead, it was his aunt Mary who first introduced him to these subjects.

Flowers were Mary's first love. By the end of the eighteenth century there was already a long tradition of female horticulturalists and botanists – women who did not necessarily commission expensive additions to their gardens, but who were nevertheless remembered for their enthusiasm for flowers. They included two sisters. Mary (1630–1715) and Elizabeth Capell (1633–1678), daughters of the Earl and Countess of Essex (both keen gardeners themselves). Mary, who became the first Duchess of Beaufort, was well known as a collector of exotic plants, whilst her younger sister, later Countess of Carnarvon, was an accomplished flower painter. In the eighteenth century the popularity of botanical studies increased, as aristocratic ladies followed the example of female members of the Royal Family. In 1759 Princess Augusta, the mother of George III, founded a botanic garden in the grounds of her summer home, the White House on Kew Green. This pleasure garden, which was laid out with the help of John Stuart, third Earl of Bute, was the beginning of the Royal Botanic Gardens. In the next generation, Queen Charlotte and several of her daughters were well known for their interest in botany. Also notable in the mid eighteenth century was the first Countess of Ilchester's acquaintance and near-contemporary, Margaret, Duchess of Portland (1715–1785), who was 'exceedingly fond of gardening' and 'a very learned botanist'. At her country house, Bulstrode in Buckinghamshire, she had 'every English plant in a separate garden by themselves'.[53] A love of flowers was considered to be a desirable feminine attribute, and botany was therefore one of the few intellectual pursuits in which, it was generally agreed, women could be permitted to excel without being unfeminine.[54] In addition to book-learning the study of plants, both wild and cultivated, encouraged country house ladies and their children to get out into the fresh air and to take exercise. It was generally agreed that this would be beneficial to them. As Henry Tilney tells Catherine Morland in *Northanger Abbey*, 'A taste for flowers is always desirable in your sex, as a means of getting you out of doors, and tempting you to more frequent exercise than you would otherwise take'.[55]

Mary Strangways's fascination with plants, which was to become an absorbing passion in later years, was already evident when she was in her teens. Her sisters regarded her as an authority on the subject, as a letter from Harriot, probably written in 1792 or 1793, shows:

> I have not been in the greenhouse [at Melbury or Redlynch] ... I never go there now for two reasons. One is, I have *nobody* to tell me the names now *you* are gone, and the other is that my charming little *bocage* takes up all my outdoor attention.[56]

Exactly how Mary acquired her knowledge of plants is not clear, but much of it must have come from the books in the libraries at Melbury and Redlynch, for Agnes Porter does not appear to have been particularly interested in the subject. Mary's interests were recognised by her husband, whose wedding presents to her in 1794 included 'all sorts of delightful books, particularly on natural history'. The satinwood bookcase in Mary's dressing room at Penrice held '*all* the birds, *all* the fishes, *all* the insects, *all* the beasts, *all* the butterflies, *all* the shells, *all* the corralines, *all* the zoophytes, *all* the fungusses and *all* the plants that ever were created, painted and described'.[57] In later years she was to acquire more books on plants and gardening. In her pocket-book of 1802 she noted, amongst a number of books that she wished to obtain, Lee's *Theory and Practice of Botany.* Mary subscribed to William Curtis's *Botanical Magazine*, and visited plant collections and nurseries whenever she had the opportunity. During a visit to London in June 1801 she noted in her pocket-book 'Walked three hours in Lee's garden'. This must have been the famous nursery and botanic garden known as the Vineyard, founded by the Scottish gardener James Lee in 1745 on a site in Hammersmith now occupied by the exhibition halls of Olympia. A week after her visit to the Vineyard, Mary went with her sister Louisa to the botanic garden at Brompton.[58]

Mary Talbot's interest in botany was shared by several members of her family, including her sister Charlotte and her future sister-in-law Caroline Murray. In the autumn of 1811 Charlotte told Mary about their investigations:

> During our other studies Caroline and I are deep in botany – that is to say, principally wild flowers, of which we have a great deal and a very pretty variety

> – and you must answer a good many questions for us. In the first place, what class of flowers the fuchsia belongs to? Can two species of the same flower be, the one perennial, the other biennial or annual? What is the English name for the canacorous, that beautiful broad-leaved thing, in full berry now in the hedges round here, and which we conclude to be a yellow flag? [59]

Encouraged by her husband Charles Lemon, who was also a keen botanist, Charlotte continued to study plants, and two years later her younger sister Louisa wrote that she was 'quite surprized to find Cha so far before me in knowledge on the subject'.[60] Charlotte also became an enthusiastic gardener, and Mary sent plants to her from time to time.

At Penrice the children helped Mary in the garden, and they all began to study the wild flowers that grew in the countryside around the house. By the age of twelve Henry Talbot was already exchanging information on plants with his aunt. He wrote from London asking his mother to:

> Tell Aunt Mary ... I have seen a species of foreign arum in bloom in Aunt Louisa's drawing room. It is a greenhouse, not a hothouse, plant. Its cylindrical blossom is of a beautiful orange colour covered with delicate white farina. It has only one blossom. There is also a beautiful rhododendron with upwards of an hundred blossoms on it. Also cineraria ... *something Japonica*, red and veined geraniums, two sorts of white heath, several other plants whose names I don't know ... Also red and white stocks, wallflowers, pinks, mignionette, roses, jonquils, geraniums, lily of the valley and a sort of red vetches in water.[61]

Two years later, Henry was able to offer a stout defence against his mother's belief that botanical studies were a waste of time, writing to her from Penrice:

> [Botany] is a science which extends pretty far, and which by no means consists entirely of nomenclature. It affords excellent exercise to the powers of discrimination and practises the memory very much. I am sure that I shall find Euclid much easier after I have accustomed myself, as I do here, to the attentive examination of plants, in the description of which every term and expression must be well weighed in the mind and throughly understood. Far from there being no *mind* in it, I think that if you ... ever read Smith's *Introduction to Botany*, you must confess that there *is* something more in botany than to know every plant when you see it. Aunt Mary says that there is a difference between a philosophical and a *stupid* botanist. The variety of wonderful contrivances which Nature employs for the protection of the flower and due ripening of the seeds etc. excite one's admiration at every step, and though not so useful, botany is as engaging as any science I have yet read about.[62]

Penrice was a particularly good place to study botany, for the Gower peninsula encompasses a wide variety of habitats within a small area. Henry and his cousins rambled around the cliffs, heathlands and woods, collecting and studying specimens of the local flora. When he was at Harrow, Henry continued to study plants with his friend Walter Trevelyan.[63] Together, the two boys compiled a list of the local flora, which Henry was able to compare with the plants that he had found in Gower. He also wrote regularly to his aunt Mary, telling her about his discoveries and sending seeds for her to try. Back at school after the summer holidays in 1814, he wrote:

> I have had a present from Trevelyan of forty-seven little packets of seeds from different parts of the world. Some are new and some are old; some are hothouse and some are not; some are rare and some are common – but which are so, he cannot tell, any more than their names, on which head we are in the dark. If you think it worth while I will send you them, or perhaps you are discouraged by the last packet's not coming up.[64]

Henry evidently did send some of the seeds, for he wrote again to Mary early in the following year: 'I hope you sowed some of the seeds I sent you by Kit. Some of them which were sown at Harrow have vegetated and look very odd'.[65] Henry and the Talbots also hunted for mosses, and Mary sent her nephew a small microscope so that he could study his collection properly.[66] Of Henry's cousins, Jane was the keenest moss-hunter: in 1815 her mother reported that 'Jane scrapes all the old walls with great perseverance', and Jane and Henry compared specimens, and notes on the mosses that they had found. Henry continued to exchange information on wild and cultivated plants with his aunt and cousins for many years, writing to Charlotte Traherne in 1835:

> I will send you a specimen of a beautiful new annual from California, the *Leptosiphon androsaceus.* I am glad to hear that the seeds I gave you of Hibiscus prospered in your stove. Would you like living plants of six of our rarer English orchises, viz. Orchis militaris, Conopsia, Fly Orchis, Man Orchis (Orchis anthropophora), Bee orchis, Orichis ustulata, all just snatched from their native soil at Cobham in Kent and Dorking in Surrey?[67]

Botany may have been Mary Talbot's main scientific interest, but it was not her only one. She shared a fascination with many aspects of the natural world with her children and nephew. When Henry Talbot was just five years old his mother wrote a letter for him to his aunt, to tell her of 'Mr Spence's', where he had seen:

> A young dried crocodile … and two peacocks stuffed whole with their feathers on, and a real bird of paradise, but not alive … and [in the next room] a large cockle shell and two beautiful green beetles and a monkey, a very very small one, and … a white rook.[68]

Mary and the children collected shells on the Gower beaches: in October

1803 they 'picked shells a great while' and, two years later, Mary and her sister Louisa 'picked shells, did not come home till dark'. In 1809, when Mary was away from home, her friend Jane King visited Penrice and found 'the three youngest with Sukey [their maid] just alighted from the little carriage, loaded with shells from the sands, rosy and hungry from the sea air'.[69] They also collected fossils and other curiosities that they found on the beach. By 1810 the collection at Penrice had grown so large that Mary Talbot decided that they would need a special cabinet to hold it. In 1810, at Abbotsbury with two of her daughters, she wrote to Charlotte who had been left at Penrice:

> There are no sands there, or shells, but a high bank of pebbles. Mary and Jane have picked up a great many, but none that are *very* beautiful. They found two animals that they mean to put in spirits of wine – they are called sea mice, though they are more like catterpillars, I think. I do not know whether you have found anything to add to our curiosities, but Mary and Jane have collected a great many fossil shells and curious flints and petrified urchins, so I think we must soon begin to have a place made to hold them, and I beg you will draw me a plan of the sort of cabinet that would be most convenient for them. I think the drawers should not be too deep, as they are then so heavy when they are loaded that they can scarcely be pulled out.[70]

Two years later Mary wrote to tell her son:

> We have been collecting more curiosities. We have some beautiful pieces of spar and manganese and a petrified leech, and Sir Christopher Cole has sent Jane two boxes (with glass covers) full of shells that he picked up in the East Indies. You can look through the glass and see them laying on the cotton. Charry has got a king bird stuffed. It is the most beautiful golden or orange colour. I think we must build a *museum*.[71]

The collection continued to grow, as Mary informed her aunt in 1817:

> Mary and Jane are busy fitting up a museum of stones and flints and dried plants, curiosities etc. etc. We have just got an old Roman *saucepan* made of silver that was ploughed up in this county, and which is so like a common one that I should have doubted its antiquity, but for the Roman letters or numerals that are on the handle, inlaid in gold, but which the learned cannot decipher.[72]

The Lemons were also interested in many aspects of natural history. Around 1811–12 Charlotte wrote that they had been attending a course of private lectures on mineralogy, and she apologised in a letter to Mary for failing to bring back 'a piece of the Land's End'.[73] In the summer of 1814 Mary and some of her daughters stayed with Charlotte and her family at their rented house, Deans Leaze near Blandford. Mary wrote from there, describing how they spent their time: 'When we have done reading, we go a jolly party in the gig – some behind, some before, and by turns running to open the gates etc. Our constant company is a hammer to crack open the odd flints we meet with.'[74] A few months later Charles Lemon wrote to his sister-in-law from Cornwall to thank her for sending him some geological information, and telling her that:

> The *pebblomania*, as Sir George Paul calls it, rages here at present very strong. We talk of another excursion to the Lizard district, and I have now got a small geological map of it which shews me we have missed a great number of things. It is only a sketch, and very imperfect, but if you would like to have it I will make one of my sisters copy it. I really think our society at Penzance will do some good. The science at present is quite in its infancy, but I really see no reason why in the present day it should seem more impossible that fifty years hence the wit of men should descend into the centre of the earth and find out the general laws and secondary agents which governed its formation than it seemed 150 years ago that Sir Isaac Newton should discover what is at least as far removed from the mind of men, namely the mechanism of the heavenly bodies.[75]

In 1824 the Lemons were 'deep in shells' and Charlotte reported that Charles was busy arranging their collection 'according to Lamark's new system'.[76]

Mary and her children were encouraged in their studies by the eminent local naturalist Lewis Weston Dillwyn, a wealthy Quaker who acquired the Cambrian pottery in 1802 and settled in Swansea a year later. In 1807 he married Mary Adams, the natural daughter and heiress of a wealthy landowner, John Llewelyn of Penllergaer, who was an old friend of the Talbots. Lewis Weston Dillwyn shared Mary Talbot's love of gardening and botany. He published a number of books and articles on British algae and wild flowers from 1802 onwards, and was elected a Fellow of the Royal Society in 1804 at the unusually young age of twenty-six. He was also in contact with many of the leading botanists of the time, including Sir Joseph Banks and William Jackson Hooker, who became the first director of Kew Gardens in 1838, in part through Henry's Talbot's influence. Dillwyn was also a zoologist. He was interested in the mammals, insects, birds and fish of the Swansea district and, like the Talbots, he collected and studied shells, of which he published a descriptive catalogue in 1817.

Lewis Weston Dillwyn and Henry Talbot began to correspond in 1814, when Henry sent Dillwyn a list of plants that he had found in Glamorgan, which had not been included in the *Botanist's Guide* that Dillwyn and his friend Dawson Turner had published nine years earlier. Dillwyn encouraged the schoolboy, and offered to help him in his study of mosses. He was as good as his word. In a letter to his aunt Mary written early in 1815 Henry said that he had just received a parcel of mosses from a Mr Traherne 'who does not know me, but he says he heard from Mr Dillwyn that I was fond of botany'.[77] The sender of the mosses was probably John Montgomery Traherne of Coedarhydyglyn near Cardiff, who was to marry Charlotte Talbot in 1830. Later in 1815, when Henry spent two months of his summer holidays at Penrice, he told his mother:

> Mr Dillwyn ... is an exceedingly clever man, and the more I see of him the more I think so, and like him ... There is so much to be learned from such a man, especially when joined to a very obliging disposition. He began his natural history with botany, then insects etc., etc., birds, and now shells, on which he is writing a book.

Later in the same letter Henry went on to describe an expedition with his cousins and Dillwyn:

> Mary, Jane, Kit, myself and Mr Dillwyn went on Thursday to Port Eynon, and were very happy, each in our way. Kit, examining the names of the vessels on the beach; Mr Dillwyn and Mary breaking stones with sledge-hammers and examining the [limestone] quarries, which indeed are well worth attention. The stalachtic incrustations (perhaps they are not so, but I am not a mineralogist) are curious and beautiful. The rocks on the beach consist (I believe generally) of petrified coralline – mind, I am *told so*, I do not vouch for the fact, and the neighbourhood abounds with rare plants, among which the bloody geranium would have delighted you.[78]

The Talbots also knew the eccentric naturalist and fossil-hunter William Buckland, who became the the first Reader in Geology at Oxford in 1819. They may have been introduced to Buckland by Lewis Weston Dillwyn, but Buckland also knew Mary Talbot's half-brother, William Fox Strangways, and Walter Trevelyan who had been at Harrow with Kit and Henry Talbot. In June 1815 Buckland wrote that he was hoping to receive some information on the geology of Glamorgan from 'Lady Mary Cole and the Misses Talbot'. This information was to be included in the Geological Society's map of England, which was already being engraved. Buckland also encouraged Jane Talbot to select 'a series of the most perfect fossil vegetables of the Welsh coal strata as her first essay in the noble art of lithography'.[79] Buckland, who corresponded with Mary Cole for several years, clearly took the Talbots' scientific studies seriously. Susan O'Brien, who met Buckland in April 1820, described him as 'a cheerfull man and, I suppose, very knowing in this new and fashionable study [geology]'.[80] Kit Talbot breakfasted with Buckland in Oxford a month later, and went to see his museum, which was soon to receive 'a petrified lady!'[81] Buckland was an entertaining, if somewhat exhausting, companion. He turned up on the Talbots' doorstep, 'bag and all', when they were staying in Bath in 1821.

He showed them the 'curiosities' in his bag, and told them that he had seen John Traherne, 'all alone in a chaise going to London'. Buckland 'thought Mr J. Traherne too grand'. 'But', Mary Theresa Talbot commented, 'I daresay [Mr Traherne] liked it better than being whisked along, as the impetuosity of Mr Buckland's temper makes him like to do, in the coach all day and all night'.[82]

A few months after his meeting with the Talbots, Buckland wrote to tell them of a collection of bones, of hyenas and other ancient animals, that he had found in a cave in a limestone quarry in Yorkshire. In response, he received a letter telling him about some bones in the 'museum' at Penrice, which had been found nearby, also in a limestone quarry, in 1792. It was as a result of the publicity given to this earlier discovery in Gower that two brothers from Reynoldston decided to investigate the cave known as Goat Hole on Paviland Farm, a few miles from Penrice. There they found a number of bones, including the teeth and part of the tusk of a mammoth. Buckland heard about the discovery from Lewis Weston Dillwyn, and wrote to Mary Cole on Christmas Eve, 1822, asking for more information. On 27 December, Dillwyn noted in his diary:

> John Traherne, Miss Talbot and I spent most of the day at a cavern which has been discovered on the coast about six miles west of Penrice, and there we found the bones of elephants.[83]

'Miss Talbot' was Mary Theresa, the eldest daughter and the most devoted 'pebblomaniac' of the family. Her mother had written in 1816 'Mary continues her *stony* heartedness, and has hardly a sigh for anything but a petrefaction'.[84] William Buckland hurried down to Gower as soon as he could after hearing about the discoveries there. On 18 January 1823 Dillwyn and John Traherne went with him to Paviland, and they were all 'engaged together geologically nearly all day'. Two days later Mary Theresa Talbot, Dillwyn, Traherne and Buckland visited Paviland again, and they also examined two further caves in the area. Their discoveries, which were described in Buckland's book *Reliquae Diluvianae*, published in London in 1823, included a human skeleton, the so-called 'Red Lady of Paviland' (actually a young man). In these pre-Darwinian days, however, the age of the bones was greatly underestimated. They belong to the Upper Palaeolothic period (*c.* 25,000 BC), and are still recognised as the earliest complete human skeleton to be found in Britain.[85]

In his book *A Plan for the Conduct of Female Education in Boarding Schools*, published in 1798, Charles Darwin's grandfather, Dr Erasmus Darwin, noted the popularity of chemistry with women. A list of books read by Elizabeth,

Lady Holland at this time includes 'some desultory chemistry'.[86] Maria Edgeworth recommended chemistry as a suitable subject for children, and suggested that chemists should make lists of experiments that could be carried out at home, and sell the necessary materials, so that parents could teach their children about 'evaporation, crystallization, calcination, detonation, effervescence and saturation'. They could also learn how to distinguish between an acid and an alkali.[87] Mary Strangways read *Elements of Chemistry* by Richard Watson, Professor of Chemistry at Cambridge, in 1793, and a few years later her sister Charlotte asked Mary to teach her 'chymistry' next time she came to Melbury.[88] A decade after this Louisa Petty told Mary that she intended to begin to study chemistry 'when they are come to an end of discoveries', for she found it 'very disheartening to find all one's studies brought to nothing by some after-discovery'.[89] Two years on, however, Louisa wrote to tell Mary that she was 'attempting a little private course of chimistry, which you would enjoy very much, as there are so few people that one can ask questions and see every experiment perfectly'.[90]

Henry Talbot showed an early fascination with chemistry, and in 1812 he wrote a long letter to his mother describing a copper-works near Swansea, which he had visited on his way back to school at Harrow after a holiday at Penrice. He had evidently taken a great interest in the precise details of the process involved. Back at school, where his housemaster Dr Butler had hitherto encouraged his chemical experiments, Henry caused an explosion by attempting to gild steel with a solution of gold in nitric and hydrochloric acid. Not surprisingly, Dr Butler then forbade him to carry out further experiments on school premises, so Henry had to resort to a nearby blacksmith's shop. It was his knowledge of chemistry that was to make possible the photographic innovations for which Henry was later to become famous.[91]

The Penrice children were also interested in astronomy, and in August 1803 they all 'got up very early to see the eclipse'.[92] Henry Talbot began to keep a notebook of astronomical drawings when he was eight or nine years old, and in the autumn of 1811 he and his cousins were excited by the appearance of a comet. They all corresponded on astronomical subjects for many years – in 1835 Henry told Charlotte Traherne that she had probably missed seeing a comet 'from not looking out early enough'.[93]

By the end of the eighteenth century visiting museums and collections of all kinds was a popular pastime. Such exhibitions stimulated and informed the visitors' own scientific enquiries, and led them into other fields of academic research, especially history and archaeology, at a time when dramatic new discoveries were being made in areas such as Greece and Egypt, which had not been on the standard route of the Grand Tour earlier in the century. Susan O'Brien went to see the Parthenon marbles in 1810, when they were displayed in a private museum in the garden of Lord Elgin's London house. She wrote afterwards in her journal:

> [The marbles are] finer than I could imagine could have been executed by the chizel. Horses quite alive; drapery and anatomy so expressed as hardly to be credible. I hope they will be purchased for the British Museum – they are too much mutilated to be ornamental in a private collection, but too fine to be allowed to go out of the kingdom, and will be a fine study for our sculptors.[94]

Susan saw the marbles again in 1818, after they had been moved to the British Museum.

In London in 1810 Susan also visited 'Mr Hope's fine house', where she saw 'Many fine and curious things – some rare busts and Egyptian statues more suitable to a museum than a drawing-room'. Susan commented that the house was 'more desirable to see than to visit'.[95] She was also impressed by Giovanni Belzoni's Egyptian Hall, an exhibition which was opened in 1821 and soon attracted great crowds. Susan's description of her visit in 1824 reminds us of the tremendous impact of such discoveries on people who had never seen anything like them before. Susan thought the Egyptian tomb 'the most astonishing sight that can be imagined':

> Three thousand years shut up. Such labour to find it, wonderfull when found. I would not but have seen it for anything. No imagination could fancy anything like its magnificence, its curious and excellent workmanship, and none will ever now understand the meaning of the emblems and hieroglyphs ... These times [are] called barbarous, but could produce such a work.[96]

At the same time, Susan and her nieces and nephews were also beginning to appreciate the importance of their own family archives. After several days spent 'reading and arranging old letters' at Melbury during the winter of 1816 to 1817, Susan wrote in her journal:

> Some letters very uninteresting, and from persons now unknown, might as well be destroyed. Some are very old and may be curious to keep, both for stile and contents on family subjects. There is something melancholy in looking at the writing of so many dead hands, and reading the same affectionate expressions we should use ourselves of our parents, children and friends. Likenesses of disposition; likenesses of amusement, as well as likenesses of countenance are very traceable in our generation to those described in our progenitors.[97]

Susan's niece Harriot Frampton also became absorbed in the study of family history. In 1819 her half-brother William Fox Strangways, far away in St Petersburg and longing for news from home, complained 'Harriot used to write to me ... but since she has taken to pedigrees, letters are neglected'.[98] During a visit to Stinsford in the following year Harriot was 'full of her pursuits, examining old books of all sorts from the library at Kingston'. Her aunt commented:

> It is surprising how much she knows and how much she does, and, I think, surprising the pursuits she has – pedigrees, antiquitys, divinity, old chronicles etc. A very uncommon variety of studys.[99]

Such subjects were, in reality, becoming increasingly popular at this time, for historical and genealogical studies, like botany, were fields in which women were allowed to play an active part without being thought unfeminine. Harriot's sister Louisa Lansdowne, who was described in an obituary as 'the animating spirit ... of Lord Lansdowne's refined and intellectual household', designed a group of armorial windows for the newly-restored chapel at Bowood in the 1820s.[100] Most of the Talbot girls, too, were interested in genealogy and heraldry. Charlotte, who was the most academic member of the family, continued with her historical studies for many years in association with her antiquarian husband John Mongomery Traherne, and it was she who was largely responsible for collecting, sorting and preserving so many of the family letters.

The legacy of Henry Talbot's early years at Penrice remained with him throughout his life. Although he became increasingly reclusive as he grew older, Henry continued to correspond with his cousins, and they all visited each other from time to time. Having spent several years abroad after graduating from Cambridge in 1821, Henry was eventually able to move into Lacock in 1827, when the tenant John Rock Grosett surrendered his lease of the Abbey. Much of Henry's time was taken up with mathematic and scientific research, and by the mid 1830s he was experimenting with the effects of light on paper treated with a variety of chemical preparations, using the camera obscura and other types of apparatus. His relations were fascinated by Henry's 'photogenic drawings', which were first exhibited at a meeting of the Royal Institution in January 1839. Shortly after this meeting Henry wrote to Charlotte Traherne, who had evidently been trying to make photogenic drawings of her own:

> As you are experimentalizing, I daresay you have already found out that in using nitrate of silver it is best to operate with gloves on, as the substance stains most unmercifully and lasts, not eternally, indeed, but sometimes for a fortnight or two. In my communication to the Royal Society I did not mention this, because it was 'beneath the dignity of science', but I hope you will be cautious with it.

At the end of the letter, almost in passing, Henry referred to his third daughter, Matilda Caroline, who had been born a few days earlier. His half-sister Horatia and cousin Harriot Mundy had evidently been teasing him about his obsession with his scientific discoveries, suggesting that the baby should be named 'Photogenia Iodine'.[101]

Charlotte's sister Emma and her husband John Dillwyn Llewelyn (the son of Henry's old friend and mentor Lewis Weston Dillwyn) tried 'sun painting' too. They kept in close touch with Henry during the next few years, as he refined and improved his photographic techniques, inventing the negative-positive system, which made it possible to produce multiple copies of a single image for the first time. Llewelyn was to become a distinguished contributor to the development of photography in the mid nineteenth century. Kit Talbot was a keen photographer, as was one of his closest and oldest friends, Calvert Richard Jones. Jones, whose parents lived on the outskirts of Swansea and were old friends of Thomas and Mary Talbot, officiated at the wedding of Kit Talbot and Lady Charlotte Butler in Ireland in 1835. The two men shared a passion for sailing, and travelled together around the coasts of Europe. A talented artist, Calvert Jones collaborated closely with Henry Talbot in the 1840s, and produced some of the earliest and most attractive photographic views of Swansea and the surrounding countryside.

Henry often referred to Penrice in his letters to his cousins, recalling with nostalgia their rambles in the park at Penrice, in Nicholaston Wood, and on Cefn Bryn and the Worm's Head. In 1835 he even told Charlotte Traherne that he had asked her sister Mary Theresa to find for him:

> A beautiful cottage in Glamorganshire with an acre of land for a beautiful garden, which is to consist of honeysuckles and sweetbriar, and eglantine (whatever that is) ... It must be the perfect image of seclusion, near a waterfall.[102]

In another letter Henry asked Charlotte to look out for 'a cottage orné or villa residence to be sold or let ... near the sea, far however from copper smoke, with a sandy coast, not muddy'.[103] Nothing came of this plan, however: in 1851 Henry said that he had not been to Penrice for twenty-two years, and asked Charlotte to give his love to 'the dear place'. But he did go there at least once more, for family letters refer to a brief visit in March 1868.[104]

12

Gardens

A few weeks after Mary Talbot's marriage in 1794 Susan O'Brien wrote to tell her niece how much she would be missed at her Dorset home:

> I have just been enjoying myself in the green house, where I have been sitting an hour or two, and which is very pleasant these fine mild mornings. Mr Greaves is here settling the little garden and putting hoops over the hyacinths. It all looks very nice, but I'm afraid will have no protection now you are gone, for though I think Harriott will succeed you in many pursuits and, I hope, practices, yet I think she does not shew any great taste for gardening or flowers. It appears a very strange thing *to me* at Melbury not to have them a very important affair.[1]

Flowers had been 'a very important affair' at Melbury and Redlynch for half a century, and a love of flowers was inherited by several members of the family. And they were not alone – or even particularly unusual. Many ladies in Georgian Britain collected porcelain decorated with flowers; they stitched elaborate, flower-strewn embroideries and tapestries; they wore flower-patterned dresses; their walls were covered with Chinese wallpaper embellished with hand-painted flowers; and their windows and beds were hung with flowery chintzes. It is hardly surprising that these ladies took an increasingly intelligent and active interest in the cultivation of living plants, both to ornament and enhance the pleasure grounds where they took the air, and to decorate the interiors of their houses.

Historians of eighteenth-century horticulture and landscape design have, until recently, paid little attention to flower-gardening.[2] The usual picture of the fashionable, late eighteenth-century country house is one of an austere building 'surrounded by the sweeping parkland, adrift in an endless sea of turf'.[3] This was the culmination of developments which had taken place during the earlier part of the century under the direction of influential designers such as Sir John Vanbrugh, Charles Bridgeman, Stephen Switzer, William Kent and, of course, Lancelot 'Capability' Brown. Such men are best remembered for large-scale plans, which involved the reorganisation and remodelling of the countryside surrounding great houses such as Blenheim, Chatsworth, Holkham, Stowe and Castle Howard. These designers were commissioned by aristocratic landowners, who were able to produce artificial landscapes by rerouting streams and creating lakes, diverting roads and moving whole villages, thus demonstrating their family's political and economic power and their own refined taste and modernity. Indeed, aristocrats such as the third Earl of Carlisle at Castle Howard, Lord Cobham at Stowe and Lord Leicester at Holkham took an active part in the replanning of their own grounds, reinforcing their claims that their superior education and breeding gave them the right to rule over more ordinary mortals.

These designers and patrons were, of course, almost all men. Social convention and their own limited education excluded women from professional garden design, and few possessed the independent financial resources that would enable them to create new gardens, or make large-scale changes to old ones. But this does not mean that the wives of eighteenth-century landowners had no interest in, or influence on, alterations to the grounds surrounding the houses where they and their children spent so much of their time. Women's interests were, however, rather different from those of their husbands and brothers. Unable, in general, to undertake expensive projects by themselves, and perhaps less interested in remodelling the landscape in order to impress their equals and social inferiors, they were more involved with everyday concerns, such as the desire to create a pleasant area within reach of the house, with shady, gravelled walks, where they might wander alone or entertain their friends. They wanted places where they could sit and read in peace, gossip or take tea. On seeing her new home, Delville near Dublin, for the first time in 1744, Mary Delany wrote to tell her sister: 'There are several prettinesses I can't explain to you – little wild walks, private seats, and lovely prospects'.[4] Ten years later, also in Ireland, Lady Louisa Conolly described her private retreat at Castletown to her sister Sarah:

> I am sitting in an alcove in my cottage with a park before it, in the wood three quarters of a mile from the house, a lovely fine day, the grass looking very green, honeysuckles and roses in abundance, mignonette coming up, seringa all out, the birds singing, the fresh air all about ... my work and my book by me, inkstand as you may perceive, and a little comfortable table and chairs, two stands with china bowls, filled with immense nosegays.[5]

If they had children, ladies wanted a place where they could play and run around, and perhaps cultivate patches of flowers and vegetables for themselves. They did not necessarily want to live in a typical Capability Brown landscape, in which their country house was turned into 'an island lapped by a sea of parkland, whose austere simplicity – mere turf, tree clumps and sheets of water – could pass for Nature, thanks to the art that concealed art'.[6] At Nuneham Courtenay in Oxfordshire, where there was a famous flower garden, Brown created a park that extended to the walls of the main building. Fanny Burney complained that she got her feet wet simply walking from the carriage to the house when she visited Nuneham in 1786.[7] The ladies who lived in Georgian country houses wanted sheltered, enclosed gardens – and they wanted flowers, which could be seen at close hand, in a place where their precious blooms would not be eaten or damaged by the animals that grazed the parkland.

It was almost expected of these ladies that they should be fond of flowers, which were often seen as the woman's particular domain. This was partly because of the association in contemporary minds between the ephemeral beauty of women and flowers, and partly because flower-gardening was thought to be a useless but decorative pursuit, appropriate for leisured, well-to-do females.[8] As early as 1717 Charles Evelyn wrote in the introduction to his book *The Lady's Recreation*:

> As the curious part of gardening in general has been always an amusement chosen by the greatest of men, for the unbending of their thoughts, and to retire from the world, so the management of the flower-garden, in particular, is oftentimes the diversion of the ladies, where the gardens are not very extensive, and the inspection thereof doth not take up too much of their time.[9]

Flower gardens continued to be the 'diversion of the ladies' throughout the eighteenth and nineteenth centuries, though it was no longer fashionable to set the flowers out in formal parterres as in earlier times. Planting became less regimented, making use of an increasingly wide variety of flowering shrubs, herbaceous plants and annuals, supplied by an ever-growing number of nurseryman and seedsman. The flower garden was, however, now less likely to be visible from the principal rooms of the house. Instead, it was often hidden away, in a secret, enclosed area which might be several hundred yards away, so that it did not impinge on the views over the landscaped parkland. As a result, the cultivation of flowering plants is largely ignored in most histories of Georgian parks and gardens. A recent account of the flower garden at Nuneham describes it as a rare feature in the eighteenth century.[10] As the history of the homes of the female members of the Fox Strangways family shows, such gardens were in fact quite common throughout the Georgian period.

A very few wealthy women were able to undertake large-scale improvements. In the early eighteenth century Sarah, Duchess of Marlborough, took an active interest in the creation of the gardens and parkland surrounding Blenheim Palace. These included a flower garden, laid out for Sarah by Henry Wise, master gardener to Queen Anne. For this garden, Wise's nursery at Brompton supplied thousands of flowers, including Brompton stocks, polyanthuses, ranunculuses, hyacinths, violets, carnations, marigolds, tulips and damask roses.[11] After her husband's death in 1722 the Duchess commissioned further work on the grounds at Blenheim. Elizabeth, Countess of Portsmouth, 'a strong and generous character', purchased the house and part of the park at Audley End in Essex in 1751. During the following decade attempts were made to make the landscape surrounding the house less formal: the kitchen gardens were moved further away, the straight drives were given more meandering routes, and remnants of the old avenues in the park were thinned out and supplemented by new planting, to create a series of informal clumps.[12] In the early 1780s the bluestocking Elizabeth Montagu of Sandleford Priory in Berkshire, recently widowed, even commissioned Capability Brown to transform her gardens into 'a lovely pastoral – a sweet arcadian scene' – though she thought it necessary to apologise for her 'paltry plans'.[13]

It may be significant that Susanna Strangways Horner was a friend of Sarah, Duchess of Marlborough. Both were forceful women who were not afraid to ignore contemporary notions of how members of their sex ought to behave. Though Susanna regarded her husband as a fool, and showed little inclination to obey him whilst he was alive, it was not until after his death in 1741 that she was entirely free to spend money on her house and grounds at Melbury. As a wealthy widow who knew her own mind, she was able to commission extensive improvements of the kind that few women of the time could even contemplate.

Little is known about the gardens at Melbury in the first half of the eighteenth century, but it is clear from the accounts of the work carried out in 1742 that they included a summer house and a bowling green. The latter was close to the house, and was surrounded by walls, as were the fountain garden and the adjoining flower garden. There was a greenhouse on the south front of the house, and an aviary in the north court. Fruit trees were planted along some of the garden walls, and in orchards around the house. Below the lawns and terraces to the south of the house was a garden canal. This sounds like a conventional late seventeenth-century plan, with rectangular, walled gardens containing flowers and fruit trees. The formal layout was ornamented with steps, pilasters and balusters of Portland and Ham Hill stone, and there were 'two lyons on pillers on each side the iron gates'.[14]

Susanna's alterations, which were well under way by the end of June 1742, included the demolition of some of the garden walls and an old summer house. By November there were twenty people at work. Some of the old formal terraces were removed or rebuilt, and several gravel walks were levelled and laid with turf. A 'grand slope' was created, leading down

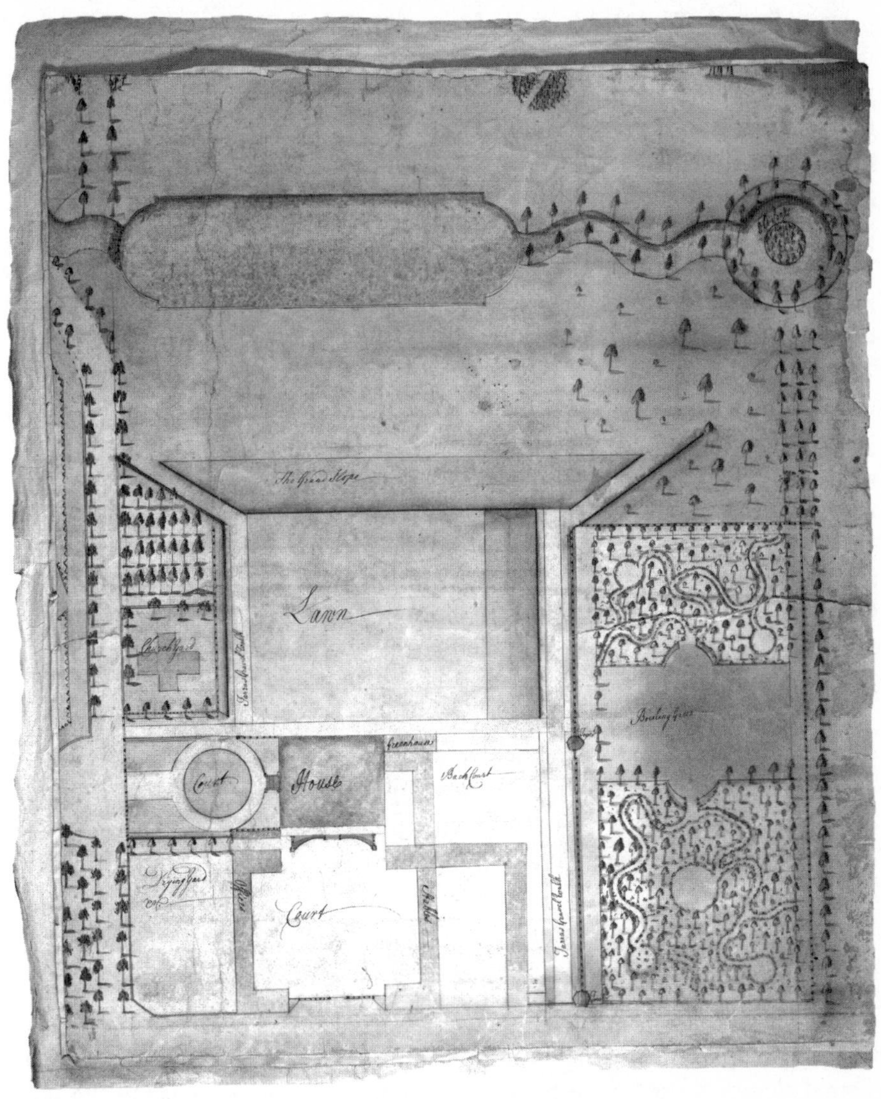

A proposal for alterations to the gardens at Melbury House (*c.* 1742). (*Reproduced with the permission of Ilchester Estates and the Dorset Archives Service, ref. D/FSI, Acc. 5294*)

to the canal in the southern garden, and the canal itself was made much larger: the estimates for the work included £76 8*s.* for 'making the laun before the house into one easey slope, that the water may be seen from the parlour floore'. The bridge to the east of the house was reconstructed, and new canals or 'pieces of water' were created on either side of it. Cascades were built, and serpentine rivers were dug between the pieces of water to the south and east of the house. New 'sunk fences' or ha-has opened up the views across the parkland surrounding the gardens. A new walled kitchen garden was created, and planted with 'espaliered hedges' made up of 'the choisest sorts of fruits agreeable to the different aspects'.[15]

Most of the work in the gardens and grounds at Melbury at this time was planned and directed by John Kininmonth, a man who is not known to have worked anywhere else.[16] His proposals for the alterations to the gardens are illustrated in a drawing, which may have been made by Kininmonth himself in association with his estimates for the work. Some earlier features, such as the canal and bowling green, are included, but the plan owes a good deal to the influence of the garden designer Batty Langley, who wrote in 1728 that there was nothing 'more shocking than a stiff regular garden'.[17] So there are winding pathways in the wilderness area or shrubbery, and serpentine rivulets, all of which sit somewhat uneasily with the more formal Baroque elements still remaining in the garden. The surviving documents do not, however, tell us how much of the work suggested in this plan was actually carried out.

During the autumn of 1742 Susanna's workmen were also busy grubbing out trees in the 'great visto' in the wood to the north east of the house. There were further payments for 'grubbing of vistos', including one near the garden, in 1743 and 1744. The eventual effect of this work was described thus by Horace Walpole when he visited Melbury in 1762, four years after Susanna's death:

> [There is] a charming wood of 200 acres cut into wild walks, with a natural water and two beautifull cascades. It rises to a very large circular field, round which is an *étoile* of six walks, commanding rich views.[18]

Layouts of this kind, which combined formal avenues and rides with informal elements such as serpentine paths, had become popular in the 1720s and 1730s under the influence of well-known designers such as Charles Bridgeman and Stephen Switzer. They were no longer in the forefront of contemporary fashion by the 1740s, but Susanna may have been influenced by her visits to her son-in-law's grounds at Redlynch, where the walks through the grove had been laid out fifteen years earlier.[19]

John Kininmonth and his workmen were at Melbury until at least 1745, when Susanna was informed that Mr Parsons had come 'with a pretty many hands and begane building', whilst Kininmonth's own men were busy pulling down the old stables and levelling the rough ground before sowing grass seeds.[20] Some further work was carried out in later years, under the direction of Francis Cartwright. A cold bath with an inlaid floor was built at some time between 1747 and 1750 at a cost of £25, and in 1748 Susanna had a sixteenth-century turret in the garden reconstructed in the 'Gothick' style popularised by Batty Langley, with an ogee arch over the entrance and six newly-carved pinnacles on the roof. Inside, this 'temple' was given a ceiling 'in the Gothic order', which was 'adorned with shields, the matches of the family',[21] emphasising its owner's ancient and illustrious lineage.[22] Susanna also had a small boat built in 1748, at a cost of at least £60. It was ornamented with a carved dragon which was painted and gilded. Paints supplied at this time by Bayly and Morgan included Spanish white, blue-black (1*s.* 2*d.* to 1*s.* 4*d.* a pound), common ochre, vermilion (6*s.* 6*d.* a pound), fine Prussian blue (30*s.* a pound), India red (8*d.* a pound), black lead (16*d.* a pound), red lead (2½*d.* a pound), white lead, and best stone ochre (3½*d.* a pound).[23]

In addition to her structural improvements to the gardens at Melbury, Susanna also bought large quantities of flowering shrubs from the Blandford seedsman and nurseryman Francis Kingston. These included fifty-four roses, forty 'lawrenistines', twenty laburnums, twenty jessamines, ten 'dwarf syringoes' (Philadelphus), and ten Hypericum fruticosum, which were probably used in a shrubbery or pleasure ground close to the house.[24] Planting of this kind continued for several years, and in 1757 Susanna's daughter wrote that 'Mama is going to put shrubs on the lawn which will, we think, improve it extremely. The borders are now earthing for that purpose.'[25]

After her mother's death in 1758, Elizabeth, Countess of Ilchester, made some further alterations to the gardens and park at Melbury, and it may have been she who created the cascades in the wood described by Horace Walpole in 1762. In a letter written in the early 1760s she informed her husband:

> Though I am busy planting, I write, which I look on as great merit, especially as you have never wrote to me ... Melbury is pleasant, the wood would be delightfull if there was a made road through it, but as it is there is no going – it is almost up to the horses' knees. The cascades are both quite clear, though the upper water looks muddy ... The green house is turned into a hot house. So many irons in the fire – I wish I am not ruined.[26]

Lady Ilchester continued to amuse herself with her improvements at Melbury for several years after this.[27] In 1767 she wrote that she was planting 'an evergreen drive round the park', which had recently been extended by taking in the fields in front of the house. She also informed George Donisthorpe that she 'intended to be very notable, and to pay the workmen herself every week'.[28] Some remnants of the old formal layout still survived in the late eighteenth century, as may be seen in the print of the house published in John Hutchins's *History of Dorset* and a plan of the grounds made around 1790,[29] but these were largely swept away during the alterations carried out by the second Earl of Ilchester after his mother's death in 1792.

When Admiral Robert Digby visited Melbury in October 1793 he found Lord Ilchester 'cutting down trees without mercy, and making great alterations'.[30] According to his granddaughter Charlotte Traherne, Lord Ilchester was seized with 'a mania for improvements' in the style of Fonthill, where the grounds around William Beckford's famous mansion had been turned into a flowering wilderness. As a result, Lord Ilchester destroyed the eastern approach to Melbury created in the late seventeenth century, together with the cut hedges and walls and terraces which had been preserved by his mother and grandmother.[31]

It was in the gardens at Redlynch and Abbotsbury that the influence of Elizabeth, Countess of Ilchester, was felt most strongly. The grounds at Redlynch, as originally laid out by Stephen Fox before his marriage, had not included a flower garden. A plan of 1738 shows the parkland studded with rectangular clumps of trees. Close to the house are a bowling green and a walled kitchen garden with four ponds, and to the east a terrace walk overlooks a rectangular grove of trees and the newly laid-out landscape beyond it. On the southern side the only informal feature is a serpentine path through a wooded area. This path led to 'Hervey's Grove', which was laid out in a geometric style, with four straight walks radiating out from a central clearing. Other features within the grounds were similarly named after Stephen's friends and relations. They included 'Digby's Walk', 'Count Coppice' (after Henry Fox, who was known to his family and friends as 'The Count') and 'Charlotte Coppice', after Stephen's sister. There is no indication that Stephen had employed a professional designer to lay out the grounds for him, but he may well have been influenced by the published works of Stephen Switzer, whose garden plans, though largely geometric, often included serpentine paths. Switzer was also fond of terrace walks, from which the surrounding landscape could be viewed. Lord Hervey had offered to send Fox a book by Switzer in 1727, when the work at Redlynch was just beginning.

Additions to the gardens at Redlynch began soon after Stephen and

Elizabeth Fox first began to live together. Nathaniel Ireson and Francis Cartwright were both employed at this time: in November 1739 Ireson was paid £41 19*s.* for 'his bill for the garden wales etc.'; and in December 1742 Cartwright received 5*s.* for 'seting up the statue on the tarrice' and 12*s.* for 'cutting a motto at the temple'. This may refer to the surviving summer-house, which is dated 1742. The orangery may also belong to this period. A payment of £10 10*s.* to 'Mr Ireson in part of Mr Cartwright's bill' in 1753 shows that both men were involved in developments at Redlynch over a period of several years, though much of the work cannot be dated precisely.[32] When Horace Walpole stayed at Redlynch in 1762 he saw 'a small wood cut into walks, a flower garden and a handsome menagerie',[33] and Samuel Donne's map of Redlynch, made in the same year, illustrates in more detail the impact both of changing fashions and of the requirements of the female members of the household. In this plan the original straight walks in Hervey's Grove have been supplemented by a number of Rococo elements, including curved paths and flower beds; there is a new temple;[34] and a pond, which is shown as a rectangle on the earlier plan, is now larger and more rounded in shape. Along one side of this pond there is a new serpentine path, and on each side of this path is a cleared area within which a 'cluster of kidney-shaped clumps' is arranged. These clumps (or beds) may have contained exotic shrubs as well as flowers, and the Redlynch accounts include several payments for flowering shrubs from 1744 onwards, mostly from Francis Kingston.[35] Significantly, the light-hearted, often fantastic style known as Rococo which was popular in the mid eighteenth century was thought by many to be essentially feminine, though it was also adopted by some men.[36]

The map of 1762 also shows a 'Ladies' Garden' beside the serpentine path which led from the house to Hervey's Grove. This was probably first laid out in 1747 or 1748, though work on it continued for several years. James Refel was paid £5 3*s.* for 'work in My Lady's garden' in November 1748, and in May of the following year there is a payment for thirty-four loads of gravel 'for a walk from My Lady's garden to the great pond'.[37] The new garden had already been planted by February 1750, when Lady Ilchester told her husband 'I am glad my garden looks so pretty and full of flowers'.[38] In locating the flower garden at Redlynch so far away from the house, Lord and Lady Ilchester may have been influenced by Dickie Bateman's *ferme ornée*, The Grove (also called Grove House) at Old Windsor.[39] Bateman was an old friend of the Fox brothers, having been their contemporary at Oxford,[40] and the Ilchesters often stayed with him for a few days on their way to or from London. A 'confirmed bachelor', Dickie Bateman was a keen gardener, and especially fond of flowers. During the 1730s he created a garden at The Grove, 'with a walk round it of about half a mile, part of which is close, in the wilderness way'. Guests who took the circuit walk could rest themselves in the self-contained flower garden, which was set in a grove, with a pedimented Ionic temple as a backdrop. Bateman's friend Horace Walpole described the gardens at The Grove as a 'kingdom of flowers', with flower-filled beds of different shapes cut into the green turf. Bateman was well known for his liking for chinoiserie, and visitors could also see 'a Chinese alcove seat, near which there is a Chinese covered bridge to an island'.[41] A 'Chinese seat' was duly constructed at Redlynch in the mid 1750s.[42]

Another old friend and Oxford contemporary was Charles Hamilton, a regular visitor to Redlynch, who had been in Rome with Henry Fox in 1732. From 1738 onwards Hamilton was busy creating his own much-admired picturesque landscape garden at Painshill in Surrey, which had a lake, a circular walk, and garden buildings including a hermitage and a temple.[43] Hamilton was a keen horticulturalist, who planted many newly-introduced species in his garden. He is also known to have advised many of his friends and acquaintances on laying out and planting their own grounds – including Henry Hoare at Stourhead and Henry Fox at Holland House. It seems likely that he advised Stephen Fox on improving his garden and parkland at Redlynch.

Lady Ilchester took an active interest in the management of her garden, though she does not appear to have worked there herself. In a letter written in the summer of 1750, when she was on her way home, she told her husband to make sure that the grass near to the house and in 'my garden' was mown. In another letter, sent from Bath in the early 1750s, she wrote:

> Tell Miss Cheeke when you see her that ... I wish she would see one of the least orange trees that I have put into the most sheltered part of my garden. Tell her the pot should be broke, but not quite taken away, and that it must thrive and be as pretty sweet dears [*sic*] as that at Old Windsor ... I also wish that Miss Cheeke would have one of the round spots in my garden where the uglyest things are planted cleared and filled with mertel cuttings, as this is the season.[44]

Work continued in the autumn of 1750, when a carpenter and a boy were paid for putting up posts and rails in 'the new garding'.[45] Further information on the Ladies' Garden is given in a letter written by Henry Fox in February 1752 after a visit to Redlynch, in which he asked his brother to 'Tell [Lady Ilchester] that the miserium trees, the white primrose and the myrtle in her flower garden looked very well'. Henry also reported that 'The holly bushes in My Lady's pleasure ground seem all alive'.[46] Whether the pleasure ground and the flower garden were two distinct areas is not clear – the two were often merged at this time.[47] By the end of 1753 there was also a 'house' in My Lady's garden, built of lath and plaster with a slate roof.[48]

The estate accounts of the 1750s and 1760s list some of the flowers that visitors would have been able to enjoy in the gardens at Redlynch. In December 1758 Francis Kingston supplied traditional flowering plants, including ranunculus roots, hyacinths, sweet peas, roses, nasturtiums, lupins, double balsams and African marigolds, in addition to newer introductions such as blue phlox and zinnias. Four years later there were further purchases from Kingston: a hundred scarlet ranunculus roots, twenty-five 'double gray vilots', one double lily of the valley, six purple lily of the valley, and twelve 'best whole blowing carnations'. The new plants were carefully tended, for payments at this time also include £1 10*s.* to a glazier for '24 hand-glasses for flowers'.[49]

Flowers were still important at Redlynch at the end of the eighteenth century. From this period there are many references to the 'shrubbery', an area planted with trees and flowering shrubs, with paths winding amongst them, where the ladies of the house and their visitors could walk in fine weather. This informal garden was probably planted in the 1780s for the second Countess of Ilchester, for the Blandford nurseryman John Kingston Galpine was paid £20 9*s.* for 'trees and shrubs sent to Redlynch' in 1783; and two years later further plants were bought from 'Mr Luccomb, nurseryman' for £15 5*s.*[50]

Mary Strangways was already beginning to show an interest in gardening by the time of her mother's death in 1790, though she was only fourteen at the time. Just over a month after the funeral, Lord Ilchester wrote to his daughter from Tunbridge Wells, asking her to take care of the garden, and warning her not 'lounge in it when the weather is either too hot or too damp'.[51] Early in the following year, Lord Ilchester left his daughters in London with their governess whilst he paid a visit to the West Country. He knew, when he wrote to Mary, how much she would be missing Redlynch:

> Notwithstanding your love of scrawling, I have not had one scratch from you, but as I am not exceedingly angry I shall write you two or three lines to tell you how garden matters are. Every thing looks vastly well in general, but I think there will [be] no good hyacynths at all. There will be, I believe, some very good auriculas, and we are making a stand for them and the carnations under the portico, which will be [a] very good place for them, not only to do well in, but also to shew themselves off. The gardiner has a new polyanthus from seed, which I think very pretty ... Every thing looks delightful, the grass coming on, the birds singing, and the bushes coming out very fast. I have been planting, that is, filling

The hothouse in Mary Talbot's garden at Penrice by Emma Talbot, (*c.* 1830). (*Private Collection*)

The rock pool in Mary Talbot's garden at Penrice by Emma Talbot (*c.* 1830). The figure glimpsed through the doorway may be Mary herself. (*Private Collection*)

up, a good deal. I am not certain, but I rather think you would prefer the gloomy horrors of this poor country life to the sunshine through a Claude in Burlington Street.[52]

In later years, after the family's regular visits to Redlynch had ceased, the gardens there became overgrown. As early as 1804, Susan O'Brien found the place 'quite ruinous'.[53] She was there again in 1819, and noted: 'Melancholy to see it so forsaken, but there's no remedy. The shrubbery might be restored in a week; the beech trees of my father's planting wonderfully fine and large.'[54]

The first Countess of Ilchester was also directly responsible for the creation of a new house and garden at Abbotsbury, on the Dorset coast, twelve miles south of Melbury. The site of the Benedictine abbey of Abbotsbury with its estates had been acquired by Elizabeth's ancestor Sir Giles Strangways in 1542, after the dissolution of the monasteries. In later years the men of the Strangways family had come to Abbotsbury to hunt and fish, staying in the building known as the 'Old Manor House' to the north west of the church. The inventory of the possessions of Thomas Strangways junior drawn up in 1727 suggests that this house was comparatively small, with only five main bedchambers. Some of the furnishings were quite expensive: there were silk hangings in the blue bedchamber over the best parlour, and brocaded hangings in another bedchamber, but the general impression is one of comfort, rather than great luxury. This fits well with the use of the house mainly as a hunting lodge. The downstairs rooms, in particular, show few signs of female occupation in 1727: there were two parlours, which contained little apart from tables and chairs, and a reference to a japanned iron punch bowl hints at long drinking sessions in the evenings.[55]

In the mid eighteenth century Lord and Lady Ilchester and their children began to visit Abbotsbury from time to time, as the popularity of sea-bathing grew and the health-giving benefits of sea air came to be appreciated. Whilst it was perfectly adequate as a shooting box, the old manor house was not an ideal house for a family with young children and a large number of servants, being cramped and old-fashioned. It was also in the middle of the village and half a mile from the sea. The house did have a garden, but this was probably very simple. In the 1760s, therefore, it was decided that a new mansion house should be built, close to the sea at one end of Chesil Beach. The architect of this house is unknown, but Charles Hamilton was certainly consulted. In 1762 George Donisthorpe told his employer that Hamilton had 'sketched out a front for Your Lordship's Abbotsbury design'.[56] Although this letter implies that the new building was being contructed for Lord Ilchester, it is apparent from subsequent references that this was really Lady Ilchester's project. In October 1762 Donisthorpe wrote from Abbotsbury to say that he was planning to go to Wyke Wood 'to mark some timber, as well for Your Lordship as for My Lady's intended buildings at this place'. A further letter, written in April 1763, suggests that work on the new house did not begin until 1764 or 1765, but it was finished by the autumn of 1766, when Lady Ilchester wrote to tell her friend Lady Hervey: 'I have been a jaunt to my new house, Pin Money Castle. It is close to the sea, which was a most noble and awfull sight as there was a most remarkable high south wind.'[57] The reference to 'Pin Money Castle' is interesting, for it suggests that Elizabeth had paid for the new house with her own money.

Before the early 1760s most houses had been built in sheltered positions away from the sea-shore. The idea of siting a house so that its occupants had a good view of the sea was something quite new. One of the earliest such structures was Lord Holland's new house at Kingsgate in Kent, which was started in 1762.[58] Lady Ilchester's 'Pin Money Castle' at Abbotsbury was therefore in the forefront of contemporary fashion. A sketch of the building made shortly after its construction shows a two-storeyed house in the Strawberry Hill Gothic style.[59] The south front, which faced the sea, was symmetrical, with broad, canted bays projecting on either side of the three-bay centre. The parapet was castellated, and the diamond-paned windows had pointed heads. In front of the house, a narrow garden was enclosed by a castellated wall, into which were set arbours, with seats sheltered from the wind. To the rear of the house, and slightly to one side, was a curious rectangular block with a pyramid-shaped roof – perhaps stables or a service wing of some kind. The house was so close to the shore that Agnes Porter, who stayed there in 1791, noted 'the sea prospect very grand, and seen from the drawing-room window as if we had been on board a ship'.[60]

The Gothic style seems to have been particularly popular with female representatives of ancient families in the mid eighteenth century. After 1741, the heiress Henrietta, Countess of Oxford and Mortimer, of Welbeck Abbey in Nottinghamshire, spent her widowhood 'in collecting and monumenting the portraits and reliquaries of all the great families from which she is descended'.[61] She showed her respect for her ancestors by adopting the Gothic style for many of her improvements at Welbeck. In the 1750s Elizabeth, Countess of Northumberland used Gothic designs when she restored her ancestral seat, Alnwick Castle. Like Susanna Strangways Horner at Melbury, she ensured that the coats of arms of her noble forebears were conspicuously displayed wherever possible.[62] But Gothic was also very fashionable in the 1760s, and Lady Ilchester was no doubt influenced by her friends too. Dickie Bateman added a Gothic cloister to his house at Old Windsor at this time, having been converted from the Chinese style by his friend Horace Walpole.[63] The choice of the Gothic style for the new house at Abbotsbury may, indeed, have been a direct result of Walpole's influence, for he visited Lord and Lady Ilchester in July 1762, just as the plans for the building were being discussed.

Lady Ilchester appears to have stayed in her new house for the first time in the summer of 1766. She took her daughters with her, and they spent some of their time 'batheing in the sea for health'.[64] At this time there was no flower garden at Abbotsbury, but in the autumn of 1767 Elizabeth wrote to tell her daughter Susan that she had 'contrived a flower garden at the bottom of the hill'.[65] Work continued in later years, apparently to create shelter-belts for the ornamental gardens: payments to Charles Hebditch for work at Abbotsbury in the years 1784 to 1787 included £10 for 'making hedges round the new plantations'.[66] The house and gardens at Abbotsbury were developed further in the early nineteenth century by Maria, Countess of Ilchester, the second wife of the second Earl. In 1816 Susan O'Brien went there for the first time for several years and wrote:

> I have been for a few days at Abbotsbury. It is quite metamorphosed since I saw it last. Really, now the house is a very good and a very pretty one, but no alteration can be made beyond the walls of the court, and it must always be *en le beau milieu d'un champ* [right in the middle of a field]. There is, however, a very good garden a quarter of a mile off, where flowers and every thing seem to flourish. It is just before you come to that hollow way between the two red banks.[67]

The relationship between the garden made in 1767 and the one described by Susan in 1816 is not totally clear. The first Countess of Ilchester is traditionally regarded as the founder of the famous 'sub-tropical' gardens at Abbotsbury, which visitors can still enjoy today, though the house built in the 1760s was burnt down in 1913.[68] The core of the garden consists of a hollow, which is far enough back from the sea for it to be sheltered from the worst of the winds and includes Abbotsbury's only patch of sandy soil. These conditions have made it possible to grow a wide variety of tender plants, many of which were first introduced in the nineteenth century.

The first Countess of Ilchester's interest in plants was inherited by her eldest daughter. As a child Susan had a garden of her own at Redlynch,[69] and she also seems to have had a garden of some kind whilst she was in America, for Lady Holland sent her a box of flower roots and seeds in 1766.[70] It was not, however, until after she and her husband left America and settled at Stinsford in the summer of 1775 that Susan's horticultural activities really began. When the O'Briens first saw Stinsford in the summer of 1774 the house had been uninhabited for a long time, and the garden was presumably in an equally neglected condition. William and Susan never had enough money to make any very expensive improvements, nor could they afford to employ more than one gardener. In 1812 Susan recorded the death of Andrew Vacher, her gardener for the past twenty-three years, and noted in her journal 'though grown useless, I feel sorry for him'.[71] Useless or not, the O'Briens and Andrew had, between them, created a beautiful garden by this time. Susan's great-niece Charlotte Talbot, who was born in 1800, visited Stinsford when she was a girl, and left the following description of the grounds there:

> A garden door led from a lobby on to the terrace, where in spring my aunt had what she called her *ribbon* – a broad border of crocuses, with large bunches of double red hepaticas at regular intervals. There were three gardens, one above the other. On the second terrace stood an oriental plane tree of great beauty and a fine magnolia. The lowest garden ended in a pond, where I have seen fine feats of skating.[72]

Spring flowers were a particular feature of the garden at Stinsford. In January 1818 Susan noted that she had crocuses and hepaticas 'blowing and very pretty', and in February 1825 'Walked on the gravel walk. Crocuses in great beauty'.[73] Later on, there were roses, stocks, carnations and pinks. The latter were popular florists' flowers, and annual 'Pink Feasts' or flower shows were held in many towns. In a letter written in June 1810 Susan asked her niece Mary if she was going to the annual Pink Feast, which was to be held at the Woolpack in Salisbury, and said that she would like to have some 'roots … cast-offs' if they could be obtained cheaply.[74] In June 1825 Susan visited the Pink Feast in Dorchester with her sister-in-law Mrs Charles Strangways. Afterwards, she commented in her journal: 'I did not think pinks would have made such a show, but since I find some of my own, if they had been so dressed and papered up, would have looked nearly as well.'[75] Susan must have had a greenhouse too, for she grew myrtles and orange trees.

Susan loved her garden and the surrounding countryside, and she missed the freedom of her life there when she was away. In June 1798 she wrote from Long Bredy, where she was staying with her friends the Brownes, to tell her niece Elizabeth that she was:

> Hotter, crosser, more out of humour and more out of every thing than words can express, in the hottest house, with the most stinking kitchen. Can I but regret my orange trees, my roses, my steps and my gravel walk? Can I be agreeable,

entertaining, conversible, sensible and a few more etceteras, which I am invited and expected to be? I answer, 'No, no, no'.[76]

Susan was particularly upset when a number of trees around the house were felled early in 1805, especially as a part of the garden wall fell down at the same time. Afterwards, she 'walked in the garden and grove, contemplating the ruinous appearance of every thing round me'.[77] One of the most notable features of the garden was a plane tree that William O'Brien had planted. Just over a year after his death, on Michaelmas Day 1816, there was a disaster, when a large branch of the tree was torn off during a storm. Susan described this event in her journal:

A loss never to be supplyed. The glory of the garden and the favorite of my heart. It was O.'s planting and he loved it much – used sometimes to say, if anything happened to it, he should hate the place. I cannot say that I have too many ties to it, but it grieves me in every way. It quite disfigures the garden, its dear shade, my summer retreat, is ruined.[78]

In a letter to Elizabeth Feilding, Susan said that her only consolation was that the tree had not been damaged until after William's death.[79] But the tree survived. A magnificent plane tree – presumably the same one – is still an important feature of the gardens at Stinsford, nearly two hundred years later.

Another important part of the garden at Stinsford was the gravel walk on the upper terrace, close to the house. A door led from the terrace into the churchyard, and it has been suggested that this was the setting for a scene in Hardy's novel *Two on a Tower*, in which Swithin St Cleeve climbs the tower of Welland church and watches Lady Constantine as she paces up and down on the terrace in front of her house.[80] In old age, William and Susan O'Brien would walk on their terrace even in the coldest weather. In August 1815 William, who had been ill for some time, was able to get as far as the gravel walk 'but was so weak he could hardly walk into the house'.[81] A week later he was dead. In 1817, when the Duke of Gloucester paid a surprise visit to Stinsford, he found Susan on the gravel walk, and offered her his arm to help her up the steps into the house 'seeing I was very infirm'. The garden was full of memories, and in later years Susan would often walk there, or sit and think of her husband and their years together. In May 1819, after visiting Redlynch and finding the gardens there neglected, she returned sadly to her empty house at Stinsford. On the following day she wrote in her journal:

Alone all day. A beautiful sunset. In the porch to look at it – here, in early days, we used to sit and contrive our little improvements: the road, the sweep etc.

> Walked up and down in it a long time, but with what different views! In idea I see all that is neat and handsome destroyed, the grass full of cart ruts, pigs grubbing about the house and shrubbery – everything obliterated but our monument in the church.[82]

In general Susan was happiest at Stinsford, and the garden there was a comfort and a distraction from other cares. But she could find no consolation when her husband fell seriously ill in 1814, and wrote sadly in her journal: 'The garden in beauty and every thing looking well, but I had no pleasure in it, or any thing.'[83] Two years later, when she was particularly depressed, she found that the garden and flowers provided 'some amusement', adding, 'All want some one to admire them – at least to say how pretty we are'. Indeed, to Susan the garden almost took on a personality of its own, particularly after her husband's death. As she wrote in May 1822: 'Quite alone. The garden a sort of companion – never saw it in so much beauty.'[84] The Stinsford garden continued to delight and interest Susan until the end of her long life. In her last surviving letter to Mary, written in February 1826 when she was eighty-three, she told her niece:

> Crocus border in its glory, and many other good symptoms of spring and very fine weather. Those, you will allow, are pleasures, and the pleasures of Nature don't depend so much on others as most other pleasures do.[85]

At Penrice, as at Redlynch half a century earlier, there is no indication that a flower garden was laid out when the grounds were landscaped for Thomas Talbot in the late 1770s. There was little new work during the 1780s, but in October 1791 work started on a small hothouse or orangery, sited near to the walled kitchen gardens, a quarter of a mile from the house. There would have been little to see, apart from the plans and perhaps the foundations of this new building, when Mary Strangways first visited Penrice with her father early in the following year. After meeting Mary, however, Thomas pressed on with his alterations to the house and grounds with enthusiasm, and in January 1793 he was able to tell his friend Michael Hicks Beach that he had 'totally changed the walks and shrubberys and begun to level and arrange the unfinished heaps of rubbish etc. etc. near the river'.[86] The hothouse or orangery at Penrice was finished later in the same year. Mary's family believed that she finally agreed to marry Thomas because she had fallen in love with his garden. And it was, as her son later wrote, the garden that sustained her during the years of her marriage to him:

> Had it not been for her garden, that never-ending, still-beginning subject of interest, it would have been impossible to have endured for nineteen years such

> an isolation as my mother was subjected to. Gardening was her passion, not her employment for employment's sake, and I do not believe the attraction of all the gaieties of London would have induced her to forego seeing the snowdrops or the crocuses at Penrice in blow for one single day! [87]

Mary divided up the year according to her own 'botanical chronology', telling William O'Brien in 1814: 'I shall be put out of my reckoning if crocus time, harebell season etc. are not in their usual routine at the usual season.' She also wrote of 'wood anemone time', 'lilac time' and 'honeysuckle time', and of the 'ranunculus and anemone season'.[88]

Few of Mary's friends and relations shared or understood her lack of interest in the outside world, as a story related by her son illustrates:

> Lady Jersey and [Aunt Lily] were staying on a visit at Penrice and, having nothing to occupy them, strolled down to the pond-side and sat down. After they had been sitting there for some time, and had exhausted their London gossip, a silence of some duration ensued, at the end of which Lady Elizabeth observed Lady Jersey to be in tears, with her handkerchief to her face. 'My dear Lady Elizabeth', she said, 'I am thinking of the dreadful fate of your poor sister, condemned to pass her life in such a hateful solitude. Why, positively, for the last twenty minutes I have not heard the sound of a living creature – one might hear a pin drop, half a mile off.' Lady Elizabeth laughed heartily, assuring Lady Jersey that her sympathy was quite thrown away, for that her sister would not exchange her ranunculas bed for all Berkeley Square, but Lady Jersey was incredulous and inconsolable.[89]

The flower garden was Mary's special domain, though her husband was happy to walk there with her, and would sometimes read to her whilst she worked. She missed her garden desperately when she was away from Penrice – almost as much as she missed any children who had to be left behind. In October 1798, after two months' absence from home, she noted in her pocket-book: 'Home. Walked to my garden the minute I got to Penrice.'[90] During a visit to Dorset in 1810 she asked her daughter Charlotte, 'Do not you long for the happy day when we shall all be gardening happily together?'[91]

Mary's friends did their best to tell her what was happening in the garden during her absences. In March 1809, when the Talbots were in Salisbury with some of the children, Mary's friend Jane King drove over from Swansea to visit Penrice, and reported:

> The next interesting subject is your garden, and I have to tell you that you will find every thing as forward as you thought them last year when you returned home. The hyacinths promise very well, and the new walk looks extremely gay with narcissus's and other flowers. Indeed, all your plants appear so highly

> cultivated and in such variety that I am quite dissatisfied with those I possess.[92]

In June 1811, when Agnes Porter was looking after the children at Penrice, she wrote to tell Mary, who was staying with her sister Harriot in Dorset:

> Your garden looks beautiful. When the weather permits I go to it, and examine the flowers to the best of my ability. I was much pleased yesterday with the balsams: Mr Ace told me they were pretty well, he could not say that he had much reason to complain of them. This I interpretted into their being very fine. The lychnadeas make a serene appearance; the roses are beginning to bloom. The kitchen garden has been the most injured by the weather. The young ladies walk whenever they can – I generally know when Miss Talbot comes from the garden by the gift of a nice little nosegay.[93]

Mary's own garden at Penrice was the area around the hothouse next to the kitchen gardens, known to later generations as the Pleasure Gardens. Here, some of the flowers were grown in beds, whilst others were planted more informally around the natural rocky outcrops of limestone. There was also a flower garden close to the house, though little information on this has survived. During the period 1811–12 another area, to the north west of the house, was developed, mainly to provide gardens for the children. The gardener, Bozman, built a rockwork well and a grotto there. In March 1813 Mary Talbot wrote to tell her son: 'The little well at the gardens is finished, and looks very pretty, as there are a great many primroses round it and the water trickles down the rock into it.'[94]

Mary kept careful records of the plants that she grew. Early in the year there were the spring bulbs to look forward to: snowdrops, crocuses ('many varieties'), narcissi, hyacinths and fritillaries, followed by lily of the valley (white, double and red) and tulips ('many fine varieties of single and double'). She grew all the old florists' flowers: auriculas, primulas (oxlips, cowslips, silver-edged and hose-in-hose), ranunculuses, carnations and pinks. Other flowering plants included anemones, snapdragons, columbines, wallflowers, delphiniums, geraniums, irises, poppies (Welsh and oriental), paeonies, lilies, lupins, tobacco plants, zinnias, violas and violets (single and double). There were flowering trees and shrubs too: *Arbutus unedo* (the strawberry-tree), azaleas, daphnes, honeysuckles, lilacs, rhododendrons, magnolias and, of course, masses of roses. In the hothouse grew varieties of tender plants such as agapanthus, amaryllis, alstromeria and camellias.[95]

A flourishing mail order business in plants and seeds had developed by the second half of the eighteenth century. Nursery gardens produced detailed catalogues, and sent items to the country by the public coaches. The pocket-books kept by Mary Talbot and her husband in the first few years of the nineteenth century give a good deal of information on the sources of the plants grown at Penrice. In 1802 Mary wanted a 'new white moss rose' sold by 'Henry Shaller, nurseryman, Little Chelsea'; and *Ferraria* or *Tigridia pavonia* from the Chelsea nursery run by the Colville family. She had been told that Loddiges of Hackney was a 'cheap place for heaths and Americans'.[96] Early in 1806 Thomas Talbot noted that he had asked the Colvilles to send 'heaths etc. in March or early in April to Bristol, to come from thence to Penrice by Swansea boat from Bristol'. In March of the same year, Thomas paid £17 1*s.* to 'Messrs Curtis and Milliken, Florists, Walworth, Middlesex to the present time', and £10 to 'Messrs Fuller and Co., Neat Houses, Chelsea, for the garden seeds as per their bill'. Mary Talbot's own pocket-book of 1806 has a list of plants 'to send for in autumn'. She wanted: 'A root of Virginian lungwort; a dozen hepaticas, blue, red and white; 6 cyclamens, sweet scented; variety of frittilaries; collection of roses; 1 dozen *Melanthium Virginicum*; 6 double scarlet lychnis; 6 *Daphne cneorum*.' In November Thomas noted that he had written 'to Curtis and Millekin about flower roots to send per mail coach', and in the following month he sent another order for garden seeds to Fuller and Co., noting that he would pay on receiving them.[97] Further payments to Curtis and Milliken, of £12 19*s.* and £11 16*s.*, were made in 1808 and 1809. In 1809 Thomas paid £19 8*s.* 6*d.* to 'Messrs Lee and Kennedy, nurserymen, Hammersmith, for dear Mary'.[98] The Talbots were also customers of Messrs Sweet and Miller, nurserymen and seedsmen at Bristol, to whom the sum of £89 10*s.* was paid by Thomas's executors after his death in 1813.[99]

Mary's friends and relations regularly asked for her advice on planting and laying out their own gardens. In 1803 she wrote from Penrice to Henrietta Hicks Beach:

> Since you went a Guernsey lily has come into blow, so I advise you to follow my example and plant a good many in sand in the natural ground in some very, very warm corner. Mine are under the kitchen garden wall, where I observed that the snow always melted first, and that made me think it the warmest place. Near the hothouse, perhaps, the fire might warm the earth so as to make it comfortable for them.

Several years later, in 1810, Mary sent Henrietta 'some roots of the yellow oxalis' with the comment that they would look very pretty in the spring, as they opened every day in the sun and shut when there was none. They would, however 'require to be tied up and to be deluged with water'.[100]

Another correspondent on gardening matters for several years was Ann

Fowler, the wife of Dr Richard Fowler of Salisbury. In August 1809 Mrs Fowler wrote to tell Mary:

> These soaking rains have been very good for gardens, to be sure, and mine as a dry soil enjoys it most particularly. You cannot think how well every thing looks, particularly my American pets, who seem to enjoy themselves very much. But I want you so much you cannot imagine, for Dr Fowler has increased my *territories* quite to the cow's house. All that ground where the potatoes were – is not that *very magnificent?* And now I want you to tell me how I shall do it, for I shall not think it right if you don't, so if you can give me a little bit of a ground plan as to the interior, I should be *so much* obliged to you. A thick plantation to hide the cow's mansion, of course? And laurels close to the pales? A sweetbriar hedge as a fence? Where shall I put the entrance? Where it is now, or at the further end? ... Had not I better leave a sort of shrubbery where my boundary is now?

The two women continued to exchange plants in later years. In 1811 Ann sent Mary 'two or three little plants' including *Crocus officinalis.* Two months later Ann wrote again to tell her friend about her own garden and the gifts that she had received:

> Thanks to you, my garden begins to cut some figure. *Your* bed looks very flourishing, and your rhododendron is in very fine bloom, but the one in the corner is entirely covered with blooms and looks beautiful. All the plants you were so kind as to send me are looking very healthy: many are in flower, some have been, and some are coming. The *Anemone hortensis* did not blow that you gave me last, but the one before did, and very pretty it was. From that I conclude they ought not to be moved.[101]

Even Dr Fowler was enlisted to help in the garden, informing Mary in a letter written in July 1811: 'My employment ... has been confined to repairing and planting hedges and rooting out weeds.'[102]

Once they had houses of their own, Mary's sisters also began to be interested in gardening. A few months after her marriage in 1808, Louisa Petty wrote from her new home, Bounds near Tunbridge Wells, with a request:

> I want you shockingly to help me set my garden to rights, for it is in such confusion I don't know where to begin. Will you impart some annual seeds for next year, for I don't know what to ask for, and at the great nursery gardens they dispise you if you ask for any thing common. I have some very pretty cornflowers in bloom, the seed of which you gave me and which, in consequence, I love very much. Have you a white cluster rose? It is single and blows profusely and grows immensely tall.[103]

In the next letter Louisa asked Mary for roses: a red musk and 'a Lord

Macartney rose'.[104] Further requests followed, together with a plan of the garden at Bounds, which was to be planted so that it would be at its best during the summer months, when the Pettys were able to spend time out of London. Mary duly sent some plants, and Louisa wrote to thank her:

> The box has arrived very safe. You have sent me a most magnificent collection. I am very sorry, however, that you sent me any precious things, for if they should die I shall be quite unhappy, as with you they would long have flourished. I have unfortunately no peat earth, as for miles around it is only sand, but having abundance of shade they can be accommodated with that, and if they will but wait till some artificial earth is ready for them which answers all the purposes of peat, they will do nicely.

In later years Louisa continued to consult Mary, whose knowledge of plants was greatly superior to her own. In 1809 she wrote:

> Almost all your plants are thriving, but the names were so washed out by the rain I am in utter ignorance what they are. There is a beautiful, white, tallish thing which I wish to know the name of particularly.[105]

At the end of 1809 Louisa became Marchioness of Lansdowne, and she and her husband subsequently took over the family seat, Bowood in Wiltshire, where the park had been laid out by Capability Brown between 1762 and 1768. Later additions had included the pleasure grounds, with flower gardens and shrubberies, and a rockwork cascade designed by Charles Hamilton. In May 1810 Louisa wrote to Mary describing her future home, which had been neglected since the death of the first Marquess five years earlier:

> The house stands upon a slope which rises from a very fine piece of water, of which the ends are admirably concealed. Behind it is the garden, or rather pleasure grounds, as they are too extensive for the former. There are some very fine shrubs and a vast number of trees of all discriptions, and a very pretty valley which runs up from the water's edge. As you walk along, thinking of nothing, you enter a thicket which presently opens, and you are in a very nice flower garden, where there still remain a great many flowers of various sorts which [we] are now fostering up and, I hope, will all forget the bad treatment they have undergone. Going on, you go down a steep hill and amongst some rocks to a pretty cascade, and farther climbing up by its side through a dark walk from overhanging trees to a pininsula, which is covered with fine beech trees and commands a fine view of the water and house and woods adjoining.[106]

The Lansdownes eventually moved into Bowood in 1812. Louisa and her husband added to the gardens there over the following decades, employing the well-known architect Robert Smirke to lay out a formal garden on a terrace in front of the house in 1818, and planting a pinetum and many other trees and shrubs in the 1840s and 1850s.[107]

Gardening was a popular activity for children long before the 1760s, when Jean-Jacques Rousseau wrote of the benefits of work in the open air. The Cust girls at Belton House in Lincolnshire all had gardens in 1740, when their mother wrote that they were all 'now mightily imployed with setting of flowers and fruit trees in them',[108] and Susan Fox had a garden at Redlynch in 1752 when she was nine. In later years Susan's nephew and nieces were all given gardens of their own. In 1788 Harriot wrote from her boarding school in Weymouth to tell Mary, 'When I go home I hope I shall have a garden, but if it is not close to yours I would not give a pin for it'.[109] A year or so later the Dowager Lady Ilchester wrote that 'Stavey [her grandson, Lord Stavordale] has a wheel-barrow and spade and seems in high good humour and happy'.[110] Not long after this, Lord Ilchester wrote that 'Stavey' was planning to plant a nut tree in each of his sisters' gardens 'the same as he has done in his own'.[111]

The Strangways children also had gardens after they moved to Melbury in 1792. In 1794 Charlotte told Mary, 'All the things in my garden grow very well. I have a little greenhouse under the trees, on a hurdle upon sticks'.[112] The children grew both vegetables and flowers: in an undated letter Louisa informed her sister: 'My garden is the prettiest place in nature. We shall have of our own planting today for dinner, onions, carrots, turnips, lettuces and potatoes.'[113] The children's garden at Melbury was still in existence a few years later, when William Fox Strangways wrote to tell his half-brother, 'My hyarcinth is very much grown, and so is Gileses ... Charlotte, me and Giles dig in our garden when it is fine to make it look nice, and the gardener has given us a rose, a carnation, a honeysuckle and a pink.'[114]

By the end of the eighteenth century writers such as Richard and Maria Edgeworth were recommending gardening as a suitable occupation for children, and the Talbot children at Penrice were encouraged to take an interest in the garden there from an early age. They would not have understood Jane Austen's heroine Catherine Morland, who 'had no taste for a garden, and if she gathered flowers at all, it was chiefly for the pleasure of mischief'.[115] In June 1801 Agnes Porter helped the two eldest girls to write a letter to their mother, who was away from home:

> Little Mary to her dear Mama:
> The yellow roses are in blow round about the basket near the rock work. There are two little red rose trees full of blossoms. The renunculuses in the kitchen

> garden have been very beautiful since you went away, and the pinks are coming out in blow.
>
> Little Jane to her dear Mama:
> Mama, the cucumbers are come, but Mary says they are *melons.* The strawberries are come. The cherries are coming. The gooseberries are come ripish, but not much.[116]

On a summer's day in the following year Agnes spent three hours in the garden with 'the dear children', who 'like their Mama, have a great taste for flowers and are always pleased to be among them'.[117] The new gardens laid out at Penrice in 1811–12 included a plot for each of Mary's children and one for their cousin Henry Talbot. They grew vegetables and flowers there, and in May 1811 Mary Theresa informed her sister Charlotte:

> Our white lilac is in blossom. Your mustard and cress is come up in a very good 'CT' and a line at the top. The birds have eaten up all our gooseberries at our new gardens and the other seeds in our gardens are beginning to make their appearance. The may trees are all white; the other lilacs are almost in blow. The ash and oak trees are coming out in leaf.[118]

The development of the children's gardens continued during the following months, and Kit Talbot, who was away at school, was given regular progress reports. In March 1812 Mary Theresa told Kit:

> Our new gardens are coming on nicely. I have planted a nut tree in yours, I hope the people will not pull it up for a weed. They are making the gravel walks round the beds now, but it has been so wet that I have not been able to go and plant in the beds a long time. I will sow seeds for you in your bed if you like it.[119]

In April Kit's mother told him that she had been watering his garden. Some of the new plants looked 'very sick' but she hoped that they could be revived. She continued, 'I shall put some more things into [your garden] tomorrow as I like to go and think of my dear boy in the spot that I hope will prove so much amusement to him'. They all enjoyed making bonfires, and Mary told Kit in the same letter that they had just burnt 'a great collection of briars', but that 'it was not near so great or beautiful a bonfire as the one we made before'.[120]

The children took a great deal of pride in their gardens, and carried out much of the work themselves. In April 1812 Mary Theresa wrote to Charlotte, who was at Margam:

> I have given your garden a piece of water-leaf. It is a plant that blows very well in the shade, and so my garden would not suit it at all. I have had a great many plants out of my old garden transplanted into my new one, and my bed

> is *stuffed full.* I am sadly afraid that I shall not be here when all my plants are in blow and my seeds come up, which will be very vexing after having had the trouble of planting and sowing, and then not see any of the beauties ... The double purple violets are charming, so sweet and so delightful.[121]

There were occasional disappointments, too, as Jane told Kit in April 1813:

> Mama has planted a great many things in your garden that will blow when you are here for the summer. I had a tulip in my garden, but some body or some *slug* gathered it, it was a beautiful red and yellow early tulip. I have got nothing in blow but lungwort, fumitory and a *poor, half-eaten* narcissus.

After her husband's death in May 1813, Mary worked even harder in Kit's garden, as Jane informed him in another letter:

> Mama takes so much pains with your garden. She rakes it continually and plants [and] hunts for slugs, which she never does without finding plenty. I wish I was at school, that I might have somebody to take so much pains with my garden for me.[122]

Their early introduction to, and love of, gardening was perhaps Mary's most enduring legacy to her children, and also to her nephew Henry Talbot.

Flowers, both painted and real, also decorated the interiors of Georgian houses. Cut flowers and potted plants were used in abundance: one of Queen Charlotte's visitors in March 1767 found that 'every room was full of roses, carnations, hyacinths, etc., dispersed in the prettiest manner imaginable, in jars and different flower pots on stands'.[123] Arrangements of flowers were displayed on tables, cornices and mantelpieces, and branches of flowering shrubs, in special vases known as bough pots, were used to decorate fireplaces in the summer when the fires remained unlit.[124] In 1759 Lord Ilchester paid 18*s.* for 'six dozen of flower pots and pans to hold water when in the howse'.[125] A supply of flowers for the house was greatly valued, especially in winter time. In February 1784 the Parkers' house at Saltram in Devon was filled with 'roses, violets, lily of the valley, minionet and everything else that is sweet and delightful'.[126] Hothouses and orangeries increased the range of flowers that could be grown, and fragrant plants such as tuberoses and orange trees could be raised in a greenhouse and then brought into the living rooms whilst they were in bloom. The greenhouse at Melbury was turned into a hothouse in the early 1760s, and there were orangeries or hothouses at Redlynch and Penrice. Sometimes, as at Melbury, the hothouse adjoined the house, so that the lady of the house could visit it even when the weather was bad. At Corby Castle in Cumbria a pair of single-storeyed arcaded conservatories, one on each side of the entrance porch, was built for the lady of the house, Catherine Howard, who was interested in plants.[127]

By the early nineteenth century special plant-stands were widely available. They were designed to be placed indoors in front of the windows, and could be used to display a succession of flowering plants. Scented flowers were particularly popular. In March 1812 Mary Theresa Talbot told Kit 'We have got a nice Persian lilac in blossom now in the morning-room, and a honeysuckle and plenty of mignionette and a great many other flowers.'[128] A few weeks later, however, there were problems, as Kit's mother informed him:

> The rabbits that I told you about have been very plaguing to me. They got out of the cage that Mary put them into, and eat up all my nice mignionette and auriculas that I had blowing in my window.

In another letter, written a year later, Mary Talbot told her son:

> In my window I have got a rose tree in full blossom, and a honeysuckle and lillies of the valley and red cowslips. Every night when I am undressing they smell delightfully sweet, for I remark they are much sweeter at night than in the day time.[129]

In December 1808 Louisa Petty was in London, pining for the countryside, when she wrote to tell Mary:

> I have a little garden in my back drawing room where I cherish my narcissus. I am trying to revive some sick geraniums, so I am very happy in spite of being confined in this smoky, dark abode.[130]

In another letter she described the 'cartloads of flowers' that she had amused herself in arranging for a London assembly: 'I made two pyramids under the arcade by the glass door into the hall, which with a light in the center had a very pretty effect.' Flowers from their gardens in the country would be sent to London when the family was away from home. In 1811–12 Louisa informed Mary that 'I get a nosegay once a week, which is a great delight as it is as fresh again as town-bred flowers'.[131]

It is clear from the letters already quoted that the gardens and parkland around their houses were important to the female inhabitants of Redlynch, Melbury, Abbotsbury, Stinsford and Penrice in a number of different ways. The first Countess of Ilchester and her mother both took a great interest in the creation and maintenance of their gardens, though they were not actively engaged in the necessary physical work. For them, the garden and grounds were a place for recreation and contemplation, and flowers were of particular importance, even when the fashion for uncluttered 'Brownian' landscapes was at its height. In this they were not particularly unusual:

though the flower gardens tended to be hidden away, they could be found all over the country in the eighteenth century. In many cases their name linked them with the lady of the house. In the 1760s Capability Brown remodelled the park at Audley End in Essex for Sir John Griffin Griffin. Much of the work involved the creation of broad views within a park enclosed by belts of trees, but there was also a 'close walk' or pleasure ground within easy reach of the house. This area, which became known as 'Lady Griffin's garden', was sited at the side of the house, where it would not interrupt the main vistas. The works listed in Brown's contract with Lord Digby for work at Sherborne, which was drawn up in 1776, include making and altering the enclosed garden ground near the house, and 'sowing grass seeds, planting trees, shrubbs [and] flowers'. 'Lady Digby's garden' is mentioned in 1788 when, according to a note in the Sherborne game books, it was infested by rabbits.[132] There are many references to flower gardens in other places too: in 1783 William Mason, the designer of the famous and influential flower garden at Nuneham Courtenay, travelled from Yorkshire to Cornwall to plan a flower garden for the Countess of Mount Edgcumbe; and at Blickling in Norfolk there was, in 1793, an enclosed garden in the woods – sited, once again, away from the house, and known as 'Lady Buckinghamshire's garden'.[133]

For much of the eighteenth century, the outdoor activities of most country house ladies were confined to walking, riding or driving around the grounds, or sitting with their friends, chatting and taking tea. In June 1750 Mary Delany and her husband planned a meal in their garden, where they had found 'a new breakfasting-place under the shade of nut-trees, impenetrable to the sun's rays in the midst of a grove of elms'. Mrs Delany wrote that she had ordered 'cherries, strawberries and nosegays to be laid on our breakfast table, and have appointed a harper to be here to play to us during our repast'.[134] Fishing was also considered to be a suitable occupation for the female members of the household. In an undated letter, written in the early 1740s, Lady Ilchester describes a fishing expedition, and says that she and Parson Hill had each caught a carp.[135] Boating on the lake was also popular. At Sherborne Castle in September 1764 everyone decided to go out in the boats one evening:

> And Mr Charles Feilding, in the little boat with Lady Heneage Finch and Miss Maria Tryon, had the misfortune to be overset and thoroughly ducked. Both the ladies went to bed at Pinford Farm and Mr Feilding, having borrowed the bayley's cloaths, came home and sent the coach with the ladys' servants and cloaths to bring them home dry.[136]

At Stinsford Susan O'Brien was much more involved in the day-to-day management of her garden than her mother or grandmother had been. In part, this may have been out of necessity, as she and William O'Brien could not afford to employ more than one gardener, but, like so many other female members of the family, she loved flowers, and this led her to take a direct interest in their acquisition and cultivation. How much work Susan herself did in the garden is unknown, but she certainly selected the plants that were to grow there. Early in 1791 she wrote to Mary Strangways, who was in London, enclosing a list of flower seeds that she wanted, and asking Mary to have them sent to the gardener at Stinsford by the Exeter coach. A month or so later Susan wrote to Mary again, to tell her that the seeds had been sown, though she had been ill and had been unable to go into the garden herself.[137] Mary sent some more seeds in the spring of 1793, but this time disaster struck, and Susan wrote to tell her: 'I am quite in dispair about my garden. We have a plague of mice which eat up every thing I plant or sow. I have not a peach or carnation left.' Conditions had not improved a month or two later:

> I quite forgot to thank you for the flower seeds. I believe they were very good, though the weather and slugs prevented many of them coming up. The tuberoses are now blowing very well. The only flowers I can have from Melbury is carnations. There used to be some pretty good, and if I can have some layers at the season I shall be glad, mine being mostly destroyed.[138]

Mary continued to supply her aunt with plants and flowers in later years. When, in April 1818, the two women went together to visit Mary's son Kit at school in Fulham, they also spent some time in the nursery gardens there, finding them 'enchanting with flowers'. Susan noted in her journal: 'Too far from home to be as extravagant as I should have liked, but could not resist one *Daphne Sneuorum*.'[139]

For Mary Talbot much of the attraction of gardening was that it enabled her to get out into the fresh air. She did not simply give orders to the gardeners at Penrice, but spent a good deal of time working in her garden. She was fortunate, in that she lived at a time when women's clothes were comparatively informal and loose-fitting – physical work would have been difficult, if not impossible, in the constricting corsets and tightly-fitting dresses that had been fashionable in the mid eighteenth century. When she was gardening, Mary often wore a 'whittle', a cloak of red flannel, as used by the local countrywomen – and recommended that her female friends and relations should do the same. She seems to have been particularly fond of digging. In April 1809, when she was pregnant, Louisa Petty wrote from London to Mary, who was staying in Salisbury with her invalid daughter Ellinor:

> I am very glad you have found a place to dig. I don't understand how you used

to manage. I have seen you garden to the very *end*, and I cannot stoop now without great pain. I have cramps, stitches, and all manner of aches if I put myself the least out of my perpendicular.[140]

Entries in Mary's diaries for 1798 and 1803 show that she did indeed garden when she was pregnant, 'to the very end':

13 April 1798
Gardened all morning, not very well at night.

14 April 1798
Little Christiana was born.

6 May 1803
Worked at my tent stitch and gardened.

9 May 1803
Very ill all day. Amused myself with crying and working tent stitch.

10 May 1803
My little boy was born at two o'clock in the morning.

In general, the physical effort of gardening was thought to be beneficial to women. In 1811 Ann Fowler wrote to tell Mary Talbot, 'I never saw Lady Charlotte look so well, enjoying her garden which had made great progess, working hard in it [and] walking four and six miles without fatigue'.[141]

Mary's pocket-books also include references to collecting and sowing seeds, and planting bulbs and flowering plants:

8 January 1798
Planted snowdrops from Pitt.

17 January 1801
Planted some frittilaries and dug up some plants for Mr Lucas.

4 March 1801
Mon Ami went to my garden with me to plant rock plants.

23 March 1802
Settling my seeds.

9 November 1803
Gathered a great many seeds.

3 November 1804
Walked about my garden and planted auriculas.

5 March 1806
Sowed wind flowers.

12 May 1806
I planted adder's tongue.

29 October 1807
Planting myrtles.

Other activities connected with the gardens are also noted in the pocket-books:

16 February 1801
Printed a great many garden sticks.

19 February 1801
Gardened. The rain washed all my printing out.

30 June 1801
Mrs Hunt and I had a nice walk in the garden.

22 March 1802
Printed garden labels all day, which little J[ane] spoiled.

22 April 1802
Gardened all day and nunched in the garden.

11 May 1804
Made rock work.

13 June 1804
Gardened, pruning trees.

26 September 1804
Gardened at my rocks.

Gardening and botany, which had so fascinated Mary as a girl and young woman, continued to occupy much of her time and attention as she grew older. It was something that she could share with friends and relatives of all ages, so many of whom were infected by her enthusiasm for horticulture. In a letter written to a cousin in 1827, she summed up the reasons why gardening was so important to her:

> I have a rose tree at the garden gate, which was dug up by my dear grandmother herself out of her garden at Capercullen which, with other memoranda of the same kind, make my garden more engaging to me than any other spot in the world, and I spend all the time I can in it, as it mends my health, as well as soothes my heart.[142]

Mary visited nurseries and botanical gardens during her her occasional stays in London, she was interested in new plant introductions, and she enjoyed comparing notes with her fellow-gardeners. A particularly welcome visitor to Penrice in the early nineteenth century was the architect and landscape-gardener John Haverfield, who was in charge of the royal gardens at Richmond and Kew.[143] Mary always loved to see other people's gardens, and she was extremely generous with gifts of seeds and plants. In return, she was often given plants by members of her family, and by friends in Glamorgan, many of whom were keen gardeners. They included several women: Jane King of Marino; Catherine Hunt of Tynycaeau, the wife of the incumbent at Margam; Fanny Llewelyn of Penllergaer; and Mary Adams, the illegitimate daughter of Fanny Llewelyn's husband. Mary Talbot also exchanged plants with her near neighbour John Lucas of Stouthall. In 1802 Mr Lucas promised to give Mary 'some red lillies of the valley and different sorts of double polyanthos', and in 1803 'snake's head iris and polyanthos's, and three bird snapdragons'.[144]

By the early nineteenth century the numerous descendants and connections of the first Earl and Countess of Ilchester who were interested in gardening and botany made up a complex and wide-ranging network. They wrote long descriptive letters to each other, they visited and stayed in each other's country houses, and they met and compared notes when they were in London. A list of these families and their estates includes many of the best-known West Country gardens of the eighteenth, nineteenth and twentieth centuries. Mary Talbot knew, or was related to, families such as the Hoares of Stourhead and the Aclands of Killerton in Devon. A list made in 1806 shows that she intended to send 'curious seeds and plants' to Highclere in Hampshire for her first cousin Kitty, Lady Porchester, who became Countess of Carnarvon a few years later.[145] Mary was related several times over to the Digbys of Sherborne and Minterne in Dorset. Sir Charles Lemon of Carclew, the husband of Mary's sister Charlotte, was a founder member and chairman of the Royal Horticultural Society of Cornwall and a keen collector, who sponsored overseas expeditions in search of new plants. Another sister, Louisa, became Marchioness of Lansdowne, and mistress of Bowood in Wiltshire. Mary's half-brother, William Fox Strangways, showed an interest in plants from an early age, and in 1808 Mary noted that she was to send him some 'curiosities'.[146] William later became a well-known authority on the flora of Europe and, in the course of his extensive overseas travels, an enthusiastic collector and introducer of new plants. He gave his name to the genus *Stranvaesia*, and was responsible for much new planting at Abbotsbury.

The network continued to expand with the next generation. Emma Talbot, Mary's youngest daughter, married John Dillwyn Llewelyn of Penllergaer near Swansea, whose interests included horticulture as well as photography. Though best known as a photographic pioneer, Mary's nephew Henry Talbot was, throughout his life, also a keen botanist and plant-collector. Henry's younger half-sister Caroline became Countess of Mount Edgcumbe in Cornwall, where a spectacular garden had been laid out in the late eighteenth and early nineteenth centuries. Many of these gardens still exist today, some still in the hands of descendants of their eighteenth-century owners, whilst others such as Lacock and Killerton belong to the National Trust.[147]

13

Travel

At a time when most people rarely ventured much more than half a day's walk from their home town or village, the ladies of the Fox Strangways and Talbot families travelled a surprising amount. Unlike the majority of their contemporaries, they had the incentive and the means to do so, though their journeys were made in conditions that their descendants two centuries later might well find intolerable.

People travelled in the Georgian period for many of the same reasons as they do today. The Strangways women and their children made regular journeys between their houses at Redlynch and Melbury – a distance of approximately twenty miles. They also visited their cousins at Sherborne Castle (conveniently situated halfway between Redlynch and Melbury), and paid occasional visits to Abbotsbury, fifteen miles from Melbury. At least once a year most members of the family travelled to London, where they stayed for several months. Even if they did not intend to spend the whole Season in London, they might go there for a week or two so that they could go shopping and see friends and family. For wealthy families, the maintenance of family connections was an important reason for travelling. Many young people met their future marriage partner in a major social centre such as London or Bath and ended up living many miles away from their parents' home. Over the generations, a wide-ranging network of family connections was built up in this way.

Of the daughters of the first Earl and Countess of Ilchester, Lucy Digby lived in, or near to, London; Harriot Acland lived in Devon and Somerset; and Fanny Quin lived in Ireland until she left her husband. One of the girls' brothers married an Irishwoman. In the next generation, Lily led a peripatetic life for several years, moving between Wiltshire, South Wales, south-west England and London, whilst Mary spent most of her time in South Wales. Only Harriot Frampton spent the whole of her married life in Dorset. Of the two youngest girls, Charlotte married a Cornishman, whilst Louisa and her husband lived in Wiltshire. The daughters of Thomas and Mary Talbot were exceptional in that they all married men who lived in Glamorganshire, but they had numerous relations in England.

Family connections were maintained by letter-writing, and also by occasional visits to each other's homes, many of which lasted for several weeks. The women met at large family parties, at Melbury, Moreton, Bowood or Penrice, and saw each other during the London Season when many branches of the family would congregate in London. Women also made journeys for health reasons, either to visit doctors in London or to take the waters or bathe at a spa or seaside resort, such as Bath, Cheltenham, Malvern or Weymouth. The therapeutic effects of such watering-places were both physical and mental, for towns such as Bath and Cheltenham provided a break from country society and a chance to enjoy oneself, seeing old friends and meeting new people, attending balls and concerts, and buying new clothes and other luxuries in the shops. Travel was also seen as healthy in itself – Celia Fiennes said that she had embarked on her excursions in the late seventeenth century 'to regain my health by variety and change of aire and exercise'.[1] During the eighteenth century, too, people began to travel purely for pleasure, and a number of well-trodden tourist trails developed as the roads improved and carriages became more comfortable.

When Thomas Strangways of Melbury made his will in 1713 he left to his wife: 'All my coaches, chariots, sheess [chaises], calash and coach horses, with all harness, bridles, horse cloathes and other furniture thereto belonging or therewith used'. Under a similar bequest in a draft will of 1728, Susanna Strangways Horner was to inherit 'all my coaches, chariotts, calashes and coach-horses' on the death of her husband Thomas Horner.[2] These wills suggest that the families at Melbury and Mells owned several vehicles in the early eighteenth century, including, perhaps, more than one coach. This underlines their great wealth at a time when few members of the lesser country gentry could afford 'the great status symbol of a crested coach and horses', the possession of which was 'a universal shorthand for wordly wealth and social prestige'.[3] A coach was the equivalent of a large saloon car such as a Rolls Royce or a Daimler. It held four to six travellers with their luggage, and showed off the wealth of its owners, whose arms would be prominently displayed. The coachman and postillion would wear their owner's own distinctive livery. A coach was, however, comparatively cumbersome and expensive to run. The coaches of the early eighteenth century were poorly sprung, and journeys in them were slow and uncomfortable, so they were used mainly for long-distance travel – and for show when the family was in London. During the course of the eighteenth century coaches became less ornate, and thus lighter. They also had better springs, which made them more comfortable. In 1742, when Lady Ilchester was pregnant for the first time and planning to travel to London for the birth, she informed her husband:

> I have tryed Mrs Digby's coach that is on springs and I think it easy, so shall borrow that and lend her mine in the stead ... Mama came yesterday in her uneasy travelling coach to carry me to London, but I desired to be excused going in it.[4]

When the family was in the country the coach would be used for formal visits, as when Lord and Lady Ilchester and their daughters Lucy and Harriot travelled to Sherborne Castle in their coach in 1770 to call on the new Lady Digby.[5] Contemporary letters and journals suggest, however, that chariots and post chaises were preferred for many journeys, especially if there were only one or two passengers. A chariot, which had four wheels, resembled a coach which had been cut in half. It had one seat which faced forwards and was lighter, and thus faster, than a coach. Chariots were mainly kept for Town use, and were drawn by two horses driven by a coachman sitting on a box, with liveried footmen riding on a dummy board at the back. For longer journeys, a post chaise would be used. These carriages resembled chariots, but the horses were controlled by mounted postillions instead of a coachman. From the 1740s onwards the Dukes of Bedford and their families generally used post chaises to travel between London and their country residences, keeping their heavier coaches for occasional journeys over rural roads.[6]

In practice, the terms 'chariot' and 'post chaise' often seem to have been interchangeable. There are occasional references to 'posting chariots', and carriages could be converted from one use to another by the addition or removal of the box. In March 1754 Charlotte Digby 'proposed setting out in her new post chaise', and in the following month Lord Digby promised to carry Lord Ilchester from Sherborne to Redlynch in his chariot. In 1758, at Sherborne, Lady Ilchester and a friend 'drove about the park in the chariot'.[7] In 1764, when William and Susan O'Brien sailed for America, they took a chariot with them. Not surprisingly, it seems to have been damaged during the long sea journey, though noblemen quite often did take their carriages with them when they travelled overseas.

A coach may have been grander, but post chaises could be quite luxurious. In London, in particular, a family needed to have a smart, up-to-date carriage, drawn by well-bred horses and attended by liveried servants. In 1771 Lord Digby paid £10 10*s*. for 'painting and gilding a Town chariot',[8] but ten years later William O'Brien reported disapprovingly to his wife that he had seen His Lordship driving about Town in 'a carriage that would discharge the lowest mountebank or quack'.[9] The Redlynch accounts record the payment of eleven guineas for 'a leopard skin for a hamar cloth for the chariot' in 1742, and £1 16*s*. for 'a black bare skin for My Lady's chariot' three years later.[10] In 1753 Lord Ilchester bought a new four-wheeled post chaise, which was ordered for him by his friend Dickie Bateman and cost £90. It was lined with cloth and had canvas window-blinds; the body was painted with 'mosaic shells and cyphers in flowers, and coronets heightened in gold' and the chaise also carried a pair of lanterns, a travelling bag and a trunk. The back and sides were 'handsomely ornamented with brass and coronets', and the whole thing was 'compleated in a very extraordinary manner'.[11] In 1805 Elizabeth Feilding claimed that she had paid £300 for a post chaise, and informed the Chancery Master who was responsible for administering the financial affairs of the Lacock estate that she needed to keep a chaise so that her five-year-old son Henry could be taken out airing when the weather was suitable.[12] If Elizabeth had really paid as much as this, the chaise must have been very luxurious indeed: in 1795 the prices for post chaises usually ranged from £93 to £108, and even a coach with painted crests and silk curtains cost only £189.[13]

A wider variety of vehicles became available during the eighteenth century. By 1742 the family at Redlynch had a landau, a four-wheeled vehicle with a folding hood in two sections.[14] The passengers sat on two cross-seats, facing each other, and the carriage would usually be drawn by a pair of horses. This may be the vehicle that Lord Ilchester had bought in June 1736 (three months after his marriage) from Budworth, a London coachmaker. It was described as a 'double chaise', and it had two 'bellows roofs', which formed a folding hood, and sliding glass windows. The 'chaise' was lined with light-coloured cloth, and the exterior was painted 'a light ground colour' with painted 'arms and crests in the pannells' and 'very handsome shields adorned with eagles and palm branches all heightened with gold'. The carriage and wheels were coloured twice with oil paint, and the wheels were 'varnished vermillion'. The cost of the new carriage was £85 8*s*., which included £8 'for the search at the Heralds' Office' to verify the details of the arms.[15] Susanna Strangways Horner also had a landau, for which she paid £129 5*s*. 10*d*. in 1749.[16]

There were also smaller carriages such as calashes, chaises and cabrioles, which were drawn by one or two horses. They were used mainly for short excursions, though two visitors to Redlynch in 1747 travelled from London in a 'one horse chair'.[17] The Digbys had a one-horse chair at Sherborne by 1764, and the Melbury accounts of 1768 record the payment of £15 12*s*. for 'a garden chaise and harness for My Lady's use'.[18] In 1761 Lord Poulett promised to have a cabriole made for Lady Ilchester. This was probably an open carriage, for use in fine weather only.[19] Cabrioles were still used in the early nineteenth century, when Lady Ilchester and two of her sons called at Stinsford in one. Susan O'Brien 'could not resist taking a round or two before the house in it'.[20] Smaller carriages of this kind were used for driving around the park surrounding the country house, or for short local excursions to local historic sites or beauty spots. Georgian ladies quite often drove themselves on these trips, especially in the lighter types of carriages. Mary Talbot drove the phaeton and the sociable at Penrice, and Susan O'Brien regularly drove herself out in her little chaise. In 1811 Charlotte Lemon told Mary, 'Mr Lemon has got me a very easy gig and a perfect horse, in which I drive myself every day'.[21] Private roads, along which these carriages could be driven, were built around country houses such as Stourhead, Redlynch and Sherborne Castle in the eighteenth century. In the early nineteenth century Thomas Talbot paid for the construction of new roads, or the improvement of old ones, around Penrice, so that his family and their visitors could drive the five miles to Worm's Head, or enjoy the invigorating air of Cefn Bryn.

By the end of the century the most fashionable carriage was the phaeton. A light carriage with four large wheels, it was the sports car of the horse-drawn carriage world, and was often driven by the owner rather than his coachman. In 1795 phaetons were described as: 'The most pleasant sort of carriages in use, as they contribute to health, amusement and fashion more than any other.'[22] There were many kinds of phaetons: some were drawn by a pair of horses, others by one horse, or even a pony. There would be one or two seats, both facing forwards and at least partly sheltered by a hood. The second Earl and Countess of Ilchester had a phaeton in the 1780s, and their daughter Mary remembered travelling in it when the family went on their annual autumn expedition to their shooting lodge at Maddington.[23] Admiral Robert Digby used his phaeton regularly in the 1790s, and Harriot Acland had one by 1792.

Other new types of carriage were also introduced at this time: in 1805 Susan O'Brien commented in a letter to her niece Elizabeth, 'You seem very *grand*. Last time I heard of your curricle, now of your barouche. The latter seems best calculated for family proceedings.'[24] A barouche was a four-wheeled carriage, with a seat in front for the driver and two seats inside, on which the passengers sat facing each other. A curricle was the successor to the earlier calash: it was a light, two-wheeled vehicle with a hood, and was usually drawn by two horses abreast. Curricles were popular with rich young men in the early nineteenth century, and in the summer of 1808 Charlotte Strangways enjoyed 'two or three delicious drives' in her brother's 'very nice' new curricle.[25]

Sedan chairs are also mentioned occasionally. These were carried by two servants, and were mainly used for short journeys in towns such as Bath or London. Susanna Strangways Horner had 'a sedan chair with poles in a case' at her London house in Albemarle Street in 1741. The Sherborne Castle accounts record the payment in 1772 of £1 13*s.* to 'Mr Vaughan, chair-maker, for repairing My Lady's sedan chair'.[26] Chairs were also used by people who suffered from gout or some other ailment that made walking difficult. In 1799, when Harriot Strangways married James Frampton at Melbury, the bride and some of the guests were carried from the house to the church in Lord Ilchester's sedan chair during a torrential downpour.[27]

Changes in a family's circumstances might lead to the acquisition of a new carriage, or the sale of an old one. In 1745, when he was temporarily hard up, Lord Ilchester talked of economising by 'parting with coach and horses and [a] great many servants'.[28] Thomas Talbot seems to have made do with a post chaise before his marriage to Mary Strangways. In 1792 he paid £64 for a new one, which was bought from the Salisbury coach-builder John Mitchell, and was made of 'the best materials', with 'best plate glass, spring curtains, plated mouldings round the leather, plated brace buckles and door locks, the leather jappaned, box under the seat, carpet at the bottom, best pipe boxes to the wheels [and] a leather platform cover and straps'.[29] When he married, however, Thomas had to buy a coach as well. In January 1794, a couple of weeks before the wedding, Thomas wrote from London to tell Michael Hicks Beach that he had got 'a decent coach and four jobb horses', and that his 'tub of a chaise' had been 'new varnished', and 'done up new and sound for the journey'. Mary was asked to choose the colour for the new coach, and decided that it should be dark green – 'one of the prettyest colours that is under the sun, in the rainbow, on the earth, etc. etc.' Thomas proposed to travel from London to Melbury in his chaise, sending his valet Merandez and the female servants in the coach with the trunks containing his bride's trousseau.[30] Additional carriages were acquired in later years to carry the Talbots' growing family: in 1804 Thomas bought a coach from William Stone of London at a cost of £136 10*s.*, minus an allowance of twenty guineas for an old coach, which had been 'made in London and never used'.[31] In 1810 a new 'posting coach', was bought from the London coachmakers Atkinson and Hopkins.[32] Such coaches were much lighter than the old, lumbering vehicles of fifty or a hundred years earlier.

The Talbots also had a variety of smaller vehicles. In 1795 Elizabeth Strangways, who was staying at Penrice, told her sister Harriot that they drove out every morning in 'a little phaeton or in an Irish car'.[33] The phaeton, which was drawn by one horse, was used mainly for short trips to Swansea and its neighbourhood, but the Talbots also used it when they went on a tour to North Wales in the summer of 1802. By this time they had also acquired a 'sociable', an open cart which was so called because it was designed to carry a comparatively large number of people. In his *Treatise on Carriages*, published in 1794, William Felton wrote of this type of carriage, 'They are intended for the pleasure of gentlemen to use in parks, or on little excursions with a whole family, and are also peculiarly convenient for the conveying of servants from one residence to another'.[34] In 1804 Thomas Talbot bought a new socialette with two wheels from Thomas Garland, a coachmaker in Monmouth Street, Bath, at a cost of fifty guineas, 'thinking it a good thing for a party to Wormshead'. A later note records that it was 'a very unpleasant carriage'. By the end of 1804 the Talbots had a total of three carriages: a coach and a phaeton, each with four wheels, and the socialette, which had two wheels.[35]

It is interesting to compare the carriages used by William and Susan O'Brien with those of their much wealthier relations. The O'Briens did not have a coach of their own, but they had a succession of chaises. These were presumably post chaises. These carriages were replaced every few years, and Susan's accounts refer to the sale of old chaises in 1780 (£12), 1794 (£15 15*s*.), 1801 (£6 6*s*.) and 1814 (£20). In 1781 she and William considered hiring a chaise instead of buying a new one. In June William, who was about to embark on a short-lived career as a barrister, wrote from London to tell his wife:

> I think, with regard to the carriage ... that it will be better to buy one entirely at once, for we want one directly very much. Ours is quite scandalous and beggarly, and if we wait, we must wait till winter, for there are no carriages to be bought at this time of year. And, as I intend you should renew your acquaintance with the Duke of Gloucester, our appearance at Weymouth should be decently handsome. A new one will cost about £90 ... If [we cannot afford this] I think I shall go by the year, and I find I can do it for £35 a year.

William also said in the same letter that he was 'trying to pick up a cabriole', and that he hoped to get one for ten or twelve pounds.[36] Later on, the O'Briens had a 'little phaeton', which was sold for £6 in 1798 when they were even shorter of money than usual.[37] The pony which had pulled the carriage was sent away at the same time. Susan, who particularly enjoyed driving herself, was upset by the loss of 'the greatest pleasure I have', and wrote in her journal, 'I think the exercise it affords me very necessary to the preserving my health at the time of life I am'. Two years later she was still 'confined for want of my poney', and thought that 'with a little contrivance and management I might still enjoy this, my *unique gratification*'.[38]

Eventually the O'Briens' financial circumstances improved and by 1803 Susan had a 'little horse' called Tiny, which she drove out, harnessed to her 'little chaise'. In May 1812, however, when she took Tiny out, she found that the horse was 'very stiff and unable to go'. She noted in her journal 'I fear I must give up driving him, which I shall be very sorry for'. Two months later, when the O'Briens returned to Stinsford after a short visit to Moreton, Susan found that Tiny had gone. She was extremely upset when her husband told her that he had arranged for Tiny to be 'put out of his pain' whilst they were away, and wrote: 'This, I daresay was kindly meant, but it adds to my regret for my poor dear little poney. I would have had more consultation on the necessity of doing it. I would have had him buried.'[39]

William O'Brien suffered badly from rheumatism during the last years of his life, and this made it difficult for him to get in and out of the little chaise. In 1812 Susan tried out a new kind of two-wheeled carrage at Melbury, a 'little gig'. She found it 'lower than mine, but not much easier, though it has sort of springs'.[40] In the following year the O'Briens bought a new chaise. This was drawn by a horse, which had been bought in 1804, and which Susan kept until 1825. Once the horse was gone, Susan had 'no way of moving out at all'. She tried hiring a horse and a little carriage from Weymouth, but 'found it very disagreeable in every respect, and not being able to drive it myself, which was my greatest amusement ... found the scheme was a bad one'.[41]

Women rode too, sometimes out of necessity but also for pleasure. When Thomas Strangways of Melbury made his will in 1713, he left (in addition to his coaches) four saddle horses to his widow Susanna 'with such proper furniture for them, viz. saddles, bridles, collars and cloathes as she shall make a choice of'. Susanna was also to choose 'three other such horses or mares as she shall make a choice of for my three daughters to ride single on, with suitable furniture'.[42] In a letter written around 1720, Charlotte Fox informed her brother Stephen that 'I ride a-horseback often'.[43] Women invariably rode side-saddle at this time, and in in 1729 the possessions of the late Duchess of Hamilton at Milton Clevedon included a side-saddle laced with silver and two old side-saddles.[44] Under the terms of the draft of her husband's will made in 1728, Susanna Strangways Horner was to have 'the horse which my wife useth for her padd, with her best side-saddle and furniture thereto belonging'.[45] A pad was an easy-paced horse, comfortable and not too high-spirited, and thus suitable for a lady rider. Such horses were still used by ladies in the mid eighteenth century in areas where the roads were unfit for carriages such as Cornwall, where women undertook long journeys on horseback, sitting 'on a pillion behind a servant, the horse being of a peculiar disposition fit to carry double and to plod on at an even trot for a certain number of hours, day after day'.[46] The Redlynch accounts for the early 1750s include a payment to a farrier for 'four new shoes [for] My Lady's pad'.[47] Other payments were made to a harness-maker for 'a new panell to a side-saddle', 'a green sursingale [surcingle] for the side-saddle' and 'a new handle to Her Ladyship's whip'.

By the middle of the century the Strangways ladies rode mainly for enjoyment and exercise. The first Countess of Ilchester was still riding in 1767, when she was in her forties, writing in November to tell her husband, 'The weather is very mild. I ride double and walk a good deal.'[48] Lady Digby was also a keen horsewoman – in 1775 Captain Robert Digby drove his sister-in-law out from Sherborne Castle in the one-horse chaise 'six mile on the Dorchester road', and she then rode home again.[49] Riding was also felt to be good for the health: when, in 1748 Caroline Fox's doctor advised her to ride, she wrote 'I own I belive 'twould do me good, because the jumbling of the journey [from London to Bath] did me a great deal for a day or two'.[50] The effects were not always beneficial – Caroline's sister Sarah Lennox, who described herself as 'horse-mad', broke her leg when she fell off a horse in 1761.[51] Sarah was much more intrepid than Caroline, who was a nervous rider. Three years after her accident Sarah went to a race meeting on the Duke of Grafton's estate at Euston in Suffolk, where she 'rid on my beautifull Weazle, who was gentle enough to let me gallop backwards and forwards, so I saw the whole course'.[52]

Towards the end of the century, with the increasing emphasis on the benefits of fresh air and exercise, girls were positively encouraged to ride. In his widely-read book *A Father's Legacy to his Daughters*, which was first published in 1774, Dr John Gregory wrote:

> I would particularly recommend to you those exercises that oblige you to be much abroad in the open air, such as walking and riding on horseback. This will give vigour to your constitutions, and a bloom to your complexions. If you accustom yourself to go abroad always in chairs and carriages, you will soon become so enervated as to be unable to go outdoors without them.[53]

In *Mansfield Park* the health of Fanny Price deteriorates when she has no horse to ride, until her cousin Edmund Bertram obtains a mare which would 'procure for [her] the immediate means of exercise, which he could not bear she should be without'.[54]

The daughters of the second Earl and Countess of Ilchester all rode: they had ponies at Maddington in the 1780s, and in 1784 the sum of £2 16*s*. was paid for 'a side-saddle for Lady Eliza'.[55] When Mary Strangways visited Penrice for the first time in 1792 she 'rode and walked about a good deal',[56] and in Ireland she rode both single and double, getting wet through on one occasion. Also in 1792, Admiral Robert Digby of Minterne noted in his journal that 'Lady Elizabeth Strangways rode here from Melbury' – a distance of six or seven miles.[57] At Penrice the Talbot children had ponies and a donkey, and they rode out whenever they could. In 1812 Jane Talbot told her brother, 'Charlotte rides my poney every fine day. She rode to Nicholaston Wood, and yesterday to the sands. It was so cold it made her cold worse.'[58] A few years later her elder sister Mary told Charlotte, who had been left behind at Penrice whilst some of the family visited relations in England:

> Mama says you are very welcome to ride, and she wishes you would ride regularly. You may ride Pitch, if you feel hardy enough, or the little long-tailed grey. Mama says perhaps Mlle Allemand [the governess] might like to ride with you, and if the groom *tames* Pitch first he would be very pleasant, though I think he would be best for you as you always ride in a string. However, you can settle among yourselves, only remember Pitch's fiery disposition when he has not been rode for some time ... Pray offer Mlle Allemand my habit.[59]

Mary Talbot continued to ride until she was in her late thirties at least, but by this time she – like most women of her age – generally travelled in a carriage. Writing in 1818, Susan O'Brien thought that the greater use of carriages meant that there were fewer good horsewomen than there had been fifty or sixty years earlier. On the other hand, more comfortable travelling conditions meant that the ladies of the early nineteenth century were 'greater rovers about the kingdom than formerly'.[60]

The aristocratic ladies of the mid eighteenth century do not appear to have walked a great deal. They might wander around the garden or pleasure grounds, admiring the flowers and stopping to sit and chat or take tea in a pavilion, but longer excursions were made on horseback or in a carriage. Many of their daughters and granddaughters were, however, keen walkers. As the Cornishwoman Loveday Sarah Gregor (born in 1792) wrote in the mid nineteenth century :

> The ladies of my generation made no objection to walking [a mile] any more than the present race would do, but *active* exercise on foot was not *then* [in her father's childhood] considered becoming to a gentlewoman.[61]

Loveday Gregor also recorded the disapproving comments of the wife of a Cornish farm bailiff on these newly-mobile ladies:

> Oh my dear, times are sadly changed! Ladies *were* ladies then, and couldn't be mistaken. They never demeaned themselves, as you do, putting on great thick boots and *stranting* about the country, up hill and down, over hedges and what not, as if you were a milkmaid![62]

At this time, of course, travelling on foot was still a necessity, rather than a pleasure, for the vast majority of country people, and it is not surprising that they found it difficult to understand why anyone should walk unless they had to, and greeted those who chose to undertake a long journey on foot with a good deal of suspicion. Long-distance walking became increasingly popular from the 1790s onwards. Most of these travellers were young men, such as the romantic poets William Wordsworth and Samuel Taylor Coleridge, who wanted to experience the countryside at first hand but could not afford to undertake a more formal tour. One such walker was Wilbraham Ford, an old friend of Mary Talbot, who arrived at Penrice in the summer of 1803. Ford, who was in his early twenties, was intended for the church 'and to fill up some vacant time became a pedestrian traveller'.[63]

The ladies of the late Georgian period did not go on long-distance hikes, but they were generally encouraged to take exercise for the good of their health. They walked around the hills, woods and coastline of their home areas, and visited areas known for their wild and picturesque scenery, such as Wales, the Lake District and the Isle of Wight, admiring the scenery, sketching and collecting shells, mosses and botanical specimens. Mary Talbot and her sisters had grown used to rambling around the woods and grounds during their childhood at Redlynch and Melbury. They had also enjoyed the freedom of the wild Irish countryside when they stayed at their mother's family home in County Limerick. Mary showed no inclination to change her ways as she grew older, complaining to her sister Harriot in a letter sent from Penrice soon after her marriage:

> We have had very little good weather since we came here and I, of course, have been out but little. He [her husband] made me go out in the post chaise one day an-airing, but it looked so pompous airing with four horses, besides, as I was in perfect health, there was no pretence for it, and I could not bear it. I had rather wet my feet every day in the year.[64]

In 1810, during a visit to Salisbury, Mary was again unhappy about the prospect of having go out in a carriage:

> It has rained so much … that we have scarcely had any comfortable walk, but if this weather continues we must go out an-airing in the carriage, which is very dull to me, who are used to scramble about in all weathers.[65]

Visitors to Penrice were taken on long walks and 'scrambles', to the Great Tor, or to Worm's Head and Mewslade Bay. In 1812 Charlotte Lemon, who had been unwell, was said to be 'walking four and six miles without fatigue'.[66] Not everyone, however, was convinced of the benefits of such long walks – Agnes Porter wrote in 1794 to beg Mary Talbot 'take care of your dear health and do not (I charge you) walk eight miles – it is suicide – never do it again'.[67] A few years later, however, when she was living in Fairford and had no carriage at her disposal, Agnes ventured out every day 'to preserve [my health] by air and exercise'. As she wrote to Mary Talbot in 1806:

> You would smile to see me ... who used to shrink so from the least particle of humidity, now mounted upon high pattens which do not preserve me from the mud, wading half a mile through the dirtiest streets to pay an afternoon visit, and return home at night with no other light than a lantern.[68]

When it came to long carriage journeys, the distance that could be covered in one day varied greatly according to the method of transport used and the state of the roads. In the winter, snow and rain frequently made even the main roads impassable, though travelling was easier if the ground had been hardened by a frost. In the more remote areas of Britain the roads remained unfit for any kind of wheeled traffic, but travel on most of the of the main routes became much easier during the second half of the eighteenth century, due to the work of numerous private trusts formed to improve the existing roads and bridges and build new ones. Long journeys by coach were divided into stages, with each stage covering approximately twelve to fourteen miles and lasting roughly two hours. It was necessary to change horses often if travellers wished to maintain a reasonable speed. If the same team of horses was used throughout a journey they would have to be rested regularly and would only be able to manage a limited distance each day, but if fresh horses were hired at each stage it was possible to cover forty or fifty miles in one day if the roads were in good condition. Journeys were, however, often taken at a fairly leisurely pace, with stops on the way to call on friends, see the local sights, or visit the shops.

When the family was travelling from Melbury or Redlynch to London they might use their own horses for the first stage, and possibly for the second, but after that they would generally hire post-horses from one stage to the next. A well-organised posting system existed by the mid eighteenth century, with teams of horses available for hire at the better-appointed inns. Each pair of horses was accompanied by a postboy or postillion, who rode the nearside horse. An outrider would usually be sent ahead of the coach on each stage of the journey, to ensure that a room, meal or fresh horses were available when his master or mistress arrived. Inevitably, the horses that were supplied were not always very satisfactory. In November 1771 Mr and Mrs Penton set out from Sherborne Castle for Winchester:

> They had very bad and resty [sluggish] horses, and were obliged to get out in the deer park and walk back to the house; got fresh horses from the Antelope and set out again a quarter before ten o'clock.[69]

Where possible, the Earls and Countesses of Ilchester and the Talbots stopped for the night at friends' houses, though it was not always possible to avoid spending a night or two in inns. In 1750 Susanna Strangways Horner visited Oxford, and decided to return home via her son-in-law's houses at Maddington and Redlynch instead of staying at the inns on the way, which her daughter described as 'intolerable'.[70] In 1796, when Mary Talbot was pregnant, she and Thomas took ten days to travel from Melbury to Penrice, 'making use of our friends' houses as inns all the way'.[71] Susan O'Brien, whose house at Stinsford was close to one of the main roads from Dorset to London, often complained that her house was treated as an inn. In July 1825, with a house full of Strangways relations, she wrote in her journal: 'The house quite full and very hot – quite a landlady, and the house compared to the White Horse Cellar.'[72] The White Horse Cellar was a well-known London coaching inn.

Most towns and large villages had several inns of varying quality. Aristocratic travellers would try to stay or dine at the best establishments, some of which catered only for people who arrived in their own private carriages. They would not usually have to sleep at an inn such as the Plough in Cheltenham, where a maidservant of the Talbots spent an uncomfortable night in 'a bed full of bugs' in 1812.[73] Many of the better inns were quite luxurious and furnished like gentlemen's houses. Thomas and Mary Talbot probably spent their wedding night at the Old Down Inn at Emborough, between Shepton Mallet and Midsomer Norton, which was a regular stopping-point on the much-travelled road from Redlynch, Melbury and Sherborne to Bath.

The Castle in Marlborough which had originally been a private house, was a particularly grand inn, catering for wealthy travellers on the road between Bath and London. In 1785 it had between 130 and 140 beds available for visitors 'and the most beautiful apartments and furnishings'.[74] In 1815 Charlotte Talbot (aged fifteen) with her sisters Mary Theresa and Emma, dined at the Castle during a journey from Bath to London with two servants. The girls were given: 'A charming room, so high, a famous fire, a great skreen, the pannels of the room were salmon colour. There was a grotto, and a fine worked picture.' On the following day the party reached Reading at dinner time. Mary Theresa told the coachman to go to the Angel, but then, according to Charlotte:

> Mary thought that it did not look like the Best Inn, and upon looking in her paper with the names of the inns we were to go to, she saw that we ought to have gone to the Sun – but we had a very good dinner, so it did not much signify.[75]

Improvements to the roads in the second half of the eighteenth century shortened the journey from Melbury to London (130 miles) by approximately one day. In the 1740s Susanna Strangways Horner's servants took four or five days, but in the 1790s the same journey usually took Agnes Porter and her pupils three days in Lord Ilchester's carriage. When Agnes returned to Melbury in the mail coach in June 1796, however, she left London in the evening, travelled all night, and reached home on the following day.[76] In the early nineteenth century it was possible to get from Stinsford to London (130 miles) in two days, spending a night at Andover on the way. Alternatively, travellers might stop in Salisbury, and then at Hartfordbridge, where there were several large coaching inns. The Talbots generally took approximately five days to travel the two hundred miles from Penrice to London. The public stagecoaches took between two and five days from Swansea to London, but they kept going during the night. The journey from Melbury to Penrice (about 170 miles) took Thomas and Mary Talbot three days after their wedding in February 1794, but in later years, when they had their children with them, they were often on the road for four or five days. On the way, they usually stayed at Margam, then at Cardiff or Newport, before continuing to the Passage across the Bristol Channel, where they might have to spend a night if the tides were not favourable. The next night would usually be spent in Bath, or at the Old Down Inn, which was an easy day's journey from Melbury.

By the late eighteenth century a number of directories, or road-books, were available to guide travellers, and gave them information about the best routes, and the towns, villages and country seats along the way. Such publications were widely used – eighteen editions of one of the most popular, *Paterson's Roads*, were published between 1771 and 1829. In 1807 Susan O'Brien received a letter from Thomas Talbot's cousin, Barbara Davenport, 'to offer me a visit in her way to Southampton, as she says her road-book tells her she goes by my abode'.[77]

Even the best-informed traveller sometimes found that all did not go according to plan, as when Thomas and Mary Talbot and two daughters stopped for a night during a journey from Bristol to Fairford in Gloucestershire in 1812:

> When we came to Tetbury, where we were to sleep, it was very late and the inn was quite full of a regiment of militia, and if one of the officers had not been absent we should not have found room. It was an old house ... and there were great chinks in the partitions. When Mary and Jane went to bed they had a dispute whether they should lock their door and, as usual, whether the pillows should be high or low, etc. When all these weighty measures were settled, and

> Eliza [the maid] was gone away, they heard an officer 'hem' two or three times through the partition, and say 'John, tell the colonel I shall come and speak to him presently'. Now, as *they* slept in the colonel's room they began to be in a great fright least he should keep his word, but it turned out he only said it to frighten them, having heard every word they had uttered.[78]

Travel with small children could be just as much of a nightmare in the eighteenth century as in the twenty-first. In December 1746 Caroline Fox endured a three-day journey from London to Bath with her son Ste, aged twenty-one months. She arrived 'excessively fatigued' and told her husband that Ste 'was as good as any child of his age could be going such a tedious journey, but not so good as he generally is at home'.[79] It is not surprising that the children were often sent in the coach with their nursemaids, whilst their parents rode in the post chaise. In the early nineteenth century the Talbot children were encouraged to keep travel diaries, in which they sketched and wrote about the sights that they passed on the way. Their other entertainments included playing games such as 'travelling picquet', singing songs and reading.

In 1815 Charlotte Talbot wrote a journal of a journey from Bath to London with her sisters Mary and Emma, and their servant Sukey:

> We left Bath about half-past one in the afternoon ... in the chariot. The roads were very dirty, so that the horses were covered with dirt ... Mary and Emma began to play at travelling piquet. Mary won, because there was a cat sitting on the ledge of the window *outside*. They played another game, which Mary won also. We stopped at a half-way house and watered the horses. Sukey sung 'Oh Neptune, oh Neptune, why are you then so cross?' We did not have 'Rochester City', but we had 'The Yorkshire bite'. We ate biscuits (Emma and me) almost the whole way. We saw a very odd building – Sukey thought it was a factory, Mary thought it was a prison.

The girls studied the houses along the way, and decided which ones they would like to live in. Between Newbury and Reading, Charlotte wrote, there was 'A fine house and a park with deer in it. It was to have been mine, but I would not have it because it was brick. Mary's house was a little way farther. It was stone, but no deer'. Later on, as the road 'grew worse and worse', they saw a woman wearing lilac stockings, and continued to look at the houses – 'every red-brick house was Sukey's, and Emma had almost all the rest'. Finally, on the last stage of the journey, from Hounslow to London,

> Sukey told me that one hundred and twenty-six stage coaches changed horses at Hounslow in the twenty-four hours. It seemed like going in a *town* the whole way: the mud was like white soup. Mary and Emma played at travelling piquet,

> they played four games and both won twice. We had two friends in a taxed cart whom we passed, and who passed us, for ever and ever. We called the fattest man, who was rather old and had a green coat on, *Verd Antique*, and the other *Corbeau* [crow] from the colour of his coat. We sung almost all the way.[80]

The children also enjoyed coach-spotting (the pre-railway version of train-spotting), and were most impressed by the sight of stagecoaches on the road. In 1813 Kit Talbot informed Charlotte:

> I saw your Mercury as we passed through Dorchester in our way from Melbury to Moreton, and we saw the Exeter and London pass through Blandford in our way to Deans Leaze where we are now. The Mercury had seven on the top, and the Exeter and London four or five.[81]

Wealthy people preferred to travel in their own carriages, though they were happy to hire the horses to pull them. Those travellers who did not have their own vehicle could hire both horses and post chaise from stage to stage. This was an inconvenient way of travelling, as any luggage had to be transferred from one chaise to another at each change-over point, and it was also quite expensive – about two shillings a mile in the early nineteenth century. But it was quick and reasonably flexible. Servants were sometimes sent from one house to another by post chaise: in 1748 Caroline Fox asked her husband to send one of their footmen from London to Bath by post, and said that she would, in return, send another footman to London in the same way.[82] The female members of the family did not usually travel in hired post chaises, and Henry Fox was surprised when his mother-in-law, the Duchess of Richmond, 'took it into her head suddenly that she would go to Goodwood, and set out the next morning in a common post chaise'.[83]

Agnes Porter used post chaises from time to time, but she usually travelled in one of the public stagecoaches which ran regularly between the towns and villages of Britain. In the first part of the eighteenth century such coaches were all privately owned, and they were slow and uncomfortable. Conditions improved with the introduction of the Post Office mail coaches in 1784. The mail coaches were more expensive than the old stagecoaches, but they were better built, better horsed and better manned.[84] They were also faster and more reliable. In 1785 François La Rochefoucauld noted that the mail took fifteen hours to travel 117 miles from London to Bath – an average of ten or twelve miles an hour, excluding the time spent at the inns whilst the horses were changed.[85] The mail coaches usually carried four people inside, whilst some of the stagecoaches had room for six, with additional passengers on the roof. Sometimes, more than four passengers were crammed into the mail coaches too – in 1819, when Kit Talbot wanted to travel from Swansea to Cardiff, he found that the mail coach was full:

> But one of the passengers, having taken his place only to Swansea (although he wanted to go to Neath), was obliged to turn out. The other passengers wanted to keep him (being, I suppose, an entertaining companion) but I refused to give up my place, for which I had paid. They then said that they would have five inside, but I said I should not go if that was the case, upon which the office clerk, fearing lest he should have to reimburse my money, stept out from his counter and forcibly expelled the Hero of the Coach, who was obliged to be contented with an outside seat, vainly muttering 'very unhandsome, very' with many other exclamations of disappointment, which plainly proved he had not been accustomed to gentlemanly society.[86]

The private stagecoaches were often poorly maintained – in 1811 Agnes Porter travelled through Glamorgan in the 'Prince Regent's coach', and wrote afterwards:

> I am sorry to remark that His Royal Highness had not a sound bottom, for the lower part of the coach was like a sieve, having round holes all over it, and I was afraid to lean my feet *at full* for fear of destroying the foundation.[87]

Travellers often complained about the people with whom they were incarcerated for several hours, but Agnes Porter usually enjoyed observing her companions. A few days before Christmas in 1789 she travelled in a coach from Wincanton (near Redlynch) to London with 'a young glover, a middle-aged hatter, and an old grocer, with the addition of a Miss from Sherbourne school'. On the next stage of her journey, from London to Norwich, her fellow travellers were three 'very agreeable men' – a ship's captain, a Yarmouth merchant and a lawyer 'who were so obliging as to [take] all the trouble of the journey off my hands as much as possible. They regulated the windows during the night at my pleasure'.[88] Inevitably, however, some journeys were more difficult. In 1803 Agnes set out from Penrice on an excursion to visit her sister and brother-in-law in Swindon. At eight o'clock on the evening of 9 February she left Swansea in the Bristol mail coach, accompanied by a lady and two gentlemen:

> They [Agnes's companions] chose the glasses to be up all night. It was insufferably close – quite a little Calcutta. A room of three feet square only for four persons would be reckoned dreadful, yet many people have no objections to that small space under the name of a carriage. What encreased my regret was its being a bright star-light, which was soon obscured by our breath on the glasses. However, I consoled my self with the thought that none of us could catch cold. The lady was very lively: she prattled and sang pretty little airs alternately, declaring it was very unsociable in any one to wish to sleep. We found it indeed not very practicable.

The coach reached Bristol at noon on the following day. After dinner

Agnes continued in a stagecoach to Bath, and then caught another coach to Marlborough, arriving there at ten at night. She slept twelve hours at the Marlborough Arms inn and, on the next day, hired a post chaise to take her the last twelve miles to Swindon. On her return journey, two months later, Agnes was taken to Marlborough by her sister and brother-in-law, but she had to spend a night there as all the stages were full. At half-past three the following morning she caught the Bristol mail coach. This time her travelling companions were a Scotsman, a 'little merry-looking woman', an Irish gentleman, and 'a very elegant-looking man who smiled but said little', who, she later discovered, was a butler who was hoping to find employment in Bath. The travellers breakfasted in Bath before continuing their journey to Bristol. At Bristol Agnes went to the Bush, 'the Swansea mail inn', only to find that she had missed the mail coach by five minutes. She had to stay overnight at the Bush, in 'a dark little apartment', the only room that was vacant. At twelve the next day Agnes finally caught the Swansea mail coach, together with an Englishman, a gentleman from Glamorgan, a banker from Carmarthen and an officer returning from the Indies. The coach arrived at Swansea at five the following morning: Agnes slept there and was then collected in the phaeton from Penrice.[89]

Two years after the Swindon trip Agnes (who was then aged about fifty) used public coaches again when she went on a marathon expedition to Scotland, to visit friends and relatives in Edinburgh. She does not appear to have considered such a long journey, on her own, to be anything very extraordinary. She left Penrice for Swansea on 16 February 1805, stayed there for two days, and then continued to London, spending one night at the Passage and one in the coach from Bristol to London. On 5 March she set off in a stagecoach from the Saracen's Head inn, and travelled all day and all night. Her fellow travellers on this journey were dismissed by Agnes as 'hums drums'. After a further day's travel, the coach arrived in York at ten in the morning of 6 March, having been on the road for thirty-seven hours out of the previous forty. After a day's rest in York – where she visited the 'Minstrel' [York Minster], 'a glorious building' – Agnes continued her journey on 8 March, and arrived in Edinburgh shortly before midnight on the ninth.

The return journey went less smoothly. Agnes spent the first night in the coach from Edinburgh to Newcastle. Her companions on this stage of the journey were 'a communicative Scotsman, a conceited Englishman, and a *mad* German, with a sulky-looking silent young man'. Agnes stayed the following night at an inn in Newcastle, but the maid forgot to call her in the morning and she missed the coach onto which her trunks had already been loaded. Agnes reported that she was 'sadly vexed', but she took this slight misadventure in her stride, even when she discovered that the 'mad' German was to travel with her to Newcastle:

> He told me that he had injured his brain by a fall from an open carriage, that his health was now better, and he was travelling in pursuit of happiness, that he had passed through France, Spain and Scotland, but with no success.[90]

Whilst it was quite usual for Agnes Porter and other female employees to use public coaches, there is no indication that any of the ladies of the Fox Strangways and Talbot families ever did so. Their male relations did, however, travel by mail coach or stagecoach from time to time. In January 1818 Sir Christopher Cole used a combination of post chaises and coaches to take him from Tredegar in Monmouthshire to London, as he wrote from Oxford to tell his wife:

> After posting from Tredegar to Cheltenham, all the coaches by the way being filled, I at last secured an outside place from Cheltenham at half-past five this cold, frosty morning, and arrived here about noon. I am now at half-past nine preparing to travel all night by mail to London, where I hope to arrive about seven tomorrow morning.[91]

Boys often travelled to and from their boarding schools by public coach. Both Kit and Henry Talbot were regular stagecoach passengers in the first decades of the nineteenth century and their descriptions of these journeys give a vivid impression of travelling conditions in general. To begin with, the boys were accompanied by an relation or a servant, but by the age of twelve or thirteen they were allowed to travel alone or with friends of their own age. In January 1812 Henry Talbot returned to Harrow from Penrice at the end of the Christmas holidays, and wrote to tell his mother about his journey:

> I will now relate to you my stagecoach adventures ... When I got into the coach there was nobody there. In the night a gentleman came in who proved to be Mr Richard Quin [a cousin]. He was excessively entertaining ... He left me at Newport, and I journeyed by myself to Bath, where I came at near seven – too late for the coaches, the latest of which sets off at six, so I took a chaise to Bath and got to Mrs Davenport's [his aunt's house] at a quarter before ten. Next day ... at four I went to the coach office, and set off at a little past five ... From Bath I went with a proud gentleman, a young lady, and an old one. In the middle of the night a gentleman came in with the consent of the rest, which made us one more than our number: thus was I poked in the middle and consequently could get no sleep. At half past twelve we stopped to sup, and at the same time next morning arrived in Sackville Street [London].[92]

Four years later Kit Talbot was sent home from Harrow for the summer holidays earlier than expected, following an outbreak of scarlet fever at the school. He and a friend travelled in a gig to London, where he stayed with his aunt Elizabeth Feilding. Kit (aged thirteen) then had to find a way of getting himself back to Penrice. With no central booking-office, the prospective traveller had to enquire at the larger inns, where the long-distance coaches were based:

> I have been to Lad Lane and to the Angel near St Clement's and to the White Horse Cellar and to the Golden Cross, and I cannot anywhere find anyone who could tell me of any Gloucester coach except the mail coach, which had all the places taken for three days, so I could not wait. I thought I should be able to get a coach somewhere in the City, so I stopped at the Turk's Head, Snow Hill, and at the Bolt-in-Tun, but there was no coach running from the Turk's Head, and the man at the Bolt-in-Tun was so impudent and surly that I could get no answer out of him, and so I was obliged to take a place in the Bristol Regulator, though I was next to certain that several coaches go to Gloucester on Monday morning from the Bolt-in-Tun.[93]

Like Agnes Porter, Kit usually enjoyed meeting a wide variety of people on his travels, though he was less than happy in 1819 when his fellow travellers on a journey from Swansea to Chippenham included 'a kind of gentleman farmer who kept up an argument about agricultural institutions which lasted thirteen miles' and 'a drunken Radical spouting "The grievances of the people" on the summit of the roof ... all the way from Bristol to Bath'.[94]

For travellers from the West Country to South Wales the River Severn was a major obstacle. If they wished to avoid crossing it in a boat, they had to go as far as the bridge at Gloucester. Some chose this route, but the roads were dreadful, especially the fifteen-mile stretch between Chepstow and Newnham, which Thomas Talbot described in 1800 as 'that great bar to neighbourhood'.[95] The Talbots and their visitors generally preferred to use one of the ferries across the mouth of the Severn near Chepstow: the Old Passage (which crossed close to the site of the first of the modern Severn Bridges, from Beachley to Aust) and the New Passage, a few miles further downstream. The crossing could take anything from ten minutes to two or three hours, depending on the state of the wind and tides, and passengers were sometimes delayed for several hours before they could embark. In March 1804 the Talbots and Agnes Porter had to wait for six hours on the English side of the Passage, and eventually endured a 'very disagreeable' crossing 'in a great boat full of cattle, men and children ... It poured rain continually and the boat was too crowded to use umbrellas'.[96] In January 1811, however, the O'Briens, who had been nervous about making the crossing, 'had the finest passage possible, neither the large nor the small boat more than twenty minutes on the water, high tide and no mud or difficultys of any sort'.[97] In 1816 Kit Talbot saw 'thousands of pigs just arrived from Cardiganshire' waiting at the Passage. He noted that the pigs were 'so tired that their feet were bleeding and the drovers were obliged to roll them to the water's edge'.[98] According to *Paterson's Roads* (1808), the cost of the passage was 12*s.* for two-wheeled vehicles; 1*s.* 6*d.* for a man and a horse; and 9*d.* for each foot passenger. The Talbots generally seem to have hired a small boat for the crossing, at a cost of 5*s.* plus 9*d.* for each passenger. Their coach had, however, to be carried across the Severn in the 'great boat'.

The Bristol Channel could also be crossed lower down. Many boats sailed between South Wales and the West Country ports, carrying farm produce, coal, limestone – and people. This route was taken only occasionally by visitors to Penrice, but 1803 Colonel Stephen Strangways chose the sea route from Somerset to South Wales when he and his sixteen-year-old nephew Harry, the Earl of Ilchester, travelled to Penrice for Kit Talbot's christening. The two travellers set off from Melbury on 15 August. At Crewkerne (ten miles from Melbury) they hired a post chaise and four horses which carried them twenty miles to Harriot Acland's home, Tetton House near Taunton. They stayed at Tetton for a night or two and then set off again, in a post chaise, to Minehead – another twenty miles. They spent the night at Minehead, embarking on a boat sailing to Wales on the following day, when Colonel Strangways paid 3*s.* 'to the men carrying the luggage to the vessel', 2*s.* 6*d.* to 'the men towing the vessel out of the harbour', and three guineas 'to the captain for the passage to Swansey'. At Swansea he paid another 3*s.* to have the luggage carried from the boat to an inn. On the next day they hired four horses to Penrice Castle, and they also paid 3*s.* 'to a person bringing the portmantuas'. They arrived at Penrice on 19 August and left again a week later.

On their return journey the Talbots' coach carried them as far as Swansea, but they almost missed the boat and had to pay 5*s.* 'for a boat and luggage to overtake the paccate'. This time they sailed to Ilfracombe. They stayed the night there and then took a chaise to Barnstaple (about twelve miles), from where they hired a chaise to South Moulton (another twelve miles) and then one to Tiverton (a little under twenty miles). At Tiverton they paid 8*s.* for 'dinners and liquor'. They did not stay at Tiverton, but continued in a chaise to Wellington (twelve miles). The final stage of this long journey took them from Wellington back to Harriot Acland's house. Altogether they had travelled between sixty and seventy miles in one day, changing chaises four times. On the journey back to Melbury they changed chaises once, at Somerton. The whole cost of the excursion was £28 8*s.*, with each chaise costing from 12*s.* 10*d.* to £1 11*s.* 6*d.* On top of this the travellers had to pay between three and four shillings to the post boy at each stage, and sixpence or a shilling to the ostlers of the inns where they changed horses. When they used turnpike roads they also had to pay something at each gate – 7*d.* between Penrice and Swansea; 2*s.* 3*d.* between Barnstaple and South Molton; and 2*s.* between South Molton and Tiverton.[99]

Road accidents were by no means uncommon. Susanna Strangways Horner's carriage was overturned at Melbury in 1746, and again in 1757 when 'the coachman drove against a pice of a rock in the side of the lane, which tossed him out of the box, and then the horses got stuck on the bank and so pulled the coach quite over'.[100] In 1792 the Digbys' coach overturned near Hawley in Hampshire and Jane Digby, one of the passengers, was afterwards reported have a badly bruised face, and to be 'muffled up and black and blue'.[101] In 1816 Sir Christopher Cole described a hazardous journey from Penrice to Swansea with some of the Talbot children, when the floods had been so high at one point that one of the carriage horses 'was thrown down and the waters passed over him'. Then 'the carriage tottered, and nothing but the most violent exertion saved us from being carried away by the flood'.[102] Mary Cole must have been worried when Kit told her about the experiences of a Mr Roby, one of his companions in the Cambrian coach travelling from South Wales to Gloucester:

> [He] said he had four tumbles lately: one the coach from Brecon was overturned between Neath and Swansea; once the coach was overturned in Cowbridge ... once in a chaise he was overturned with Mr Haynes; and once his horse fell upon him.[103]

Sometimes, if the roads were particularly bad, the passengers had to get out and walk. In 1737 Susanna Strangways Horner and her companion Dr John Wigan had to alight from their coach 'in a dangerous place' near Sandy Lane in Wiltshire, on the road from London to Bath, 'but it was so slippery she fell into the dirt and besmeared very much her Norwich crape and, what was worse, hurt her wrist a little'. During the same journey the travellers saw someone who looked like a highwayman:

> One in woman's clothes appeared, who had such broad shoulders and fetched such large strides, and gave Mrs Horner such a bold nod while she was contemplating her figure, that we agreed it must be [Dick] Turpin making his escape in disguise.[104]

The ladies and gentlemen of the Fox Strangways and Talbot families were always accompanied by several manservants on their journeys, and there is no indication that any member of the family was ever attacked, but they were always on the look-out for highwaymen. In the mid eighteenth century Lady Ilchester and Joanna Cheeke had a worrying journey to London, as the latter informed Lord Ilchester:

> My Lady desires me to tell your Lordship of the two odd men that overtook us yesterday upon Bagshot Heath, which we realy think were highwaymen. They both rode as near the coach as they could for the servants and looked like very impudent, ill-looked people. They stoped a little, let us come before, and then went to the second coach and said 'how-de-do, pretty Master'. They then rode to Harvey, who was before the coach, and said to him 'I see you are very well armed, and your men know how to ride, for they keep close on each side of the coach'. By this time we came to Bagshot, where we stayed to get rid of them, and there hierd [hired] another long gun and put Harvey behind the coach and left his horse at Bagshot. However, we heard no more from them.[105]

Bagshot Heath, about twenty miles from London, was described by Daniel Defoe as a 'great black desart', 'horrid and frightful to look on'.[106] It was a notorious haunt of highwaymen.

A few hardy souls, such as Celia Fiennes and Daniel Defoe, undertook extensive tours around Britain before the 1730s, though journeying for pleasure was still quite unusual at this time. But in the middle of the eighteenth century, and again between 1793 and 1815, travel on the Continent was disrupted by war, and wealthy people who might otherwise have gone to France or Italy began to explore their own country instead. The roads were improving by this time, and carriages were becoming more comfortable, though travellers could still be 'shook to death' – as Mary Talbot was when she went to visit friends in Gower in 1803.[107] A letter written by George Eden to Ellinor Talbot includes a graphic description of road conditions in the more remote areas in the early nineteenth century. Eden had travelled from London to Manchester, Durham, Newcastle and Carlisle. The letter was written in 'a snug little village on the banks of the lake of Wyndermere':

> My poor little bones have been so jostled and jolted, so jumbled and tumbled, over mountains and vallies, high country and low country, through villages, towns, cities and countries, on good roads and bad roads, muddy roads and dusty roads, smooth roads and rough roads, with ruts and without ruts, that they have almost shaken all my little sense out of my little body.[108]

In spite of these discomforts British travellers began to study the country houses and ruined medieval castles and abbeys of their own country with the interest that previous generations had devoted to the remains of the

Greek and Roman civilisations that they found on the Continent. The craze for country house visiting was already well developed by the mid eighteenth century.[109] Sometimes, as at Stowe, Castle Howard and Stourhead, the park and gardens were at least as much of an attraction as the house. Aristocratic visitors would be allowed to wander around the grounds, and might well be able to enter the house to be shown around by the housekeeper or by the owner himself. In many cases the owner was an acquaintance, or least the friend of a friend. In July 1750 Lady Ilchester and her mother visited Oxford together. They travelled from Salisbury, stopping on the way to see the Earl of Shaftesbury's grounds at St Giles's House, Wimborne. Susanna and Elizabeth evidently appreciated these Rococo gardens, with their serpentine river, cascade, pavilions and a Chinese bridge, all of which was very much in line with their own taste.[110] Lady Ilchester found the gardens 'large and very pretty, a vast deal of water, which I liked', and Susanna 'walked almost over them'. In Oxford the two women visited Christ Church and All Souls, and tried to decide which college would be most suitable for Lord and Lady Ilchester's eldest son. They also drove out of the city to see Cornbury Park, which Elizabeth described as 'very pleasant'. They then saw Blenheim, which seems to have disappointed them, though Elizabeth found it 'noble'.[111]

Stourhead, one of the most famous pleasure gardens in England, is fifteen miles from Sherborne and only five from Redlynch, and visitors were often taken there. The Foxes and Digbys knew the banker Henry Hoare, who had begun to develop the gardens at Stourhead after his mother's death in 1741. By 1762, when Horace Walpole visited Stourhead, there was a private carriage road six miles long 'cut through farms, that look like a paddock', linking it with Redlynch, and constructed at Lord Ilchester's expense.[112] At this time the layout of the pleasure grounds was virtually complete, and visitors could admire the chain of lakes and the circuit walk, with a grotto and temples designed by Henry Flitcroft. Walpole wrote after his visit to Stourhead that 'the whole composes one of the most picturesque scenes in the world'.[113] There was also an inn, built by Henry Hoare, where visitors could get a meal or stay overnight. In September 1768 Lord Digby, with Sir Brook and Lady Bridges and Miss Feilding, 'went in the coach to see Mr Hoare's at Stowerhead, dined at the inn there and returned to Sherborne in the evening'.[114] Three years later Lord and Lady Digby and four friends drove from Sherborne to Redlynch, where they spent the night. On the following day 'They drove up Lord Ilchester's new road over the terrass to King Alfred's Tower, and then to Mr Hoare's house; saw that and the gardens [and then] dined at the inn'. After dinner, they 'drove to see the Convent, and then back to Redlynch'.[115] Alfred's Tower, which was also designed by Flitcroft, had been erected to commemorate the accession of George III in 1760. The 'Convent', which was quite new at this time, was a folly, a bizarre cottage-like building in the Gothick style, with a thatched roof, turrets and spires.

Stourhead was still popular at the end of the eighteenth century, but by this time tourists were also beginning to develop a passion for wild, unspoilt countryside ornamented with romantic ruined castles and abbeys. The public's appetite for such sights was whetted by the writings of men such as Edmund Burke and William Gilpin; by published travel journals and prints; and by exhibitions of paintings of romantic landscapes by Richard Wilson and other artists. In 1774 Henry Penruddocke Wyndham found that the Welsh tour was still 'strangely neglected', though the English roads were already 'crowded with travelling parties of pleasure',[116] but this was all to change within a couple of decades. The picturesque scenery that attracted these travellers might be entirely natural, as in the Wye Valley and the Lake District, or 'improved', as at Hawkstone in Shropshire and Mount Edgcumbe in Cornwall. Although no classical education was needed to appreciate these landscapes – unlike the carefully-designed scenes at Stourhead and Stowe – travellers in the second half of the eighteenth century were still taught that the discerning visitor should observe the countryside in a certain way. When Mary Strangways travelled to Wales and Ireland in 1792, William O'Brien told her what she should look out for. That O'Brien had absorbed many of William Gilpin's 'principles of picturesque beauty'[117] is clear from his wife's letter to her sixteen-year-old niece:

> Your uncle says he only meant to give you an idea of *what* you should observe in looking at a country, that you might give the better account of it when he talked to you about it. He would have you observe what's called the *face* of the country – how it lies; the gentle slopes down to a river or a plain; how it swells into eminences, then to hills and mountains; the quantity of wood; the neatness of fields and hedges; the appearance of the people, their dress and their comforts; whether they appear busy and cheerfull, and in what they differ in going about the same things that we do.[118]

The influence of writers on the picturesque such as Gilpin, Uvedale Price and Richard Payne Knight is also evident in a letter written *circa* 1815 by Jane Talbot, aged about nineteen, to her younger sister Charlotte:

> We left Bowood this morning. I think the woods etc. we came through are very much improved indeed by what they are cutting down. I cannot help wishing for you to *lecture* to upon the picturesque when I see a place like Bowood, which wants so much to make it anything like pretty. Spy Park is *very picturesque*, but it is *too much so* for enclosed ground round a house – it is perfectly rugged and

wild, and I think the soil being so poor gives you a disagreeable, *damp* idea, which takes off from the pleasure the picturesque would otherwise give. We came very near Longleat – I should have liked to see it very much, but I hope if we return that way I shall. From Stourton here we came through Sir Richard Hoare's grounds [Stourhead]. They are very beautiful for, besides having large timber trees, it is full of evergreen shrubs. The Temple of the Sun stands on the top of a steep bank covered quite thick with short laurels which look exceedingly green and pretty. The inn and all the houses about there are all ornamented with nice stone window frames etc. etc. I like them better than cottage fashion. There is a cross, which Sir Richard brought from some village in Somersetshire. It is very beautiful, but should have been left in its native place, I think.[119]

William and Susan O'Brien were keen sightseers, and they often went on tours in the summer and early autumn. In 1792 they 'took a week's tour' to Deans Leaze, near Wimborne,[120] Crichel, 'Mr Banks's' [Kingston Lacy] and 'Lord Bute's near Christchurch [Highcliffe]'. Susan noted in her journal that the tour 'amused us, and was of use to my spirits, which were indeed very low'.[121] Two years later they went to Blandford Races and West Lodge near Iwerne Minster, and then embarked on 'a tour into Devonshire' with some friends.[122] In 1811, when they were both nearly seventy, the O'Briens paid a long-promised and frequently-postponed visit to Penrice. They set out from Melbury on 11 January, and drove forty miles to Bristol 'without any delay or accident'. It rained all the following morning, and Susan complained that she was 'out of patience to be confined at the White Lion [the inn where they had stayed overnight] when I wanted to see the town and go to Clifton'. The Talbots arrived that afternoon, and they all travelled eight or so miles to the inn at the New Passage over the Bristol Channel, where they spent the next night. On the following morning they crossed 'very pleasantly', with a favourable wind and tide. They continued on their journey to Cardiff (thirty miles from the Passage), where they walked from their inn (probably the Angel) to see Cardiff Castle. After spending a night in Cardiff, they travelled another twenty-five miles to Margam. Unfortunately, the weather was terrible: 'Lady Mary came in our chaise to shew us the country, and to name the places as we passed, but the weather was so foggy we could see nothing.' On 14 January, after staying a few days at Margam, they travelled the remaining twenty-five miles to Penrice, arriving in time for dinner. Susan described the final stage of the journey in a letter to her niece Elizabeth Feilding:

The road from Margam was in all respects quite new to me. The picturesque scenes about Britton Ferry and the infernal ones at Neath greatly exceeded my expectation. Pluto's realms cannot be better represented – black figures, black roads, black trees, every thing black ... Swansea seems a thriving town, and everything in Wales in the travelling way is much better than some who have been here described.[123]

The bad weather continued during the first weeks of the O'Briens' stay at Penrice, but they nevertheless managed to see something of the surrounding countryside. After they had been there for a month, Susan wrote to Elizabeth again:

> I continue to admire this place as much as possible in this wintry season and constant bad weather. The snowdrops begin to appear – they revive Mary and give hopes of spring. We went Saturday to the sands, which are delightfull, but as there is only one lame horse we can do but little yet in the driving way, and, being so much older than the rest of the party, Mr O'Brien and I are rather confined. However, he finds great provision of scenes for his *picturesque eye*, as I do for my philosophical reflexions, one of which is that remoteness ... is more calculated for young than old minds.[124]

In March the weather began to improve, and the O'Briens went out 'airing and seeing innumerable beauties – Nicholson Wood, the Great Tor, Keven Brin, sands, rocks of every shape and size'. Susan regretted that 'age and rheumatism' prevented them from enjoying all the sights – 'ruins, rocks etc. etc.', which were more suited to 'youth and activity'. In April the O'Briens spent a few days in Swansea with the Talbots, and visited the pottery there. They also travelled around Swansea Bay to see Oystermouth Castle:

> We set out in our chaise, and were to meet the tram coach and the rest of our party on the sands. It was quite new, and very amusing, to me to go in this extraordinary carriage, which is fitted to the tram-roads or railways on wheels.[125]

The O'Briens stayed at Penrice for more than three months and eventually returned home in May. They visited Chepstow Castle on the way, and crossed the Bristol Channel via the Old Passage, sleeping at the passage house 'the worst we have met with'. After parting with the Talbots at Clifton, the O'Briens continued to the inn at Old Down, where they slept for one night. They then returned home to Stinsford, calling on Joanna Melliar at Castle Cary on the way.

Susan O'Brien continued to travel after her husband's death in 1815. In September 1823, at the age of eighty, she went on an excursion to Hampshire, to stay with her nephew Richard Quin and his wife who were living at Chilworth near Southampton, 'a very pretty place'. From there she went to Cowes on the Isle of Wight, and stayed overnight with an old friend and distant relation, Lady Hippisley. Susan visited other places from Chilworth too, including Romsey Abbey; Grove Place, a red-brick Elizabethan house in the parish of Nursling, which Susan described as 'a fine old house, and the finest avenue to it I ever saw'; and the romantic, ivy-covered ruins of Netley Abbey. She also saw Winchester Cathedral, and thought it 'very fine'. The cathedral was being restored 'repairing and ornamenting in the best taste – restoring the Gothic screen and banishing Grecian and all manner of trumpery fancys that had been crammed into it'.[126]

Thomas and Mary Talbot also enjoyed travelling in the early years of their marriage. At the end of 1794 they visited Croome in Worcestershire, where Capability Brown been commissioned to design a new house for the sixth Earl of Coventry in 1750. Brown had also laid out the grounds around the house, and it was these that brought the Talbots to see the place. They enjoyed the gardens at Croome, where they 'daudled in the greenhouses etc. full five hours'. They then went on to the Worcester china factory, where, Thomas said, he 'could not help being extravagant', though his wife 'almost insisted' that he should not. He left orders for 'some dozens of plates with the views of gentlemen's seats etc. etc. in the center, and ornamented with an oak wreath round the edge, with a very narrow gold border'.[127] In 1797 the Talbots took two of their daughters to Ireland, and in the summer of 1802 – when Mary was, for once, not pregnant – they went on a tour of North Wales. They travelled 850 miles in fifty-four days 'in an open phaeton with one horse and two out-riders', though one of the horses sometimes helped to pull the phaeton up hills. The tour took them to Brecon, Gloucester, Cheltenham, Worcester, Kidderminster, Shrewsbury, Whitchurch, Nantwich, Chester, Liverpool, Wrexham, Llangollen, Conway, Anglesey, Bala ('dreadful bad road'), Dollgellau, Barmouth, Machynlleth, Aberystwyth ('very bad road'), Lampeter and Llandeilo ('shocking road'). On the way, they visited sights such as Croome Court (again), Coalbrookdale, Hawkstone, Erddig, Wynnstay, Chirk Castle, Vale Crucis Abbey, Plas Newydd, Llanberis (where they went for a boat trip on the lake, and had to take an old woman with them as an interpreter), Beddgelert, Snowdon (where they walked to the top and back in the rain), Devil's Bridge (they stayed at the Hafod Arms), Hafod and Dynevor Castle. Where possible, they avoided travelling on Sundays. The longest day's journey was thirty miles, but on many days they covered only ten or twelve miles.

Mary Talbot spent her second honeymoon, in 1815, on the Isle of Wight, which was a popular destination at this time. Mary's sister Charlotte had been there in 1808 with her brother and a friend, Alicia Campbell, and other members of the family were to go there in later years. Several of them visited Cornwall too – Sir Charles Lemon, the husband of Charlotte

Strangways, was a Cornishman, as was Mary Talbot's second husband Sir Christopher Cole. Some ventured as far as the Lake District. Richard Quin and his wife were there in 1814, 'all in raptures with the beauty of all sorts and kinds'.[128]

The Talbots often broke their journeys by stopping for a day or two to see the local sights. In 1814 Mary visited Blenheim Palace (as her grandmother and great-grandmother had done over sixty years earlier) with three of her daughters. They admired the gardens, especially the aviary where they saw 'Some gold and silver pheasants, and doves and Spanish pigeons, and Puter's Curasoa birds, which made a dismal moan'. In Oxford they saw the students in their gowns and caps, 'which set us laughing so immoderately – Mary [Theresa] particularly – that it was long before we could stop ourselves'. They also saw the Radcliffe Camera and the library of All Souls, where they 'stayed three or four hours looking at beautiful prints'.[129] In the following year, on the way from Penrice to London, Mary and her children stopped at the inn on the Welsh side of the New Passage in the early afternoon and ordered dinner 'and while it was getting ready we got into a hackchaise and went to see Caldicot Castle'. After visiting the dentist in Bristol, they stopped in Bath to see friends and do some shopping. On the way from Bath to Bowood they passed 'an exhibition of wild beasts' at Chippenham. The children were disappointed when their mother refused to allow them to stop to see the animals.[130]

Several members of the family also travelled in Ireland at different times, usually to visit relations. Though Ireland was a part of the United Kingdom, it was just as remote as continental Europe, and almost as foreign. Civil unrest was common, and the Anglo-Irish and their English visitors had many reasons to feel nervous in the wake of the French Revolution. Nevertheless, the second Earl of Ilchester chose to take his only son and one of his daughters to Ireland with him in 1792, and Thomas and Mary Talbot took their two little daughters there in 1797, just a few months before the rising of the United Irishmen.[131] Neither group seems to have met with any hostility from the Irish people. In August 1798, however, Agnes Porter wrote that two 'worthy friends' had been forced to flee from Dublin to North Wales – they 'locked up their house and, with their only child, were glad to escape with their lives'.[132] In subsequent years the families at Melbury and Penrice were kept up-to-date with developments in the country by their Irish friends and relations.

Simply getting to and from Ireland could be a problem. From south-western England this usually involved an overland journey to one of the Welsh ports, and then a long – and invariably uncomfortable – sea crossing.

In 1764 Louisa Conolly, attempting to cross from Ireland to the mainland had 'a shocking expedition'. According to her sister Sarah Bunbury:

> She was fifty hours at sea in the packet and in a violent storm, and she was so ill they thought she would have died, and they persuaded the packet to go back to Ireland, and are now coming by Scotland.[133]

In 1792 the crossing from South Wales to Cheekpoint near Waterford took Lord Ilchester and his party twenty-two hours. Five years later, when Thomas and Mary Talbot took their two little daughters to Ireland, the passage from Milford Haven to Waterford lasted thirty-nine hours 'with contrary winds most of the time, and a very tempestuous sea'. Thomas hired a packet-boat for himself and his family at a cost of twenty guineas excluding tips to the captain, cabin steward and crew. The coach, which was to carry the family around Ireland, was ferried over from Wales in another ship.[134] The third Earl of Ilchester was more fortunate in 1807: after getting 'very safe through all the very bad roads of South Wales', he and his party had 'a tolerable passage of eighteen hours'.[135] In 1809 his sister Louisa Petty, also travelling to Ireland, 'made a very good sailor and was only moderately sick, though we were becalmed and had a gale in our passage also'. She was, however 'not moderately glad to get on shore'.[136]

Having landed safely, usually at Waterford, travellers from Wales to the west of Ireland still had a journey of several days in front of them. It look Lord Stavordale three days to get to Limerick in 1771, as he told his father:

> I am at last, after a most tedious journey of three days, in one and the same bad vehicle all the way, with tired, jaded horses, without having it either in my power to change horses or get fresh ones, should those I have had expired on the road, or a fresh carriage should mine [have] broke in the journey, which last indeed I thought would happen perpetually, arrived at Limerick.[137]

When Lord Stavordale (now the second Earl of Ilchester) made this journey again in 1792, with his son and daughter, the roads were better, and it took them only two days to cover the seventy miles from Waterford to Limerick. They stopped for one night at Caher on the way. On their return journey a few months later, the travellers took a different route, covering the fifty miles from Adare to Cork in one day, and then sailing from Cork to Minehead. They dined on deck during the passage, and Mary noted in her journal 'very sick, obliged to sing songs in the gun-room'.[138] Once they had arrived in Ireland, the English visitors admired the scenery, and complained about the weather, the roads or the inns – or all three.

The third Earl of Ilchester, who had been only five years old when he travelled to Ireland with his father and sister in 1792, was there again in 1807. He summed up his impressions of the country in a letter to Mary:

> The cove of Cork is a very find thing ... [We] went from there to Killarney ... staid there a week and wished to stay another, but saw it very well. I wish you had seen it, or had been of our party, as it [is] just the sort of place you would like – *magnificent* mountains, some of them covered with wood; *grand* waterfalls; *sublime* sheets of water; excellent roads; bad inns ...[139]

Two years later, Louisa Petty, visiting her husband's estate at Kenmare in County Kerry, was 'delighted with Ireland' and found the Irish inns 'very good'. Her picture of Ireland is, it must be admitted, more than a little idealised:

> The people are so cordial it does one good to be amongst them, and the part of the country this place is in is so delightfully wild, it suits my taste to a T ... I saw the cove of Cork in my way here. There is a fair today in the village. It is a gay and pleasant sight. There are large droves of Kerry cows sold at it – they are very small and mostly black, and form beautiful groups. I long to buy a dairy of them and carry them to England.[140]

Foreign travel was more usual for men than for women in the eighteenth century. For a wealthy young male aristocrat, a Grand Tour on the Continent was the summit of his education – a time when he could broaden his horizons, improve his manners and sow a few wild oats, in addition to learning a foreign language or two and collecting paintings, antique statues and objets d'art with which to embellish his family seat. Stephen and Henry Fox both travelled abroad, as did several of their sons, and a number of their Digby cousins. For most of the young ladies of the family, however, a foreign jaunt of this kind was quite out of the question. It was not felt to be necessary for their education, and it would not generally have been considered proper for a young lady to travel abroad accompanied only by a tutor and a servant or two. Women did, however, go on journeys overseas for other reasons. Some, like Lady Mary Wortley Montagu, one of the best-known female travellers of the eighteenth century, went because their husbands were sent abroad in connection with their work. Some travelled for the good of their health – though it is clear that this was often just an excuse.[141] Others escaped from their parents or husbands and ran off to the Continent with their lovers. Poor health was the ostensible reason for Susanna Strangways Horner's decision to leave England and spend several years on the Continent with her daughter in the 1730s, but it is clear from subsequent events that foreign travel also held out other attractions for her.

One of the most popular destinations for British tourists was Spa, a village in the Ardennes famous for the health-giving properties of its waters. Susanna and Elizabeth Strangways Horner were there for several months in 1731 and 1732, and other friends and relations visited the watering-place in later years. Sarah Bunbury stayed in Spa in 1767, and found that the place was 'detestable' if the weather was bad, but 'if it's fine, and your health admits of it, 'tis impossible to resist entering into the good-humoured idleness of the place'. The informality of life in the resort made a refreshing change:

> You may walk out in the street, or in a promenade close by, all the morning, and buy your own greens and fruit, read the papers at the bookseller's, go a-shopping or make parties for the evening. After dinner you go on foot to the Rooms, play, ball or walks, make your own party, and walk home (or in a chair if sick) at 9, 10, 11 or 12 o'clock.[142]

William and Susan O'Brien went to Spa in 1785 after William had been seriously ill. The resort had been recommended by a friend, who claimed that the Spa waters had effected 'the most perfect cure' of his 'most obstinate and extraordinary illness'. The O'Briens travelled first to Aix-la-Chapelle, where William 'used the baths and the waters as a preparation for Spa'. They then travelled to Spa itself, where they stayed for about three months, and where William 'experienced all the benefit that we had hoped for from this journey'.[143] Spa was still popular in the following century, when the Lemons planned to take their invalid daughter Augusta there.[144]

The O'Briens spent several years in North America, but the decision that they should leave England was made not by them but by Susan's family, after their elopement in April 1764. Susan's younger sister Harriot visited America too, but in rather different circumstances. By 1776 the discontent of the American colonists, described by Susan ten years earlier, had turned to open revolt, and General Burgoyne was sent to Canada, at the head of an army, to reinforce the British troops already based in the colony and prevent the Americans from taking over Canada. John Dyke Acland went with Burgoyne as major of the Twentieth Foot, leaving his wife, who had just given birth to a daughter, with her family at Redlynch. When the baby was two weeks old, however, Harriot set off for Cork, from where the fleet was to sail, accompanied by her monthly nurse 'in case she should fall ill by the way'. As she later told her niece Mary:

> She was in an agony of apprehension the whole journey, by Dublin to Cork, lest the fleet should have sailed, but it took near a fortnight to reach her destination owing to various difficulties and delays, and she arrived at two o'clock in the morning, having had such tired horses [during] the last stage that she had to walk up every hill.

Harriot's husband, though 'no doubt flattered by her strong attachment', was 'very averse to her scheme of accompanying him', and she later told Mary that she had spent 'hours persuading him even on her knees'. At last he was forced to agree that she could sail with him.[145] The fleet sailed out of Cork harbour on 8 April 1776. The five companies of the Twentieth Foot, consisting of approximately 250 men and fifteen officers, were on the *Kent*, a square-rigged East Indiaman. Some of the soldiers were accompanied by their wives and children, but Harriot was the only officer's wife on board. They also took with them a cow to provide milk. This much-travelled cow, which was named Kent after the ship, subsequently returned to Devon with the Aclands, and Mary Talbot later remembered seeing her at Pixton, where, aged eighteen or nineteen, she 'regularly attended the other dairy cows when they came from the field to be milked'. Like her sister before her, Harriot 'suffered much' from seasickness on the voyage. Crossing the Atlantic took six weeks. The fleet then sailed up the St Lawrence river to Quebec, finally anchoring there on 27 May. The Americans had already been driven from Quebec and, with the help of Burgoyne's troops, General Carleton was able to retake Montreal. The British army then chased the Americans into the forts on Lake Champlain. Harriot stayed in Montreal, apart from a brief and characteristically intrepid excursion by sledge to nurse John through an illness in a remote outpost. Prevented from travelling by the snow and ice of the Canadian winter, the Aclands then spent several months in Montreal with the rest of the army.

Burgoyne set off from Montreal again in June 1777 with an army of 10,000 men. The plan was that they should travel down the Champlain-George-Hudson waterway to Albany, where they were to meet two other British armies, one from New York and the other from the west. The American colonies would then, it was thought, be divided, and the British would be victorious. Unfortunately, this plan was hopelessly over-ambitious. Major Acland refused to let his wife accompany him on this ill-fated expedition, and she stayed in Montreal 'presenting him and all the other officers with half a Cheshire cheese each to augment their rations'. In July the British army took the fort of Ticonderoga and Acland was wounded. His wife commandeered a boat, and sailed down Lake Champlain to nurse him. After her husband's recovery Harriot stayed with him, and she travelled down the Hudson valley at the rear of the army, 'insisting on going forward every night to share her husband's tent, which was always in the most advanced position, because he commanded the Grenadiers'.[146] The nights in the Canadian wilderness were disturbed by the sounds of shooting, the yells of Indians dispatching enemy stragglers and the howling of wolves. But Harriot was not, apparently, put off, even when she and her husband were almost burned to death when their dog upset a candle which set fire to their tent.

The British advance was eventually halted on 7 October 1777 at the second battle of Saratoga. John Dyke Acland was shot in both legs and taken prisoner. Harriot again insisted on going to nurse her husband, though she was pregnant by this time. She made the journey down the river in an open boat, with two servants and a chaplain, carrying a flag of truce. The American commander, General Gates, allowed her to stay with her husband, and she nursed him for several months whilst he remained a prisoner at Albany. Gates was evidently impressed by Harriot, noting in a letter to his wife that she was 'sister to the famous Lady Susan' and describing her as 'the most amiable, delicate little piece of quality you ever beheld'.[147] When John Dyke Acland was well enough to travel, he and his party were exchanged for a number of Americans who had been taken prisoner by the British. The Aclands then returned to England, arriving in time for the birth of their son in February 1778. The story of Harriot's exploits travelled with them, and she was greeted as a heroine. Robert Pollard's imaginary painting of her, with her maid and chaplain, standing in the open boat as they were rowed along the Hudson River, was exhibited at the Royal Academy. An engraving, taken from this picture, was much in demand at the time.

Other women travelled for more conventional reasons. After the Peace of Paris of 1763, which brought an end to the Seven Years War, many English aristocrats embarked on European tours. They included Lord and Lady Holland, who visited Brussels before moving on to Paris, where they stayed for several months. They also spent some time at Spa during this trip. Caroline, Lady Holland, who spoke fluent French, enjoyed Parisian society. She and Henry also shopped enthusiastically, buying clothes, china and furniture for themselves and for their friends and relations at home in England. Further visits to the Continent, to Paris again, and also to Florence, Rome and Naples, followed during the next few years. Caroline's sister Sarah Bunbury visited Paris for the first time in 1765, and found the town 'beautifull, the people so genteel that it's a real amusement to drive about the streets'.[148] These were rich, aristocratic women. Their less wealthy contemporaries were far less likely to travel abroad in the eighteenth century, though Agnes Porter, spent some time in Boulogne with her sister Fanny, probably in the 1770s. Their father was never particularly well-off, and it is not clear if the whole family went to Boulogne, where there was a large English community at the time. It is possible that Agnes and Fanny were sent there by themselves, to learn French. Other women travelled with their employers – even Susan O'Brien took her maid to America with her.

In the second half of the eighteenth century more and more people – both men and women – began to undertake expeditions for pleasure, to see new scenes and enjoy the more agreeable climate of southern Europe. The number of British tourists travelling in Europe fell sharply during the French Wars from 1793 to 1815, but when peace was restored after the battle of Waterloo more travellers ventured overseas, and many of the Fox Strangways and Talbot ladies spent long periods of time on the Continent, often with their families. Mary Talbot 'never would go abroad, though fond of reading books of travel',[149] but her sisters Elizabeth, Louisa and Charlotte all went on long expeditions, mainly to France, Italy and Switzerland. Elizabeth Feilding and her sixteen-year-old son Henry were in Paris in May 1816, and Henry wrote in great excitement to his cousin Mary Theresa Talbot to tell her about his first visit to a foreign country:

> You cannot think how odd it seems on entering Calais to hear everybody talking French; all the shops with French inscriptions, and French handbills stuck up everywhere ... I should never finish my letter if I were to tell you all the things which I have seen, therefore I think it will be wisest to say nothing about them. However, I must tell you that you would like the *Cabinet d'Histoire Naturelle* amazingly. I never saw anything more nicely arranged: birds, fishes, insects, butterflies, shells and minerals in long cabinets, all with their names and in order.[150]

From the 1820s onwards whole families travelled, and many stayed in areas such as Switzerland or Tuscany for months, or even for several years. In many cases they went because a member of the family was suffering from an illness such as consumption, though residence on the Continent also had the advantage of being cheaper than living in England. In 1822 Charlotte Lemon (who had married in 1810) wrote after spending several months in Europe with her sickly daughter Augusta:

> I can imagine nothing of external pleasure so great as travelling without care, not caring whether the bread, or the water, or the beds are good. I always regretted that the war prevented my touring abroad when I married, and I now do so more than ever, being quite aware what extreme amusement it would be to me under other circumstances.[151]

In general, travelling conditions improved greatly during the Georgian period, so that by the beginning of the nineteenth century the Earls of Ilchester and the Talbots did not view even long journeys to and from London, South Wales and the West Country as major undertakings. Susan O'Brien continued to travel until she was well into her eighties: in April 1825, at the age of eighty-two, 'after a long deliberation', she 'took courage and set out for London to see my friends there and the world once more'.[152]

The most dramatic changes were to come in the mid nineteenth century, with the construction of the railways, but the impact of new technology was felt even in the early 1800s. In 1823 Susan O'Brien travelled to the Isle of Wight in the steam packet, which she found 'very convenient and pleasant'.[153] Two years later, Henry Talbot told his cousin Mary that he might 'run down and pay you a week's visit [at Penrice] by the Bristol steam boat'.[154] By 1830 the *Palmerston*, a steam packet, was sailing from Bristol to Swansea twice a week.[155] Inevitably, the reactions to such improvements to the transport system were mixed. Turnpike roads made journeys easier but, like modern road-building, they were not always popular with local property-owners. In 1825 Susan O'Brien noted that Lord Ilchester and his brother-in-law Edward Murray, the vicar of Stinsford, had been discussing 'the alteration talked of in the turnpike road, which I feared may affect my gate, road and trees, which I hope they may prevent'. Susan added, 'But the odious inventions of rail ways and canals leave no place in any degree secure'.[156] Twenty years later Susan's great nephew Kit Talbot became chairman and principal shareholder of the South Wales Railway Company. In 1890 the value of his investments in the railways was estimated at three million pounds. He had, however, managed to ensure that his own homes were not blighted by the railway: he prevented the main Cardiff to Swansea line from running too close to his mansion at Margam, and blocked attempts to build a railway into Gower, insisting that 'We can come and enjoy the country; the rail would destroy it all'.[157] Kit's mother was eight years old in 1784 when the first mail coaches began to run. She was seventy-four when the first section of the South Wales Railway through Monmouthshire and Glamorgan was opened. Where travel was concerned, the changes in her lifetime could truly be described as a revolution.

14

Patronage

Some historians have seen the eighteenth century as a period when the day-to-day lives of men and women diverged to an increasing extent, so that they came to live in 'separate spheres'. We are told that gentlemen monopolised the public sphere of business and politics at this time, whilst their wives became ornamental status objects, who spent most of their time sitting around at home without anything useful to do, having handed the management of their household over to servants. These delicate creatures depended on men to look after them; they had no independent lives of their own and remained 'immured in the private sphere' until they were liberated by the rise of feminism in the twentieth century.[1]

Having studied of the lives of the 'genteel' ladies of Georgian Lancashire in considerable detail, Amanda Vickery concluded that this picture represents a gross oversimplication. It is equally inaccurate where the ladies of the Fox Strangways family are concerned. Inevitably, they spent a good deal of their time at home, and much of their attention was absorbed by their children and domestic affairs: domains in which a woman was well advised to keep control, as Susan O'Brien advised her niece Elizabeth in 1796, shortly before the latter's marriage:

> Should your husband be inclined to take the trouble from you, do not suffer it in the interior regulation of your house, or what is called *the woman's province.* He will probably do it ill, and reluctantly, and if he does it well it will only produce a *pettitesse d'esprit* [littleness of spirit] that you will not like ... *Chacun doit garder le ton de son sexe* [everyone must protect the character of their sex].[2]

But neither a great country mansion nor a landed family's London house, was an entirely private space. Such buildings were also used to impress and entertain important visitors, including the Royal Family: King George III and Queen Charlotte were at Redlynch in 1789, and in October 1817 the recently-married Duke and Duchess of Gloucester spent three nights at Melbury. On the latter occasion a total of 114 people were lodged and fed in the house, and there were twenty-two horses in the stables in addition to Lord Ilchester's own.[3] By the early nineteenth century it was quite usual for ladies to involve themselves in more public entertainments too: in May

1812 Harriot Frampton was in Blandford, pursuing 'her military career' and presiding over the Dorset Yeomanry's ball and review. A few months later Harriot's mother-in-law held an 'assizes assembly for the lawyers, grand jury and other *beaux esprits*' in Dorchester.[4] With more and more women becoming interested in academic subjects such as botany, chemistry and geology, there was an increasing demand for lectures and meetings where they could exchange information and find out about the latest discoveries. The Royal Institution, which was founded in 1799, was open to both men and women from the outset and proved to be an immediate success.[5] At the London Botanic Garden in Sloane Street in 1810, lectures on botany alternated with 'concerts of instrumental musick' on summer evenings: both men and women were admitted, though the 'intrusion of improper persons' was prevented by asking members to pay an annual subscription of one or two guineas, with an admission fee of 2*s.* 6*d.* for guests.[6]

An aristocratic woman also had a considerable amount of economic power, even if she did not have sole possession of a landed estate. The Fox Strangways ladies are not remembered as great patrons of the arts, but all purchased clothes, books, china and other luxury goods for themselves and their children; they furnished their homes and ornamented their gardens; and they had overall responsibility for running large and complex households. They employed large numbers of people on a regular basis and bought services from many others, from innkeepers to dancing-masters. Such women's access to patronage and their ability to devote money to charitable uses had a direct impact on the lives of their neighbours and tenants. And although, like all other females in Georgian England, the ladies of the Fox Strangways family were theoretically subject to the authority of their fathers, husbands and brothers, they were quite capable of asserting themselves if they chose to do so. More so, perhaps, than many of their contemporaries: in 1783 Sarah Lennox told Susan O'Brien that although women were generally supposed to be 'of a more pliable nature' than men, 'my argument hardly holds good to *your* family, as you are all of so *firm* a disposition that it greatly resembles that of men'.[7]

Susanna Strangways Horner's unnamed obituarist wrote that 'Her temper was irresistibly sweet and engaging and such, accordingly, as never failed to gain the affection, and command at the same time the respect, of all that approached her'.[8] Few of her contemporaries found her quite so engaging: a historian sympathetic to the Horner family described her as 'A most engaging woman, a false wife, and a monster of hypocrisy and dissimulation'.[9]

Susanna's own authority, and the independence with which she was able to pursue her own objectives, were greatly enhanced by her status as an heiress. From the time of her sister's death in 1729, Susanna alone controlled one half of the Melbury estate, though she had to share the other half with her husband. In 1737 she also inherited the Foxley estate in Wiltshire from her friend and cousin Judith Ayliffe. Like Susanna's sister, Judith had shown her sympathy with her cousin by ensuring that Thomas Horner could not 'intermeddle' in the property, and by appointing Stephen and Henry Fox and their brother-in-law Edward Digby to be her executors and trustees.[10] The estate accounts suggest that Susanna received a gross income of between £5000 and £6000 a year in the 1740s and 1750s, and it was she who decided how this was spent. She showed no inclination to allow her son-in-law to take over the running of the Melbury estate: it was Susanna who met and corresponded with the steward George Donisthorpe, made all the decisions, and signed leases and other documents. Donisthorpe made it his business to keep on the right side of his often cantankerous employer, and his letters appear excessively obsequious to modern eyes, but even he protested from time to time. In 1743 he apologised for a delay in submitting the estate accounts for Susanna's approval. This had come about because:

> The method which you have been pleased to prescribe for making up my accounts being different from any I ever yet see, and being desirous to make them as compleat as I can, has occasioned me to be somewhat longer about them.[11]

Perhaps inevitably, Susanna's determination to have her own way eventually led to a deterioration in her relationship with her son-in-law. The two did not agree on political matters: having been brought up in a strongly Tory family, Susanna could not bring herself to support the Whigs as Lord Ilchester and his brother did. When the Foxes tried to persuade their nephew Lord Digby to stand for the Whigs in the election of 1754, Susanna remained determinedly neutral.[12] Like all great landowners at this period, Susanna had the power to influence the way in which her tenants voted, even though, as a woman, she had no vote of her own.

Financial matters were, however, the main cause of disputes between Susanna and her son-in-law. Throughout the years of her widowhood Susanna probably spent most of her annual income. The total cost of the repairs and alterations carried out at Melbury after Thomas Horner's death in 1741 is unknown, but by 1745 Lord Ilchester was beginning to complain about his mother-in-law's extravagance. In July 1745 he told his brother that he had written to Mrs Horner 'very seriously' and that she had assured him that she would do very little more at Melbury.[13] Susanna's expenditure on her house and gardens was, indeed, less in later years, but she began instead to devote large sums of money to various charitable pursuits.

A particular cause of friction was Susanna's resolute refusal to allow any part of the Strangways estates to be sold to pay off debts. Her determination arose, she said 'from tender motives ... because it touches me to the quick to have any of my family property parted with'. She did not, however, see any reason why Lord Ilchester should not sell his own estates for the same purpose, telling him:

> It touches me to the quick to have any part of my family property parted with ... therefore, for God [sic] sake, think no more of selling or exchanging but, as you used to say was your ambition, keep the Strangways estate entire for the object of our hopes, I mean your eldest son.

Lord Ilchester retorted that Susanna was 'of so happy a temper as seldom to see the strength of the arguments that make for that side of the question you don't relish', and he accused her of acting unreasonably.

Susanna also accused Lord Ilchester of being less than honest about his own financial situation when he married her daughter. He reminded her that she had demanded that he should draw up a statement 'specifying what my estate was, where it lay, what money I had, and where it was' at the time of the marriage. Susanna usually avoided open confrontation by the simple expedient of refusing to discuss business when she and her son-in-law were together, informing him in 1747 that at their next meeting she would 'most likely be unfit to discompose myself about anything that requires serious thinking'. Later in the same year relations broke down completely, when Susanna complained that the annuity due to her from Lord Ilchester had not been paid on time. In a letter which began 'Madam', rather than 'Dear Madam' as usual, her son-in-law replied that the payments had never been more than a month in arrear. 'I must have been more than blind' he continued 'not to have perceived for a long time that there has been a great alteration in your disposition towards me'. Nevertheless, he wrote, he knew that it was his duty to behave 'in the most respectful manner' towards his mother-in-law, and he was 'resolved never to swerve' from this duty.[14] A truce seems to have been negotiated after this, and in the following years Lady Ilchester attempted to keep the peace between her husband and her increasingly capricious mother with varying degrees of success.

Susanna's reluctance to defer to – or even to consult – the members of her closest family ultimately had unfortunate consequences. In 1745 or 1746 Susanna's friend and cousin Sir Robert Long introduced her to an impoverished country schoolmaster called John Ayliffe, who was then aged about twenty-five. Ayliffe, who claimed to be the rightful heir to the Foxley estate, persuaded Susanna that he was 'a disinherited person' and was 'entituled in conscience to the whole Wiltshire estate'.[15] Susanna decided that she should 'make [Ayliffe] some compensation for the injury he had sustained', and she therefore took him into her service as a bailiff and house steward. Within a short while Ayliffe had:

> Acquitted himself so much to her satisfaction that she frequently shewed him acts of friendship, and he was in great confidence with her, as was also Sarah his wife, whom she intrusted with the management of many of her private concerns and family secrets.

Unwisely, as it turned out, Susanna signed any papers that Ayliffe brought to her 'without reading or knowing the contents otherwise than from what he was pleased to tell her'. As a witness later testified:

> Her estate made it necessary for her to execute great number of leases. Her sex and bad health made it troublesome for her to look into them herself, and it was natural she should have that confidence in her steward as to rely upon his judgment and integrity.

Early in 1750, Susanna granted John Ayliffe a lease of one of her farms in Wiltshire, which would give him approximately £30 a year. It was later claimed that she had also executed a deed under which Ayliffe and his wife and son were to receive an annuity of £420 after her death, and had charged her estates with the payment of a lump sum of £3000 to Ayliffe, or to his widow or son. The Ayliffes alleged that Lord and Lady Ilchester knew nothing of this arrangement, because Susanna had

> enjoined the said John Ayliffe to keep the said deed secret and not divulge it to any person whomsoever, alledging that the discovery of it would create an uneasiness in her family, and would prejudice his [Ayliffe's] interest with the Right Honourable Stephen, Earl of Ilchester, and his lady.

In the event, it was not Susanna's daughter and son-in-law but Sir Robert Long who began doubt Ayliffe's honesty. He informed Susanna of his suspicions, and she assured him that she had merely promised to give the Ayliffes a lease of a farm worth £30 a year. In 1753, however, she sacked Ayliffe, having become convinced that he was 'a rogue' who had imposed upon her. If he was related to Judith Ayliffe, Susanna declared, 'he was only a bastard of one of the family'. But Susanna still retained some regard for Ayliffe's wife, and her dying request to Henry Fox (to whom she intended to leave the Foxley estate) was that he should give the Ayliffes £30 a year for their lives.

Susanna was not alone in being taken in by John Ayliffe. In 1750 she had asked Henry Fox to procure 'some genteel office that might enable him in all events to support his wife and child in a decent matter'. Fox had used his interest to get the post of Commissary of the Muster for Ayliffe, at a salary of about £200 a year; he also employed him as steward of his own estates in Wiltshire. Even after Long and Susanna had turned against Ayliffe, Fox made him his Deputy Receiver of the Crown Rents in Wales, 'imputing his disgrace to ill offices done him with Mrs Horner by some about her who envied the favor [Ayliffe] was in'. After Susanna's death early in 1758, Fox recommended Ayliffe to his friend John Calcraft, and to his brother-in-law the Duke of Richmond. He fulfilled his promise to Susanna by offering Ayliffe a farm on his own estate, for which the rent was to be £35 a year. At this point, however, Ayliffe – who was close to bankruptcy by this time – overreached himself. In November 1758 he took the lease to Henry Fox at the Pay Office in London. Fox signed the document without noticing that Ayliffe had altered it so that the annual rent appeared to be £5, rather than £35. Ayliffe then borrowed £1700 on the security of this lease and the earlier lease from Susanna Strangways Horner, but failed to make the interest payments as they became due. When the mortgagee applied to Henry Fox, the lease supposedly granted by him was carefully examined and found to be a forgery. John Ayliffe was tried for fraud at the Middlesex Assizes in October 1759. He was found guilty and sentenced to death. On 19 November 1759 he was carried from Newgate gaol to Tyburn in an open cart, and executed.

The dead man's creditors subsequently tried to claim the annuity of £420 and lump sum of £3000, supposedly granted by Susanna to the Ayliffes in 1750. When Lord Ilchester refused to pay anything, claiming that the deed was not valid in law, and had been obtained from Susanna 'by fraud and imposition', the creditors petitioned the Court of Chancery. Their claims were eventually dismissed.[16] It is difficult to blame Susanna for being deceived by John Ayliffe, but Henry Fox – a Member of Parliament and government minister – should have known better. This episode does, however, underline the mistrust and secrecy which did so much to undermine the relationship between Susanna and her son-in-law in the last years of her life.

Elizabeth, Countess of Ilchester, was a much less forceful character than her mother had been, and she was usually content to leave the running of the Melbury and Redlynch estates to her husband. But she could act independently when she chose to do so. Her mother had left her a capital sum of £1000, together with an income of £600 a year out of the Melbury estate, and she was also entitled to £1000 from the Horners.[17] Elizabeth's letters make it clear that it was she who was responsible for initiating alterations to the grounds at Melbury in the 1760s, and it was for her, rather than her husband, that a new house was built at Abbotsbury at the same time. Though Lord Ilchester refused to have any direct contact with Susan O'Brien after her elopement in 1764, his wife wrote regularly to their daughter whilst she was in America, and she also gave her money: £200 before she left England, and £100 a year whilst she was overseas. But Elizabeth's gifts to Susan were never entirely without strings, as became clear from a conversation which Sarah Bunbury reported in 1767:

> [Lady Ilchester] said that she never would agree to your having a *certain* income (from your relations) because that would make you independent of *her* [and] that it was the only power or tie by which she could direct your way of life.

Lady Ilchester also promised that she would insist that her husband gave Susan an income if Lord Holland were to die and 'that even if that failed, she might out of her own money give you what she liked'. This, however, 'intirely depended on yours and Mr O'Brien's merits towards her'.[18] Lady Ilchester continued to support the O'Briens after their return from America, giving her daughter £2000 to pay off her debts in 1773. Two years later she paid for the house at Stinsford to be renovated so that Susan and her husband could live there.

After her husband's death, Lady Ilchester had an annual income of approximately £4500 to £5000, out of which she gave the O'Briens £400 a year. She also gave £200 to her son Charles, and paid the costs of running the household at Melbury. Her conservative instincts led her to resist major changes, and she shared her mother's reluctance to allow the Strangways estates to be broken up. She was also quite capable of standing up to her son when she chose to do so. The first Earl had left his widow the family's London house in Old Burlington Street for life, but by the early 1780s the second Earl was pressing his mother to make the house over to him. Lady Ilchester replied firmly:

> Was you my only child, I should have great pleasure from assisting you, but as I have a large family, many of them much poorer than yourself, in justice I ought not to give up any right that I can claim whereby they may be benefited ... I endeavour to conform in most things to your requests, and am sorry when my reason tells me I must not comply.

And when Lord Ilchester told his mother that he wished to close the inn at Bexington near Abbotsbury, she replied:

> For my own part, I am against it ... for I think it of great use to the fisher people, and to anyone that may be in distress on that road. Besides, I don't chuse to make alterations in my time. When it's yours, you may do as you like.[19]

Although Susan O'Brien was not an heiress like her mother and grandmother, it was she who held the purse-strings in her marriage. Having been forced to give up the stage after eloping with Susan in 1764, William O'Brien never succeeded in finding a way of making a living that would make him financially independent of his wife's family. He was bored by country life and uninterested in country sports and farming, and a disastrous attempt to become a barrister in the 1780s brought him to a state of nervous collapse. He also seems to have been hopeless with money: Susan wrote of his 'disposition to expence', and she kept the household accounts. She foresaw problems when William was appointed Receiver General of Taxes for the county of Dorset in 1802, noting in her journal in the following year that a meeting with his bankers had 'quite discomposed' her husband, who was 'so little acquainted with business and accounts that everything alarms him'. His health began to deteriorate again, and he eventually resigned in 1811. Susan claimed that it was only by resorting to her 'book and memorandums' that William's business affairs were eventually sorted out, for he had always refused to keep an account book of his own.[20]

Susan O'Brien's financial and legal position was not greatly affected by her husband's death. Other widows were less fortunate, and some found themselves at a considerable disadvantage because of the way in which their husband's will had been drawn up – or because the will had not been amended as the family's circumstances had changed. It was by no means a foregone conclusion that they would be appointed guardian to their own children. After William Davenport Talbot's death 'in insolvent circumstances' in 1800, it was discovered that his will made no provision for the management of the Lacock estate, or for an income for his wife Lily and baby son Henry until the latter came of age. Chaos reigned until matters were referred to the Court of Chancery, but it was not until 1805 that Lily was officially judged to be 'a fit and proper person' to be appointed guardian to her son, with £400 a year for herself and £500 a year for Henry's support and maintenance.[21]

Lily's stepmother Maria, Countess of Ilchester, was confronted by a similarly difficult situation after her husband's death in 1802. It was discovered that the Earl's will had been written in 1778, long before the death of his first wife. There were several codicils, but there was no reference to an income for Maria, and her three young sons (one born after his father's death) were not mentioned at all.[22] As the surviving executor, the Earl's brother Colonel Stephen Strangways was appointed guardian to those of the children who were under age. Maria's petition to the Lord Chancellor for the custody of her own children was unsuccessful, placing her in a situation that she found 'mortifying'.[23] The widespread fear that a wealthy widow would be preyed upon by a fortune-hunter who would disinherit the children of her first marriage could cause problems if she chose to remarry. After her first husband's death in 1813, Mary Talbot had the right to live at Penrice only so long as she remained a widow.[24] Her second husband, Sir Christopher Cole, therefore had to rent the house from the trustees of the Penrice and Margam estates.

The ladies of the Georgian country house may not have been able to vote in elections or hold public office, but this did not mean that they were ignorant of national affairs. Susan O'Brien and Sarah Lennox often discussed contemporary politics in their letters, and Susan's later journals bear witness to her continuing interest in the subject, and her strongly-held views. She mistrusted politicians, but she was in general a supporter of the status quo, writing after the outbreak of the French Revolution in 1789:

> Publick affairs this summer were very new and interesting. The violent conduct of the French, and the admiration which their distruction of the Bastile and other insults on their government has occasioned, and been expressed by the Dissenters here, make many thinking people uneasy. But, as we have no Bastile, nor no want of liberty to say, write or do what we please, I hope we shall continue sensible of the blessings we enjoy, and continue to enjoy them as long as we have already done.[25]

Newspapers were an essential means of keeping in touch with the wider world, though Susan regarded them with a certain amount of cynicism, as she noted in her journal one day in 1813:

> Studyed the newspapers. Nothing can be as mischievous as they are grown, publishing all the dinners, and speeches made at them in praise of Catholicks, Dissenters, Luddites, and every description of person that attacks the government, the establishment, or the quiet of the country.[26]

The O'Briens' friendship with their near neighbour, the philanthropist and prison reformer William Morton Pitt, gave them a direct interest in the politics of the county of Dorset, which he represented in the House of Commons from 1790 to 1826. In the general election of 1806 there was a contest for the two Dorset seats for the first time for eighty years. Susan went to Dorchester to hear the candidates' speeches, and she and Mrs Pitt then attended the poll, a scene of 'fine confusion'. Pitt was duly re-elected, together with Edward Berkeley Portman of Bryanston.[27] Susan was also at the election ball a fortnight later, and wrote afterwards, 'never was at one before, very amusing, all sorts of freeholders and their friends and familys dancing most merrily and happyly'.[28] When another election was called six months later, Susan again went to the hustings in Dorchester, and she was there to see the scaffolding collapse whilst the speakers were in full flow. Nobody was hurt, and all 'removed to the leads of the church opposite, which is a much better place'.[29]

According to her son, Mary Talbot 'took no interest in public affairs',[30] and she refused to accompany her second husband during his visits to London after he was elected Member of Parliament for Glamorgan in 1817. Mary's lack of involvement was not, however, shared by her elder sister Lily, a passionate Whig who was on the periphery of the Prince of Wales's disreputable set. Susan O'Brien, whom Lily resembled in many ways, thoroughly disapproved of her niece's behaviour. In August 1798 Lily stayed with the O'Briens at Stinsford:

> [She] came from Winchester, where she had been racketting for two months. Foolish proceedings – more than one quarrell about it. Gave the best advice in my power. The danger of the society she was in there: Sheridans and Ogles the worst company *she* can keep. Very clever, very flattering, very pleasant, but very bad. Fortune and reputation may be hurt by folly, as well as by vice.[31]

As usual, Lily took little notice of her aunt's advice. In 1811 she wrote to Susan describing the grand fête held at Carlton House to celebrate the Prince's appointment as Regent, and her aunt replied with the warning that 'the heart and mind is contaminated, as well as the manners, by evil communication'.[32]

As the wife of a Member of Parliament and government minister, another sister, Louisa Lansdowne, presided over house parties at Bowood at which the guests included many of the most prominent figures from the worlds of the arts and Whig politics. In September 1822 Susan O'Brien was at one such gathering, together with Lord and Lady Holland, the well-known wit and essayist Sydney Smith and his family, and Samuel Rogers, the 'pale poet':

> Dinner very agreeable. Had much conversation both with Lord and Lady Holland. He, I knew, was (politicks excepted), everything likeable and lovable ... Mr Sidney Smith excessively entertaining, [in] great spirits and saying a thousand odd and unexpected things – keeping everyone laughing and merry, which is not always the case in such large partys.

At the age of almost eighty, however, Susan found gatherings of this kind hard work, commenting on the following evening:

> Though the conversations are often lively, generally instructive to me who know so little of what is passing in the great or literary world, yet they seem long, and want music, cards or chess – some *point d'appui* [prop] for the elderlys.[33]

Kit Talbot, who stayed at Bowood often, remembered his aunt Louisa as 'a handsome and most dignified looking person'. He thought, however, that she 'would have been happier in a humbler position than that of a Marchioness, the wife of a leading politician', and liked her the least of his aunts: 'She was so exclusively devoted to her husband that it always seemed to me that the rest of the world was a blank to her'.[34]

The relationship between the British aristocracy and the established church was a close one in the eighteenth century. With approximately half of the benefices in the country in the gift of private landowners, most great families had at least one or two livings at their disposal.[35] Without such a patron, many a clergyman was doomed to spend his life as a poorly-paid curate or schoolmaster, or riding around from parish to parish taking occasional services for the incumbents. Such a man was Francis Porter, the father of the governess Agnes Porter. The son of a Yarmouth beer brewer, and lacking any influential connections, Francis Porter did not gain a parish of his own until he was sixty, and he died only four years later.[36]

In 1817 the third Earl of Ilchester was the patron of at least fourteen livings in Dorset, Somerset and Wiltshire.[37] Such livings could be used to assist friends and dependants, or to provide for the patron's younger sons: the first Earl's youngest son Charles Redlynch Fox Strangways was rector of the family parish of Maiden Newton in Dorset from 1787 until his death in 1836, and he also had Kilmington in Somerset from 1811, succeeding his first cousin Charles Digby, who had been presented to the living by his uncle in 1767. Lay patrons also built and rebuilt churches and established charitable institutions such as schools and almshouses. Many incumbents acted as private chaplains to their patrons; they also taught in their schools and ministered to the poor and sick among the estate's tenants. In return for the favours shown to them, the clergymen were expected to support the established order and to encourage their parishioners to be sober, dutiful and respectful.

Few of the women described in this book wrote much about their religious beliefs, but there is little sign that they were dissatisfied with the Church of England, which provided employment for so many of their male relations. Most would have agreed with Lady Harriot Acland when she asked: 'Why can't they let one alone to believe the things we were taught in our youth, and do all the good we can to merit the favor of God?'[38] Most, if not all, attended church regularly as a matter of course, and read sermons and other devotional works. They were aware of the growth of nonconformity during the second half of the eighteenth century, though they were only indirectly affected by it. Moderation was felt to be important, and ostentatious displays of sentimental or religious feelings were frowned on. Susan

O'Brien disapproved of her friend Margaret Pitt's behaviour after the death of her daughter Sophia, Lady Romney, in 1812:

> Mrs Pitt went into Lady Romney's room, and would sit by the coffin. She will not spare her feelings – on the contrary [she] forces and encourages them. No principles of religion, no degree of affection, require or recommend such exertions. It is not a strong mind that seeks to do more than is required, where so much is required. It is rather a symptom of weakness and enthusiasm, but quite in poor Mrs Pitt's character, who feels and sees everything in [the] utmost degree.[39]

Having shown few obvious signs of piety in her youth, Susanna Strangways Horner took to religion in the latter part of her life – in an attempt, perhaps, to atone for the sins of her earlier years. That her closest relations found this new addiction to holiness somewhat trying is evident from a letter written by her daughter during a stay in Bath in 1752:

> I am just come home from Mama's, which I do with as much pleasure as many people would go to the prettiest entertainment in the world, for really she talks more of religion than ever. I often feel ready to rebell, and my patience will scarse hold out, but to be sure it's my duty to bear it all, and as I am doing my duty, that is my only comfort. I hope this will serve as a penance for all my faults. I don't think there can be a more severe one.[40]

After her death, Susanna's obituarist wrote with a degree of hyperbole which must have surprised anyone who had actually known her:

> What ... distinguished Mrs Horner, and left her with but few equals, and it may be without a rival, were her benevolence toward man and her piety towards Almighty God. These swallowed up and absorbed the whole woman ... She appeared to injoy [her large fortune] only in proportion to the good she was enabled to perform. Her benevolence was as unbounded as the nature she shared and extended to all of her fellow kind, whose miseries she really felt, and endeavoured as much as possible to alleviate.[41]

This may well have been composed by the Revd Marrian Feaver, Susanna's 'unworthy chaplain' and the rector of Melbury for over forty years. Susanna came to rely on Feaver's advice more and more as she grew older. Inevitably, his influence was resented, both by Susanna's own family and by other people who felt that Feaver had turned Susanna against them. In 1757 a clergyman, Thomas Edwards, wrote to Henry Fox asking for his help in obtaining the living of Brinkworth in Wiltshire, and claiming that Susanna had previously promised him a parish, but had gone back on her word due to 'groundless and malicious' imputations by Feaver, who had 'basely stabbed me in the dark'. According to Edwards, Susanna had told him 'with an open frankness and ingenuity ... that she could not think of giving me a living, if I had been her own brother, for that she heard I was not orthodox'. Edwards had no doubt that Feaver was responsible, and that 'the same skillfull engineer' was continuing to work in order to complete his ruin.[42]

From 1745 onwards Susanna spent considerable sums of money on repairs and gifts to the churches with which her ancestors had been associated. According to a memorial at Melbury Osmond erected by Marrian Feaver, the old church, which was in a ruinous state, was 'wholly taken down, and rebuilt on the same foundation' in 1745 by Susanna, who adorned it with 'pews, font, altar-piece, communion plate etc.'[43] Much of this work was directed by Francis Cartwright, whose estimate for the work on the church came to £252 16*s.* 8*d.* 'exclusive of timber, sawing and carriage etc.', with a further £82 9*s.* 1*d.* for the tower.[44] In 1748 a Mr Greenaway was paid £6 6*s.* for gilding and painting the altarpiece in the church.

Some work was also carried out in the church at Melbury Sampford. Here, Susanna was able to indulge her taste for sumptuous Rococo decoration – rather to the dismay of some of her descendants. Writing in the mid nineteenth century, Charlotte Traherne commented:

> Mrs Horner ornamented the chancel of Melbury church with carved seats and a very fine red velvet altar cloth and reredos, richly adorned with gold lace and gilt carving. The whole is in a debased taste, but very handsome in its way. She probably took the idea from some of the Belgian churches she saw in her visit to Spa.[45]

Payments for work at Melbury Sampford in 1748–49 included £32 5*s.* 8*d.* for pulling down and rebuilding the aisle; £24 9*s.* for new pews and paving for the chancel; £4 for making a new bell-cage wheel and hanging the bell; and £15 for a new pulpit . The family tombs were also cleaned, repaired and regilded, and the church itself was whitewashed. Cartwright directed work at Abbotsbury too: in 1749 John Ford was paid £1 2*s.* 6*d.* for taking down the screen whilst the chancel there was being altered; and a new reredos with Corinthian columns was erected two years later.[46]

Susanna's expenditure was not limited to the buildings themselves. In 1748–49 she bought a number of prayer books and Bibles for the churches at Melbury. The bill for these, which was presented by Samuel Gould in 1749, came to £51 5*s.* 6*d.*, and included £36 10*s.* for twelve Common Prayer Books and £7 7*s.* for a Bible. These books were all covered in blue Turkey leather, and the Bible also had blue ribbons and a fringe of gold wire.[47] Even more was spent on gifts of communion plate to several churches in parishes where Susanna's estates lay. Many of these were from the workshop of the highly-regarded silversmith Paul de Lamerie, one of the first in England to work in the Rococo style. Earlier, in 1737, Susanna had given a silver-gilt cup, paten and flagon by de Lamerie to Stinsford church. Between 1748 and 1755 she made several further purchases for the churches at Melbury Osmond, Melbury Sampford, Abbotsbury and Mells. One of de Lamerie's accounts was presented in September 1748. It came to £130 4*s.* 7*d.*, and included £63 15*s.* 7*d.* for two flagons, two chalices, two patens and two salvers. 'Engraving all the arms, glory etc. on the aforesaid plate' cost £6 18*s.*, and de Lamerie charged £23 18*s.* for gilding the plate, and £2 4*s.* for 'two neat wainscott cases for the two setts of plate, partitioned and lined; locks, keys and hinges and a large outpacking case'.[48]

Hutchins recorded in 1774 that Susanna Strangways Horner had devoted herself during the latter part of her life to 'acts of piety, charity and generosity'.[49] She was certainly remembered for her gifts to a wide variety of good causes, at a time when such liberality was becoming less and less common. In the sixteenth and seventeenth centuries the honour and reputation of landowning families had been maintained by displays of hospitality and generosity to their neighbours, both rich and poor. From the reign of Queen Elizabeth onwards, however, complaints about the decay of housekeeping became increasingly vociferous, and by the early eighteenth century many people felt that wealthy families were opting out of their responsibilities by spending too much of their time (and money) in London or in spa towns such as Bath. When they were in the country, such people were increasingly likely to spend their time isolated, both socially and geographically, from the majority of their neighbours. Susan O'Brien expressed the nostalgia for the 'old times' felt by so many of her contemporaries when she wrote in 1801 after a visit to Wherwell Priory in Hampshire, the home of Joshua Iremonger:

> The place and family quite a specimen of an old country gentleman's manner of living. So good, so happy, so beneficial to the neighbouring inhabitants, that one cannot but regret that is is now so rarely to be met with.[50]

In their wills, Susanna's father and brother had left money to the poor of several parishes in which their lands lay. Where Melbury Osmond and Evershot were concerned, the sums thus bequeathed (a total of £80 to each parish) were retained by the later owners of the Melbury estate, who paid out the interest to the rector and the parish officials responsible for levying the statutory poor rates. By the mid 1740s Susanna was paying £4 interest to the poor of each parish at Christmas.[51] By 1747, however, this had been increased to £8 5*s.* a year for the poor of Melbury Osmond. Most English parishes had two Overseers of the Poor at this time, chosen by the inhabitants and responsible for levying a rate and distributing the money that they collected. In the parish of Melbury Sampford, however, the situation was different: no Overseers were appointed, presumably because the whole parish belonged to the Strangways family and the inhabitants were all dependent on them for their livelihood. Anyone who was too old, too young or too sick to work had to look to the inhabitants of Melbury House for support. In 1728, shortly after Susanna and her sister inherited the estate, regular payments included a shilling each a week to nine poor women, and two shillings a week to a blind man called William Watts.[52] The household accounts of the 1740s record several payments to individuals such as Mary Hodges, who received two shillings a week until she died in 1749. In her will, Susanna provided for such payments to continue after her death by leaving £50 to the poor of Melbury Sampford, though this, too, was to be held by her successors, who were to pay out the intererest every year.[53] She also left £50 to the poor of Melbury Sampford and Osmond; £100 to the poor of Abbotsbury; £50 to each of the parishes of Stinsford, Evershot and Foxley; and £20 to Mells.

When he visited Melbury, Horace Walpole was shown a 'cell' near the kitchen and servants' hall which, he was told, had been built by Susanna 'to receive beggars'.[54] He was also told that she had given away £3000 a year in charity.[55] This was probably an exaggeration, but she does appear to have been unusually generous, both to people who lived on the estate and also to casual callers at the house, giving them food, money, clothes and medicine. Typical payments include 2*s.* 6*d.* 'to a poor woman that brought a foolish child' in 1743. In the late 1740s Susanna was giving up to £1 14*s.* a week to the poor at Melbury, and she also paid £25 4*s.* a year for 'charity cloaths' for the poor in Evershot and Melbury. The bill for 'medicines for Mrs S. Horner's servants, paupers etc.' from July 1749 to December 1750 came to a total of £72 7*s.* 6*d.*[56] Codicils to Susanna's will included bequests of £6 a year to William Sparrow, 'a poor blind man of the city of Bath', to whom Susanna had already been giving a shilling a week for some years; and two shillings a week to Henry Chubb, 'a poor blind man of Evershot'.

Susanna also supported schools for poor parishioners, as her ancestors had done. In 1728 Mr Harding was paid £3 a year to teach poor children in Evershot, whilst Edward Godfrey, the schoolmaster at Melbury Osmond, received an annual salary of £10.[57] John Houlton, the Melbury schoolmaster in 1748, was still paid £10 a year. In her will Susanna said that she wished to establish a perpetual free school for the poor children of the parishes of Melbury Osmond and Melbury Sampford, and to provide a school-house and residence for the master, who was to be paid £15 a year. John Houlton was to continue as master for his life, 'if he shall behave well', and he was to teach twenty poor children to read, write and cast accounts.[58]

In his will, written in 1726, Susanna's brother had asked his sisters to erect a charity school for twenty boys at Abbotsbury, and by 1745 Susanna was paying the schoolmaster there an annual salary of £12 12*s.*[59] A new schoolhouse was built in the village in 1748 and 1749 at a cost of approximately £170.[60] Susanna stipulated in her will that the schoolmaster should be paid £20 a year, and also that thirty poor children should be taught to 'read, write, and cast accounts, and to understand the art of navigation so as to render them fit for the sea service'.[61]

Other occasional payments are recorded too. From 1748 to 1751 Susanna paid a subscription of £10 10*s.* a year to the Westminster Infirmary.[62] At about this time, too, a deed was drawn up under which she proposed to set up a trust to produce a regular income for the Society for the Propagation of the Gospel in Foreign Parts. The impetus for this may have come from Marrian Feaver, who left £5 to the society in his own will.[63] Henry Fox tried to persuade Susanna to change her mind, telling her that the money would be used not to convert 'infidels' but to increase the stipends of clergymen in the colonies. In Henry's opinion, moreover, charity should begin at home, and Susanna should put the interests of her own granddaughters first. He begged her to 'think it part of your duty and to make it your pleasure too, to save some money for those pretty ones who may, or may not, be happy wives and mothers'.[64] Henry's arguments were only partly effective: Susanna did not go ahead with the gift to the S.P.G., choosing instead to set up an endowment under which the stipend of the vicar of Abbotsbury was to be increased by £20 a year 'for ever'.[65] Susanna's expenditure on charitable projects continued unabated during the last years of her life. When grain prices rose sharply in 1756 she gave 'a great deal' of corn to the inhabitants of the towns and villages around Melbury, and asked her son-in-law to do the same for the poor people in the neighbourhood of Redlynch, telling him that it was 'a proper and a great charity' and that she always wished him to do right.[66]

The level of expenditure no doubt fell after Susanna's death in 1758, but the household accounts of the 1760s nevertheless give the impression of an almost continuous stream of lame, indigent and unfortunate men, women and children making their way to the back door at Melbury. Payments in September 1760 include 3*s.* 6*d.* 'to three poor people who were strangers', and 4*s.* 'to a poor man at Lower Melbury almost dead in a consumption'. In October the housekeeper paid 6*d.* to 'a half dozen of lemons to make jelly for the keeper and a poor woman of Lower Melbury'. She also gave 1*s.* 'to a poor man that played on the Welsh harp who used to come in the late Mrs Horner's time', and 5*s.* 'to two poor girls of Lower Melbury to have wrens in their necks cured'.[67] In November 'a poor man who was a sufferer by fire' received 2*s.* 6*d.*; 'Sarah Marshall, who is very poor' had 6*d.*; and 'a poor crazy man that used to come' received 1*s.* Payments in 1761 included 2*s.* 6*d.* 'to a poor woman who was servant to Mr Strangways'; 1*s.* 'to two poor men who had been confined in a French prison'; 1*s.* 'to a poor blind woman'; 1*s.* 'to a poor man that was out of his mind'; 2*s.* 6*d.* 'to a poor woman of Lower Melbury that keeps her bed'; 6*d.* 'to a poor man that was a stranger'; and 1*s.* 'to a very poor sailor'. In March of the following year 'a poor black man that had no legs' was given 6*d.* During the colder months of the year the housekeeper often bought oatmeal to make caudle (gruel) for villagers who were poor or sick. There were also regular payments to poor women for weeding the courtyards around the house (they received 5*d.* each for a day's work).

As the wealthiest landowning family in Gower, the Talbots received frequent requests for contributions to good causes. Kit Talbot remembered that his father had been generous to the poor:

> But [he] did not use much discrimination in his alms-giving. Latterly it used to be his daily custom, first to feed the peacocks at the window of the breakfast-room, and afterwards to distribute half-crowns to the beggars in front of the house.[68]

His wife's charitable efforts were better directed. Mary seems to have been extremely conscientious and anxious to do right from an early age, and she had inherited strong principles from her beloved mother, to whom religion had been the 'comfort and guide'. For the rest of her life, Mary remembered her mother's words, spoken shortly before her early death: 'What should I do now if I had not prepared for this hour when I had health and strength?' Every Sunday, Mary noted the subject of the sermon that she had just heard in her pocket-book. At the end of her copy of Mrs William's 'Thoughts on Education', she added the words 'O God, hear the prayer of an anxious mother: "Let my children be perfect Christians"'.[69] Mary was also influenced by Hannah More, whose own ideal of useful womanhood was summed up by Mrs Stanley, a character in More's didactic novel *Coelebs in Search of a Wife*, who declared: 'Charity is the calling of a lady; the care of the poor is her profession.'[70]

Mary Talbot's own religious views, according to her son, were 'practical', and she was 'not fond of discussing dogmas or sectarian differences'.[71] As a strong supporter of the established church, she was dismayed by the attempts of a reforming newcomer, Diana, Lady Barham, to 'Methodize' her neighbours in Gower after 1813.[72] Mary was also violently anti-Catholic, and she was deeply distressed when one of her grandsons 'turned to Romanism' and was 'admitted into that detestable and deceitful church'.[73]

For several years in the early nineteenth century Mary supported members of the Stote family, who lived near Penrice. The father may have been the musician (probably a fiddler) 'poor blind Stote', who was engaged to play at the party given at Penrice to celebrate the birth of Jane Talbot in 1796.[74] Over the next few years, Mary gave Stote money from time to time. He was probably dead by April 1805, when Mary began to make regular payments towards the support of his children. In that month she paid £3 6*s.* 8*d.* for 'clothes for Stote's children', and a further 5*s.* for a 'hat for Jane Stote'. Shifts and stockings for Jane Stote a year later cost 14*s.* Mary appears to have paid for the board and lodging of three Stote girls, Jane, Elizabeth and Sarah, for several years after this. She continued to buy clothes for them, and she also gave clothes to other poor villagers from time to time, paying £2 6*s.* 8*d.* for 'printed cotton for the poor' in April 1806.[75]

By the beginning of 1801 Mary Talbot was also paying £5 5*s.* a year towards the costs of running a Sunday school at Penrice.[76] Such schools had become increasingly popular in the 1780s and 1790s as a means of improving the morals and behaviour of the lawless, uneducated poor by inculcating the socially desirable virtues of punctuality, cleanliness and honesty.[77] Prominent advocates included Hannah More and Sarah Trimmer, another writer admired by Mary Talbot and her friends.

The Talbot girls inherited their mother's philanthropic inclinations, teaching in the Sunday school at Penrice, and conceiving a somewhat hare-brained project for the education of a number of poor children, enthusiastically described in a letter from Jane to Charlotte in 1821:

> Bella, Emma and I are going to live some day or other in the middle of Dartmoor ... We are to have an enormous house to accomodate a hundred boys and a hundred girls, who are to be educated according to a plan I have made up from M. Fellenburg, Dr Bell etc. etc. We mean to travel about England and Wales for a year or so with a waggon behind us to collect children in, for as we do not wish them to return to their parents we shall kidnap them very young. We are to have a large farm for the boys to cultivate, and nothing is to be bought after the first year, for the girls will spin everything for themselves and the boys; the boys will make shoes and hats, and tailor for themselves. In short, it will be the happiest establishment ... It is to be a Gothic building [with an] ornamental garden. We mean to have no servants to wait on us after the girls have been instructed in the art of cookery, washing, etc. etc. [They] will do everything, and the boys are to take care of the plantations and are to be taught morris-dancing and mumming ... Part of the plan is for one of us to marry a clergyman who is to serve in our chapel.[78]

Not surprisingly, the girls' mother was not optimistic that the scheme would achieve the desired result, telling Charlotte:

> As for Jane's Utopia, I am obliged to turn the conversation, for she gets *really* angry at the fancied objections which we make, so that I think she is getting a little maddish. Not only would her pupils be utterly ignorant of the world (which I doubt sometimes is any misfortune) but they would lose all family and filial ties, which I feel *would* be a great misfortune.[79]

In 1852, towards the end of her life, Mary followed her great-grandmother's example and built a schoolroom and schoolmaster's house in Marazion in Cornwall, the birthplace of her second husband Sir Christopher Cole.[80] Other members of the family shared Mary's charitable interests: at Bowood Louisa Lansdowne devoted much of her time to improving the tenants' cottages, building schools and 'comforting the sick, instructing the young and feeding the hungry'.[81]

The importance of lay patrons in appointing men to positions within the Church of England has already been mentioned. Similarly, advancement in royal and government service, as in the army and navy, was heavily dependent on knowing the right people. It was as a result of pressure from his brother and his friends Lord Hervey, Thomas Winnington and Charles Hanbury Williams that Stephen Fox was appointed a Joint Secretary of the Treasury in 1739, with an annual salary of £3000. His elevation to the peerage in 1741, as Lord Ilchester, Baron of Woodford Strangways in Dorset, was again largely due to Hervey's machinations, rather than to his own ability or conscientious service to the Crown. As Stephen told Lord Hervey at this time, his main object was 'to pass my life with tranquillity and obscurity'.[82] The price of his title was a bribe to the King's mistress, the Countess of Yarmouth, and the resignation of his Treasury post. Henry Fox obtained a second barony for his brother in 1747, this time with a remainder to Henry himself and to his sons if Stephen had no legitimate male issue.[83] Eventually, in 1756, Stephen became Earl of Ilchester, with the help of his brother's influence and his mother-in-law's money.[84] A day after she became the first Countess of Ilchester, Elizabeth wrote from Melbury to tell the new Earl how delighted everyone was by their new title:

> This afternoon I, the Horners, and the children visited Mr Fever, who received us with the utmost respect ... The bells rung [and] he lorded and ladyed us vastly. I wish we had been together to have some fun out of our new tittle. Pray, how do you like being an Earl? ... Mama is, I think, very kind about the patent, but [I] don't think she will quite like to give more than five hundred toward it, so if you could bring what she pays within that, it would be best.[85]

Having secured his brother's appointment as Joint Comptroller of the Army accounts in 1747,[86] Henry tried to find another post for him ten years later. In his reply Stephen thanked his brother for his 'kind intentions', and continued:

> Of the three places you mention, I should like Treasurer of the Chambers best. The Jewel Office, I believe, is not worth above £200 more than the employment I now have, so I won't think of that. What sort of employment the Wardrobe is, I don't guess either. For profit or agreeableness, what I wish is that while I stay in the employment I have, which I am far from disliking, the £400 additional salary I received may be encreased [by] 600 and made up to one thousand; then I shall receive near 18 hundred a year.[87]

In the end, Stephen was not appointed to any of these posts. His financial problems were relieved by the death of his mother-in-law early in the following year, and he no longer felt the need to look for additional sources of income.

Many aristocratic ladies had a considerable amount of patronage at their disposal. Women, as well as men, could present clergymen to livings. Susanna Strangways Horner presented Marrian Feaver to Melbury Sampford in 1739, and he held it until his death in 1783, after which Susanna's daughter presented William Jenkins. Elizabeth also presented Jenkins to Abbotsbury in 1786, and he held both livings until his death in 1822. At Stinsford Susanna Strangways Horner appointed John Randall in 1750, and her daughter chose William Floyer after Randall's death in 1784. Floyer was a friend of the O'Briens, and was presented on William O'Brien's recommendation.[88]

Anyone, male or female, who was thought to have any access to patronage was likely to receive begging letters from time to time. Sometimes these came from poor relations: in 1816 Louisa Lansdowne described a distressing visit from an Irish cousin, who had brought a letter from her late mother's brother, the Revd Thomas Grady, who was 'in a great state of embarrassment' and hoped that Lord Lansdowne might be able to procure some church preferment in Ireland for him. Louisa had promised to do what she could, and told her sister Mary, 'I am going to ask Lord Ossory if he has any livings in Ireland, but it is very hopelessly, I own, and I know no one else I can apply to'.[89] Twenty years later Mary Cole asked another Irish cousin for a copy of her mother's family tree, which her brother needed, because he was 'continually called on for pecuniary assistance' by people claiming to be related to his mother. 'Last year', Mary wrote 'two ladies at [Saint] Petersburg applied through the Russian ambassador, declaring they were my mother's nieces and in great distress, their mother having married a Russian merchant.'[90]

Often, the writers of begging letters hoped that the recipient would intercede with an influential friend or relative to obtain some office or favour for them. The attention with which members of the aristocracy and gentry followed the ups and down of contemporary governments owed less to their political beliefs than to the hope that, if their friends were in power, they would have places and pensions at their disposal. As Secretary at War from 1746 to 1755, Henry Fox received numerous letters asking for military employment. In 1750 his sister-in-law Lady Ilchester wrote to tell him:

> I have long had a request from Mrs Ridley, in which Mama and I join, that, if you could do anything in the army way for young Stradick's brother, we should be very glad – not him you have already got into the army ... I should be obliged to you greatly if, when you see the Duke of Marlborough, you would remind him of poor Sam Rogers, who I wish vastly could get a little place. The Duke said, when he had provided for two or three of his own people, he would give him one.[91]

Two years later, Lord Ilchester asked his brother to find a place for Tom Cheeke, a cousin of his old friend Joanna Cheeke, 'because at present Miss Cheeke, in a manner, keeps him and his two sisters, who are as near coming to the parish as possible'.[92] A further request, in 1757, was for a pension of two hundred pounds a year for Miss Cheeke herself 'who, without something of that sort, is undone'.[93] In 1764 Henry Fox (now Lord Holland) received a letter from his sister Charlotte Digby, asking him to secure the promotion of Mr Brightman, a lieutenant in the army whose wife had lived with Mrs Digby whilst her husband was abroad. Mr Brightman was said to be 'hopeless of getting a step higher; everything being sold in the regiment, and he having no money to buy'.[94] A year later Charlotte told her brother that she had 'no hopes of anything being got' for her sons, William and Stephen, but through him.[95] Charlotte had six sons: the eldest had succeeded his grandfather as Lord Digby in 1752, but the provision for his five younger brothers had been comparatively modest: they had received capital sums of £2000 each, and annuities of £100 a year.[96] The second son, Henry, inherited his brother's title in 1757, and the others found employment with the help of their friends and family: one went into the army; one into the navy, then the royal household; and two into the church. The youngest son, Charles, was presented to the living of Kilmington by Lord Ilchester in 1766.

William and Susan O'Brien looked to Susan's uncle for help after their elopement in 1764. But Lord Holland, who was out of office by this time, could do much less for them than he might have done a year earlier.[97] In November 1765 he wrote to William, sending him his commission as Barrack-Master at Quebec, with the words 'I wish what I sent you were better, but I have found it so difficult that I am glad to get anything'.[98] In the event, it was Susan's mother who obtained another office for William, who was appointed Provost Marshal of Bermuda in 1768 on the recommendation of her friend Lord Hillsborough.

After the O'Briens returned to England from America, they hoped for patronage and assistance from Holland's son Charles James Fox, who had been such a close friend of Susan before her marriage. Having been elected Member of Parliament for Midhurst in 1768, Charles Fox, had been appointed a Junior Lord of the Admiralty in 1770, a few weeks after his twenty-first birthday. At first he promised great things, and claimed that he was trying to obtain a post that would give William O'Brien an adequate income, but by the end of 1772 Susan was complaining of his 'marked neglect of me and coolness in all our interests'. It was, she concluded, 'obvious to me that I had little to hope from any exertions of his'.[99]

Charles Fox was out of office for eight years from 1774, but he returned to government in 1782 as one of the two Principal Secretaries of State. Susan O'Brien wrote of her hopes in her journal:

> This spring ... Mr Fox came into the Ministry. This event, which we had waited for with anxious expectation and hope for so many years, gave us the greatest pleasure. Mr O'Brien thought he had very reasonable expectations that [Charles] would soon make some provision for him.

But Susan was again to be disappointed, and by the middle of the year she was writing:

> [My hopes] had declined so rapidly that I was quite ill with the loss of them, and could hardly support my spirits enough to bear the daily congratulations I received on the success of the party; on my friend and relation being Minister; and on the near approach of some agreeable and permanent settlement.[100]

The O'Briens never lost hope entirely: Charles continued to make vague promises, but he failed to do anything for them, and it was through the influence of their friend William Morton Pitt that William was eventually appointed Receiver General for Dorset in 1802.

Though she was not as successful as she had hoped in obtaining a post for her husband, Susan O'Brien herself received requests for assistance from other people. In 1821 her doctor Adair Hawkins asked her to apply to Lord Lansdowne for help in obtaining a travelling fellowship for his son. Later in the same year Susan asked for the help of the Duchess of Gloucester, whom she had recently met, in obtaining a naval promotion for her nephew Charles Strangways. Susan was not, however, optimistic that her letter would produce the desired result:

> I felt very unwilling to engage in such a correspondence, but the fear that poor Charles might lose by my scruples made me, after much hesitating, take courage,

> and I wrote, more for the sake of my conscience than from much hope of success. I thought it could do no harm, if it did no good ... It is like a lottery ticket: little chance of a prize, but no chance without trying.

Susan received a 'gracious' reply from the Duchess, but her application was unsuccessful. Four years later she was still trying to help Charles, this time with the assistance of her cousin Lord Holland.[101]

Even Agnes Porter did her best to promote the interests of people who applied to her. In 1810 she wrote to her former pupils Mary Talbot and Harriot Frampton to ask for their help in finding pupils for her sister Fanny, who had a small private school.[102] In the following year Agnes asked Mary to assist two of her acquaintances: 'Miss Elbury', a former governess who wished to 'return to the more pleasing care of instructing little children', and a younger girl, a 'poor cottager's daughter', who could 'handle her needle uncommonly well for a cottager' and was 'very innocent and sweet-tempered'.[103]

Royal service could also bring rich rewards, though the duties were often tedious, as the writer Fanny Burney (Keeper of the Robes to Queen Charlotte from 1786 to 1791), discovered. In a world in which so few women of the aristocracy and gentry had any opportunity at all for paid employment, places at Court were keenly sought. Not only would a girl who secured such a place have a home and a salary (Fanny Burney was paid £200 a year, and had her own apartment, maid and footman, and the use of a carriage), but she would also be well placed to find a wealthy and well-connected husband.[104] Any woman who was offered a place at Court would be under considerable pressure to accept it, and would then be expected to promote the interests of her friends and family.

Several of Charlotte Digby's numerous children and grandchildren held posts within the Royal Household. Her third son Admiral Robert Digby was a groom of the Bedchamber in 1792, whilst his younger brother Colonel Stephen Digby (Fanny Burney's friend), was Vice-Chamberlain to the Queen from 1783 to 1792, and then Ranger and Keeper of Richmond Park from 1792 to 1800. Stephen's daughter Charlotte Elizabeth (Lilley) Digby, was a Maid of Honour to the Queen for a few months in 1802. In November Agnes Porter wrote to Lilley to ask her 'to use her interest with the Queen to procure me to be of St Catherine's Bounty'.[105] Unfortunately Lilley had already resigned her post by the time she received the letter, having become engaged to her cousin the Revd William Digby. One of the latter's sisters, Julia Digby, was a Maid of Honour to Queen Charlotte from 1789 until she married in 1794, and a Woman of the Bedchamber from 1805; another sister,

Maria, Countess of Ilchester, was a favourite Lady of the Bedchamber to Queen Charlotte from 1804 until the Queen's death in 1818, apart from a period from 1814 to 1816 when she was 'lent' to the Queen's granddaughter Princess Charlotte. Maria's close friend Alicia Campbell was another friend at Court: she was appointed Sub-Governess to Princess Charlotte in 1805 and became Keeper of the Privy Purse to the Princess when she married in 1816. Mrs Campbell was still with Princess Charlotte when the latter died in childbirth in the following year. As a result of Lady Ilchester and Mrs Campbell's appointments, the two youngest daughters of the second Earl of Ilchester spent much more time at Court than their elder sisters had done, and the youngest, Louisa Lansdowne, was to become Principal Lady of the Bedchamber for a year from 1837 to 1838. None of her sisters or aunts, however, was employed at Court, presumably because they were better provided for than the Digbys.

How did the lives of country house women and children change in the hundred years covered by this book? In what way did the life of Mary Talbot at Penrice in the early nineteenth century resemble that of her great-grandmother Susanna Strangways Horner at Melbury in the second quarter of the previous century? Some allowances must be made for differences of temperament: the two women were quite unalike, and would probably have had little in common, even if they had both lived at the same time. In many ways the changes were more apparent than real, a belief expressed by Susan O'Brien in 1817 when her own memories stretched back over sixty years or more:

> As for my ancestors, as well as everybody else's, I never thought they were better, or more moral, than their descendants ... What I think is that manners are more altered than morals; conversation than practice. What was coarsely and openly abused is now palliated, admired and immitated, and fashion, that great leader, now leads Hercules down the hill instead of up it.[106]

The ladies of the late Georgian period travelled more than their grandmothers and great-grandmothers had done. They were better educated, though their schooling was still greatly inferior to that of their brothers. They had many more opportunities to make up the deficiencies in their formal education by reading, and they were beginning to show that they could make a real contribution to academic studies in fields such as botany and geology – but they were still advised to be modest about their own achievements, and always to defer to men, even if they thought they were wrong. They were probably healthier than their predecessors had been, though this owed less to medical improvements than to the fact that they took more exercise. Their clothes were less constricting – though by the late 1820s the fashion for tiny waists meant that many women had to wear tight corsets for much of the time. Their homes were more comfortably furnished, and less formally arranged. The provision of separate sleeping accommodation for servants brought increased privacy for their employers, as did the construction of secondary staircases and the tendency to locate kitchens and other office buildings in a structure that was separate from the main mansion. Better transport brought more visitors, thus relieving the tedium and isolation of life in the depths of the country. At the same time, the social life in provincial towns and the surrounding countryside was improving, with race-meetings, balls and assemblies.

Much more was written about romantic love in the early nineteenth century than fifty or a hundred years earlier, but men and women continued to choose their marriage partners for a variety of reasons. Writers of sermons and conduct books may have laid less emphasis on submissiveness, but Hannah More and the preachers of the evangelical movement brought new burdens for women: whilst they still had to be obedient to their husbands, they were also under a moral obligation to be good, and to improve their children and menfolk by example. It would be difficult to claim that the married couples of the reign of George IV were significantly happier together than those of the reign of George II. But the more relaxed atmosphere of the last quarter of the eighteenth century certainly brought benefits for their offspring: writers such as Rousseau and the Edgeworths taught parents to enjoy their children's company and to value them as individuals, rather than as miniature adults who should be encouraged to grow up as quickly as possible.

Social divisions were accentuated by the physical separation of employers and servants. The old medieval and Tudor idea of a household as a family had largely broken down, and parents were discouraged from allowing their children to spend too much time in the 'vulgar' company of the lower orders. Servants were less likely to spend most of their working life in one household, though there were few opportunities for paid work outside domestic service and farming for those who chose to remain in rural Dorset or Somerset. Many headed for London in the hope of bettering themselves. Those of their employers who spent more time in Bath or London, or travelling in Europe, were less likely to be involved in their local community, or to take an interest in the management of their estates or the lives of their tenants.

In many ways the inhabitants of the late Georgian country house remained isolated in their own comfortable environment. But the world outside their park walls was changing, and unsettling – even dangerous – events sometimes intruded on their day-to-day lives. The French Revolution shook everyone, and many viewed the activities of radicals and political activists at home with fear and suspicion. In 1792 Susan O'Brien expressed the opinion of many when she wrote:

> When we know the pains that are taken by books, and a thousand other ways, to corrupt and alienate the people's minds, it is a proof of our happy and prosperous state that such bewitching notions as those of equality must be to the common people, have not gained more prosolites [proselytes], though they certainly have made some progress.[107]

Several Digby and Fox Strangways relatives were actively involved in the Napoleonic Wars, which brought military and naval personnel to the Dorset coast and South Wales in large numbers, and there was a real threat of invasion for several years. In 1794 Susan O'Brien told Mary Talbot than such an invasion was 'really so much and so universally talked of that one hardly knows what to think', and said that she might flee to Wales 'on a poney' if the French landed at Weymouth. Three years later Susan noted in her journal: 'Nothing talked of but military preparations, invasion and deffence. The situation of the country but too alarming'. In February 1797 a French force numbering 1400 landed at Fishguard, eighty miles from Penrice. They soon surrendered, but the Talbots, at home with two small daughters, were 'in a fright' for several days.[108]

The French were eventually defeated, but there were problems at home too. Dorset was one of the poorest counties in England, and rural society, as portrayed in Thomas Hardy's novels, such as *Tess of the d'Urbervilles*, *The Mayor of Casterbridge* and *The Woodlanders*, was beginning to disintegrate.[109] Alone at Stinsford, Susan O'Brien was more conscious of day-to-day happenings in the surrounding countryside than her wealthier contemporaries. In the summer of 1818 she was disturbed by the information that many gardens in the area had been robbed. Her friend Francis Browne of Frampton advised her to put 'detonating balls' under her fruit trees.[110] The fire at Stinsford in 1825 was thought to have been started deliberately, though the target seems to have been the farmer, rather than Susan herself.[111] In 1826, a few months before Susan's death, she wrote of her distress on hearing that her pet cat, Myrtle, had been killed by a dog:

> Have ascertained the circumstances of poor Myrtle's death. All as affecting and grievously provoking as it is possible to be. The sheppard's boy set his dog at him. Ten thousand lies told by the whole tribe at the cottages: the sheppards and some of the others denying they knew anything about it, when the man had skinned it, and it was found with his sheepskins. Then pretending it had attacked

> his dog. Poor little thing! It was afraid of our own dogs, and never attacked anything ... I have been punishing these liars and concealers with a prohibition of coming to this house or having anything from it. I will not reward those that torment me and are so cruel. What did it signify whose cat it was? Is not a cottager's wife as fond of her cat as My Lady, as they call me? But human nature is cruel, and cats the most persecuted of all the animals we have, though one of the most useful.[112]

By the late 1820s there was serious unrest in southern Britain. Many thought that the nation was on the brink of a revolution: there were political disturbances associated with demands for parliamentary reform, and widespread distress in rural areas resulting from the long-term effects of the agricultural depression which had had followed the end of the Napoleonic Wars in 1815. Wiltshire and Dorset were particularly badly affected: at the end of 1830 trouble was reported around Lacock, and bands of rioting farm labourers roamed the Dorset countyside. They demanded that wages should be raised and rents lowered, set fire to hay and corn ricks, and destroyed the hated threshing machines which had deprived them of their traditional winter's work. One group turned up at West Stafford House, the home of Susan O'Brien's old friend Elizabeth Floyer, but went away empty-handed.[113] Threatening letters signed by 'Captain Swing' were sent to farmers and landowners, and the Dorset Militia was called out to protect Moreton House, the home of Susan O'Brien's niece Harriot Frampton, whose husband had been prominent in resisting the labourers' demands and was said to be 'a marked man'.[114] The doors and lower windows of the house were barricaded, and Harriot and her husband and son took turns in sitting up to keep watch during the night. Four years later, in 1834, James Frampton was to become notorious as the magistrate who prosecuted the Tolpuddle Martyrs, six Dorset labourers who were transported to Australia for seven years after joining an illegal trades union.[115] The Martyrs were eventually pardoned, and they returned to England in 1838, having done little to improve the pay and working conditions of their contemporaries. In common with other areas where there was little employment outside farming, living conditions for the rural poor in Dorset were to see little improvement until well into the twentieth century.

At the beginning of the twenty-first century life in the countryside has changed out of all recognition. Many of the labourers' cottages of Thomas Hardy's day have been demolished or gentrified and turned into weekend retreats for city-dwellers. Many great country houses have gone too, though several of the homes of the Georgian ladies who feature in this book are still lived in by the same family. Much of Susanna Strangways Horner's inheritance has survived at Melbury: the house and estate still belong to her descendants, and the Strangways lions continue to greet visitors as they approach the house.[116]

Biographical Notes

This is a selective list, which is designed to help readers to identify the people mentioned in the text. With one or two exceptions, men and women are indexed under their surnames at birth, with cross-references to the names by which they were later known.

Acland, Elizabeth Kitty (1772–1813). Only surviving child of John Dyke Acland and his wife Lady Harriot. Usually called Kitty. In April 1796 she married Henry George, Lord Porchester (1772–1833), who became the second Earl of Carnarvon in 1811.

Acland, Harriot, see **Strangways, Lady Christiana Caroline Henrietta.**

Acland, John Dyke (1747–1778). Son and heir of Sir Thomas Dyke Acland of Killerton, Devon. In 1771 he married Lady Christiana Caroline Henrietta Fox Strangways.

Adare, Lady, see **Strangways, Lady Frances Muriel** (1755–1814).

Beach, Henrietta Maria Hicks (1760–1837). Born Henrietta Maria Beach. First cousin of Thomas Mansel Talbot. In 1779 she married Michael Hicks.

Beach, Michael Hicks (1760–1830). Friend of Thomas Mansel Talbot. Of Beverstone Castle, Gloucestershire. In 1779 he married Henrietta Maria Beach. Took the additional name of Beach in 1790 after the death of his father-in-law William Beach of Fittleton, Keevil and Netheravon, Wiltshire, and Williamstrip, Gloucestershire.

Bunbury, Sarah, see **Lennox, Lady Sarah.**

Campbell, Alicia (1768–1829). Daughter of Thomas Kelly of Dawson's Grove, County Armagh. Widow of Major William Campbell of the Twenty-Fourth Regiment of Foot (d. 1796). An old friend of the Fox Strangways family. From 1818 she lived mainly with Maria, Countess of Ilchester.

Cole, Captain Sir Christopher (1770–1836). Sixth son of Humphrey Cole of Marazion, Cornwall. A captain in the Royal Navy, and a colonel of Marines. In 1815 he married, as her second husband, Lady Mary Lucy Talbot, widow of Thomas Mansel Talbot.

Cole, Mary, see **Strangways, Lady Mary Lucy Fox.**

Digby, Charlotte, between 1729 and 1778, see **Fox, Charlotte.**

Digby, Charlotte, between 1790 and 1794, see **Gunning, Charlotte Margaret.**

Digby, Charlotte Elizabeth (1778–1820). Usually called Lilley. Daughter of Colonel Stephen and Lady Lucy Digby. In 1803 she married her cousin the Revd William Digby (1774–1848), the second son of the Very Revd William Digby, Dean of Durham.

Digby, Edward (d. 1746). Second surviving son, but heir (due to his elder brother's incapacity) to his father William, fifth Baron Digby, whom he predeceased. In 1729 he married Charlotte, daughter of Sir Stephen Fox.

Digby, Edward (1730–1757). Eldest son of Edward Digby and Charlotte Fox. He succeeded his grandfather as sixth Baron Digby of Geashill, King's County, in 1752 and died unmarried.

Digby, Henry (1731–1793). Second son of Edward Digby and Charlotte Fox. He succeeded his brother as seventh Baron Digby of Geashill in 1757. In 1763 he married Elizabeth, daughter of the Hon. Charles Feilding, who died in 1765. In 1770 he married Mary, daughter and heiress of John Knowler. Created first Baron Digby of Sherborne, Dorset, in 1765; Viscount Coleshill and Earl Digby in 1790.

Digby, Lil[le]y, see **Digby, Charlotte Elizabeth.**

Digby, Lord, between 1752 and 1757, see **Digby, Edward** (1730–1757).

Digby, Lord, between 1757 and 1793, see **Digby, Henry.**

Digby, Lucy, see **Strangways, Lady Lucy Fox.**

Digby, Maria (1771–1842). Daughter of the Very Revd William Digby, Dean of Durham. In 1794 she married, as his second wife, her first cousin the second Earl of Ilchester.

Digby, Admiral Robert (1732–1814). Third son of Edward Digby and Charlotte Fox. In 1784 he married Eleanor, daughter of Andrew Elliot, Governer of New York, and widow of James Jauncey of New York.

Digby, Colonel Stephen (1742–1800). Fifth son of Edward Digby and Charlotte Fox. In 1771 he married his first cousin, Lady Lucy Fox Strangways, who died in 1787. In 1790 he married Charlotte Margaret Gunning.

Eden, George (1784–1849). Son (and heir, after the suicide of his brother in 1810) of William Eden, first Baron Auckland. Friend of the Fox Strangways family. Governor-General of India, 1835–41; created first Earl of Auckland in 1839.

Feilding, Captain Charles (1780–1837). A great-grandson of the fourth Earl of Denbigh. In 1804 he married, as her second husband, Lady Elizabeth Theresa Talbot, widow of William Davenport Talbot.

Feilding, Elizabeth, see **Strangways, Lady Elizabeth Theresa Fox.**

Fowler, Dr Richard (1765–1863). Physician to the General Infirmary in Salisbury, 1796–1841. Consulted by the Fox Strangways family and by the Talbots. In 1805 he married Ann, daughter of William Bowles of Heale House, Wiltshire.

Fox, Caroline, between 1744 and 1762, see **Lennox, Lady Caroline.**

Fox, Charles James (1749–1806). Second surviving son of Henry Fox, first Lord Holland. His family called him Charles. An eminent statesman and politician. In 1795 he married Elizabeth Armistead, with whom he had lived since 1783.

Fox, Charlotte (1707–1778). Only surviving daughter of Sir Stephen Fox by his second marriage, and sister of Stephen Fox, first Earl of Ilchester, and Henry Fox, first Baron Holland. In 1729 she married Edward Digby, son and heir of William, fifth Baron Digby.

Fox, Elizabeth, see **Horner, Elizabeth.**

Fox, Henry (1705–1774). Younger son of Sir Stephen Fox by his second marriage. In 1744 he married Lady Caroline Lennox, who was created Baroness Holland in 1762. In 1763 Henry Fox was created Baron Holland of Foxley, Wiltshire.

Fox, Miss, between 1743 and 1758, see **Strangways, Lady Susanna Sarah Louisa Fox.**

Fox, Stephen (1704–1776). Elder son of Sir Stephen Fox by his second marriage. In 1736 he married Elizabeth Strangways Horner. Created Lord Ilchester, Baron of Woodford Strangways, Dorset, in 1741; Lord Ilchester and Stavordale, Baron of Redlynch, 1747; and first Earl of Ilchester in 1756. He took the additional name of Strangways after the death of his mother-in-law Susanna Strangways Horner in 1758.

Fox, Stephen (1745–1774). Eldest son of Henry and Caroline Fox. Usually called Ste. In 1766 he married Mary, eldest daughter of John Fitzpatrick, first Earl of Upper Ossory. He became second Baron Holland when his mother died in 1774, but died shortly afterwards.

Fox, Susan, between 1743 and 1758, see **Strangways, Lady Susanna Sarah Louisa Fox.**

Frampton, Harriot, see **Strangways, Lady Harriot Fox.**

Frampton, James (1769–1855). Son and heir of James Frampton of Moreton, Dorset. In 1799 he married Lady Harriot Fox Strangways.

Frampton, Mary (1773–1846). Sister of James Frampton (1769–1855). She never married. Her journal for the period 1779 to 1846 was edited by her niece Harriot Georgiana Mundy and published in 1885.

Grady, Mary Theresa (*c.* 1755–1790). Daughter of Standish Grady of Cappercullen, County Limerick. In 1772 she married Henry Thomas Fox Strangways, Lord Stavordale. She was Lady Stavordale 1772–76, then second Countess of Ilchester.

Gunning, Charlotte Margaret (1759–1794). Daughter of Sir Robert Gunning, first Baronet, of Horton, Northants. In 1790 she married Colonel Stephen Digby, as his second wife.

Hervey, John, Lord (1696–1743). Friend of Stephen and Henry Fox. Eldest surviving son of John Hervey, first Earl of Bristol. In 1720 he married Mary (Molly) Lepell. Lord Hervey predeceased his father, whom his son George William succeeded as Earl of Bristol in 1751.

Hicks Beach, see **Beach.**

Holland, Lady, between 1762 and 1774, see **Lennox, Lady Caroline.**

Holland, Lord, between 1763 and 1774, see **Fox, Henry.**

Horner, Elizabeth (1723–1792). Only surviving child of Thomas Horner and Susanna Strangways. Called Elizabeth Strangways Horner from 1726. In 1736 she married Stephen Fox. Her husband was created a baron in 1741, and she became Lady Ilchester. In 1756 she became first Countess of Ilchester; dowager Countess of Ilchester from 1772 when her eldest son married.

Horner, Elizabeth Strangways, see **Horner, Elizabeth.**

Horner, Susanna Strangways, see **Strangways, Susanna.**

Horner, Thomas (1688–1741). Eldest surviving son, and heir, of George Horner of Mells, Somerset. In 1713 he married Susanna Strangways of Melbury. In 1726 they took the additional surname of Strangways.

Ilchester, Countess of, between 1756 and 1772, see **Horner, Elizabeth.**

Ilchester, Countess of, between 1772 and 1790, see **Grady, Mary Theresa.**

Ilchester, Countess of, between 1794 and 1812, see **Digby, Maria.**

Ilchester, Countess of, between 1812 and 1819, see **Murray, Caroline Leonora.**

Ilchester, Dowager Countess of, between 1772 and 1792, see **Horner, Elizabeth.**

Ilchester, Dowager Countess of, between 1812 and 1842, see **Digby, Maria.**

Ilchester, first Earl of, between 1756 and 1776, see **Fox, Stephen.**

Ilchester, second Earl of, between 1776 and 1802, see **Strangways, Henry Thomas Fox.**

Ilchester, third Earl of, between 1802 and 1858, see **Strangways, Henry Stephen Fox.**

Ilchester, Lady, between 1741 and 1772, see **Horner, Elizabeth.**

Ilchester, Lady, between 1772 and 1790, see **Grady, Mary Theresa.**

Ilchester, Lady, between 1794 and 1812, see **Digby, Maria.**

Ilchester, Lady, between 1812 and 1819, see **Murray, Caroline Leonora.**

Ilchester, Lord, between 1741 and 1776, see **Fox, Stephen.**

Ilchester, Lord, between 1776 and 1802, see **Strangways, Henry Thomas Fox.**

Ilchester, Lord, between 1802 and 1858, see **Strangways, Henry Stephen Fox.**

Ilchester, Maria, Countess of, see **Digby, Maria.**

Lansdowne, Louisa, see **Strangways, Lady Louisa Emma Fox.**

Lemon, Lady Charlotte, see **Strangways, Lady Charlotte Anne Fox.**

Lemon, Sir Charles (1784–1868). Son and heir of Sir William Lemon, first Baronet, of Carclew, Cornwall. In 1810 he married Lady Charlotte Anne Fox Strangways.

Lennox, Lady Caroline (1723–1774). Eldest daughter of Charles, second Duke of Richmond. In 1744 she married Henry Fox. Caroline Fox was created Lady Holland, Baroness Holland, in her own right in 1762.

Lennox, Lady Sarah (1745–1826). Fourth daughter of Charles, second Duke of Richmond. In 1762 she married Sir Charles Bunbury. Divorced 1776, and reverted to her maiden name. In 1781 she married Colonel George Napier.

Murray, Caroline Leonora (1788–1819). Daughter of Lord George Murray, Bishop of St David's. In 1812 she married Henry Stephen Fox Strangways, third Earl of Ilchester.

Napier, Sarah, see **Lennox, Lady Sarah.**

O'Brien, Susan, see **Strangways, Lady Susanna Sarah Louisa Fox.**

O'Brien, William (*c.* 1738–1815). An actor of Irish origin, who eloped with Lady Susan Fox Strangways in 1764. Of Stinsford, Dorset, 1775–1815.

Paul Sir George Onesiphorus (1746–1820). Of Rodborough, Gloucestershire. He was a friend of the Fox Strangways family; a landowner, philanthropist and prison reformer.

Petty, Louisa, see **Strangways, Lady Louisa Emma Fox.**

Porter, Ann Agnes (*c.* 1750–1814). Daughter of the Revd Francis Porter. Governess at Melbury, 1784 to 1797, and at Penrice, 1799–1806.

Quin, Fanny, see **Strangways, Lady Frances Muriel Fox.**

Stavordale, Lady, between 1772 and 1776, see **Grady, Mary Theresa.**

Stavordale, Lord, between 1756 and 1776, see **Strangways, Henry Thomas Fox.**

Stavordale, Lord, between 1787 and 1802, see **Strangways, Henry Stephen Fox.**

Strangways, Revd Charles Redlynch Fox (1761–1836). Third son of the first Earl of Ilchester. He went into the church and was rector of Maiden Newton, Dorset, from 1787, and of Brimpton, Somerset, from 1788. From 1811 to 1836 he was rector of Kilmington, Somerset. In 1787 he married Jane (*c.* 1770–1830), daughter of the Revd Dr Nathan Haines.

Strangways, Lady Charlotte Anne Fox (1784–1826). Fourth daughter of the second Earl of Ilchester. In 1810 she married Sir Charles Lemon.

Strangways, Lady Christiana Caroline Henrietta Fox (1750–1815). Fifth-born, but third surviving, daughter of the first Earl of Ilchester. Sometimes called Kitty when she was young, but usually called Harriot. Her surname was Fox until 1758. In 1771 she married John Dyke Acland.

Strangways, Lady Elizabeth Theresa Fox (1773–1846). Eldest daughter of the second Earl of Ilchester. Sometimes known as Lily or Eliza. She usually seems to have signed Elisabeth, but other members of her family wrote Elizabeth, and this has been preferred here for the sake of consistency. In 1796 she married William Davenport Talbot, who died in 1800. In 1804 she married Captain Charles Feilding.

Strangways, Lady Frances Muriel Fox (1755–1814). Youngest daughter of the first Earl of Ilchester. Known as Fanny. Her surname was Fox until 1758. In 1777 she married Valentine Richard Quin of Adare, County Limerick (1752–1824), whom she left in 1793. Valentine Quin became Baron Adare in 1800 and first Earl of Dunraven in 1822.

Strangways, Lady Harriot Fox (1778–1844). Third daughter of the second Earl of Ilchester. In 1799 she married James Frampton of Moreton, Dorset.

Strangways, Henry Stephen Fox (1787–1858). Only surviving son of the second Earl of Ilchester by his first wife, Mary Theresa Grady. Known as Lord Stavordale until 1802, when he succeeded his father as third Earl of Ilchester. In 1812 he married Caroline Leonora Murray.

Strangways, Henry Thomas Fox (1747–1802). Eldest son and heir of the first Earl of Ilchester. Known as Lord Stavordale from 1756 until 1776 when he became second Earl of Ilchester. In 1772 he married Mary Theresa Grady, who died in 1790. In 1794 he married Maria Digby.

Strangways, Lily, see **Strangways, Lady Elizabeth Theresa Fox.**

Strangways, Lady Louisa Emma Fox (1785–1851). Fifth daughter of the second Earl of Ilchester. In 1808 she married Henry Petty (1780–1863), who became third Marquess of Lansdowne in 1809.

Strangways, Lady Lucy Fox (1748–1787). Second surviving daughter of the first Earl of Ilchester. Her surname was Fox until 1758. In 1771 she married her first cousin Colonel Stephen Digby.

Strangways, Lady Mary Lucy Fox (1776–1855). Second daughter of the second Earl of Ilchester. In 1794 she married Thomas Mansel Talbot, who died in 1813. In 1815 she married Captain Sir Christopher Cole (1770–1836).

Strangways, Colonel Stephen Strangways Digby Fox (1751–1836). Second son of the first Earl of Ilchester. Known as Tangy when he was a boy. He never married.

Strangways, Susanna (1689–1758). Eldest surviving daughter, and eventually sole heiress, of Thomas Strangways of Melbury Sampford, Dorset. In 1713 she married Thomas Horner of Mells, Somerset. In 1726 she and her husband took the additional surname of Strangways.

Strangways, Lady Susanna Sarah Louisa Fox (1743–1827). Eldest daughter of the first Earl of Ilchester. Known as Susan. Her surname was Fox until 1758. In 1764 she married William O'Brien.

Strangways, William Thomas Horner Fox (1795–1865). Eldest son of the second Earl of Ilchester by Maria Digby. Succeeded his elder half-brother as fourth Earl of Ilchester in 1858.

Strangways Horner, Thomas, see **Horner, Thomas.**

Talbot, Charlotte Louisa (1800–1880). Fourth-born, but third surviving daughter of Thomas Mansel Talbot. In 1830 she married the Revd John Montgomery Traherne of Coedarhydyglyn, Glamorgan (1788–1860).

Talbot, Christiana Barbara (1798–1808). Third daughter of Thomas Mansel Talbot. Often called Tina.

Talbot, Christopher Rice Mansel (C. R. M.) (1803–1890). Only son and heir of Thomas Mansel Talbot. MP for Glamorgan 1830–1890. Called Kit by his family. In 1835 he married Lady Charlotte Jane Butler (1809–1846), daughter of Richard Butler, first Earl of Glengall.

Talbot, Elizabeth, see **Strangways, Lady Elizabeth Theresa Fox.**

Talbot, Ellinor Sybella (1801–1810). Fifth daughter of Thomas Mansel Talbot.

Talbot, Emma Thomasina (1806–1881). Youngest daughter of Thomas Mansel Talbot. In 1833 she married John Dillwyn Llewelyn of Penllergaer, Glamorgan (1810–1882).

Talbot, Henry, see **Talbot, William Henry Fox.**

Talbot, Isabella Catherine (1804–1874). Sixth daugher of Thomas Mansel Talbot. In 1830 she married Richard Franklen of Clemenstone, Glamorgan (*c.* 1801–1883).

Talbot, Jane Harriot (1796–1874). Second daughter of Thomas Mansel Talbot. In 1821 she married John Nicholl of Merthyr Mawr, Glamorgan (1797–1853).

Talbot, Kit, see **Talbot, Christopher Rice Mansel.**

Talbot, Lily, see **Strangways, Lady Elizabeth Theresa.**

Talbot, Mary, see **Strangways, Lady Mary Lucy Fox.**

Talbot, Mary Theresa (1795–1861). Eldest daughter of Thomas Mansel Talbot. She never married.

Talbot, Thomas Mansel (1747–1813). Son of the Revd Thomas Talbot and grandson of John Ivory Talbot of Lacock Abbey, Wiltshire. Owner of the Penrice and Margam estates in Glamorgan. In 1794 he married Lady Mary Lucy Fox Strangways.

Talbot, William Davenport (1763–1800). Son of the Revd William Davenport and grandson of John Ivory Talbot of Lacock Abbey, Wiltshire; first cousin of Thomas Mansel Talbot. In 1796 he married Lady Elizabeth Theresa Fox Strangways.

Talbot, William Henry Fox (W.H.F.) (1800–1877). Only child of William Davenport Talbot. Usually known as Henry. In 1832 he married Constance, daughter of Francis Mundy of Markeaton, Derbyshire.

Traherne, Charlotte, see **Talbot, Charlotte Louisa.**

Notes

Notes to Introduction

1. Hardy owned the third edition, published in London, 1861–74, with additions by W. Shipp and J. W. Hodson.
2. Amanda Vickery, *The Gentleman's Daughter: Women's Lives in Georgian England* (New Haven and London, 1998), p. 37.
3. J. V. Beckett, *The Aristocracy in England* (Oxford, 1986), pp. 16–58.
4. Thomas Hardy, *A Group of Noble Dames* (first published 1891, this edition, with a preface of 1896, published Stroud, 1983), p. xi.
5. Neither the Fox Strangways family nor the Horners were pleased with Hardy's version of their family history. Sir John Horner, who died in 1927, vowed that he would never speak to Hardy again after the story was published. The fifth Earl of Ilchester, who died in 1905, destroyed letters that he had received from Hardy, though his widow was later reconciled with the author, who stayed at Melbury in 1915. Information from the Earl of Oxford and Asquith and the Hon. Mrs Townshend. See also V. Meynell (ed.), *Friends of a Lifetime: Letters to S. C. Cockerell* (London, 1940), p. 282.
6. Those who have read Stella Tillyard's *Aristocrats* will already have met Susan O'Brien, whose closest female friend was Lady Sarah Lennox, with whom George III is thought to have been in love before his marriage to Charlotte of Mecklenburg-Strelitz in 1761. See Stella Tillyard, *Aristocrats: Caroline, Emily, Louisa and Sarah Lennox, 1740–1832* (London, 1994).
7. Gervase Jackson-Stops, 'Temples of the Arts', in *The Treasure Houses of Britain* (New Haven and London, 1985), pp. 14–21. A recent book by Rosemary Baird, *Mistress of the House: Great Ladies and Grand Houses, 1670–1830* (London, 2003) concentrates almost exclusively on this aspect of country house history.
8. Vickery, *The Gentleman's Daughter*, pp. 10–11.

Notes to Chapter 1: Susanna

1. The main sources for the early history of Melbury House are: Royal Commission on Historical Monuments, England (RCHME), *An Inventory of the Historical Monuments in the County of Dorset*, i, *West Dorset* (second impression, London, 1974), pp. 164–67; John Newman and Nikolaus Pevsner, *The Buildings of England: Dorset* (London, 1972), pp. 273–77; Arthur Oswald, *Country Houses of Dorset* (London, 1935), pp. 118–22; and John Hutchins, *The History*

and Antiquities of the County of Dorset, ii (3rd edn, with additions by W. Shipp and J. W. Hodson, London, 1863), pp. 672–74. See also Maurice Howard, *The Early Tudor Country House: Architecture and Politics, 1490–1550* (London, 1987), especially pp. 93–95, 178, 203.

2. Some kind of family arrangement also appears to have been involved, for Henry Strangways's Stafford ancestry meant that he was a potential heir to the Melbury estate when the Browning line became extinct.
3. Now best known as the location of HM Prison, Strangeways. The senior branch of the Strang[e]ways family died out in the male line early in the seventeenth century; the family seat, Strangeways Hall, then changed hands several times, and was finally demolished in 1864.
4. Alionor's mother was Alice, daughter and coheiress of Sir Humphrey Stafford of Hooke. Alionor also inherited from her cousin, Humphrey Stafford, Earl of Devon, who was beheaded in 1469.
5. Giles Strangways was admitted to the Middle Temple in 1504.
6. For a biography of Sir Giles Strangways, see S. T. Bindoff, *The History of Parliament: The House of Commons, 1509–1558*, iii (London, 1982), pp. 395–97.
7. Lucy Toulmin Smith (ed.), *The Itinerary of John Leland in or about the Years 1535–1543*, iii (London, 1907), pp. 247–48. See also John Chandler (ed.), *John Leland's Itinerary* (Stroud, 1993), pp. 133–34. Leland's word *quadrato* has been interpreted to mean either 'with squared stone' or 'in the form of a quadrangle', but the latter seems more likely. See Oswald, *Country Houses of Dorset*, p. 119.
8. Wadham, who married but had no children, was killed in the Duke of Monmouth's rebellion in 1685, when he was thirty-nine.
9. It is not clear from the Melbury register if they married in 1674 or 1675.
10. Quoted in Basil Duke Henning, *The History of Parliament: The House of Commons 1660–1690*, iii (London, 1983), p. 498, under John Strangways.
11. Eveline Cruickshanks, Stuart Hadley and D. W. Hayton (ed.), *The History of Parliament: The House of Commons, 1690–1715*, v (Cambridge, 2002), p. 585.
12. See below, p. 79, for further details of the house.
13. They were part of a country-wide phenomenon, in a period when, for reasons which are still not fully understood, an exceptionally large number of wealthy and long-established landowning families died out in the direct male line. T. H. Hollingsworth, 'Demography of the British Peerage', *Population Studies*, supplement, 18 (1964); Lloyd Bonfield, 'Marriage Settlements and the Rise of Great Estates: The Demographic Aspect', *Economic History Review*, second series, 32 (1979), pp. 483–94.
14. BL, Add. MS 51396, fols 108–9, Lord Hervey to Henry Fox, 13 September 1733.
15. BL, Add. MS 51340, fols 33–34, Charlotte Digby to Lord Ilchester, 17 December 1748; fols 75–76, Edward Digby to Lord Ilchester, 24 March 1750.
16. Sherborne Castle MSS, Fox correspondence, Lord Ilchester to Lord Digby, 13 August 1755.
17. PP, Thomas Mansel Talbot to Henrietta Maria Hicks Beach, 20 December 1796; Thomas Mansel Talbot to Michael Hicks Beach, 4 April 1798.

18. DRO, D/FSI, box 241B, Maria, Countess of Ilchester, to third Earl of Ilchester [12 May 1803].
19. DRO, D/FSI, box 225, marriage settlement of Thomas Horner and Susanna Strangways, 14 November 1713. The early versions of Thomas Horner's will are in D/FSI, box 232; the final version is PRO, PROB 11/717/139, will of Thomas Horner of Mells, Somerset, 1742. See below, p. 26, for further information.
20. BL, Add. MS 51404, fols 27–28, John Wigan to Henry Fox, 21 February 1729.
21. BL, Add. MS 51353, fols 23–27, Sarah Lennox to Susan O'Brien, 20 December 1761.
22. BL, Add. MS 51352, fols 70–71, Caroline Fox to Susan Fox, 4 February 1762.
23. Suffolk Record Office, Bury St Edmunds, Ickworth MSS, 941/47/4, fols 310–13, Lord Hervey to Stephen Fox, 4 December 1731. The Duchess and Southcote eventually married 'about 5 August 1733'. See GEC, *The Complete Peerage*, iii, p. 283, under Cleveland.
24. BL, Add. MS 51357, fol. 26, Charlotte Digby to Susan O'Brien, 7 January 1765; fols 32–33, Charlotte Digby to Susan O'Brien, 1 September 1765.
25. BL, Add. MS 51353, fols 109–10, Sarah Bunbury to Susan O'Brien, 8 March 1766.
26. BL, Add. MS 51359, Susan O'Brien's journal, 21 July 1806.
27. Fox Talbot Museum, Lacock, Susan O'Brien to Elizabeth Feilding, 24 July [1806].
28. BL, Add. MS 51354, fols 94–97, Sarah Lennox to Susan O'Brien, 21 April 1779.
29. BL, Add. MS 51386, fols 8–12, Sarah, Duchess of Marlborough to Henry Fox, 23 November 1732.
30. BL, Add. MS 51386, fols 3–4, Sarah, Duchess of Marlborough to Susanna Strangways Horner, 14 July 1732. See also GEC, *The Complete Peerage*, viii, p. 499, under Marlborough.
31. BL, Add. MS 51352, fols 116–17, Lady Holland to Susan O'Brien [*c.* June 1766].
32. Quoted in GEC, *The Complete Peerage*, vi, p. 326, under Harrington.
33. BL, Add. MS 51353, fols 96–103, Sarah Bunbury to Susan O'Brien, 9 January 1766; fols 109–10, Sarah Bunbury to Susan O'Brien, 8 March 1766. Isabella married Charles, Viscount Molyneux, later first Earl of Sefton, in 1768.
34. Lawrence Stone, *The Family, Sex and Marriage in England, 1500–1800* (London, 1977), pp. 7–8.
35. Amanda Vickery, *The Gentleman's Daughter* (New Haven and London, 1998), p. 40.
36. BL, Add. MS 51396, fols 129–30, Lord Hervey to Henry Fox, 9 June 1734.
37. BL, Add. MS 51353, fols 35–39, Sarah Lennox to Susan O'Brien, 14 September 1776.
38. The marriage took place at Melbury Sampford on 17 November 1713: Melbury Sampford parish register, DRO, PE/MBO: RE 1/2.
39. Between the late sixteenth and early eighteenth centuries the median age at first marriage for wealthy brides was nineteen to twenty-three. Amy Louise Erickson, *Women and Property in Early Modern England* (London and New York, 1993), p. 120.

40. Mells Manor, MS 576. The author 'A.B.', has been identified by Michael McGarvie as the Revd Henry Harris (*c.* 1706–1786), vicar of Norton St Philip, Somerset, from 1739 to 1786.
41. DRO, D/FSI, box 225, marriage settlement of Thomas Horner and Susanna Strangways, 14 November 1713.
42. PP, Charlotte Traherne, 'Family Recollections'.
43. Susanna and Charlotte were second cousins: Susanna's paternal great-aunt, Howarda Strangways, had married Sir Lewis Dyve of Bromham, Bedfordshire. Charlotte Clayton (*née* Dyve) was Sir Lewis's granddaughter. Charlotte's husband, William Clayton, was created first Baron Sundon in 1735, and Charlotte is better known as Lady Sundon. See Katherine Thomson (ed.), *Memoirs of Viscountess Sundon, Mistress of the Robes to Queen Caroline* (London, 1847), especially pp. 344–61.
44. PP, Charlotte Traherne, 'Family Recollections'.
45. PRO, PROB 11/635/10, will of Elizabeth, Duchess of Hamilton and Brandon, 1730. She died on 3 November 1729, 'on the road from Bath': GEC, *The Complete Peerage*, vi, p. 270, under Hamilton.
46. Thomson (ed.), *Memoirs of Viscountess Sundon*), pp. 346–49, Susanna Strangways Horner to Mrs Clayton, 10 August [1730–31]. The letter, which was sent from Spa is dated only '10 August', but it must have been written before 1732.
47. Jeremy Black, *The British and the Grand Tour* (London, 1985), p. 8.
48. Francesco Solimena (1657–1747) is known to have painted a number of British visitors to Naples around this time.
49. R. A. Roberts (ed.), *Diary of the First Earl of Egmont*, ii, *1734–38* (London, 1923), p. 150; and Fourth Earl of Chesterfield, *Characters of Eminent Persons of his own Time* (London, 1777), p. 38.
50. DRO, D/FSI, box 240A, bundle 2, Susanna Strangways Horner to Stephen Fox, 23 January 1735.
51. Romney Sedgwick, *The History of Parliament: the House of Commons 1715–1754*, i (London, 1970), p. 347. Hindon's two MPs were elected by approximately 120 voters.

Notes to Chapter 2: Elizabeth

1. PP, Charlotte Traherne, 'Family Recollections'. The Mells parish registers record only the burials of two boys, and Elizabeth's baptism. The other children may have been still-born and not baptised. The burials of still-born children rarely appear in parish registers at this period.
2. PP, MS account of 'The Four Countesses of Ilchester', by Susan O'Brien, 1817.
3. See Katherine Thomson (ed.), *Memoirs of Viscountess Sundon, Mistress of the Robes to Queen Caroline* (London, 1847), p. 350, Susanna Strangways Horner to Lady Sundon, 21 July [1735]. Susanna's cousin Charlotte Clayton had become Lady Sundon in May 1735, when her husband was made an Irish baron.
4. Ibid., p. 355, Susanna Strangways Horner to Lady Sundon, 31 July [1735].

5. DRO, D/FSI, box 240A, bundle 2, Susanna Strangways Horner to Stephen Fox, 23 January 1735.
6. Charlotte Fox had married Edward Digby, son of William, fifth Baron Digby, in 1729. Charlotte's doubts appear to have been expressed in a letter to Lord Hervey, in which she accused Hervey of 'assisting the tempter' – probably Henry or Susanna. Charlotte's letter has not survived, but Lord Hervey's reply is included in Earl of Ilchester, *Lord Hervey and his Friends, 1726–1738* (London, 1950), pp. 231–33.
7. Thompson, *Viscountess Sundon*, p. 354, Susanna Strangways Horner to Lady Sundon, 15 December [1735].
8. PP, Charlotte Traherne, 'Family Recollections'.
9. Later 31 Old Burlington Street. The house had been built by Lord Hervey around 1722. Hervey had then sold it to Stephen Fox in 1730. Ilchester, *Lord Hervey and his Friends*, p. 28.
10. PP, Charlotte Traherne, 'Family Recollections'.
11. Or Villemain. Stephen Fox presented Willemin to the living of Eisey, near Cricklade in Wiltshire, on 26 October 1737. Halsband says that he was a Frenchman, educated at the University of Paris: see Robert Halsband, *Lord Hervey, Eighteenth-Century Courtier* (Oxford, 1973), p. 343.
12. DRO, D/FSI, box 240A, bundle 3.
13. BL, Add. MS 27735, fol. 123, quoted in Halsband, *Lord Hervey*, p. 190.
14. DRO, D/FSI, box 240A, bundle 3.
15. Christopher Clay, *Public Finance and Private Wealth: The Career of Sir Stephen Fox, 1627–1716* (Oxford, 1978), p. 328–29.
16. BL, Add. MS 51337, fols 169–71, Lord Ilchester to Susanna Strangways Horner, 15 January 1747.
17. Clay, *Public Finance and Private Wealth*, pp. 1–18, 246.
18. BL, Add. MS 51345, fols 95–95, Lord Ilchester to Lord Hervey, 13 November 1742.
19. BL, Add. MS 51345, fols 81–82, Lord Hervey to Stephen Fox, 15 October 1737.
20. See Lucy Moore, *Amphibious Thing: The Life of Lord Hervey* (London, 2000), pp. 37–39.
21. Third Baron Holland (ed.), *Memoirs of the Reign of King George the Second by Horace Walpole*, i (London, 1846), p. 174.
22. He became third Duke of Marlborough in 1733.
23. Eveline Cruckshanks, Stuart Hadley, and D. W. Hayton (ed.), *The History of Parliament: The House of Commons, 1690–1715*, iv (Cambridge, 2002), p. 392.
24. Suffolk Record Office, Bury St Edmunds, Ickworth MSS, 941/47/4 , fols 533–38, Lord Hervey to Charlotte Digby, 13 November 1735.
25. BL, Add. MS 51337, fol. 156, Elizabeth Fox to Thomas Strangways Horner [*c.* 1 April 1736].
26. Robert Dunning, *Somerset Families* (Somerset County Council, 2002), p. 68.
27. From a contemporary translation of the epitaph in Melbury Sampford church, BL, Add. MS 51337, fol. 243.

28. In the coat of arms of the first Earl of Ilchester in Melbury church, Strangways quarters Fox, with Strangways appearing in the quarters of the shield which usually belong to the male line, rather than the female. Later generations of the family bore the same arms. See below, p. 347, for further details of the peerages.
29. See, for example, the first and second editions of John Hutchins's *History of Dorset*, published in 1774 and 1796.
30. A similar take-over can be seen in the ancestors of the Dukes of Northumberland. The first Duke was Sir Hugh Smithson, a Yorkshire baronet whose ancestors had been haberdashers. In 1740 he married Elizabeth Seymour, who became the heiress to the Percy family when her brother died four years later. Smithson inherited the title of Earl of Northumberland from his father-in-law in 1750, and was made a Duke in 1766. In 1750 he took the surname Percy in lieu of Smithson.
31. BL, Add. MS 51337, fol. 6, Elizabeth Fox to Stephen Fox, 3 October 1736.
32. BL, Add. MS 51337, fol. 8, Elizabeth Fox to Stephen Fox [1736–39].
33. BL, Add. MS 51419, fols 37–38, Lord Ilchester to Henry Fox, 27–28 October 1748; Add. MS 51359, Susan O'Brien's journal, 1789.
34. BL, Add. MS 51347, fols 95–96, Lord Ilchester to Lord Hervey, 13 November 1742.
35. DRO, D/FSI, box 232, George Donisthorpe to Susanna Strangways Horner, 3 December 1739.
36. Quoted in Sedgwick (ed.), *The History of Parliament: The House of Commons, 1715–1754*, ii, pp. 48–49.
37. BL, Add. MS 51360, Susan O'Brien's journal, 24 September 1820.
38. PRO, PROB 11/717/139, will of Thomas Horner of Mells, Somerset, 1742.
39. DRO, D/FSI, box 335, legal opinions, 1747–53.
40. DRO, D/FSI, box 191, 'A particular of Sir Stephen Fox's goods [at Redlynch]', 15 May 1683.
41. Clay, *Public Finance and Private Wealth*, pp. 206–11.
42. Howard Colvin, *A Biographical Dictionary of British Architects, 1600–1840* (3rd edn, New Haven and London, 1995), pp. 370–71.
43. R. W. Dunning (ed.), *The Victoria History of the Counties of England: A History of the County of Somerset*, vii (London, 1999), pp. 26–28.
44. Clay, *Public Finance and Private Wealth*, p. 320.
45. DRO, D/FSI, box 170B, 'A particular of the Right Hon. Sir Stephen Fox his estate in the county of Somerset', September 1712.
46. Samuel Donne's map of Redlynch 1762 shows 'the water house which supplies the mansion house and offices with water'. It is not clear when this was built. See DRO, D/FSI, Acc. 5294.
47. DRO, D/FSI, box 207, estate accounts (Redlynch), 1716–25.
48. The Melbury accounts show that Ireson was paid £200 for a monument to Thomas Strangways junior early in 1728: DRO, D/FSI, box 187, household accounts (Melbury), 1726–28.

49. Edward was the second surviving son, but heir to his father due to the insanity of his elder brother.
50. BL, Add. MS 51404, fols 27–28, John Wigan to Henry Fox, 21 February 1729.
51. BL, Add. MS 51340, fols 21–22, Charlotte Digby to Lord Ilchester, 3 December [1746].
52. See below, pp. 86–88, for further details.
53. BL, Add. MS 51415, fols 91–92, Henry Fox to Caroline Fox, 23 April 1761; fols 77–78, Caroline Fox to Henry Fox [13 July 1751].
54. BL, Add. MS 51421, fols 76–77, Lord Ilchester to Lord Holland [*c.* 1767].
55. BL, Add. MS 51347, fols 58–60, Lord Stavordale to Lord Ilchester, 24 September 1767.
56. BL, Add. MS 51341, fols 93–94, Lord Digby to Lord Ilchester, 20 November 1770; Add. MS 51350, fol. 74, fifth Earl of Bristol to Lord Ilchester, 20 November 1770.
57. PP, John Dyke Acland to Lord Ilchester, 22 June 1771.
58. See below, pp. 324–27, for details of the Aclands' American expedition.
59. BL, Add. MS 51340, fols 17–18, Charlotte Digby to Lord Ilchester, 11 October [1746].
60. BL, Add. MS 51341, fol. 146, Stephen Digby to Lady Ilchester, 2 May 1771.
61. BL, Add. MS 51337, fol. 147, Lady Ilchester to Lord Ilchester [*c.* 8 May 1771].
62. BL, Add. MS 51356, fols 113–14, notes by an unnamed cousin.
63. See Hester Davenport, *Faithful Handmaid: Fanny Burney at the Court of King George III* (paperback edn, Stroud, 2003), especially pp. 103–55.
64. BL, Add. MS 51353, fols 113–16, Sarah Bunbury to Susan O'Brien, 8 May 1766.
65. Sons of Henry Fox and his wife Caroline. See below, p. 36.
66. BL, Add. MS 51421, fols 78–79, Lord Ilchester to Lord Holland, 6 November 1764; Add. MS 51341, fol. 80, Lord Digby to Lord Ilchester, 23 November 1766, and fols 85–86, Lord Digby to Lord Ilchester, 6 December 1766. The second girl may have been a member of the Fane family.
67. *Letters of Horace Walpole to Sir Horace Mann, 1760–1785*, ii (London, 1843), pp. 81–82.
68. DRO, D/FSI, box 241A (1), bundle 3/14, John Dyke Acland to Lord Stavordale [1772].
69. A romanticised, (and largely apocryphal) account of the events leading to their marriage was later given by the Irish writer William Le Fanu, the brother of Joseph Sheridan Le Fanu, the author of *Uncle Silas.* See W. R. Le Fanu, *Seventy Years of Irish Life* (London, 1893), pp. 22–26.
70. DRO, D/FSI, box 240B, bundle 5, Lady Ilchester to Lord Stavordale, 11 November [1774].
71. PP, Susan O'Brien to Mary Strangways [May 1792].
72. BL, Add. MS 51359, Susan O'Brien's journal, 1794.
73. WSRO, Lacock Abbey MSS, Acc. 2664, box of miscellaneous correspondence (Feilding, Strangways, Talbot), Elizabeth Talbot to Harriot Strangways, 27 May 1799; BL, Add. MS 51359, Susan O'Brien's journal, 26 July 1810.

74. BL, Add. MS 51359, Susan O'Brien's journal, 2 April 1801.
75. A. P. W. Malcolmson, *The Pursuit of the Heiress: Aristocratic Marriage in Ireland, 1750–1820* (Ulster Historical Foundation, 1982), p. 35.
76. PP, Harriot Strangways to Mary Strangways [1791].
77. PP, MS account of 'The Four Countesses of Ilchester', by Susan O'Brien, 1817.
78. Charles Spence (1786–1840), a lieutenant in the Royal Navy from 1802, and his sister Harriot: DRO, D/FSI, box 241A(1), bundle 3/6.

Notes to Chapter 3: Susan

1. W. S. Lewis, Warren Hunting Smith and George L. Lam, *The Letters of Horace Walpole*, xxii (London, 1960), pp. 218–19.
2. BL, Add. MS 51344, fols 6–16, letters from Susan Fox to Lord Ilchester, *c.* 1756–58.
3. Earl of Ilchester, *Henry Fox, First Lord Holland: His Family and Relations*, i (London, 1920), p. 55.
4. BL, Add. MS 51352, fol. 60, Susan Fox to Henry Fox [*c.* 1745]. Charlotte was Susan's younger sister, born in 1744. Henry was a Lord of the Treasury at this time, and the Treasury was presumably the source of the red tape. 'Gimcrack' means showy but worthless.
5. BL, Add. MS 51414, fols 1–2, Caroline Lennox to Henry Fox [28 April 1744].
6. The second son is now usually known as Charles James Fox, but his family always called him Charles.
7. BL, Add. MS 51420, fols 118–20, Henry Fox to Lord Ilchester, 4 November 1760.
8. BL, Add. MS 51421, fols 13–14, Henry Fox to Lord Ilchester, 20 May 1762.
9. Brian Fitzgerald (ed.), *The Correspondence of Emily, Duchess of Leinster*, ii (Dublin, 1953), p. 85, Sarah Lennox to Countess of Kildare, 26 January 1760. Lady Caroline Russell (*c.* 1743–1811) was the daughter of the Duke of Bedford. She married George, fourth Duke of Marlborough, in 1762.
10. BL, Add. MS 51337, fol. 134, Lady Ilchester to Lord Ilchester, 6 February [1760].
11. BL, Add. MS 51344, fols 36–37, Susan Strangways to Lord Ilchester [*c.* 1 January 1761].
12. BL, Add. MS 51420, fols 127–28, Henry Fox to Lord Ilchester, 1 January 1761.
13. W. S. Lewis and Ralph S. Brown junior (ed.), *The Letters of Horace Walpole*, ix (London, 1941), p. 335, Horace Walpole to George Montagu, 22 January 1761.
14. PP, 'J'ai vu', MS recollections of Susan O'Brien.
15. BL, Add. MS 51420, fols 157–58, Henry Fox to Lord Ilchester, 30 July 1761.
16. PP, 'J'ai vu', MS recollections of Susan O'Brien.
17. BL, Add. MS 51353, fols 21–22, Sarah Lennox to Susan Strangways, 15 December 1761.
18. See above, p. 36.
19. BL, Add. MS 51358, fols 119–20, biographical note by William O'Brien [*c.* 1808].

20. BL, Add. MS 51422, fols 192–93, Charlotte Digby to Lord Holland, 13 April 1764.
21. BL, Add. MS 51361, fol. 1, 'To Lady Susan Strangways, 1762'.
22. BL, Add. MS 51422, fols 192–93, Charlotte Digby to Lord Holland, 13 April 1764.
23. BL, Add. 51361, fol. 2.
24. BL Add. MS 51352, fols 29–30, William O'Brien to Susan Strangways, 21 July. Added later are the dates '1762 or 1763'. 1763 must the the correct date: Susan did go to Barton in 1762, but she did not get there until September. O'Brien also refers to his forthcoming visit to Ireland in the letter of 21 July, and this visit probably took place in the summer of 1763.
25. BL, Add. MS 51360, Susan O'Brien's journal, 10 March 1818.
26. BL, Add. MS 51420, fols 174–75, Henry Fox to Lord Ilchester, 28 November 1761.
27. BL, Add. MS 51350, fols 12–13, Lord Ilchester to Sarah Bunbury, 8 April 1764.
28. She was born on 1 February 1743, but the change from the Julian calendar to the Gregorian meant that she celebrated her birthday on 12 February from 1752 onwards.
29. BL, Add. MS 51352, fol. 36, William O'Brien to Susan Strangways [early April 1764]; Mrs Paget Toynbee (ed.), *The Letters of Horace Walpole, Fourth Earl of Orford*, vi (London, 1903–5), pp. 49–50, Horace Walpole to Earl of Hertford, 12 April 1764.
30. BL, Add. MS 51350, fols 12–13, Lord Ilchester to Sarah Bunbury, 8 April 1764.
31. BL, Add. MS 51352, fols 84–85, Susan Strangways to Lord Holland, 6 April 1764.
32. BL, Add. MS 51344, fol. 47, Lady Ilchester to Susan O'Brien [April-May 1764].
33. BL, Add. MS 51357, fols 18–21, Louisa Conolly to Susan O'Brien, 12 May 1764.
34. BL, Add. MS 51352, fols 101–3, Lord Holland to Susan O'Brien, 8 March 1765.
35. BL, Add. MS 51405, fols 120–21, Clotworthy Upton to Lord Holland, 29 June 1764.
36. Charles Lee to Sir William Johnson, 25 July 1764, quoted in Charlotte Wilcoxen, 'A Highborn Lady in Colonial New York', *New York Historical Society Quarterly* (1979), p. 320.
37. BL, Add. MS 51352, fols 88–89, Susan O'Brien to Lord Holland, 19 August [1764].
38. BL, Add. MS 51425, fols 109–12, Samuel Touchet to Lord Holland, 3 and 10 October 1764; Add. MS 51353, fols 72–73, Sarah Bunbury to Susan O'Brien, 4 November 1764; Add. MS 51356, fols 161–63, Samuel Touchet to Susan O'Brien, 10 November 1764.
39. BL, Add. MS 51356, fols 161–63, Samuel Touchet to Susan O'Brien, 10 November 1764.
40. BL, Add. MS 51425, fols 107–8, Samuel Touchet to Lord Holland, 29 September 1764.
41. BL, Add. MS 51425, fols 105–6, Samuel Touchet to Lord Holland, 29 August 1764.
42. Letter in Forster Collection, Victoria and Albert Museum, quoted in

P. H. Highfill et al., *A Biographical Dictionary of Actors and Actresses, Musicians, Dancers, Managers and Other Stage Personnel in London, 1660–1800*, ii (Illinois, 1987), p. 91.

43. Oliver DeLancy to Adam Drummond, 8 November 1764, quoted in Wilcoxen, 'A Highborn Lady in Colonial New York', p. 328.
44. BL, Add. MS 51352, fols 92–93, Susan O'Brien to Lord Holland, 10 November [1764].
45. BL, Add. MS 51356, fols 161–63, Samuel Touchet to Susan O'Brien, 10 November 1764.
46. BL, Add. MS 51353, fols 72–73, Sarah Bunbury to Susan O'Brien, 4 November 1764; fols 74–78, Sarah Bunbury to Susan O'Brien, 16 December 1764.
47. BL, Add. MS 51357, fol. 26, Charlotte Digby to Susan O'Brien, 7 January 1765.
48. BL, Add. MS 51352, fols 101–3, Lord Holland to Susan O'Brien, 8 March 1765.
49. BL, Add. MS 51356, fols 170–71, Samuel Touchet to Susan O'Brien, 9 February 1765; fols 181–82, Samuel Touchet to Susan O'Brien, 8 June 1765.
50. BL, Add. MS 51353, fols 113–16, Sarah Bunbury to Susan O'Brien, 8 May 1766.
51. BL, Add. MS 51356, fols 125–30, Susan O'Brien to Clotworthy Upton, 13–14 April 1765.
52. BL, Add. MS 51353, fols 120–21, Sarah Bunbury to Susan O'Brien, 7 July 1766.
53. BL, Add. MS 51352, fols 125–26, Susan O'Brien to Lady Holland, 14 May 1769.
54. BL, Add. MS 51344, fols 72–73, Lady Ilchester to Susan O'Brien, 18 June 1769.
55. BL, Add. MS 51359, Susan O'Brien's journal, 1769 [written 1787].
56. BL, Add. MS 51356, fols 125–30, Susan O'Brien to Clotworthy Upton, 13–14 April 1765.
57. BL, Add. MS 51356, fols 92–93, Susan O'Brien to Miss Fox, 1 June 1824.
58. BL, Add. MS 51357, fols 39–40, Harriot Acland to Susan O'Brien, 9 February [1771].
59. BL, Add. MS 51357, fols 42–43, Susan O'Brien to Harriot Acland [*c.* 11 February 1771].
60. BL, Add. MS 51354, fols 1–10, Sarah Bunbury to Susan O'Brien, 23 June 1775.
61. BL, Add. MS 51359, Susan O'Brien's journal, 1772.
62. See below, pp. 271–73, for Abbotsbury.
63. BL, Add. MS 51359, Susan O'Brien's journal, 1774.
64. His will was dated 18 December 1484 and proved 24 March 1485: PRO, PROB 11/7/21. See above, p. 3, for further details.
65. John Coker, *A Survey of Dorsetshire* (London, 1732), pp. 70–71. Originally attributed to John Coker of Mappowder, Dorset, but thought to have been written by Thomas Gerard of Trent, in the time of Charles I.
66. John Hutchins, *The History and Antiquities of the County of Dorset*, ii (3rd edn, with additions by W. Shipp and J. W. Hodson, London, 1863), p. 561.
67. PRO, PROB 11/612/245, Thomas Strangways of Melbury Sampford, 1726; PROB 11/614/52, Mary Strangways of Stinsford, 1727.
68. BL, Add. MS 51359, Susan O'Brien's journal, 1775 and 14 May 1819.
69. BL, Add. MS 51359, Susan O'Brien's journal, 1787.

70. BL, Add. MS 51357, fols 175–84, 'Account of Money Received by Mr O'Brien and Lady Susan since their Marriage, 1764'.
71. BL, Add. MS 51354, fols 19–25, Sarah Bunbury to Susan O'Brien, 29 July [1775].
72. BL, Add. MS 51354, fols 128–34, Sarah Lennox to Susan O'Brien, 14 May 1781.
73. BL, Add. MS 51359, Susan O'Brien's journal, 20 October 1812.
74. By the time of her death in 1827, Susan had received at least £40,000 from her family, including £2000 to equip her for her trip to America; a bequest of £500 in her father's will; and £2500 paid to her in 1779 under the terms of her parents' marriage settlement: BL, Add. MS 51357, fols 175–84, 'Account of Money Received by Mr O'Brien and Lady Susan since their Marriage, 1764', written in 1826–27.
75. BL, Add. MS 51359, Susan O'Brien's journal, 14 August and 1 September 1800; BL, Add. MS 51358, fols. 38–39, Lord Ilchester to William O'Brien, 11 August [1800], fols 40–41, William O'Brien to Lord Ilchester [18 August 1800].
76. BL, Add. MS 51359, Susan O'Brien's journal, 2 April 1801.
77. BL, Add. MS 51359, Susan O'Brien's journal, July-September 1803.
78. BL, Add. MS 51352, fols 54–55, William O'Brien to Susan O'Brien, 21 October 1804.
79. BL, Add. MS 51359, Susan O'Brien's journal, December 1804.
80. BL, Add. MS 51359, Susan O'Brien's journal, 1805.
81. Fox Talbot Museum, Lacock, Susan O'Brien to Elizabeth Feilding, 13 May 1805; and [September] 1805.
82. There are some hints that Susan may have been pregnant in the summer of 1764: BL, Add. MS 51405, fols 139–42, Clotworthy Upton to Lord Holland, 26 July and 11 August 1764. This is, however, denied in another letter written at the same time: BL, Add. MS 51421, fols 64–65, Lady Ilchester to Lord Holland [8 August 1764]. There is no indication that Susan ever gave birth to a living child.
83. PP, Susan O'Brien to Mary Cole, 18 September 1816.
84. Florence Emily Hardy, *The Early Life of Thomas Hardy, 1840–1891* (London, 1928), pp. 11–12.
85. John Newman and Nikolaus Pevsner, *The Buildings of England: Dorset* (London, 1972), pp. 398–99.
86. *Dorset County Chronicle*, 17 March 1825; BL, Add. MS 51360, Susan O'Brien's journal, 17 March 1825. An examination of the house whilst it was being renovated suggested that much of the surviving structure dates from the seventeenth century or earlier, though there were clearly many alterations and additions in the eighteenth and nineteenth centuries. The house was used as a school in the mid twentieth century, and was then empty – and in a state of increasing dereliction – for several years. In the 1990s it was divided into several units. Unfortunately the formerly remote and tranquil setting has now been destroyed, firstly by the opening of the Dorchester bypass to the west of the house, and then by the construction of no fewer than twelve new houses in the grounds.

Notes to Chapter 4: Mary

1. DRO, D/FSI, box 240B, bundle 6, Lady Ilchester to Lord Ilchester, 9 June [1772].
2. DRO, D/FSI, box 329, post-nuptial settlement of second Earl and Countess of Ilchester, 1782.
3. PRO, PROB 11/1384/908, will of Henry Thomas Fox Strangways, Earl of Ilchester, 1802.
4. DRO, D/FSI, box 241A(1), 'Statement of the late Earl of Ilchester's Concerns' [*c.* 1802].
5. Joanna Martin, *The Penrice Letters, 1768–1795* (Cardiff and Swansea, 1993), p. 83, Thomas Mansel Talbot to William Beach, 3 January 1773. The information on the building and furnishing of Penrice may be presumed to come from the Penrice Papers unless otherwise stated.
6. Nicholas Kingsley thinks that 'The most striking thing about the house is its panache. There is a cool sophistication about the seaward-facing south front ... It is a wholly neo-Classical vision'. Nicholas Kingsley, 'Vision of Villas: The Work of Anthony Keck II', *Country Life*, 182, no. 43 (27 October 1988), p. 127.
7. H. Skrine, *Two Successive Tours throughout the Whole of Wales* (London, 1798), pp. 69–70.
8. For the orangery, see P. Moore, *Margam Orangery, West Glamorgan* (Glamorgan Archive Service, 1986), p. 3. See also the Royal Commission on Ancient and Historical Monuments in Wales, *An Inventory of the Ancient Monuments in Glamorgan*, iv, *Domestic Architecture from the Reformation to the Industrial Revolution, part I: The Greater Houses* (Cardiff, 1981), pp. 325–31. For the Pyle Inn, see Benjamin Heath Malkin, *The Scenery, Antiquities and Biography of South Wales*, ii (2nd edn, London, 1807), pp. 517–18. The accounts for the building of the inn are in West Glamorgan Archive Service (Swansea), D/DMa 38–40.
9. PP, Frances Richards to Henrietta Maria Hicks Beach, 10 February 1794.
10. PP, Frances Richards to Henrietta Maria Hicks Beach, 11 July 1793.
11. Martin, *The Penrice Letters*, pp. 129–30, Thomas Mansel Talbot to Mary Strangways, 18 December 1793.
12. DRO, D/FSI, box 241A(1); and West Glamorgan Archive Service (Swansea), D/DMa 40–41.
13. DRO, D/FSI, box 195. Mary was entitled to £3200 under her parents' marriage settlement, but she and her sisters appear to have received £3500 each.
14. BL, Add. MS 51357, fols 74–75, Kitty Acland to Susan O'Brien, 22 February 1794; PP, Mary Grady to Mary Talbot, 3 April [1794].
15. BL, Add. MS 51359, Susan O'Brien's journal, 1794.
16. PP, C. R. M. Talbot, 'Characters of Some Members of His Family'.
17. See Martin, *The Penrice Letters*, p. 47, for a list.
18. Martin, *The Penrice Letters*, pp. 130–39, Mary Strangways to Harriot Strangways, 6, 13, 20 and 23 January 1794.
19. Martin, *The Penrice Letters*, p. 143, Mary Talbot to Harriot Strangways, 5 February 1794.

20. Martin, *The Penrice Letters*, p. 144, Mary Talbot to Harriot Strangways [February 1794].
21. PP, Thomas Mansel Talbot to Mary Talbot [before 17 August 1797].
22. National Library of Wales, MS 11981E, Sydney Smith to Henrietta Maria Hicks Beach, 17 September 1799. Smith was tutor to the Hicks Beachs' two sons from 1798 to 1803.
23. PP, C. R. M. Talbot, 'Characters of Some Members of His Family'.
24. PP, Charlotte Traherne, 'Family Recollections'. Charlotte excludes the two children who died young.
25. Thomas and William were first cousins: Thomas's father was a brother of William's mother Martha, the wife of the Revd William Davenport.
26. In a letter written in 1790 Thomas Mansel Talbot refers to 'my wild cousin Will Talbot': Martin, *The Penrice Letters*, p. 103, Thomas Mansel Talbot to Michael Hicks Beach, 24 August 1790.
27. National Library of Wales, MS 11981E, Sydney Smith to Henrietta Maria Hicks Beach, 17 September 1799.
28. PP, Susan O'Brien's portrait of her niece Elizabeth Strangways, October 1792.
29. PP, C. R. M. Talbot, 'Characters of Some Members of His Family'.
30. PP, Frances Richards to Henrietta Maria Hicks Beach, 11 July 1793.
31. PP, Thomas Mansel Talbot to Michael Hicks Beach, 7 February 1796.
32. Most of the family called her Lily, but Susan O'Brien usually called her Eliza.
33. PP, Susan O'Brien to Mary Talbot, 12 December 1795.
34. DRO, D/FSI, box 241, Elizabeth Strangways to Lord Ilchester [1795–96].
35. Joanna Martin, *A Governess in the Age of Jane Austen* (London and Rio Grande, Ohio, 1998), p. 154, Agnes Porter's journal, 17 April 1796.
36. BL, Add. MS 51359, Susan O'Brien's journal, April 1796.
37. PP, Thomas Mansel Talbot to Michael Hicks Beach, 21 February 1798.
38. Fox Talbot Museum, Lacock, Susan O'Brien to Elizabeth Talbot [21 June 1798].
39. Fox Talbot Museum, Lacock, Susan O'Brien to Elizabeth Talbot, 8 November 1798.
40. BL, Add. MS 51359, Susan O'Brien's journal, 1 August 1799. James Frampton's father, who died in 1784, had an income of £4000 a year. Harriot Georgiana Mundy (ed.), *The Journal of Mary Frampton* (London, 1885), p. 5.
41. BL, Add. MS 51359, Susan O'Brien's journal, 10 August 1799.
42. WSRO, Lacock Abbey MSS, Acc. 2664, box of miscellaneous correspondence (Feilding, Strangways, Talbot), Susan O'Brien to Elizabeth Talbot, 9 September [1799]. The Revd Charles Fox Strangways, who performed the ceremony, was the bride's uncle.
43. Mundy (ed.), *The Journal of Mary Frampton*, p. 106, Phillis Frampton to Mary Heberden, 12 September 1799.
44. DRO, D/FSI, box 241B, Louisa Strangways to Lord Stavordale, 10 September 1799.
45. Fox Talbot Museum, Lacock, Susan O'Brien to Elizabeth Feilding, 13 May 1805; BL, Add. MS 51360, Susan O'Brien's journal, 23 February 1819.
46. PP, C. R. M. Talbot, 'Characters of Some Members of His Family'.

47. BL, Add. MS 51359, Susan O'Brien's journal, 25 July 1800.
48. BL, Add. MS 51359, Susan O'Brien's journal, 30 July 1800.
49. BL, Add. MS 51357, fols 89–90, Agnes Porter to Susan O'Brien, 3 August 1800.
50. BL, Add. MS 51359, Susan O'Brien's journal, 6 August 1800.
51. BL, Add. MS 51357, fols 107–8, Harriot Frampton to Susan O'Brien, 2 September 1800.
52. BL, Add. MS 51357, fols 97–98, Susan O'Brien to Agnes Porter, 15 August 1800.
53. Lacock Abbey was let until 1827. See H. J. P. Arnold, *William Henry Fox Talbot: Pioneer of Photography and Man of Science* (London, 1977), pp. 45–46.
54. BL, Add. MS 51359, Susan O'Brien's journal, 25 April 1804.
55. BL, Add. MS 51359, Susan O'Brien's journal, 5 September 1806.
56. See further below, pp. 246–58, for Henry Talbot and Penrice.
57. BL, Add. MS 51359, Susan O'Brien's journal, 16 December 1802, 16–17 October 1802.
58. BL, Add. MS 51359, Susan O'Brien's journal, 21 March 1804. Captains Stephen and George were both Digbys.
59. BL, Add. MS 51359, Susan O'Brien's journal, 24 May 1804.
60. BL, Add. MS 51359, Susan O'Brien's journal, 21 October 1804.
61. BL, Add. MS 51359, Susan O'Brien's journal, 4 April 1806.
62. BL, Add. MS 51359, Susan O'Brien's journal, 6 December 1806, 7 January 1807.
63. Lord Henry was connected to Louisa by marriage, as he was a nephew of Lady Mary Fitzpatrick, the wife of Ste Fox, second Lord Holland.
64. BL, Add. MS 51359, Susan O'Brien's journal, 12 January 1808.
65. PP, Louisa Strangways to Mary Talbot, 7 May 1807.
66. PP, Louisa Strangways to Mary Talbot, 6 July 1807.
67. BL, Add. MS 51359, Susan O'Brien's journal, 15 December 1807.
68. PP, Louisa Strangways to Mary Talbot, 30 March 1808.
69. PP, C. R. M. Talbot, 'Characters of Some Members of His Family'.
70. PP, Louisa Lansdowne to Mary Talbot, 3 November 1810.
71. BL, Add. MS 51359, Susan O'Brien's journal, 11 March 1806.
72. PP, Charlotte Strangways to Mary Talbot, 4 July 1808. He was the second son of George, second Marquess Townshend.
73. Later first Earl of Auckland; Governor-General of India 1835–41.
74. BL, Add. MS 51359, Susan O'Brien's journal, 3 September 1810.
75. BL, Add. MS 51359, Susan O'Brien's journal, 28 August 1812.
76. PP, C. R. M. Talbot, 'Characters of Some Members of His Family'. See also below, p. 187–88.
77. Earl of Ilchester (ed.), *The Journal of the Hon. Henry Edward Fox, 1818–1830* (London, 1923), p. 29; and BL, Add. MS 51359, Susan O'Brien's journal, 1 December 1811.
78. Tina and Ellinor had died in 1808 and 1810 respectively. See below, pp. 173–74, 186.
79. BL, Add. MS 51359, Susan O'Brien's journal, 27 May 1813.
80. PP, Revd Dr John Hunt to Mary Talbot [October-November 1814].

81. PP, Mary Talbot to Revd Dr John Hunt, 8 November 1814.
82. PP, Sir Christopher Cole to Mary Talbot, 27 December 1814.
83. PP, Lord Ilchester to Mary Talbot, 23 February 1815.
84. BL, Add. MS 51360, Susan O'Brien's journal, 18 April and 2 June 1815.
85. PP, C. R. M. Talbot, 'Characters of Some Members of His Family'.
86. BL Add. MS 51360. Susan O'Brien's journal, 5 May 1821.
87. PP, Mary Cole to Sir Christopher Cole, 16 May 1821 and 14 March 1823.
88. PP, C. R. M. Talbot, 'Characters of Some Members of His Family'.
89. Martin, *A Governess in the Age of Jane Austen*, p. 298, Agnes Porter to Harriot Frampton, 21 September 1810.
90. Martin, *A Governess in the Age of Jane Austen*, p. 286, Agnes Porter to Mary Talbot, 20 July 1809.
91. Martin, *A Governess in the Age of Jane Austen*, p. 298, Agnes Porter to Harriot Frampton, 21 September 1810.
92. PP, note by Florence Franklen.
93. PP, Mary Cole to Mrs St George, 31 August 1827.
94. PP, C. R. M. Talbot to Mary Theresa Talbot, 11 December 1829, and C. R. M. Talbot to Mary Cole, 6 May [1830].
95. The house now belongs to Thomas Methuen-Campbell, a four-times-great grandson of Thomas and Mary Talbot.

Notes to Chapter 5: Country Houses

1. Although Hutchins refers in 1774 to a 'large canal', formed from a rivulet in 1742, it is possible that the rivulet had first been dammed to form a canal in the 1690s: canals were very fashionable at the time: John Hutchins, *The History and Antiquities of the County of Dorset*, i (first edn, London, 1774), p. 513.
2. There is a portrait of the architect at Melbury. He may be John Watson, 'architect of Glashampton' who died in 1707 and is commemorated by a tombstone in Astley church, Worcestershire. Howard Colvin, *A Biographical Dictionary of British Architects, 1600–1840* (3rd edn, New Haven and London, 1995), p. 1026.
3. See below, pp. 113–14, for further details of the dressing rooms.
4. Charlotte Smith, *The Old Manor House* (first published 1793; paperback, Oxford, 1989), pp. 7, 190.
5. DRO, D/FSI, box 186, Melbury inventory, 12 July 1727. Sarsnet is a fine, soft silk material.
6. Probably the structure referred to as 'long row' in the household accounts.
7. The area behind the eastern block is called the 'drying yard' in the early 1740s, so this structure probably included the laundry.
8. DRO, D/FSI, box 232, George Donisthorpe to Susanna Strangways Horner, 3 December 1739.
9. See below, pp. 262–65, for the work on the grounds at this time.
10. DRO, D/FSI, box 188, general disbursements (Melbury), 1742–44. Susanna left

£5 in her will to 'Joseph Child, my carpenter': PRO, PROB 11/837/115, will of Susanna Strangways Horner of Melbury Sampford, 1758.

11. Payments in 1750 included £8 8*s.* for 'a marble cistern for the water closet with brass work to it': DRO, D/FSI, box 188, household accounts (Melbury), 1747–51.
12. PRO, PROB 11/837/115, will of Susanna Strangways Horner of Melbury Sampford, Dorset, 1758.
13. John Dixon Hunt (ed.), 'Horace Walpole's Journals of Visits to Country Seats', in *The History of the Modern Taste in Gardening* (New York and London, 1982), pp. 47–48.
14. DRO, D/FSI, box 241, Elizabeth Strangways to second Earl of Ilchester, 12 March [1794]. The Wadhams and Ayliffes were ancestors, and Elizabeth is presumably referring to their portraits.
15. DRO, D/FSI, box 195, estate accounts (Melbury) to Michaelmas 1792.
16. BL, Add. MS 51373A, fols 80–95, catalogue of Melbury sale, 1801. Though there appears to be no definite evidence that the carvings were by Gibbons, the prices paid for them indicate that they were of very high quality. Similar carvings from the breakfast room were bought in at £64 1*s.*
17. BL, Add. MS 51359, Susan O'Brien's journal, 18 August 1803.
18. BL, Add. MS 51359, Susan O'Brien's journal, 20 October 1812. The 'family picture' must be the large portrait of Susan's great-grandfather Thomas Strangways and his family on the main staircase.
19. BL, Add. MS 51359, Susan O'Brien's journal, 1789. The Royal Family visited Redlynch on 14 September.
20. BL, Add. MS 51418, fols 34–35, Lord Ilchester to Henry Fox, 26 July 1746.
21. Suffolk RO, Bury St Edmunds, Ickworth MSS, 941/47/4, fols 51–53, Lord Hervey to Stephen Fox, 1 June 1727. Stephen Switzer (1682–1745), the writer and garden designer, published *The Nobleman, Gentleman and Gardener's Recreation* in 1715. *Vegetable Statisticks* by Stephen Hales was published in 1727. I have been unable to identify 'Hubbard upon Agriculture'.
22. Suffolk RO, Bury St Edmunds, Ickworth MSS, 941/47/4, fols 77–78, Lord Hervey to Stephen Fox, 18 June 1728.
23. BL, Add. MS 51417, fols 19–20, Henry Fox to Stephen Fox [*c.* 16 June 1729].
24. DRO, D/FSI, box 189, general day book (Redlynch), 1735–54; box 218, general household accounts (Redlynch), 1730–43; Lord Hervey to Stephen Fox, 7 November 1732, letter (then at Melbury) quoted in Ilchester, *Lord Hervey and his Friend*, pp. 146–47; BL, Add. MS 51396, fols 127–28, Lord Hervey to Henry Fox, 11 May 1734.
25. BL, Add. MS 51373A, fols 37–40, 'Work Done for the Right Honourable Lord Ilchester, 1751, 1752, 1753, 1754 and 1755 by Nathaniel Ireson'.
26. BL, Add. MS 51374, fols 52–53 'Plan of the Offices at Redlynch'.
27. BL, Add. MS 51418, fol. 8, Henry Fox to Lord Ilchester, 15 May 1746.
28. See below, pp. 266–67.
29. BL, Add. MS 51417, fols 133–34, Lord Ilchester to Henry Fox, July 1745.
30. BL, Add. MS 51348, fols 44–45, E. Berkeley to Lord Ilchester, 22 July 1745.

31. BL, Add. MS 51417, fols 210–12, Henry Fox to Lord Ilchester, 8 February 1746, and fols 224–25, Henry Fox to Lord Ilchester, 1 March 1746.
32. BL, Add. MS 51417, fols 210–12, Henry Fox to Lord Ilchester, 8 February 1746. In a letter dated 21 July 1753, Fox told Lord Digby that 'Mr Flitcroft knows nothing ... of true architecture'. Sherborne Castle MSS, Fox correspondence.
33. In 1762 this building held 'a fine collection of foreign and English pheasants'. See DRO, D/FSI, Acc. 5294.
34. BL, Add. MS 51373A, fols 37–40; DRO, D/FSI, box 218, private disbursements 1732–64. There is a payment of 1*s.* 10*d.* for hinges for the water closet in D/FSI, box 189, general day book (Redlynch), 1735–54.
35. Harateen is a woollen material.
36. DRO, D/FSI, box 218, accounts of Samuel Severn, 1746–50.
37. DRO, D/FSI, box 189, general day book (Redlynch), 1735–54.
38. BL, Add. MS 51337, fol. 43, Lady Ilchester to Lord Ilchester [*c.* 19 July 1750]. The Longs, of Draycot Cerne, Wiltshire, were cousins of Susanna Strangways Horner. Marrian Feaver, the rector of Melbury Sampford and Osmond, was Susanna's chaplain, and James Canelle was one of her servants.
39. Hunt, 'Horace Walpole's Journals of Visits to Country Seats', pp. 44–45.
40. DRO, D/FSI, box 340, Redlynch sale catalogue, 1912.
41. In 1749 the upholsterer Samuel Severn had supplied ninety-one and three quarters yards of 'Saxon green silk and worsted damask, sent into the country' at a cost of £29 1*s.* 1*d.*: DRO, D/FSI, box 218.
42. See below, pp. 112–13, for further details of this room.
43. DRO, D/FSI, box 183, Redlynch inventory, 10 August 1793.
44. RCHME, *An Inventory of the Historical Monuments in the County of Dorset*, i, *West Dorset* (second impression, London, 1974), p. 166.
45. BL, Add. MS 51373A, fols 96–103; also DRO, D/FSI, box 241A (1), 3/5, Redlynch sale catalogue, 1801.
46. Fox Talbot Museum, Lacock, Susan O'Brien to Elizabeth Talbot, 23 August 1804.
47. The service block was subsequently repaired, and it and the nearby stable block were divided into flats and maisonettes in the 1980s.
48. National Library of Wales, Penrice and Margam MS 6126. The water for the house came from the same source until 1987. By the 1820s it was possible to have plumbed-in bathrooms with hot and cold water, and the architect John Soane had one in his London house by 1825. See Susan Palmer, *The Soanes at Home* (London, 1997), p. 3. No separate bathroom is listed in the 1890 inventory of Penrice. Instead, there were japanned hip-baths in most of the bedrooms.
49. National Library of Wales, Penrice and Margam MSS 5622 and 2305.
50. Moreen is a stout material, of wool or wool and cotton, which was often used for curtains.
51. See below, p. 114, for further details of these items.
52. The letters are in Martin, *The Penrice Letters*, pp. 142–45.
53. Malkin, *Scenery, Antiquities and Biography of South Wales*, ii, pp. 491–92.

54. PP, Thomas Mansel Talbot's pocket-book, 18 February 1806.
55. PP, Mary Theresa Talbot to C. R. M. Talbot 17 March [1813].
56. Fox Talbot Museum, Lacock, Elizabeth Feilding to W. H. F. Talbot, 4 November 1836.
57. Cheney or cheyney is a woollen material.
58. DRO, D/FSI, box 186, Stinsford inventory, 21 July 1727.
59. PP, Charlotte Traherne, 'Family Recollections'.
60. Richard H. Taylor (ed.), *The Personal Notebooks of Thomas Hardy* (London, 1978), pp. 26–27.

Notes to Chapter 6: Country House Life

1. Unlike the 'genteel families' of northern England studied by Amanda Vickery, who did not in general 'expect to decamp to London for the Season'. Amanda Vickery, *The Gentleman's Daughter* (New Haven and London, 1998), p. 32.
2. BL, Add. MS 51344, fols 84–85, Harriot Acland to Lord Ilchester [January-February 1771].
3. Of sixty-four sessions between 1740 and 1800, sixty began between the last week in October and the last week in January. Thirty-four began in November.
4. *Gentleman's Magazine*, 8 (1738), p. 30, 'Advice to the Fair on their Return to London'.
5. Sherborne Castle MSS, game book, 24–31 January 1775.
6. PP, Susan O'Brien to Mary Talbot, 17 January 1814.
7. DRO, D/FSI, box 218, household accounts (Redlynch), 1730–43; box 189, ledger (Redlynch), 1743–64.
8. DRO, D/FSI, box 173A, household accounts (Redlynch), 1750–51.
9. Robert Halsband, *Lord Hervey, Eighteenth-Century Courtier* (Oxford, 1973), p. 104.
10. DRO, D/FSI, box 186, bundle of inventories.
11. Harriot Georgiana Mundy (ed.), *The Journal of Mary Frampton* (London, 1885), p. 2.
12. PP, Thomas Mansel Talbot to Michael Hicks Beach, 19 January 1794.
13. PP, Mary Strangways to Harriot Strangways, 20 January 1794.
14. PP, Maria Mauleverer to Mary Talbot, 16 September 1814.
15. PP, Susan O'Brien to Mary Cole, 6 July 1816.
16. Fox Talbot Museum, Lacock, Susan O'Brien to Elizabeth Feilding [September 1816].
17. Suffolk RO, Bury St Edmunds, Ickworth MSS, 941/47/4, fols 484–88, Lord Hervey (for Charlotte Digby) to Henry Fox, 13 January 1735.
18. BL, Add. MS 51337, fol. 130, Lady Ilchester to Lord Ilchester, 19 December [1756–61].
19. BL, Add. MS 51353, fols 113–116, Sarah Bunbury to Susan O'Brien, 8 May 1766.
20. BL, Add. MS 51354, fols 52–55, Sarah Lennox to Susan O'Brien, 3 December 1777.

21. BL, Add. MS 51354, fols 186–87, Sarah Napier to Susan O'Brien, 10 May 1785.
22. PP, Louisa Lansdowne to Mary Talbot, 3 November 1810.
23. Earl of Ilchester (ed.), *The Journal of Elizabeth, Lady Holland, 1791–1811*, i (London, 1908), p. 194.
24. BL, Add. MS 51357, fol. 74, Kitty Acland to Susan O'Brien, 22 February 1794.
25. DRO, D/FSI, box 241, Elizabeth Strangways to second Earl of Ilchester, 12 March [1794].
26. Suffolk RO, Bury St Edmunds, Ickworth MSS, 941/47/4, fol. 45, Lord Hervey to Henry Fox, 30 May 1727. The King's birthday was on 28 May.
27. BL, Add. MS 51345, fols 5–8, Lord Hervey to Stephen Fox, 9 January 1728.
28. BL, Add. MS 51344, fol. 19, Susan Fox Strangways to Lord Ilchester, 9 February 1758. Leicester House was the home of Princess Augusta, the mother of the Prince of Wales (later George III). Susan's father took the additional name of Strangways in this month.
29. PP, Susan O'Brien to Mary Strangways [April-May 1793].
30. Joanna Martin, *A Governess in the Age of Jane Austen* (London and Rio Grande, Ohio, 1998), pp. 177–78, Agnes Porter's journal, 27 April 1797. 'Laylock' is lilac, and 'bugles' are beads.
31. DRO, D/FSI, box 218, household accounts (Redlynch), 1747–52; box 188, household accounts (Melbury), 1747–51; box 217, household accounts (Melbury), 1760–70.
32. DRO, D/FSI, box 186, Melbury and Stinsford inventories, 1727; box 166B, Mells inventory, 1741.
33. DRO, D/FSI box 218, accounts of Samuel Severn, 1746–50; box 186, Redlynch inventory, 1793; box 217, household accounts (Melbury), 1760–70; box 189, ledger (Redlynch), 1743–64; box 189, general day book (Redlynch, 1735–54. I have no idea what this machine was!
34. Pamela A. Sambrook, *The Country House Servant* (Stroud, 1999), pp. 85–86.
35. Fox Talbot Museum, Lacock, Susan O'Brien to Elizabeth Feilding [June-July 1806].
36. BL, Add. MS 51354, fols 150–52, Sarah Napier to Susan O'Brien, 11 September 1782; fols 166–67, Sarah Napier to Susan O'Brien, 22 September 1783.
37. Martin, *A Governess in the Age of Jane Austen*, p. 214, Agnes Porter's journal, 7 October 1802.
38. John Calcraft, MP (1726–72) was related to the Fox brothers: his mother Christian (Burslem) was a daughter of their mother's sister Jane.
39. See below, pp. 312–13, for the Passage.
40. BL, Add. MS 51360, Susan O'Brien's journal, 26 April 1826.
41. BL, Add. MS 51360, Susan O'Brien's journal, 31 October 1824.
42. BL, Add. MS 51360, Susan O'Brien's journal, 28 August 1824.
43. BL, Add. MS 51360, Susan O'Brien's journal, 18 June 1816, 3 June 1822, 1 June 1824.
44. BL, Add. MS 51360, Susan O'Brien's journal, 17 October 1818.
45. BL, Add. MS 51359, Susan O'Brien's journal, 6 January 1811.

46. Joanna Martin, *The Penrice Letters* (Cardiff, 1993), p. 109, Mary Strangways to Harriot Strangways, 5 January 1792. The 'pupils' were Adèle, the legitimate daughter of the Duke of Orléans; Pamela, whom contemporaries believed to be the Duke's illegitimate daughter by Madame de Genlis; and the latter's niece Henriette de Sercey.
47. PP, Mary Talbot's pocket-book, 26 August 1803; Martin, *A Governess in the Age of Jane Austen*, p. 231, Agnes Porter's journal, 26 August 1803.
48. BL, Add. MS 51359, Susan O'Brien's journal, 28 February 1808; PP, Mary Talbot's pocket-book, 29 February 1808.
49. BL, Add. MS 51360, Susan O'Brien's journal, 7 July 1814.
50. BL, Add. MS 51360, Susan O'Brien's journal, 19 July and 15 August 1821.
51. Sherborne Castle MSS, game book, 8 November 1763. Isabella Feilding was the sister of the new Lady Digby.
52. BL, Add. MS 51359, Susan O'Brien's journal, 30 May 1813.
53. Georgina Blakiston, *Lord William Russell and his Wife, 1815–1846* (London, 1972), p. 123, letter of Lady William Russell to old Lord William Russell, 6 October [1824]. See further below, p. 115, for the Russells. The boulevards referred to here are the tree-lined Walks, planted in the eighteenth century, which follow the line of the old town walls.
54. BL, Add. MS 51359, Susan O'Brien's journal, 28–30 July 1803.
55. BL, Add. MS 51359, Susan O'Brien's journal, 19 June 1804.
56. BL, Add. MS 51359, Susan O'Brien's journal, 19 June 1804; PP, Susan O'Brien to Mary Talbot, 30 May [1812].
57. BL, Add. MS 51359, Susan O'Brien's journal, 25 October 1809.
58. BL, Add. MS 51359, Susan O'Brien's journal, 29 October 1803.
59. PP, Louisa Strangways to Mary Talbot [September 1805].
60. BL, Add. MS 51360, Susan O'Brien's journal, 4 August 1819.
61. Martin, *A Governess in the Age of Jane Austen*, p. 230, Agnes Porter's journal, 14 August 1803.
62. PP, Thomas Mansel Talbot's pocket-book, 1804.
63. Sixth Earl of Ilchester, *Henry Fox, First Lord Holland, His Family and Relations*, i (London, 1920), p. 47; and Suffolk RO, Bury St Edmunds, Ickworth MSS, 941/47/4, fol. 174, Lord Hervey to Stephen Fox, 11 September 1731.
64. Ilchester, *Henry Fox*, i, p. 52.
65. PP, Charlotte Traherne, 'Family Recollections'.
66. Sherborne Castle MSS, game book, 7 September 1764.
67. Fox Talbot Museum, Lacock, Susan O'Brien to Elizabeth Feilding, 29 October 1817.
68. DRO, D/FSI, box 217, household accounts (Melbury), 1760–70.
69. DRO, D/FSI, box 218, private disbursements (Redlynch), 1732–64.
70. DRO, D/FSI, box 218, household accounts (Redlynch), 1781–87.
71. PP, Thomas Mansel Talbot to Michael Hicks Beach, 6 December 1794; Jane King to Mary Talbot [January 1795]; Fanny Collins to Mary Talbot [January 1799].

72. BL, Add. MS 51359, Susan O'Brien's journal, Christmas 1809.
73. Or their fathers: *Under the Greenwood Tree* was first published in 1872, but was set 'within living memory'.
74. BL, Add. MS 51359, Susan O'Brien's journal, 25 December 1810; Add. MS 51360, Susan O'Brien's journal, 25 December 1819.
75. PP, Jane Talbot to Charlotte Talbot, 11 January 1813; Mary Theresa Talbot to Charlotte Talbot, 18 January 1813.
76. PP, C. R. M. Talbot to Charlotte Talbot, 9 January 1815. The cake usually had beans or coins in it. Whoever found them would become king and queen.
77. Sara Paston-Williams, *The Art of Dining* (London, 1993), p. 243.
78. BL, Add. MS 51414, fol. 2, Caroline Lennox to Henry Fox [29 April 1744].
79. Martin, *A Governess in the Age of Jane Austen*, p. 85, Agnes Porter's journal, 27 August 1790.
80. Sherborne Castle MSS, game books, 24 December 1763, 14 September 1764 and 3 December 1772.
81. PP, Thomas Mansel Talbot's pocket-book, 11 March and 25 April 1806.
82. Martin, *A Governess in the Age of Jane Austen*, pp. 208–9, Agnes Porter's journal, 23–24 May 1802; Fox Talbot Museum, Lacock, W. H. F. Talbot to Elizabeth Feilding, 25 August 1815.
83. PP, Mary Theresa Talbot to Charlotte Talbot [January 1813].
84. See below, pp. 218–25, for further information on governesses.
85. Mark Girouard, *Life in the English Country House* (London, 1978), p. 286.
86. DRO, D/FSI, box 186, Melbury inventory, 1727; Redlynch inventory, 1793.
87. DRO, D/FSI, box 186, Melbury inventory, 1727.
88. Suffolk RO, Bury St Edmunds, Ickworth MSS, 941/47/4, fols 122–24, Lord Hervey to Stephen Fox, 26 August 1730; fols 296–98, Lord Hervey to Stephen Fox, 18 November 1731.
89. BL, Add. MS 51419, fols 45–46, Lord Ilchester to Henry Fox, 8 November [1748].
90. DRO, D/FSI, box 186, Melbury and Stinsford inventories 1727.
91. PP, miscellaneous accounts.
92. Martin, *The Penrice Letters*, pp. 144–45, Mary Talbot to Harriot Strangways [March-April 1794].
93. Fox Talbot Museum, Lacock, Susan O'Brien to Elizabeth Feilding, 24 January 1811.
94. PP, C. R. M. Talbot to Mary Cole, 25 January 1836.
95. BL, Add. MS 51359, Susan O'Brien's journal, 20 October 1812.
96. BL, Add. MS 51419, fols 120–21, Lord Ilchester to Henry Fox, 31 August 1750.
97. BL, Add. MS 51359, Susan O'Brien's journal, 1789.
98. Sherborne Castle MSS, game book, 30 November 1770.
99. BL, Add. MS 51360, Susan O'Brien's journal, 9 November 1824.
100. Blakiston, *Lord William Russell and his Wife*, p. 130. Major-General George William Russell (1790–1846), the second son of the sixth Duke of Bedford, was the commander of the Eighth Hussars, who were stationed in Dorchester

at this time. The Russells took lodgings in Weymouth to begin with, then moved to Dorchester in November.

101. Sherborne Castle MSS, game book, 28 August 1755.
102. Fox Talbot Museum, Lacock, Elizabeth Talbot to Harriot Strangways), 1 May [1798].
103. Martin, *A Governess in the Age of Jane Austen*, p. 209, Agnes Porter's journal, 28 May 1802.
104. Martin, *A Governess in the Age of Jane Austen*, p. 240, Agnes Porter's journal, 25 June 1804.
105. DRO, D/FSI, box 232, George Donisthorpe to Lord Ilchester, 19 March 1760.
106. Harriot Georgiana Mundy (ed.), *The Journal of Mary Frampton* (London, 1885), p. 5.
107. DRO, D/FSI, box 186, Melbury and Stinsford inventories, 1727.
108. DRO, D/FSI, box 186, Redlynch inventory, 1793.
109. Suffolk RO, Bury St Edmunds, Ickworth MSS, 941/47/4, fols 242–43, Lord Hervey to Stephen Fox, 14 October 1731; BL, Add. MS 51419, fols 45–46, Lord Ilchester to Henry Fox, 8 November [1748].
110. PP, Mary Talbot's pocket-book, 20 October 1801.
111. BL, Add. MS 51360, Susan O'Brien's journal, 25 August 1825.
112. Martin, *A Governess in the Age of Jane Austen*, p. 126, Agnes Porter's journal, 20 November 1791.
113. Martin, *A Governess in the Age of Jane Austen*, p. 211, Agnes Porter's journal, 14 June 1802.
114. Sherborne Castle MSS, game book, 31 December 1770.
115. PP, Mary Talbot's pocket-book, 22 April 1802.
116. Martin, *A Governess in the Age of Jane Austen*, p. 238, Agnes Porter's journal, 24 March 1804; Fox Talbot Museum, Lacock, W. H. F. Talbot to Elizabeth Feilding, 25 August 1815; BL, Add. MS 513460, Susan O'Brien's journal, 22 October 1817.
117. Martin, *A Governess in the Age of Jane Austen*, pp. 208–9, Agnes Porter's journal, 23 May 1802.
118. Martin, *A Governess in the Age of Jane Austen*, p. 123, Agnes Porter's journal, 30 July 1791; PP, Harriot Strangways to Mary Strangways, 18 March [1793].
119. Martin, *A Governess in the Age of Jane Austen*, p. 242, Agnes Porter's journal, 14 August 1804.
120. Martin, *A Governess in the Age of Jane Austen*, p. 83, Agnes Porter's journal, 14 and 15 August 1790.
121. BL, Add. MS 51360, Susan O'Brien's journal, 26 September 1823.

Notes to Chapter 7: Servants

1. PRO, PROB 11/13/7, will of Alionor Strangways of Stinsford, Dorset, 1501.
2. Mark Girouard, *Life in the English Country House* (New Haven and London, 1978), p. 208; J. Jean Hecht, *The Domestic Servant in Eighteenth-Century England* (London, Boston and Henley, 1980), p. 6.

3. Norman Scarfe (ed.), *A Frenchman's Year in Suffolk, 1784*, Suffolk Records Society, 30 (Woodbridge, 1988), p. 19.
4. At Sherborne Lord Digby had twenty-four servants in 1770: fifteen men and nine women. Sherborne Castle MSS, household accounts, 1764–82.
5. J. T. Cliffe, *The World of the Country House in Seventeenth-Century England* (New Haven and London, 1999), p. 84.
6. DRO, D/FSI, box 232, list of Melbury servants, 1715.
7. PRO, PROB 11/566/225, will of Susanna Strangways of Milton, Somerset, 1718.
8. DRO, D/FSI, box 187, household accounts (Melbury), 1726–28.
9. DRO, D/FSI, box 232, George Donisthorpe to Susanna Strangways Horner, 3 December 1739.
10. From a note written by Thomas Hardy in the margin of p. 680 of his copy of the second volume of John Hutchins's *History of Dorset.* See above, p. xv, for details.
11. DRO, D/FSI, box 186, Melbury inventory, 1727; box 166B, Stinsford inventory, 17 May 1737.
12. PRO, PROB 11/903/429, will of Edward Hiett of Redlynch, Somerset, 1764.
13. DRO, D/FSI, box 188, household accounts (Chiswick and Whitehall), 1713–15.
14. DRO, D/FSI, box 188, household accounts (Melbury), 1728–29. A 'leash' was a term for three pheasants, hares etc.
15. DRO, D/FSI, box 189, general day book (Redlynch), 1735–54.
16. BL, Add. MS 51417, fols 133–34, Lord Ilchester to Henry Fox, July 1745.
17. DRO, D/FSI, box 240B, bundle 1, directions for upper servant (Redlynch), undated.
18. PRO, PROB 11/903/429, will of Edward Hiett of Redlynch, Somerset, 1764.
19. PRO, PROB 11/1003/434, will of Mary Fenn of Redlynch, Somerset, 1774.
20. DRO, D/FSI, box 186, Redlynch inventory, 1793.
21. DRO, D/FSI, box 218, household accounts (Redlynch), 1781–87.
22. BL, Add. MS 51358, fol. 24, Mr O'Brien's terms to Parkinson, 26 April 1797.
23. I have been unable to discover if this Jourdan (who was born *c.* 1761) was the same man as the Jourdan who was butler at Penrice until he was dismissed in 1800 (see below, pp. 150–51). The information on his age and place of birth is taken from his gravestone at Stinsford.
24. She may be Hannah Butt, who started work at Redlynch in 1755, and was described as 'Lady Susan's maid' in 1762; DRO, D/FSI, box 189, ledger (Redlynch), 1754–64.
25. BL, Add. MS 51360, Susan O'Brien's journal, 21–25 October 1822.
26. DRO, D/FSI, box 166B, Mells inventory, 1741.
27. DRO, D/FSI, box 189, general day book (Redlynch), 1735–54.
28. DRO, D/FSI, box 247, legal papers concerning John Ayliffe. The duties of Ellis Dawe senior seem to have included house-painting, at Melbury and Redlynch, and elsewhere.
29. DRO, D/FSI, box 217; BL, Add. MS 51357, fols 34–35, Mary Fenn to Susan O'Brien, 9 July 1766.
30. PP, Louisa Petty to Mary Talbot, 25 January 1809.

31. BL, Add. MS 51417, fols 125–26, Henry Fox to Susanna Strangways Horner, 14 November 1744.
32. DRO, D/FSI, box 189, general day book (Redlynch), 1735–54.
33. This John Debrett, who died in London a few months after leaving Melbury, was the father of John Debrett, bookseller, who was the founder of *Debrett's Peerage*: Frances-Jane French, 'The Debrett Family: Ancestors and Descendants of John Debrett', *Debrett's Peerage and Baronetage, 1995*, pp. 17–21. I am indebted to Susan Morris of Debrett's Ancestry Research for this reference.
34. PP, Thomas Mansel Talbot to Michael Hicks Beach, 7 February 1796.
35. PP, Thomas Mansel Talbot to Michael Hicks Beach, 6 October 1796.
36. If she is the cook who arrived in 1806 (in which case she had actually been at Penrice for twenty-six years), she probably married a Gower man, for Ace is a local name. I am indebted to Joy Cooke for transcripts of the gravestones at Penrice.
37. Amanda Vickery, *The Gentleman's Daughter* (New Haven and London, 1998), passim.
38. PP, MS account of 'The Four Countesses of Ilchester', by Susan O'Brien, 1817.
39. DRO, D/FSI, box 329, Susan O'Brien's advice to a niece, 1796.
40. DRO, D/FSI, box 217, servants' wages (Melbury), 1748–52.
41. Sherborne Castle MSS, household accounts, 1764–82; DRO, D/FSI, box 217, servants' wages (Redlynch), 1764.
42. BL, Add. MS 51337, fol. 43, Lady Ilchester to Lord Ilchester, *c.* 19 July [1750].
43. DRO, D/FSI, boxes 187, 188, 232, household accounts (Melbury).
44. DRO, D/FSI, boxes 188 and 217, household accounts (Melbury and Abbotsbury).
45. PP, Louisa Lansdowne to Mary Cole, 27 December 1815.
46. PP, Sir Christopher Cole to Mary Cole, 22 May 1817.
47. DRO, D/FSI, box 186, Redlynch inventory, 1793.
48. DRO, D/FSI, box 189, general day book (Redlynch), 1735–54.
49. DRO, D/FSI, box 232, account of servant's mourning (Melbury and Abbotsbury), 1758.
50. These rates seem to have been marginally more generous than was usual in rural areas in southern England. See Pamela Horn, 'Georgian Domestic Servants and Poor Law Settlement', *Genealogists' Magazine*, vol. 27, no. 9 (March 2003), pp. 399–405.
51. The information on wages in this section is taken from DRO, D/FSI, boxes 188, 217, 218, household accounts (Melbury and Redlynch).
52. Monument to Samuel Guy in church of Melbury Sampford.
53. DRO, D/FSI, box 166B, Stinsford inventory, 17 May 1737.
54. BL, Add. MS 51360, Susan O'Brien's journal, 7 June 1814.
55. DRO, D/FSI, box 240B, bundle 1, directions for upper servant (Redlynch), undated.
56. PRO, PROB 11/1384/908, will of Henry Thomas Fox Strangways, Earl of Ilchester, 1802.

57. DRO, D/FSI, box 186, Milton Clevedon inventory, 1729.
58. DRO, D/FSI, box 186, 'inventory of Mrs Horner's house in Albemarle Street', 1741.
59. BL, Add. MS 51337, fol. 43, Lady Ilchester to Lord Ilchester [*c.* 19 July 1750].
60. BL, Add. MS 51337, fol. 116, Lady Ilchester to Lord Ilchester, 18 January [1759].
61. BL, Add. MS 51337, fol. 116, Lady Ilchester to Lord Ilchester, 18 January [1759].
62. BL, Add. MS 51428, fols 1–2, Ann Fannen to Henry Fox, 4 February 1748.
63. BL, Add. MS 51414, fols 83–84, Caroline Fox to Henry Fox [2 February 1748].
64. BL, Add. MS 51414, fols 90–91, Henry Fox to Caroline Fox, 5 February 1748.
65. BL, Add. MS 51414, fols 88–89, Caroline Fox to Henry Fox, 4 February [1748].
66. Quoted (without reference) by Stella Tillyard in *Aristocrats* (London, 1994), pp. 222–23. Tillyard does not appear to have realised that Milward and Mrs Fannen were one and the same person.
67. DRO, D/FSI, box 217, servants' wages (Melbury), 1771–92.
68. PRO, PROB 11/1384/908, will of Henry Thomas Fox Strangways, Earl of Ilchester, 1802.
69. DRO, D/FSI, box 240B, bundle 8. Two years later her salary was £9 a year, and by 1748 she was paid £14: D/FSI, box 189, general day book (Redlynch), 1735–54.
70. DRO, D/FSI, box 218, general household accounts (Redlynch), 1730–43.
71. BL, Add. MS 51337, fol. 97, Lady Ilchester to Lord Ilchester, 22 February [*c.* 1748–49]. Molly's aunt Ann Fenn also appears to have lived at Redlynch in the 1740s. She died there in 1748, and was buried at Bruton, where she is named as 'Mrs Fenn the elder' in the parish register. References to 'Mrs Fenn' in the household records are ambiguous and it is difficult to work out exactly what duties either woman performed.
72. PRO, PROB 11/1003/434, will of Mary Fenn of Redlynch, Bruton, 1774.
73. DRO, D/FSI, box 240B, bundle 5, Lady Ilchester to Lord Stavordale, 11 November [1774] and Lady Ilchester to Lady Stavordale, 21 November [1774].
74. BL, Add. MSS 51359 and 51360, Susan O'Brien's journal, 25 September 1803 and 1 April 1817.
75. BL, Add. MS 51337, fol. 27, Lady Ilchester to Lord Ilchester, 29 December [1747]. A 'bean' was a young man, a *beau.*
76. BL, Add. MS 51337, fol. 29, Lady Ilchester to Lord Ilchester [*c.* 8 January 1748].
77. BL, Add. MS 51419, fols 29–31, Lord Ilchester to Henry Fox, 17 October [1748].
78. BL, Add. MS 51419, fols 37–38, Lord Ilchester to Henry Fox, 27–28 October 1748.
79. BL, Add. MS 51419, fols 79–80, Henry Fox to Lord Ilchester, 19 August 1749.
80. BL, Add. MS 51419, fols 79–80, Lord Ilchester to Henry Fox [23 August 1749].
81. BL, Add. MS 51414, fol. 168, Caroline Fox to Henry Fox [*c.* 10 September 1749].
82. BL, Add. MS 51414, fols 171–74, Caroline Fox to Henry Fox [14 September 1749].
83. BL, Add. MS 51337, fol. 71, Lady Ilchester to Lord Ilchester, 3 January 1755.
84. BL, Add. MS 51354, fols 72–76, Sarah Lennox to Susan O'Brien [*c.* September 1778].

85. Somewhat bizarrely, a lesbian relationship with a woman (unrelated to the Foxes) is also hinted at. See Roy Winstanley, 'Some Letters of Joanna Cheeke (Mrs Melliar)', *Parson Woodforde Society*, 30, no. 4 (Winter, 1997), pp. 14–33; Derek Matthews, 'The Relationship between Joanna Cheeke (Melliar) and the Ilchester and Holland Families', *ibid.*, 32, no. 2 (Summer, 1999), pp. 18–31; Derek Matthews, 'Joanna Cheeke and the Quest for 'The Foxhunter', *ibid.*, 33, no. 2 (Summer, 2000), pp. 11–22.
86. BL, Add. MS 51415, fols 232–33, Henry Fox to Caroline Fox, 16 February 1756.
87. BL, Add. MS 51415, fol. 239, Henry Fox to Caroline Fox [25 February 1756].
88. Roy Winstanley, 'Notes towards a Social History of Castle Cary in the Eighteenth Century', *Parson Woodforde Society Quarterly*, 9, no. 3 (Winter, 1976), p. 27.
89. Sherborne Castle MSS, Fox correspondence, Lord Ilchester to Lord Digby [*c.* 1755].
90. PRO, C38/943, Chancery Master's reports and exhibits, Hilary Term 1805.
91. M. and R. L. Edgeworth, *Practical Education*, i (London, 1798), pp. 121–32.
92. PP, Mary Talbot to Henrietta Maria Hicks Beach, 24 June [1806].
93. Joanna Martin, *A Governess in the Age of Jane Austen* (London and Rio Grande, Ohio), p. 99, Agnes Porter's journal, 2 January 1791.
94. PP, C. R. M. Talbot, 'Characters of Some Members of His Family'.
95. Martin, *A Governess in the Age of Jane Austen*, p. 204, Agnes Porter to Mary Talbot, 23 November [1800].
96. PP, Charlotte Talbot's account of a journey from Bath to London, February 1815.
97. I am indebted to Joy Cooke for a transcript of the inscription.
98. PP, Mary Theresa Talbot to C. R. M. Talbot [17 March 1813].
99. PP, Jennet Ace to Charlotte Talbot, 13 July [1814] and 8 May 1815.
100. BL, Add. MS 51354, fols 35–39, Sarah Lennox to Susan O'Brien, 14 September 1776.
101. PP, MS account of 'The Four Countesses of Ilchester', by Susan O'Brien, 1817.
102. Fox Talbot Museum, Lacock, Susan O'Brien to Elizabeth Talbot [4 April 1797].
103. BL, Add. MS 51359, Susan O'Brien's journal, 28 January 1797.
104. BL, Add. MS 51360, Susan O'Brien's journal, 23 September 1826.
105. DRO, D/FSI, box 232, account of servants' mourning (Melbury and Abbotsbury), 1758.
106. Scarfe (ed.), *A Frenchman's Year in Suffolk*, p. 19.
107. Edward Moore (ed.), *The World, by Adam Fitz-Adam*, 157 (1 January 1756), p. 15.
108. DRO, D/FSI, box 188, household accounts (Melbury), 1746–49.
109. DRO, D/FSI, box 217, board wages (Melbury), 1777–92; box 228, household accounts (Redlynch), 1781–87.
110. Hecht, *The Domestic Servant*, pp. 154–55.
111. DRO, D/FSI, boxes 173A, 186, household accounts (Melbury and Redlynch).
112. This is the more usual spelling.
113. DRO, D/FSI, box 218, general household accounts (Redlynch), 1730–43.

114. DRO, D/FSI, box 218, private disbursements, 1732–64. Mrs Hiett died in 1752.
115. BL, Add. MS 51360, Susan O'Brien's journal, May 1817.
116. DRO, D/FSI, box 240A, bundle 5, household accounts (Melbury), 1747–51.
117. DRO, D/FSI, box 173A, household accounts (Redlynch), accounts of Thomas Clarke, apothecary. See below, pp. 208–9, for details of some items from these accounts. Sherborne Castle MSS, household accounts, 1764–82.
118. E. S. Turner, *What the Butler Saw: Two Hundred and Fifty Years of the Servant Problem* (first published 1962; reprint London, 2001), p. 28.
119. DRO, D/FSI, boxes 217 and 218, household accounts (Melbury and Redlynch).
120. DRO, D/FSI, box 232, George Donisthorpe to Susanna Strangways Horner, 24 September 1742.
121. See above, p. 129.
122. DRO, D/FSI, box 217, money advanced to servants, 1789–96.
123. PP, Mary Talbot's pocket-book, January 1801.
124. DRO, D/FSI, box 218, household accounts (Redlynch), 1747–52 and 1781–87; box 217, household accounts (Melbury), 1760–70; Gloucester Record Office, Hicks Beach (St Aldwyn) papers, D2440, box 53, accounts of Thomas Mansel Talbot's executors.
125. Elizabeth, widow of Edward Richard Montagu, Viscount Hinchingbrooke, married Francis Seymour of Sherborne in July 1728.
126. Clifton Maybank near Yeovil, the seat of Michael Harvey (1694–1748), who was one of the Duchess's trustees and executors.
127. DRO, D/FSI, box 188, household accounts (Melbury), 1728–29.
128. PP, Thomas Mansel Talbot to Michael Hicks Beach, 19 January 1794.
129. PP, Harriot Strangways to Mary Strangways, 19 January 1794.
130. Presumably the proprietor of Reddish's Hotel, where Hicks Beach often stayed when he was in London.
131. PP, Thomas Mansel Talbot to Michael Hicks Beach, 6 October 1796.
132. PP, Mary Talbot to Henrietta Maria Hicks Beach [October to November 1803].
133. Brett Harrison, 'The Servants of William Gossip', *Georgian Group Journal*, 6 (1996), pp. 141–42.
134. As Amanda Vickery has written, 'To say that female servants constituted a supremely unreliable workforce is to offer a fatuous understatement': Vickery, *The Gentleman's Daughter*, p. 135.
135. BL, Add. MS 51353, fols 90–91, Susan O'Brien to Lord Holland, 1 September [1764].
136. BL, Add. MS 51352, fols 101–3, Lord Holland to Susan O'Brien, 8 March [1765].
137. PP, Thomas Mansel Talbot to Michael Hicks Beach, 16 February 1800.
138. PP, Thomas Mansel Talbot to Michael Hicks Beach, 7 February 1796.
139. PP, Sir Christopher Cole to Mary Cole, 22 May 1817.
140. Eliza Haywood, *A New Present for a Servant Maid* (London, 1771), p. 15. This is a revised version of *A Present for a Servant Maid*, published in 1743.
141. PP, Mary Talbot's pocket-book, 1798.
142. Several editions of this book were published in the seventeenth and eighteenth

centuries. See Martin, *A Governess in the Age of Jane Austen*, p. 89, Agnes Porter's journal, 10 October 1790.

143. John Brewer, *The Pleasures of the Imagination* (London, 1997), pp. 167–68.
144. DRO, D/FSI, box 217, Mrs Strangways Horner's receipt book for servants' wages, 1754–78.
145. See below, p. 343, for further details of this school.

Notes to Chapter 8: Household Management

1. DRO, D/FSI, box 217, Melbury housekeeping book, 1748–50.
2. Most information in this chapter is taken from the Redlynch household accounts, DRO, D/FSI, boxes 173A and 173B; and the Melbury household accounts, DRO, D/FSI, boxes 187, 188, 193 and 217.
3. Hotspur, a type of early pea.
4. DRO, D/FSI, box 173A, accounts (Redlynch), 1750–51; box 189, general day book (Redlynch), 1735–54; box 173B, accounts (Redlynch) 1756.
5. DRO, F/FSI, box 189, ledger (Redlynch), 1754–64.
6. There are regular payments at this time for loads of tanners' bark for the pine-apples in DRO, D/FSI, box 188, household accounts (Melbury), 1747–51. Tan was being used in the hothouses at Sherborne Castle in 1764: Sherborne Castle MSS, household accounts, 1764–82. The bark provided heat by fermenting.
7. DRO, D/FSI, box 217, household accounts (Melbury), 1760–70.
8. Sherborne Castle MSS, game book, 11 October 1772; BL, Add. MS 51360, Susan O'Brien's journal, 15–16 August 1826.
9. DRO, D/FSI, box 193, estate accounts (Melbury), 1749–53; box 188, household accounts (Melbury), 1747–51. 'Sparked' was a West Country dialect word for dappled or parti-coloured.
10. DRO, D/FSI, box 189, general day book (Redlynch), 1735–54.
11. DRO, D/FSI, box 189, ledger (Redlynch), 1754–64. 'Alderney' was a general term for cattle from the Channel Islands at this time.
12. John Dixon Hunt (ed.), 'Horace Walpole's Journals of Visits to Country Seats', in *The History of the Modern Taste in Gardening* (New York and London, 1982), p. 44.
13. A painting of these cows is reproduced in Stephen J. G. Hall and Juliet Clutton-Brock, *Two Hundred Years of British Farm Livestock* (London, 1995), p. 72.
14. BL, Add. MS 51373A, fols 96–103, Redlynch sale catalogue, 1801.
15. DRO, D/FSI, box 188, household accounts (Melbury), 1747–51.
16. DRO, D/FSI, box 217, household accounts (Melbury), 1760–70. Gurgeons were coarse meal.
17. DRO, D/FSI, box 189, ledger (Redlynch), 1754–64.
18. DRO, D/FSI, box 217, household accounts (Melbury), 1760–70.
19. DRO, D/FSI, box 207, estate accounts (Redlynch), 1740–45.
20. Sherborne Castle MSS, game book, 11 November 1766.

21. DRO, D/FSI, box 217, Melbury housekeeping book, 1748–50.
22. Turbot, a large flat fish, was highly prized.
23. Such as Elizabeth Shackleton of Barrowford in Lancashire. See Amanda Vickery, *The Gentleman's Daughter* (New Haven and London, 1998), p. 153.
24. DRO, D/FSI box 166B, Mells inventory, 1741.
25. DRO, D/FSI, box 188, household accounts (Melbury), 1747–51.
26. DRO, D/FSI box 189, general day book (Redlynch), 1735–54.
27. West Glamorgan Archive Service (Swansea), D /DP 882, miscellaneous accounts, 1792.
28. DRO, D/FSI, box 189, ledger (Redlynch), 1743–64.
29. Purchases in the late 1740s included saltpetre, which was used for preserving meat.
30. DRO, D/FSI, box 188, household accounts (Melbury), 1747–51. Baskets of fine salt were also bought, for use in the dairy and the parlour.
31. See Rob David, 'Ice-Getting on the Country House Estate', in Pamela A. Sambrook and Peter Brears (ed.), *The Country House Kitchen* (Stroud, 1996), pp. 216–17, for the use of salt in ice houses.
32. PP, Thomas Mansel Talbot's pocket-book, November and December 1807.
33. In the latter part of the eighteenth century the male household servants of James and Susanna Whatman of Turkey Court, Kent, were allowed a pint of ale a day, whilst the women were allowed half a pint. In addition, they were allowed small beer 'as much as they chuse'. Christina Hardyment (ed.), *The Housekeeping Book of Susanna Whatman, 1776–1800* (London, 2000), p. 57.
34. DRO, D/FSI, box 217, housekeeping book (Melbury), 1748–50.
35. Christina Hardyment, *Home Comfort: A History of Domestic Arrangements* (London, 1992), p. 87.
36. DRO, D/FSI box 189, general day book (Redlynch), 1735–54. A buck was a tub used for brewing or washing.
37. DRO, D/FSI, box 217, household accounts (Melbury), 1760–70. A huckmuck was a type of strainer used in brewing.
38. Fox Talbot Museum, Lacock, W. H. F. Talbot to Elizabeth Feilding, 4 September 1808.
39. Florence Emily Hardy, *The Early Life of Thomas Hardy, 1840–1891* (London, 1928), pp. 213–14.
40. DRO, D/FSI, box 217, household accounts (Melbury), 1760–70. John Swetman, who died in 1822 aged 89, was the author Thomas Hardy's great-grandfather.
41. DRO, D/FSI, box 217, Melbury housekeeping book, 1748–50.
42. DRO, D/FSI, box 188, household accounts (Melbury), 1747–51; box 217, household accounts (Melbury), 1760–70.
43. DRO, D/FSI, box 217, household accounts (Melbury), 1760–70.
44. DRO, D/FSI, box 173B, household accounts (Redlynch), 1759–63. For the dairy at Sherborne, which may have been designed by Capability Brown, see Ann Smith and Michael Hall, 'Sherborne Castle, Dorset, I', *Country Life*, 194, no. 32 (10 August 2000), pp. 38–41.

45. DRO, D/FSI, box 188, household accounts (Melbury), 1728–29.
46. DRO, D/FSI, box 188, household accounts (Melbury), 1747–51; box 217, household accounts (Melbury), 1760–70.
47. DRO, D/FSI, box 188, household accounts (Melbury), 1728–29.
48. 'Common tea', bought for the servants at Melbury, cost 4*s.* 8*d.* a pound in 1762 and 3*s.* in 1768.
49. PP, Thomas Mansel Talbot's pocket-books, especially 3 December 1806.
50. A hogshead was a large cask, which held 52½ imperial gallons; a pipe was equivalent to two hogsheads.
51. DRO, D/FSI, box 173A, accounts (Redlynch), 1750–51. A quart is two pints, so each bottle held approximately one litre.
52. Bucellas came from Portugal.
53. DRO, D/FSI box 188, household accounts (Melbury), 1747–51.
54. DRO, D/FSI, box 189, ledger (Redlynch), 1743–64. Silesia holland was a fine quality linen cloth.
55. DRO, D/FSI, box 217, household accounts (Melbury), 1760–70.
56. Blue powders were used to brighten white fabrics. The powder was added to the water used for rinsing.
57. DRO, D/FSI, box 217, household accounts (Melbury), 1760–70.
58. DRO, D/FSI, box 188, household accounts (Melbury), 1728–29. Drums, or thrums, were short pieces of yarn.
59. A pope's head was a round brush with a long handle, used for sweeping ceilings etc.
60. DRO, D/FSI, box 189, ledger (Redlynch), 1743–64.
61. Rush lights cost 5½*d.* a pound in 1752; DRO, D/FSI, box 218, household accounts (Redlynch), 1747–52.
62. Fire-dogs raised the logs above the floor, thus improving the draught.
63. The 1737 inventory of Stinsford refers to coal-grates instead of stove-grates; DRO, D/FSI, box 166B.
64. DRO, D/FSI, box 217, household accounts (Melbury), 1760–70.
65. DRO, D/FSI, box 189, ledger (Redlynch), 1743–64.

Notes to Chapter 9: Health

1. DRO, D/FSI, box 173A, accounts of Thomas Clarke, 1750–52.
2. Cornwall RO, Lemon Family Papers, DDG 1952, memoirs of Loveday Sarah Gregor.
3. Nigel Surry (ed.), *Your Affectionate and Loving Sister: The Correspondence of Barbara Kerrich and Elizabeth Postlethwaite, 1733 to 1751* (Dereham, Norfolk, 2000), pp. 86–92.
4. Eliza Haywood, *A New Present for a Servant Maid* (London, 1771), pp. 234–41.
5. Sherborne Castle MSS, game book, 17 November 1766, 1 September 1769; BL, Add. MS 51359, Susan O'Brien's journal, May 1788, 1 January 1807.
6. PP, Mary Talbot's pocket-books, 6 October 1801, 12 December 1808.

7. BL, Add. MS 51359, Susan O'Brien's journal, 14 November 1808; PP, Alicia Campbell to Mary Talbot [1808]; Charlotte Strangways to Mary Talbot, 16 November, 21 November, 8 December 1808.
8. BL, Add. MS 51418, fols 78–79, Lady Ilchester to Henry Fox, 7 November 1746.
9. Countess of Ilchester and Lord Stavordale, *The Life and Letters of Lady Sarah Bunbury* (London, 1902), p. 30. See also Stella Tillyard, *Aristocrats* (London, 1994), pp. 129–30.
10. See below, p. 314, for further details of accidents on the road.
11. PP, Mary Talbot's pocket-book, 9 November 1805; BL, Add. MS 51359, Susan O'Brien's journal, 9 October 1810; PP, Louisa Lansdowne to Mary Talbot, 31 October 1811.
12. Obituary quoted in Lettice Digby, *My Ancestors: Being the History of the Digby and Strutt Families* (London, 1928), p. 87.
13. GEC, *The Complete Peerage*, vii, p. 47.
14. Joanna Martin, *A Governess in the Age of Jane Austen* (London and Rio Grande, Ohio, 1998), pp. 231–32, Agnes Porter's journal, 15 August to 16 November 1803.
15. PP, Charlotte Traherne, 'Family Recollections'. An eighteenth-century version of a zimmer-frame.
16. Fox Talbot Museum, Lacock, Susan O'Brien to Elizabeth Feilding, 16 May 1811.
17. WSRO, Lacock Abbey MSS, Acc. 2664, box of miscellaneous correspondence (Feilding, Strangways, Talbot), Susan O'Brien to Elizabeth Feilding, 25 October [1811].
18. BL, Add. MS 51419, fols 86–87, Lord Ilchester to Henry Fox, 19 October 1749; DRO, D/FSI, box 240B, bundle 5, Lady Ilchester to Lord Stavordale, 11 November [1774].
19. BL, Add. MS 51359, Susan O'Brien's journal, 1784.
20. PP, Thomas Mansel Talbot to Henrietta Maria Hicks Beach, 7 February 1796.
21. PP, Richard Fowler to Mary Talbot, 10 September 1813.
22. PP, Louisa Lansdowne to Mary Talbot [1811]; Fox Talbot Museum, Lacock, Susan O'Brien to Elizabeth Feilding [March 1815].
23. BL, Add. MS 51359, Susan O'Brien's journal, 15 October 1808.
24. PP, Ann Fowler to Mary Talbot, 28 May 1811.
25. PP, C. R. M. Talbot to Jane Talbot, 25 November 1813.
26. PP, W. H. F. Talbot to Mary Theresa Talbot, 27 July 1805; Mary Cole to Charlotte Talbot, 10 February [1818].
27. BL, Add. MS 51422, fols 33–34, Charlotte Digby to Henry Fox, *c.* 1746–47.
28. PP, Countess of Ilchester to Mary Talbot [1810].
29. PP, C.R.M. Talbot's 'Memoranda from 1803'.
30. DRO, D/FSI, box 240A, bundle 4, Henry Fox to Lord Ilchester [1746].
31. BL, Add. MS 51419, fols 17–18, Lord Ilchester to Henry Fox, 2 July 1748.
32. BL, Add. MS 51422, fols 59–60, Charlotte Digby to Henry Fox, 13 July 1748.
33. PP, Mary Talbot to Henrietta Maria Hicks Beach, 3 September [1804].
34. Martin, *A Governess in the Age of Jane Austen*, pp. 245–46, Agnes Porter's journal, 16 November to 13 December 1804.

35. BL, Add. MS 51414, fols 92–93, Caroline Fox to Henry Fox [6 February 1748].
36. PP, Mary Cole to Frances St George, 10 June 1836, quoted in Charlotte Traherne, 'Family Recollections'.
37. Fox Talbot Museum, Lacock, Susan O'Brien to Elizabeth Feilding, 15 February 1815.
38. PP, C. R. M. Talbot to Mary Cole, 19 and 20 July 1816.
39. Thomas Dormandy, *The White Death: A History of Tuberculosis* (London and Rio Grande, Ohio, 1999), p. 73.
40. PP, Mary Talbot's pocket-book, 27 December 1807.
41. This belief persisted in northern Europe for much of the nineteenth century. In southern Europe the contagious nature of the disease was better understood. See Dormandy, *The White Death*, pp. 52–54.
42. PP, Mary Talbot's pocket-book, 23 May and 20 December 1808.
43. BL, Add. MS 51359, Susan O'Brien's journal, 23 February 1809.
44. BL, Add. MS 51359, Susan O'Brien's journal, 19 April 1809.
45. PP, Mary Talbot to Harriot Frampton [1809].
46. Cinchona (or Peruvian) bark was the source of quinine.
47. PP, Richard Fowler to Mary Talbot, 25 July 1809.
48. PP, Thomas Mansel Talbot's pocket-book, 16 January 1810.
49. PP, Louisa Petty to Mary Talbot, 19 August 1809.
50. PP, Mrs Burgh to Mary Cole, 9 August 1832.
51. One daughter, Christiana, died before Ellinor.
52. PP, Charlotte Lemon to Mary Cole, August [1820].
53. Roy Porter, *The Greatest Benefit to Mankind* (London, 1997), pp. 174–75; GEC, *The Complete Peerage*, vi, p. 46.
54. Isobel Grundy, *Lady Mary Wortley Montagu* (Oxford, 1999), p. 162.
55. BL, Add. MS 51414, fols 4–5, Caroline Fox to Henry Fox, 8 December 1746.
56. BL, Add. MS 51418, fols 52–53, Lord Ilchester to Henry Fox, 4 October 1746.
57. BL, Add. MS 51422, fols 48–49, Charlotte Digby to Henry Fox, 2 April 1748.
58. BL, Add. MS 51419, fols 131–32, Lady Ilchester to Henry Fox. The letter is dated 31 December 1751, but other letters referring to Harry's inoculation indicate that it took place in January 1751.
59. Martin, *A Governess in the Age of Jane Austen*, p. 173, Agnes Porter's journal, 29 January 1797.
60. Porter, *The Greatest Benefit to Mankind*, pp. 276–77.
61. BL, Add. MS 51357, fols 107–8, Harriot Frampton to Susan O'Brien, 2 September 1800.
62. PP, Mary Talbot's pocket-book, 15 October 1805. The inoculation in 1803 was carried out by 'Mr Collins'. This could be John Charles Collins or his father Charles Collins.
63. BL, Add. MS 51417, fols 133–34, Lord Ilchester to Henry Fox, July 1745.
64. PP, Sir Christopher Cole to Mary Talbot [7–24 January 1815].
65. Randolph Trumbach, *The Rise of the Egalitarian Family* (New York, 1978), pp. 208–9.

66. BL, Add. MS 51354, fols 186–87, Sarah Napier to Susan O'Brien, 10 May 1785.
67. Fox Talbot Museum, Lacock, Susan O'Brien to Elizabeth Feilding, 3 October 1805.
68. BL, Add. MS 51423, fols 9–10, Edward Digby, Rome, to Henry Fox, 21 January 1750 and passim. See also Lawrence Stone, *The Family, Sex and Marriage in England, 1500–1800* (London, 1977), pp. 415–24.
69. BL, Add. MS 51337, fol. 53, Lady Ilchester to Lord Ilchester, 14 November [?1752].
70. BL, Add. MS 51414, fol. 40, Caroline Fox to Henry Fox, 10 January 1747; fols 47–48, Caroline Fox to Henry Fox, 15 January 1747; fols 49–52, Caroline Fox to Henry Fox [16 January 1747].
71. Trumbach, *The Rise of the Egalitarian Family*, p. 209.
72. Parish registers, the main source of statistics relating to infant mortality, do not in most cases record miscarriages or still-births, so the information given in the Fox Strangways family letters is particularly useful here.
73. BL, Add. MS 51418, fols 108–9, Lord Ilchester to Henry Fox, 13 January 1747; fols 112–13, Henry Fox to Lord Ilchester, 15 January 1747.
74. BL, Add. MS 51349, fols 149–50, Richard Bateman to Lord Ilchester, 12 September [1759].
75. PP, Susan O'Brien to Mary Talbot, 21 November 1814.
76. PP, Charlotte Lemon to Mary Cole, 6 February [*c.* 1820].
77. PP, Louisa Petty to Mary Talbot, 21 November 1808.
78. 'Lying upon a couch [or a sofa]' was a expression that was frequently used when referring to a woman who resting more than usual because she was pregnant.
79. PP, Alicia Campbell to Mary Talbot, 3 December 1808.
80. Dorothy Porter and Roy Porter, *Patients' Progress: Doctors and Doctoring in Eighteenth-Century England* (Cambridge and Oxford, 1989), pp. 174–75.
81. He arrived within three hours. The Aclands were at Combe House, near Honiton, so Mr Patch may have come from Exeter.
82. William Hunter was a well-known surgeon who specialised in obstetrics.
83. BL, Add. MS 51344, fols 90–91, John Dyke Acland to Lord Ilchester [1771]; fols 104–5, Thomas Dyke Acland to Lord Ilchester, 24 November 1771.
84. BL, Add. MS 51418, fols 52–53, Lord Ilchester to Henry Fox, 4 October 1746.
85. BL, Add. MS 51418, fols 84–85, Lord Ilchester to Henry Fox, 22 November 1746.
86. DRO, D/FSI, box 240A, bundle 5, Lady Ilchester to Lord Ilchester, 22 October [1751].
87. PP, Louisa Petty to Mary Talbot, 11 April 1809.
88. BL, Add. MS 51419, fols 48–49, Henry Fox to Lord Ilchester, 14 January 1749. Charles Fox was the third son to be born, but the second to survive, as his eldest brother had died when only a few months old.
89. BL, Add. MS 51344, fols 86–87, John Dyke Acland to Lady Ilchester [1771].
90. PP, Louisa Petty to Mary Talbot, 28 February 1809.
91. BL, Add. MS 51353, fol. 79, Sarah Bunbury to Susan O'Brien, 23 January 1765.

92. BL, Add. MS 51357, fols 32–33, Charlotte Digby to Susan O'Brien, 1 September 1765.
93. BL, Add. MS 51359, Susan O'Brien's journal, 8 January 1819; PP, Susan O'Brien to Mary Cole [January 1819].
94. PP, Mary Talbot to Harriot Strangways, 11 September 1795.
95. BL, Add. MS 51353, fols 74–78, Sarah Bunbury to Susan O'Brien, 16 December 1764.
96. BL, Add. MS 51360, Susan O'Brien's journal, 'Changes between 1760 and 1818'.
97. PP, Thomas Mansel Talbot to Michael Hicks Beach, 10 October 1796. The word *accouchement* was also used at this time.
98. BL, Add. MS 51344, fols 90–91 and 93–94, John Dyke Acland to Lord Ilchester [1771].
99. BL, Add. MS 51337, fol. 13, Lady Ilchester to Lord Ilchester [1742].
100. J. S. Lewis, *In the Family Way: Childbearing in the British Aristocracy, 1760–1860* (New Brunswick, New Jersey, 1986), pp. 200–2.
101. PP, Mary Talbot's pocket-book, 1801.
102. PP, Thomas Mansel Talbot to Henrietta Maria Hicks Beach, 20 May 1803.
103. DRO, D/FSI, box 241B, Countess of Ilchester to Earl of Ilchester [8 June 1803].
104. PP, Thomas Mansel Talbot to Michael Hicks Beach, 16 February 1800.
105. BL, Add. MS 51359, Susan O'Brien's journal, 22 January, 22 February 1808.
106. BL, Add. MS 51419, Lord Ilchester to Henry Fox, 17 October [1748].
107. Fox Talbot Museum, Lacock, Elizabeth Talbot to Harriot Strangways, 14 August 1796. The words in italics are underlined in the original letter.
108. PP, Thomas Mansel Talbot to Michael Hicks Beach, 19 March 1798.
109. PP, Mary Talbot's pocket-book, 1798.
110. PP, Louisa Petty to Mary Talbot, 11 and 30 April 1809.
111. PP, Louisa Petty to Mary Talbot, 20 November 1809.
112. PP, Charlotte Lemon to Mary Talbot, 23 October 1811.
113. PP, Charlotte Lemon to Mary Cole, 25 December 1815.
114. Trumbach, *The Rise of the Egalitarian Family*, pp. 197–208.
115. PRO, PROB 11/1232/265, will of Elizabeth, Countess Dowager of Ilchester, 1793.
116. Trumbach, *The Rise of the Egalitarian Family*, pp. 215–17.
117. DRO, D/FSI, box 240B, bundle 5, Lady Ilchester to Lady Stavordale, 21 November [1774].
118. PP, Mary Talbot to Harriot Strangways, 11 September [1795].
119. PP, Mary Talbot to Harriot Strangways, 7 February [1796].
120. PP, Thomas Mansel Talbot to Mary Talbot [*c.* February 1796].
121. PP, Harriot Strangways to Mary Talbot, 8 August 1797.
122. Fox Talbot Museum, Lacock, Susan O'Brien to Elizabeth Feilding, 24 July [1806].
123. Trumbach, *The Rise of the Egalitarian Family*, p. 227.
124. DRO, D/FSI, box 240A, bundle 5, Charlotte Digby to Lord Ilchester, 7 November 1748.

125. DRO, D/FSI, box 240B, bundle 5, Lady Ilchester to Lady Stavordale [*c.* 1774].
126. PP, Mary Talbot's pocket-book, 23 September, 24 December 1806.
127. Fox Talbot Museum, Lacock, Susan O'Brien to Elizabeth Feilding, 21 February and 8 March 1816.
128. Martin, *A Governess in the Age of Jane Austen*, p. 89, Agnes Porter's journal, 9 October 1790.
129. PP, Countess of Ilchester to Mary Strangways, 5 April [1791].
130. Martin, *A Governess in the Age of Jane Austen*, p. 130, Agnes Porter's journal, 7 January 1792.
131. PP, Mary Talbot to Harriot Strangways, 11 September [1795].
132. See above, p. 172.
133. PP, Thomas Mansel Talbot's pocket-books, 24 January 1804 and, in 1808, note on memorial inscription for Christiana to be erected in Lacock church; Mary Talbot's pocket-books, 4 December 1803, and 8 February, 8–9 March 1808.
134. Martin, *A Governess in the Age of Jane Austen*, p. 288, Agnes Porter to Mary Talbot, 6 October 1809.
135. PP, Charles Lemon to Mary Talbot, 27 November [1812].
136. PP, Charlotte Lemon to Mary Cole, 21 September 1816, 4 April 1819, 4 January [1824].
137. Cornwall Record Office, DDT 2751, J. H. Tremayne to Revd H. H. Tremayne [31 May 1825].
138. Cornwall Record Office, DDT 2759A/1.
139. PP, Mary Cole to Mrs St George, 31 August 1827; quoted in PP, Charlotte Traherne, 'Family Recollections'.
140. Stone, *The Family, Sex and Marriage in England*, pp. 70–71. The pattern in the Fox and Strangways families appears to be similar, though the sample is too small to be statistically significant. Towards the end of the seventeenth century, between 40 and 60 per cent of the children in these families died before they reached their fifteenth birthday. For the children of Thomas and Susanna Horner, born in the early eighteenth century, the mortality rate was 75 per cent. But in the next generation only 15 per cent of Sir Stephen Fox's grandchildren died young. In the subsequent two generations, born in the last three decades of the eighteenth century and the first two of the nineteenth century, the mortality rate of those aged under fifteen was approximately 20 per cent.
141. Trumbach, *The Rise of the Egalitarian Family*, pp. 187–88.
142. Of the fifty ladies studied by J. S. Lewis, the average age at death was nearly sixty-nine, if seven women with 'significant health problems' are excluded: Lewis, *In the Family Way*, p. 149.
143. BL, Add. MS 51337, fol. 53, Lady Ilchester to Lord Ilchester, 14 November [1752].
144. BL, Add. MS 51359, Susan O'Brien's journal, 1791.
145. BL, Add. MS 51359, Susan O'Brien's journal, 1792.
146. BL, Add. MS 51359, Susan O'Brien's journal, 14 February 1810; Add. MS 51360, Susan O'Brien's journal, 20 March 1819.

147. BL, Add. MS 51360, Susan O'Brien's journal, 23 August 1819.
148. BL, Add. MS 51359, Susan O'Brien's journal, 31 July 1815.
149. BL, Add. MS 51359, Susan O'Brien's journal, 20 August 1820.
150. BL, Add. MS 51359, Susan O'Brien's journal, 31 October 1824.
151. BL, Add. MS 51360, Susan O'Brien's journal, 21 June 1825.
152. PP, Susan O'Brien to Mary Cole, 14 February 1826.
153. BL, Add. MS 51359, Susan O'Brien's journal, 1772 and 1774.
154. BL, Add. MS 51359, Susan O'Brien's journal, 1776.
155. BL, Add. MS 51359, Susan O'Brien's journal, 25 January 1806.
156. PP, C. R. M. Talbot, 'Characters of Some Members of His Family'.
157. PP, William O'Brien to Mary Talbot, 15 December 1810.
158. BL, Add. MS 51359, Susan O'Brien's journal, 29 October 1813.
159. DRO, D/FSI, box 240A, bundle 6, Lady Ilchester to Lord Ilchester, 28/29 November [1747–49]; BL, Add. MS 51414, fols 79–80, Caroline Fox to Henry Fox, [31 January 1748].
160. BL, Add. MS 51422, fols 61–62, Charlotte Digby to Henry Fox, 16 July 1748.
161. BL, Add. MS 51419, fol. 210, Henry Fox to Lord Ilchester, 23 June 1753; Add. MS 51428, fols 55–56, Mr Middleton's report on opening the body of Miss Digby, 16 June 1753.
162. BL, Add. MS 51359, Susan O'Brien's journal, July 1800.
163. BL, Add. MS 51359, Susan O'Brien's journal, 15 November 1808.
164. Sherborne Castle MSS, game book, 6 April 1756. Lord Digby died eighteen months after the operation.
165. Sherborne Castle MSS, Fox correspondence, Lord Ilchester to Lord Digby, 20 March 1756.
166. BL, Add. MS 51419, fols 123–24, Lord Ilchester to Henry Fox, 12 October 1750.
167. BL, Add. MS 51359, Susan O'Brien's journal, April 1798 to 17 June 1799.
168. BL, Add. MS 51359, Susan O'Brien's journal, 15 November 1813.
169. BL, Add. MS 51414, fols 81–82, Caroline Fox to Henry Fox, 1 February 1748.
170. PP, Charlotte Traherne, 'Family Recollections'.
171. PP, Thomas Mansel Talbot's pocket-book, 9 March–9 June 1806.
172. Fox Talbot Museum, Lacock, Susan O'Brien to Elizabeth Feilding, 13 April [1807]; PP, Mary Talbot's pocket-book, 14 April to 1 May 1807; PP, Maria Burgh to Mary Talbot, 4 May 1812, 26 July 1812; BL, Add. MS 51359, Susan O'Brien's journal, 21 October 1814.
173. BL, Add. MS 51337, fol. 24, Lady Ilchester to Lord Ilchester, 22 December [1747].
174. BL, Add. MS 51422, fols 166–67, Charlotte Digby to Henry Fox, 29 December 1750.
175. PP, Richard Fowler to Mary Talbot, 17 December 1810.
176. BL, Add. MS 51359, Susan O'Brien's journal, 29 August 1813, 15 November 1813.
177. BL, Add. MS 51346, fols 1–2, Joanna Cheeke to Lord Ilchester [*c.* 1745–47]; fol. 3, Joanna Cheeke to Lord Ilchester, 20 June [1747]; DRO, D/FSI, box 240A, bundle 5, Lady Ilchester to Lord Ilchester, 13 February [1750]; BL, Add. MS

51337, fol. 46, Lady Ilchester to Lord Ilchester, 22 July [1750]; Add. MS 51421, fol. 61, Lady Ilchester to Lord Holland, 14 July [1764].

178. BL, Add. MS 51359, Susan O'Brien's journal, 16 July 1808, 11 February 1811.

179. BL, Add. MS 51359, Susan O'Brien's journal, 23 February 1808; PP, Richard Fowler to Mary Talbot, 17 December 1810.

180. BL, Add. MS 51422, fols 56–58, Charlotte Digby to Henry Fox, 9 July 1748.

181. PP, Mary Talbot to Henrietta Maria Hicks Beach, 27 February [1804].

182. PP, Lady Ilchester to Lord Ilchester [1777].

183. BL, Add. MS 51417, fol. 191, Henry Fox to Lord Ilchester, 26 December 1745.

184. BL, Add. MS 51414, fols 83–84, Caroline Fox to Henry Fox [2 February 1748].

185. PP, Lady Ilchester to Lord Ilchester [1777].

186. BL, Add. MS 51359, Susan O'Brien's journal, 5 November 1813 and 29 August 1815; PP, Charlotte Lemon to Mary Cole, 4 April 1819. Iceland moss is *Cetraria islandica*, a species of edible lichen with medicinal properties.

187. PP, Louisa Lansdowne to Mary Talbot, 17 March 1810; Richard Fowler to Mary Talbot, 30 May 1811; Charlotte Lemon to Mary Cole, 25 July 1822.

188. BL, Add. MS 51414, fols 43–44, Caroline Fox to Henry Fox, 12 January 1747.

189. DRO, D/FSI, box 218, private disbursements (Redlynch), 1732–64; BL, Add. MS 51337, fol. 46, Lady Ilchester to Lord Ilchester, 22 July [1750]; Add. MS 51349, fol. 141, Mary Fenn to Lord Ilchester, 29 May [1756–62]; Add. MS 51359, Susan O'Brien's journal, 2 June 1814.

190. BL, Add. MS 51414, fols 79–80, Caroline Fox to Henry Fox, [31 January 1748].

191. PP, Mary Talbot to Henrietta Maria Hicks Beach [July 1803].

192. PP, Alicia Campbell to Mary Talbot, 22 [November] 1808.

193. Fox Talbot Museum, Lacock, Mary Talbot to W. H. F. Talbot, 19 September 1814.

194. BL, Add. MS 51359, Susan O'Brien's journal, October 1801.

195. BL, Add. MS 51353, fols 118–19, Sarah Bunbury to Susan O'Brien, 7 June [1766].

196. PP, Richard Fowler to Mary Talbot, 24 July 1811.

197. Haywood, *A New Present for a Servant Maid*, pp. 40–41; BL, Add. MS 51414, fols 99–100, Caroline Fox to Henry Fox [9 February 1748].

198. BL, Add. MS 51414, fols 97–98, Henry Fox to Caroline Fox [8 February 1758].

199. PP, Richard Fowler to Mary Talbot, 18 September 1810.

200. PP, Richard Fowler to Mary Talbot, 24 July 1811.

201. BL, Add. MS 51404, fols 35–36, John Wigan to Henry Fox, 30 January 1729.

202. DRO, D/FSI, box 173A and box 173B, accounts (Redlynch).

203. WSRO, Lacock Abbey MSS, Acc. 2664, box of miscellaneous correspondence (Feilding, Strangways, Talbot), Elizabeth Talbot to Harriot Strangways, 22 February 1798.

204. PP, Richard Fowler to Mary Talbot, 24 July 1811.

205. David Gadd, *Georgian Summer: The Rise and Development of Bath* (Newbury, Berkshire, 1987), pp. vii and passim.

206. Lucy Moore, *Amphibious Thing: The Life of Lord Hervey* (London, 2000), p. 37.

207. DRO, D/FSI, box 187, accounts (Melbury), 1726–28.
208. GEC, *The Complete Peerage*, vi, p. 270.
209. BL, Add. MS 51337, fol. 53, Lady Ilchester to Lord Ilchester, 14 November [*c.* 1752].
210. BL, Add. MS 51337, fol. 57, Lady Ilchester to Lord Ilchester, 27 November [1752].
211. BL, Add. MS 51337, fol. 59, Lady Ilchester to Lord Ilchester, 8 December [1752].
212. BL, Add. MS 51337, fol. 61, Lady Ilchester to Lord Ilchester [*c.* 1752].
213. BL, Add. MS 51337, fol. 96, Lady Ilchester to Lord Ilchester [*c.* July 1756].
214. DRO, D/FSI, box 240B, bundle 5, Lady Ilchester to Lady Stavordale [1774–75]; BL, Add. MS 51359, Susan O'Brien's journal, 1779.
215. Harriot Georgiana Mundy (ed.), *The Journal of Mary Frampton* (London, 1885), pp. 103–5, Catherine Gumbleton to Harriot Strangways, 29 January 1799.
216. BL, Add. MS 51359, Susan O'Brien's journal, 28 February 1810.
217. BL, Add. MS 51359, Susan O'Brien's journal, 16 April 1819.
218. BL, Add. MS 51337, fols 188–89, Joanna Cheeke to Susanna Strangways Horner, 25 August [1754].
219. David Selwyn, *Jane Austen and Leisure* (London and Rio Grande, Ohio, 1999), p. 44.
220. PP, John Hunt to Mary Talbot, 20 March [1812].
221. PP, George Eden to Mary Talbot, 28 May 1810.
222. PP, Maria Burgh to Mary Talbot, 26 July 1812.
223. PP, Mary Cole to Sir Christopher Cole, 22 and 27 June 1822. The Sherborne Spa (later renamed the Imperial Spa) was constructed in 1818 on the site of the present Queen's Hotel.
224. Fox Talbot Museum, Lacock, Susan O'Brien to Elizabeth Feilding, 19 July 1812.
225. BL, Add. 51419, fols 17–18, Lord Ilchester to Henry Fox, 2 July 1748.
226. BL, Add. MS 51359, Susan O'Brien's journal, 1789.
227. PP, Harriot Strangways to Mary Strangways, 12 October 1792.
228. Fox Talbot Museum, Lacock, Susan O'Brien to Elizabeth Feilding, 15 February 1815.
229. DRO, D/FSI box 241B, Mary Talbot to Lord Stavordale, 7 April 1802.
230. BL, Add. MS 51359, Susan O'Brien's journal, July to September 1802.
231. See below pp. 323–24, for further details.
232. D/FSI box 189, general day book (Redlynch), 1735–54. The cold bath at Melbury was built 1747–50: DRO, D/FSI, box 188, household accounts (Melbury), 1747–51. The bath at Redlynch was there by 1738, when it is shown on E. Grant's map of Redlynch, BL, King's Top., K38.16.
233. John Hutchins, *The History and Antiquities of the County of Dorset*, 3rd edn by W. Shipp and J. W. Hodson, ii (London, 1861–74), p. 73.
234. PP, Thomas Mansel Talbot to Henrietta Maria Hicks Beach, 10 October 1796.

235. PP, Mary Talbot to Henrietta Maria Hicks Beach, 3 September [1804].
236. Martin, *A Governess in the Age of Jane Austen*, p. 245, Agnes Porter's journal, 17 November 1804.
237. DRO, D/FSI, box 218, private disbursements (Redlynch), 1732–64; box 188, household accounts (Melbury), 1747–51.
238. BL, Add. MS 51359, Susan O'Brien's journal, April 1791.
239. BL, Add. MS 51337, fol. 61, Lady Ilchester to Lord Ilchester [*c.* 1752]; Add MS 51420, fols 99–100, Henry Fox to Lord Ilchester, 24 October 1758; Add. MS 51415, fols 5–6, Caroline Fox to Henry Fox [9 December 1750].
240. BL, Add. MS 51359, Susan O'Brien's journal, 27 and 30 March 1799.
241. Joan Lane, 'The Medical Practitioners of Provincial England in 1783', *Medical History*, 28 (1984), pp. 353–71.
242. DRO, D/FSI, box 187, estate accounts (Melbury), 1725–27.
243. BL, Add. MS 51422, fols 133–34, Charlotte Digby to Henry Fox, 7 June 1750.
244. PP, Charlotte Strangways to Mary Talbot, 14 January 1809.
245. BL, Add. MS 51360, Susan O'Brien's journal, 20 March and 10 November 1823.
246. BL, Add. MS 51360, Susan O'Brien's journal, 5 April 1826.
247. William Munk, *The Roll of the Royal College of Physicians of London*, iii, *1801–25* (London, 1878), p. 68.
248. *Gentleman's Magazine*, new series, 14 (1863), pp. 796–98, obituary of Dr Fowler of Salisbury.
249. PP, Ann Fowler to Mary Talbot, 25 July 1809.
250. PP, Richard Fowler to Mary Talbot, 21 September 1809.
251. *Dictionary of National Biography*, xlvii (London, 1896), pp. 267–68.
252. DRO, D/FSI, box 240A, bundle 5, Lady Ilchester to Lord Ilchester, 13 February 1750.
253. DRO, D/FSI, box 240A, bundle 5, Edward Digby to Lord Ilchester, 19 October [1751]; Sherborne Castle MSS, Fox correspondence, Henry Fox to Lord Digby, 21 July 1753.
254. *The Medical Register for the Year 1779* (London, 1779), p. 18.
255. DRO, D/FSI, box 240A, bundle 5, Joanna Cheeke to Lord Ilchester, 15 October [1751].
256. Stella Tillyard, *Aristocrats* (London, 1994), p. 109.
257. Sherborne Castle MSS, household accounts, 1764–82.
258. BL, Add. MS 51359, Susan O'Brien's journal, 31 May 1799.
259. PP, Charlotte Lemon to Mary Cole, August [*c.* 1820].
260. PRO, C38/943, Chancery Masters' reports and certificates, 27 April 1805.
261. DRO, D/FSI, box 173A, accounts (Redlynch).
262. Probably 'medicated' or 'medicative'.
263. 'Fumigant' or 'fumigatory'.
264. BL, Add. MS 51419, fols 102–3, Lord Ilchester to Henry Fox, 16 June 1750. 'Mr Thomas Clarke, apothecary', was buried at Bruton on 25 May 1762.
265. DRO, D/FSI, box 240B, bundle 5, Lady Ilchester to Lady Stavordale [1774–75]; box 173B, accounts of Somerset estate, 1759–63.

266. BL, Add. MS 51359, Susan O'Brien's journal, 1784; Martin, *A Governess in the Age of Jane Austen*, p. 84, Agnes Porter's journal, 23 August 1790.
267. Fox Talbot Museum, Lacock, Susan O'Brien to Elizabeth Feilding [September] 1805].

Notes to Chapter 10: Education

1. Alison Sim, *The Tudor Housewife* (Stroud, 1996), pp. 31–33; J. T. Cliffe, *The World of the Country House in Seventeenth-Century England* (New Haven and London, 1999).
2. BL, Add. MS 51337, fol. 243.
3. DRO, D/FSI, box 186, Melbury inventory, 1727.
4. Isobel Grundy, *Lady Mary Wortley Montagu* (Oxford, 1999), p. 15.
5. DRO, D/FSI, box 232, 'Mrs Horner's character', 1758.
6. PP, MS account of 'The Four Countesses of Ilchester', by Susan O'Brien, 1817.
7. DRO, D/FSI, box 187, household accounts (Melbury), 1726–28.
8. There is one more reference to Aminta: shoes were bought for her in December 1728; D/FSI, box 188, household accounts (Melbury), 1728–29.
9. Letters (for which no dates are given) quoted in Earl of Ilchester, *Henry Fox, First Lord Holland, His Family and Relations*, i (London, 1920), pp. 41–44.
10. PP, MS account of 'The Four Countesses of Ilchester', by Susan O'Brien, 1817.
11. Lady Sarah Pennington, *An Unfortunate Mother's Advice to her Absent Daughters in a Letter to Miss Pennington* (London, 1761), pp. 20–25.
12. Quoted in Carola Hicks, *Improper Pursuits: The Scandalous Life of Lady Di Beauclerk* (London, 2001), p. 52.
13. Quoted in Dorothy Gardiner, *English Girlhood at School* (Oxford, 1929), pp. 393–94.
14. PP, MS account of 'The Four Countesses of Ilchester', by Susan O'Brien, 1817.
15. She was discharged in July 1753, but she appears to have been employed again for eighteen months in 1758–59, perhaps as a companion, as she was paid only £10 a year.
16. BL, Add. MS 51357, fols 114–15, John Delafons to Susan O'Brien, 6 June 1808.
17. Gladys Scott Thomson, *The Russells in Bloomsbury, 1669–1771* (London, 1940), p. 203.
18. PP, Charlotte Traherne, 'Family Recollections'.
19. Daughter of Wills Hill, later first Marquess of Downshire. She married Viscount Cranborne, later first Marquess of Salisbury.
20. Fox Talbot Museum, Lacock, Susan O'Brien to Elizabeth Feilding, 8 September 1810.
21. PP, Charlotte Traherne, 'Family Recollections'.
22. DRO, D/FSI, box 173B, household accounts (Redlynch), 1755–63.
23. Claire Harman, *Fanny Burney* (London, 2000), p. 65.
24. Joyce Hemlow et al. (ed.), *The Journal and Letters of Fanny Burney*, iv (Oxford, 1972–84), p. 254.

25. Pennington, *An Unfortunate Mother's Advice to her Absent Daughters*, p. 25.
26. Thomson, *The Russells in Bloomsbury*, pp. 203–4.
27. DRO, D/FSI, box 218, private disbursements (Redlynch), 1732–64; box 217, household accounts (Melbury), 1760–70. A spinnet resembled a small harpsichord.
28. Pennington, *An Unfortunate Mother's Advice to her Absent Daughters*, p. 27.
29. Harriot Georgiana Mundy (ed.), *The Journal of Mary Frampton from the Year 1779, until the Year 1846* (London, 1885), pp. 18–20.
30. BL, Add. MS 51344, fol. 46, Lady Ilchester to Susan O'Brien, 9 May [1764].
31. BL, Add. MS 51353, fols 109–10, Sarah Bunbury to Susan O'Brien, 8 March 1766.
32. Jacqueline Pearson, *Women's Reading in Britain, 1750–1835* (Cambridge, 1999), p. 48.
33. BL, Add. MS 51354, fols 15–18, Sarah Bunbury to Susan O'Brien, 6 July 1775.
34. PP, MS account of 'The Four Countesses of Ilchester', by Susan O'Brien, 1817.
35. Anna Jameson, 'On the Relative Social Position of Mothers and Governesses' in *Memoirs and Essays Illustrative of Art, Literature, and Social Morals* (London, 1846), p. 255.
36. Kenneth Neill Cameron, *Shelley and his Circle, 1773–1822*, ii (London and Cambridge, Massachusetts, 1961), pp. 936–82). I am grateful to Janet Todd for identifying Miss Arden.
37. DRO, D/FSI, box 218, household accounts (Redlynch), 1781–87.
38. They were old friends of her father, who had been born in Yarmouth.
39. PP, Charlotte Traherne, 'Family Recollections'.
40. Joanna Martin, *A Governess in the Age of Jane Austen* (London and Rio Grande, Ohio, 1998), p. 84, Agnes Porter's journal, 21 August 1790.
41. PP, Louisa Fox Strangways to Mary Talbot, 3 August 1796
42. Martin, *A Governess in the Age of Jane Austen*, p. 105, Agnes Porter's journal, 5 February 1791.
43. Martin, *A Governess in the Age of Jane Austen*, p. 114, Agnes Porter's journal, 26 April 1791; DRO, D/FSI, box 217, accounts (Redlynch), 1789–92.
44. DRO, D/FSI 217, 'money advanced to servants', 1789–96.
45. Martin, *A Governess in the Age of Jane Austen*, pp. 79–80, Agnes Porter's journal, 1788; DRO, D/FSI, box 217, 'money advanced to servants', 1789–96.
46. PP, Charlotte Digby to Mary Strangways, 30 July 1790.
47. DRO, D/FSI, box 194, accounts of Earl of Ilchester's estates, 1789–90.
48. PP, C. R. M. Talbot to Charlotte Traherne, 29 May 1851.
49. Martin, *A Governess in the Age of Jane Austen*, p. 96, Agnes Porter's journal, 2 December 1790.
50. BL, Add. MS 51357, fols 107–8, Harriot Frampton to Susan O'Brien, 2 September 1800.
51. PP, Mary Talbot to Henrietta Maria Hicks Beach [early 1806].
52. PP, Mary Talbot to Henrietta Maria Hicks Beach, 24 June [1806].
53. University of Wales, Swansea, Collins letters, Revd John Collins, 24 October 1806.

54. PP, Mary Talbot's pocket-book, 4 March 1807.
55. Alice Renton, *Tyrant or Victim: A History of the British Governess* (London, 1991), pp. 60–61. See also Martin, *A Governess in the Age of Jane Austen*, p. 269, Agnes Porter to Mary Talbot, 22 October 1807.
56. University of Wales, Swansea, Collins letters, Revd John Collins, 19 May 1808. See also above, p. 173, for Miss Smith.
57. Martin, *A Governess in the Age of Jane Austen*, p. 269, Agnes Porter to Mary Talbot, 22 October 1807.
58. Martin, *A Governess in the Age of Jane Austen*, p. 272, Agnes Porter to Mary Talbot, 17 August 1808.
59. PP, Emily Raines to Charlotte Talbot [*c.* 1808–9].
60. PP, Louisa Petty to Mary Talbot, 21 December 1808 and 25 January 1809.
61. Martin, *A Governess in the Age of Jane Austen*, p. 299, Agnes Porter to Mary Talbot, 21 September 1810.
62. PP, Thomas Mansel Talbot to Michael Hicks Beach, 7 February 1796.
63. PP, Susan O'Brien to Mary Talbot, 6 July 1816.
64. PP, Thomas Mansel Talbot to Henrietta Maria Hicks Beach, 7 February 1796.
65. PP, Susan O'Brien to Mary Strangways, 21 March 1791.
66. DRO, D/FSI, box 194, accounts of Earl of Ilchester's estates, 1788–91.
67. PP, Harriot Strangways to Mary Strangways, n.d.; Susan O'Brien to Mary Strangways, 16 July [1792].
68. Martin, *A Governess in the Age of Jane Austen*, p. 97, Agnes Porter's journal, 16 December 1790.
69. WSRO, Lacock Abbey MSS, Acc. 2664, box of miscellaneous correspondence (Feilding, Strangways, Talbot), Elizabeth Strangways to Harriot Strangways, 21 January 1792.
70. Frances Power Cobbe, *The Life of Frances Power Cobbe, as Told by Herself* (London, 1904), p. 59.
71. PP, Mary Talbot to Harriot Strangways, 12 April [1798].
72. DRO, D/FSI, box 241B, Lady Ilchester to Lord Stavordale, 20 May 1799.
73. See below, pp. 240–41, for further information on books on education.
74. The book was first published in France in 1791.
75. Maria and Richard Lovell Edgeworth, *Practical Education*, ii (London, 1798), p. 529.
76. Peter Ackroyd, review (in *The Times*, 15 January 2003) of Anne Stott, *Hannah More: The First Victorian* (Oxford, 2003).
77. Hannah More, *Essays on Various Subjects, Principally Designed for Young Ladies* (Cork, 1778), pp. 84–85. 'Tambour work' is embroidery.
78. The book was first published in 1779.
79. WSRO, Lacock Abbey MSS, Acc. 2664, box of miscellaneous correspondence (Feilding, Strangways, Talbot), Elizabeth Talbot to Harriot Strangways, 27 May 1799.
80. First published in 1805.

81. Jean-Jacques Rousseau, *La Nouvelle Héloïse* (1761) and *Emile: sur l'éducation* (1762).
82. BL, Add. MS 51359, Susan O'Brien's journal, 9 March 1811.
83. The book is still at Penrice.
84. Martin, *A Governess in the Age of Jane Austen*, p. 210, Agnes Porter's journal, 7 June 1802.
85. Edgeworth, *Practical Education*, i, pp. 167–68.
86. Nowell C. Smith (ed.), *The Letters of Sydney Smith*, i (Oxford, 1953), pp. 8–9.
87. PP, 'Thoughts on Education by Mrs Williams, Governess at Williamstrip'.
88. PP, Agnes Campbell to Mary Talbot, 3 December [1808]; Charlotte Lemon to Mary Talbot, 23 October 1811.
89. PP, C. R. M. Talbot to Jane Talbot, 23 June 1816.
90. PP, Jane Talbot to Charlotte Talbot, *c.* 1820. The 'foul deeds' included the Margam Abbey manuscripts, one of the most extensive collections of medieval documents in Wales.
91. PP, Mary Strangways to Harriot Strangways, 23 January 1794.
92. PP, C. R. M. Talbot to Mary Cole, 30 October 1818. They would not have had many opportunities to practise, for Penrice is not in a Welsh-speaking region of Wales.
93. PP, Susan O'Brien to Mary Strangways, 19 August 1792. To 'hansel' means to wear for the first time. Such aprons were decorative, rather than functional. 'Harriott' refers to Mary's younger sister.
94. PP, Louisa Lansdowne to Mary Talbot, 10 September 1811.
95. PP, Charlotte Lemon to Mary Talbot, 19 March 1819.
96. PP, Mary Theresa Talbot to C. R. M. Talbot, 7 May [1813].
97. PP, Susan O'Brien to Mary Cole, 25 December 1815.
98. BL, Add. MS 51360, Susan O'Brien's journal, 22 May 1821.
99. PP, Thomas Mansel Talbot's pocket-book, 1811.
100. PP, Thomas Mansel Talbot's pocket-book, 1812. The turning-room, a small building close to Mary's garden, is still there and has recently been restored.
101. PP, Townshend Selwyn to Mary Talbot, 19 October 1811.
102. PP, Mary Cole to Charlotte Talbot [*c.* 1820].
103. PP, Harriot Strangways to Mary Strangways, 12 April 1791.
104. PP, Mary Talbot to Harriot Strangways [early 1794].
105. PP, Mary Talbot to C. R. M. Talbot, 21 February 1812.
106. PP, Mary Talbot to Henrietta Maria Hicks Beach, 27 February [1804].
107. PP, Mary Talbot's pocket-book, 1792.
108. DRO, D/FSI, box 241B, Lady Ilchester to Lord Stavordale, 20 May 1799.
109. WSRO, Lacock Abbey MSS, Acc. 2664, box of miscellaneous correspondence (Feilding, Strangways, Talbot), Elizabeth Strangways to Harriot Strangways, 22 February 1795.
110. PP, Thomas Mansel Talbot's pocket-books, 15 January 1807; 21 October 1812.
111. PP, Mrs Burgh to Mary Talbot, 26 November 1811.
112. PP, Jane King to Mary Talbot, 31 May [1809].

113. PP, Mary Cole to Charlotte Talbot, 10 February [1818].
114. PP, Mary Talbot's pocket-book, 18 April 1804.
115. BL, Add. MS 51360, Susan O'Brien's journal, 24 September 1814.
116. PP, Charlotte Strangways to Mary Talbot [1810]; Charlotte Talbot to Mary Talbot, 28 October [1812].
117. PP, George Eden to Mary Talbot, 12 March 1810.
118. BL, Add. MS 51360, Susan O'Brien's journal, 13 April 1821.
119. PP, C. R. M. Talbot, 'Characters of Some Members of His Family'.
120. Elizabeth Hamilton, *Letters on Education* (Dublin, 1801), p. 185.
121. BL, Add. MS 51359, Susan O'Brien's journal, 19 January 1813.
122. BL, Add. MS 51360, Susan O'Brien's journal, 11 February 1819.
123. BL, Add. MS 51360, Susan O'Brien's journal, 26 April 1821.
124. BL, Add. MS 51360, Susan O'Brien's journal, 30–31 October 1823.
125. PP, 'Thoughts on Education by Mrs Williams, Governess at Williamstrip'.
126. Martin, *A Governess in the Age of Jane Austen*, p. 287, Agnes Porter to Mary Talbot, 17 September 1809.
127. BL, Add. MS 51359, Susan O'Brien's journal, 19 January 1810.
128. BL, Add. MS 51360, Susan O'Brien's journal, 28 February 1826.

Notes to Chapter 11: Literature and Science

1. DRO, D/FSI box 238, bundle 14, account of Lady Christian Fox's books in her closet at Whitehall (undated).
2. BL, Add. MS 51361, fols 73–80, list of books read by Susan O'Brien, 1792–1815.
3. BL, Add. MS 51415, fols 23–24, Caroline Fox to Henry Fox [28 February 1751].
4. BL, Add. MS 51354, fols 150–52, Sarah Napier to Susan O'Brien, 11 September 1782.
5. Lady Sarah Pennington, *An Unfortunate Mother's Advice to her Absent Daughters in a Letter to Miss Pennington* (London, 1761), p. 39.
6. PP, Harriot Strangways to Mary Strangways, 28 December [1789].
7. PP, Harriot Strangways to Mary Strangways [summer 1792].
8. BL, Add. MS 51360, Susan O'Brien's journal, 28 March 1815.
9. BL, Add. MS 51360, Susan O'Brien's journal, 20 February 1820.
10. BL, Add. MS 51360, Susan O'Brien's journal, 24 February 1814.
11. PP, Susan O'Brien to Mary Cole, 6 July 1816.
12. PP, Alicia Campbell to Mary Talbot, 14 November 1812.
13. PP, C. R. M. Talbot to Mary Cole, 11 February 1817.
14. PP, W. H. F. Talbot to Mary Theresa Talbot, 16 April 1824.
15. BL, Add. MS 51360, Susan O'Brien's journal, 5 February 1817.
16. BL, Add. MS 51360, Susan O'Brien's journal, 13 August 1819.
17. BL, Add. MS 51360, Susan O'Brien's journal, 30 December 1826.
18. BL, Add. MS 51360, Susan O'Brien's journal, 16 April 1816.
19. Joanna Martin, *A Governess in the Age of Jane Austen* (London and Rio Grande, Ohio, 1998), p. 150, Agnes Porter to Mary Talbot, 11 September 1794; p. 236, Agnes Porter's journal, 2 February 1804.

20. PP, Townshend Selwyn to Mary Talbot, 19 September 1809.
21. See below, p. 248, for further details.
22. Joanna Martin, *The Penrice Letters* (Swansea and Cardiff, 1993), p. 145, Mary Talbot to Harriot Strangways, [March-April 1794].
23. M. and R. L. Edgeworth, *Practical Education*, ii (London, 1798), p. 536.
24. Thomas Gisborne, *An Enquiry into the Duties of the Female Sex* (7th edn, London, 1806). This book is still at Penrice. See also Leonore Davidoff and Catherine Hall, *Family Fortunes* (London, 1987), p. 170.
25. PP, Thomas Mansel Talbot to Michael Hicks Beach, 12 January 1800.
26. PP, Thomas Mansel Talbot's pocket-book, May 1809.
27. PP, Mary Talbot's pocket-book, 1806.
28. PP, Louisa Petty to Mary Talbot, 12 August 1808.
29. PP, George Eden to Mary Talbot, 28 May 1810.
30. PP, George Eden to Mary Talbot, 27 November 1810.
31. BL, Add. MS 51414, fols 73–74, Caroline Fox to Henry Fox, 27 January 1748.
32. PP, Thomas Mansel Talbot's pocket-book, 18 January 1806.
33. BL, Add. MS 51354, fols 94–97, Sarah Lennox to Susan O'Brien, 21 April 1779.
34. PP, Susan O'Brien to Mary Talbot, 30 May [1812].
35. PP, Mary Talbot's pocket-books, 2–3 March 1801, 7 January 1802, 18 July 1804.
36. PP, Louisa Petty to Mary Talbot, 28 October 1808, 10 November 1808.
37. Fox Talbot Museum, Lacock, Susan O'Brien to Elizabeth Feilding, 11 February 1811; Susan O'Brien to Elizabeth Feilding, 8 March 1811; BL, Add. MS 51359, Susan O'Brien's journal, 10–24 March 1811.
38. PP, William O'Brien to Mary Talbot, 24 July 1811.
39. Martin, *A Governess in the Age of Jane Austen*, p. 141, Agnes Porter to Mary Strangways, 12 March 1793.
40. PP, C. R. M. Talbot, 'Characters of Some Members of His Family'.
41. Martin, *A Governess in the Age of Jane Austen*, p. 322, Agnes Porter to Mary Talbot, 7 November 1812.
42. BL, Add. MS 51359, Susan O'Brien's journal, 1787.
43. BL, Add. MS 51360, Susan O'Brien's journal, 31 October 1824.
44. BL, Add. MS 51359, Susan O'Brien's journal, 16 January 1813.
45. PP, Susan O'Brien to Mary Cole, 18 September 1816.
46. Patricia Phillips, *The Scientific Lady: A Social History of Woman's Scientific Interests, 1520–1918* (London, 1990), pp. ix–x.
47. Leonard Jenyns, *Memoir of the Revd John Stevens Henslow* (London, 1862), quoted in S. M. Walters and E. A. Stow, *Darwin's Mentor: John Stevens Henslow, 1796–1861* (Cambridge, 2001), p. 5; Adrian Desmond and James Moore, *Darwin* (London, 1991), pp. 12–13.
48. Fox Talbot Museum, Lacock, Jane Talbot to W. H. F. Talbot, 17 October 1811.
49. Fox Talbot Museum, Lacock, Mary Cole to W. H. F. Talbot [*c.* 1820].
50. BL, Add. MS 51357, fol. 124, Mary Talbot to Susan O'Brien [*c.* 20 July 1814].
51. Fox Talbot Museum, Lacock, W. H. F. Talbot to Elizabeth Feilding, 6 September 1814.

52. Though she seems to have taken to gardening later on, in her sixties. See H. J. P. Arnold, *William Henry Fox Talbot: Pioneer of Photography and Man of Science* (London, 1977), p. 94.
53. E. J. Climenson (ed.), *Passages from the Diaries of Mrs Phillip Lybbe Powys, 1756–1808* (London, 1899), p. 121. The Duchess, who was born in 1715, was eight years older than Elizabeth.
54. Not everyone agreed, however: conservative writers such as the Revd Richard Polwhele thought that botanical studes were unsuitable for women because they encouraged an indelicate interest in sex. See Ann B. Shteir, *Cultivating Women, Cultivating Science: Flora's Daughters and Botany in England, 1760 to 1860* (Baltimore and London, 1996), pp. 27–29.
55. Jane Austen, *Northanger Abbey* (first published 1818; Penguin Classics edition, 1985), p. 179.
56. PP, Harriot Strangways to Mary Strangways, n.d. [*c.* 1792–93].
57. Martin, *The Penrice Letters*, p. 145, Mary Talbot to Harriot Strangways [March-April 1794].
58. PP, Mary Talbot's, pocket-book, 3 June 1801, 9 June 1801.
59. PP, Charlotte Lemon to Mary Talbot, 23 October 1811.
60. PP, Louisa Lansdowne to Mary Talbot, 25 March [1813].
61. Fox Talbot Museum, Lacock, W. H. F. Talbot to Elizabeth Feilding, 18 April 1812.
62. Fox Talbot Museum, Lacock, W. H. F. Talbot to Elizabeth Feilding, 6 September 1814.
63. Later Sir Walter Trevelyan. He was to become an eminent botanist, whose major work on *The Vegetation of the Faroe Islands* was published in 1837.
64. PP, W. H. F. Talbot to Mary Talbot, 19 October 1814.
65. PP, W. H. F. Talbot to Mary Talbot, 20 January 1815.
66. PP, Mary Talbot to W. H. F. Talbot, 28 January 1815.
67. PP, W. H. F. Talbot to Charlotte Traherne, 2 June 1835.
68. PP, W. H. F. Talbot to Mary Talbot, 27 July 1805.
69. PP, Mary-Talbot's pocket-books, 6 October 1803, 9 December 1805; Jane King to Mary Talbot, 4 May [1809].
70. PP, Mary Talbot to Charlotte Talbot, 24 December 1810.
71. PP, Mary Talbot to C. R. M. Talbot, 5 November 1812.
72. BL, Add. MS 51357, fols 150–52, Mary Cole to Susan O'Brien [18 August 1817].
73. PP, Charlotte Lemon to Mary Talbot, 11 August 1811, and *c.* 1811–12.
74. PP, Mary Talbot to Charlotte Talbot [July 1814]. The inventory of the contents of Penrice drawn up after the death of Kit Talbot in 1890 lists 'a quantity of fossils, shells, eggs etc. in cupboards fitted with trays', and 'an oak cabinet fitted with five drawers and a collection of shells'.
75. PP, Sir Charles Lemon to Mary Talbot, 3 October 1814.
76. PP, Charlotte Lemon to Mary Cole, 4 January [1824]. Jean-Baptiste Lamarck, a professor at the Natural History Museum in Paris, was an early evolutionist who had revolutionised the study of the lower invertebrates.

77. Fox Talbot Museum, Lacock, Lewis Weston Dillwyn to W. H. F. Talbot, 28 October 1814; PP, W. H. F. Talbot to Mary Talbot, 20 January 1815.
78. PP, W. H. F. Talbot to Elizabeth Feilding, 13 August 1815. Port Eynon is about three miles from Penrice.
79. Letter quoted in *The Life and Correspondence of William Buckland, DD, FRS: By His Daughter, Mrs Gordon* (London, 1894), p. 16. For Buckland see also Deborah Cadbury, *The Dinosaur Hunters* (London, 2000).
80. BL, Add. MS 51360, Susan O'Brien's journal, 20 April 1820.
81. PP, C. R. M. Talbot to Mary Cole, 18 May 1820.
82. PP, Mary Theresa Talbot to Charlotte Talbot, 3 February 1821.
83. Henry J. Randall and William Rees, *Diary of Lewis Weston Dillwyn*, South Wales and Monmouth Record Society publication, 5 (1963), p. 54.
84. Fox Talbot Museum, Lacock, Mary Cole to W. H. F. Talbot, 10 October 1816.
85. See also F. J. North, 'The "Red Lady" of Paviland', in *Stewart Williams' Glamorgan Historian*, iii (Cowbridge, Glamorgan, 1966), pp. 123–37.
86. Sixth Earl of Ilchester (ed.), *The Journal of Elizabeth, Lady Holland, 1791–1811*, i (London, 1908), p. 192.
87. Edgeworth, *Practical Education*, i, p. 26.
88. PP, Charlotte Strangways to Mary Talbot, 30 September 1799.
89. PP, Louisa Petty to Mary Talbot, 31 August [1808].
90. PP, Susan O'Brien to Mary Strangways [spring 1793]; Louisa Lansdowne to Mary Talbot [*c.* 1811].
91. Fox Talbot Museum, Lacock, W. H. F. Talbot to Elizabeth Feilding, 16 April 1812. See also Arnold, *William Henry Fox Talbot*, p. 34.
92. PP, Mary Talbot's pocket-book, 17 August 1803.
93. PP, W. H. F. Talbot to Charlotte Traherne, 21 October 1835. See also Arnold, *William Henry Fox Talbot*, pp. 246–47.
94. BL, Add. MS 51359, Susan O'Brien's journal, 16 April 1810.
95. BL, Add. MS 51359, Susan O'Brien's journal, 21 April 1810.
96. BL, Add. MS 51360, Susan O'Brien's journal, 18 May 1824.
97. BL, Add. MS 51360, Susan O'Brien's journal, 31 December 1816, 11 January 1817.
98. BL, Add. MS 51352, fols 127–28, William Fox Strangways to Susan O'Brien, 22 January [1819].
99. BL, Add. MS 51360, Susan O'Brien's journal, 22 August 1820. The pedigree of the Strangways and Fox Strangways families published in the third edition of Hutchins's *History of Dorset* was 'compiled from family documents, public records, and other authentic sources by the Lady Harriot Frampton of Moreton': John Hutchins, *The History and Antiquities of the County of Dorset*, ii (3rd edn, with additions by W. Shipp and J. W. Hodson, London, 1863), p. 662.
100. Doreen Slatter, 'The Third Marquess of Lansdowne and his Family at Bowood, 1810–40', *Wiltshire Archaeological and Natural History Magazine*, 84 (1991), p. 132; *Gentleman's Magazine*, new series, 36 (1851), p. 81.

101. PP, W. H. F. Talbot to Charlotte Traherne, 4 March 1839.
102. PP, W. H. F. Talbot to Charlotte Traherne, 2 June 1835.
103. PP, W. H. F. Talbot to Charlotte Traherne, 21 October 1835.
104. Fox Talbot Museum, Lacock, C. R. M. Talbot to W. H. F. Talbot, 5 March 1868; W. H. F. Talbot to Amélina Petit de Billier, 27 March 1868.

Notes to Chapter 12: Gardens

1. PP, Susan O'Brien to Mary Talbot, 18 February [1794].
2. Recent exceptions include Tom Williamson, *Polite Landscapes: Gardens and Society in Eighteenth-Century England* (Baltimore, Maryland, and Stroud, 1995); Mark Laird, *The Flowering of the Landscape Garden: English Pleasure Grounds, 1720–1800* (Philadelphia, 1999); and Penelope Hobhouse, *Plants in Garden History* (London, 1992).
3. Williamson, *Polite Landscapes*, p. 88.
4. Ruth Hayden, *Mrs Delany: Her Life and Her Flowers* (London, 1980), pp. 85–86.
5. Quoted in Stella Tillyard, *Aristocrats* (London, 1994), p. 210.
6. Roy Porter, *Enlightenment: Britain and the Creation of the Modern World* (London, 2000), p. 312.
7. Austin Dobson (ed.), *Diaries and Letters of Madame D'Arblay*, ii (London, 1904), p. 447.
8. Keith Thomas, *Man and the Natural World* (London, 1983), pp. 238–39.
9. Charles Evelyn, *The Lady's Recreation* (London and Dublin, 1717), p. 1.
10. Mavis Batey in Geoffrey and Susan Jellicoe et al. (ed.), *The Oxford Companion to Gardens* (Oxford, 1986), p. 402.
11. Jane Brown, *The Pursuit of Paradise* (London, 1999), p. 94, quoting David Green, *Gardener to Queen Anne: Henry Wise* (Oxford, 1956), p. 102.
12. Michael Sutherill, *The Gardens of Audley End* (English Heritage, 1995), p. 25.
13. Sue Bennett, *Five Centuries of Women and Gardens* (London, 2000), p. 48; Dorothy Stroud, *Capability Brown* (London, 1975), p. 196.
14. DRO, D/FSI, box 232, George Donisthorpe to Susanna Strangways Horner, 26 June and 27 November 1742, 12 January and 13 March 1743.
15. The main sources of information on the work carried out at this time are: DRO, D/FSI, box 156B, estimates of John Kininmonth; box 232, George Donisthorpe to Susanna Strangways Horner, 26 June 1742 to 26 January 1743, and John Kininmonth to Susanna Strangways Horner, 13 March 1745. See also D/FSI, box 188, general disbursements (Melbury), 1742–44, and household accounts (Melbury), 1747–51.
16. Little is known about John Kininmonth, and I have not been able to trace any other work for which he was responsible. Dr Timothy Mowl says that he was a Sherborne nurseryman, but I have not been able to verify this. Kininmonth is a Scottish name, and he may have been born in Scotland. In 1739 John Kininmonth was of Stinsford when he married Anna Davie of Dorchester. He may have been employed by Lora, widow of George Pitt, who had built a new

house at Kingston Maurward (in the parish of Stinsford) between 1717 and 1720. Kininmonth died in 1754, and was buried in the parish of All Saints, Dorchester. He left a will, DRO, DA/1754/W/22, in which he left 'all my mathematical and surveying instruments' to his nephew John Mackentosh.

17. Batty Langley, *New Principles of Gardening* (London, 1728), p. xi. Tim Mowl first pointed out the influence of Batty Langley on the gardens at Melbury in *Historic Gardens of Dorset* (Stroud, 2003), pp. 59–63. The plan is in D/FSI, Acc. 5294.
18. John Dixon Hunt (ed.), 'Horace Walpole's Journals of Visits to Country Seats', in *The History of the Modern Taste in Gardening* (New York and London, 1982), pp. 47–48. The wood is also shown in the map of the grounds at Melbury of *c.* 1790: DRO, D/FSI, MC9/4.
19. See below, p. 266, for Redlynch.
20. DRO, D/FSI, box 232, George Donisthorpe to Susanna Strangways Horner, 26 June 1742 to 26 January 1743; John Kininmonth to Susanna Strangways Horner, 13 March 1745.
21. Hunt, 'Horace Walpole's Journals of Visits to Country Seats', p. 44. The shields appear to have been copied from those on the monuments in the church: DRO, D/FSI, box 188, household accounts (Melbury), 1747–51.
22. There is a photograph of the 'temple' in RCHME, *West Dorset*, i, plate 141. In *Historic Gardens of Dorset*, Tim Mowl draws attention to the use of Batty Langley's patterns for the arch and pinnacles, as published in *Ancient Architecture Restored and Improved* (London, 1742; republished in London, 1747, as *Gothic Architecture*).
23. DRO, D/FSI, box 188, household accounts (Melbury), 1747–51. The accounts do not say what the paints were for – some may have been for the boat; others for painting the coats of arms.
24. DRO, D/FSI, box 188, household accounts (Melbury), 1747–51. 'Lawrenistines' are probably the winter-flowering shrub *Laurustinus* or *Viburnum tinus*.
25. BL, Add. MS 51337, fol. 102, Lady Ilchester to Lord Ilchester, 3 October [1757].
26. DRO,D/FSI, box 240A, bundle 6, Lady Ilchester to Lord Ilchester, 5 October [1760–63].
27. In 1780 Sarah Lennox asked Susan O'Brien if her mother still enjoyed 'her former amusements at Melbury in improving the place': BL, Add. MS 51354, Sarah Lennox to Susan O'Brien, 24 July 1780.
28. BL, Add. MS 51346, fols 183–84, George Donisthorpe to Lord Ilchester, 16 May 1767; Add. MS 51344, fols 63–64, Lady Ilchester to Susan O'Brien, 17 October [1767].
29. John Hutchins, *The History and Antiquities of the County of Dorset* (1st edn, London, 1774). The Melbury estate accounts record the payment in 1774 of £51 15*s.* 8*d.* 'to Dr Cuming for the copper plate of Melbury': DRO, D/FSI, box 194, estate accounts (Melbury); DRO, D/FSI, MC9/4.
30. Minterne MSS, Admiral Robert Digby's journal, 10 October 1793.
31. PP, Charlotte Traherne, 'Family Recollections'.

32. D/FSI, box 189, general day book (Redlynch), 1735–54.
33. Hunt, 'Horace Walpole's Journals of Visits to Country Seats', p. 44.
34. The temple was certainly built before 1753, when there is an account for 'mending the temple': DRO, D/FSI box 173B, accounts (Redlynch), 1753–56. Further work was done in 1755, when an account from Nathaniel Ireson for work at Redlynch refers to 'taking down part of the end of the temple in the wood and setting it up again'; BL, Add. MS 51373A, fols 39–40.
35. DRO, D/FSI, box 189.
36. Michael Symes, *The English Rococo Garden* (Princes Risborough, 1991), p. 4.
37. DRO, D/FSI, box 173A, accounts (Redlynch), 1748–50; box 189, general day book (Redlynch), 1735–54.
38. DRO, D/FSI, box 240, bundle 5, Lady Ilchester to Lord Ilchester, 13 February 1750.
39. The plans are reproduced and discussed in Laird, *The Flowering of the Landscape Garden*, pp. 234–37. Hervey's Grove is mentioned in a letter from Lord Hervey to Stephen Fox, dated 18 June 1728: Suffolk Record Office, Bury St Edmunds, Ickworth MSS, 941/47/4, fols 77–78.
40. He may have known them even earlier: in his will Lord Ilchester left £100 to Bateman 'as a small remembrance of the strict friendship subsisting between us, and begun in our earliest youth', PRO, PROB 11/1025/463, will of Stephen, Earl of Ilchester, 1776.
41. W. S. Lewis et al. (ed.), *The Yale Edition of Horace Walpole's Correspondence*, xxxi (Yale, 1937–84), pp. 35–36, Horace Walpole to Lady Hervey, 11 June 1765; James Joel Cartwright (ed.), *The Travels through England of Dr Richard Pococke*, (Camden Society, London, 1888–89), p. 64.
42. The sum of 10*s.* 5*d.* was paid for 'slating and plastring the Chineas sate' in September 1756: DRO, D/FSI box 173B, accounts (Redlynch), 1753–56; box 189, 'ledger', Redlynch, 1754–64. See also BL, Add. MS 51373A, fols 39–40, work done by Nathaniel Ireson for Lord Ilchester, 1751–55.
43. The Fox brothers were at Christ Church, Oxford, with Bateman and Hamilton. Hamilton matriculated there on 4 November 1720, Stephen and Henry Fox on 20 February 1721, and Bateman on 13 October 1722.
44. BL, Add. MS 51337, fol. 43, Lady Ilchester to Lord Ilchester, July [?1750]; fol. 65, Lady Ilchester to Lord Ilchester, 21 June [1750–1752].
45. DRO, D/FSI, box 173A, accounts (Redlynch) 1750–51.
46. BL, Add. MS 51419, fols 152–53, Henry Fox to Lord Ilchester, 25 February 1752. A year earlier, William and Richard Bradshall had supplied Lord Ilchester with '8000 of birch, alder and holly at 1*s.* per hundred' for £4, in addition to three bushels of holly-berries for £1: DRO, D/FSI 173A, accounts (Redlynch), 1750–51. 'Miserium' was probably *Daphne Mezereum.*
47. DRO, D/FSI, box 240A, bundle 1, Susan Fox to Lord Ilchester, 29 April 1752.
48. DRO, D/FSI, box 173B, accounts (Redlynch), 1753–56.
49. DRO, D/FSI, box 173B, accounts (Redlynch), 1759–63. A hand-glass was a portable cloche for protecting delicate plants.

50. DRO, D/FSI, box 194, accounts (Redlynch), 1783–85. The Lucombe family had a well-known nursery in Exeter. It is just possible that Capability Brown helped to plan this area, for he visited the second Earl and Countess of Ilchester at Redlynch in October 1777: Sherborne Castle MSS, game book, 16–17 October 1777.
51. PP, Lord Ilchester to Mary Strangways, 25 July 1790.
52. PP, Lord Ilchester to Mary Strangways, 25 March [1791].
53. BL, Add. MS 51359, Susan O'Brien's journal, 13 August 1804.
54. BL, Add. MS 51360, Susan O'Brien's journal, 18 April 1819.
55. DRO, D/FSI, box 186, Abbotsbury inventory, 1727.
56. BL, Add. MS 51346, fols 142–43, George Donisthorpe to Lord Ilchester, 14 March 1762.
57. DRO, D/FSI, box 240B, bundle 11, George Donisthorpe to Lord Ilchester, 27 October 1762 and 11 April 1763; box 240B, bundle 3, Lady Ilchester to Lady Hervey, 17 November 1766.
58. Michael Hunter, 'The First Seaside House?', *Georgian Group Journal*, 8 (1998), pp. 135–142.
59. Reproduced in John Fair and Don Moxom, *Abbotsbury and the Swannery* (Wimborne, Dorset, 1993), p. 55. There is also a illustration of the house in the first (1774) edition of Hutchins, *History and Antiquities of the County of Dorset.*
60. Joanna Martin, *A Governess in the Age of Jane Austen* (London and Rio Grande, Ohio, 1998), p. 126, Agnes Porter's journal, 17 October 1791.
61. Horace Walpole, quoted in Peter Smith, 'Lady Oxford's Alterations at Welbeck Abbey, 1741–55', *Georgian Group Journal*, 11 (2001), p. 134.
62. Rosemary Baird, *Mistress of the House* (London, 2003), pp. 153–56.
63. David Jacques, *Georgian Gardens: The Reign of Nature* (London, 1983), p. 49.
64. BL, Add. MS 51344, fols 57–58, Lady Ilchester to Susan O'Brien, 30 July [1766]; fols 59–60, Lady Ilchester to Susan O'Brien [September 1766].
65. BL, Add. MS 51344, fols 63–64, Lady Ilchester to Susan O'Brien, 17 October [1767].
66. DRO, D/FSI, box 194, accounts of Lord Ilchester's estates, 1784–87.
67. PP, Susan O'Brien to Mary Cole, 18 September 1816.
68. The house was rebuilt in 1915, but the new building proved to have severe structural faults and it was demolished in 1934.
69. DRO, D/FSI, box 240A, bundle 1, Susan Fox to Lord Ilchester, 29 April 1752.
70. BL, Add. MS 51356, fols 211–12, Samuel Touchet to Susan O'Brien, 27 September 1766.
71. BL, Add. MS 51359, Susan O'Brien's journal, 26 September 1812.
72. PP, Charlotte Traherne, 'Family Recollections'.
73. BL, Add. MS 51360, Susan O'Brien's journal, 19 January 1818, 9 February 1825.
74. PP, Susan O'Brien to Mary Talbot, 16 June [1810].
75. BL, Add. MS 51360, Susan O'Brien's journal, 27 June 1825.

76. Fox Talbot Museum, Lacock, Susan O'Brien to Elizabeth Talbot, 21 June 1798.
77. BL, Add. MS 51359, Susan O'Brien's journal, 30 January 1805, 11 February 1805.
78. BL, Add. MS 51360, Susan O'Brien's journal, 29 September 1816.
79. Fox Talbot Museum, Lacock, Susan O'Brien to Elizabeth Feilding, 9 October 1816.
80. Thomas Hardy, *Two on a Tower* (first published 1882; Oxford World Classics edition, 1998), pp. 174–75; Denys Kay-Robinson, *The Landscape of Thomas Hardy* (Exeter, 1984), p. 30.
81. BL, Add. MS 51359, Susan O'Brien's journal, 24 August 1815.
82. BL, Add. MS 51360, Susan O'Brien's journal, 13 September 1817, 14 May 1819.
83. BL, Add. MS 51359, Susan O'Brien's journal, 1 June 1814.
84. BL, Add. MS 51360, Susan O'Brien's journal, 19 May 1816, 19 May 1822.
85. PP, Susan O'Brien to Mary Cole, 14 February 1826.
86. Joanna Martin, *The Penrice Letters* (Swansea and Cardiff, 1993), p. 124, Thomas Mansel Talbot to Michael Hicks Beach, 27 January 1793.
87. PP, C. R. M. Talbot, 'Characters of Some Members of His Family'.
88. BL, Add. MS 51358, fols 114–15, Mary Talbot to William O'Brien, 23 January 1814.
89. PP, C. R. M. Talbot, 'Characters of Some Members of His Family'.
90. PP, Mary Talbot's pocket-book, 22 October 1798.
91. PP, Mary Talbot to Charlotte Talbot, 24 December 1810.
92. PP, Jane King to Mary Talbot, 20 March [1809].
93. Martin, *A Governess in the Age of Jane Austen*, p. 312, Agnes Porter to Mary Talbot, 9 June 1811. Thomas Ace was the gardener at Penrice. *Lychnadeas* are lychnideas or phlox.
94. PP, Mary Theresa Talbot to C. R. M. Talbot, [17 March 1813]; and Mary Talbot to C. R. M. Talbot, 29 March 1813.
95. PP, list of plants at Penrice, 1799–1829. Camellias now flourish outside at Penrice, but in Mary's day they were thought to need extra heat and shelter in the winter.
96. The nurserymen Henry Shailer senior (fl. 1775–1822) and Henry Shailer junior (fl. 1810–52) specialised in roses. James Colville senior (*c.* 1746–1822) and James Colville junior (*c.* 1777–1832) had a nursery in Chelsea. In the early nineteenth century they specialised in supplying plants to wealthy collectors and specialists. *Tigridia pavonia*, a bulbous plant, had been introduced to Britain from Mexico only a few years earlier, in 1796. Conrad Loddiges (*c.* 1743–1826), a German nurseryman, and his two sons had a nursery garden in Hackney, famous for rare plants.
97. PP, Mary Talbot's pocket-book, 1806; Thomas Mansel Talbot's pocket-books, 1806, 1809.
98. PP, Thomas Mansel Talbot's pocket-books, 1808, 1809. Lewis Kennedy and James Lee founded the famous Vineyard nursery at Hammersmith in the mid eighteenth century.
99. Gloucester Record Office, Hicks Beach (St Aldwyn) papers, D2440, box 53, accounts of Thomas Mansel Talbot's executors.

100. PP, Mary Talbot to Henrietta Maria Hicks Beach [October-November 1803], 12 October 1810.
101. PP, Ann Fowler to Mary Talbot, 17 August 1809, 23 March 1811, 28 May 1811.
102. PP, Richard Fowler to Mary Talbot, 24 July 1811.
103. PP, Louisa Petty to Mary Talbot, 12 August 1808.
104. PP, Louisa Petty to Mary Talbot, 31 August [1808]. The 'Macartney Rose', *Rosa bracteata*, an evergreen climber, was brought to this country from China by the diplomat and plant collector Lord Macartney in the late eighteenth century.
105. PP, Louisa Petty to Mary Talbot, 21 November 1808, 31 July 1809.
106. PP, Louisa Lansdowne to Mary Talbot, 2 May 1810.
107. D. A. Crowley (ed.), *The Victoria History of the Counties of England: A History of the County of Wiltshire*, xvii (Woodbridge, 2002), pp. 120–21.
108. Trevor Lummis and Jan Marsh, *The Woman's Domain: Women and the English Country House* (London, 1993), pp. 54–55.
109. PP, Harriot Strangways to Mary Strangways, 24 December 1788.
110. DRO, D/FSI, box 240B, bundle 5, first Countess of Ilchester to second Countess of Ilchester [*c.* 1789–90].
111. PP, Lord Ilchester to Mary Strangways, 25 March [1791].
112. PP, Charlotte Strangways to Mary Talbot, 3 October 1794.
113. PP, Louisa Strangways to Mary Talbot [*c.* 1795–99].
114. DRO, D/FSI, box 241B, William Fox Strangways to Lord Ilchester [*c.* 1805].
115. Jane Austen, *Northanger Abbey* (first published 1818; Penguin Classics edition, 1985), p. 37.
116. PP, Agnes Porter to Mary Talbot, 4 June 1801.
117. Martin, *A Governess in the Age of Jane Austen*, p. 212, Agnes Porter's journal, 7 July 1802.
118. PP, Mary Theresa Talbot to Charlotte Talbot, 15 May 1811.
119. PP, Mary Theresa Talbot to C. R. M. Talbot, 22 March 1812.
120. PP, Mary Talbot to C. R. M. Talbot, 18 April 1812.
121. PP, Mary Theresa Talbot to Charlotte Talbot, 23 April 1812.
122. PP, Jane Talbot to C. R. M. Talbot, 16 or 17 April [1813], 7 June 1813.
123. Emily J. Climenson (ed.), *Passages from the Diaries of Mrs Philip Lybbe Powys* (London, 1899), p. 116.
124. See Mary Rose Blacker, *Flora Domestica: A History of Flower Arranging, 1500–1930* (London, 2000), especially chapters 2–4.
125. DRO, D/FSI box 173B, accounts (Redlynch), 1758–59.
126. Quoted in Lummis and Marsh, *The Woman's Domain*, p. 74.
127. Catherine Howard was related by marriage to the Fox Strangways ladies. She was a daughter of Sir Richard Neave of Dagnam Park, Essex, and sister of Sir Thomas Neave, who married Frances Caroline Digby (a sister of Maria Digby, the second wife of the second Earl of Ilchester, and a great-granddaughter of Sir Stephen Fox).
128. PP, Mary Theresa Talbot to C. R. M. Talbot, 22 March 1812.

129. PP, Mary Talbot to C. R. M. Talbot, 18 April 1812, 29 March 1813.
130. PP, Louisa Petty to Mary Talbot, 21 December 1808.
131. PP, Louisa Lansdowne to Mary Talbot [*c.* 1811–12], [*c.* 1811].
132. Ann Smith, 'Sherborne Castle: From Tudor Lodge to Country House', *Local Historian*, 25 (November, 1995), p. 238; Janet Waymark, 'Sherborne, Dorset', *Garden History*, 29 (Summer 2001), pp. 78–79.
133. Douglas Ellory Pett, *The Parks and Gardens of Cornwall* (Penzance, 1998), pp. 230–31; Gervase Jackson-Stops, *Blickling Hall* (National Trust Guide, 1980), p. 49.
134. Angélique Day (ed.), *Letters from Georgian Ireland: Mary Delany, 1731–68* (Belfast, 1991), p. 186.
135. BL, Add. MS 51337, fol. 18, Lady Ilchester to Lord Ilchester, n. d.
136. Sherborne Castle MSS, game book, 7 September 1764.
137. PP, Susan O'Brien to Mary Strangways, 15 February 1791, 21 March 1791.
138. PP, Susan O'Brien to Mary Talbot, [April-May 1793], [summer 1793].
139. BL, Add. MS 51360, Susan O'Brien's journal, 16 April 1818. *Daphne cneorum*, also known as the 'garland flower' was introduced to Britain around 1750. Its fragrant, pink flowers would have been out in April.
140. PP, Louisa Petty to Mary Talbot, 11 April 1809.
141. PP, Ann Fowler to Mary Talbot, 6 May 1812. Lady Charlotte [Lemon] was Mary's sister.
142. PP, Mary Cole to Mrs St George, 31 August 1827, quoted in Charlotte Traherne, 'Family Recollections'.
143. John Haverfield (1744–1820) visited Penrice in 1801, and he was there again in 1804 and 1805. He was involved in the restoration of the abbey church at Margam. The work, which was paid for by Thomas Talbot, was carried out between 1805 and 1810. See D. John Adams, *The Mansel-Talbots and their Tombs* (Margam, Port Talbot, 2003), pp. 3–4; and Howard Colvin, *A Biographical Dictionary of British Architects* (New Haven and London, 1995), pp. 472–73.
144. PP, Mary Talbot's pocket-books, 1802 and 1803.
145. PP, Mary Talbot's pocket-book, 1806.
146. PP, Mary Talbot's pocket-book, 1808.
147. Many are now regularly open to the public, including Abbotsbury, Bowood, Highclere, Killerton, Lacock, Minterne, Mount Edgcumbe, Sherborne and Stourhead.

Notes to Chapter 13: Travel

1. Christopher Morris (ed.), *The Illustrated Journeys of Celia Fiennes, 1685 to c. 1712* (London, 1982), p. 32.
2. PRO, PROB 11/539/77, will of Thomas Strangways of Melbury Sampford, 1714; DRO, D/FSI, box 232, draft will of Thomas Strangways Horner, dated 29 January 1728.

3. Amanda Vickery, *The Gentleman's Daughter* (New Haven and London, 1998), p. 31.
4. BL, Add. MS 51337, fol. 13, Lady Ilchester to Lord Ilchester [1742].
5. Sherborne Castle MSS, game book, 30 November 1770.
6. Gladys Scott Thomson, *The Russells in Bloomsbury, 1669–1771* (London, 1940), pp. 234–35.
7. Sherborne Castle MSS, Fox correspondence, Henry Digby to 'Dear Brother', 20 March 1754; BL, Add. MS 51340, fol. 107, Lord Digby to Lord Ilchester, 6 April [1754]; Sherborne Castle MSS, game book, 2 September 1758.
8. Sherborne Castle MSS, accounts 1764–82.
9. BL, Add. MS 51352, fols 43–44, William O'Brien to Susan O'Brien, 28 June 1781.
10. DRO, D/FSI, box 218, household accounts (Redlynch), 1730–43; box 189, ledger (Redlynch), 1743–64. A hammer-cloth covered the driver's seat or box in a private coach.
11. BL, Add. MS 51373A, fol. 34. The total of £90 for this carriage included the cost of some items of harness, unlike the £85 8*s*. for the chaise bought in 1736, which was for the chaise only.
12. PRO, C/38/943, Chancery Masters' reports and certificates, 27 April 1805.
13. William Felton, *A Treatise on Carriages*, ii (London, 1795), pp. 9 and 49.
14. DRO, D/FSI, box 189, general day book (Redlynch), 1735–54.
15. DRO, D/FSI, box 240B, bundle 8.
16. DRO, D/FSI, box 188, household accounts (Melbury), 1747–51. This payment was for 'the landau etc.', so the price probably included other items such as harness.
17. BL, Add. MS 51419, fol. 22, Henry Fox to Lord Ilchester, 19 July 1748.
18. DRO, D/FSI, box 193, estate accounts (Melbury), 1767–68.
19. DRO, D/FSI, box 240A, bundle 1, Lord Poulett to Lord Ilchester, 21 October 1761.
20. BL, Add. MS 51360, Susan O'Brien's journal, 17 January 1820.
21. PP, Charlotte Lemon to Mary Talbot, 23 October 1811.
22. Felton, *A Treatise on Carriages*, p. 85.
23. PP, Charlotte Traherne, 'Family Recollections'.
24. Fox Talbot Museum, Lacock, Susan O'Brien to Elizabeth Feilding, 3 October 1805.
25. PP, Charlotte Strangways to Mary Talbot, 4 July 1808.
26. Sherborne Castle MSS, accounts, 1764–82.
27. DRO, D/FSI, box 186, inventory of household furniture, Albemarle Street, 10 December 1741; WSRO, Lacock Abbey MSS, Acc. 2664, box of miscellaneous correspondence (Feilding, Strangways, Talbot), Susan O'Brien to Elizabeth Talbot, 9 September [1799].
28. BL, Add. MS 51417, fols 133–34, Lord Ilchester to Henry Fox, July 1745.
29. PP, account of John Mitchell, 1792.
30. PP, Thomas Mansel Talbot to Michael Hicks Beach, 19 January 1794 and

25 January 1794; Mary Strangways to Harriot Strangways 23 January 1794. A 'job horse' was one that had been hired.

31. PP, Thomas Mansel Talbot's pocket-book, 1804.
32. Gloucester Record Office, Hicks Beach (St Aldwyn) papers, D2440, box 53, accounts of Thomas Mansel Talbot's executors.
33. WSRO, Lacock Abbey MSS, Acc. 2664, box of miscellaneous correspondence (Feilding, Strangways, Talbot), Elizabeth Strangways to Harriot Strangways, 22 February 1795.
34. Felton, *A Treatise on Carriages*, pp. 106–7.
35. PP, Thomas Mansel Talbot's pocket-book, 1804.
36. BL, Add. MS 51352, fols 43–44, William O'Brien to Susan O'Brien, 28 June 1781.
37. BL, Add. MS 51357, fols 175–84, 'accounts of money received by Mr O'Brien and Lady Susan'.
38. BL, Add. MS 51359, Susan O'Brien's journal, January 1798, 1 April 1800.
39. BL, Add. MS 51359, Susan O'Brien's journal, 15 July and 24 September 1803, 6 May and 8 July 1812.
40. BL, Add. MS 51359, Susan O'Brien's journal, 14 October 1812.
41. BL, Add. MS 51360, Susan O'Brien's journal, 1 June 1825, 12 June 1826.
42. PRO, PROB 11/539/77, will of Thomas Strangways of Melbury Sampford, 1714.
43. BL, Add. MS 51340, fols 3–4, Charlotte Fox to Stephen Fox, 9 September [1719–20].
44. DRO, D/FSI, box 186, Milton Clevedon inventory, 1729.
45. DRO, D/FSI, box 232, draft will of Thomas Strangways Horner, dated 29 January 1728.
46. Cornwall RO, FS/3/1126/1,2, typescript of memoirs of Loveday Sarah Gregor (*c.* 1851), p. 60.
47. DRO, D/FSI, box 173A, accounts (Redlynch), 1752–53.
48. BL, Add. MS 51344, fols 65–66, Lady Ilchester to Lord Ilchester, 20 November [1767]. 'Riding double' meant sitting on a pillion behind a male rider.
49. Sherborne Castle MSS, game book, 16 October 1775.
50. BL, Add. 51414, fols 88–89, Caroline Fox to Henry Fox, 4 February [1748].
51. See above, p. 169, for further details.
52. BL, Add. MS 51353, Sarah Bunbury to Susan O'Brien, 11 October 1764.
53. Dr John Gregory, *A Father's Legacy to his Daughters* (first published 1774; this edition Dublin, 1790), p. 20.
54. Jane Austen, *Mansfield Park* (London, Penguin Classics, 1986), p. 70.
55. DRO, D/FSI, box 194, estate accounts, 1783–84.
56. PP, Mary Strangways to Harriot Strangways, 24 January 1792.
57. Minterne MSS, Admiral Robert Digby's journal, 1792–1800.
58. PP, Jane Harriot Talbot to C. R. M. Talbot, 25 February 1812.
59. PP, Mary Theresa Talbot to Charlotte Talbot, 7 March [*c.* 1816].
60. BL, Add. MS 51360, account of changes between 1760 and 1818 by Susan O'Brien.

61. Cornwall RO, FS/3/1126/1,2, typescript of memoirs of Loveday Sarah Gregor, p. 50.
62. Ibid., p. 119.
63. Joanna Martin, *A Governess in the Age of Jane Austen* (London and Rio Grande, Ohio, 1998), p. 230, Agnes Porter's journal, 14 August 1803.
64. PP, Mary Talbot to Harriot Strangways [early 1794].
65. PP, Mary Talbot to Charlotte Talbot [1810].
66. PP, Ann Fowler to Mary Talbot, 6 May 1812.
67. Martin, *A Governess in the Age of Jane Austen*, p. 147, Agnes Porter to Mary Talbot, 1 August 1794.
68. Martin, *A Governess in the Age of Jane Austen*, pp. 263–64, Agnes Porter to Mary Talbot, 11 December 1806.
69. Sherborne Castle MSS, game book, 14 November 1771. The Antelope is an inn in Sherborne.
70. BL, Add. MS 51337, fol. 43, Lady Ilchester to Lord Ilchester [*c.* 19 July 1750].
71. PP, Thomas Mansel Talbot to Michael Hicks Beach, 6 October 1796.
72. BL, Add. MS 51360, Susan O'Brien's journal, 9 July 1825.
73. PP, Jennet Flew to C. R. M. Talbot, 21 October 1812.
74. Norman Scarfe (ed.), *Innocent Espionage: The La Rochefoucauld Brothers' Tour of England in 1785* (Woodbridge, 1995), p. 143.
75. PP, Charlotte Talbot's 'Journal from Bath to London in the Year 1815'.
76. Martin, *A Governess in the Age of Jane Austen*, pp. 153–55, Agnes Porter's journal, 7 March to 13 June 1796.
77. PP, Susan O'Brien to Mary Talbot, 26 August 1807.
78. PP, Mary Talbot to Charlotte Talbot, 22 October 1812.
79. BL, Add. MS 51414, fols 4–5, Caroline Fox to Henry Fox [8 December 1746].
80. PP, Charlotte Talbot's 'Journal from Bath to London in the Year 1815'. A taxed cart was a two-wheeled open cart drawn by one horse, used mainly for agricultural or trade purposes, so called because a reduced rate of tax was levied on these carts.
81. PP, C. R. M. Talbot to Charlotte Talbot, 24 January 1813.
82. BL, Add. MS 51414, fols 132–33, Caroline Fox to Henry Fox, 1 March 1748.
83. BL, Add. MS 51414, fols 86–87, Henry Fox to Caroline Fox, 3 February 1748.
84. E. W. Bovill, *English Country Life, 1780–1830* (London, 1962), p. 141.
85. Scarfe (ed.), *Innocent Espionage*, p. 158.
86. PP, C. R. M. Talbot to Mary Theresa Talbot, October 1819.
87. Martin, *A Governess in the Age of Jane Austen*, p. 313, Agnes Porter to Mary Talbot, 4 July 1811.
88. Martin, *A Governess in the Age of Jane Austen*, pp. 81–82, Agnes Porter to Mary Strangways, 21 December 1789.
89. Martin, *A Governess in the Age of Jane Austen*, pp. 219–225, Agnes Porter's journal, February to April 1803.
90. Martin, *A Governess in the Age of Jane Austen*, pp. 248–57, Agnes Porter's journal, February to April 1805.

91. PP, Sir Christopher Cole to Mary Cole, 27 January 1818.
92. Fox Talbot Museum, Lacock, W. H. F. Talbot to Elizabeth Feilding, 20 January 1812.
93. PP, C. R. M. Talbot to Mary Cole, 20 July 1816.
94. PP, C. R. M. Talbot to Mary Theresa Talbot, October 1819.
95. PP, Thomas Mansel Talbot to Michael Hicks Beach, 19 March 1798, 12 January 1800.
96. Martin, *A Governess in the Age of Jane Austen*, p. 237, Agnes Porter's journal, 2 March 1804.
97. Fox Talbot Museum, Lacock, Susan O'Brien to Elizabeth Feilding, 24 January 1811.
98. PP, C. R. M. Talbot to Mary Cole, 16 February 1816.
99. DRO, D/FSI, box 241A(1), bundle 3/11, travelling expenses to Wales, August 1803; Mary Talbot's pocket-book, 1803; Martin, *A Governess in the Age of Jane Austen*, p. 231, Agnes Porter's journal, 19–26 August 1803.
100. BL, Add. MS 51337, fol. 106, Lady Ilchester to Lord Ilchester [*c.* 5 November 1757].
101. Minterne MSS, Admiral Robert Digby's journal, 7 July 1792; PP, Susan O'Brien to Mary Strangways, 16 July 1792.
102. PP, Sir Christopher Cole to Mary Cole, 10 September 1816.
103. PP, C. R. M. Talbot to Mary Cole, 14 January 1817.
104. BL, Add. MS 51404, fols 39–40, John Wigan to Henry Fox, December 1737.
105. DRO, D/FSI, box 240A, bundle 5, Joanna Cheeke to Lord Ilchester, 12 October [?1751].
106. P. N. Furbank, W. R. Owens and A. J. Coulsons (ed.), *Daniel Defoe: A Tour Through the Whole Island of Great Britain* (New Haven and London, 1991), pp. 58–60.
107. PP, Mary Talbot's, pocket-book, 4 April 1803.
108. PP, George Eden to Ellinor Talbot, 13 August 1809.
109. Adrian Tinniswood, *A History of Country House Visiting* (Oxford, 1989), p. 89.
110. Timothy Mowl describes the grounds at St Giles's House as 'one of the most committed Rococo parks in the country': Timothy Mowl, *Historic Gardens of Dorset* (Stroud, 2003), p. 71.
111. BL, Add. MS 51337, fol. 43, Lady Ilchester to Lord Ilchester [*c.* 19 July 1750].
112. This may be the 'new roade' for which £108 13*s.* 2*d.* was paid in 1745–46: DRO, D/FSI, box 189, general day book (Redlynch), 1735–54.
113. John Dixon Hunt (ed.), 'Horace Walpole's Journals of Visits to Country Seats', in *The History of the Modern Taste in Gardening* (New York and London, 1982), p. 43.
114. Sherborne Castle MSS, game book, 28 September 1768.
115. Sherborne Castle MSS, game book, 29, 30 August 1771.
116. H. P. Wyndham, *A Gentleman's Tour through Monmouthshire and Wales in June and July 1774* (2nd edn, London, 1781), pp. i–ii.
117. Malcolm Andrews, 'A Picturesque Template: The Tourists and their Guide-books',

in Dana Arnold (ed.), *The Picturesque in Late Georgian England* (London, 1995), p. 4.

118. PP, Susan O'Brien to Mary Strangways, 22 May 1792.
119. PP, Jane Talbot to Charlotte Talbot, *c.* 1815. The cross referred to here is presumably the Bristol High Cross, which was erected by Henry Hoare in 1764. It still stands, between the bridge and the church.
120. Deans Leaze belonged to the Binghams of Bingham's Melcombe. They leased it out from time to time: Susan O'Brien's niece Charlotte Lemon and her husband rented Deans Leaze for several years from 1811.
121. BL, Add. MS 51359, Susan O'Brien's journal, summer 1792.
122. BL, Add. MS 51359, Susan O'Brien's journal, June-July 1794.
123. Fox Talbot Museum, Lacock, Susan O'Brien to Elizabeth Feilding, 24 January 1811. 'Pluto's realms' at Neath were the copper-works.
124. Fox Talbot Museum, Lacock, Susan O'Brien to Elizabeth Feilding, 11 February 1811.
125. BL, Add. MS 51359, Susan O'Brien's journal, 11 January to 13 May 1811. The Oystermouth tramroad, later known as the Mumbles railway, began to carry passengers in 1807. It was the first passenger railway in the world.
126. BL, Add. MS 51360, Susan O'Brien's journal, 29 September to 10 October 1823.
127. PP, Thomas Mansel Talbot to Michael Hicks Beach, 6 December 1794.
128. Fox Talbot Museum, Lacock, Susan O'Brien to Elizabeth Feilding, 4 September [?1814].
129. PP, Charlotte Talbot's, 'Journal from Penrice to London', 1814.
130. PP, C. R. M. Talbot's 'Journal from Penrice to London', 1815.
131. One of the leaders of the rising was Lord Edward Fitzgerald (1763–1798), son of the Duke and Duchess of Leinster, and nephew of Sarah Napier.
132. Martin, *A Governess in the Age of Jane Austen*, p. 198, Agnes Porter to Mary Talbot, 14 August 1798.
133. BL, Add. MS 51353, fols 74–78, Sarah Bunbury to Susan O'Brien, 16 December 1764.
134. University of Wales, Swansea, Collins letters, Thomas Mansel Talbot to Revd John Collins, 1 September 1797.
135. PP, Lord Ilchester to Mary Talbot, 6 August 1807.
136. PP, Louisa Petty to Mary Talbot, 16 September 1809.
137. BL, Add. MS 51342, fol. 54, Lord Stavordale to Lord Ilchester, 19 September 1771.
138. PP, Mary Strangways's pocket-book, 1792.
139. PP, Lord Ilchester to Mary Talbot, 6 August 1807.
140. PP, Louisa Petty to Mary Talbot, 16 September and 21 September 1809.
141. Brian Dolan, *Ladies of the Grand Tour* (London, 2001), pp. 160–61. Dolan cites several examples, including Elizabeth, Lady Webster, who claimed that she was too ill to return to England with her husband in 1795, and so stayed in Italy with her lover Lord Holland.

142. BL, Add. MS 51354, fols 186–87, Sarah Napier to Susan O'Brien, 10 May 1785 (the letter describes conditions eighteen years earlier).
143. BL, Add. MS 51359, Susan O'Brien's journal, 1785.
144. PP, Charlotte Lemon to Mary Cole, 25 July 1822.
145. PP, Charlotte Traherne, 'Family Recollections'.
146. Anne Acland, *A Devon Family: The Story of the Aclands* (London and Chichester, 1981), p. 33.
147. J. H. Jesse, *Memoirs of the Life and Reign of King George the Third*, ii (London, 1867), p. 181.
148. BL, Add. 51353, fol. 82, Sarah Bunbury to Susan O'Brien, 5 May 1765.
149. PP, C. R. M. Talbot, 'Characters of Some Members of His Family'.
150. PP, W. H. F. Talbot to Mary Theresa Talbot, 2 May 1816.
151. PP, Charlotte Lemon to Mary Cole, 25 July 1822.
152. BL, Add. MS 51360, Susan O'Brien's journal, 8 April to 26 May 1825.
153. BL, Add. MS 51360, Susan O'Brien's journal, 3 October 1823.
154. PP, W. H. F. Talbot to Mary Theresa Talbot, 7 May 1825.
155. Pigot & Co., *National Commercial Directory of Gloucestershire* (1830), p. 123.
156. BL, Add. MS 51360, Susan O'Brien's journal, 9 September 1825.
157. John Vivian Hughes, *The Wealthiest Commoner: C. R. M. Talbot* (Port Talbot, 1977), pp. 26–28.

Notes to Chapter 14: Patronage

1. The arguments are summarised by Amanda Vickery in the introduction to *The Gentleman's Daughter* (New Haven and London, 1998), pp. 1–12. See also Lawrence Stone, *The Family, Sex and Marriage in England* (London, 1977), pp. 396–97; and Robert B. Shoemaker, *Gender in English Society, 1650–1850* (London, 1998).
2. DRO, D/FSI, box 329, Susan O'Brien's advice to a niece, 1796.
3. BL, Add. MS 51360, Susan O'Brien's journal, 22–25 October 1817. The Duke was the son of George III's younger brother, Prince William Henry, who had been created Duke of Gloucester in 1764. The Duchess was George III's fourth daughter, Princess Mary.
4. PP, Susan O'Brien to Mary Talbot, 19 May [1812]; Fox Talbot Museum, Lacock, Susan O'Brien to Elizabeth Feilding, 29 May and 19 July 1812.
5. Patricia Phillips, *The Scientific Lady* (London, 1990), pp. 193–99.
6. *Gentleman's Magazine*, 80 (1810), pp. 113–15, 'Plan of Mr Salisbury's Botanic Garden explained'.
7. BL, Add. MS 51354, fols 168–71, Sarah Napier to Susan O'Brien, 10 November 1783.
8. DRO, D/FSI, box 232, 'Mrs Horner's character'.
9. Mells Manor, MS 576, 'History of the Horner Family' by 'A.B.' (Revd Henry Harris).
10. PRO, PROB 11/688/83, will of Judith Ayliffe of Foxley, Wiltshire, 1738. Judith also left £2000 to Henry Fox 'in return for his friendship to me'.

11. DRO, D/FSI, box 232, George Donisthorpe to Susanna Strangways Horner, 2 March 1743.
12. Sherborne Castle MSS, Fox correspondence, Lord Ilchester to Lord Digby [*c.* 1753–54]; BL, Add. MS 51419, fols 213–14, Henry Fox to Lord Ilchester, 21 July 1753; fols 215–16, Henry Fox to Lord Ilchester, 28 July 1753.
13. BL, Add. MS 51417, fols 133–34, Lord Ilchester to Henry Fox, July 1745.
14. BL, Add. MS 51337, fols 167–81, letters between Lord Ilchester and Susanna Strangways Horner, 1747. See also DRO, D/FSI, box 240B, bundle 1, Susanna Strangways Horner to Lord Ilchester, 31 January 1747.
15. He does appear to have been related to Judith Ayliffe, but more distantly than he claimed.
16. DRO, D/FSI, box 247, bundle of legal papers concerning John Ayliffe. See also BL, Add. MS 51416, fols 65–66, Henry Fox to Caroline Fox, 19 November 1759, and *Gentleman's Magazine*, 29 (1759), pp. 496 and 548.
17. PRO, PROB 11/837/115, will of Susannah Strangways Horner of Melbury Sampford, 1758; and PROB 11/1025/463, will of Stephen, Earl of Ilchester, 1776.
18. BL, Add. MS 51353, fols 138–44, Sarah Bunbury to Susan O'Brien, 7 May 1767.
19. DRO, D/FSI, box 242A(1), Dowager Countess of Ilchester to Lord Ilchester [c. 1783] and [November 1783].
20. BL, Add. MS 51359, Susan O'Brien's journal, 1775, 3 August 1803, 24 July 1812.
21. PRO, C38/943, Chancery Master's Report, 27 April 1805; C38/959, Chancery Master's Report, 2 July 1806.
22. PRO, PROB 11/1394/908, will of Henry Thomas Fox Strangways, Earl of Ilchester, 1802.
23. BL, Add. MS 51359, Susan O'Brien's journal, September and October 1802, 21 February 1803; DRO, D/FSI, box 241B, Countess of Ilchester to Earl of Ilchester [May 1803].
24. PRO, PROB 11/1546/389–90, will of Thomas Mansel Talbot of Penrice Castle, 1813.
25. BL, Add. MS 51359, Susan O'Brien's journal, 1789.
26. BL, Add. MS 51359, Susan O'Brien's journal, 12 June 1813.
27. The other candidate was Henry Bankes of Kingston Lacy.
28. BL, Add. MS 51359, Susan O'Brien's journal, 6–26 November 1806.
29. BL, Add. MS 51359, Susan O'Brien's journal, 13 May 1807.
30. PP, C. R. M. Talbot, 'Characters of Some Members of His Family'.
31. BL, Add. MS 51359, Susan O'Brien's journal, August 1798. They were in Winchester because Lily's husband was an officer in the militia at the time. The dramatist and politician Richard Brinsley Sheridan had married Esther Jane Ogle, daughter of the Dean of Winchester, in 1795.
32. Fox Talbot Museum, Lacock, Susan O'Brien to Elizabeth Feilding [June-July 1811].
33. BL, Add. MS 51359, Susan O'Brien's journal, 12–13 September 1822.
34. PP, C. R. M. Talbot, 'Characters of Some Members of His Family'.
35. Irene Collins, *Jane Austen and the Clergy* (London, 1994), pp. 24–25.

36. See Joanna Martin, *A Governess in the Age of Jane Austen* (London and Rio Grande, Ohio, 1998), pp. 4–10, for Francis Porter.
37. *The Clerical Guide* (London, 1817), and *Patroni Ecclesiarum* (London, 1831). The livings were Abbotsbury, Bridport, Maiden Newton, Melbury Osmond, Melbury Sampford, Stinsford and Winterborne Monkton in Dorset; Kilmington, Middle Chinnock, Milton Clevedon, Shepton Montague and Somerton in Somerset; and Little Somerford and West Grimstead in Wiltshire. In addition, Lord Ilchester was one of two or more patrons in the parishes of Chiselborough with West Chinnock in Somerset and Rewe, Lustleigh and Silverton in Devon who presented in turn.
38. BL, Add. MS 51360, Susan O'Brien's journal, 29 July 1815.
39. BL, Add. MS 51359, Susan O'Brien's journal, 19 September 1812.
40. BL, Add. MS 51337, fol. 53, Lady Ilchester to Lord Ilchester, 14 November [1752].
41. DRO, D/FSI, box 232, 'Mrs Horner's character', 1758.
42. BL, Add. MS 51430, Thomas Edwards to [Henry Fox], 14 August 1757.
43. John Hutchins, *The History and Antiquities of the County of Dorset* (3rd edn, with additions by W. Shipp and J. W. Hodson, London, 1863), iv, p. 440.
44. DRO, D/FSI, box 188, household accounts (Melbury), 1747–51. The new marble font cost £6 6*s*. Exactly how much the work cost altogether is unclear, but Cartwright was paid £140 for the tower, and £70 for new seating and paving in 1747–49.
45. PP, Charlotte Traherne, 'Family Recollections'. Horace Walpole, who visited the church in 1762, thought that the altarpiece was 'the only thing unworthy this venerable little temple': 'Horace Walpole's Journals of Visits to Country Seats', in *The History of the Modern Taste in Gardening* (New York and London, 1982), p. 48.
46. DRO, D/FSI, box 188, household accounts (Melbury), 1747–51; John Newman and Nikolaus Pevsner, *The Buildings of England: Dorset* (London, 1972), p. 72. Cartwright's estimate for the work on the chancel came to £99.
47. DRO, D/FSI, box 188, household accounts (Melbury), 1747–51.
48. DRO, D/FSI, box 188, household accounts (Melbury), 1747–51. The Strangways family had a long-standing tradition of patronising Lamerie, for a chalice with cover, paten and flagon, all by him, had been given to Milton Clevedon church – presumably by Susanna's mother – back in 1717. In 1727 Susanna's cousin, Judith Ayliffe, gave a silver-gilt set of chalice, paten and flagon, also by Lamerie, to the church at Foxley, Wiltshire.
49. John Hutchins, *The History and Antiquities of the County of Dorset*, i (1st edn, London, 1774), p. 512.
50. BL, Add. MS 51359, Susan O'Brien's journal, 3 August 1801.
51. At 5 per cent, this was close to the average for the time.
52. DRO, D/FSI, box 188, household accounts (Melbury), 1728–29.
53. At the rate of 4 per cent. In 1760 the 'poor's weekly allowance' was 16*s*. and one of the villagers, 'old Francis', was also given 4*s*. 6*d*. a week: DRO, D/FSI, box 217, household accounts (Melbury), 1760–70.

54. The accounts suggest that this was built in 1747 and 1748. In 1748–49 Mr Greenaway was paid 5*s.* 10*d.* 'for cutting 70 letters at 1*d.* each over the poor house door' at Melbury: DRO, D/FSI, box 188, household accounts (Melbury), 1747–51.
55. 'Horace Walpole's Journals of Visits to Country Seats', p. 48.
56. DRO, D/FSI box 188, household accounts (Melbury), 1747–51.
57. DRO, D/FSI, box 188, household accounts (Melbury), 1728–29.
58. John Houlton remained as schoolmaster until 1766, at a salary of £15 a year. He had an assistant. From 1760 to 1768 Mary Coombs of Melbury Osmond was paid £2 10*s.* a year for teaching at the school there. At midsummer 1768 she was replaced by a new schoolmistress, Mary Childs, who received the same salary. These women may have been teaching girls, rather than boys: in 1793 Mrs Fiander was paid £2 10*s.* a year 'for instructing poor girls at Melbury'. Mr Fiander was the schoolmaster in the 1790s, still with a salary of £15 a year: DRO, D/FSI, box 195, accounts (Melbury), 1792–94.
59. The next master, Mr Bond, who arrived *c.* 1752, was paid £20 a year: DRO, D/FSI, box 193, estate accounts (Melbury), 1752–53.
60. DRO, D/FSI, box 188, household accounts (Melbury), 1747–51. Francis Cartwright was responsible for this building too.
61. PRO, PROB 11/837/115, will of Susanna Strangways Horner, 1758.
62. DRO, D/FSI, box 188, household accounts (Melbury), 1747–51
63. PRO, PROB 11/1101/125, will of Marrian Feaver of Melbury Osmond, 1783.
64. BL, Add. MS 51419, fols 6–7, Henry Fox to Susanna Strangways Horner [early 1748].
65. Susanna stated in her will that her ancestors had given £20 a year to the vicar of Abbotsbury 'for many years'.
66. DRO, D/FSI, box 240A, bundle 6, Lady Ilchester to Lord Ilchester [November 1756].
67. 'Wrens' are presumably wens or lumps.
68. PP, C. R. M. Talbot, 'Characters of Some Members of His Family'.
69. See above, p. 230, for Mrs Williams.
70. Hannah More, *Coelebs in Search of a Wife: Comprehending Observations on Domestic Habits … Religion, and Morals*, ii (9th edn, London, 1809), p. 20, quoted in Anne Stott, *Hannah More: The First Victorian* (Oxford, 2003), p. 276. *Coelebs* was first published in 1808.
71. PP, C. R. M. Talbot, 'Characters of Some Members of His Family'.
72. PP, Louisa Lansdowne to Mary Cole, 10 December 1815. Lady Barham, who lived at Fairy Hill, a few miles from Penrice, was a follower of the Countess of Huntingdon. She built six Methodist chapels in Gower between 1813 and 1823. See Gary Gregor, 'William Griffiths: "The Apostle of Gower"', *Gower*, 54 (2001), pp. 54–66.
73. Letter from Mary Cole to Kitty St George, 27 November 1852, quoted in Charlotte Traherne, 'Family Recollections'. The grandson concerned was Iltyd, son of Jane Nicholl.

74. PP, Thomas Mansel Talbot to Henrietta Maria Hicks Beach, 20 December 1796.
75. PP, Mary Talbot's pocket-books, 1805–8.
76. I am assuming that this was at Penrice, though the records of the payments in Mary's pocket-books do not give the location of the school. The only likely alternative would be Oxwich.
77. Stott, *Hannah More*, pp. 105–6.
78. PP, Jane Talbot to Charlotte Talbot, 15 January 1821. Andrew Bell (1753–1832) developed the 'Madras system' of education, which was based on mutual instruction: children were both tutors and scholars.
79. PP, Mary Cole to Charlotte Talbot, 18 January 1821.
80. They are still standing, though now converted into two private houses.
81. Doreen Slatter, 'The Third Marquess of Lansdowne and his Family at Bowood, 1810–40', *The Wiltshire Archaeological and Natural History Magazine*, 84 (1991), p. 134.
82. BL, Add. MS 51345, fols 95–96, Lord Ilchester to Lord Hervey, 13 November 1742.
83. Lord Ilchester's first son was not born until the following year. The new title, Lord Ilchester and Stavordale, Baron of Redlynch, Somerset, is referred to irrevently in a letter from Joanna Cheeke in 1747 as 'My Lord Invention and Stuff': BL, Add. MS 51346, fols 2–3, Joanna Cheeke to Lord Ilchester, 20 June [1747].
84. Robert Halsband, *Lord Hervey, Eighteenth-Century Courtier* (Oxford, 1973), pp. 239, 276–77; *Diary of the First Earl of Egmont*, iii (London, 1923), pp. 259–60. In this instance, too, Henry and his sons would inherit the title if Stephen died without male heirs of his own. In the event, Henry's last descendant in the male line was his great-grandon, who died in 1859; the Earldom of Ilchester still exists.
85. BL, Add. MS 51337, fol. 94, Lady Ilchester to Lord Ilchester, 18 June [1756]. 'Mr Fever' is the Revd Marrian Feaver.
86. Stephen held this post until his death in 1776.
87. BL, Add. MS 51420, fols 54–56, Lord Ilchester to Henry Fox [*c.* 17 March 1757].
88. BL, Add. MS 51360, Susan O'Brien's journal, 31 December 1826.
89. PP, Louisa Lansdowne to Mary Cole, 1 March 1816.
90. PP, Mary Cole to Frances St George, December 1835.
91. BL, Add. MS 51419, fols 118–19, Lady Ilchester to Henry Fox, 29 August [1750].
92. BL, Add. MS 51419, fols 174–76, Lord Ilchester to Henry Fox, [17] December 1752.
93. BL, Add. MS 51420, fols 54–56, Lord Ilchester to Henry Fox, [c. 17 March 1757].
94. BL, Add. MS 51422, fols 197–98, Charlotte Digby to Lord Holland, 8 October 1764.
95. BL, Add. MS 51422, fols 201–22, Charlotte Digby to Lord Holland, 4 June 1765.
96. BL, Add. MS 51340, fols 17–18, Charlotte Digby to Lord Ilchester, 11 October 1746.

97. Having been Paymaster General from 1757 to May 1765.
98. BL, Add. MS 51352, fols 109–10, Lord Holland to William O'Brien, 30 November 1765.
99. BL, Add. MS 51359, Susan O'Brien's journal, 1772.
100. BL, Add. MS 51359, Susan O'Brien's journal, 1782.
101. BL, Add. MS 51360, Susan O'Brien's journal, 20 June to 9 July 1821; 5 May 1825.
102. Martin, *A Governess in the Age of Jane Austen*, p. 295, Agnes Porter to Mary Talbot, 12 June 1810.
103. Martin, *A Governess in the Age of Jane Austen*, p. 317, Agnes Porter to Mary Talbot, 7 December 1811. 'Miss Elbury' was probably Jane Elborough, who had been a governess at Penrice for a few months in 1806 and 1807.
104. Hester Davenport, *Faithful Handmaid: Fanny Burney at the Court of King George III* (Stroud, 2000), p. 33.
105. Martin, *A Governess in the Age of Jane Austen*, p. 217, Agnes Porter's journal, 7 November 1802.
106. Fox Talbot Museum, Lacock, Susan O'Brien to Elizabeth Feilding, 31 January 1817.
107. BL, Add. MS 51359, Susan O'Brien's journal, September 1792.
108. PP, Susan O'Brien to Mary Talbot, 18 February 1794; BL, Add. MS 51359, Susan O'Brien's journal, February 1797; PP, Mary Talbot to Harriot Strangways, 26 February 1797.
109. Hardy researched this period by reading editions of the *Dorset County Chronicle* published in the 1820s. A book, based on one of his notebooks and edited by William Greenslade, is due to be published soon. See 'Hardy, the Copycat of Casterbridge', *Sunday Times*, 3 August 2003.
110. BL, Add. MS 51360, Susan O'Brien's journal, 12 July 1818.
111. *Dorset County Chronicle*, 17 March 1825.
112. BL, Add. MS 51360, Susan O'Brien's journal, 26 October 1826.
113. Jo Draper, *Discover Dorset: Regency Riot and Reform* (Wimborne, 2000), pp. 46–47.
114. Fox Talbot Museum, Lacock, Elizabeth Feilding to W. H. F. Talbot, 27 November 1830.
115. They were actually prosecuted for swearing an illegal oath, part of the initiation rite for new members of the Union.
116. The name Fox Strangways survives too, though not at Melbury: the house now belongs to the Hon. Mrs Townshend, a descendant of the second Earl of Ilchester by his second wife. Mrs Townshend's mother was a daughter of the seventh Earl of Ilchester.

Bibliography

MANUSCRIPT SOURCES

British Library, London, Department of Manuscripts
Holland House Collection: Additional MSS 51318–52254

Dorset County Record Office, Dorchester
Fox Strangways/Ilchester estates collection
Sherborne Castle collection

Fox Talbot Museum, Lacock, Wiltshire
Letters of William Henry Fox Talbot and Lady Susan O'Brien

Gloucestershire Record Office, Gloucester
Hicks Beach/St Aldwyn estates collection

Minterne, Dorset
Digby family papers (private collection)

National Library of Wales, Aberystwyth
Penrice and Margam manuscripts

Penrice Castle, Gower, South Wales
Talbot family papers (private collection)

Public Record Office (National Archives) London
Records of the Court of Chancery
Probate records of the Prerogative Court of Canterbury

Sherborne Castle, Dorset
Sherborne Castle archives (private collection)

Suffolk Record Office, Bury St Edmunds
Ickworth estate collection: letters of John, Lord Hervey

Swansea University Library
Collins family papers

West Glamorgan Archive Service, Swansea
Penrice and Margam estates collection

Wiltshire and Swindon Record Office, Trowbridge
Lacock Abbey collection

PUBLISHED SOURCES

Acland, Anne, *A Devon Family: The Story of the Aclands* (London and Chichester, 1981).

Arnold, Dana (ed.), *The Georgian Country House: Architecture, Landscape and Society* (Stroud, 1998).

Arnold, H. J. P., *William Henry Fox Talbot: Pioneer of Photography and Man of Science* (London, 1977).

Ashelford, Jane, *The Art of Dress: Clothes and Society, 1500–1914* (London, 1996).

Austen, Jane, *Mansfield Park* (first published 1814).

Austen, Jane, *Northanger Abbey* (first published 1818).

Baird, Rosemary, *Mistress of the House: Great Ladies and Grand Houses, 1670–1830* (London, 2003).

Beckett, J. V., *The Aristocracy in England, 1660–1914* (Oxford, 1986).

Bennett, Sue, *Five Centuries of Women and Gardens* (National Portrait Gallery, London, 2000).

Black, Jeremy, *The British and the Grand Tour* (London, 1985).

Blacker, Mary Rose, *Flora Domestica: A History of Flower Arranging, 1500–1930* (London, 2000).

Blakiston, Georgina, *Lord William Russell and his Wife, 1815–1846* (London, 1972).

Bonfield, Lloyd, *Marriage Settlements, 1601–1740: The Adoption of the Strict Settlement* (Cambridge, 1983).

Boorman, David, *The Brighton of Wales: Swansea as a Fashionable Seaside Resort, c. 1780-c. 1830* (Swansea, 1986).

Bovill, E. W., *English Country Life, 1780–1830* (London, 1962).

Brewer, John, *The Pleasures of the Imagination* (London, 1997).

Brown, Jane, *The Pursuit of Paradise* (London, 1999).

Buck, Anne, *Clothes and the Child: A Handbook of Children's Dress in England, 1500–1900* (Carlton, Bedford, 1996).

Burke's Landed Gentry (various editions).

Burke's Peerage (various editions).

Cadbury, Deborah, *The Dinosaur Hunters: A Story of Scientific Rivalry and the Discovery of the Prehistoric World* (London, 2000).

Cannon, John, *Aristocratic Century: The Peerage of Eighteenth-Century England* (Cambridge, 1984).

Clarke, Norma, *Dr Johnson's Women* (London and New York, 2000).

Clay, Christopher, *Public Finance and Private Wealth: The Career of Sir Stephen Fox, 1627–1716* (Oxford, 1978).

Cliffe, J. T., *The World of the Country House in Seventeenth-Century England* (New Haven and London, 1999).

Climenson, Emily, *Passages from the Diaries of Mrs Philip Lybbe Powys* (London, 1899).

Cockayne, George Edward, *The Complete Peerage* (new edn, edited by Vicary Gibbs and H. A. Doubleday, 13 vols, London, 1910–59).

Collins, Irene, *Jane Austen and the Clergy* (London, 1994).

Collinson, John, *The History and Antiquities of the County of Somerset* (3 vols, Bath, 1791).

Colvin, Howard, *A Biographical Dictionary of British Architects, 1600–1840* (third edn, New Haven and London, 1995).

Crowley, D. A. (ed.), *The Victoria History of the Counties of England: A History of the County of Wiltshire*, xiv, xv and xvii (Oxford, 1991–95, and Woodbridge, 2002).

Davenport, Hester, *Faithful Handmaid: Fanny Burney at the Court of King George III* (Stroud, 2000).

Davidoff, Leonore, and Hall, Catherine, *Family Fortunes: Men and Women of the English Middle Class, 1780–1850* (London, 1987).

Day, Angélique (ed.), *Letters from Georgian Ireland: Mary Delany, 1731–68* (Belfast, 1991).

Desmond, Adrian, and Moore, James, *Darwin* (London, 1991).

Dictionary of National Biography (London, 1885–1900).

Digby, Lettice, *My Ancestors, Being the History of the Digby and Strutt Families* (London, 1928).

Dolan, Brian, *Ladies of the Grand Tour* (London, 2001).

Dormandy, Thomas, *The White Death: A History of Tuberculosis* (London and Rio Grande, Ohio, 1999).

Draper, Jo, *Discover Dorset: The Georgians* (Wimborne, 1998).

Draper, Jo, *Discover Dorset: Regency Riot and Reform* (Wimborne, 2000).

Dunning, R. W, *Somerset Families* (Somerset County Council, 2002).

Dunning, R. W., *The Victoria History of the Counties of England: A History of the County of Somerset*, vii (London, 1999).

Edgeworth, Maria and Richard Lovell, *Practical Education* (London, 1798).

Erickson, Amy Louise, *Women and Property in Early Modern England* (London and New York, 1993).

Evelyn, Charles, *The Lady's Recreation* (London and Dublin, 1717).

Felton, William, *A Treatise on Carriages* (London, 1795).

Fitzgerald, Brian (ed.), *The Correspondence of Emily, Duchess of Leinster* (Dublin, Stationery Office, 1953).

Fletcher, Anthony, *Gender, Sex and Subordination in England, 1500–1800* (New Haven and London, 1995).

Foreman, Amanda, *Georgiana, Duchess of Devonshire* (London, 1998).

Foster, Joseph, *Alumni Oxonienses, 1715–1786* (London and Oxford, 1887–88).

Fowler, John and Cornforth, John, *English Decoration in the Eighteenth Century* (London, 1974).

Furbank, P. N., Owens, W. R., and Coulson, A. J. (ed.), *Daniel Defoe: A Tour Through the Whole Island of Great Britain* (New Haven and London, 1991).

Gadd, David, *Georgian Summer: The Rise and Development of Bath* (Newbury, Berkshire, 1987).

Gardiner, Dorothy, *English Girlhood at School* (Oxford, 1929).

Girouard, Mark, *Life in the English Country House* (New Haven and London, 1978).

Gisborne, Thomas, *An Enquiry into the Duties of the Female Sex* (7th edn, London, 1806).

Gore, Alan and Ann, *The History of English Interiors* (Oxford, 1991).

Gregory, John, *A Father's Legacy to his Daughters* (first edn, 1774).

Grundy, Isobel, *Lady Mary Wortley Montagu: Comet of the Enlightenment* (Oxford, 1999).

Hall, Michael (ed.), *Gothic Architecture and its Meanings, 1550–1830* (Reading, 2002).

Halsband, Robert, *Lord Hervey, Eighteenth-Century Courtier* (Oxford, 1973).

Hamilton, Elizabeth, *Letters on Education* (Dublin, 1801).

Hardy, Florence Emily, *The Early Life of Thomas Hardy, 1840–1891* (London, 1928).

Hardy, Thomas, *A Group of Noble Dames* (first published 1891).

Hardy, Thomas, *Two on a Tower* (first published 1882).

Hardyment, Christina, *Home Comfort: A History of Domestic Arrangements* (London, 1992).

Hardyment, Christina (ed.), *The Housekeeping Book of Susanna Whatman*, 1776–1800 (London, 2000).

Harvey, John, *Early Gardening Catalogues* (London and Chichester, 1972).

Harvey, John, *Early Nurserymen* (London and Chichester, 1974).

Hayden, Ruth, *Mrs Delany: Her Life and Her Flowers* (London, 1980).

Haywood, Eliza, *A New Present for a Servant Maid* (London, 1771).

Hecht, J. Jean, *The Domestic Servant in Eighteenth-Century England* (London, Boston and Henley, 1980).

Hemlow, Joyce, et al. (ed.), *The Journal and Letters of Fanny Burney (Madam d'Arblay)* (Oxford, 1972–84).

Hibbert, Christopher, *George III: A Personal History* (London, 1998).

Hicks, Carola, *Improper Pursuits: The Scandalous Life of Lady Di Beauclerk* (London, 2001).

Hill, Bridget, *Servants: English Domestics in the Eighteenth Century* (Oxford, 1996).

Hill, Bridget, *Women Alone: Spinsters in England, 1660–1850* (New Haven and London, 2001).

History of Parliament (various editions).

Hobhouse, Penelope, *Plants in Garden History* (London, 1992).

Howard, Maurice, *The Early Tudor Country House: Architecture and Politics, 1490–1550* (London, 1987).

Hufton, Olwen, *The Prospect Before Her: A History of Women in Western Europe, 1500–1800* (London, 1995).

Hughes, John Vivian, *The Wealthiest Commoner: C. R. M. Talbot* (Port Talbot, 1977).

Hughes, Kathryn, *The Victorian Governess* (London and Rio Grande, Ohio, 1993).

Hunt, John Dixon (ed.), 'Horace Walpole's Journals of Visits to Country Seats', in *The History of the Modern Taste in Gardening* (New York and London, 1982).

Hutchins, John, *History and Antiquities of the County of Dorset* (first published 1774; 2nd edn 1796; 3rd edn, with additions by W. Shipp and J. W. Hodson, London, 1861–74).

Ilchester, Countess of, and Stavordale, Lord, *The Life and Letters of Lady Sarah Bunbury* (London, 1902).

Ilchester, 6th Earl of, *Henry Fox, First Lord Holland, His Family and Relations* (London, 1920).

Ilchester, 6th Earl of (ed.), *The Journal of Elizabeth, Lady Holland, 1791–1811* (London, 1908).

Ilchester, 6th Earl of (ed.), *The Journal of the Hon. Henry Edward Fox, 1818–1830* (London, 1923).

Ilchester, 6th Earl of, *Lord Hervey and his Friends, 1726–1738* (London, 1950).

Jackson-Stops, Gervase (ed.), *The Treasure Houses of Britain* (New Haven and London, 1985).

Jacques, David, *Georgian Gardens: The Reign of Nature* (London, 1983).

Jellicoe, Geoffrey and Susan, et al. (ed.), *The Oxford Companion to Gardens* (Oxford, 1986).

Jones, Vivien (ed.), *Women and Literature in Britain, 1700–1800* (Cambridge, 2000).

Kay-Robinson, Denys, *The Landscape of Thomas Hardy* (Exeter, 1984).

Laird, Mark, *The Flowering of the Landscape Garden: English Pleasure Grounds, 1720–1800* (Philadelphia, 1999).

Langford, Paul, *Public Life and the Propertied Englishman, 1689–1798* (Oxford, 1991).

Laurence, Anne, *Women in England, 1500–1760: A Social History* (London, 1994).

Le Fanu, W. R., *Seventy Years of Irish Life* (London, 1893).

Le Faye, Deirdre (ed.), *Jane Austen's Letters* (Oxford, 1997).

Lewis, J. S., *In the Family Way: Childbearing in the British Aristocracy, 1760–1860* (New Brunswick, New Jersey, 1986).

Lewis, Wilmarth S., the Yale edition of *Horace Walpole's Correspondence*, 48 vols (New Haven and London, 1937–83).

Lummis, Trevor, and Marsh, Jan, *The Woman's Domain: Women and the English Country House* (London, 1993).

Malcolmson, A. P. W, *The Pursuit of the Heiress: Aristocratic Marriage in Ireland, 1750–1820* (Ulster Historical Foundation, 1982).

Malkin, Benjamin Heath, *The Scenery, Antiquities and Biography of South Wales* (2nd edn, London, 1807).

Martin, Joanna, *A Governess in the Age of Jane Austen: The Journals and Letters of Agnes Porter* (London and Rio Grande, Ohio, 1998).

Martin, Joanna, *Henry and the Fairy Palace: Fox Talbot and Glamorgan* (Aberystwyth, 1993).

Martin, Joanna, *The Penrice Letters: 1768–1795* (Swansea and Cardiff, 1993).

Millgate, Michael, *Thomas Hardy: A Biography* (Oxford, 1982).

Moore, Lucy, *Amphibious Thing: The Life of Lord Hervey* (London, 2000).

More, Hannah, *Essays on Various Subjects, Principally Designed for Young Ladies* (Cork, 1778).

Morris, Christopher (ed.), *The Illustrated Journeys of Celia Fiennes, 1685 to c. 1712* (London, 1982).

Morris, Richard, *Penllergare: A Victorian Paradise* (Llandeilo, 1999).

Mowl, Timothy, *Historic Gardens of Dorset* (Stroud, 2003).

Mowl, Timothy, and Earnshaw, Brian, *An Insular Rococo: Architecture, Politics and Society in Ireland and England, 1710–1770* (London, 1999).

Mundy, Harriot Georgiana, *The Journal of Mary Frampton from the Year 1779 until the Year 1846* (London, 1885).

Myers, Sylvia Harcstark, *The Bluestocking Circle: Women, Friendship and the Life of the Mind in Eighteenth-Century England* (Oxford, 1990).

Newman, John, and Pevsner, Nikolaus, *The Buildings of England: Dorset* (London, 1972).

Newman, John, *The Buildings of Wales: Glamorgan* (London, 1995).

Oswald, Arthur, *Country Houses of Dorset* (London, 1935).

Painting, David, *Swansea's Place in the History of Photography* (Swansea, 1982).

Paston-Williams, Sara, *The Art of Dining* (London, 1993).

Pearson, Jacqueline, *Women's Reading in Britain, 1750–1835* (Cambridge, 1999).

Pennington, Lady Sarah, *An Unfortunate Mother's Advice to her Absent Daughters in a Letter to Miss Pennington* (London, 1761).

Pevsner, Nikolaus, *The Buildings of England: South and West Somerset* (London, 1958).

Phillips, Patricia, *The Scientific Lady: A Social History of Woman's Scientific Interests, 1520–1918* (London, 1990).

Pitfield, F. P., *Hardy's Wessex Locations* (Wincanton, 1992).

Porter, Dorothy and Porter, Roy, *Patients' Progress: Doctors and Doctoring in Eighteenth-Century England* (Cambridge and Oxford, 1989).

Porter, Dorothy, and Porter, Roy, *In Sickness and in Health: The British Experience, 1650–1850* (London, 1988).

Porter, Roy, *Disease, Medicine and Society in England, 1550–1860* (Cambridge, 1995).

Porter, Roy, *Enlightenment: Britain and the Creation of the Modern World* (London, 2000).

Porter, Roy, *The Greatest Benefit to Mankind: A Medical History of Humanity from Antiquity to the Present* (London, 1997).

Randall, Henry J., and Rees, William, *Diary of Lewis Weston Dillwyn*, South Wales and Monmouth Record Society, 5 (1963).

Renton, Alice, *Tyrant or Victim: A History of the British Governess* (London, 1991).

Royal Commission on Historical Monuments, England, *An Inventory of the Historical Monuments in the County of Dorset* (London, 1952–70).

Royal Commission on Historical Monuments in Wales, *An Inventory of the Ancient Monuments in Glamorgan*, iv, *Domestic Architecture from the Reformation to the Industrial Revolution, part I: The Greater Houses* (Cardiff, 1981).

Sambrook, Pamela, *The Country House Servant* (Stroud, 1999).

Sambrook, Pamela, *The Country House at Work: Three Centuries of Dunham Massey* (London, 2003).

Sambrook, Pamela, and Brears, Peter, *The Country House Kitchen, 1650–1900* (Stroud, 1996).

Scarfe, Norman (ed.), *A Frenchman's Year in Suffolk, 1784*, Suffolk Records Society, 30 (Woodbridge, 1988).

Schaaf, Larry J., *Out of the Shadows: Herschel, Talbot and the Invention of Photography* (New Haven and London, 1992).

Selwyn, David, *Jane Austen and Leisure* (London and Rio Grande, Ohio, 1999).

Seymour-Smith, Martin, *Hardy* (London, 1994).

Shoemaker, Robert B., *Gender in English Society, 1650–1850* (London, 1998).

Sim, Alison, *The Tudor Housewife* (Stroud, 1996).

Skrine, Henry, *Two Successive Tours throughout the Whole of Wales* (London, 1798).

Smith, Ann, 'Sherborne Castle: From Tudor Lodge to Country House. New Evidence from the Archives', *Local Historian*, 25, no. 4 (November, 1995).

Smith, Charlotte, *The Old Manor House* (first edition, 1793).

Smith, D. J. M., *A Dictionary of Horse-Drawn Vehicles* (London, 1988).

Smith, Nowell (ed.), *The Letters of Sydney Smith* (Oxford, 1953).

Somerset, Anne, *Ladies in Waiting: From the Tudors to the Present Day* (London, 1984).

Southam, Brian, *Jane Austen and the Navy* (London and New York, 2000).

Stone, Lawrence, *The Family, Sex and Marriage in England, 1500–1800* (London, 1977).

Stott, Anne, *Hannah More: The First Victorian* (Oxford, 2003).

Strong, Roy, *The Artist and the Garden* (New Haven and London, 2000).

Stroud, Dorothy, *Capability Brown* (London, 1975).

Symes, Michael, *The English Rococo Garden* (Princes Risborough, 1991).

Thomas, Keith, *Man and the Natural World* (London, 1983).

Thomson, Gladys Scott, *The Russells in Bloomsbury, 1669–1771* (London, 1940).

Thomson, Katherine (ed.), *Memoirs of Viscountess Sundon, Mistress of the Robes to Queen Caroline* (London, 1847).

Tillyard, Stella, *Aristocrats: Caroline, Emily, Louisa and Sarah Lennox, 1740–1832* (London, 1994).

Tinniswood, Adrian, *A History of Country House Visiting* (Oxford, 1989).

Tomalin, Claire, *Jane Austen: A Life* (London, 1997).

Tomalin, Claire, *The Life and Death of Mary Wollstonecraft* (London, 1974).

Toulmin-Smith, Lucy (ed.), *The Itinerary of John Leland in or about the Years 1535–1543*, iii (London, 1907).

Trumbach, Randolph, *The Rise of the Egalitarian Family* (New York, 1978).

Turner, E. S., *What the Butler Saw: Two Hundred and Fifty Years of the Servant Problem* (first edition, 1962; reprint London, 2001).

Williamson, Tom, *Polite Landscapes: Gardens and Society in Eighteenth-Century England* (Stroud, 1995).

Wilson, Richard, and Mackley, Alan, *Creating Paradise: The Building of the English Country House, 1660–1880* (London and New York, 2000).

Vickery, Amanda, *The Gentleman's Daughter: Women's Lives in Georgian England* (New Haven and London, 1998).

Virgin, Peter, *Sydney Smith* (London, 1994).

Wallis, P. J. and R. V., *Eighteenth-Century Medics* (Newcastle-upon-Tyne, 1988).

Waterson, Merlin, *The Servants' Hall: A Domestic History of Erddig* (London and Henley, 1980).

Wilcoxen, Charlotte, 'A Highborn Lady in Colonial New York', *New York Historical Society Quarterly* (1979).

Williamson, Tom, *Polite Landscapes: Gardens and Society in Eighteenth-Century England* (Baltimore, Maryland, and Stroud, 1995).

Index